Peter Ackroyd

Shakespeare

Peter Ackroyd is a bestselling writer of both fiction and nonfiction. His most recent books include *The Lambs of London* and *J.M.W. Turner*, the second biography in the Ackroyd Brief Lives series. He has also written full-scale biographies of Dickens, Blake, and Thomas More and the novels *The Clerkenwell Tales*, *The Trial of Elizabeth Cree*, *Milton in America*, and *The Plato Papers*. He has won the Whitbread Award for Biography, the Royal Society of Literature Award under the William Heinemann Bequest (jointly), the Somerset Maugham Award, the South Bank Award for Literature, the James Tait Black Memorial Prize, and The Guardian fiction prize. He lives in London.

Also by Peter Ackroyd

FICTION

The Great Fire of London
The Last Testament of Oscar Wilde
Hawksmoor
Chatterton
First Light
English Music
The House of Doctor Dee
Dan Leno and the Limehouse Golem
Milton in America
The Plato Papers
The Clerkenwell Tales

NONFICTION

Dressing Up: Transvestism and Drag: The History of an Obsession
London: The Biography
Albion: The Origins of the English Imagination

BIOGRAPHY

Ezra Pound and His World
T.S. Eliot
Dickens
Blake
The Life of Thomas More

POETRY

Ouch!
The Diversions of Purley

CRITICISM

Notes for a New Culture
The Collection: Journalism, Reviews, Essays, Short Stories, Lectures
(edited by Thomas Wright)

Shakespeare

THE BIOGRAPHY

Shakespeare

THE BIOGRAPHY

Peter Ackroyd

Anchor Books
A Division of Random House, Inc.
New York

FIRST ANCHOR BOOKS EDITION, NOVEMBER 2006

Copyright © 2005 by Peter Ackroyd

All rights reserved. Published in the United States by Anchor Books, a division
of Random House, Inc., New York. Originally published in hardcover in the United
Kingdom by Chatto & Windus, London, in 2004, and subsequently in hardcover in the
United States by Nan A. Talese, an imprint of Doubleday, a division of
Random House, Inc., New York, in 2005

The Library of Congress has cataloged the Nan A. Talese / Doubleday edition as follows:
Ackroyd, Peter, 1949–
Shakespeare : the biography / Peter Ackroyd. —1st ed.
p. cm.
Originally published : Great Britain : Chatto & Windus, 2005.
1. Shakespeare, William, 1564–1616. 2. Dramatists, English—
Early modern, 1500–1700—Biography. I. Title.
PR2894.A26 2005
822.3'3—dc22
[B]   2005043903

Anchor ISBN-13: 978-1-4000-7598-0
Anchor ISBN-10: 1-4000-7598-X

www.anchorbooks.com

146938060

Contents

Stratford-Upon-Avon

New Place

The Globe

The King's Men

Blackfriars

$\mathcal{L}$ist of $\mathcal{I}$llustrations

ILLUSTRATIONS IN THE TEXT

Title page from *The Bishops' Bible*, quarto edition 1569. G 12188. *By permission of the British Library*

The Elizabethan clown, Richard Tarlton, depicted as part of a decorated initial. *Harley 3885 f. 19. By permission of the British Library*

One of Nicholas Visscher's panoramas of London and the Thames. *Guildhall Library, Corporation of London, UK/Bridgeman Art Library*

From Robert Greene's autobiographical pamphlet, *Groats-worth of Witte, bought with a million of Repentance* (1592). *The Folger Shakespeare Library*

The comedian William Kempe. From his *Nine Daies Wonder* (printed in 1600) in which he described how he had morris-danced all the way from London to Norwich. *Bodleian Library*

Rough sketch (1602) of the proposed Shakespeare coat of arms. *The Folger Shakespeare Library*

The Globe Theatre on Bankside, after an engraving of the time of James I. *Bridgeman Art Library/private collection/The Stapleton Collection*

Title page to *Mischeefes Mysterie or Treasons Master-peece, the Powder Plot.* Wood cut by John Vickars. *Bridgeman Art Library/private collection*

Ben Jonson's *Oberon, the Fairy Prince*: designs by Inigo Jones (1611). *The Courtauld Institute/The Devonshire Collection, Chatsworth. Reproduced by permission of the Duke of Devonshire and the Chatsworth Settlement Trustees*

ILLUSTRATIONS IN THE INSERTS

Seventeenth-century gloves. *V & A images, Victoria and Albert Museum*

Hornbook. *The Folger Shakespeare Library*

The nave of Stratford's Guild Chapel. *Maya Vision International*

Queen Elizabeth I. *National Portrait Gallery, London*

Edmund Campion. *By permission of the Governors of Stonyhurst College*

Lord Strange (Ferdinando Stanley, the fifth Earl of Derby). Oil on canvas, Marcus Gheeraerts the Younger. © *The Right Hon the Earl of Derby/ Bridgeman Art Library*

Thought to be Christopher Marlowe. *The Master and Fellows of Corpus Christi College, Cambridge*

Titus Andronicus (1594). *By permission of the Marquess of Bath, Longleat House, Warminster, Wiltshire, Great Britain*

Frontispiece to *The Spanish Tragedy* by Thomas Kyd, printed by Augustine Mathewes, 1633 (woodcut). *Private collection/Bridgeman Art Library*

Dedicatory epistle to *The Rape of Lucrece. The Folger Shakespeare Library*

Henry Wriothesley, third Earl of Southampton. Nicholas Hilliard. Gouache on vellum. © *Fitzwilliam Museum, University of Cambridge, UK/Bridgeman Art Library*

William Herbert, third Earl of Pembroke. Studio of Daniel Mytens. *Philip Mould, Historical Portraits Ltd, London, UK/ Bridgeman Art Library*

Mary Herbert, Countess of Pembroke (c. 1590). *National Portrait Gallery, London*

The Swan Theatre, Southwark. Ink on paper, English school, seventeenth century. *Private collection/Bridgeman Art Library*

The Hall of the Middle Temple, London. *Photographed by A. F. Kersting*

Author's Note

Certain questions of nomenclature arise. The earliest publications of Shakespeare's plays took the form of quartos or of the Folio. The quartos, as their name implies, were small editions of one play characteristically issued several years after its first production. Some of the more popular plays were reprinted in quarto many times, whereas others were not published at all. About half of Shakespeare's plays were printed during his lifetime by this means. The results are good, clumsy or indifferent. There has been a division made between "good quartos" and "bad quartos," although the latter should really be known as "problem quartos" since textual scholars are uncertain about their status and provenance. The Folio of Shakespeare's plays is an altogether different production. It was compiled after Shakespeare's death by two of his fellow actors, John Heminges and Henry Condell, as a commemorative edition of Shakespeare's work. It was first published in 1623, and for approximately three hundred years remained the definitive version of the Shakespearian canon.

The earliest biographical references to Shakespeare deserve mentioning. There are allusions and references in various published sources, during his lifetime, but there were no serious descriptions or assessments of his plays. Ben Jonson ventured a brief account in *Timber: or, Discoveries Made upon Men and Matter* (1641) and some biographical notes were composed by John Aubrey without being published in his lifetime. The first extended biography was Nicholas Rowe's prefatory *Life* in Jacob Tonson's edition of the *Works*

of Shakespeare (1709), and this was followed by the various surmises of eighteenth-century antiquarians and scholars such as Samuel Ireland and
Edmond Malone. The vogue for Shakespearean biography itself arose in the
mid- to late nineteenth century, with the publication of Edward Dowden's
Shakespeare: A Critical Study of His Mind and Art (the first edition of which
was published in 1875), and has not abated since.

Part 1

Stratford-upon-Avon

The title page of this edition of *The Bishops' Bible* shows the enthroned Queen Elizabeth I surrounded by the female personifications of Justice, Mercy (Temperance), Prudence and Fortitude. During his schoolboy years, Shakespeare would have become familiar with the vigorous language of the Bible recently translated into English.

CHAPTER 1

There Was a Starre Daunst, and Vnder That Was I Borne

illiam Shakespeare is popularly supposed to have been born on 23 April 1564, or St. George's Day. The date may in fact have been 21 April or 22 April, but the coincidence of the national festival is at least appropriate.

When he emerged from the womb into the world of time, with the assistance of a midwife, an infant of the sixteenth century was washed and then "swaddled" by being wrapped tightly in soft cloth. Then he was carried downstairs in order to be presented to the father. After this ritual greeting, he was taken back to the birth-chamber, still warm and dark, where he was laid beside the mother. She was meant to "draw to her all the diseases from the child,"[1] before her infant was put in a cradle. A small portion of butter and honey was usually placed in the baby's mouth. It was the custom in Warwickshire to give the suckling child hare's brains reduced to jelly.

The date of Shakespeare's christening, unlike that of his birth, is exactly known: he was baptised in the Church of the Holy Trinity, in Stratford, on Wednesday 26 April 1564. In the register of that church, the parish clerk has written *Guilelmus filius Johannes Shakespere*; he slipped in his Latin, and should have written *Johannis*.

The infant Shakespeare was carried by his father from his birthplace in Henley Street down the High Street and Church Street into the church itself. The mother was never present at the baptism. John Shakespeare and his newborn son would have been accompanied by the godparents, who were other-wise known as "god-sips" or "gossips." On this occasion the godfather was William Smith, a haberdasher and neighbour in Henley Street. The name of the infant was given before he was dipped in the font and the sign of the cross marked upon his forehead. At the font the gossips were exhorted to make sure that William Shakespeare heard sermons and learned the creed as well as the Lord's Prayer "in the English tongue." After the baptism a piece of white linen cloth was placed on the head of the child, and remained there until the mother had been "churched" or purified; it was called the "chrisom cloth" and, if the infant died within a month, was used as a shroud. The cere-mony of the reformed Anglican faith, in the time of Elizabeth, still favoured the presentation of apostle-spoons or christening shirts to the infant, given by the gossips, and the consumption of a christening cake in celebration. They were, after all, celebrating the saving of young William Shakespeare for eternity.

Of his earthly life there was much less certainty. In the sixteenth century, the mortality of the newly born was high. Nine per cent died within a week of birth, and a further 11 per cent before they were a month old;[2] in the decade of Shakespeare's own birth there were in Stratford 62.8 average an-nual baptisms and 42.8 average annual child burials.[3] You had to be tough, or from a relatively prosperous family, to survive the odds. It is likely that Shakespeare had both of these advantages.

Once the dangers of childhood had been surmounted, there was a further difficulty. The average lifespan of an adult male was forty-seven years. Since Shakespeare's parents were by this standard long-lived, he may have hoped to emulate their example. But he survived only six years beyond the average span. Something had wearied him. Since in London the average life expectancy was only thirty-five years in the more affluent parishes, and twenty-five years in the poorer areas, it may have been the city that killed him. But this roll-call of death had one necessary consequence. Half of the population were under the age of twenty. It was a youthful culture, with all the vigour and ambition of early life. London itself was perpetually young.

The first test of Shakespeare's own vigour came only three months after his birth. In the parish register of 11 July 1564, beside the record of the burial of a weaver's young apprentice from the High Street, was written: *Hic incipit pestis.* Here begins the plague. In a period of six months some 237 residents of Stratford died, more than a tenth of its population; a family of four ex-pired on the same side of Henley Street as the Shakespeares. But the Shakespeares survived. Perhaps the mother and her newborn son escaped to her old family home in the neighbouring hamlet of Wilmcote, and stayed there until the peril had passed. Only those who remained in the town succumbed to the infection.

The parents, if not the child, suffered fear and trembling. They had already lost two daughters, both of whom had died in earliest infancy, and the care devoted to their first-born son must have been close and intense. Such children tend to be confident and resilient in later life. They feel themselves to be in some sense blessed and protected from the hardships of the world. It is perhaps worth remarking that Shakespeare never contracted the plague that often raged through London. But we can also see the lineaments of that fortunate son in the character of the land from which he came.

CHAPTER 2

Shee Is My Essence

Warwickshire was often described as primeval, and contours of ancient time can indeed be glimpsed in the lie of this territory and its now denuded hills. It has also been depicted as the heart or the navel of England, with the clear implication that Shakespeare himself embodies some central national worth. He is central to the centre, the core or source of Englishness itself.

The countryside around Stratford was divided into two swathes. To the north lay the Forest of Arden, the remains of the ancient forest that covered the Midlands; these tracts were known as the Wealden. The notion of the forest may suggest uninterrupted woodland, but that was not the case in the sixteenth century. The Forest of Arden itself included sheep farms and farmsteads, meadows and pastures, wastes and intermittent woods; in this area the houses were not linked conveniently in lanes or streets but in the words of an Elizabethan topographer, William Harrison, "stand scattered abroad, each one dwelling in the midst of his own occupying."[1] By the time Shakespeare wandered through Arden the woods themselves were steadily being reduced by the demand for timber in building new houses; it required between sixty and eighty trees to erect a house. The forest was being stripped, too, for mining and subsistence farming. In his survey of the region, for his *Theatre of the Empire of Great Britaine* of 1611, John Speed noticed "great and notable destruction of wood." There never has been a sylvan paradise in England. It is always being destroyed.

Yet the wood has always been a token of wildness and resistance. In *As You Like It* and *A Midsummer Night's Dream*, in *Cymbeline* and *Titus Andronicus*, it becomes a symbol of folklore and of ancient memory. The great prehistoric forest of the Arden gave refuge to the British tribes against the Roman invaders of their land; the name of Arden itself derives from Celtic roots, meaning high wooded valleys. It was the Celts who named the Ardennes in the region of north-eastern France and Belgium. The same woods provided cover for the Celtic people from the marauding Saxon tribes of the Hwiccas. The legends of Guy of Warwick, imbibed by Shakespeare in his infancy, tell of the knight's hermitic concealment in the forest. His sword, used in his fight against the encroaching Danes, was kept as a memorial in Warwick Castle.

So Arden was a place of concealment as well as of industry; it was an area that outlaws and vagrants might enter with impunity. That is why wood-dwellers were regarded with some disfavour by those from more open habitations. Wood-dwellers were "people of lewd lives and conversation";[2] they were "as ignorant of God or any course of civil life as the very savages amongst the infidels."[3] Thus the history of rebellion mingles with that of savagery and possible insurrection. The history runs very deep, and is inseparable from the land itself. When in *As You Like It* Touchstone enters the wood, he declares that "I, now am I in Arden, the more foole I" (761). Shakespeare's mother was Mary Arden. His future wife, Anne Hathaway, dwelled in the outskirts of the forest. His consciousness of the area was close and intense.

Beyond the Wealden, in the south of the county, lay the Fielden. In Saxton's map of Warwickshire, issued in 1576, this region is almost wholly devoid of trees except for those growing in groves and small woods. The rest of the land had been changed to scrub and pasture, with the arable territory sweeping across the hills. In his *Britannia* William Camden described it as "plain champaign country, and being rich in corn and green grass yieldeth a right goodly and pleasant prospect." John Speed saw the view from the same spot as Camden, on the summit of Edgehill, and noticed "the medowing pastures with their green mantles so imbrodered with flowers." It is the quintessential picture of rural England. It was as much part of Shakespeare's vision as the forests beyond. It has been surmised that the Fielden was rich and

Protestant, while the Wealden was poor and Catholic. This is the shorthand of popular prejudice, but it suggests a context for that balancing of oppositions that came so instinctively to Shakespeare.

The climate of Stratford was of a mild temper, protected by the Welsh hills. There was much moisture in the land and in the air, as the various streams running through Stratford itself would have testified. The clouds from the south-west were known as "Severn Jacks" and presaged rain. Only "the Tyrannous breathing of the North," as Imogen remarks in *Cymbeline*, "Shakes all our buddes from growing" (257–8).

But what, in the larger sense, has this landscape to do with Shakespeare or Shakespeare with the landscape? Some future genius of topography may elucidate what has become known as the territorial imperative, the sense of place that binds and determines the nature of those who grow up on a certain spot of ground. Yet, in relation to Shakespeare, we may already venture one conclusion. The evidence of his work provides unequivocal proof that he was neither born nor raised in London. He does not have the harshness or magniloquence of John Milton, born in Bread Street; he does not have the hardness of Ben Jonson, educated at Westminster School; he does not have the sharpness of Alexander Pope from the City or the obsessiveness of William Blake from Soho. He is of the country.

CHAPTER 3

Dost Thou Loue Pictures?

tratford is a meeting place of roads crossing the Avon river; afon is the Celtic name for river. The area had been settled from the Bronze Age. There were barrows and stone circles, lying now neglected, and there were "lowes" or graves where meets or open courts once gathered. A Romano-British village was established on the outskirts of the present town, lending weight and substance to the weathered and enduring atmosphere of the place.

Stratford means a Roman *straet*, a paved road or highway, crossing a ford. In the seventh century a monastery was established, by the banks of the river; this was first in the possession of Aethelard, subordinate king of the Hwiccas, but was then transferred into the ownership of Egwin, Bishop of Worcester. Since this was soon after the conversion of the Saxons to the Christian faith, we may say that Stratford had a connection with the old religion from the earliest times. The church in which Shakespeare was baptised was erected on the site of the old monastery, and the dwellings of the monks and their servants were once on land now known as "Old Town." The *Domesday* surveyors of 1085 carefully noted the presence of a village on this spot, comprising farmers and labourers as well as the ecclesiastical community; there was a priest, together with twenty-one "villeins" and seven "bordarii" or cottagers.

It began to prosper in the thirteenth century. A fair of three days was instituted in 1216; it was supplemented by four other fairs held at various times of the year, one of which lasted for fifteen days. A survey of 1252 reports 240 "burgages," or properties held on a yearly rental from the lord of the manor, as well as numerous shops, stalls and tenements. Here were shoemakers and fleshmongers, blacksmiths and carpenters, dyers and wheelwrights, engaged in trades that Shakespeare would still have seen on the streets of his childhood. The medieval town itself was approximately the same size as it was at the time of Shakespeare's birth. To be aware of continuity—to be settled within it—was in a real sense his birthright.

The open country beyond the town has been described as "tumbled down," covered with thorn bush and populated by rabbits. There were few trees and no hedges, but flat land all around sprinkled with cowslips and clover and yellow mustard. This unenclosed territory comprised meadow land, arable land and rough pasture stretching towards the hills. Of all writers, Shakespeare has the widest vocabulary on the variety of weeds to be found in such places, disentangling the hemlock from the cuckoo-flower, the fumiter from the darnel.

There had been a church in Stratford, dedicated to the Holy Trinity, since the early thirteenth century. It was erected beside the river, of local undressed stone and yellow stone from the Campden quarries, in the utmost harmony with the landscape; it possessed a wooden steeple and was surrounded by elm trees, with an avenue of lime trees leading to the north porch.

Shakespeare would have known the ancient bone-house on the north side of the chancel, where the skeletons of the long-dead had been deposited; it had also been a dormitory for the singing boys and a study for the minister. Shakespeare and his contemporaries were familiar with death, although this did not prevent Juliet from crying out against the "Charnel house" with its "reekie shanks and yealow chaples sculls" (2259). Local legend suggests that the playwright had this bone-house in mind when he wrote this passage in *Romeo and Juliet*, and local legend may be right. His own grave was to be situated just a few feet from it, within the church itself, and his solemn curse against anyone who "moves my bones" acts as a reminder. There were other intimations of mortality: a college, or house for chantry priests praying in perpetual intercession for the dead, had been erected on the western side of the churchyard in 1351.

Of equal antiquity was the Guild of the Holy Cross, established in Stratford at the beginning of the thirteenth century. This was a society of lay people devoted to the festivals and institutions of their faith; it was a "friendly society" where, by payment of an annual subscription, its members would be assured of a fitting funeral. But it was also a communal society, with its own wardens and beadles who supervised the interests of the town as well as the benefactions of the church.

If Shakespeare knew one public building in Stratford thoroughly well, it was the chapel of this guild; it was erected beside the school where he was taught, and each weekday morning he attended prayers here. And then there were the bells. The little bell called the boy to school in the morning; the great bell tolled at dawn and dusk, and was "the surly sullen bell" of the sonnet that tolled at the time of dying and the time of burial. It eventually tolled for Shakespeare when he was laid in the Stratford ground.

CHAPTER 4

For Where Thou Art, There Is the World It Selfe

hakespeare was born five years after the coronation of Elizabeth I, and much of his life was spent within the constraints and uncertainties of her highly individualistic reign. Her principal concern was always for the stability and solvency of the country (and of her own position), so that all the imperiousness and ingenuity of her character were dedicated to the avoidance of civil disturbance and external conflict. She feared disorder more than anything else, and fought only when it became absolutely necessary to do so. An unmarried queen also created an inherently unstable polity, especially when she created competing "favourites" at her court, but Elizabeth managed to thwart or divert a number of conspiracies against her throne. Her impatient and often indecisive rule lifted the horizons of the country. It was an age of exploration, of renewed commerce and of literature. In retrospect it has even been called the age of Shakespeare. There is no reason to assume, however, that Shakespeare himself either liked or admired her. As a child, of course, he was part of a quite different world.

Stratford lay on the north bank of the Avon. The river was the most familiar presence in a landscape filled with trees, with orchards and with gardens. When it was in flood, whether in summer or in winter, it could be heard in every street. When "Avon was up," according to Leland, the people attempting a crossing "stood in jeopardy of life." In the summer of 1588, for example, it rose 3 feet an hour continuously for eight hours. A prominent local gentleman, Sir Hugh Clopton, financed the building of the stone bridge that survives still. But the flooded river has another important memorial. No Elizabethan dramatist invokes the river more often than Shakespeare; and, of the fifty-nine separate references, twenty-six concern the river in flood.[1] The river was part of his imagination. There is a particular and peculiar image in *The Rape of Lucrece*, where an eddy of water is forced back by the current in the same direction from which it came; the phenomenon can be observed from the eighteenth arch of the stone bridge[2] at Stratford.

The bridge led by a walled causeway into Bridge Street, running through the middle of the town. It was part of a matrix of six or seven streets that supported 217 houses and two hundred families; the population of Stratford in the late sixteenth century has been estimated at approximately nineteen hundred. The streets themselves retained their medieval identity, as Sheep Street and Wood Street and Mill Lane still testify. Rother Street was named after the *rother* or local cattle that were sold there. Yet the majority of the houses were of relatively recent construction, having been erected in the fifteenth century by the close-timbered method. The timber was oak, felled in the adjacent forest, and the wooden frame was filled with the familiar wattle-and-daub. The foundations were of lias stone quarried in the neighbouring village of Wilmcote, from which Mary Arden came, and the roofs were of thatch. The windows were not glazed but were protected by thick wooden bars. These were natural and local dwellings in every sense.

It was a well-watered town with various streams or streamlets running through the streets, with adjacent wells and ponds as well as standing water and cess-pools. Two doors down from Shakespeare's house was a smithy that made use of the water from a stream called the Mere. He was never very far from the sound of water. The streets of Stratford were wide enough for wagons to pass each other, yet not so wide that they were not pestered by dunghills and gutters, ditches and mud walls. They were "paved" or cobbled on each side, but anything might flow down the middle channel. They were also encroached upon by uncultivated land, marked by makeshift and shapeless roads.

Pigs, geese and ducks were not supposed to wander freely through the town but the presence of the pigs, in particular, was signalled by the numerous sties and yards in every street. There were many goodly houses, to use the expression of the day, but there were also hovels and tenements for the poorer sort, thatched barns for the storage of corn and many decayed outbuildings. There were stone crosses to show humankind the way; there was a pillory, stocks and a whipping post for those who defied the authority of the town's governors, one of whom was Shakespeare's father; there was also a gaol, a structure known as "the cage," and a ducking stool. This was no Tudor idyll. The engravings of Stratford—of the mills and the market crosses, the church and the chapel—naturally display a world of stillness and of silence, populated by merchants or labourers in picturesque costume. The earliest photographs also show a world preternaturally solemn and still, the wide streets almost bare of human habitation. They do not evoke the pressing and chaotic life that was Shakespeare's reality.

Each trade had its own place and station. Pigs were sold in Swine Street, and horses in Church Way; sellers of hides took their place at the cross in Rother Market, while the salters and sugarers put up their stalls in Corn Street. The ironmongers and ropers were to be found in Bridge Street, while the "fleshers" or butchers were at the top of Middle Row. There were various markets for corn, cattle and cloth. When Shakespeare returned to Stratford in later life, there was a butter and cheese market at the White Cross just outside his front door.

By four o'clock in the morning, the town had awakened; by five, the streets were filled with people. The traders and labourers breakfasted at eight, and took their dinner or nuncheon at noon; they finished their work at seven in the evening, at the end of a fourteen-hour day. The Statute of Artificers, however, promulgated in 1563, allowed one hour of sleep after the noonday meal. There were no holidays but the various holy days.

Many of the Stratford trades had been followed for centuries. A survey of occupations, from 1570 to 1630, shows that the town had twenty-three butchers, twenty weavers, sixteen shoemakers, fifteen bakers and fifteen carpenters.[3] These were "primary" occupations; townspeople, such as Shakespeare's own father, engaged in a variety of different trades. John Shakespeare's principal occupation was that of glover, one of twenty-three in the town, but he also earned his living as a trader in wool, a money-lender and a maker of malt. The brewing and selling of ale was a speciality in Stratford; no fewer than sixty-seven households were involved in the trade.[4]

Yet underlying these trades, and the whole of the town's economy, was the larger rhythm of the agricultural year with the February sowing and harrowing, the March pruning, the June haymaking, the reaping of August, the threshing of September and the pig-killing of November. There were horses and sheep and pigs and cattle and bees. There was tillage land and fallow land, meadow and pasture. "Again, sir, shal we sow the hade land with wheate?" a servant asks Justice Shallow in the second part of *King Henry IV*. "With red wheat, Dauy" (Part Two, 2704–5). Shakespeare evidently understood the language of the land.

In 1549 the Bishop of Worcester was obliged to cede his manorial rights over Stratford to John Dudley, Earl of Warwick; the town was in that sense secularised. In 1553 it was granted a charter whereby the erstwhile officers of the Guild of the Holy Cross became aldermen; fourteen townsmen were given this role, and out of their number a bailiff or mayor was to be elected. They in turn chose fourteen other "burgesses," and together they comprised the town council.

They met in the old guildhall beside the chapel where their duties included the supervision of the bridge, the school and the chapel itself; the properties that once belonged to the guild were now used to garner income for the council. Although many regretted the demise of church authority, it represented a signal advance in local self-government. The bailiff and a chosen alderman acted as Justices of the Peace in place of the church court. There were two chamberlains and four constables, all appointed from this oligarchy of the more respectable townsmen. This was the world in which Shakespeare's father flourished for a time; it was part of the fabric of Shakespeare's childhood.

The stocks and the pillory of Stratford, not to mention the gaol and the ducking stool, afford good reason to believe that the way of life in the town itself was thoroughly supervised. It has become customary to describe the England of Elizabeth I as a "police state," but that is an anachronism. Yet it was a world of strict and almost paternal discipline. It was in other words still governed by medieval prescription. There was a keen sense of the difference between social classes and of the power granted to those who owned land. These were principles observed faithfully by Shakespeare himself. It was a world of patronage and prerogative, of customary observance and strictly local justice. Anyone who spoke disrespectfully of a town officer, or who disobeyed a municipal order, was placed in the stocks for three days and three nights. No one could lodge a stranger without the mayor's permission. No servant or apprentice could leave the house after nine in the evening. Bowling was permitted only at certain times. Woollen caps were to be worn on Sundays, and it was obligatory to attend church at least once a month. There were no secrets in Stratford; it was an open society in which everyone knew everybody else's business, where marital or familial problems became the common gossip of the immediate neighbourhood. There was no notion of "private" life in any sense that would now be recognised. It is suggestive, therefore, that Shakespeare has often been credited with the invention of private identity within his dramas. He was keenly aware of its absence in the town of his birth.

It is generally assumed that the nature or atmosphere of the town did not alter in Shakespeare's lifetime, and did not materially change until well into the nineteenth century, but this is incorrect. Changing agricultural methods brought their own problems and uncertainties; in particular the enclosure of common fields, and the intensive rearing of sheep, sent many labourers away from the land. There were more vagrants and landless workers in the streets of the town. In 1601 the overseers of Stratford remarked upon the presence of seven hundred poor people, and these would in large part comprise labourers coming from the surrounding countryside. The migration of the poor also increased underlying social tensions. Between 1590 and 1620 there was a rapid increase in "serious offences" tried at the county assize.[5]

The presence of the landless and unemployed exacerbated a problem that at the time seemed insoluble. How to prevent the poor from becoming ever more destitute? It was a period of rising prices. Sugar was 1s 4d a pound in 1586, 2s 2d in 1612. Barley was sold at 13s 3d a quarter in 1574, but by the mid-1590s this price had risen to £1 6s 8d. The increase of population also depressed the earnings of wage labourers. A mason was paid 1s 1d a day in 1570 but thirty years later, after a time of steeply rising prices, he was earning only 1s. These conditions were rendered ever more severe with a succession of four bad harvests after 1594; in the latter half of 1596, and the first months of 1597, there were many Stratford deaths that seem directly related to malnutrition. It was a time of famine. The mutinous citizens of *Coriolanus*, "in hunger for Bread" (21), were not some historical fantasy.

Yet as the poor were reduced to the level of subsistence, or worse, yeomen and landowners became steadily richer. The growing population, and the demand for wool in particular, favoured land speculation on a large scale. It was a means of making easy profit that Shakespeare himself enjoyed, and he can in fact be cited as a major beneficiary of the economic change that proved so disadvantageous to the labouring poor. He was not in the least sentimental about such matters, and arranged his finances with the same business-like acumen that he applied to his dramatic career. But he saw what was happening.

The nature of the new secular economy was becoming increasingly clear, in any case, and many studies have been devoted to Shakespeare's expression of the change from medieval to early modern England. What happens when old concepts of faith and authority are usurped, when old ties of patronage and obligation are sundered? It is the transition from Lear to Goneril and Regan, from Duncan to Macbeth. There also emerged a disparity between polite and popular traditions that grew ever more pronounced; Shakespeare was perhaps the last English dramatist to reconcile the two cultures.

CHAPTER 5

Tell Me This: Who Begot Thee?

here were two cultures in a more particular sense: old and reformed. The English Reformation of religion was begun in
fury and in greed; such violent origins beget violent deeds. It
was only during the cautious and pragmatic reign of Elizabeth that a form of
compromise or settlement was reached.

As a result of his anger and impatience with the Pope, Henry VIII had
proclaimed himself to be the head of the Church in England, despatching
several churchmen to their deaths for daring to deny his supremacy. His more
ardent advisers, moved by the prospect of enrichment as much as by religious fervour, suppressed the monasteries and confiscated the monastic
lands. It was the single largest blow to the medieval inheritance of England.
The king was also responsible for the introduction of the English Bible into
parish churches, an innovation which had more beneficent effects.

Edward VI, after the death of his father, was more eagerly devoted to
the destruction of Catholicism. He was the young Josiah, ready to tear down
the idols. In particular he was emboldened to reform the prayer book and the
liturgy, but his early death interrupted his programme of renewal. His
measures were then reversed during the equally brief reign of Mary I, leaving the English people in some doubt as to the nature and direction of the
nation's faith. It was Mary's successor, Elizabeth, who successfully found a
middle path. She seemed intent upon placating as many factions as possible.

It was part of her church "settlement" in which the vagaries of Catholicism and Protestantism were chastened. She ordained that church services should be held in English, but permitted the use of such papist tokens as the crucifix and the candlestick. By the Act of Supremacy she affirmed her position as the head of the Church of England, and by the Act of Uniformity she installed the Book of Common Prayer in every church. It was a somewhat rickety structure, stitched together by compromise and special pleading, but it held. She may have underestimated the power of the Puritan factions, as well as the residual Catholicism of the people themselves, but her control of religious affairs was never seriously in doubt.

The Virgin Queen, however, was not necessarily mild with her more recalcitrant subjects. Recusants as they were known—those who refused to attend the services of the Church of England—were fined, arrested or imprisoned. They were considered to be traitors to their sovereign and their realm. Catholic priests and missionaries were tortured and killed. Commissioners made periodic and much advertised "visits" to towns where the old faith was said to persist, while the bishops made regular inspections of their dioceses in pursuit of renegade piety. It was perilous to be a Catholic, or a suspected Catholic.

All these conflicts and changes found a vivid reflection in the life of John Shakespeare. The father of the dramatist was described in later life as "a merry Cheekd old man—that said—Will was a good Honest Fellow, but he durst have crackt a jeast with him at any time."[1] Since this sketch was first published in the mid-seventeenth century, from an ambiguous source, it need not be taken with any high degree of literalness. It is perhaps too close to the image of Falstaff, although we may surmise that the merry-cheeked roisterer of the history plays may bear some passing resemblance to a domestic original. What we know about Shakespeare's father, and forefathers, can be more carefully measured by documentary reports.

The ancestry of the Shakespeares stretches far back. Shakespeare's own name had more than eighty different spellings—including Sakspere, Schakosper, Schackspere, Saxper, Schaftspere, Shakstaf, Chacsper, Shasspeere—perhaps testifying to the multifarious and polyphonic nature of his given identity. The variations suggest prolificity and universality. In Stratford documents alone there are some twenty different and separate spellings.

The original family may have been of Norman derivation. In the Great

Rolls of Normandy, dated 1195, there is found "William Sakeespee"; a late thirteenth-century Norman romance, *Le Chatelain de Couci*, was composed by "Jakemes Sakesep." It is also true that the Shakespeare families of England preferred Christian names that were characteristically Norman. The surname itself seems to have had some militaristic association, and in Shakespeare's lifetime there were some who were impressed by its martial ring. An early sixteenth-century text suggests that it was "imposed upon the first bearers . . . for valour and feats of arms."[2] It is suggestive, then, that when Shakespeare's father applied for a coat of arms, he claimed that his grandfather had been rewarded by Henry VII for "faithfull & valeant service."[3] Shakespeare was also used as a nickname "for a belligerent person, or perhaps a bawdy name for an exhibitionist."[4] For this reason it was sometimes regarded as a "base" name. In 1487 Hugo Shakespeare wished to change his surname because "*vile reputatum est*"[5] (it was considered "low"). Similar obloquy was later heaped upon the name of Dickens.

The first mention of the name in English records is of "William Sakspeer" in 1248; he came from the village of Clopton, just a few miles outside Stratford. From the thirteenth century the name often occurs in Warwickshire records; it was a family name of long local settlement, in a literal sense part of the landscape. This may help to explain the rootedness of Shakespeare himself within English culture. Thomas Shakespere was living in Coventry in 1359. William Shakespere dwelled in the southern part of Balsall in 1385. Adam Shakespere was part of the manor of Baddesley Clinton in 1389. The religious guild of Knowle had as its members Richard and Alice Shakspere, in 1457, subsequently joined by Ralph Schakespeire in 1464. Thomas and Alice Shakespere, of Balsall, entered the same guild in 1486.

There are many other Shakespeares of later date in Balsall, Baddesley, Knowle, Wroxall and neighbouring villages; the names and dates provide clear evidence of an extended family of siblings and cousins living within a geographical area a few miles in extent. Many of them were part of the guild of Knowle, fulfilling certain secular and religious obligations, and can therefore be considered good and observant Catholics. The prioress of the nuns' house in Wroxall in the first years of the sixteenth century was Isabella Shakespeare; in 1526 that position, in characteristically medieval fashion, was in turn granted to Jane Shakspere. It was from this cluster of Shakespeares that William Shakespeare's immediate ancestors came.

His grandfather, Richard Shakespeare, was a farmer of Snitterfield, a village four miles north of Stratford. He was the son either of John

Shakeschaffte of Balsall, or of Adam Shakespere of Baddesley Clinton; whatever his exact paternity, his origin is clear. He was an affluent farmer, commonly known as a husbandman, with two sets of land in the vicinity. Snitterfield itself was a scattered parish with a church and manor-house, ancient farmhouses and cottages, presiding over a mixed landscape of woodland and pasture, heath and meadow. This was the landscape for part of the dramatist's childhood.

There was a further familial bond. Richard Shakespeare's house and grounds were leased from Robert Arden, the father of Mary Arden, whom John Shakespeare later married. The dramatist's mother and father knew each other from an early age, therefore, and doubtless met in Richard Shakespeare's old house on the High Street whose land stretched down to a little brook. It had a hall and several bedchambers; by the standard of the time it was an imposing dwelling. John Shakespeare himself grew up in the life and atmosphere of the farm. He was born in 1529, the year that his father is first known in Snitterfield, and it seems likely that Richard Shakespeare moved to this area with his new wife and anticipated family.

Richard Shakespeare left in his will the sum of £38 17*s* 0*d*, which demonstrates that he was by the standard of his age and position living in modest affluence. He was fined on occasions, for not attending the manorial court and for not controlling his livestock or yoking his swine, but he was a man of some substance in the little community of Snitterfield. A friend of his living in Stratford, Thomas Atwood, bequeathed him a team of oxen. He sat on juries in order to appraise his neighbours' goods, and seems to have also been enrolled in the religious guild of Knowle. He was in that sense the image of the Shakespeare family itself, in its affluence, in its solidity, and also in its occasional recklessness. It is sometimes conjectured that Shakespeare sprang from a race of illiterate peasants, but that is emphatically not the case.

Shakespeare's father, John Shakespeare, embarked at an early age on a prosperous career. Although there were already Shakespeares settled in Stratford, he was a native of Snitterfield. His younger brother, Henry, remained a Snitterfield farmer, but John did not choose to work only in the family business. He wished to pursue other trades as well. He was, in the tradition of striving first sons, moving upwards through the world. His own son would follow him. John Shakespeare left the farm in order to be enrolled as an apprentice to a glover in Stratford. The most plausible candidate for his master is Thomas Dixon, who was the innkeeper of the Swan, at the bottom of Bridge Street, as well as a master glover. His wife came from Snitterfield.

John Shakespeare's apprenticeship lasted for seven years, and in the Stratford records of 1556 he was listed as a "glover." He was then twenty-seven, and he would already have pursued the trade for a few years. In later documents he is described as a "whittawer" or dresser of "tawed" or un-tanned white leather. He soaked and scraped the skins of horses and deer, sheep and hounds, before softening them with salt and alum; they were placed in pots of urine or excrement before being laid out in the garden to dry. It was a messy and smelly business. From the evidence of his drama Shakespeare had a pronounced aversion to unpleasant smells. When the skins had been rendered tender and pliant they were cut to pattern with knife and scissors as they assumed the shape of gloves, purses, belts and bags. They were then hung on a rod by the window in order to attract custom. Shakespeare often mentions the trade, and its products, in his plays. He knows the varieties of leather, from dog-skin to deer-skin, and lists the assortment of items that his father sold, from shoes of neat's leather to bridles of sheep's leather and the bags of sow-skin carried by tinkers. "Is not Parchment made of sheepe-skinnes?" Hamlet's question is answered by Horatio with a further refinement: "I, my Lord, and of Calues-skinnes to" (3082–3). Gloves, particularly those made of cheveril or kid-skin, are praised by Shakespeare for their softness; there are references to a "soft chiuerell Conscience" (*All Is True*, 996) and "a wit of cheuerell, that stretches from an ynch narrow, to an ell broad" (*Romeo and Juliet*, 1139–40). Shakespeare describes gloves continually, whether worn in the hat or thrown down as a pledge. In *The Merry Wives of Windsor*, Mistress Quickly remarks upon "a great round Beard, like a Glouer's pairing-knife." This is the language of close observation.

John Shakespeare had a ground-floor shop at the front of his house, looking out upon Henley Street, with outbuildings at the back for stretching and drying. He found employment here for one or two apprentices or "stitchers." His "sign" was a pair of glover's compasses. He also set up a stall on market-days by the High Cross, where the cheapest gloves sold at 4 pence a pair; lined and embroidered items were of course far more expensive. It would be interesting to see his eldest son helping to attract custom at this Thursday morning market; but on most weekday mornings he was at school. Nevertheless every business was in some sense a family business.

John Shakespeare was a member of the glovers' guild. The making and selling of gloves was a well-developed and thriving Stratford trade. Between 1570 and 1630, there were some twenty-three glovers in the town. But he had other occupations as well. He was still a yeoman farmer, and farmed land with his father in Snitterfield and with his younger brother in the neighbouring village of Ingon. Here he reared and slaughtered the animals whose skins were later converted into leather; hence derive later Stratford reports that Shakespeare's father was a butcher and that the young Shakespeare had become a butcher's apprentice. Behind all local legends, there lies a modicum of ascertainable fact. There are indeed a number of references to butchers and to butchery in Shakespeare's dramas, most notably connected with the relationship between sons and fathers; Shakespeare knows the various shades and textures of blood, as well as the "uncleanly sauours of a Slaughterhouse" (*King John*, 2002). There is a suggestive connection.

John Shakespeare, recorded in an official document as *"agricola"* or farmer, dealt in barley and in wool. He also traded in timber. It was perfectly natural, and proper, that a man should be possessed of many skills and trades. Of his business in wool-dealing, there is ample evidence. Like many other glovers he needed the skins and wished to pass on the fleece. Part of the house in Henley Street was known as "the Woolshop," and when a later tenant "re-laid the floors of the parlour, the remnants of wool, and the refuse of wool-combing, were found under the old flooring, imbedded with the earth of the foundation."[6] John Shakespeare sold 28-pound parcels of wool, or "tods," to mercers and clothiers in surrounding towns. The clown in *The Winter's Tale* does his arithmetic—"Let me see, euery Leauen-weather toddes, euery tod yeeldes pound and odde shilling: fifteene hundred shorne, what comes the wooll too?" (1508–9).

But, like other glovers, John Shakespeare also acted as an unlicensed wool-broker or "brogger"; information was laid against him in court that on two occasions he had illegally purchased wool at 14 shillings per "tod." His actions were illegal because he was not a member of the wool "Staple," a kind of guild, but more importantly he laid down the sums of £140 for one transaction and £70 for the other. These were very large amounts indeed. They suggest that John Shakespeare was a wealthy man.

That is why he could afford to speculate in property. He bought a house in Greenhill Street, just down the road from Henley Street, and rented it out. He bought two further houses, with gardens and orchards, for £40. He rented another house to one William Burbage, who may or may not have been related to the London acting family. Ordinary life is filled with coincidence.

He also lent money at an illegal rate of interest to his neighbours, a trade which passed under the unhappy name of "usury." The legal rate was 10 per cent, but John Shakespeare lent £100 to a business colleague at interest of 20 per cent, and a further £80 to another contemporary at the same rate. He charged the excess because it had become standard practice. He could get away with it, in other words. Money-lending was itself widely accepted, in a period where there were no banks or credit facilities, and it was even one in which his son engaged from time to time. According to one social historian such financial dealings were "extremely widespread,"[7] and in fact necessary for the smooth running of the community. Of usury William Harrison wrote that it is "practiced so commonly that he is accounted a fool that doth lend his money for nothing."[8] The sums in which John Shakespeare dealt were nevertheless very large. When observing his payment of £210 for wool, and his loans of £180, a contrast might be made with his father's entire estate amounting to less than £40. The son had far outstripped the affluence of his father. It was a tradition of striving that his own son would inherit.

So John Shakespeare was a canny and prosperous businessman. There has been much speculation, however, about his literacy. He signed with a mark rather than a signature, which suggests that he could not write. There is something deeply satisfying, to some commentators, in the prospect of the greatest writer in the history of the world springing from an illiterate family. It adds to the supposed drama. The fact that John Shakespeare could not write, however, does not necessarily imply that he could not read. Reading and writing were taught separately, and were considered to be different skills. It would in any case have been difficult for him to engage in his multifarious trades and businesses without being able to read. He was also left some books, in a bequest, which points towards the same conclusion.

And then there is the vexed question of his religion. For centuries scholars have argued over the possibility that Shakespeare's father was a secret adherent of the old faith. The question is confused by the perplexing circumstances of the time, when a person's professed faith might not have been his or her real faith and when there were nice distinctions and gradations in any religious observance. There were conflicting loyalties. You might be a Catholic who attended the reformed services for the sake of propriety, or to escape a fine; you might be a member of the new communion, yet one who loved the rituals and festivals of the old Church. You might be undecided, leaning one way and then another in the quest for certainty. You might have no real faith at all.

The evidence for John Shakespeare is similarly equivocal. He had his son baptised within the rites of the Anglican communion, and the minister Bretchgirdle was a Protestant. But John Shakespeare might also have concealed within the rafters of the roof at Henley Street an explicit "spiritual testament." There are many scholars who doubt the authenticity of this document, believing it to be a fabrication or a plant, but its provenance seems genuine enough. It has been shown to be a standard Roman Catholic production, distributed by Edmund Campion, who journeyed to Warwickshire in 1581 and stayed just a few miles from Stratford-upon-Avon. Campion himself was a Jesuit priest who had travelled from Rome on a secret and ultimately fatal mission to England, both to bolster the faith of native Catholics and to convert those who were wavering in their allegiance. Jesuit missionaries were not welcome in England, especially after the Pope's excommunication of Elizabeth in 1570, and Campion was eventually apprehended, tried and sentenced to death.

The spiritual testament found in Henley Street included John Shakespeare's obedience to "the Catholike, Romaine & Apostolicke Church" and invocations to the Virgin Mary and "my Angell guardian," as well as to the succour of "the holy sacrifice of the masse." It could not be a more orthodox or pious document. It was printed or transcribed, with blanks left for the specific details of the testator. Here John Shakespeare's mark or signature appeared, as well as the information that his particular patron saint was "saint Winifrede." This saint had her shrine in Holywell, Flintshire, which was a place of pilgrimage for the wealthier Catholic families of Warwickshire. If the testament is a forgery, only a well-informed forger would know the details of a local saint. More doubts are raised by the notation. If John Shakespeare could not write, then who added the reference to Winifred? Was there another member of the Shakespeare family who could read and write by 1581? There is one clue. In this Catholic testament there is reference to the danger that "I may be possibly cut off in the blossome of my sins." In *Hamlet* the ghost laments that he was "Cut off euen in the blossomes of my sinne" (693) and invokes the Catholic doctrine of purgatory. This ghost is of course that of the father.

The identity of the amanuensis must, however, remain a matter for speculation. But if we believe that the testament was signed by John Shakespeare, and then concealed in the attic of his house, the suggestion is that he was or had become a secret and practising Catholic. There are other pieces of evidence. His family history included pious ancestors, among them Dame Isabella and Dame Jane of the nuns' house in Wroxall. His wife, Mary Arden, also came from an old Catholic family. On several occasions he himself was included in lists of recusants "presented for not comminge monethlie to the Churche according to hir Majesties lawes." In this context, he may also have conveyed his properties to members of his family to avoid the possibility of confiscation.

On the other side of the argument is the contention that he would have subscribed to the oath of supremacy in order to take up various official posts in Stratford; he was also instrumental in ordering and overseeing the lime-washing of the religious imagery in the guild chapel as well as the removal of the "rood loft" or crucifixion scene. But he was an ambitious man, one of many sixteenth-century officials who continually balanced their careers against their convictions. He could fulfil his administrative duties on these occasions without necessarily compromising or admitting any deeply held private faith.

By 1552 John Shakespeare is recorded as a tenant or householder in Henley Street; at the age of twenty-three he had passed through his apprenticeship, and had set up business on his own account. In 1556 he purchased the ad-joining house in Henley Street that has since become known as the "Wool-shop." The two houses were eventually knocked together to create the comfortable and commodious house that survives still. In the same year he bought the tenement and garden in neighbouring Greenhill Street. He was expanding.

In the spring or summer of the following year he married Mary Arden, the daughter of his father's old landlord. In 1556, too, he began his slow rise in the Stratford hierarchy when he was appointed one of two "tasters." These were the borough officials who ensured the quality of the bread and ale purveyed in the district. He was moving forward on all fronts with his family, his business, and his civic career, being organised simultaneously.

He was fined for missing three meetings of the Stratford court, but that did not prevent him from being appointed as one of four "constables" in 1558. He was obliged to supervise the night watch, quell disturbances in the street and disarm those bent on an affray. It was not a sinecure and suggests that, at the age of twenty-nine, John Shakespeare was a person of consider-able respect among his neighbours. His judicial duties increased in the fol-lowing year, when he was appointed to be "affeeror" or fixer of fines. Within a short space of time came a greater honour, when he was elected as a burgess of Stratford; he now attended the monthly council meeting and was permitted to educate any of his sons at the King's New School free of charge. His first son, however, would not be born for another six years.

In 1561 he was elected as chamberlain, in charge of the property and revenues of the Stratford corporation; he filled that office for four years, in which period he supervised the building of a new schoolroom in the upper storey of the guildhall, where his son would one day be taught.

He was appointed as one of fourteen aldermen in 1565, the year after his son's birth. From this time forward he was addressed as "Master Shakespeare." On holy days and days of public festival he was obliged to wear a black cloth gown faced with fur; he also wore an aldermanic ring of agate that his young son knew very well. In *Romeo and Juliet* the playwright refers to "an Agot stone / on the forefinger of an Alderman" (515–16). And then in 1568 John Shakespeare reached the height of his civic ambition, when he was elected bailiff or mayor of Stratford. He exchanged his black robe for a scarlet gown. He was led to the guildhall by a serjeant bearing the mace of office. He sat with his family, now including the four-year-old William Shakespeare, in the front pew of the Church of the Holy Trinity. He was also a Justice of the Peace, presiding over the Court of Record. When his term of office expired in 1571 he was appointed high alderman and deputy to his successor as mayor; he was clearly held in great respect. The extant and sporadic records of council business suggest a man of tact and moderation–referring to his colleagues, for example, as a "brotherhode"–as well as one of sound judgement. We will see some of those virtues in his son. Like many other "self-made" men, however, he may also have been excessively confident in his own abilities. This was also a familial trait.

His younger brother, Henry, continued the family tradition of farming; he rented land in Snitterfield and in a neighbouring parish. What little is known of him suggests pugnacity and a certain independence of mind. He was fined for assaulting one of his close relations–the husband of one of Mary Arden's sisters–and in his eighties he was excommunicated from the church for failing to pay his tithes. He was also fined for breaching the Statute of Caps; he refused, in other words, to wear a cap on Sundays. He was fined on other occasions for various agricultural misdemeanours, and gaoled at different times for debt and for trespass. He was, perhaps, a "black sheep" in the Stratford farm landscape. But he exhibited a fierceness and hardiness that would inspire any young relative. Shakespeare might have inherited the vices of his uncle as well as the virtues of his father. Despite his reputation as a bad debtor Henry Shakespeare was good at acquiring and keeping his money. At his death a witness deposed that there was "plenty of money in his coffers"; his barns, too, were filled with corn and hay "of a great value."[9] Shakespeare came from a family of undoubted affluence, with all the ease and self-confidence that such affluence encourages.

CHAPTER 6

A Witty Mother, Witlesse Else Her Sonne

I *t is an undoubted fact,"* Charles Dickens once wrote, that "all remarkable men have remarkable mothers." In the lineaments of the mature William Shakespeare, then, we might see the outline of Mary Arden. She is a formidable figure. She could plausibly claim to be part of a family that extended beyond the Norman Conquest. The Ardens had been "Lords of Warwick" and one of their number, Turchillus de Eardene, was credited in the *Domesday Book* with vast extents of land.[1] The immediate beneficiaries of this wealth and gentility were the Ardens of Park Hall, in the north of the county of Warwickshire. They were a strongly Catholic family who were eventually harried and persecuted for their faith.

There is no proof that the Ardens of the village of Wilmcote were related to the wealthy landowners of Park Hall. In matters of lineage, however, what can be asserted or suggested is more important than that which can be proved. The shared surname was probably enough. It seems likely that the Ardens from whom Mary Arden was descended considered themselves to be connected, in however distant a fashion, with other branches of the Ardens and indeed with the grand families who were related to other Ardens—families such as the Sidneys and the Nevilles.

It has often been suggested that male actors are prone, in their earliest years, to identify with the mother; they internalise her behaviour and adopt her values. This at least is one explanation for the overriding concern for nobility and gentility in Shakespeare's subsequent drama; he was known for playing kingly roles, and the aristocratic world is at the heart of his design. Could his mother have taught him his fastidiousness and his disdain? In the quest for an alternative Shakespeare, it has often been suggested that the dramatist was actually a well-known aristocrat; among these hypothetical aliases can be found the seventeenth Earl of Oxford and the sixth Earl of Derby. So it is a matter of the greatest irony that Shakespeare may have already considered himself to be of noble stock. He may even be alluding to his parents' marriage at the beginning of *The Taming of the Shrew* (82–3):

> Since once he plaide a Farmers eldest sonne,
> "Twas where you woo'd the Gentlewoman so well.

Mary Arden's father, Robert Arden, was an affluent yeoman farmer who owned two farmhouses and possessed more than 150 acres of land. Of such farmers William Harrison wrote that they "commonlie live wealthilie, keepe good houses, and travel to get riches . . . and with grazing, frequenting of markets and keeping of servants do come to great welthe."[2] Robert Arden was in fact the most prosperous farmer, and the largest landowner, in Wilmcote. The village itself was three miles from Stratford, situated in cleared woodland; it was close to the very edge of the forest from which the family derived its name. The Ardens were nourished with a specific sense of belonging.

They lived here in a single-storey farmhouse, built at the beginning of the sixteenth century, with its barns and its cowsheds, its dovecote and its woodpiles, its pump and its apiary. Robert Arden possessed oxen and bullocks, horses and calves and colts and sheep, bees and poultry. There were plentiful quantities of barley and oats. Shakespeare's mother, just like Shakespeare's father, was brought up as an integral part of a working farm. This may be the best way of describing Robert Arden himself: he was of ancient farming stock, with pretensions to gentility.

An inventory of his possessions has survived. Among these were the farmhouse at Snitterfield, where Richard Shakespeare and his family had recently lived, as well as the house in Wilmcote. In that household there was a hall and a second chamber for sleeping, as well as a kitchen, but the accommodation was still somewhat cramped; Mary Arden had six sisters, and she grew up in an environment where there was much competition for attention and affection. In the inventory, too, there are references to table-boards and benches, cupboards and little tables in the hall or principal room; there were shelves, too, and three chairs. From these bare memoranda we can fill a sixteenth-century room in imagination. The second chamber contained a feather bed, two mattresses and seven pairs of sheets, as well as towels and tablecloths kept in two wooden coffers.

In the rooms were hung painted cloths for decoration and edification. These depicted classical or religious scenes, such as Daniel in the Lions' Den or the Siege of Troy, and would have dominated the interiors of this relatively modest farmhouse. Mary Arden was bequeathed at least one of these painted tapestries in her father's will, and it is most likely to have ended up on a wall in Henley Street. In *Macbeth* Shakespeare refers to the "Eye of Child-hood that feares a painted Deuill" (595–6), and Falstaff mentions "Lazarus in the painted cloth" (*1 Henry IV*, 2287).

When Mary Arden brought the painted cloth with her from her family home, and became the mistress of Henley Street, she was probably in her seventeenth or eighteenth year. Her husband was a decade older and already, as we have seen, a rising man. She was the youngest of Robert Arden's daughters, and may have some claim to being the most favoured. Alone among her kin she was left a specific piece of land. Her father bequeathed to her "all my lande in Willmecote cawlid Asbyes and the crop apone the grounde sowne and tyllide as hitt is."[3] From this we may deduce that she was dependable and practical. No farmer would leave land to an incompetent daughter. She was also healthy and vigorous, giving birth to many children and living to the age of sixty-eight. We may plausibly imagine her also to be energetic, intelligent and quick-witted; in a household of seven sisters she would also have learnt the virtues of tact and compliance. It is not known whether she was literate, but her mark upon a bond is well formed and even graceful. She could wield a pen in a single movement. Her private seal was of a galloping horse, an emblem of agility and industry. The fact that she had a seal at all is a sign of affluence and respectability. Shakespeare has left no record of her, but it has been surmised that her outlines can be glimpsed in a number of strong-minded mothers who appear in his dramas—Volumnia extolling Coriolanus's achievements, the Countess reminding Bertram of his duty, the Duchess of York berating King Richard. It is also possible, and indeed plausible, that the high-spirited and intelligent young women of the comedies owe something to the memories of his mother.

The family house in Henley Street can even now be seen; it is much changed, but still recognisable. It was originally two (or perhaps three) houses, each with a garden and an orchard. It was on the northern side of Henley Street, at the edge of the town, with its narrow rooms looking directly on to the thoroughfare; there was very little privacy. At the back of the house, beyond the garden, was an area known as the "Guild Pits" that was essentially a stretch of waste ground with a ramshackle road threading within it.

The house itself was erected at the beginning of the sixteenth century in the usual mode of oak timber frame with wattle-and-daub, and with a roof of thatch. The ceilings of the interiors were lime-washed, and the walls decorated with painted cloths or patterned all over with the use of wood-blocks. Its timbers were much lighter in colour than the "mock-Tudor" beams now characteristically stained black or dark brown. The plaster work would have been of light beige. The whole effect was of brightness or, at least, of lightness. The stark black and white of restored Tudor interiors is wrong; Shakespeare's contemporaries used much paler colours, and more subtly graded shades. The wooden furniture was of the standard household type, as already exemplified by Robert Arden's inventory—chairs and plain tables and jointstools (so called because the separate parts were joined together). The floors were of broken Wilmcote limestone, covered by rushes. If there were "carpets," they were used as covers for the table. There may have been a wall-cupboard to display dishes or plate. In *Romeo and Juliet* a servant calls out, "Away with the ioyntstooles, remove the Courtcubbert [cupboard], looke to the plate" (579–80).

It was a commodious house with six separate chambers, the lower and upper storeys connected with a ladder rather than a stairway. The hall was the principal room of the house, next to the front door and the cross-passage; there was a large fireplace here, and the Shakespeare family sat for their meals in front of it. There was a kitchen at the back of the house with its usual complements of a hand-turned spit, brass skillets and leathern bottles. Beside the hall was the parlour, a combined sitting room and bedroom where the bed itself was displayed as a prize specimen of household furniture. The walls here were heavily patterned and decorated. Across from the hall, on the other side of the passage, was John Shakespeare's workshop, where the labour of stitching and sewing was undertaken by him and his apprentices. It was also a shop trading with the outside world, with a casement opening on to the street, and as such had a different atmosphere from the rest of the house. From an early age Shakespeare knew all about the demands of the public. On the floor above there were three bedchambers. Shakespeare would have slept on a mattress of rush, stretched on cords between the wooden frame of the bed. In the attic rooms slept the servants and the apprentices. It was a large house for a tradesman and reinforces the note of affluence in all his father's affairs.

It was also a noisy house, a wooden sound-box in which a conversation in one part of the house could clearly be heard in another. The creaking of timber, and the noise of footsteps, would have been a constant accompaniment to household tasks. From Shakespeare's dramas, too, come the unmistakable impressions of childhood in Henley Street. There are images of stopped ovens and smoking lamps, of washing and scouring, of dusting and sweeping; there are many references to the preparation of food, to boiling and mincing and stewing and frying; there are allusions to badly prepared cakes and unsieved flour, to a rabbit being turned upon a spit and a pasty being "pinched." There are many references to what was considered to be women's work within the home, to knitting and to needlework. But there are also images of carpentering, of hooping and of joinery; these were the activities of the yard or of the outhouses at the back of John Shakespeare's property. No other Elizabethan dramatist employs so many domestic allusions. Shakespeare maintained a unique connection with his past.

That is why the natural world seems to impinge so directly upon him. The house in Stratford, like most others in the vicinity, had a garden and an orchard. The image of the garden occurs to him in many different contexts, whether that of the body or of the state. An ill-weeded garden is an image of decay. He knows of grafting and pruning, of digging and dunging. In *Romeo and Juliet* there is an image of a trailing plant being pressed down to the ground so that it will put forth fresh roots. This is not a scene, perhaps, that would have readily occurred to an urban writer. In all he alludes to 108 different plants. In his orchards hang apples and plums, grapes and apricots.

The flowers of his plays are native to the soil from which he came; the primrose and the violet, the wallflower and the daffodil, the cowslip and the rose, sprang up wild all around him. He need only shut his eyes to see them again. He uses the local names for the flowers of the meadow, such as Ophelia's crow-flowers and Lear's cuckoo-flowers; he uses the Warwickshire word for the pansy, love-in-idleness. He employs the local names of bilberry for the whortleberry and honey-stalks for stalks of clover. In that same dialect, too, a dandelion is a "golden lad" before becoming a "chimney sweeper" when its spore is cast upon the breeze. Thus, in *Cymbeline* (2214–15),

Golden Lads and Girles all must,
As Chimney-Sweepers, come to dust.

The words of his childhood surround him once more when he contemplates meadows and gardens.

No poet besides Chaucer has celebrated with such sweetness the enchantment of birds, whether it be the lark ascending or the little grebe diving, the plucky wren or the serene swan. He mentions some sixty species in total. He knows, for example, that the martlet builds its nest on exposed walls. Of the singing birds he notices the thrush and the ousel or blackbird. More ominous are the owl and raven, the crow and the maggot-pie. He knows them all, and has observed their course across the sky. The spectacle of birds in flight entrances him. He cannot bear the thought of their being trapped, or caught, or snared. He loves free energy and movement, as if they were in some instinctive sympathy with his own nature.

$\mathcal{B}$ut $\mathcal{T}$his $\mathcal{I}$s $\mathcal{W}$orshipfull $\mathcal{S}$ociety

here was a world beyond the house and garden of Henley Street. Stratford remained a deeply conservative and traditional society. At its centre was the small nuclear family, like that of the Shakespeares, which was closely knit and self-sustaining. Yet family was linked to family, and neighbour to neighbour, in organic fashion. A neighbour was more than the man, woman or child who lived in the same street. A neighbour was the one to whom you turned for support, in times of distress, and the one to whom you offered help in return. A neighbour was expected to be thrifty, hard-working and reliable.

Many inhabitants of Stratford were connected by marriage and kinship alliances so that the town itself might be viewed as an extended family. Friends were often known as "cousins" so that, for example, Shakespeare is noticed as "cousin Shakespeare" by those with whom he seems to have had no blood relationship. This also encouraged the ties of patronage and local community. In his capacity as mayor John Shakespeare was "father" to the town as well as to his more immediate progeny. The inheritance of place was a very powerful one. It encouraged a deep sense of settlement and of possession.

Henley Street may serve as an image of this relatively small and enclosed community. The traveller reached it from Bridge Street, passing the Swan and the Bear inns on either side of the thoroughfare; Bridge Street was divided into two by a line of buildings known as Middle Row. Fore Bridge Street and Back Bridge Street contained some of the more commodious shops as well as inns. By the High Cross, where John Shakespeare kept his stall on market-days, the street branched into Henley Street and a little south-ward into Wood Street. Henley Street itself contained shops, like that of John Shakespeare, cottages and houses. Like medieval streets in general, it was of mixed occupancy.

Shakespeare's immediate neighbour, east towards Bridge Street, was the tailor William Wedgewood. His tailor's shop was next to the glover's, in other words. He owned two other houses in the same stretch of street, but was eventually compelled to leave Stratford when it was discovered that he had "there married an other wife his first wife yet living." He was also ac-cused of being "very contencious prowde & slaunderous oft buseing himself with noughty matters & quarrelling with his honest neighbours."[1] So, living next door, he may have been difficult. The young Shakespeare must have soon become acquainted with the vagaries of human conduct.

Next to Wedgewood's house was the smithy of Richard Hornby who, among other things, forged the iron links to fasten local prisoners. He made use of the stream that ran past his house. The tailor Wedgewood and the smith Hornby seem to make an appearance in Shakespeare's *King John* (1815–18) when a citizen, Hubert, remarks that

> I saw a Smith stand with his hammer (thus)
> The whilst his Iron did on the Anuile coole,
> With open mouth swallowing a Taylors newes,
> Who with his Sheeres, and Measure in his hand . . .

It is a moment of observation snatched out of time.

Hornby had five children, and indeed the street was altogether filled with children. One Henley Street family had seven, and another had fourteen. As an infant Shakespeare could never have been alone. It is the open life of the towns memorialised in *Romeo and Juliet*, *The Two Gentlemen of Verona*, *The Taming of the Shrew*, and *The Merry Wives of Windsor*. It irradiates the Venice of *Othello* and the Ephesus of *The Comedy of Errors*.

On the further side of the stream resided another glover, Gilbert Bradley. Since he became godfather to one of John Shakespeare's other sons, it may be assumed that theirs was a friendly rivalry. Further down the street lived George Whateley, a woollen-draper, who was wealthy enough to en-dow a small school at the time of his death. He was a Roman Catholic, and two of his brothers became fugitive priests. Next to him was the haberdasher, and Shakespeare's godfather, William Smith, who had five sons. Just beyond his shop, across the road at the corner of Fore Bridge Street, was the Angel Inn. It was owned and managed by the Cawdrey family, who were also staunch Catholics; one of their sons trained as a Jesuit priest in exile. This was a close community in every sense.

So the northern side of Henley Street was populated by clothiers of one kind or another, and is a token of that clustering of trades that took place in most market towns. Shakespeare grew up in an atmosphere of animated business. On the western end of the street John Shakespeare's closest neighbour was another Catholic, George Badger, a woollen-draper whose principal business was in Sheep Street. He was elected as an alderman but was deprived of his office; he was even sent to prison because of his staunch Catholicism. His was not a model that John Shakespeare chose to follow. Beyond Badger lived a yeoman farmer, John Ichiver, about whom little is known. There were other neighbours in Henley Street. There were six shepherds' families, for example, two of whom, the Cox and the Davies families, lived directly opposite the Shakespeares. John Cox was well known to the Hathaways, soon to be mingled with the Shakespeares. The shepherds in Shakespeare's plays are not some pastoral invention.

On the same side of the street resided Thomas a Pryce, a "mettle-man" or tinker. John Shakespeare stood surety for his son when the young man was charged with a felony. Here also lived John Wheeler, an alderman and recusant Catholic; he owned four houses in the street as well as tenements elsewhere. There was also a wool merchant, Rafe Shaw, whose goods John Shakespeare appraised, and Peter Smart, whose son became a tailor. Already we can see the outlines of a close community, with many familial as well as religious and mercantile ties.

It would be otiose to prepare a roll-call of the townspeople of Stratford, except to the extent that they emerge in Shakespeare's own life. So we find the Quineys, for example, visiting the dramatist in London and calling him "loving good friend and countryman." One of them eventually married Shakespeare's younger daughter, Judith, and so we can presume some degree of intimacy. They were fierce Catholics married into the Badger family who, as we have seen, owned a house next door to John Shakespeare. Adrian Quiney was a grocer who lived on the High Street and who was three times mayor of Stratford. In that capacity he knew John Shakespeare very well. It was his son, Richard, who formed the friendship with Shakespeare; the dramatist was probably godfather to his child, baptised William.

The Quineys also married into another family, the Sadlers, who were in turn closely connected with the Shakespeares. John Sadler, who lived in Church Street, was the owner of several mills and barns in Stratford; he was also a landowner and proprietor of the Bear Inn in Stratford. He had been bailiff of the town, and John Shakespeare voted for his second term.

The Bear Inn was eventually sold to the Nash family of Stratford; they too were Catholic, and they also married into the Shakespeare family. The host of the Bear Inn, Thomas Barber, was also a Catholic. A few months before his death Shakespeare was concerned to protect "Master Barber's interest." It is important to recognise the line of sympathies and affiliations beneath the surface of Stratford life. A kinsman of John Sadler, Roger Sadler, was also a baker; when he died, money was owed to him both by John Shakespeare and by Thomas Hathaway.

A member of the Combe family left money to Shakespeare in his will, and in turn Shakespeare bequeathed another Combe his sword. It may have been the ceremonial sword that he wore on state occasions, in his somewhat unlikely position as Groom of His Majesty's Chamber, and therefore of some value. The Combes sold land to the dramatist, and shared with him an income from certain tithes. It was, in other words, a close-knit collaboration between two families. The Combes were described as "one of the leading Catholic families of Warwickshire,"[2] but they also serve as an example of the conflicting religious commitments of the era; of two brothers, one was a Catholic and one a Protestant. There was also a family tradition of money-lending, not unknown among wealthy Stratfordians, as we have seen, and Shakespeare is popularly believed to have written some doggerel on the subject that was placed on the grave of John Combe.

In his last will and testament, drawn up as he lay dying in his home town, Shakespeare left 26s 8d each to Anthony Nash and John Nash, for the purchase of memorial rings. Anthony Nash farmed the tithe land that Shakespeare owned, and was close enough to him to act as his representative in various Stratford dealings. John Nash, too, acted as a witness on his behalf. They were Catholics who in characteristic fashion entered the network of marriage and kinship with the Quineys and the Combes and of course the Shakespeares. Anthony Nash's son married Shakespeare's granddaughter.

The dying dramatist left the same amount to "Hamlett" Sadler, as he calls him, and to William Reynolds. Reynolds was a fervent Catholic who shared prison with George Badger for his beliefs. A priest in disguise found refuge from his pursuers in Reynolds's house. Shakespeare also left 20 shillings in gold to his godson, William Walker; he was the son of Henry Walker, a mercer and alderman who lived on the High Street. In the way of such things, his grandfather was very well acquainted with Shakespeare's grandfather. Among the witnesses to the will was one Julius or July Shaw, a trader in wool and malt who lived on Chapel Street. His father, also a wool-dealer, had known John Shakespeare very well. So we have a group of generally affluent and no doubt sharp-witted businessmen, bluff enough but straightforward and practical. They must have been shrewd judges of markets and of people, used to saving money and driving bargains. This was the solution in which Shakespeare was formed.

So Stratford contained a very large Catholic constituency of which the Shakespeares were a part. This does not necessarily imply that Shakespeare himself professed that faith–assuming that he professed any–only that he found the company of Catholics familiar. It seems in certain respects to have been a clannish society. The family of Nicholas Lane, a Catholic landowner who lent money both to John and to Henry Shakespeare, bought their clothes from a Catholic tailor in Wood Street.[3] In the same context, therefore, it also seems likely that affluent Catholics preferred to lend money to their co-religionists. In later years Shakespeare purchased his great house from a Catholic, William Underhill, who was compelled to sell as a result of the vast sums of money he had expended on recusancy fines. We may see in Shakespeare's purchase a mixture of shrewd commercial calculation and semi-fraternal sympathy.

On any conservative reckoning it is possible to identify some thirty Catholic families within the town, and of course the available records are by their nature incomplete and inconclusive. There would have been many more papists, who concealed their private beliefs from the local authorities. They became, in the language of the day, "church papists" whose attendance at the Protestant churches masked their true faith. It has been speculated that the majority of churchgoers in Stratford were of this sort.

The religious situation in Stratford was in any case well known. Hugh Latimer, the reformer and Bishop of Worcester, declared that Stratford lay at "the blind end" of his diocese, and one of Latimer's colleagues confirmed that in Warwickshire "great Parishes and market Townes [are] utterly destitute of God's word."[4] One of his successors, John Whitgift, complained in 1577 that in the area around Stratford he could obtain no information on recusants; in a tolerant and like-minded community, neighbour would not denounce neighbour. The papistical images in the guild chapel were lime-washed, on the orders of John Shakespeare, more than four years after a royal injunction had ordered their removal. It only finally occurred after the leading Catholic family in the town, the Cloptons, had fled abroad for safety. In any case the lime-washing of the offending images was hardly in direct obedience with the administrative injunction to "utterly extinct and destroy" such images so that "there remains no memory of the same." John Shake-speare merely covered them over, perhaps in the hope of better days.

Lying concealed upon the walls of the chapel were depictions of two lo-cal Saxon saints, Edmund and Modwena, for those who wished to celebrate the blessedness of their region; there was a fresco of the martyrdom of Thomas Becket, while kneeling at the altar of St. Benedict in Canterbury; there was a painting of St. George in mortal combat with the dragon, a princess standing behind him. Here also were images of angels and of dev-ils, saints and dragons, monarchs and armed men in battle. Here in this Strat-ford chapel were hidden the images of the Catholic world. We will see some of them freshly revealed within Shakespeare's plays.

Certain of Shakespeare's schoolteachers were Catholic. If John Shake-speare had indeed espoused Catholicism, his example shows there was no hindrance to high office in the town, which in turn suggests a measure of qui-escence or even sympathy among its leading citizens. But it represented a fragile compromise. External legislation, and the presence of religious com-missioners, could create tensions within the community. Overtly partisan steps, like the concealment of renegade priests, could cause serious problems for those concerned. And in any case the general drift of the time was to-wards a grudging acceptance of the new religion and the steady abandon-ment of the practices of the old faith. By the early seventeenth century Stratford had become notably more Protestant in tendency. The town was never ruled by "precise fools" or "Scripture men," as the more formidable Puritans were known, but it eventually came to accept the ambiguous ortho-doxy of the Church of England. Yet in the latter half of the sixteenth century, despite royal injunctions and local purges, fines and sequestrations and imprisonments, the persistence of the Catholic faith in the town can clearly be seen.

This might have had a direct effect upon the Shakespeare household in one important sense. The dislike of the reformed religion meant that piety was transferred from the Church to the family. The children might now be obliged to attend the new forms of worship and listen to Elizabethan homilies. But the lessons of the old faith, and the rites of the once popular religion, might still be taught and practised in the home. It was the place of safety. Since Shakespeare's eldest daughter, Susannah, remained a firm and prominent Catholic all of her life, can it be assumed that the Shakespeares themselves retained this familial tradition of inherited piety? It has been inferred that the community of Catholics was matriarchal in tendency, and that the woman's "inferior legal and public identity afforded her a superior devotional status, a fuller membership of the Catholic Church."[5] Since the old faith is likely to have been transmitted through the women of the household, it throws an interesting light upon Shakespeare's attitude towards his closest female relations.

CHAPTER 8

I Am a Kind of Burre, I Shal Sticke

here are some human beliefs that lie below the level of professed faith and orthodoxy. As a child Shakespeare learned of the witches who created storms and of the Welsh fairies who hid in foxgloves. "Queene Mab" of *Romeo and Juliet* is derived from the Celtic word, *mab*, meaning infant or little one. There is a Warwickshire term, "mab-led," signifying madness. Shakespeare knew of the toad with the medicinal jewel in its head, and of the man in the moon who carried a bundle of thorns. In the Forest of Arden, as his mother might have told him, there were ghosts and goblins. "A sad Tale's best for Winter," says the unfortunate child Mamillius in *The Winter's Tale*, "I haue one of Sprights and Goblins" (538–9). All his life Shakespeare had a very English sense of the supernatural and the marvellous, a predilection that goes hand in hand with a taste for horror and sensationalism in all of its forms. He brings ghosts into the history plays, and witches into *Macbeth*. The plots of the fairy stories can be glimpsed in his adult drama. *Pericles* is one of the old tales told round the hearth. In similar fashion ballads and folk tales charge the plot of *The Taming of the Shrew*. They were part of his Stratford inheritance.

The zealots of the reformed Church were not well disposed towards such idolatrous relics as maypoles and church ales, but local observances survived their displeasure. The bells rang out on Shrove Tuesday, and on the feast of St. Valentine the boys sang for apples; on Good Friday the labourers planted their potatoes and on the morning of Easter Day the young men went out to hunt hares. There were "whitsun lords" in Warwickshire as late as 1580, together with all the panoply of mumming and morris-dancing. The pageant of St. George and the Dragon, for example, was performed on the streets of Stratford every year. Shakespeare saw the sheep-shearing feasts at Snitterfield, and resurrected one of them in *The Winter's Tale*. The May-games of his youth return in *A Midsummer Night's Dream*. This is not some saga of "merry England," but the very fabric of life in a conservative and rit-ualised society immediately before the permanent changes induced by the re-formation of religion.

The stray details of that enduring life emerge in a hundred different con-texts. Real names of places and of people are enlisted in Shakespeare's drama. His aunt lived in the hamlet of Barton-on-the-Heath, and it rises again as Burton-Heath in *The Taming of the Shrew*; Wilmcote becomes Win-cot. The names of William Fluellen and George Bardolph are found in a list of Stratford recusants, beside that of John Shakespeare. His father also en-gaged in business with two wool-dealers, George Vizer of Woodmancote (locally pronounced Woncote) and Perkes of Stinchcombe Hill, and they reappear in a line from *Henry IV, Part Two*. "I beseech you sir to countenance William Visor of Woncote against Clement Perkes a' th hill" (2725–6). In the play Visor is described as an "arrant knave," which may suggest some famil-ial dispute with him.

The words and phrases of Shakespeare's childhood are recalled in his writing. He uses "fap" to mean drunk, "third-borough" for constable, and "aroynt" for leave. There is also the matter of pronunciation. The sound of the language spoken by Shakespeare in his native county was nearer to Saxon than to Norman French, as if its original powers had not been dispelled by the culture of the conquerors. You would have heard the Saxon origins in words pronounced as "blewe" and "deawe," "emonges" and "ouglie," "to-gyther" and "woork." Extra consonants were added to lend emphasis to cer-tain words, in "chardge" and "mariadge," "priviledge" and "pidgeon," "sutch" and "druncke." They appear, too, in "whote" and "womand," "dogge" and "dinne," "drumme" and "sinne." The language of Shake-speare's region was thicker and more resonant than that of London. Vowels were lengthened, too, in "hond" and "husbond," "tyme" and "wyde," "fair-nesse" and "wantonesse." A similar variousness and richness are found in "marrie" and "wittie," "dutious" and "outragious," "heretique" and "reumatique."

This was the language that Shakespeare spoke as a child. It was immediately recognisable as a country accent, and he may have endeavoured to lose it on his arrival in London. His characters are, after all, engaged in a perpetual act of performance and re-invention. But there was then no "standard" English. He used his Stratford idiom in his writing, for example, although the fussiness of successive printers and editors has curbed and flattened his native sonority. Any standardisation or modernisation of Shakespeare's language robs it of half its strength; a shadow is not as dim and veiled as a "shaddowwe," a cuckoo does not sing like a "kuckow," and music is not as enchanting as "musique." In the old language we can still hear Shakespeare talking.

Shakespeare understood the country very well, with what Edgar in King Lear calls its "low fermes / Poore pelting villages, sheep-coates and milles" (1190–1), but his debt to the Stratford of his childhood is particular and profound. He knew the channels that drew off the Avon floods and the conies that come out of their burrows after the rain, the fragile mulberries and the "Tradesmen singing in their shops." The fact that, all his life, he invested in the lands and properties of the immediate neighbourhood testifies to the hold Stratford exerted upon him. It was the site of his earliest ambitions and expectations and, as we shall see, he wished to restore the fortunes of the Shakespeares there through his personal achievement. He wanted to reassert his father's name among his fellow townsmen. Stratford was also the permanent home of his family, and the place to which he returned at the end of his life. It remained the centre of his being.

CHAPTER 9

This Prettie Lad Will Proue Our Countries Blisse

n the late sixteenth century, children were customarily trained by means of strict discipline. A boy would take off his cap before addressing his elders and would wait upon his parents at table, standing rather than sitting during the meal. He rose early and recited the morning's prayers; he washed his hands and face, combed his hair, and then went downstairs where he knelt for his parents' blessing before breakfast. He would commonly address his father as "sir," although "dad" does appear in one of Shakespeare's plays. "Dad" is in fact the formal Welsh word for father, and therefore part of the border patois that Shakespeare knew very well.

Twentieth-century sociologists have emphasised the severity of the sixteenth-century household, where patriarchal authority was dominant and where repression or punishment was the most convenient means of dealing with children of either sex. There must be room for doubt in such a broad analysis, however, and Shakespeare's plays themselves are often concerned with the failure of parental authority. The children can become "unruly" or "unbridled"; the rod of birch is "more mock'd than fear'd." Shakespeare's children are in any case observant and serious, sharp-eyed and often sharp-tongued; they demonstrate respect and obedience, but there is no hint of fear or subservience. In his drama, too, father and son are generally placed in amicable or idealised relationship. So we may prefer the testimony of the dramatist to the speculations of the sociologist.

If there is one aspect of a writer's life that cannot be concealed, it is childhood. It arises unbidden and unannounced in a hundred different contexts. It cannot be denied or misrepresented without severe psychic disturbance on the surface of the writing. It is the very source of the writing itself, and must necessarily remain undefiled. It is of the utmost interest, then, that the children of Shakespeare's plays are all equally precocious and acute, possessing great confidence in themselves. They are sometimes "wayward" and "impatient." They are also oddly aware and articulate, talking to their elders without any sign of strain or inferiority. In *Richard III* one of the little princes, soon to be despatched to an unhappy end, is described (1580–1) by his malevolent uncle as

> Bold, quicke, ingenious, forward, capable,
> He is all the mothers, from the top to toe.

It has become customary to place the young Shakespeare in the conventional Elizabethan world of childhood, engaged in games such as penny-prick or shovel-board, harry-racket or barley-break; in his own plays Shakespeare mentions football and bowls, prisoner's base and hide-and-seek, as well as the rural games of muss and dun in the mire. He even mentions chess, although he does not appear to know its rules. But it is likely that he was in certain respects an odd child. He was precocious, too, and observant; but he was one who stood apart.

There can be no doubt at all that he devoured books. Much of his early reading comes back in his drama. Has there ever been a great writer who did not spend a childhood in books? He alludes to Malory's *Morte d'Arthur*, so beloved by Mistress Quickly, and the old English romances of Sir Degore and Sir Eglamour and Bevis of Southampton. Master Slender lends Alice Shortcake *The Book of Riddels* and Beatrice refers to *The Hundred Merry Tales*. Some of his earlier biographers concur that he possessed a copy of William Painter's *The Palace of Pleasure* and Richard Robinson's translation of *Gesta Romanorum*, the legends of which form the staple of some of his plots. For similar reasons the young Shakespeare has been pictured turning the pages of Copland's *Kynge Appolyne of Thyre*, Hawes's *Pass Tyme of Pleasure* and Bochas's *The Tragedies of all such Princes as fell from theyr Estates*. There were also the folk stories and the fairy tales of his neighbourhood, given so long a lease on life in his late plays.

· · ·

Mary Arden's own role in Henley Street was of course central. With the help of a servant she was obliged to wash and to wring, to make and to mend, to bake and to brew, to measure the malt and the corn, to tend to the garden and the dairy, to spin with her distaff, to clothe the children and to prepare the meals, to distil the wines and dye the cloths, to "dresse up thy dysshe bord, and set al thynges in good order within thy house."[1] As a girl growing up on the Arden farm she would have in addition been accustomed to milk the cows, to skim the milk, to make butter and cheese, to feed the pigs and the poultry, to winnow the corn and make hay. She would have been expected to be practical and capable.

A brother was born in Shakespeare's third year. Gilbert Shakespeare was baptised in the autumn of 1566, and nothing much more is ever heard of him. He died at the age of forty-five, having had an unremarkable life as a trades-man in Stratford; it was inevitable that he followed his father's profession as a glover. He was in essence the dutiful son. But how much more formidable and threatening might he have seemed to the infant Shakespeare on his first appearance into the world? Other sons followed with the curiously coinci-dental names of two of Shakespeare's villains, Richard and Edmund, and there were two daughters, Joan and Anne.

More than any other dramatist of his period Shakespeare is concerned with the family; the nature and continuity of the family are invested with the utmost resonance, and can become a metaphor for human society itself. In his plays violence erupts between brothers more frequently than between fathers and sons. The father may be weak or self-serving, but he is never the target of hostility or revenge.

Much attention has been paid instead to the nature of sibling rivalry in Shakespeare's plays, more specifically to the pattern of the younger brother usurping the place of the older. Edmund replaces Edgar in his father's affec-tions, and Richard III mounts upon the bodies of his siblings. The Wars of the Roses, as recounted by Shakespeare, can be regarded as a war between brothers. Claudius murders his brother, and Antonio conspires against Pros-pero. There are other variations upon this sensitive subject. Shakespeare refers to the murder of Abel by his younger brother, Cain, on twenty-five separate occasions. There is also the pervasive presence of envy and jealousy, most aptly captured in the fear of betrayal manifested by characters as di-verse as Leontes and Othello. It is one of Shakespeare's great themes. The biographer should resist the comfortable position of an armchair psycholo-gist, but the connections are at least suggestive. Rivalry between brothers emerges as effortlessly and instinctively in his drama as if it were a principle of composition.

The conditions in the Shakespeare household were of course wrapped in the vital tedium of daily life, beyond the purview of the dramatic imagination. There are, however, stray intimations of status and aspiration. In 1568, the year he became mayor or bailiff of Stratford, John Shakespeare applied for a coat of arms. It was natural, and practical, for a mayor to have a coat of arms for various memorials and banners. Now that he was appointed to high civic office he was able to seal his prominence by becoming a gentleman. Those known as gentlemen were "those whome their race and blood or at least their virtues doo make noble and knowne."[2] They comprised some 2 per cent of the population.

John Shakespeare wished to be enlisted in this "register of the Gentle and Noble"[3] and, to qualify, he would need to demonstrate that he owned property and goods to the value of £250 and that he lived without the taint of manual labour; his wife was supposed to "dress well" and "to keep servants."[4] He presented a pattern for his coat of arms to the College of Heralds, and his application was duly noted. The formula for his arms contained a falcon, a shield and a spear embossed in gold and silver; the falcon is shaking its wings, and holds a spear of gold in its right talon. Hence we interpret "shake spear." The motto accompanying the device is "*Non Sanẑ Droict*" or "Not Without Right." It is a bold assertion of gentility. For unknown reasons, however, John Shakespeare did not proceed with his application. He may have been unwilling to pay the heralds' large fees. Or he may have had only a passing interest in what seems essentially to have been a civic duty.

But then, twenty-eight years later, his son arranged it for him. William Shakespeare renewed his father's application, with the original coat of arms, and succeeded. At last his father was a gentleman. But if it had been a long-cherished ambition, it may have been done partly to please his mother. He was upholding his mother's claims to gentility.

What Sees Thou There?

n 1569 the theatre came to Stratford. Under the auspices of John Shakespeare, the mayor, the new players of London were allowed to perform in the guildhall and in the inn-yards of the town. It is an important moment in Shakespeare's own history, too, when the five-year-old boy was first able to witness the world of pageantry and seeming. His father invited two sets of players to entertain the town, the Queen's Men and the Earl of Worcester's Men. It would indeed have been all-round entertainment complete with music and dancing, singing and "tumbling"; actors were also expected to be minstrels and acrobats. There were dumb-shows, and speeches, and pageants with drums and trumpets. There were duels and wrestlings. How much the young Shakespeare saw, or remembered, is an open question. But there is testimony from an exact contemporary who witnessed the players in Gloucester. He recalled that "at suche a play, my father tooke me with him and made mee stand between his legges, as he sate upon one of the benches, where we saw and heard very well." It was a play of king and courtiers, of songs and transformations and colourful costumes. This contemporary goes on to say that "this sight took such impression in me that when I came towards mans estate, *it was as fresh in my memory as if I had seen it newly acted.*"[1]

There were many more opportunities for Shakespeare and his contemporaries to see the London players. Ten groups of them came to Stratford over the next few years, as part of their touring "circuit." In one year alone five companies passed through. The Queen's Men visited the town three times, and the Earl of Worcester's Men travelled here on six separate occasions. There were performances by the Earl of Warwick's Men, the Earl of Oxford's Men, the Earl of Essex's Men and several other groups of travelling players. They generally comprised companies of seven or eight, unlike the earlier players who numbered three men, a boy and a dog. The young Shakespeare would have been able to watch the best of the London troupes, therefore, imbibing the poetry and the spectacle of the emerging stage. The names of some of the plays in performance convey perhaps the atmosphere of the period—*A Marriage Between Wit and Wisdom, Cambises, Horestes, Enough Is as Good as a Feast, Damon and Pithias, The Longer Thou Livest The More Fool Thou Art* are only some of a number of dramas that poured forth from the newly secularised profession of play-writing. The playwrights took their material from anything and everything—from histories to collections of romance, from the classical plays performed at the Inns of Court to popular burlesque, from spiritual allegory to fantastic legend. It was a world of witty repartee and declamation, but it was also a world of imaginary countries and mysterious islands, of strange seas and caverns, of unvarnished evil and unearthly goodness, of dramatic lament and generally exaggerated feeling. The young Shakespeare could watch these plays unfolding before him. He would inevitably, if unconsciously, acquire a sense of dramatic space and an ear for heightened dialogue or for declamations. It is appropriate that the English drama was coming to slow maturity in the same period as Shakespeare himself; they were both children of their time, sharing a newly awakened sense of possible achievement.

There were other forms of dramatic entertainment in Stratford. Whitsun "pastimes," for example, were still being devised in 1583 by Davy Jones, a relative of the Shakespeares by marriage. These were mumming plays with plenty of ritual and symbolic action. Costumes and masks were worn; the characters were given names such as Big Head or Pickle Herring, while the action itself was concerned with slayings and miraculous healings. In *Return of the Native* Thomas Hardy describes what must have been one of the last true mummers' plays, with a battle between St. George and a Turkish knight.

It is also likely that John Shakespeare took his son to Coventry, only twenty miles away, to witness the celebrated cycle of mystery plays performed in that city. They were not formally discontinued until Shakespeare had reached his fifteenth year. In five separate dramatic passages Shakespeare mentions the performances of the popular stage villain of these religious entertainments, King Herod. He also uses the expression "All hail" as a harbinger of unfortunate events. In the New Testament Jesus uses this form of address as a blessing. But in the mystery plays it is given to Judas as a sign of threat, on greeting Christ before betraying him. We can infer that Shakespeare has picked up the unhappy connotations of the phrase from watching the mystery plays. So he was acquainted with the pageant wagons and their epic cycle, from Creation to Judgement. He heard the vulgar comedy of the "low" characters and the refined sentiments of their superiors. He saw the characteristic mingling of farce and spirituality, piety and pantomime; he listened to the mixture of lyrical songs and pounding pentameter, of Latinate diction and Anglo-Saxon demotic. It was an inclusive drama containing no less than the history of the world and the character of its peoples, played out against the background of eternity. It has often been suggested that some of the power of Shakespeare's history plays is derived from his use of the elements of Christ's Passion that he would have witnessed in the mysteries; the whole notion of his cyclical dramas, taking in so much of the history of the kingdom, seems a direct reflection of his earliest dramatic experiences.

Shakespeare himself refers to the "Death Mouth," the portal of Hell constructed for the mingled fascination and alarm of the populace. The "Porter of Hell," who played a large part in the mystery plays, re-emerges as the Porter in *Macbeth*. Critics have discerned parallels between the mystery plays and the plots of *Lear*, *Othello* and *Macbeth*. The baiting of Jesus reappears in *Julius Caesar* and *Coriolanus*. Shakespeare's was the last era of the medieval mysteries. Yet throughout the history of English culture we see continuity rather than closure. Part of that continuity lies in the achievement of Shakespeare himself, who conveyed all the enchantment, ambiguity and passion of the old religious drama within the new forms of theatre. The masques in his plays are medieval in inspiration, as are the names of such characters as Slender and Shallow and Benvolio. One of Shakespeare's last plays, *Pericles*, reverts to the medieval pageant form of the miracles. If he had not seen one when he was a child, then his is indeed a miracle of reinvention.

CHAPTER 11

ℐ Sommon 𝒰p ℛemembrance
of 𝒯hings 𝒫ast

And when Davy Jones performed the Whitsun pastimes in front of
the people of Stratford, was his young relative a part of the
cast? The first accounts of his life suggest that in his youth
Shakespeare was already an aspiring actor. In 1681 John Aubrey reports that
"I have been told heretofore by some of the neighbours, that when he was a
boy he exercised his father's Trade, but when he kill'd a Calfe, he would do
it in a *high style*, and make a Speech."[1] The "neighbours" may by the time
of Aubrey's visit have realised that their town had harboured a famous
actor and tragedian, and shaped their memories accordingly; Aubrey
himself is in any case a most unreliable narrator. It has often been proved,
however, that behind the most fanciful account there lies a substratum of
truth. And there may be a piece of authenticity even here. The act of
"killing a calf" was in fact a dramatic improvisation performed by itin-
erant players at fairs or festivals; it was a form of shadow-play behind a
cloth and in the accounts of the royal household in 1521 there is a payment to a man for "killing of a calfe before my ladys grace behynde a
clothe." (It is interesting that the image of the arras or cloth is a
leitmotif in Shakespearian drama.) If there is a true memory in the neighbours' reminiscences, therefore, it would be that of the young Shakespeare
acting.

There is nothing so unusual in that. We are told that the young Molière–the actor and dramatist whom Shakespeare most closely resembles–was a "born actor."[2] Dickens, with whom there are other similarities to Shakespeare, confessed that he had been an actor from his earliest childhood. The idea of acting here is not simply one of histrionics or bravado; it means the ability and the desire to perform in front of other people. It may represent a longing to be free of restricting circumstance, an urge towards more powerful or more interesting status, what Ulysses in *Troilus and Cressida* describes as the "spirit" that "in aspiration lifts him from the earth" (2453–4). That is why there are various speculations about the young Shakespeare joining a group of travelling players, during one of their sojourns in Stratford, before accompanying them to London.

There was a tradition and an expectation, however, that the son of a "rising" family would attend the local petty or elementary school as preparation for more orthodox educational advancement. There seems no reason to doubt that this was the case with the five- or six-year-old Shakespeare, who would then become acquainted with the delights of reading, writing and arithmetic. In later life he generally practised a "secretary hand" very close to the one used as a model in the first English book on handwriting. If his mother had already taught him to read, then he could go on to sample the primer and the catechism. These were primarily works of moral and religious instruction, containing the Lord's Prayer and the Creed, the Ten Commandments and daily prayers, as well as assorted graces and metrical psalms. It is interesting that the schoolmaster or "pedant" he satirises in *Love's Labour's Lost* is the master of a petty school who "teaches boyes the Horne-booke" (1649). A hornbook was used in the very first stages of learning. It was a wooden tablet, supporting a paper protected by thin horn, on which were printed the alphabet, the vowels, certain syllables and the Lord's Prayer. Shakespeare's imagination reverts to this early schooling also in *Twelfth Night*, where Maria refers to "a Pedant that keepes a Schoole i' th' Church" (1419–20). The petty school at Stratford was in fact held in the guild chapel, and was supervised by the assistant to the schoolmaster known as the usher.

The church was the site of his early learning. At the age of five or six he would have been expected to attend the sermons and the reading of the homilies, about which he might be questioned by his master; these latter were the doctrines of the Church and state as approved by the queen and privy council. They were essentially lessons in good Elizabethan citizenship and, as such, were later redeployed by Shakespeare in his history plays. In the *Book of Homilies*, published in 1574, there is, for example, an oration "Against Disobedience and Wilful Rebellion" which might be the sub-text for the three dramas concerning Henry VI. Even as a small boy Shakespeare must have been aware of the disparity between his familial religion and the orthodox pieties of the Stratford church; it was a difference of atmosphere more than doctrine, perhaps, but when two faiths compete the alert child will learn the power as well as the emptiness of words.

Somehow or other, he came to know the Bible very well. He may have been blessed with a singularly retentive memory rather than any more religious capacity, but it is one of his most significant sources. He knew the popular Geneva Bible and the later Bishops' Bible, with a marked preference for the vigorous expressiveness of the former. It was known to be the household Bible, familiar to the folk of Stratford, and many phrases from his plays bear a striking resemblance to the language of this version. It has been calculated that he refers to forty-two of its books, but there is one anomaly. He prefers the beginnings of books, or scriptures, to their conclusions. He quotes extensively from the first four chapters of Genesis and in the New Testament he is most familiar with chapters 1 to 7 of Matthew. The same is often true of his secular reading—he is most at home with the first two books of Ovid's *Metamorphoses*—and it leads to the conclusion that he did not necessarily persevere in his study of the various texts he employed. He imbibed a great deal at the beginning, and then tailed off. He was an opportunistic reader, who gathered quickly what he needed. Even at this early age he may have possessed an instinctive grasp of structure and of narrative.

It has often been suggested that the scriptural "colouring" of Shakespeare's language comes from a dedicated reading of the Old and New Testaments; but it is more likely that he adopted them almost instinctively as the most readily available form of sonorous language. He was entranced by the sound and by the cadence. Of course he was not just a purloiner of local effects. The evidence of his drama suggests that he was also impressed by the book of Job and by the parable of the Prodigal Son; in each case the workings of Providence solicited his interest. Phrases and images returned to him when he needed them, so that the Bible became for him an echo-chamber of the imagination. It is perhaps ironical that the Bible was translated into English at the insistence of religious reformers. The reformers, as it were, gave the sacred book to Shakespeare. He returned the compliment with his own plangent and resourceful language.

CHAPTER 12

A Nowne and a Verbe and Such Abhominable Wordes

From the petty school Shakespeare advanced to the King's New School, where he received a free education by right as the son of a Stratford alderman. Shakespeare's first biographer, Nicholas Rowe, writing at the beginning of the eighteenth century, states that John Shakespeare "had bred him, 'tis true, for some time at a Free-School, where 'tis probable he acquir'd that little Latin he was Master of . . ."[1] The school assembled in a classroom behind the guild chapel; it was on the floor above the guildhall itself, and was reached by means of a tile-covered staircase of stone. It is in use to this day, a longevity that suggests the prevalence of tradition and continuity in Stratford life. A long and narrow room with a very high oaked-timbered ceiling, strong and many-beamed with bosses in the middle where the beams join, its windows overlook Church Street, which may have afforded a distraction. Certainly the sound of the world could not be kept out.

One engraving illustrating an Elizabethan schoolroom, dating from 1574, shows a master behind a desk, with a book opened in front of him, while the pupils sit on wooden benches in various stages of attention and inattention. On the floor, curiously enough, lies a dog gnawing a bone. There is no sign of the birch or rod that is supposed to have been so prevalent in sixteenth-century school life. The amount of discipline may have

been exaggerated by those who like to emphasise the cruelties of Elizabethan life.

Before he entered this new domain the young Shakespeare would have to
demonstrate that he could read and write English, that he was "fit" to study
the Latin tongue, and that he was "ready to enter into his Accidence and
Principles of Grammar."[2] He was about to be introduced to the language of
the educated world. He and his father climbed upstairs to the schoolroom
where the master read out the statutes of the school, to which the boy agreed
to conform; for the sum of 4 pence William Shakespeare was then enrolled in
the register. He brought with him candles, fuel, books and writing materials;
these would have included a writing book, a glass of ink, an ink horn, and
half a quire of paper. He could not have inherited a set of school texts from
his father, and so they would also have been purchased. It was an undertak-
ing close to a rite of passage.

The school day was strictly controlled and supervised. It was, after all,
the training ground of society itself. The young Shakespeare was present at
six or seven in the morning, summer or winter, and replied "*adsum*" when his
name was called. The prayers of the day were then recited, and a psalm sung,
succeeded by lessons that continued until nine. There may have been parti-
tions to segregate boys of different ages or different abilities; Shakespeare
himself was part of a class of approximately forty-one others at their desks.
There was a short space for breakfast of bread and ale, and then more lessons
until eleven. Shakespeare then walked home for dinner, and returned on the
ringing of the bell at one. During the course of the afternoon fifteen minutes
were allotted for game or play, such as wrestling or shooting with a bow and
arrow. The school was closed at five. This routine was followed for six days
out of seven.

The curriculum of the Stratford school was based upon a thorough
grounding in Latin grammar and in rhetoric, inculcated through the arts of
reading, memorisation and writing. The first stage of this process consisted
in learning simple Latin phrases which could be applied to the ordinary conditions of life and, through an understanding of their construction, in recognising the elementary grammar of the language. To a young child this would
be a bewildering and painfully exacting task—to conjugate verbs and to decline nouns, to understand the difference between the accusative and the ab-
lative cases, to alter the normal structure of language so that the verb came
at the end of a sentence. How strange, too, that words might have masculine

and feminine genders. They became living things, dense or slippery according to taste. Like Milton and Jonson Shakespeare learned, at an early age, that it was possible to change their order for the sake of euphony or emphasis. It is a lesson he did not forget.

In the first months the schoolboy learned the eight parts of Latin speech, before being moved on to a book that Shakespeare invokes on many occasions. William Lilly's *Short Introduction of Grammar* is a text on which children have been shipwrecked. Lilly explained the simple grammatical formulations, and then illustrated them with examples from Cato, Cicero or Terence. The children would be expected to imitate these masters by writing very simple Latin sentences. It has been demonstrated that Shakespeare's punctuation is derived from that of Lilly and that, when he quotes from classical authors, he often uses passages that he read and memorised in Lilly. His spelling of classical names is determined by Lilly. There are many allusions to this process in his drama, not the least being the interrogation in *The Merry Wives of Windsor* of a pupil named William by a pedagogue of the strictest type. "I pray you haue your remembrance (childe) *Accusatiuo hing, hang, hog*" (1897–8). This *Short Introduction of Grammar* was a book that, approached with trepidation as well as concentration, burned itself within his memory.

Shakespeare's own references to schooldays are not entirely happy. The whining schoolboy creeping like snail unwillingly to school is well enough known, but there are other allusions to the plight of the pupil forced to labour over his texts. In *Henry IV, Part Two* there is a line concerning "a schoole broke vp," when each child "hurries towards his home, and sporting place" (2177–8). It is a stray reference but it is, for that reason, even more suggestive. Yet there is a paradox here. Of all the dramatists of the period Shakespeare is the one who most consistently draws on schoolboys, schoolmasters and school curricula as matters for comedy or comment. The notion of schooling was central to him. Perhaps, like most adults, he dreamed of early days.

In the second year the young Shakespeare's understanding of grammar was put to the test in collections of phrases, aphorisms and commonplaces carefully selected to edify as well as to instruct. These were cast into the memory, also, and it is perhaps worth noting that the child was being continually instructed in the art of remembrance. It was the ground of his education, but of course it proved fruitful in his later career as an actor. The brief sentences were laid out in *Sententiae Pueriles*, a book to which Shakespeare alludes on more than two hundred occasions. These were dry sayings that, in the alchemy of Shakespeare's imagination, are sometimes changed into the strangest poetry. "*Comparatio omnis odiosa*" becomes in the mouth of Dogberry "Comparisons are odorous," and "*ad unguem*" turns into Costard's "ad dunghill." In this same year of his education he was introduced to selections from the plays of Plautus and of Terence, dramatic episodes that may have quickened his own dramatic spirit. In his account of the proper education for children Erasmus recommends that the master take his pupils through a complete play by Terence, noting the plot and the diction. The master might also explain "the varieties of Comedy."[3] From these authorities, too, Shakespeare gathered some dim intimation of scenes within a five-act structure.

In his third year he read the stories of Aesop in simple Latin translation. He must have memorised these because, in later life, he was able to repeat the story of the lion and the mouse, of the crow with borrowed feathers, of the ant and the fly. There are altogether some twenty-three allusions to these classical fables in his drama. By this time Shakespeare would have been able to compose English into Latin and to translate Latin into English. He scanned the colloquies of Erasmus and Vives in search of what Erasmus called "*copia*" or plenty. He learned how to pile phrase upon phrase, to use metaphor to decorate an argument or simile to point a moral. He rang changes upon chosen words, and variations upon selected themes. He learnt the art of richness and elaboration from these scholars, whose purpose was to bring classical education into the living world. In Shakespeare, at least, they triumphantly succeeded.

For out of imitation, as he was taught to understand, came invention. It was possible, in the course of a school exercise, to take phrases from a variety of sources and in their collocation to create a new piece of work. It was possible to write a letter, or compose a speech, from a wholly imagined point of view. The imitation of great originals was an essential requirement for any composition; it was not considered to be theft or plagiarism, but an inspired act of adaptation and assimilation. In later life Shakespeare rarely invented any of his plots, and often lifted passages verbatim from other books. In his mature drama he took plots from a variety of sources and mingled them, creating out of different elements a new compound. There is an old medieval saying, to the effect that he who learns young never forgets. Shakespeare was introduced to this method in the fourth year of his schooling, when he was given a selection from the Latin poets, *Flores Poetarum*; from the study of these flowers of the poets he was supposed to compose his own verses. In the process he became acquainted with Virgil and with Horace, whose words resurface in his own works.

But, more significantly, he began to read the *Metamorphoses* of Ovid. At an early age he was introduced to the music of myth. He quotes from Ovid continually. In one of his earliest plays, *Titus Andronicus*, one of the characters brings a copy of the *Metamorphoses* on to the stage. It is one of the few literary "props" in English drama, but it is a highly appropriate one. Here were Jason and Medea, Ajax and Ulysses, Venus and Adonis, Pyramus and Thisbe. It is a world in which the rocks and trees seem to possess consciousness, and where the outline of the supernatural world is to be seen in hills and running brooks. Ovid celebrates transience and desire, the nature of change in all things. In later life Shakespeare was said to possess the "soul" of Ovid in his own mellifluous and sweetly sounding verses; indeed there is some close affinity. Something in Shakespeare's nature responded to this swiftly moving landscape. It took him out of the ordinary world. He was entranced by its fantastic artifice, its marvellous theatricality, and what can only be described as its pervasive sexuality. There is little reason to doubt that Shakespeare was a thoroughly sexual being. Ovid was the favourite writer both of Christopher Marlowe and of Thomas Nashe. But *Metamorphoses* became Shakespeare's golden book. The words of Ovid entered him and found some capacious residence within him.

In succeeding years, in the classroom above the guildhall, he studied Sallust and Caesar, Seneca and Juvenal. Hamlet is found reading from the tenth satire of Juvenal, which he dismisses as "Words, words, words." It was a basic grammar-school text. Shakespeare may even have had a slight brush with the Greek authors, although any evidence for this is marginal at best. What is not in doubt, however, is his Latinity. He uses a Latinate vocabulary with consummate ease and proficiency; he writes of "intermissive miseries" and "loathsome sequestration." He can use the language of the scholar and the pedagogue. It could be claimed that he simply had a good ear, and a poet's instinct for the succinct and shaping word, but it seems unlikely that this "too ceremonious and traditional" language (to use his own phrase in *King Richard III*) came to him by nature. Samuel Johnson, who was learned enough to recognise learning in others, remarked that "I always said that Shakespeare had Latin enough to grammaticise his English." We may see the young Shakespeare, therefore, spending thirty or forty hours of each week in memorising, construing, parsing and repeating prose and verse in Latin. We may hear him talking the language, to his schoolmaster and to his fellow pupils. It may seem an odd perspective in which to place him–especially to anyone accustomed to him warbling "native wood-notes wild"–but Shakespeare is as much part of the revival of Latin culture in the Renaissance as Francis Bacon or Philip Sidney. One formidable scholar of Shakespeare has even suggested that "if letters written by Shakespeare ever turn up, they will be in Latin."[4]

On the question of Shakespeare's education, Ben Jonson was decidedly superior. He was "frequently reproaching him with the want of Learning, and Ignorance of the Ancients,"[5] by which he meant that Shakespeare chose not to follow classical models. Jonson was confusing negligence with ignorance. And when he declared that Shakespeare had "small Latine and lesse Greeke" he was overstating the case for the sake of a phrase. Shakespeare's Latin was as good as that of any other grammar-school boy, and would rival the knowledge shown by any undergraduate of classics in a modern university. Jonson may also have been implicitly comparing the curriculum of the King's New School with that of his own Westminster School; but, to judge by the educated and professional schoolmasters of Stratford, the comparison may not all be in Jonson's favour.

The final stages of Shakespeare's education were perhaps the formative ones. He moved from grammar to oratory, and learned the arts of elocution. What we call creative writing, the Elizabethans called rhetoric. In the schoolroom Shakespeare was obliged to learn the elementary laws and rules of this now arcane subject. He read a smattering of Cicero and Quintilian. He learned the importance of *inventio* and *dispositio*, *elocutio* and *memoria*, *pronunciatio* or action and delivery; he remembered these principles for the rest of his life. He knew how to invent variations upon a theme, and how to ring changes on the sound as well as the sense of words; he knew how to compose themes and to write out formal orations. He also learned how to avoid hyperbole and false rhetoric; in his plays, he gave them to his comic characters. For the alert child it becomes a wonderful means of composition itself. Rhetoric, and the devices of rhetoric, then become a form of creation.

He was trained, as part of this act of creation, to take both sides of any question. The ancient habit of the philosophers and rhetoricians was to argue *in utramque partem*–on either side of the argument. Any event or action can thus be viewed from a variety of different perspectives. The artist must, like Janus, look in two directions at once. In the process language itself became a form of contest or competition. But, equally importantly for the young Shakespeare, the truth of any situation becomes infinitely malleable and wholly dependent upon the speaker's eloquence. What better preparation for a dramatist? And what better training could there have been for the making of Mark Antony's oration in *Julius Caesar* or the pleading of Portia in *The Merchant of Venice*?

There were specific lessons in action and in delivery. In one text for use in grammar schools it was ordained that the pupils "be taught to pronounce every thing audibly, leisurely, distinctly & naturally; sounding out especially the last syllable, that each word may be fully understood."[6] It was important to cultivate "sweete pronunciation." In the same book it is demanded that the pupils "utter every dialogue lively, as if they themselves were the persons which did speake in that dialogue."[7] It is a good training for the theatre. It was also a curriculum that encouraged self-assertion. In his later life Shakespeare was not averse to staking his claim to dramatic pre-eminence, and we may imagine him to have been a singularly competitive small boy. He may not have become embroiled in fights, like the juvenile Keats, but he was fast and full of furious energy. He was, we surmise, easily bored.

It was not necessarily a print culture. It was also a culture of the voice, its exponents being primarily preachers, divines and actors. That is why the theatre rapidly became the supreme art form of the age. This oral culture was of necessity deeply connected with the old medieval culture of England, encompassing storytellers, poetical reciters, ballad singers and minstrels. Shakespeare is much more likely to have heard, than to have read, poetry. An oral culture relies, also, upon the formation of strong memories. If you cannot consult a book, you must perforce remember. Schoolboys were trained in systems of memory or "mnemonics." Ben Jonson declared that "I can repeate whole books that I have read,"[8] and this was not a singular accomplishment. It is the context for the feats of memory exemplified in the ability of Elizabethan actors to perform several plays in one week.

Plays were regularly performed in the grammar schools of England, with Plautus and Terence as the staple of the juvenile repertoire. In the grammar school of Shrewsbury the pupils were obliged, each Thursday morning, to perform one act of a comedy. The boys of King's School, Canterbury–among them Christopher Marlowe–put on plays each Christmas in a tradition that must have reached many other grammar schools. It is important to remember that drama was one of the foundations of Elizabethan teaching. From the smallest grammar school to the "moots" in the Inns of Court, debate and dialogue were the staple of learning. It is no accident that much of the earliest English drama derives from the Inns, where the legal training of "putting the case" developed into sheer theatre. In the school of Stratford speeches were learned and delivered, and conversations were often treated as contests of wit. "A delivery & sweet action," it was written, "is the glosse and beauty of any discourse that belongs to a scholler."[9] We may believe that it was one in which Shakespeare excelled. It is unlikely that the man who was known for his grace and fluency did not demonstrate those virtues at an early age. We do not know whether plays were performed at the King's New School, but there is evidence in Shakespeare's drama of a favourite school play entitled *Acolastus*. Children have a natural gift for dramatisation, and they are fully able to imagine scenes and characters taken from their reading; Shakespeare was exceptional only in preserving these abilities to the end of his life. It suggests some profound irritation, or dissatisfaction, with the limitations of the adult world.

There is further evidence of his dramatic education in the careers of the schoolmasters of Stratford. Two of them, Thomas Jenkins and John Cottam, had been educated at Merchant Taylors' School under the tutelage of Richard Mulcaster; Mulcaster's pedagogic system "advocated teaching through drama, more specifically through acting."[10] What more natural than that they should continue the theatrical tradition created by their famous teacher?

The first of the school masters, Walter Roche, is the one about whom least is known. He resigned his post in the year that Shakespeare joined the school, but lived in Stratford for the rest of his life. He has the distinction in any case of formally introducing the young boy to the schoolroom. The career of the next master of the Stratford school is of more interest. Simon Hunt was schoolmaster for the first four years of Shakespeare's education and, although much of that schooling was no doubt undertaken by his assistant, he remained a powerful presence in Shakespeare's young life. It is significant, then, that he reverted to his old Catholic faith; he left Stratford in order to train at the seminary in Douai as a Jesuit priest and missionary to England. Whether his Catholic sympathies had any material effect upon the young boy is another matter; but it would surely have compounded the family's own piety and bolstered what seems to have been the Catholic environment of his growing-up.

Simon Hunt was succeeded by Thomas Jenkins, a Londoner and son of a "poor man" and "old servant" of Sir Thomas White; he had been a student of Latin and Greek at St. John's College, Oxford, which had been established by the very same Sir Thomas White. White was a Roman Catholic, and St. John's College was known to be sympathetic to Catholic undergraduates. Edmund Campion, Catholic saint and martyr, was attached to St. John's College, and taught Thomas Jenkins there. Jenkins can therefore be considered to be indulgent, at the very least, to the Catholic cause. He can also be considered an expert classicist, and it was he who first introduced Shakespeare to the work of Ovid. He was in every sense a dedicated teacher; he had requested two years' absence from his Oxford college "that he may give himself to teach children."[11]

When Jenkins resigned in 1579 he found his own replacement in John Cottam, a fellow scholar from Merchant Taylors' and Oxford University. Cottam's younger brother, Thomas Cottam, was a Jesuit priest and missionary who resided at Douai with Simon Hunt. There they were joined by a fellow pupil of Shakespeare, Robert Debdale, the son of a Catholic farmer from Shottery. The associations with Shakespeare are close, therefore, and almost pressing. Thomas Cottam returned to England with a letter from Robert Debdale to his father. Both Thomas Cottam and Robert Debdale were later arrested, for their proselytising activities in England, and executed. From allusions in his plays it is clear that Shakespeare followed the career of his erstwhile schoolfellow with some interest. He was, you might say, one of the fraternity.

John Cottam left the King's New School in the year of his brother's execution. The last connection with Shakespeare's schooldays was another master, Alexander Aspinall, popularly supposed to be the model for the pedantic dunce Holofernes. And so the unfortunate man entered the creative imagination of the English. But since he did not enter the school until Shakespeare was eighteen, the connection may not be a close one. The young man no longer attended the New School; but he did know Aspinall, and may have observed his pedagoguery with an eye more objective than that of a schoolboy. He is even believed to have written a set of verses, to accompany Aspinall's present of gloves (bought from John Shakespeare) to an intended bride:

> The gift is small
> The will is all:
> Asheyander Asbenall.

Funnily enough, the little poem sounds like Shakespeare, and may count as some amends for Holofernes.

CHAPTER 13

That's Not So Good Now

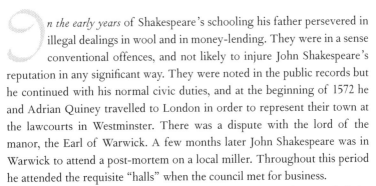

In the early years of Shakespeare's schooling his father persevered in illegal dealings in wool and in money-lending. They were in a sense conventional offences, and not likely to injure John Shakespeare's reputation in any significant way. They were noted in the public records but he continued with his normal civic duties, and at the beginning of 1572 he and Adrian Quiney travelled to London in order to represent their town at the lawcourts in Westminster. There was a dispute with the lord of the manor, the Earl of Warwick. A few months later John Shakespeare was in Warwick to attend a post-mortem on a local miller. Throughout this period he attended the requisite "halls" when the council met for business.

There is a pretty story concerning another journey, during which he might have been accompanied by his son. Elizabeth I was engaged in one of her periodic progresses when, in the summer of 1575, she arrived at Kenilworth Castle; this castle was only twelve miles from Stratford, and the dignitaries of the locality were no doubt asked to attend in honour of Her Majesty. The Earl of Leicester's Men were here to entertain her, but there were also various masques and pageants, dramatic spectacles and games, performed before her. One of these theatrical interludes included the presentation of a mermaid and various nymphs upon an artificial lake, followed by Arion riding upon a dolphin. It was part of the general extravagance of allegory and classical reference employed on such occasions, but many of Shakespeare's biographers have insisted that it inspired a reference in *Twelfth Night* to "*Arion* on the Dolphines backe" (54) and a speech by Oberon from *A Midsummer Night's Dream* (504–6):

> . . . thou remembrest
> Since once I sat vpon a promontory,
> And heard a Mearmaide on a Dolphins backe . . .

It is at least suggestive. And a pretty story does no harm.

It cannot be said that John Shakespeare's fortunes in this period were in any way declining. In 1575 he purchased two houses, with gardens and orchards, in Stratford for £40. It seems likely that these were contiguous to the dwelling in Henley Street, which he could now enlarge for his ever-growing family. He had also purchased land in Bishopton and Welcombe, which he later bequeathed to his son. He had already leased a house to William Burbage, and had also stood surety for two debts incurred by Richard Hathaway. His relative affluence makes his subsequent conduct all the more puzzling.

At the beginning of 1577, he left the borough council precipitately and abruptly. He had been present at its deliberations for the last thirteen years; after this date, he reappears in "hall" only once. This strange withdrawal does not seem to have been prompted by personal animosities. Indeed he was treated by his erstwhile colleagues with patience and forbearance. He was excused the fines generally levied for being absent, and he remained on the list of aldermen for a further ten years. His gown of office was not confiscated or "deprived."

Many reasons have been adduced for his decision, ranging from ill-health and a possible stroke to drunkenness. It is unlikely that he was in any financial trouble; he seems to have remained prosperous throughout his son's time in Stratford. There has been speculation that he avoided paying certain rates, or was deliberately under-assessed upon them, for reasons of penury. But this may simply be a misunderstanding of the difference between rates in the borough, and rates in the parish, of Stratford. A far more likely cause has been found in his espousal of the old religion. The year before his withdrawal a grand ecclesiastical commission was established by the Privy Council to investigate the religious affairs of the nation. Among its ordinances was one established to inquire into "all singular, heretical, erroneous and offensive opinions," and "to order, correct, reform and punish any persons wilfully and obstinately absenting themselves from church and service."[1] The members of the borough council were no doubt asked to expedite these matters, perhaps even to draw up lists of recusants who "obstinately" refused to attend church service. To whom else could the commissioners turn? And so John Shakespeare, recusant, absented himself.

Later that year Whitgift was nominated to be the new Bishop of Worcester, in which see Stratford lay. Whitgift was known to be assiduous in the pursuit and prosecution of those who held "erroneous and offensive opinions." In the year of John Shakespeare's resignation, he arrived in Stratford on a religious visitation to hunt out heretics. At that time, he must have requested the help of the Stratford council. But John Shakespeare had gone nine months before.

John Shakespeare's position was all the more precarious because through marriage he had become part of the Arden affinity; in this period the Catholic, Edward Arden, was engaged in full feud with the Protestant Earl of Leicester, who had charge of the county and who sent sectarian preachers to Stratford. Any member of the Arden family, however removed, could become an object of suspicion. So the world of religious politics conspired against Shakespeare's father and obliged him to withdraw from public life. His colleagues were reluctant to see his departure, but they understood his reasons. This can be no more than a guess, but it does at least make sense of his subsequent behaviour.

Shakespeare was thirteen at the time of his father's relinquishment of public duty and honour. Any effect upon his son can only be supposed, but the boy was of an age when rank and status are important among his fellows. In such a small and deeply hierarchical society, it seems likely that he felt his father's departure most keenly. When we try to measure his response it is best to trust the tale rather than the teller. The plays of Shakespeare are filled with authoritative males who have failed. That may of course be a definition of tragedy itself; in which case it will be one of the reasons for Shakespeare's intense engagement with it. Many of the central male characters of his drama have been disappointed in the practical business of the world; we may adduce here Timon and Hamlet, Prospero and Coriolanus. This failure does not engender aggression or bitterness on the dramatist's part; quite the contrary. It is invariably the case that Shakespeare sympathises with failure, with Antony or Brutus or Richard II. As his first biographer, Nicholas Rowe, put it of Wolsey in *All Is True*, "he makes his Fall and Ruin the Subject of general Compassion."[2] As soon as the male protagonists begin to lose their status, Shakespeare invests them with all the poetry of his being. It may be that John Shakespeare's decline also became the context for his son's preoccupation both with gentility and with the restoration of family honour. It will also help to elucidate, if not to explain, his unprecedented interest in the figure of the king. If the nominal head of the family has failed, it becomes quite natural to create an idealised patriarchy or an idealised relationship between father and son. In any case, Shakespeare himself made sure that he would never suffer his father's failure.

In the course of the next four years John Shakespeare became enmeshed in further difficulties and negotiations. In 1578 he refused to pay a levy for six additional soldiers, equipped at Stratford's expense. In the same year he did not attend the meetings on election day. He was not asked to pay the requisite fines for these offences. He was also involved in complicated land deals concerning some Arden property bequeathed to his wife. On 12 November he sold off 70 acres of Arden property in Wilmcote, the ancestral home of the Ardens, to Thomas Webbe and his heirs; the terms were that, after a period of twenty-one years, these lands would revert to the Shakespeare family. Thomas Webbe was a relative of some kind; Robert Webbe was Mary Arden's nephew. Just two days later John Shakespeare mortgaged a house and 56 acres at Wilmcote to Edmund Lambert, Mary Arden's brother-in-law. This was security on a loan by Lambert to Shakespeare of £40. The loan was to be repaid two years later, in 1580, when the property would be handed back to the Shakespeares. As it turned out Edmund Lambert never returned the house and land, citing various unpaid loans, and John Shakespeare sued him. It is a confusing history but the pattern is clear: the Shakespeares were selling land to relatives while arranging for its later reversion to them. In the following year they sold their portion of the property in Snitterfield, once belonging to Robert Arden, to their nephew.

The most plausible explanation for these complicated arrangements lies in John Shakespeare's difficult position as a known recusant. Whitgift had made his visitation to Stratford, and the erstwhile alderman would soon be cited as one who refused to attend church services. One of the penalties of recusancy was the confiscation of land. An official report, published at a slightly later date, noted how recusants employed "preventions commonly . . . in use to deceive." One subterfuge or "prevention" was detailed thus—"Recusants convey all their lands and goods to friends, and are relieved by those which have the same lands." Others "demise their land to certain tenants."[3] The strategy is clear. A recusant such as John Shakespeare could convey his property to safe hands, to relatives rather than to "friends," and thus avoid the prospect of confiscation. After an agreed interval the property was then returned. The conduct of Edmund Lambert, however, acts as a reminder that events did not always turn out as happily as they had been planned. His refusal to hand over the property at Wilmcote may lie behind some terse words from Horatio in *Hamlet* concerning "those foresaid lands / So by his father lost" (102–3). John Shakespeare was specifically "losing" lands once bequeathed to Mary Arden. It does not take an expert in marital relations to conclude that there was some unacknowledged tension between wife and husband, the inheritors of the Arden and Shakespeare names. As the example of D. H. Lawrence may suggest, these tensions may be bad for the child but good for the writer.

The whole imbroglio emphasises the increasing difficulty of John Shakespeare's position, and no doubt the increasing anxiety of his family. The situation was compounded by the death in the spring of 1579 of Shakespeare's sister. Anne Shakespeare was only eight years old. There is an item in the parish register concerning "the bell & paull for Mr. Shaxpers dawghter." The sorrows of the Shakespeare family are not open to inspection.

CHAPTER 14

Of Such a Mery Nimble Stiring Spirit

hakespeare himself was fifteen in that year, 1579, and entering that period of life when, according to the shepherd in *The Winter's Tale,* there is nothing "but getting wenches with childe, wronging the Auncientry, stealing, fighting" (1313–14). He committed at least one of these offences, and is popularly supposed to have been guilty of two others. But we may prefer to see him as Goethe saw the young Hamlet, as "a good companion, pliant, courteous, discreet, and able to forget and forgive an injury." If he was also "able to discern and value the good and the beautiful in the arts,"[1] then he reached the borders of manhood at an appropriate time. In this year were published North's translations of Plutarch, from which he would later borrow, as well as the *Euphues* of John Lyly and *The Shepheardes Calender* of Edmund Spenser. New forms of prose, and new kinds of poetry, were all around him.

It is possible that his father paid the £5 necessary for his son to continue his schooling after the age of fourteen; only after that age, according to the conventional school curriculum, could he have acquired even the "lesse Greeke" of which Ben Jonson accused him. The age of fourteen, however, was that hard year when boys became apprentices. The young Shakespeare may have started working for his father in some capacity; this was the standard practice of those who were not apprenticed elsewhere. Nicholas Rowe states that after school his father "could give him no better education than his own employment";[2] this surmise is confirmed by John Aubrey, who wrote that "when he was a boy he exercised his father's Trade."[3] Rowe assumes that John Shakespeare was in poverty, however, and Aubrey assumes that he was a butcher. These assumptions are not correct.

It has also been suggested that the young Shakespeare worked as a lawyer's clerk, or that he found employment as a schoolmaster in the country, or that he was called up for military service–a duty for which he would have been liable after the age of sixteen. It is perhaps significant that the only form of recruitment known to Shakespeare was that of impressments, and that there are many allusions in his plays to archery. But his extraordinary capacity for entry into imagined worlds has misled many scholars. His apparent knowledge of the technical terms of seamanship–even to the details of dry ship-biscuits–has, for example, convinced some that he served in the English navy. You can never overestimate his powers of assimilation and empathy.

In the absence of certainty, there have emerged many legends concerning Shakespeare's early years. The most famous of these is his aptitude for poaching. The story concerns his encroachment upon the estate of a local dignitary, Sir Thomas Lucy, and is first mentioned in print by Rowe. Rowe himself gathered it from the actor, Thomas Betterton, who had travelled to Stratford in order to pick up any Shakespearian lore. "He had," Rowe writes,

> by a Misfortune common enough to young Fellows, fallen into ill Company; and amongst them, some that made a frequent practice of Deer-stealing, engag'd him with them more than once in robbing a Park that belong'd to Sir Thomas Lucy of Cherlecote, near Stratford. For this he was prosecuted by the Gentleman, as he thought, somewhat too severely; and in order to revenge that ill Usage, he made a Ballad upon him. And tho' this, probably the first Essay of his Poetry, be lost, yet it is said to have been so very bitter, that it redoubled the Persecution against him to that degree, that he was oblig'd to leave his Business and Family in Warwickshire, for some time, and shelter himself in London.[4]

The ballad itself was, according to one elderly Warwickshire resident, "stuck upon the park gate, which exasperated the knight to apply to a lawyer at Warwick to proceed against him."[5] And then, at a later date, two versions of the ballad itself were fortuitously discovered, one of them ringing the changes on the consonance of "Lucy" and "lowsie." It might all be dismissed as minor literary speculation–or indeed fabrication, as many scholars believe–

except that, quite apart from the testimony of Rowe, the same story was re-peated by a clergyman in the late seventeenth century. Richard Davies told the antiquarian Anthony à Wood that Shakespeare "was much given to all unluckinesse in Stealing venison & Rabbits particularly from Sir —— Lucy who had him oft whipt and Sometimes Imprisoned & at last made Him fly his Native Country . . ."[6] Two independent accounts, employing approximately the same facts, deserve attention. But there are difficulties with the story as it stands. There was no park in the grounds of Sir Thomas Lucy's house, Charlecote; it was then a "free warren," and deer were not brought onto the estate until the eighteenth century. As a result of this discovery the site of Shakespeare's alleged misdeed was moved, two miles away across the Avon, to another of Lucy's parks called Fullbrooke. Yet it has been pointed out that the Lucys did not have proprietary rights in Fullbrooke until the last years of Shakespeare's life. Even if Shakespeare had been able to poach the non-existent deer in a non-existent park, he could not have been whipped for the offence; he would have been fined or imprisoned. Shakespeare does indeed make the allusive connection between "Lucy" and "lowsie," through the happy medium of Justice Shallow in *The Merry Wives of Windsor*. But the target of his humour is much more likely to have been a bailiff of Southwark, William Gardiner, a notorious hater of the theatre who had threatened Shakespeare with arrest. He had married Frances Lucy, and on his coat of arms were impaled three "lucies" or fish. In any event Shakespeare refers with great respect to one of Sir Thomas Lucy's ancestors, William Lucy, in the first part of *Henry VI*.

But there may be a certain truth at the bottom of this well of conjecture. Sir Thomas Lucy was, in Shakespeare's adolescence, a notable persecutor of Catholics. He was an ardent Protestant, a pupil of John Foxe, famous for Foxe's *Book of Martyrs*, and as high sheriff and deputy lieutenant of War-wickshire he inflicted his zeal upon the recusants of that county.

In Warwickshire, too, Catholicism was the faith of the gentry and what has been called a "seigneurial" religion in which clients and retainers es-poused the old faith as a matter of duty as well as piety. That is why the high politics of the county can be analysed in religious terms, with reforming families like the Lucys and the Dudleys and the Grevilles pitted against such proponents of the old faith as the Ardens and the Catesbys and the Somervilles.

Thomas Lucy visited Stratford on many occasions, and he was the prin-cipal signatory on two documents accusing John Shakespeare of refusing to attend church services. He was also granted lands confiscated from Catholics. It should also be noted that he had introduced a bill into Parliament, turning the trespass of poaching into a felony. In 1610 his son, another Sir Thomas Lucy, did prosecute poachers. It is not difficult to observe the stages of legendary change, whereby enmity between the Lucys and the Shakespeares became transformed into the story of young Shakespeare being whipped and imprisoned for poaching Lucy's deer.

There is another authentic note: the many allusions in his poetry and drama to poaching. "Chasing the deer," as it was called, was a normal pursuit for young men of the period. In *May-Day* Sir Philip Sidney describes deer-stealing as a "pretty service." The Elizabethan occultist and physician Simon Forman relates how students prefer "to steal deer and conies."[7] In Shakespeare's work the chase is a consistent theme, whether in the form of metaphor or simile or allusion. It is an obsession common to the period, but no other Elizabethan dramatist is so acquainted with all the details of the hunt. He knows the technical language of the sport with such terms as "recheat" and "embossed," using them as effortlessly and instinctively as any other household words. He has many references to the bow and the crossbow; he knows that the noise of the crossbow will scare the herd. He accompanies the hunter and runs with the hunted, his extraordinary powers of empathy turning the chase into a masterwork of the imagination. He knows about the dogs and the horses; he names the canine breeds from brach to mastiff. In *Titus Andronicus* (584–5) can be found the lines:

> What hast not thou full often stroke a Doe
> And borne her cleanlie by the Keepers nose?

Yet in other passages he laments the plight of the "sobbing deer" and the stricken deer who seeks the water. These were commonplaces of Renaissance literature, of course, but they may also reflect his instinctive attitude.

The allusions to hunting also carry a different significance in late sixteenth-century England, where it was still considered to be primarily an aristocratic pursuit. It was a mimic war and, perhaps more significantly for Shakespeare, an exercise for nobility and for gentlemen. In that sense it suited Shakespeare's abiding preoccupation with gentility. His hunters are noblemen, such as the Lord in *The Taming of the Shrew* and the Duke of Athens in *A Midsummer Night's Dream*. It may also be significant that, in both of these plays, the hunt acts as a prelude and context for theatrical performances. The hunt is itself a form of theatre. The lord of the hunt might also be the patron of a group of players, confirming the strangely disconcerting association. The hunt and the theatre both present ritualised forms of conflict and violence, and the killing of the noble stag to the sound of horns may be compared to the mimic murder of a king. The hands of the hunters in the field, and the hands of the assassins in *Julius Caesar*, are similarly dyed in blood. The writer of the plays confesses to a "dyer's hand." The mature Shakespeare has often been described as a poacher of other men's plays or plots. It is impossible to untangle the web of associations and resemblances that may be glimpsed here. But we may be sure that we are looking into the heart of Shakespeare's design. The stray story of the poacher Shakespeare has carried us a long way.

There are many other references to outdoor pursuits that suggest the presence of personal experience. He could have played bowls, for example, and the language of falconry becomes almost his private possession. One book upon his imagery fills no fewer than eight pages with his references to trained hawks and hawking, to the "check" and the "quarry," the "haggard" and the "jesse." There are eighty separate and technical allusions to the sport in his published writing, whereas there are very few in the work of any other dramatist of the period. *The Taming of the Shrew* uses the taming of the falcon as a metaphor throughout. The process of stitching up a bird's eyelids was known as "seeling." Thus in *Macbeth* (991–2) occurs the imprecation—

> Come, seeling Night,
> Skarfe vp the tender Eye of pittifull Day

Nor does he commit errors or solecisms. His references may of course have been derived from book-learning, or from his attempts to internalise what was in large part an aristocratic sport; but he speaks the language of practice, much of which is still in use.

He alludes to the hunting of hares, and of foxes, on several occasions. It was the practice of countrymen then to hunt hares on foot, with nets at the ready. Shakespeare notes how the quarry "outruns the wind," and "crankes and crosses with a thousand doubles" (*Venus and Adonis*, 681–2). In this context he uses the very specific term of "musit" for a round hole in a hedge or fence through which the hare escapes; he could not have learned this from any book.

On the basis of dramatic references one early biographer has also safely concluded that Shakespeare "was an angler" who "did not use a fly but was familiar with bottom-fishing";[8] the Avon was close by, but it is hard to imagine a still and patient Shakespeare. He seems preoccupied, too, with the liming of birds. This was the practice of the fowler, who smeared twigs and branches with the white glutinous paste of bird-lime in order to capture his terrified prey. It is one of those images particularly favoured by Shakespeare; it emerges in a variety of contexts and situations, and represents some primitive or primary scene of his imagination. He responds eloquently to the idea of speed being checked or free flight being hampered; the picture of a bird struggling to be free impressed itself upon him. It lies behind the "limed soul" of Claudius in *Hamlet*, or the bush "limed" for the Duchess of Gloucester in the second part of *Henry VI*. Shakespeare was familiar with all the sports of the field and the open air—which is, perhaps, no more than to say that he had a conventional rural boyhood.

There is another legend of this period, confirming Shakespeare's status as a rustic cavalier of free and manly disposition who was shaped by nature rather than by art. It concerns his drinking, that English token of virile and unaffected behaviour. The story goes that he visited the neighbouring village of Bidford, whose male inhabitants were supposed to be "deep drinkers and merry fellows"; he wanted to "take a cup" with them but was told that they were absent. Instead he was invited to join "the Bidford sippers" (could they perhaps have been female?) and became so drunk in their company that he had to sleep beneath a tree. This hallowed crab-tree was, by the eighteenth century, shown to visitors as "Shakespeare's canopy" or "Shakespeare's Crab."[9] The story has the advantage of being entirely unprovable. But it also has an inherent significance. It displays an instinctive tendency, among literary mythographers, to identify Shakespeare with his native soil and to portray him as a kind of *genius loci*. This is not in itself unwelcome, as long as it does not ignore all the sophistication and wit that Shakespeare brought to his unmistakable rural inheritance.

CHAPTER 15

At Your Employment, at Your Seruice Sir

ohn Aubrey remarked that Shakespeare "had been in his younger yeares a Schoolmaster in the Countrey." In the margin the diarist writes "from Mr. Beeston," who was in certain respects a reliable source; William Beeston, actor, was the son of one Christopher Beeston, who had been a player in Shakespeare's own company in the writer's lifetime. Aubrey interviewed him towards the end of his life, but it seems to be an authentic piece of information. It would not be at all unusual for a clever young man of fifteen or sixteen to be employed as an "usher" or teacher for younger children.

There is some allusive contemporary evidence also. In one of a trilogy of plays published in 1606 and entitled *The Return to Parnassus*, a character based upon Shakespeare, Studioso, is parodied as a "schoolmaster" who teaches Latin to children in the country. The reference would have no point if it were not based upon prior information. There are so many references to schoolmasters and school curricula in his plays, far more than in those of any contemporary, that one scholar has been moved to describe Shakespeare as "the schoolmaster among dramatists."[1] In his plays, too, the quotations and references often derive from passages that were used by masters as illustrations of grammatical rules. When he was laughing at Holofernes the master, perhaps he was also laughing at his own old self. But, if the tradition is correct, the inevitable question then arises. Where in the "countrey" was the young Shakespeare a schoolmaster?

Various locations have been suggested, from Berkeley Castle in Gloucestershire to Titchfield in Hampshire. His schoolmastering has also been placed closer to home, under the patronage of Sir Fulke Greville of Beauchamps Court twelve miles from Stratford; Greville, the father of the poet of the same name, was a local dignitary who took a great interest in matters of education. He was also related to the Ardens. It is interesting conjecture, but conjecture still.

In more recent years, in any case, the favoured locale for Shakespeare's career as a young teacher has become Lancashire. The omens are good. Turn first to the last will and testament of a local grandee, Alexander Hoghton, of Hoghton Tower and Lea Hall near Lea in that county. Hoghton's wife was a devout Catholic, and his brother was in exile as a result of his espousal of the old faith. In this will–executed on 3 August 1581–he leaves his musical instruments and players' costumes to his half-brother, Thomas Hoghton, with this proviso.

> And yf he wyll not keppe and manteyne playeres, then yt ys my wyll that Sir Thomas Heskethe, knyghte, shall haue the same Instrumentes and playe clothes. And I most herteleye requyre the said Sir Thomas to be ffrendlye unto ffoke Gyllome and William Shakeshafte nowe dwellynge with me, and eyther to take theym unto his Servyce or els to helpe theym to some good master, as my tryste ys he wyll.[2]

Ever since this will was discovered in the mid-nineteenth century (and later given prominence in a publication of 1937) it has provoked a great deal of interest and controversy. If the reference is indeed to William Shakespeare, why is his name spelled in so peculiar a fashion? Why at the early age of seventeen has he been singled out in this pronounced manner? In a subsequent part of the will he was also left 40 shillings a year; he is named among forty other household servants, but the bequest does suggest some form of special recognition. How had he come to deserve this? If he had already spent two years in Hoghton Tower, of course, his remarkable gifts would already have become apparent. If we leave aside these doubts and misgivings, however, then we have a description of the young Shakespeare as an actor in a Catholic household where he may have been introduced as a schoolmaster. It is an intriguing possibility.

Many scholars disagree. The movements of the young Shakespeare have become the subject of serious debate, related to the vexed question of his religious allegiances. Was he actually a crypto-Catholic or even a sympathiser with and friend of Catholics? Was he ever in the north of England at all? There can be no certainty in these matters.

But, if the account is accurate, there are further ramifications. The Hoghton and Hesketh families were very well acquainted with the household of the earls of Derby, who exercised enormous influence in Lancashire. In his history plays Shakespeare emphasises the truth and loyalty of the Stanleys, the surname of the Derby family, in defiance of the facts of their actual conduct–in *Richard III* Sir William Stanley tears the crown from the villainous king's prostrate head–and it is widely believed that Shakespeare composed epitaphs for two members of the same household. Lord Strange (Ferdinando Stanley, the fifth earl of Derby) was a Catholic or crypto-Catholic nobleman of great wealth and power. He patronised a group of players known naturally enough as Lord Strange's Men. Some biographers have enrolled Shakespeare in this acting company during the time that he dwelled at Hoghton Tower. Lord Strange's Men toured the country and were also well known in London. With one deft explanation we can move the young Shakespeare from provincial schoolmastering to the stages of the innyards in the capital.

It may be convenient, but it is not necessarily unlikely. There is a long tradition in the Hoghton family that Shakespeare served them in some capacity. This in itself is by no means conclusive, but it is bolstered by other evidence. In the immediate vicinity of the Hoghtons of Lea Hall, near Preston, lived the Cottam family; the Hoghtons and the Cottams, both Catholic, were thoroughly intimate. One of the members of that family, John Cottam, has already entered this history as Shakespeare's schoolmaster in Stratford. Cottam is mentioned in Alexander Hoghton's will as his "servant." It seems to be more than coincidence. What would be more natural than that Cottam should recommend his most brilliant pupil, also a Catholic, to be schoolmaster to the Hoghton children? Alexander Hoghton was named by an apostate priest as one of the Lancastrian gentry who kept "recusants as schoolmasters."[3]

So, at the age of fifteen or sixteen, the young Shakespeare may have journeyed away from home. Once you understand the Catholic network of late sixteenth-century England, it seems to be an entirely sensible and explicable course of action. The connection between Lancashire and Stratford-upon-

Avon has already been observed, with four out of five schoolmasters at the New School coming from that most strongly Catholic of all English counties. It has been calculated that "nine out of the twenty-one Catholic schoolmasters executed under Elizabeth were Lancastrians."[4] Thomas Cottam, the Jesuit priest and brother of John Cottam, stayed in secret at the house of Alexander Hoghton's cousin, Richard Hoghton; Edmund Campion, the Catholic missionary and proselytiser, in the spring of 1581 visited Hoghton Tower, where he left certain books and papers. He never had the opportunity of reclaiming them, the gallows preventing him. There are deep affiliations here which cannot at this late date be properly or fully recovered.

From the evidence of his will Alexander Hoghton also employed "players." It has been objected that "players" may simply mean musicians, but the reference is ambiguous. In any case actors were often required to perform music. It may also be significant that schoolmasters in this period were supposed to teach their charges the art and practice of music. There are some lines in *The Taming of the Shrew* (367–9) that reveal this connection:

> And for I know she taketh most delight
> In Musicke, Instruments, and Poetry,
> Schoolemasters will I keepe within my house . . .

The young usher would also have been expected to teach Latin from the dramatic passages of Plautus and of Terence. It is easy to see how Shakespeare's rhetorical and theatrical gifts might find expression in such an atmosphere. There was a Catholic tradition of plays written for schoolboys, exemplified by Campion himself, who wrote a devotional school-play entitled *Ambrosia*. Fulke Gillam, mentioned with "William Shakeshafte" in Hoghton's will, came from a family of pageant masters who organised the mystery plays at Chester. So the young Shakespeare was entering a world of Catholic dramaturgy, rehearsed and performed clandestinely in the halls of the Lancastrian recusant gentry.

After the death of Alexander Hoghton, the young Shakespeare might then have been recruited into Sir Thomas Hesketh's company of players at Rufford Hall. Both Hoghton Tower and Rufford Hall had banqueting halls, with a screen and a dais, where plays were performed; Hesketh also possessed a stage orchestra, complete with "vyolls, vyolentes, virginals, sagbutts, how-boies and cornets, cithron, flute and tabor pypes."[5] It has often been remarked how intimately and precisely Shakespeare in his plays traces the life of noble households, with their servants and their banquets. We may be able to find a source for that knowledge in the noble families of Lancashire, well known throughout England for their local power and authority in an area where the majesty of the Crown was only a distant reality. Was it here that the young man acquired that gentility of manner and address that so impressed his contemporaries?

Once again there is a tradition in the vicinity, dating from the early nineteenth century, of Shakespeare living and working in Rufford Hall. In this house, too, there is a Tudor tapestry that depicts the fall of Troy; in *The Rape of Lucrece* the heroine inspects "a peece of skilfull painting, made for Priams Troy" (1366–7). At a later date Shakespeare helped to choose, as one of the trustees of the Globe Theatre, a native of Rufford itself.

If Hesketh recognised the extraordinary abilities of the young actor (and possibly, even at this early age, already an aspiring dramatist) it is likely that, according to the injunctions of the will, he recommended Shakespeare "to some good master"–namely Lord Strange and his well-known company of talented players. It should be noted here that Lord Strange's Men performed at least two of Shakespeare's earliest plays. Everyone agrees that Shakespeare must have had some full and proper training as an actor before emerging, fully armed, upon the London stage in 1592, when he is described as "excelent in the qualitie he professes." Every actor in the professional companies had some apprenticeship or previous training. Why could this not have been achieved by Shakespeare with Strange's Men?

A stray piece of research serves to deepen, if not necessarily to strengthen, the picture. Fifty years ago two Shakespearian scholars, Alan Keen and Roger Lubbock, discovered a copy of Hall's *Chronicles* which had been heavily annotated in an unknown hand. Hall's *Chronicles* was an indispensable source book for Shakespeare's history plays, but this particular copy has an independent interest. The annotations have been made in a youthful hand, and display "sympathy with Hall's patriotic enthusiasm and fury at his anti-Catholicism";[6] there are also notes and marginal comments on such matters as the resignation of Richard II. A graphologist, inspecting this handwriting, has concluded that the letterings "indicate the probability that Shakespeare and the annotator were the same man, but do not by any means prove it."[7] None of this would be of the slightest consequence were it not for the fact that Keen and Lubbock, pursuing their investigations, discovered that this particular volume was in the joint or communal possession both of Thomas Hoghton and of Thomas Hesketh.

A chronology of the salient events in the summer and autumn of 1581 will create a context for the young Shakespeare. Edmund Campion was arrested on 16 July, and was taken to the Tower for torture on 31 July. On 5 August, two days after Alexander Hoghton had made his will, the Privy Council issued an order for the search of "certain books and papers which Edmund Campion has confessed he left at the house of one Richard Hoghton in Lancashire." Richard Hoghton was then arrested. Could it be that Alexander Hoghton had made his will because he knew by then that he might be arrested and that perhaps he did not expect to live for very long? On 21 August the Privy Council congratulated the loyal magistrates of Lancashire for seizing Campion's hosts and for taking "certain papers, in Hoghton House."

On 12 September Alexander Hoghton died in what appear to have been suspicious circumstances. Then, at the close of this year, Sir Thomas Hesketh—to whom Hoghton had recommended "Shakeshafte"—was consigned to prison on the grounds that he had failed to curb the practice of the Catholic faith amongst his servitors. All of his friends and retainers would naturally come under renewed suspicion from the queen's emissaries. The net of suspicion was being drawn tightly over these Lancastrian households, and it was perhaps high time that the young Shakespeare made a convenient departure. By the summer of 1582, at the very latest, he is to be found once more in Stratford.

CHAPTER 16

Before I Know My Selfe, Seeke Not to Know Me

He came back to a larger but not necessarily happier family. In the spring of 1580 John Shakespeare had been summoned to the Queen's Bench in Westminster and, when he did not appear, was fined the large sum of £40. He was not alone in his transgression, since approximately two hundred men and women from different counties were caught up in the same punitive action and fined various amounts to a maximum of £200. The supposition must inevitably be that these "malcontents" were brought to the bar of justice for recusancy or refusal to attend church services. In the following year it was formally proclaimed that those who did not conform to the prescriptions of the Act of Uniformity would be fined the sum of £20 per month, rising to "all their goods and a third part of their land." For Catholics there was now the clear danger of financial ruin. Half of John Shakespeare's fine was levied because of his reluctance or inability to ensure that a Nottinghamshire hat-maker, John Audley, came to court. On the same day Audley himself was in turn fined £10 for not bringing John Shakespeare to the Queen's Bench. Historians have inferred that this system of mutual bail, uniting people from various regions and different jurisdictions, was an attempt by Catholics to circumvent the collection of any fines. Yet Shakespeare's father did pay his fine, as recorded in the Coram Regina Roll, suggesting that he lived still in relative affluence.

When Shakespeare returned to Stratford in 1582, it was in the face of an uncertain future. At the age of eighteen, what likely career might have been open to him? In recent years there has grown an abiding, if not universal, belief that he had some training as a lawyer's clerk in Stratford. It was not an unnatural progress. For a quick and intelligent young man there were many possible "openings" in his home town. One of the old schoolmasters at the Free School, Walter Roche, had a lawyer's practice in Chapel Street. John Shakespeare used the services of William Court in the same street. If he was not clerk to a solicitor, he might have been a copyist or even a scrivener's apprentice. It is also possible that as a result of his father's influence he worked in the office of Henry Rogers, the town clerk of Stratford, situated in Wood Street.

His drama is striated with legal terminology, particularly with that concerning property law. There is scarcely a play in which words or phrases from the courts are not employed. The sonnets are filled with similar references, to such an extent that it has even been supposed that they were addressed to a member of one of the Inns of Court. It could just as well be argued that the age of Shakespeare was excessively litigious, and that any Elizabethan would of necessity have acquired a great deal of knowledge about the law. As one contemporary put it, "now every Raskall will tak upon to knowe the laws as well as the best gentleman."[1] The law was an inevitable part of ordinary social life.

But the most important Shakespearian scholar of the eighteenth century, Edmond Malone, remarked that "his knowledge of legal terms is not merely such as might be acquired by the casual observation of even his all-comprehending mind; it has the appearance of technical skill."[2] More significantly, perhaps, it emerges in the very texture of his writing. He writes of warrants and conveyances, leases and inventories, presentments and suits, fines and recoveries. There is such a multitude of examples that it is almost absurd to single out any of them. Mistress Page says of Falstaff in *The Merry Wives of Windsor* (2132–4), "If the diuell haue him not in fee-simple, with fine and recouery, he will neuer (I think) in the way of waste, attempt vs againe." It would take an expert in Tudor law to explain the remark, which may not in any case have come naturally to a wife of Windsor. Lady Macbeth consoles her husband, on the ticklish matter of Banquo and Fleance, with the sentence (983) that "in them Natures coppie's not eterne," a reference to the law of copia or copyhold. In *The Rape of Lucrece* the unfortunate heroine "folds shee vp the tenure of her woe" (1310); "tenure" is the technical legal term for a correctly completed statement. In *All's Well That Ends Well* Parolles says of his erstwhile master (2220–1), "for a Cardecue he will sell the fee-simple of his saluation, the inheritance of it, and cut th'intaile from all remainders." But enough is enough. It need only be said that it is a mark of his "all-comprehending" imagination that the language of law comes to him as effortlessly and as instinctively as the language of nature. In the larger sense he places all his characters before the Court of Equity, where justice is tempered by mercy.

There is other evidence concerning Shakespeare's early career. The first references allude to him somewhat slightingly as a former "noverint" or legal scrivener. Several palaeographers have agreed that the available remnants of his handwriting, particularly in his signatures, give clear indication of a legal training. One of those signatures appears in a volume entitled *Archaionomia*, found in 1939. It is a legal text, composed by William Lambarde, which contains a Latin translation of Anglo-Saxon edicts. The signature of "Wm Shakspere" within it is the object of considerable scholarly debate. But Lambarde was an officer of the court in Westminster Hall during the period when John Shakespeare was filing a bill of complaint at the Queen's Bench. At a later date Lambarde was Master of Chancery when another of John Shakespeare's fifty separate suits was entered there. He was also Master of the Revels at Lincoln's Inn, one of whose duties was the staging of appropriate dramas. There was every reason why Shakespeare would have been acquainted with him.

John Shakespeare's relatively late appearance as a plaintiff at Westminster suggests another explanation for Shakespeare's knowledge of the law—he may have been assisting his father in the various legal manoeuvres in which the Shakespeare family was engaged. That might explain the dramatist's excellent knowledge of property law. He could have been working for his father. There is a strange note, in the copy of *Archaionomia* possibly signed by Shakespeare, to the effect that "Mr. Wm Shakspeare Lived at No 1 Little Crown St. Westminster"; it is in an eighteenth-century hand, and the location is genuine. The information may be spurious, or it may apply to quite another William Shakespeare. In a certain set of circumstances, however, it would make perfect sense. If he had lived close to the courts of justice, while pursuing a familial suit, he may have acquired *Archaionomia* in order to impress Lambarde with ancient precedents. Lambarde's volume also acted as a source book for the play entitled *Edmund Ironside*, the surviving manuscript of which (to be found in the Manuscript Collections of the British Library) is written in an unmistakably legal hand and contains many legal abbreviations. The authorship of the play is contested, but some have ascribed it to Shakespeare himself. The connections and associations are there, for those who care to find them. The biographer can thus explore a number of possible Shakespearian identities without traducing the essential nature of the man.

One other quasi-legal digression is of some pertinence. If the young Shakespeare had indeed been working in the office of Stratford's town clerk, he would have become fully acquainted with the case of a young woman who in 1580 drowned in the Avon. The inference was that she had committed suicide but her family, intent upon giving her a proper Christian burial, insisted that she had fallen accidentally into the river while going down to the bank with her milk-pail in order to draw water. The Avon at this juncture, by Tiddington, is known for its overhanging willows and coronet weeds. If she had been found guilty of "*felo de se*" or suicide, she would have been buried in a hole by a crossroads, at a spot where local folk were permitted to throw stones or broken pots. Henry Rogers conducted the inquest, and arrived at the conclusion that she had indeed met her death "*per infortunium*" or accidentally. If this suggests images of Ophelia, then it is interesting that the name of the girl was Katherine Hamlett.

All this is speculation, but—if he did begin his career in a lawyer's office—he did not particularly care for the work. His emergence in London as an actor and dramatist suggests that, at an early stage, he willingly abandoned it. There was another change. A short while after his return to Stratford in 1582, he was courting Anne Hathaway.

CHAPTER 17

ℐ Can See a Church by Day-Light

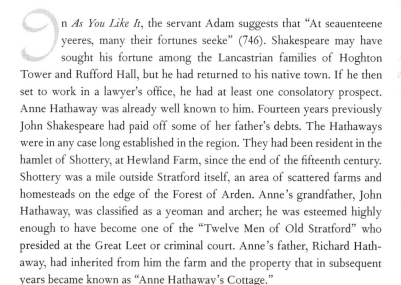

ℐn *As You Like It*, the servant Adam suggests that "At seauenteene yeeres, many their fortunes seeke" (746). Shakespeare may have sought his fortune among the Lancastrian families of Hoghton Tower and Rufford Hall, but he had returned to his native town. If he then set to work in a lawyer's office, he had at least one consolatory prospect. Anne Hathaway was already well known to him. Fourteen years previously John Shakespeare had paid off some of her father's debts. The Hathaways were in any case long established in the region. They had been resident in the hamlet of Shottery, at Hewland Farm, since the end of the fifteenth century. Shottery was a mile outside Stratford itself, an area of scattered farms and homesteads on the edge of the Forest of Arden. Anne's grandfather, John Hathaway, was classified as a yeoman and archer; he was esteemed highly enough to have become one of the "Twelve Men of Old Stratford" who presided at the Great Leet or criminal court. Anne's father, Richard Hathaway, had inherited from him the farm and the property that in subsequent years became known as "Anne Hathaway's Cottage."

Richard Hathaway was also a farmer and substantial householder. By his first wife, who came from Temple Grafton, he had three children one of whom was Anne herself. He married again, and had further children. He was eventually "honestly buried" in the manner of the reformed faith, but he named a prominent recusant as an executor of his will; so the religious affiliations of the family, like those of so many other households in the neighbourhood, may have been mixed and ambiguous.

Anne Hathaway was the eldest daughter of the house and as such incurred a fair number of household duties, chief among them the care of her younger siblings. As the daughter of a farming family, too, she learned how to bake bread, to salt meat, to churn butter and to brew ale. In the yard outside the house were poultry and cows, pigs and horses to be fed and reared. Far from being a *mésalliance* or forced marriage, as some have suggested, the partnership of William Shakespeare and Anne Hathaway could have been an eminently sensible arrangement. He may even have exercised a good deal of caution, or common sense, in his choice of lifelong partner. This was thoroughly in keeping with his practical and business-like approach to all the affairs of the world.

She was eight years his senior—in the year of their marriage he was eighteen and she was twenty-six—but, in a period of shorter life expectancy, the disparity in age would have seemed greater then than now. It was an unusual arrangement, since in the sixteenth century it was customary for the man to marry a younger woman. The difference in age has of course aroused much speculation, primarily concerned with the wiles of an older female in coaxing an inexperienced young man into bed and eventual marriage. Yet it might, on the contrary, suggest sexual self-confidence on Shakespeare's part. In any case the suspicion does less than justice to Shakespeare's judgement and intelligence which, even at the age of eighteen, might have been acute. It is also an insult to Anne Hathaway who, like many of the silent wives of famous men, has endured much obloquy. Those biographers who enjoy dramatic speculation, for example, have noted that Shakespeare's history plays harbour many manipulative older women, whose beauty seems mysteriously to wither on the vine. In *A Midsummer Night's Dream* (138) Hermia cries out, "O spight! too olde to be ingag'd to young" and the Duke in *Twelfth Night* offers some advice—"Let still the woman take / An elder then her selfe"—and goes on to caution (1896–9):

> Then let thy Loue be yonger then thy selfe,
> Or thy affection cannot hold the bent;
> For women are as Roses, whose faire flowre
> Being once displaid, doth fall that verie howre.

But it is probably best to refrain from maladroit interpretation. In the Duke, Shakespeare has created a notorious sentimentalist. It could just as well be argued that, because the females in Shakespeare's drama are literate, so must have been the women around him.

It is not known whether Anne Hathaway could read or write. There was no real opportunity which would have enabled her to learn how to do so and, in any case, 90 per cent of the female population of England were illiterate at that time. It has often been supposed that Shakespeare's two daughters were also illiterate, and so we are faced with the irony of the greatest dramatist in the history of the world surrounded by women who could not read a word he wrote.

There is a sonnet placed as the 145th in Shakespeare's sonnet sequence, which seems oddly situated and out of context. The last two lines suggest that it was in fact composed for Anne Hathaway and has some claim to being the first extant work of William Shakespeare—

> "I hate" from "hate" away she threw,
> And saued my life, saying "not you."

Hate away is equal to Hathaway. The entire poem is a conventional and youthful paean to a kind and loving mistress, with "lips that Loues owne hand did make." It is interesting as a token of Shakespeare's early ambitions as a poet. He must have borrowed the sonnet form from a contemporary collection such as *Tottel's Miscellany*, where the work of Wyatt and Surrey was to be found, or perhaps from the first published sonnet sequence in English, Thomas Watson's *Hekatompathia*, which was published in the summer of 1582. It may have proved the spur to Shakespeare's invention. He reached for the form naturally and instinctively; this early poem is fluent and forceful, a harbinger of his triumphant mastery of that genre.

It is to be hoped that "Loues owne hand" had something to do with the match, since Anne Hathaway was four months pregnant by the time of their marriage day. It was not unusual in this period for couples to cohabit before their wedding. Their Stratford neighbours, George Badger and Alice Court, Robert Young and Margery Field, had a similar arrangement. It was also customary for both parties to make a "troth-plight," a verbal contract of marriage before witnesses which was also known as "hand-fasting" or "making sure." So Alice Shaw of Warwickshire declared to William Holder, of the same county, that "I do confesse that I am your wief and have forsaken all my frendes for your sake and I hope you will use me well."[1] The man took the woman's hand, and repeated the same pledge. Only after such a "troth-plight" could the woman give up her virginity. The marriage ceremony came later. It was a code of honour, marked out by both social and sexual discipline; there were of course different forms of "making sure," varying from a private pledge to a ceremony with a prayer book. But its ubiquity can be measured in the fact that between 20 and 30 per cent of all brides bore children within the first eight months of marriage.

This informal contract remained firmly in Shakespeare's consciousness. There are many allusions to it in his plays, ranging from Claudio's plea in *Measure for Measure* that "she is fast my wife" to Olivia's demand to Sebastian in *Twelfth Night* that he "Plight me the full assurance of your faith." It would also have affected the Elizabethan understanding of dramatic action. When Troilus and Cressida plight themselves, Pandarus exclaims: "Go to a bargaine made, seale it, seale it ile bee the witnes here I hold your hand, here my Cozens" (1768–70). He is effectively sealing a "hand-fasting," thus rendering Cressida's subsequent unfaithfulness more execrable. When Orlando declares to Rosalind, in the guise of Ganymede, "I take thee *Rosalind* for wife" he is committing himself much further and more deeply than he supposes. It is a social custom, now long since discarded and forgotten, but it had profound implications for Shakespeare and for Shakespeare's audience.

There was also a custom of exchanging rings during this informal ceremony (other pre-contract gifts included a bent sixpence and a pair of gloves), a charming ritual which anticipates a no less charming "find" in the early nineteenth century. In 1810 the wife of a Stratford labourer was working in a field, next to the churchyard, when she found a heavily encrusted ring. It was of gold and, when it was cleaned, it was discovered to bear the initials "W S" separated by a lover's knot. The dating is that of the sixteenth century, and a local antiquarian believed that "no other Stratfordian of that period [was] so likely to own such a ring as Shakespeare."[2] There is one other intriguing connection. Shakespeare may have owned a seal-ring, but his will has no seal. The phrase "in witness whereof I have hereunto set my hand and seal" has been altered; the word "seal" has been struck out, as if Shakespeare had lost his ring before signing the document.

· · ·

The "cottage" in which William Shakespeare and Anne Hathaway are popularly supposed to have courted was in fact a relatively large farmhouse
constructed of timber and of wattle-and-daub (hazel twigs and dried mud
can still be seen embedded within the walls) with rooms at different levels,
low ceilings and uneven floors. Its timber construction means that it is a box
of noise, so courtship would have been untenable as well as uncomfortable.
From the upstairs bedchambers you can hear everything in the rooms below
and, through the cracks in the floorboards, see everything as well. It was
fortunate that there were meadows, and a forest, nearby. He may not have
visited her there in the crucial period, in any case, since after the death of
her father in 1581 she went to live with her mother's family in the nearby
village of Temple Grafton. She may have wished to remove herself from
the company of her stepmother and four surviving children. The absence of
paternal watchfulness, however, may have hastened the fruition of the
match.

There is one odd incident concerning the wider family in this year of
betrothal and marriage. In September 1582, John Shakespeare attended a
council meeting in the guildhall in order to vote for his friend, John Sadler,
as mayor of Stratford. Sadler declined to serve, on the grounds of ill-health
(he died six months later), but John Shakespeare's reappearance after an absence of almost six years is somewhat puzzling. It may have been a sudden
decision, or a desire to be seen to support an old friend, but it may conceivably be connected with his other appearance in the public records at this time.
Three months previously he had entered a petition against four men—Ralph
Cawdrey the butcher among them—"for fear of death and mutilation of his
limbs." This was a ritual formula and need not be taken as token of a literal
threat to John Shakespeare's life, but the circumstances are obscure. It could
not have been a partisan religious quarrel, since Cawdrey himself was a
staunch Catholic. It is more likely to have been some kind of trade or financial dispute. One of the other men, against whom John Shakespeare complained, was a local dyer. By attending the council meeting John Shakespeare
may have hoped to revive something of his old authority.

· · ·

The first child of William Shakespeare and Anne Hathaway was probably conceived in the last two weeks of September, for at the end of November the young man or Anne Hathaway's guardians hastened to Worcester in order to obtain a special marriage licence. Anne Hathaway had been left £6 13*s* 4*d* by her father, equivalent to a blacksmith's or a butcher's annual wage and enough for her dowry. The licence permitted marriage after a single publication of the banns, and did not specify any particular parish in which the ceremony must take place. The haste was necessary since the period of Advent was at hand, in which marriages were very largely restricted. Another period of prohibition began on 27 January and lasted until 7 April. It was possible, then, that their child might be born when its parents were not formally wedded. Anne's interesting condition may have become evident, and neither she nor her guardians may have wished her child to be illegitimate.

So on 27 November 1582, William Shakespeare or Anne's representatives rode to Worcester, and visited the consistory court at the western end of the south aisle of the cathedral there. The fee for this special licence, allowing for a marriage in haste or in privacy, varied from 5 to 7 shillings. Anne Hathaway's home was given as Temple Grafton, but by some strange slip of the pen she was given the surname of Whateley. So the licence reads as *"inter Willelmum Shaxpere et Annam whateley de Temple Grafton."* There has been some unnecessary speculation about an unknown young woman named Anne Whateley, but it is likely that the clerk had simply misheard or misread the name; there was a Whateley appearing at the court on the same day, so the official's confusion is understandable. Since Shakespeare himself was under the age of twenty-one, he was obliged to swear that his father had given consent to the match. On the following day two of Anne Hathaway's neighbours in Shottery, both farmers, Fulke Sandells and John Richardson, stood surety of £40 in the event of some "lawful impediment" being later discovered. It is not surprising that John Shakespeare did not sign this surety, since he was a known recusant intent upon concealing his wealth and property.

The banns were published on Friday 30 November, and the marriage took place on that or the following day. The most likely venue for the ceremony was Anne Hathaway's parish church at Temple Grafton, some five miles west from Stratford. The absence of parish records makes it clear that it was not performed in Stratford, where the vicar was strongly attached to the reformed faith. Some scholars place it at Luddington, a village three miles from Temple Grafton where other relatives of Anne Hathaway lived. One old resident claimed to have seen the parish record of the marriage, but the curate's housekeeper is supposed to have burnt that register subsequently on a cold day in order "to boil her kettle."[3] This does not, on the face of it, seem very likely. Others claim the site of the wedding to be St. Martin's Church, in Worcester, where the pages of the parish register for the marriages of 1582 have been carefully cut out.

The church of Temple Grafton, however, was convenient in more ways than one. The priest here was a remnant of Mary's Catholic reign, an old man who according to an official report was "unsound in religion" and who could "neither preach nor read well." But he was well versed in the practice of hawking and could cure those birds "who were hurt or diseased: for which purpose many do usual repair to him."[4]

It is not known whether an approximation to the Catholic marriage service took place in the ancient church of Temple Grafton. Given the affinities of the priest, however, this seems likely. If so, the ceremony was conducted in Latin and took place between the canonical hours of eight and twelve in the morning. The favoured day was Sunday. It began at the church porch, where the banns were recited three times. Anne Hathaway's dower, of £6 13s 4d, was then displayed and exchanged. She was no doubt "given" by Fulke Sandells or John Richardson who had stood surety in Worcester. The woman stood on the left side of the groom, in token of Eve's miraculous delivery from Adam's left rib; they held hands as a symbol of their betrothal. In the church porch the priest blessed the ring with holy water; the bridegroom then took the ring and placed it in turn on the thumb and first three fingers of the bride's left hand with the words "*In nomine Patris, in nomine Filii, in nomine Spiritus Sancti, Amen.*" He left it on this fourth finger, since the vein in that finger was supposed to run directly to the heart. The couple were then invited into the church, where they knelt together in order to partake in the nuptial Mass and blessing; they wore linen cloths or "care cloths" upon their heads to protect them from demons. It was also customary for the bride to carry a knife or dagger suspended from her girdle, the reasons for which are uncertain. (Juliet possesses a dagger, with which she stabs herself.) The bride's hair was unbraided, hanging loose about her shoulders. After the Mass it was customary for a festive procession to return from the church to the house where a wedding feast, or "bride-ale," was prepared. The newly joined couple might then receive gifts of silver, or money, or food. The guests were in turn often given presents of gloves—since Shakespeare's father was a glove-maker, there was no great difficulty in procurement. So we leave them on this apparently auspicious day.

Part II
The Queen's Men

Richard Tarlton, the most popular comedian of the Elizabethan age.

CHAPTER 18

To Tell Thee Plaine, I Ayme to Lye with Thee

t some point after the wedding Shakespeare made his way to London. We do not know the year of this very significant transition, but he must have left Stratford by 1586 or 1587.

There are references in several of his plays to an unhappy separation immediately after a wedding, but these may all be wholly dramatic devices. John Aubrey has a note on the subject. "This Wm being inclined naturally to Poetry and acting, came to London I guesse about 18, and was an Actor at one of the Play-houses and did act exceedingly well."[1] Aubrey would then "guesse" his removal to London just after his marriage, as others have also supposed, but this seems to defy common sense and practical decency. We may give him the benefit of a little time with his bride. The probability must be that William Shakespeare and Anne Hathaway, with their expected child, returned to the bridegroom's home in Henley Street. It was customary for a newly married couple to set up house with their own resources but, if that were not possible, the groom's father would offer lodging. With such a young bridegroom as Shakespeare, this must have been a necessity.

It has been supposed that the newly married couple moved into the back extension of the house, with its own solar (or upstairs room) and staircase. But this was probably not constructed until 1601, so the available space in Henley Street was even by Elizabethan standards nicely filled. There was not much privacy, but privacy was not itself considered essential or even particularly important. It was already a large family, with Shakespeare's four younger siblings—Gilbert, Joan, Richard and Edmund, whom we may safely call the forgotten family of the dramatist—as well as four adults, but this was the kind of household to which Mary Arden and Anne Hathaway were accustomed. The ménage was soon enlarged by three children of Shakespeare's own, so it would have been crowded and noisy. And what of Shakespeare himself? In the sixteenth century a married man could not enter a university or be formally apprenticed to a trade. Before his removal to London we may imagine that he led an ordinarily conventional outward life as a lawyer's clerk.

His first daughter, Susannah, was born in May 1583; the name itself, suggesting purity and spotlessness, derives from the Apocrypha. It may have been an assertion of virtue after a birth perilously close to the wrong side of marriage. Although the name later became popular in the circles of the religious reformers, at least if Puritan literature is anything to go by, it was already familiar enough in Stratford itself. Three female children were baptised with that name in the spring of 1583.

The cause of religion manifested itself in a more public, and more dangerous, context in the autumn of that year. Margaret Arden, the daughter of Edward and Mary Arden of Park Hall, with whom Shakespeare's mother claimed some affinity, had married a Catholic gentleman from Warwickshire. This young man, John Somerville of Edstone, was of extreme views. On 25 October 1583, he set out with the express intention of killing Elizabeth I. He announced this ambition to anyone who cared to listen and, as a result of his indiscretion, was arrested on the following day and taken to the Tower of London. He may have been mentally deranged, but the plea of insanity was not enough to excuse an aspiring royal assassin. Somerville's expedition was seen as the prelude to a foreign invasion and the resurgence of a Catholic regime in England.

The consequences were felt by his unfortunate family. A few days later a warrant was issued for the search of all suspected houses in Warwickshire and the arrest of suspicious persons. This investigation was considered urgent because, in the words of the officer in charge, "the papists in this county greatly do work upon the advantage of clearing their houses of all shows of suspicion."[2] Edward Arden was taken at the London house of the Earl of Southampton; Mary Arden and others of her family were arrested by Sir

Thomas Lucy. The Ardens were tried at the Guildhall in London, and were found guilty of treason. Mary Arden was pardoned, but her husband was hanged, drawn and quartered in Smithfield and his head placed on a pole at the southern end of London Bridge. John Somerville hanged himself in Newgate, but his head joined that of his kinsman in its prominent position. And with them was decapitated the Arden family of Warwickshire.

Did John Shakespeare, husband of another Mary Arden and putative kindred of the martyred Ardens, come under suspicion? Did his son? It was a time of terror for anyone even peripherally concerned or related. The key-cold stone of the Tower, torture and a horrible death, were genuine possibilities. It may well have been at this juncture that John Shakespeare concealed his Catholic testament in the rafters of Henley Street. We know only that when the Shakespeares submitted their coat of arms to the College of Heralds, some sixteen years after the events here related, the device of "ermine fess checky"[3] used by the Ardens of Park Hall had been removed. There is one other stray fact. In *Henry VI, Part Three*, Shakespeare invents a native of Warwickshire and gives him the name of John Somerville.

If ever there was a time when William Shakespeare might have appreciated the relative anonymity of the capital, then this was it. But he chose to remain with his family in Stratford for the duration. In February 1585 his twins, Hamnet and Judith Shakespeare, were baptised in the parish church. They were named after Hamnet and Judith Sadler, friends and neighbours who owned a baker's business at the corner of High Street and Sheep Street. When the Sadlers had a son, they named him William. The young Shakespeare, despite his immortal longings, was still very much part of the local community. The name of the boy, so fraught with association, could have been pronounced and spelled Hamblet (chimney was pronounced as chimbley) or of course Hamlet. The mystery of twinship, unique and indissoluble, also provokes Shakespeare to dramatic speculation; in two of his plays, *The Comedy of Errors* and *Twelfth Night*, a twin is confronted by his or her lost counterpart in some dream-like landscape.

The birth of the twins in the early spring of 1585 suggests that, despite Aubrey's "guesse," Shakespeare was still with his wife in the spring of 1584. But no children were conceived by the Shakespeares after that date. In this he did not follow the pattern of his parents, who produced eight children over twenty-two years. He did not even follow the pattern of the time, in which large families were common. At the birth of her twins Anne Shakespeare was only thirty years old, and well within the age of child-bearing. It may have been that the birth of Hamnet and Judith was in some way injurious.

In the conditions of Henley Street, however, it would have been inevitable that Anne and her husband slept in the same bed; in this period, too, there were no properly effective means of birth control. They may have abstained by mutual consent from sexual intercourse. All the evidence suggests, however, that Shakespeare was of a highly sexual nature; it is unlikely that, in his early twenties, he could have abstained without very good reason. The better explanation is also the more obvious one. He was not there. So where was he?

This Way for Me

It has become a commonplace of Shakespearian biography that, from roughly his age of twenty to his age of twenty-eight, we encounter the "lost years." But no years are ever wholly lost. There may be a gap in the chronology, but the pattern of a life may be discerned obliquely and indirectly. It is known that he became a player. It has been surmised that he joined a company of travelling players, perhaps when they were passing through Stratford. It has been suggested that he journeyed to London in the hope or expectation of joining one of the companies already performing there. His previous association with Sir Thomas Hesketh's players, and with Lord Strange's Men, may have facilitated some form of introduction. A clever young actor, and an aspiring dramatist, might have been welcome.

Did he join a company of travelling players when such a group was performing in Stratford? There is no record of this, and it is in any case an unlikely form of recruitment. But, in the seasons from 1583 to 1586, at least eight sets of players performed in the guildhall at Stratford–among them the Earl of Oxford's Men, Lord Berkeley's Men, Lord Chandos's Men, the Earl of Worcester's Men, and the Earl of Essex's Men. Among Worcester's players was Edward Alleyn, sixteen months younger than Shakespeare, who became a formidable presence on the London stage and a direct rival of Shakespeare's own company. But it has also been argued that Shakespeare joined the Earl of Leicester's Men, in part because of a remark in a letter from Sir Philip Sidney referring to "William my Lord of Leicester's jesting player." Sidney, however, may have been alluding to the celebrated William Kempe.

One other company of players, who came to Stratford in 1587, deserves further notice. The Queen's Men had been re-established four years before by the Lord Chamberlain and the Master of Revels, partly in order to provide what might now be called dramatic propaganda on behalf of Elizabethan polity. They were a privileged group of players who were formally chosen to play before the monarch at court. They were paid wages as the queen's servants and granted liveries as "grooms of the chamber"; Shakespeare was to receive a similar honour in later years. The twelve actors had been selected from other companies, and were considered to be at the height of their profession–among them two comic wits, Robert Wilson "quick, delicate, refined" and Richard Tarlton "wondrous plentiful and pleasant."[1]

Tarlton epitomises the nature of the theatre which Shakespeare joined. He was the first great English clown, and the most popular comedian of the Elizabethan age. As a fellow actor put it, "There will never come his like, while the earth can corn. O passing fine Tarlton!"[2] He was said to have been discovered by the Earl of Leicester while keeping swine for his father, and the earl was so delighted with his "happy unhappy answers" that he enlisted him in his service. His jigs and ballads became famous in the 1570s, and he became attached to Queen Elizabeth's Men on the formation of the group in 1583. There can be no doubt that Shakespeare witnessed his elaborate and idiosyncratic performances. Tarlton was also a playwright and wrote a comic drama entitled *Play of the Seven Deadly Sins*. He was a favourite of the queen, and became her unofficial court jester. After his death in Shoreditch in 1588, an anthology entitled *Tarlton's Jests* became a popular favourite. In his will he named as his trustee a fellow actor, William Johnson; Johnson also became in turn Shakespeare's trustee for the purchase of a house in Blackfriars. There is a connection, in other words, and it has often been suggested that Hamlet's reminiscence of Yorick is a recollection of Tarlton himself.

Tarlton's costume was a suit of russet and a buttoned cap; he carried a great bag by his side and wielded a large bat; he played on the tabor and pipe; he had a squint eye, a moustache and a flat nose. He was, according to Stow, a "man of wondrous plentifull pleasant extemporal wit"; he was "the wonder of his time."[3] He was material for endless anecdotes and allusions, he was the subject of nursery rhymes, and many alehouses were named after him complete with his portrait. It was said that the sight of his face alone, peeping from behind the stage, was enough to send audiences into hysterics; he played the role of the country innocent in the city, complete with what might be called physical comedy. It meant that the comic actor became more important than any character or role he was performing. Tarlton would break off from his part and indulge in improvised repartee with the audience, for example, and would introduce jigs or comic business in the middle of the dramatic action. He specialised in grotesque faces, and would pull them at inappropriate moments. He can claim to be the first "star" of the English stage.

The stage clown had a long pedigree. He was related to the Lord of Misrule who presided over the festival rituals of medieval England. He was also connected to the fools and jesters of the court but, more importantly, he also derived from the tradition of the Vice on the medieval stage. The Vice is preeminently the character who works with, rather than before, the spectators. Where the actors see only each other, he observes the audience. He is part of its life; he shares asides and jokes with it; he colludes with it. For him the play is a game in which everyone can participate. He is representative of all the vices of humankind and, as such, is both impresario and conspirator. He is the showman of the medieval theatre, who feigns tears or sympathy and who persuades or cajoles the actors into sin. He sings and rhymes and jokes; he often plays a musical instrument such as a gittern. He indulges in physical comedy such as tumbling or dancing. He engages in soliloquies filled with puns and double entendres. Shakespeare often mentions the fact that he carries a wooden dagger, with which he pares his nails. It is obvious that he is the source of much English humour, and the inspirer of much stagecraft. He is a paradigm for the variegated clowns and fools of Shakespearian drama, and the prototype of villains such as Iago and Richard III. He is one of the primal characters of the theatre, with an ancestry buried far back in folk ritual and a heritage stretching forward to the nineteenth-century music hall and the latest television comedy. He is part of Shakespeare's inheritance.

The Queen's Men began touring almost as soon as they were formed, in the first months journeying to Bristol, Norwich, Cambridge and Leicester. In the summer they travelled; in the winter they returned to London, where they performed at the Bell and the Bull in the City and at the Curtain or the Theatre in the suburbs. From the end of December to February they played at court. As the sovereign's own men they were welcomed wherever they went, and were well recompensed for their trouble. They seem to have earned almost double the amount of other companies. They were not just actors in the contemporary sense but acrobats and comics; they hired a Turkish rope-dancer, and there is a reference of payment "to the queens men that were tumblers." Richard Tarlton had his own "act," like that of any modern comedian.

It is an indication of the hardness or roughness of the travelling life, however, that at Norwich there was an affray in which several of the actors joined and in which one man bled to death, having been struck by a sword. The testimony of witnesses brings the incident to life before us, with a participant crying out: "Villan wilt thowe murder the quenes man?"[4] It seems that the fight started when one of the crowd demanded to see the play before he would pay for his ticket or token, a reminder of a more primitive era of the English theatre. Five years later one member of the company killed another in a brawl. Despite the patronage of the queen, actors still had an unenviable reputation.

Their name has been associated with that of William Shakespeare because of the remarkable coincidence of the plays that they performed, plays that still have a distinctly familiar ring. They include *The Famous Victories of Henry the Fifth*, *King Leir*, *The Troublesome Reign of King John* and *The True Tragedy of Richard III*. The supposition has been, therefore, that Shakespeare somehow joined himself with the Queen's Men in 1587, when they came to Stratford, and that these plays are his early versions of ones that he subsequently revised. The theory has the merit of simplicity, although the world of Elizabethan playing companies is not in itself a simple one: it displays a history of splits and amalgamations, quarrels and reconciliations, hiring and firing.

In 1588 the Queen's Men were divided into two separate groups, with separate repertoires. They were sadly depleted with the death of Richard Tarlton. One group then joined forces with the Earl of Sussex's Men. It may be that, at this time, Shakespeare also left them for another company. But this is to move too far ahead in this history that now, in 1586 and 1587, must first bring the young William Shakespeare to London.

Part III
Lord Strange's Men

Panorama of London and the Thames, showing the Tower and the church of St. Olave. The Tower is mentioned in Shakespeare's work more frequently than any other building.

CHAPTER 20

To Morrow, Toward London

t was an explosion of human energy. He had to reach it. Scholars and biographers have argued about the exact date of his arrival, but his destination was not in doubt. Others had made the journey from Stratford to London in the same period. His contemporary Richard Field had gone from the King's New School to be enrolled as an apprentice. Roger Lock, son of John Lock the glover, had also taken up an apprenticeship in the city. Richard Quiney became a London merchant, as did his cousin John Sadler. Another native of Stratford, John Lane, journeyed from London to the Levant on a merchant ship. They may all have agreed that "Home-keeping youth, haue euer homely wits" (*The Two Gentlemen of Verona*, 2).

In Shakespeare's plays, too, young men often chafe and complain at being kept "rustically at home"; they wish to speed away and be free, on the wind of their instinct and ambition. Goethe once wrote that "in stillness talent forms itself, but character [is created] in the great current of the world." The case of William Shakespeare, however, is singular in more than one sense. None of his contemporaries made their departures from wives or children. It was in fact almost unprecedented for a young man to leave behind his young family. It was unusual even in aristocratic households. It suggests, at the very least, strong determination and single-mindedness on Shakespeare's part. He had to leave.

He was a very practical person. So it seems unlikely that he abandoned his family in some indeterminate or undetermined way. It is also improbable that he decided to seek his fortune in London on the basis of some irrational impulse. Some have suggested that he was fleeing from a bad or forced marriage. There is no evidence for this. Nevertheless he can hardly have been part of a completely successful or happy marriage, for the very good reason that he would not then have considered leaving it. What contented husband would have left his wife and children for an unknown future in an unknown city? It is the merest common sense, then, to imagine him in some respects restless or dissatisfied. Some force greater than familial love drove him onward. He left with a plan, and a purpose. He may conceivably have been accepting an invitation from a group of players, and the prospects of making money as a player were greater than those currently available for a provincial lawyer's clerk. It was soon commonly reported of players that some "have gone to London *very meanly* and have come in time to be exceeding wealthy."[1] If the best means of supporting his young family were to be found in London, then to London he must go. In the lives of great men and women, however, there is a pattern of destiny. Time and place seem in some strange way to shape themselves around them as they move forward. There would be no Shakespeare without London. Some oblique or inward recognition of that fact spurred his determination. In his *Observations on Translating Shakespeare*, Boris Pasternak wrote that at this time Shakespeare was "led by a definite star which he trusted absolutely." That is another way of putting it.

James Joyce noted that "banishment from the heart, banishment from home" is a dominant motif in Shakespeare's drama. The perception may better fit Joyce's own exilic status, but it has an authentic note. Shakespeare's "star" may have led him from home, but it would still be natural to look back at what had been lost. Joyce could only write about Dublin after he had left it. Did Shakespeare have a similar relation to the fields and forests of Arden?

There were two roads to London. The shorter route would have taken him through Oxford and High Wycombe; the other arrived in the capital by way of Banbury and Aylesbury. John Aubrey connects him with a small village on a side-road of the Oxford route. In Grendon Underwood, the dramatist is supposed to have found the model for Dogberry. But any talk of "models" is misplaced. Shakespeare would in subsequent years, however, become thoroughly familiar with the wooded regions and ridges of the Chilterns, the valley of the Great Ouse, the villages and market towns that characterise these journeys. The modern roads follow much the same path, through a transformed landscape.

As sensible as Shakespeare was, he would have set out in late spring or early summer. It was good travelling weather. He might have gone in company, as a safeguard against thieves, or travelled with the Stratford–London "carriers." The principal one of these, William Greenaway, was a neighbour in Henley Street; on his pack-horses he took cheese and brawn, lamb-skins and linseed oil, woollen shirts and hose, to the capital, where he exchanged them for city goods such as spices and silverware. The journey by foot lasted for four days; by horse it took only two.

And then, as Shakespeare approached the city, he saw the pall of smoke. He heard it, a confused roar striated with bells. He smelled it, too. The distinct odour of London penetrated some twenty-five miles on all sides. One route took him to the north by way of Highgate, but the more direct led him into the heart of the capital. It passed the hamlet of Shepherd's Bush and the gravel pits at Kensington, crossing the Westburne brook and the Maryburne brook, until it reached the hanging-tree of Tyburn. Here the road parted, one path going towards Westminster and the other towards the City itself. If Shakespeare had chosen the City route, as is most likely, he travelled down the Oxford Road to the church and village of St. Giles-in-the-Fields. It was his first sight of the London suburbs or in the words of John Stow's *Survey of London*, published in 1598, here "have ye many fair houses builded, and lodgings for Gentlemen, Innes for Travellers, and such like, up almost (for it lacketh but little) to St. Giles in the Fields." But the suburbs also had a reputation for lawlessness where "a great number of dissolute, loose, and insolent people harboured in such and the lyke noysom and disorderly houses, as namely poor cottages, and habitacions of beggars and people without trade, stables, inns, alehouses, taverns, garden-houses converted to dwellings, ordinaries, dicyng houses, bowling-allies and brothel houses."[2] The young Shakespeare had never seen anything like it before; he must have found it, in the phrase Charlotte Brontë used when she first entered the City, deeply exciting. Then onwards towards the bars of Holborn, past straggling lines of shops and tenements, yards and inns, and towards the terrible prison of Newgate. This was the gateway of London, "the floure of cities alle."

A traveller entering the city for the first time could not help but be profoundly moved or disturbed by the experience. It assaulted all of the senses with its stridency and vigour. It was a vortex of energy. It was voracious. The traveller was surrounded by street-traders or by merchants beseeching him to buy; he was hustled and jostled. It was a city of continuous noise–of argument, of conflict, of street-selling, of salutations such as "God ye good morrow" and "God ye good den"–and more often than not it smelled terribly of dung and offal and human labour. Some of the phrases of the streets are deeply redolent of London life–"goe too you are a whore of your tung," and "as much worth as a piss in the Thames." If you were "snout-fair" you were good-looking, and to have sex was "to occupy." There were merchants standing in the doorways of their shops, lounging about, picking their teeth; their wives were inside, sitting on joint-stools, ready to bargain with the customers. Apprentices stood outside the workshops of their masters, calling out to passers-by. Householders, as often as not, took up position on their doorsteps where they might trade gossip or insults with their neighbours. There was no privacy in the modern sense of that word.

There were rows of shops, all in one vicinity selling the same limited range of goods–cheeses, pickles, gloves, spices. There were dimly lit basements, entered by stone steps from the street, where sacks of corn or malt were stacked up for sale. There were old women crouched upon the ground with parcels of nuts, or withered vegetables, spread out around them. There were street-sellers with their goods piled high on wooden trays hung about their necks. There seemed to be endless numbers of men carrying sacks and burdens on their backs, weaving through the crowds that packed the narrow streets. The children were busily at work alongside the adults, too, wheeling barrows or calling out for trade. People ate pies or small roasted birds as they walked, throwing the bones of the thrush into the roadway. There were literally hundreds of ballad-sellers, "singing men" or "singing women" who stood at street-corners or on barrels to advertise their wares. There were alleys that seemed to lead nowhere, ruinous gates and tenements encroaching upon the streets, sudden flights of steps, gaping holes and rivulets of filth and garbage.

It was already an ancient place, inhabited for more than fifteen hundred years, and it savoured of age and decay. John Stow loved to survey the ruins of ancient times in the sixteenth-century streets through which he walked; in shape and texture it was still the medieval city, with the old walls and gatehouses, chapels and barns. The sites of the monasteries and priories, some of them dismantled as a result of Henry's "dissolution" but others put to new use, were still marked out as precincts and liberties. The palace of the Savoy, linked with the French wars of Edward III, survived. The Earl of Warwick's house, in Dowgate between Walbrook and the Thames, still stood. The Tower of London, to which Shakespeare adverted more than to any other edifice in his plays, still watched over the city. Stone House in Lombard Street was known as King John's House. Crosby Hall, where Richard III was supposed to have accepted the crown of England, endured. It was only to be expected that Shakespeare's history plays would be imagined within the very heart of the city where he lived and worked.

But the miracle of late sixteenth-century London lay in the fact that it was renewing itself. Its vigour and energy came from a fresh access of youthfulness. It has been estimated that half of the urban population was under the age of twenty years. This is what rendered it so strident, so tough, so excitable. Never again would it be so young. Apprentices made up 10 per cent of its population, and apprentices were known for their high spirits and for their occasional tendency towards violence. Londoners were often compared to a swarm of bees, quick to congregate and to act in instinctive union.

There is another aspect to this youthful city. The average expectancy of life in the parishes of London, rich or poor, was very low. An early sixteenth-century diarist noted that he was "growing towards the age of forty, at the which year begins the first part of the old man's age."[3] The expectation of a relatively short life must have affected the conduct and attitude of many Londoners. They were consigned to a short burst of existence with the evidence of disease and mortality all around them. Their experience was all the more vital and intense. This is the proper context for the growth of drama. Elizabethan Londoners acquired, or amassed, experience with more eagerness and expedition. They were quicker, sharper, more colourful, than their contemporaries elsewhere in the kingdom. The reign of Elizabeth has often been seen as that of an ageing monarch surrounded by foolish and headstrong boys; strange though it may seem, it is part of an authentic historical picture. But the boys—and girls—were also on the streets of London, buying and selling, conversing and fighting.

That is why this is properly seen as the age of the adventurer and the projector, the dreamer of vast schemes. The formation of joint stock companies and the promotion of colonialist enterprises, the voyages of Martin Frobisher and Francis Drake, were all part of the same quickening energy and activity. It was a young man's world in which aspiration and ambition might lead anywhere and everywhere. This was where Shakespeare belonged.

𝒯he 𝒮pirit of the 𝒯ime 𝒮hall 𝒯each 𝒲e 𝒮peed

𝒯*he city was expanding* quickly. It lured both the poor and the wealthy, the immigrant and the agricultural labourer. The aspiring youth of the country came to the Inns of Court, while the gentry haunted the legal courts and royal court of Westminster. The London "season," for gentry and nobility, really only developed between 1590 and 1620. But there were also more beggars in London than in the rest of the country combined. The city was in a ferment of building and rebuilding, with tenements being erected on any and every vacant spot or spare piece of land. Proclamations of 1580 and 1593 attempted to halt the spread of new construction, but they might as well have tried to halt the tides. Houses and hovels were built away from the streets and the alleys, in gardens or in courtyards, and existing houses were divided up into smaller and smaller dwellings. The graveyards had houses built upon them. A population of approximately fifty thousand in 1520 had reached two hundred thousand by 1600. The shock of the new, for the young Shakespeare, was in part the shock of great numbers of people huddled together in a vast effusion of life.

That is why the city was pushing westward and eastward, too, beyond the city walls. The road between London and Westminster was as busy as the streets within the City, filled with litters and hackney coaches, carts and drays, wagons and pack-horses and four-wheeled carriages called "caroches." Shakespeare may have been surprised by the narrowness of some of these streets that had not been built for the access of new traffic: the principal streets of Stratford were wider.

London was unique. It was the only city of its kind, and of its size, in England. So there grew a unique form of self-awareness among Londoners. It would be absurd to suppose some sudden change of consciousness—most citizens were too busy to be reflective in that manner—but there was an instinctive awareness that they were engaged in forms of life that had no real precedent. This was no longer a medieval city. It had suffered a sea-change. It was a new kind of thing, an urban mass comprised of people who related to each other in specifically urban ways. It is of vital consequence in the context of Shakespeare's plays.

The city created, and existed upon, confusion. Thomas Dekker, in *The Honest Whore*, asked: "Is change strange? 'Tis not the fashion unless it alter . . ." The rise of the gentry and the merchant class steadily eroded the position and privileges of the old nobility. Kinship counted for less, and civic society for more; privately sworn obedience gave way to more impersonal bonds. It has been described as the transition from a "lineage society" to a "civil society."

Costume is of the utmost significance in determining the quality of the Elizabethan urban world. Appearance indicated status and position as well as wealth. The emphasis among all groups of citizens—apart, that is, from the Puritan elect and the more staid members of the merchant aristocracy—was upon brightness or originality of colour and upon the wealth of minute detail lavished upon each article. One fashion was that of wearing a very large rose, made of silk, on each shoe. The nature of your dress also indicated the nature of your profession. Even street-sellers dressed in the clothing that would signify their role. Prostitutes made use of blue starch to advertise their trade. Apprentices wore blue gowns in winter and blue cloaks in summer; they were also obliged to wear blue breeches, stockings of white cloth and flat caps. Beggars and vagrants dressed in a way that would elicit pity and alms. In the theatres themselves infinitely more money was spent on costumes than on hiring playwrights or actors. It was a young city in this sense, too. More and more significantly the city itself became a form of theatre. London was a forcing house for dramatic improvisation and theatrical performance. It encompassed the ritual recantation of the traitor at the scaffold and the parade of the merchants in the Royal Exchange. It was the world of Shakespeare.

. . .

The city became the home of the pageant, in which all the spectacle and colour of the urban world were on display. On these festival occasions, arches and fountains were especially built, thereby turning London into a piece of moving scenery; the members of the various guilds and the aldermen, the knights and the merchants, dressed in their appropriate costume and were accompanied by ensigns and bannerets. There were platforms and stages upon which tableaux were performed. There was no real distinction between those who participated in, and those who watched, the moving displays. It was a piece of intense theatricality in which life and art were lit by the same pure, bright flame. It was also a means of expressing the power and wealth of the city. In the same spirit an historian has noted, of Elizabethan style, that "it was magnificent by design and saw magnificence the sum of all virtues" with "a glorious ostentation of random craftsmanship" that endlessly diverts: "it never rests; it demands response and elicits pleasure; there is no concession to order or to simplicity."[1] It might in part be a definition of Shakespeare's own art. The predilection was for bold colour, and intricate pattern, all designed to elicit wonder or amazement. These were also the characteristics attributed to Shakespearian drama. In any one period, all the manifestations of a culture are of a piece.

This sense of magnificence was particularly pertinent to royalty. Elizabeth I declared that "we Princes are set as it were upon stages in the sight and view of the world," an opinion echoed by Mary Queen of Scots who at her trial explained to her judges that "the theatre of the world is wider than the realm of England." Shakespeare, with sure dramatic instinct, populated his stage with monarchs and courtiers. It is the world of his history plays, where ritual and ceremonial play so large a part. But there are surely risks in such an enterprise. A player can be a king, or a queen. What if the sovereign herself were no more than a player? It is a potentially delicate question that he broaches in *Richard II* and *Richard III*.

As the Church became desacralised, its candles and its images removed, so urban society became more profoundly ritualistic and spectacular. This is of the utmost importance for any understanding of Shakespeare's genius. He thrived in a city where dramatic spectacle became the primary means of understanding reality. The pulpit just outside St. Paul's Cathedral, known as Paul's Cross, was defined as "the very stage of this land"[2] where the preacher played his part, and John Donne declared that "this City is a great Theatre." An early dramatist, Edward Sharpham, echoed this sentiment with his observation that "the Cittie is a Commedie, both in partes and in apparel, and your Gallants are the Actors."[3] Just as in more recent times New York has become a cinematic city, known primarily through the images in film and television, so London was the first theatrical city. The success of the drama in London, whether presented at the Globe or at the Curtain, had no parallel in any other European capital. From the production in 1581 of Robert Wilson's *The Three Ladies of London*, there were innumerable plays that used the city as their setting.

The London playhouse was a new kind of building, erected for the first time in this period. People watched the actors in order to learn how to behave, how to speak and how to bow; the audience applauded individual speeches. The drama was also used as a means of conveying a social or political message to those assembled. A preacher complained that "plays are grown nowadays into such high request, as that some profane persons affirm they can learn as much both for edifying and example at a play, as at a sermon."[4] For the majority of the English, the drama of the mystery plays and the morality plays had until recent times been the major vehicle for spiritual instruction and doctrinal fable. It still retained its authority as an instructor. It was not simply an entertainment in the modern sense.

There was a profound recognition of life as a play. Jaques's metaphor, "All the world's a stage . . ." in *As You Like It*, was already a Renaissance commonplace. In sixteenth-century London, however, the truism acquired a more powerful resonance. For some the conflation of life and theatre was a source of comedy and high spirits; for others, like the Duchess of Malfi in Webster's melodrama, it provoked sadness rather than mirth. Whatever its precise connotation, it consorted with what may be called the London vision. This has a direct bearing on Shakespeare's drama. If life was a play, then what was a play but heightened life? The action on stage might be artificial, and might even draw attention to its artificiality, but it was still deeply authentic.

What were the characteristics of this London vision? It combined mockery and satire, discontinuity and change. It included cruelty and spectacle, where bears were tied to the stake and baited until death. It was mixed and variable, conflating satire and tragedy, melodrama and burlesque. It was the context for what Voltaire described as "*les farces monstrueuses*" of Shakespeare. It often depended upon coincidence and chance encounter. It was interested in the behaviour of crowds. It was bright and garish. It jostled for attention: Walt Whitman believed that Shakespeare "painted too intensely." It was also implicitly egalitarian. Once the actors had taken off the robes of king or common soldier, all were equal. On the stage itself the queen shared the same space–had the same presence–as the clown. As Hazlitt said at a later date, "it raises the great, the remote, and the possible to an equality with the real, the little and the near." This was Shakespeare's experience of the city.

CHAPTER 22

There's Many a Beast Then in a Populous City

isitors to London registered their surprise or disapproval at the level of intimacy between the sexes. Erasmus mentions that "wherever you come, you are received with a kiss by all; when you take your leave, you are dismissed with kisses."[1] It was customary, at the end of the sixteenth century and the beginning of the seventeenth century, for women to wear dresses in public that exposed their breasts.

The proximity of brothels and playhouses was always a matter for comment among contemporary moralists; they were both erected beyond the strict jurisdiction of the city, outside the walls or on the south bank, but there was a closer connection. The owners of the playhouses, the respected Henslowe and Alleyn among them, were also the owners of brothels. Alleyn's wife was paraded in an open cart because of her connection with one such place of assignation. There were over one hundred bawdy-houses in the suburbs, and Shakespeare mentions the sign of the blind Cupid over their doors. Near the theatres, too, were "garden walks" and "garden alleys" where prostitutes gathered. The young women came from all over England. Contemporary legal documents reveal that two young girls, contemporaries of Shakespeare, had come from Stratford-upon-Avon to find an illicit income. There is a clear association between play-going and sexual indulgence, perhaps because both represented a temporary relief from the usual world. The theatre and the brothel both offered a release from conventional ethics and social morality. Shakespeare's plays are filled with bawdy and sexual innuendo. He was catering to the tastes of a large section of the crowd.

Of disease, there was no end. The playhouses were closed down at the time of plague, precisely because they were considered to be the prime agent of infection. Waves of epidemic illness swept away the urban crowd in the most terrible ways. In 1593 more than 14 per cent of the population died of plague, and twice that number were infected. Sex and disease were closely associated. The plague was ascribed by some to "sodomitical sins."[2] Plague was also associated with the characteristic smell of the city, so that London became an organism of death as well as depravity. Few could ever have been wholly well. Mortality and anxiety were part of the air that the citizens breathed. The frontispiece of a production by Thomas Dekker in 1606 reads as *The Seven Deadlie Sinns of London: Drawn in seven severall Coaches, Through the seven severall Gates of the Citie*. All of Shakespeare's plays allude to disease in one or other of its myriad forms, to agues and fevers, to palsy and sweating-sickness. In his drama, the notion of infection is associated with breathing itself.

The poor and the vagrant, also, have always been part of London's life. They are the shadow that the city casts. In this period they comprised some 14 per cent of the population. There were the labouring poor who eked out their livings as porters or sweepers or water-bearers. There were the "sturdy beggars" who as often as not were whipped out of the city; a second or third appearance would incur the penalty of death. There were the masterless men who earned a small living by plastering or building or other casual trades. There were the destitute who lived off the parish and begged in the streets. These are "the famisht beggers" in *Richard III* (3374) who are "wearie of their liues." Shakespeare was acutely aware of this group of the dispossessed who appear, appropriately enough, in the margins of his plays; but, unlike the pamphleteers and the divines, he did not launch any great invectives against the conditions of the time. The parlous conditions of the poorer sort emerge fitfully in *Coriolanus*, for example, but without any great expressions either of pity or contumely.

The presence of these outcasts, who had little or nothing to lose, encouraged crime and violence on a large scale. It has been estimated that there were thirty-five serious disturbances or riots in the city between 1581 and 1602. There were food riots, riots between apprentices and the gentlemen of the Inns of Court, threats of riots against immigrants or "aliens." In the first part of *Henry IV* the king blames "moody beggars staruing for a time" for causing "pell-mell hauocke and confusion" (2578). Of course in a city where male citizens customarily carried daggers or rapiers, apprentices had knives, and females were armed with bodkins or long pins, there was a constant danger of violence. Daggers were generally worn on the right hip. Shakespeare would have carried a rapier or a broadsword as a matter of habit. Cases of violent assault, brought before one of the under-sheriffs, were as common as cases of theft or over-pricing. There were criminal gangs, difficult to distinguish from gangs of disbanded soldiers, threatening the stability of certain areas of the city such as the Mint by the Tower and the Clink in Southwark.

In the course of his life Shakespeare came to know this city very well. He resided at various times in Bishopsgate, in Shoreditch, in Southwark and in Blackfriars. Well known to his neighbours and fellow parishioners, and recognisable by sight to the citizens who crowded the public theatres, he was in no sense an anonymous person. He knew the bookshops of St. Paul's Churchyard and Paternoster Row; the title pages of his plays published in quarto list some sixteen different premises, from the sign of the Fox near St. Austin's Gate to the sign of the White Hart in Fleet Street. He knew the taverns, where Rhenish and Gascony wines were sold, and the inns where beers and ales were purveyed. He knew the eating houses, or banqueting houses, such as the Oliphant in Southwark and Marco Lucchese's in Hart Street. He knew the Royal Exchange, where free concerts were held on Sunday afternoons in the summer. He knew the fields to the north of the walls, where wrestling and archery contests were held. He knew the woods that encircled the city and, when in his plays he arranged meetings in the woods outside the town, the majority of his audience would have thought of London's retreats. He also became very well acquainted with the Thames in all of its moods. He crossed it continually, and it became his primary form of transport. It was shallower, and wider, than it is now. But in the stillness of the night it could distinctly be heard, rushing between its banks. "Tut, man, I mean thou'lt loose the flood, and in loosing the flood, loose thy voyage." So speaks Panthino in *The Two Gentlemen of Verona* (607–8). Shakespeare did not need to address London directly in his work; it is the rough cradle of all his drama.

CHAPTER 23

Sir I Shall Study Deserving

✳

n his first arrival in London, how did he appear to his contemporaries? When in *The Taming of the Shrew* Lucentio leaves
Pisa to "plunge" into Padua, that "nurserie of Arts," he arrives
expectantly and "with sacietie seekes to quench his thirst" (298). The young
Shakespeare was eager for experience, in all of its forms; in some way he
wished for "satiety" in the manifold life of London. In his fancy, or fantasy,
he might "heare sweet discourse, conuerse with Noble-men" (*The Two Gentlemen of Verona*, 318). His aspiring spirit might there find its true setting. He
also wished to test himself in the forcing house of thought and drama. This
youthful ambition emerges in the most surprising contexts. In *Antony and
Cleopatra* (2120–1) Antony remarks of the morning that it resembles:

> . . . the spirit of a youth
> That meanes to be of note.

Was he then eager for the fame that, as the King of Navarre puts it, "all hunt
after in their lyues" (*Love's Labour's Lost*, 1)? Many have assumed it, but the
fame of an actor or a dramatist was in this period a highly perishable commodity. He would have felt the mental power of the city, however, and with
it an inkling of his own destiny.

We might remark upon Shakespeare's intense and overwhelming energy.

It manifests itself at all stages of his career, and in his youth it must have been irrepressible. We might also remark upon his buoyancy, an inward easiness of spirit. As an actor he was trained to be quick and nimble, but that vitality was an essential part of his being; the images of his plays are filled with flight and with swift action, with movement and lightness. He is the poet of speed and agility. His characters are not of the study or the library but of the busy and active world. His is a drama of the sudden moment or change, and one of his most powerful images is that of the lightning strike "which doth cease to bee / Ere one can say, it lightens" (*Romeo and Juliet*, 892–3). All the myriad imagery, from the social as well as the natural world, suggests that he was a man of preternatural alertness. And he was known, like the characters within his comedies, for the quickness of his repartee. John Aubrey, acquiring his information from the theatrical Beeston family, noted that Shakespeare possessed "a very readie and pleasant smooth Witt" and also scribbled down that "he was a handsome well-shap't man."[1] Actors, with the exception of those who specialised in comic roles, were expected to be handsome and well shaped.

No remarkable young man or woman is devoid of energy, but many are also beset by self-consciousness and embarrassment. It is the price of eminence. There are many passing references in Shakespeare's drama to blushes and to flushed faces, when emotions suffuse the countenance in unanticipated ways; it is an almost unwitting habit of Shakespeare to include such details. Charles Lamb mentions his "self-watchfulness." There are also references in his dramas to stage-fright.

Everyone remarked upon his sweetness and courtesy. He was variously called "ciuill," "generous" and, most often, "gentle." Despite spiteful allusions to his past as a law-writer or country schoolmaster he was generally considered to be well bred and indeed "gentle"–not meaning mild or tender, in the modern sense, but possessing the virtues and attributes of a gentleman. He would later demonstrate to the world that he was indeed "well bred."

Gentility implies instinctive courtesy towards those of inferior rank or position, pleasing modesty towards those of equal status, and proper respect towards superiors. Bernard Shaw put the point differently when he speculated that Shakespeare "was a very civil gentleman who got round men of all classes."[2] The vogue for Castiglione's *The Courtyer*, published in English translation in 1561, had not yet passed; it was a manual of civil conduct to which all gentlemen (including lawyers and the wealthier merchants) subscribed. It is clear, from many allusions, that Shakespeare had read it. His own plays have indeed been read as a "pattern book" in courteous speech. That is why he was described by his contemporaries as "mellifluous" and "honie-tongued." Castiglione himself recommends one who is "in companie with men and women of al degrees [and who] hath in him a certaine sweetnes, and so comely demeanour, that who so speaketh with him, or yet beholdeth him, must needes beare him an affection for ever."[3] Did this come to Shakespeare instinctively, as most have surmised, or was it in part the result of practice and education?

This view of his character was in any case established very early when, in 1709, Nicholas Rowe depicted him as "a good-natur'd Man, of great sweetness in his Manners, and a most agreeable Companion."[4] This comes as a surprise to those romantics who believe that he must have shared the horrors of Macbeth or the torments of Lear. He is not jealous Othello, nor rumbustious Falstaff, except in the moment of conceiving them. Sophocles, the author of some of the most desperate Greek tragedies, was known as the happy playwright. Authors, at least when they are in the company of other people, can be most "unlike" their work—and Shakespeare generally was in company. It was not an age of privacy.

John Aubrey also passed on the information that he was "very good company." He was affable and convivial, according to contemporary testimony. He was amiable, and undoubtedly funny. Much of the surviving testimony concerns his sudden jokes, and a prevailing wit which tended towards irony. He manifested a continual subtle humorousness, like some stream of life. J. B. Yeats passed on a remarkable insight to his son, W. B. Yeats, in a letter of 1922. "I bet that the gentle Shakespeare," he wrote, "was not remarkable for his gravity, and I think that in his plays, he is always maliciously on the watch for grave people as if he did not like them."[5]

He did not stand out as a man of eccentric or extraordinary character, and it seems that his contemporaries sensed a deep equality with him. He effortlessly entered the sphere of their interests and activities. He was in that sense infinitely good-natured. The apparent ordinariness of extraordinary men and women is one of the last great taboos of biographical writing. It would not do to admit that nineteen-twentieths of a life, however great or enchanted, is plain and unexciting and not to be distinguished from the life of anyone else. But there should be a further admission. The behaviour and conversation of even the most powerful writer, or statesman, or philosopher, will in large part be no more than average or predictable. There is not much to differentiate the mass of humankind, except for some individual action or production. Shakespeare seems to embody the truth of this.

That is why his contemporaries came away from Shakespeare's company with no overwhelming sense of his personality. Would he have recounted his sexual conquests or commented upon other writers? Would he have become drunk, in an effort to douse his furious energy? Ben Jonson remarked upon his "open, and free nature," echoing Iago's description of Othello. Open may mean accessible and transparent; but it can also mean receptive, like an open mouth. His amiability may not have been so apparent in his professional capacity. It has often been pointed out that he did not become engaged in the more pugnacious writers' quarrels of the period, and seems in general to have steered clear of public conflict and controversy. They were a waste of time and energy. But he parodied his contemporaries' styles in his plays, and caricatured their persons in figures such as Moth. It is easy to exaggerate Shakespeare's poise and detachment; he may not have been argumentative in public, hating controversy of every kind, but he may have been sharp and acerbic in private.

Much speculation has been devoted to his "feminine" characteristics and, in particular, to his extraordinary compassion and sensitivity. Yet many men have been known for their yielding sympathy and consideration; as attributes, these are not sexually exclusive. It was not because he had some "soft" aspect of his character that he chose not to enter into fights and disagreements, but because he could see every side of every argument. It was once said of Henry James that he had a mind so fine that no idea could violate it; we might say of Shakespeare that he had a sympathy so fine that no belief could injure it.

But, when he left the company of others, what then? In remarkable people there is always an inward power propelling them forward. Shakespeare was very determined. He was very energetic. You do not write thirty-six plays in less than twenty-five years without being driven. So, on his first arrival in London, his contemporaries would have encountered a highly ambitious young man. He was ready to compete with his more educated contemporaries, from Marlowe and Chapman to Greene and Lyly. In certain respects he resembles the adventurers in other fields of Elizabethan endeavour, and he would come to master the contemporary drama in all of its forms. To succeed in Elizabethan society, too, it was necessary to be quick, shrewd and exceedingly determined. We may assume that he was not sentimental. The young men in his early plays are remarkable for their humour and their energy, amounting almost to self-assertion; they are not troubled by inward doubt. Shakespeare himself had a sure sense of his own worth. One of the themes of his sonnets, for example, lies in the full expectation that his verse would be read in succeeding ages. It is hard to believe, however, that he was free from interior conflict. His plays are established upon it. He was a man who had left behind his wife and children, and whose plays are filled with images of loss, exile and self-division. He had a desire to act, even at the cost of his reputation as a poet, and the sonnets are in any autobiographical reading touched by melancholy brooding and even self-disgust.

Yet he was also exceedingly practical. He could not otherwise have written, acted in, and helped to "direct" dramas that appealed to all of the people. It is a matter of common observation that a "genius" in one field is likely to be supremely able in other spheres of life. Turner was a sterling businessman. Thomas More was an expert lawyer. Chaucer was an excellent diplomat. Shakespeare was skilful, not to say hard-headed, in money matters. He acquired a reputation among his fellow countrymen as a money-lender. He bought up properties and tithes. He speculated on corn and malt at times of dearth. His will is an eminently pragmatic and unsentimental document. And, by the time of his death, he had become a very rich man.

CHAPTER 24

I Will Not Be Slack to Play My Part in Fortunes Pageant

here were innumerable inns where he could have lodged, on his first arrival in London. The Bell Inn, in Carter Lane by St. Paul's Cathedral, was the inn used by such Stratfordians as William Greenaway, but it is just as likely that he stayed with a fellow countryman who had been approached in advance. The Quineys or the Sadlers may even have written for him letters of introduction to friends or relatives in the city; Bartholomew Quiney, for example, was a rich cloth-maker who had settled in the capital. It is even possible that he stayed with his friend Richard Field; but Field was still an apprentice, and may not have been able to offer suitable accommodation.

His first employment was in the theatre, but it is not clear in what capacity. His earliest biographer states that "he made his first Acquaintance in the Play-house . . . in a very mean Rank."[1] This has been variously construed as meaning that he became a prompter, a call-boy, a porter or a patcher-up of other men's plays. It could also imply that he began as a young actor or "hired man." The tradition in Stratford itself was of the same import. A visitor to the town in 1693 records that "the clerke who shew'd me this church is above eighty years old" and that this old man recalled how the young Shakespeare had gone to London "and there was received into the play-house as a serviture."[2]

A lineal descendant of Joan Shakespeare, the poet's sister, stated "that

Shakespeare owed his rise in life, and his introduction to the theatre, to his accidentally holding the horse of a gentleman at the door of the theatre on his first arriving in London; his appearance led to enquiry and subsequent patronage."[3] This sounds too good to be true. But flesh was added to these bones in the eighteenth century by Samuel Johnson, who repeated the story that the young Shakespeare earned his living by holding the horses of theatrical patrons. In *The Plays of William Shakespeare*, published in 1765, he added the information that many such patrons "came on horseback to the play" and when Shakespeare arrived in London "his first expedient was to wait at the door of the play-house, and hold the horses of those who had no servants, that they might be ready again after the performance. In this office he became so conspicuous for his care and readiness, that in a short time every man as he alighted called for *Will Shakespear*."[4] It is true that two of the earliest theatres, the Theatre and the Curtain, were best reached on horseback. But the only real evidence for this claim lies in the fact that Shakespeare did indeed know a great deal about horses and could distinguish a Neapolitan from a Spaniard; he even knew the slang of the horse-yard. Since horses were the primary means of transport, however, that knowledge was widely shared. There are other reasons for Shakespeare's interest in horsemanship; it was considered to be an intrinsic part of gentlemanly and especially noble conduct.

The authority of Samuel Johnson was not, in any event, sufficient to sway other commentators. The Shakespearian scholar and editor Edmond Malone stated that "there is a stage tradition that his first office in the theatre was that of Call-boy or prompter's attendant; whose employment it is to give the performers notice to be ready to enter."[5]

There is no reason to suppose that a "call-boy," if such a post existed, or a horse-minder would automatically rise very high in the theatrical profession. Common sense suggests that he was hired as an actor, in which capacity he later emerges in the public record. By this time acting was a profession to which it was customary to become informally "apprenticed." Certainly it required an intense and specific training, in the arts of deportment and vocal technique as well as swordsmanship, memory and dancing. There are two principal candidates for the honour of first employing him, the Queen's Men and Lord Strange's Men. Some of the earliest versions of his plays were the property of the Queen's Men, as we have observed, and it is likely that he joined them for a limited period. He may well have been looking around for the best possible opportunities, in any case, and moved from company to company. There is evidence that he joined Lord Strange's Men, perhaps as early as 1588. Certain juvenile plays of his were also performed by that company. They were established in Lancashire, and we may conjecture that he was taken on by players who already knew or recognised his abilities.

Lord Strange–Ferdinando Stanley, later the fifth Earl of Derby–was one of the wealthiest and most influential of the English nobility. The earls of Derby, whose family name was Stanley, based their power in Lancashire. Henry VII, to whom Lord Strange was related, had modelled his palace at Richmond upon the Stanley castle at Lathom. Strange had his own court, retinue and, of course, players. It is known that he delighted in drama, and that he witnessed the last performance of the Chester mystery cycle. Even though the presentation of these religious plays had been banned by official interdict, since they were considered too close to the dramatic rituals of the old faith, the mayor of Chester ordained in 1577 a special production for the grandees "at the hie Crosse."[6] It is an indication of Lord Strange's affinity with the old faith and suggests, too, that for him drama was more than mere tumbling. His own players were no doubt largely occupied in performing at one or another of the various great houses of the Stanleys in Lancashire, which is where the young Shakespeare, in service with the Hoghtons or the Heskeths, is likely to have encountered them.

Lord Strange was only five years older than Shakespeare, and from a relatively early age gained a reputation for learning and for artistry. In *Colin Clout's Come Home Again* (442–3), a poem in which Shakespeare himself is mentioned, Edmund Spenser refers both to Lord Strange's munificent patronage and to his native abilities:

> Both did he other, which could pipe, maintaine,
> And eke could pipe himself with passing skill.

It is not at all unlikely that he might have spotted the superlative talents of young Shakespeare.

Lord Strange has also been associated with a group of noblemen and scholars who have become known as "the school of night." It met at Sir Walter Raleigh's London dwelling, Durham House, and included among its members Raleigh himself, the Earl of Northumberland, George Chapman, George Peele, Thomas Heriot, John Dee and perhaps even Christopher Marlowe. This esoteric group of projectors and speculators engaged in discussion of sceptical philosophy, mathematics, chemistry and navigation. They were taunted with atheism and blasphemy, but they were in effect part of the speculative and adventurous spirit of the period in which mathematics and occultism were seen as aspects of the same great design. Shakespeare possibly alludes to them in *Love's Labour's Lost*, a play that was written as a kind of "in-house" entertainment. Although he was not a member of the "school of night," he knew its purposes.

Lord Strange had been a contemporary of the precocious and witty playwright John Lyly, at Oxford, and numbered among his acquaintance what might be called a theatrical "set." Christopher Marlowe claimed to be "very well known" to him.[7] This is not hard to believe, since Lord Strange's Men performed Marlowe's *The Jew of Malta* and *The Massacre at Paris*. Thomas Nashe in *Pierce Penniless* praised Strange as "this renowned Lord, to whom I owe the utmost powers of my love and duty." Strange was also well acquainted with Thomas Kyd, whose *The Spanish Tragedy* was part of his players' repertoire. Since versions of Shakespeare's plays also became part of that repertoire, we may safely conclude that there is some connection between these playwrights. It seems likely that Shakespeare acted in *The Jew of Malta* and *The Spanish Tragedy*. He was part of the same group.

It was perhaps a chance of cultural history that this particular collection of young men arose in the same period, and became dedicated to the same new profession. There are other parallels to this sudden burst of efflorescence and magnificent achievement—among English poets, for example, in the late fourteenth century and in the late eighteenth century. In the popular imagination Shakespeare stands alone and inviolable among his contemporaries—quiet, gentle, modest, perhaps rather retiring. But is the popular imagination altogether correct? Instead we will begin to see him as part of a competitive and restless world, where the palm was awarded to the shrewdest, the most energetic and the most persevering.

Strange was also considered to be Catholic or crypto-Catholic, and around him grew a network of suspicion, espionage and intrigue. In 1593 Richard Hesketh delivered a letter to Strange, by then Earl of Derby, asking him to stand as leader of a plot against the queen; Strange surrendered Hesketh to the authorities, but died suddenly in the following year. His unexpected death was popularly ascribed to witchcraft or to poisoning. Is it any wonder that Shakespeare steered clear of contemporary factions and quarrels?

CHAPTER 25

As in a Theatre. Whence They Gape and Point

n 1572 *two Acts* of Parliament materially affected the status of the players. The earlier of them, promulgated in January, restricted the number of retainers that any nobleman might keep in his service. It was a device by which Elizabeth and her advisers hoped to curb the power of over-mighty lords, but it had an effect upon certain troupes of actors who were cut adrift from noble patronage. So James Burbage wrote to the Earl of Leicester, asking him to reaffirm his patronage of his players.

The urgency of his request is explained by the second Act of Parliament of 1572, which set down conditions for "the punishment of Vagabondes"; among such vagabonds were included "all fencers, bear-wards, common players in interludes, & minstrels, not belonging to any Baron of the realm or towards any other personage of greater degree."[1] If you were not a retainer of a great lord, you could be whipped and burned through the ear. So these were the conditions that created the new world of players that Shakespeare entered. By force of necessity they had grouped themselves around certain settled employers or patrons. They were also searching for fixed and stable premises where they might perform in London. It was a way of acquiring respectability and of escaping legal punishment. The stratagem was not completely successful–actors and playwrights were routinely hauled before investigations or consigned to prison–but in hindsight it can be seen as a first step in the creation of the London theatrical world and the eventual emergence of the "West End."

When Shakespeare arrived in London there were several familiar venues for theatrical performances. The oldest of them were the inns or, rather, large rooms within inns which would otherwise have been used for meetings or assemblies. There is a belief that inn-yards, with covered galleries all around them, were the first public theatres; but a moment's consideration reveals the impracticality of such an arrangement. Inn-yards were places where travellers arrived, where horses were tethered, and where supplies were delivered: places of public ingress and egress. These are not the ideal circumstances for public performances. The only exception occurred in an inn such as the Black Bull, where there was an extra yard connected to the rear yard by a covered alley.

There must have been many more places for performance than are currently known, but a few have been recorded for posterity. The Cross Keys was in Gracechurch Street, where Lord Strange's Men performed, and the Bell Inn was on the same street. The Belsavage was located on Ludgate Hill, the Bull in Bishopsgate Street and the Boar's Head was on the north side of Whitechapel Street beyond Aldgate. It is not clear how much they resembled theatres rather than inns; it seems likely, given the continuities of London life, that they were close to the early nineteenth-century "musical saloons" or "music halls" where drink or "wet money" was served to paying customers. Certainly it would be a mistake to think of them as inns that simply put on plays as additional entertainment. The Boar's Head, for example, had erected a permanent theatrical space on its premises, and for the Earl of Worcester's Men "the house called the Bores head is the place they haue especially vsed and doe best like of."[2] Some of the earliest companies employed, for a stage, wooden planks placed across beer barrels that had been roped together. The great companies worked in the inns, and one contemporary described "the two prose books played at the Bel-savage, where you shall never find a word without wit, never a line without pith, never a letter placed in vain."[3] These are precisely the places where Shakespeare learned his craft at first hand.

By the time of Shakespeare's arrival, however, there were at least four large structures built as general resorts for entertainment in which the theatre took its place alongside wrestling and bear-baiting. The first ever recorded in London documents, the Red Lion at Mile End, had been con-

structed in 1567 by John Brayne, citizen and grocer, as a financial speculation. Since he was also brother-in-law to James Burbage, there may have
been some family interest in profiting from various forms of public entertainment. James Burbage began as a player but, in the changed circumstances of city life, he became a noted theatrical entrepreneur and father of
the celebrated actor who played many of Shakespeare's most important
roles. He was one of those skilful businessmen who seem to sense the movement of the time.

The growth of the city, and the increasing appetite for urban entertainment, presented Brayne and Burbage with an opportunity. The Red Lion
sounds like an inn but it was in fact a permanent playhouse, attached to an old
farmhouse. Its stage was 40 feet wide and 30 feet deep; there was a trap-door
for special effects, and an 18-foot "turret of Tymber" was built above the
stage for scenic ascents and descents. The coherence of its design suggests
that it was based upon previous models, and was therefore not the first of its
kind. It is sometimes suggested that the drama before Shakespeare's arrival
was coarse and rudimentary, complete with wooden daggers and bladders of
ox blood. But that is not necessarily so. Of course there must have been much
trash, as there has always been–trashy plays were known colloquially as
"Balductum" plays–but it would be unwise to underestimate the skill and
subtlety of early writers and performers. There is no progress or evolution
in theatrical matters–the nineteenth-century theatre is signally worse than
the sixteenth-century theatre–and plays now lost were no doubt excellent of
their kind.

The Red Lion was followed by a joint venture between John Brayne and
James Burbage. They picked another spot outside the city walls, in Shoreditch, and there in 1576 erected a public building known as the Theatre. They
deliberately chose the name from the Latin "*theatrum*," and may have hoped
that the classical connotation would augment the status of their enterprise;
they could not have anticipated that the word would take on generic status. It
was a large building, with capacity for some fifteen hundred people seated in
three levels of galleries around an open yard; the yard was also used by members of the audience, and the stage was set against one side. This fixed stage
had a roof, supported by pillars, and a "tiring-house" at the back that was
used for exits, entrances and changes of costume. It resembled the general
shape of all future public theatres of the period, in other words. It became the
formal setting for Shakespeare's own plays. Its coherent design again sug-

gests, however, that it was based upon lost originals. It was polygonal in structure, plastered black and white, with a tiled roof. There was a principal entrance, but two external staircases led to the different levels.

It was located in the ancient land of Halliwell or Holy Well, so named from a holy well harboured within a Benedictine nunnery in the vicinity. The name of Holywell Street survives to this day. It marks an interesting association, since other theatrical sites have sprung up beside holy wells. The first miracle plays in London were performed at Clerkenwell beside the clerks' well, for example, and the Sadlers Wells theatre was erected beside a healing well of the same name. The association has never been properly examined, but it suggests that the theatre was still in a subliminal sense seen as a sacred or ritual activity.

The Theatre itself was erected on the site of the convent, just west of its old cloister. It was close to a horse pond and a great barn. Bordered on its southern and western sides by the Finsbury fields and open ground, it had Shoreditch High Street to the east and private gardens to the north. A ditch and a wall separated it from the fields, and a breach was made into the wall to allow the citizens to walk or ride up to the playhouse. Two years after the establishment of the Theatre a preacher asked: "Will not a fylthye playe with the blast of a trumpette [sooner] call thither a thousande . . . so full as possible they can thronge?"[4] At the blast of a trumpet, then, the people gathered. It is depicted as if it were a relatively new phenomenon, the urban crowd out in force to seek entertainment. In *Tarlton's News out of Purgatory,* Richard Tarlton narrated how "I would needs to the Theatre to a play, where when I came, I founde such concourse of unrulye people, that I thought it better solitary to walk in the fields, then to intermeddle myselfe amongst such a presse." He fell asleep close by, in Hoxton, and when he awoke "I saw such a concourse of people through the fields that I knew the play was doon."[5]

Where there were crowds, there were also riots and affrays. Four years after the construction of the Theatre, Brayne and Burbage were indicted for causing "tumults leading to a breach of the peace" as a result of showing "playes or interludes."[6] In 1584 there was a serious riot involving gentlemen and apprentices. The official documents of the period constantly refer to "the baser sorte of people," "the refuse sorte of evill disposed and ungodly people," "maisterles men and vagabond persons,"[7] who haunted the vicinity of the Theatre.

And what were the entertainments on display there? There were "playes, beare-bayting, fencers and prophane spectacles." Among the "playes" were *The Blacksmith's Daughter*, *Catiline's Conspiracy*, *The History of Caesar and Pompey*, and *The Play of Plays*. It was the occasion for spectacle and melodrama as well as stage fighting and bawdry. Mention is made of "a baudie song of a maide of Kent and a litle beastly speech of the new stawled roge."[8] Yet this was also the setting for some of Shakespeare's earliest plays. There is an allusion to "the visard of the ghost which cries so miserably at the Theator, like an oister-wife, *Hamlet, revenge!*." The playwright, Barnaby Rich, wrote of "one of my divells in Dr. Faustus, when the olde Theatre crackt and frighted the audience."[9] Marlowe and Shakespeare were on the same ground as the fencers and bear-baiters. They had to match them.

It was a commercial venture by Brayne and Burbage, and was so successful that only the year after it opened another Londoner, Henry Laneham, built a new playhouse a few hundred yards away. This was named the Curtain—not after any theatrical curtain, which did not exist in the period, but after a wall on its ground that offered some relief from wind and bad weather. It was built on the same plan as the Theatre, with three tiers of galleries surrounding an open yard and raised scaffold as stage. A foreign visitor noted that it cost a penny to stand in the yard, and a further penny to sit in the gallery. It cost 3*d*, however, for the most comfortable seats with cushions. There is an engraving of the period, "View of London from the North," showing both theatres with flags flying from their roofs; there are fields to the south of them but, to the east, are closely congregated thatched dwellings and barns. These were the suburbs of Shoreditch, where Shakespeare would dwell.

The Curtain and the Theatre soon ceased to compete with one another, and came to a profit-sharing arrangement whereby the Curtain became an "easer" or second home for the theatrical companies. With the presence of two playhouses Shoreditch enjoyed a novel reputation as a place of resort and entertainment, on a larger and more garish scale than any other part of London. It was a centre for passing trade of every description—for sales of food and beer, for trinkets and playbills—and the site of taverns and of brothels. It became a fairground and a market, quite unlike anything else, and was no doubt deeply unpopular with the older residents of the area.

The playhouses themselves were decorated and gilded; the wooden pillars upon the stage were painted so that they resembled gold and marble, while all the accoutrements were designed to be as gaudy and as elaborate as possible. There were painted walls, carvings and plaster modellings. If the Theatre itself was named after alleged classical predecessors, then it was important that it had the air of glamorous antiquity. When Thomas Nashe attempts to describe a Roman banqueting house in *The Unfortunate Traveller*, he says that "it was builte round of greene marble, like a Theatre without." In that respect the sixteenth-century playhouses were close in spirit to late nineteenth-century music halls or to early twentieth-century picture palaces. A new communal art demanded new and enticing surroundings. These were the circumstances in which some of Shakespeare's dramas were performed. *Romeo and Juliet* "won Curtain plaudities,"[10] and when the Prologue in *Henry V* refers to "this wooden O" he is alluding to the Curtain. It is often suggested that Shakespeare himself played the part of the Prologue, in *Henry V*, and so we can place him on the creaking boards of this theatre.

There was at least one older playhouse south of the river, on the road leading from Southwark High Street and crossing St. George's Fields. It was erected in 1575 or 1576 and is known to historians only as the playhouse at Newington Butts, after the locality in which it was built. It does not seem to have been as great a success as the Theatre and the Curtain in the north. Nevertheless this southern playhouse was the home of the Earl of Warwick's Men for four years from 1576, after which it was leased to the Earl of Oxford's Men.

Even as Shakespeare made his way through London, a new theatre called the Rose was being erected on the south bank of the river by Paris Garden. It seemed to be a harbinger of popular and successful times for plays and players. The Rose itself was being financed and managed by one of a new breed of theatrical entrepreneurs. Philip Henslowe plays a large role in Elizabethan cultural history, in part because of the survival of his "diaries" or registers of payment. In true sixteenth-century fashion the dry account of receipts and payments is interrupted by notations on magical spells and astrological matters. He was a merchant and commercial speculator, only thirty-two at the time of the building of the Rose. It might seem that the Elizabethan theatre was a young man's game and opportunity, especially when the average age of mortality was forty. Henslowe owned much property in Southwark already, having married a wealthy widow of that neighbourhood, and earned his living from starch-making and money-lending as well as the theatre. But he was another of those businessmen who sensed the direction of their time; he became involved in the building and leasing of three other theatres. It was the "growth industry" of the period that also became a highly profitable one.

The Rose itself was situated on Bankside in Southwark, close to the High Street and in the parish of St. Saviour's. It was smaller than its predecessors, in large part because of the premium on building land. Its walls were of lath and plaster, its galleries roofed with thatch. It was situated beside two houses for the baiting of bulls and bears, suggesting that it harboured a distinct but associated activity. The discovery of a bear skull and other bones, in recent excavations, does suggest that it also reverted to type. The actors performed among the very reek of animals. The theatre itself was built upon the site of a former brothel, "rose" being the slang name for a prostitute as well as an heraldic emblem, and there were many houses of assignation in the vicinity. Philip Henslowe owned some of them.

In his contract for the theatre there was a clause concerning the repair of bridges and wharves that were part of the property, suggesting the marshy and riverine nature of the area. The excavations have revealed that the Rose was a fourteen-sided polygon, which was the closest approximation to a circle then possible. The advantages of a "wooden O" had become obvious from the success of the Curtain. The archaeologists have come to the provisional conclusion that the theatre was in fact built without a stage, suggesting that Henslowe conceived a multitude of purposes for the space. But then in the course of the first year a stage was added. It stretched out into the yard, and was so located that it received the full light of the afternoon sun; the yard itself was "raked" or sloped downwards, presumably to allow a better angle of vision for the audience congregated there. When the site was investigated in 1989 it revealed, among other items, "orange pips, Tudor shoes, a human skull, a bear skull, the sternum of a turtle, sixteenth-century inn tokens, clay pipes, a spur, a sword scabbard and hilt, money boxes, quantities of animal bones, pins, shoes and old clothing."[11] So the life of the period is retrieved.

It has been calculated that in its original form the Rose held some nineteen hundred people and, after a remodelling of its interior five years later, some 2,400 customers. But the diameter of the theatre measured only 72 feet, roughly the size of London's smallest contemporary theatres. The diameter of the inner yard itself was some 46 feet. When it is recalled that one of London's largest theatres, the Theatre Royal in Drury Lane, has a maximum capacity of less than nine hundred, the sheer accumulation of people in the Rose is little short of astonishing. It was jammed at least three times as full as any modern place of entertainment. It smelled of rank human odours, of bad breath and of sweat, of cheap food, of drink. The theatres were open to the air in part to expel this miasma of noisome savours. That is perhaps why Hamlet, when meditating upon the stage scenery of the world with its "majestical roof fretted with golden fire," then alludes suddenly to "a foule and pestilent congregation of vapoures" (1233–4). This was the atmosphere in which the young Shakespeare acted and in which the plays of Marlowe were performed.

These theatres, north and south of the river, north and east of the city walls, varied in size and in construction. It has long been debated whether they were built upon classical principles, or whether they were modelled upon the more impromptu art of the street theatre. Theatrical historians have reached some consensus, however, that these buildings represented the first public theatres in London. But there is reason to doubt that claim. There were certainly public theatres in Roman London, and it seems likely that there were popular venues in the period after the re-emergence of London in the ninth century. In the early twelfth century William Fitzstephen, the first historian of London, noted the prevalence of dramatised saints' lives in public places. There are also references to "*spectaculis theatralibus*" and "*ludis scenicis.*"[12] In 1352 Bishop Grandisson of Exeter referred to "*quondam ludum noxium,*" a certain unpleasant entertainment, "*in theatro nostrae civitatis,*" in the theatre of our city.[13] This plainly suggests that there was a building in Exeter which was popularly known as a "*theatrum.*" If there was one in a provincial city, it seems likely that there was also one and perhaps more in London itself. All the evidence suggests that there was much more secular dramatic activity than is generally recognised, and that certain places in the city were designated as playing areas. Why not, for example, the old amphitheatre that has recently been discovered by the Guildhall? There was also an amphitheatre at Southwark at a very early date.

It has also been argued that the *mimi* and *histriones* of medieval provenance continued their work well into Shakespeare's own period. The *mimus* put on an ass's head, as did Bottom in *A Midsummer Night's Dream*; he worked with a dog, as did Launce in *The Two Gentlemen of Verona*. Thus Shakespeare, and other sixteenth-century dramatists, emerged from many hundreds of years of cultural practice. What could be more natural—inevitable, almost–than continuity rather than abrupt or unanticipated change? Life is a process rather than a hurdle race. It is wrong to assume that somehow the English drama began with the emergence of Shakespeare. He entered what was already a swiftly flowing stream.

CHAPTER 26

This Keene Incounter of Our Wits

S hakespeare arrived in the city at the most opportune possible moment, when the drama of Peele and Lyly had become highly fashionable and the new drama of Kyd and Marlowe was just emerging. By the late 1580s and early 1590s the theatrical companies were performing six days a week with a different play each day. The Admiral's Company launched twenty-one new plays in one season, and performed thirty-eight plays in all. The Queen's Men were performing on different occasions and in different seasons at the Bull in Bishopsgate Street, the Belsavage on Ludgate Hill, the Theatre and the Curtain. Lord Strange's Men were at the Cross Keys in Gracechurch Street, the Theatre and then the Rose. There was much movement and change in the theatrical world. The Queen's Men lost their position of primacy in 1588, as we have observed, and were supplanted by the combined talents of the Lord Admiral's Men and Lord Strange's Men. This may have been the moment when Shakespeare himself joined Strange's company.

There were, in addition, such groups as the Earl of Warwick's Men, the Earl of Essex's Men and the Earl of Sussex's Men; they made extended tours of the country, but of course they also performed in London. Gabriel Harvey, a close companion of Edmund Spenser, wrote to Spenser of "freshe starteupp comedanties" with "sum newe devised interlude, or sum malt-conceivid comedye fitt for the Theater or sum other paintid stage whereat thou and thy lively copesmates in London maye lawghe ther mouthes and bellyes full for a pence or twoepence apiece."[1] We may assume that all the possible venues for theatrical performance were fully booked, by the companies then being formed or consolidated, and that Shakespeare had stepped into an environment where his talents could be fully exploited.

The principal theatrical companies themselves were significantly larger than they were at a later date, but this may in part have been the result of loose associations and amalgamations. The number of players in each company, men and boys, rose from an average of seven or eight to more than twenty. A play like Peele's *The Battle of Alcazar* demanded a stage company of some twenty-six players. As a result of larger companies, too, there was more ingenuity in staging, with rapid scene-changing and more spectacular effects. The playwrights themselves grew more ambitious, and began working on a larger scale; by some strange natural process, too, the plays themselves grew longer. All of these forces helped to create a truly popular drama, of which Shakespeare was the principal beneficiary. It was a small world, comprising no more than two or three hundred people at most, but it had a disproportionately large effect upon the London public. It was the most urgent and the most popular form of artistic expression, and in that sense helped to create the new atmosphere of urban life.

The boys' companies were the darlings of the hour, taking their roles in allegorical drama, classical drama and satirical drama. It may now seem to be an odd taste, among the Elizabethans, for child actors rather than adult actors; but it is connected with the sacred origins of the drama and with the desire to purge it from all associations with vulgarity or vagabondage. Theirs was a form of "pure" theatre in every sense. There were the Children of St. Paul's, who performed in the precinct of the cathedral, and the Children of the Chapel Royal, who made use of rooms in the old monastery of Blackfriars by the river. They became part of the theatrical ferment of the time. After James Burbage had erected the Theatre in 1576 a musician and playwright, Richard Farrant, rented a hall in the Blackfriars which became known as "the private house in the Blackfriars"; here, under the pretext that they were rehearsing for the queen's court performances, the Children of the Chapel Royal could attract high-paying customers. From so early a date, therefore, there was in London an "indoor" as well as an "outdoor" playhouse. It would have been inconceivable at the time that the "indoor" theatre would eventually become the choice of the world.

In 1583—through the agency of the Earl of Oxford—the Children of the

Chapel Royal secured the services of John Lyly who, with euphonious and stylised dramas such as *Campaspe* and *Sapho and Phao*, diverted the more discerning playgoer with displays of courtly dialogue and intricate plots. Lyly had already gained a considerable reputation with his narratives *Euphues: The Anatomy of Wit* and *Euphues and His England*, two prose romances which with their intricate and rhetorical style created the literary fashion known as "euphuism"; it was a style that Shakespeare imitated and parodied in equal measure, but it is true to say that none of his comedies is unaffected by it. It was the modern style. Anyone who wished to be contemporary, and of the moment, used it. Like all egregiously modern styles it faded very rapidly.

The residents of Blackfriars were not happy with the press of people who attended the productions of the Chapel Royal Children, however, and in 1584 the owner of the building forced out the boys and masters. So Lyly transferred his attentions to the Children of St. Paul's, and for some years his "court comedies" continued to charm private audiences. More importantly, for him if not for posterity, his plays were also regularly performed at court, where Elizabeth herself was entertained by the classical allegories he devised. His was in a sense a royal art. When Shakespeare arrived in London Lyly was reaching the height of his success; the most distinguished and artful of all his productions, *Endimion*, was performed in 1588. He wrote about the mysteries and possibilities of love, both in comic and in sentimental manner; he employed pastoral settings; he created intricate patterns of human behaviour as if they were part of a measured dance; he mixed farce and bawdry with romance and mythology; he charmed audiences with the beauty of his expression; he infused his plots with comedy and with an overwhelming geniality of mood. It is easy to understand the effect upon the young Shakespeare, who had never before seen such plays. It was a new dramatic world of lyrical statement and romantic intrigue. Where would *Love's Labour's Lost* and *A Midsummer Night's Dream* be without the influence of Lyly? There are many passages in Shakespeare's plays that are strikingly reminiscent of Lyly. Shakespeare was indeed a great cormorant of other writers' words. Moreover Lyly, just ten years older than Shakespeare, was already a fashionable and relatively wealthy man who was about to be appointed as a Member of Parliament. There was no better advertisement for the rewards of the theatre, albeit of the courtly or private kind. He spurred Shakespeare's ambition as well as his creation.

Yet the rise of the professional adult companies, employing young playwrights and larger bands of actors, steadily eclipsed the popularity of the boys and displaced the reputation of John Lyly. By 1590 the children had effectively disappeared, only to emerge a decade later under the guidance of yet another new wave of playwrights. Lyly spent his last years vainly seeking court preferment, as aspiring Master of the Revels, and living in what might be called genteel poverty. He wrote nothing for the last twelve years of his life, since the wheels of fashion and literary taste had turned a revolution. "I will cast my wits in a new mould," he wrote in 1597, "for I find it folly that one foot being in the grave, I should have the other on the stage."[2]

The luxury of choice was not given to another contemporary dramatist, George Peele, of whom there is a memorable image in a small volume entitled *The Merry Conceited Jests of George Peele*. He is described in this catchpenny pamphlet as lodging with his wife and family in Southwark beside the playhouses; here he is to be seen wrapped in a blanket, writing furiously, while his wife and young daughter cook larks for supper. He is also described as "of the poeticall disposition, never to write so long as his mony lasted." The real and historical Peele became acquainted with Shakespeare soon after Shakespeare's arrival in London. Peele had a measure of success with drama, but he was equally well known to his contemporaries as an inventor of street pageants and other public shows. That is why his plays were notable for their ceremonial and ritual aspects, and for the expressive clarity of their language. He also catered to the popular taste in blood and gore, in murder and madness. One of his stage directions records the entry of "Death and three Furies, one with blood, one with Dead mens heads in dishes, another with Dead mens bones." Shakespeare is widely credited for having taken over the first act of *Titus Andronicus* from Peele and completing the play, while elaborating upon the older writer's sensationalistic effects. This was the theatrical world that Shakespeare inherited.

Shakespeare was later to parody Peele's bombast in his history plays, and there may have been some cause for disagreement between the two men. Peele, the son of a London charity school clerk, was proud of his education at Oxford and his status as Master of Arts. Yet it was difficult for even a university-educated dramatist to make his way in the capital; there were too many clerkly writers and too many claimants to noble purses. There is every reason to suppose that young writers were attracted to London because of the rise of the playhouses there, but expectations of plenty are not always rewarded. So Peele tried his hand at various kinds of verse and drama—translations, university plays, pastorals, patriotic shows, biblical plays and comedies. Like literary young men of any and every period, he had to make money whatever way he could; he could have come out of George Gissing's *New Grub Street* rather than a sixteenth-century chapbook.

Like literary young men in London, too, he and his contemporaries tended to congregate together. In his lifetime Peele was associated with Christopher Marlowe, Thomas Nashe and Robert Greene—all of them "university wits," spirited, reckless, drunken, promiscuous, wild, and in the case of Marlowe dangerous. As Nashe said of his erstwhile companions, "wee scoffe and are iocund, when the sword is ready to goe through us; on our wine-benches we bid a Fico for tenne thousand plagues."[3] They were the roaring boys of the 1580s and 1590s, doomed to early deaths from drink or the pox. It would be mistaken to view them as some coterie, but they were part of the same literary (and social) tendency. Shakespeare knew them well enough, but there is no evidence that he consorted with them. He had too great a respect for his own genius, and thus a much greater sense of self-preservation. He was too sane to destroy himself—or, rather, he had a much greater need for permanence and stability. It is not known how Peele reacted to a collaboration with this apparently uneducated young actor from the country, but it provoked fury and resentment in at least one of his university colleagues.

So the stage was always ready for new voices. Even as Lyly was being performed at court and in the undercroft of St. Paul's Cathedral, there were new dramas and new dramatists coming into the ascendant. Shakespeare entered London at a moment of dramatic revelation. Thomas Kyd's *The Spanish Tragedy* had caused something of a sensation, and it was swiftly followed by Christopher Marlowe's *Tamburlaine*. *The Spanish Tragedy* inaugurated the fashion for revenge tragedy on the London stage; it directly inspired a very early version of *Hamlet*, which there is some reason to suppose was written by the young Shakespeare. *The Spanish Tragedy* has many parallels with the more famous play. It has a ghost; it has a variety of murders; it has scenes of madness, real and feigned; it stages a play within a play that promotes revenge; it has a great deal of blood. Unlike the later version of *Hamlet*, however, it is suffused by an unvarying rhetoric of vengeance and retribution that thrilled its first auditors. It was an immensely powerful and seductive language filled with sensationalist imagery. It became a form of secular liturgy. When Hieronimo advances upon the stage, in a state of undress, he calls out (II, v, 1–2):

> What outcries pluck me from my naked bed,
> And chill my throbbing heart with trembling fear?

The lines became catchphrases, repeated and parodied by other dramatists. They were picked up and redeployed by Shakespeare in *Titus Andronicus*, when Titus appears in a similarly discomposed state to cry: "Who doth molest my contemplation?" (2106).

Kyd himself was still a young man when he wrote the play. He was born in 1558, just six years before Shakespeare, and was the son of a London scrivener; like Shakespeare he endured a relatively brief education at grammar school, and seems then to have entered his father's trade. Little is known about him because, as a writer for the playhouses, little was required to be known. One of the few references to him is that of "industrious Kyd," which suggests that he wrote a great deal for his daily bread. He seems to have begun his career as a playwright for the Queen's Men in 1583, but by 1587 he and Christopher Marlowe had both entered the service of Lord Strange's Men. Shakespeare may have followed them. *The Spanish Tragedy* was enacted by that company, as was Marlowe's *The Jew of Malta* and *The Massacre at Paris*.

It is important to note that playwriting was a young man's occupation–Kyd and Marlowe being no more than twenty-three or twenty-four (and perhaps even younger) when they began their work. "My first acquaintance with this Marlowe," Kyd later wrote in an exculpatory letter, "rose upon his bearing name to serve my Lord [Strange] although his Lordship never knewe his service, but in writing for his pliers."[4] This immediately raises an intriguing possibility. If Shakespeare joined Lord Strange's Men in 1586, then he would very soon have become acquainted with Thomas Kyd and Christopher Marlowe; he would, as it were, be part of the same affinity of writers. He acted in their plays. He may even have collaborated with them. It has often been observed how, in his earliest dramas, Shakespeare seems alternately to imitate and parody both dramatists. What could be more natural in a junior member of this confraternity than to copy those whom he was ambitious to succeed? It was the time, after all, of their maximum effectiveness and success. *The Spanish Tragedy* was so popular that it propagated a number of imitations and was revised in 1602, after the playwright's death, with additions by Ben Jonson. So for almost twenty years it remained part of the staple fare of theatrical entertainment. What else would the young Shakespeare do but copy it?

There was one other association between Kyd and Shakespeare. Neither had been to university. As products of the grammar school only, they were both criticised by the "university wits" for their lack of learning. They were condemned by Nashe, Greene and other graduates as ex-scriveners or ex-schoolmasters, in terms that make it very difficult to know which of the two is being addressed. So there was a connection.

It was a small and intense world. These young dramatists stole lines and characters from one another. They criticised one another. Their plays were put on in competition, one with another, like the works of the Greek tragedians. The success of *The Spanish Tragedy* in 1586 seems to have inspired, or provoked, Marlowe into writing another play of bombastic eloquence. The two parts of *Tamburlaine* were acted at the end of the following year, but the speed of production and performance suggests that Marlowe had already written the plays in outline. They did constitute a revolution in English drama, however, but like other young artists Marlowe quickly acquired notoriety for his life as much as for his art. He was generally regarded as an atheist, a blasphemer and a pederast. He had become, after his first success upon the stage, a notorious renegade.

He was the son of a Canterbury shoemaker who was first shaped by the same kind of grammar-school training that Shakespeare experienced at Stratford; but, unlike Shakespeare, he moved on to university. Even before he attained his degree, however, he was involved in some kind of clandestine government activity. Like the salamander he seemed to live and thrive in fire. His comments, repeated at second hand, were themselves incendiary. He is supposed to have said that "all protestantes are Hypocritical asses" and "all they love not Tobacco and Boies were fooles." He has been associated with the "school of night," as we have observed, and is reported to have remarked that "Moyses was but a Jugler & that one Heriots being Sir W Raleighs man Can do more than he." Heriot and Raleigh were members of that esoteric society. Marlowe was also engaged in various forms of surveillance activity, particularly in regard to Catholics, but it is not at all clear whether he was a government agent, a double agent, or both. He was not in any case someone to be trusted. In 1589 he and another "university wit," Thomas Watson, were assailed by the son of an innkeeper; Watson stabbed the man to death, with the result that Watson and Marlowe were consigned to prison. Both Watson and Marlowe lived and worked in the theatre district of Shoreditch, which is perhaps where the young Shakespeare encountered them.

Marlowe was in one sense the marvellous boy of English drama. He was the same age as Shakespeare and made the journey to London at approximately the same time. It is convenient to consider Shakespeare as somehow "after" Marlowe, but it is more appropriate to see them as exact contemporaries, with Shakespeare having fewer obvious advantages.

The success of the two parts of Marlowe's *Tamburlaine*, for example, was immediate and profound. It was an act of dramatic independence on his part to present a pagan protagonist without in any sense disavowing him. Since it is in large measure a drama of conquest and success, it has been suggested that there is no play of contraries to enliven the action; but the contraries exist in the relationship between author and audience. He is perhaps the first dramatist in English to assert himself in the manner of the poets. The drama of the preceding period had remained to a large extent communal or impersonal; but Marlowe changed all that. He introduced a personal voice. It is the voice of Tamburlaine, but within its register there is the unmistakable accent of Marlowe himself (I, ii, 175–8):

> I hold the Fates bound fast in yron chaines,
> And with my hand turne Fortunes wheel about;
> And sooner shall the sun fall from his Spheare
> Than Tamburlaine be slaine or overcome.

It excited the audience because it caught the burgeoning mood of ambitious purpose and spirited individualism. It was an Elizabethan voice. If Tamburlaine was guilty of hubris, then so were many other Elizabethan adventurers. It was the penalty of "aspiring minds," to use Tamburlaine's own phrase. The thumping rhythm of the verse, comprised of what were called "high astounding terms," earned the rebuke of a young playwright clearly envious of Marlowe's sudden success. In a pamphlet published the year after the productions of *Tamburlaine*, Robert Greene complained that he was being criticised "for that I could not make my verses jet upon the stage in tragical buskins, every word filling the mouth like the fa-burden of Bow Bell, daring God out of heaven with that atheist Tamburlan . . ."[5] Another Elizabethan pamphleteer, Thomas Nashe, was also caustic about Marlowe's declamatory verse, describing it as "the spacious volubility of a drumming decasyllabon."[6] It was such a new voice that it had suddenly become disconcerting.

It was a voice that Shakespeare heard and internalised; it became one of the many voices that he could call upon at will. In such a relatively small and enclosed world, of course, influences and associations can be traced in every direction. *Tamburlaine* influenced the shape of Shakespeare's history plays, and the history plays in turn seem to have affected Marlowe's composition of *Edward II*. It is even possible that they collaborated on aspects of the trilogy concerning Henry VI. As has already been observed, the young Shakespeare no doubt also acted in *The Jew of Malta* and *The Massacre at Paris*. That he was mightily impressed and influenced by Marlowe is not in doubt; it is also clear that in his earliest plays Shakespeare stole or copied some of his lines, parodied him, and generally competed with him. Marlowe was the contemporary writer who most exercised him. He was the competitor. He was the antagonist to be mastered. He haunts Shakespeare's expression, like a figure standing by his shoulder. But Shakespeare's muse was an envious one, ready to deflate or destroy any contestant.

It is possible, however, that the young Shakespeare kept his personal distance from Marlowe. Marlowe's reputation always preceded him. In the language of another era, he was generally considered to be mad, bad, and dangerous to know. But there was another distinction between the two playwrights. Marlowe, like the other writers trained at university, came to the theatre from the outside. Shakespeare was the first who emerged as a writer through the ranks of a company. He came from the inside, as a fully theatrical professional. He did not consider actors to be hirelings, or servants, but as companions. It is a fundamental difference. In a later play, *The Second Return to Parnassus*, the actors Burbage and Kempe criticise the "university wits" for writing plays that "smell too much of that writer Ovid, and talk too much Proserpina and Jupiter." In contrast to these allegorising and mythologising writers "our fellow Shakespeare . . . it's a shrewd fellow indeed . . . puts them all down." The emphasis here is upon "our fellow," one of the actors, an integral part of the company rather than some hired hand. It is significant that at first Shakespeare surpassed his university contemporaries in stagecraft rather than in plot. His association with Kyd and Marlowe, through Lord Strange's Men, nourished strange rivalries.

CHAPTER 27

My Sallad Dayes

ithin a few years Lord Strange's Men had acquired an enviable reputation. This can be measured by the fact that when Leicester's Men were disbanded, on that nobleman's death in 1588, many of the players chose to join Strange's Men. They had good material with which to work. Two of Shakespeare's earliest plays were already part of the repertoire. We can trace some of their tours in this early period–Coventry in 1584, Beverley in 1585, and Coventry again in 1588–and their likely London venues are well known. In the 1580s, with Shakespeare as one of their number, they played at the Cross Keys Inn, the Theatre and the Curtain. The eclipse of the Queen's Men after 1588 helped Lord Strange's Men rise to eminence, and by 1590 they were sometimes acting jointly with the Admiral's Men as the paramount companies of the period. This meant that they had also acquired the services of Edward Alleyn, the prime actor of the Admiral's Men and already regarded as the great tragedian of the period. It was he who made such a success of Marlowe's plays, having taken the leading parts in *Tamburlaine*, the *Jew of Malta* and *Doctor Faustus*. Since he acted with Shakespeare, and may have played Talbot in *King Henry VI* as well as the title role in *Titus Andronicus*, his acting style is of some interest.

He was very tall, and at a height of over 6 feet towered over contemporaries who were on average 6 inches shorter than their counterparts in the twenty-first century. As a result he was very striking, and excelled in what were known as "majesticall" parts; Ben Jonson alluded to him at a later date in *Discoveries* with references to "*scenicall* strutting and furious vociferation." His role in *Tamburlaine*, for example, became a byword for "passionate" or "stalking" action–a success all the more remarkable because he was only twenty-one at the time. Nashe said of him that "not Roscius and Aesop, those tragedians admired before Christ was born, could ever perform more in action than famous Ned Allen."[1] He was in the tradition of non-naturalistic acting, grand and exaggerated. He could, in the phrase of the time, tear a cat upon the stage. It is likely that Shakespeare condemned his style in the words of Hamlet, where "it offends mee to the soule, to heare a robustious perwig-pated fellowe tere a passion to totters, to very rags . . . it out Herods Herod" (1736–7); and indeed Alleyn was better suited to Kyd or to Marlowe. Shakespeare worked much more successfully with Richard Burbage; Burbage was a tragic actor who may have rendered character and feeling with less circumstance and, as it were, subdued himself to his parts. But it would be unwise and unhistorical to draw too broad a distinction between the two actors. Both were conventionally compared to Proteus for their ability to assume a part, and Elizabethan acting was never–and never could have been–"naturalistic" in the contemporary sense. It was always in part a rhetorical performance. The playhouses exhibited the art of speech. The twin reputations of Burbage and Alleyn also throw an interesting light on the larger conditions of the theatre. The 1570s and the 1580s had been the decades of the comic actors, Tarlton and Kempe principal among them, while the 1590s and early 1600s witnessed the rise of the tragic actor as a symbol of Elizabethan drama itself.

In 1590 the Lord Admiral's Men and Lord Strange's Men had come to some reciprocal arrangement whereby the Admiral's performed at the Theatre and Strange's at the adjacent Curtain. In plays that required a large number of performers, they acted together in one or the other of the playhouses which were both now owned by James Burbage. In the following season of 1591–2 the joint company was commanded to perform six times at court. Since Lord Strange was related to the Master of the Revels, Edmund Tilney, there may have been some prejudice in their favour. But they could not have been a disappointment; they returned to court in the following Christmas season, with three separate performances. We have a picture, then, of the young Shakespeare acting before the queen. Among the other twenty-seven actors in Lord Strange's company, and thus Shakespeare's colleagues, were Augustine Phillips, Will Sly, Thomas Pope, George Bryan, Richard

Cowley and of course Burbage himself. The remarkable fact is that all of these actors worked with Shakespeare for the rest of his life, and that their names are appended to the First Folio of his work published in 1623. They eventually joined the Lord Chamberlain's Company with him, and stayed within it. It is a plausible supposition that they formed a small body of talent that remained relatively stable in very difficult circumstances. Shakespeare was loyal to them, remembering some of them in his will, and they remained loyal to him.

The titles of some of their early plays have survived, and we can assume that the young Shakespeare at some point acted in such popular dramas as *The Seven Deadly Sins*, *A Knack to Know a Knave*, *Friar Bacon*, *Orlando Furioso* and *Muly Molloco*. There is a "plot" or stage précis of one of these plays, *The Seven Deadly Sins*, in which many of the actors are named–among them Pope, Phillips, Sly and Burbage. There is also a stray reference to the actors who played female parts–among them Nick, Robert, Ned and Will. "Will" is interesting. It may seem implausible that an actor, now in his midtwenties, would play a female role; but it is not inconceivable. It is, in any case, intriguing.

In these early years Shakespeare's relationship with Lord Strange himself may have been amplified by a poem. "The Phoenix and Turtle" has puzzled many critics and scholars with its recondite meaning and esoteric vocabulary; but its purpose has also proved perplexing. It is not known to whom it is addressed or upon what occasion. It might have been written for Lord Strange's sister upon her marriage in 1586.[2] If that is indeed the case, then the young dramatist's relationship with this noble family was equivalent to that of a household poet. It has sometimes been suggested that Lord Strange himself directly commissioned Shakespeare to compose the cycle of history plays, as a tribute to Elizabeth and the nation equally. Shakespeare, in his historical narratives, awarded Lord Stanley's ancestors with notably patriotic and benevolent roles. Lord Strange's relatives, the Stanleys and the Derbys, are prominent in all three parts of *Henry VI*; in *Richard III* the victorious Henry Bolingbroke is crowned by the Earl of Derby. The praise of Clifford in *Henry VI*, for example, may well be a reflection of the fact that Lord Strange was the son of Margaret Clifford. What better way of acknowledging a patron?

It is not at all clear, however, when Shakespeare began writing these histories, or when he embarked upon comedies such as *The Two Gentlemen of Verona* and melodramas such as *Titus Andronicus*. Biographers and scholars have argued over these dates for years, if not for centuries, and there is still no agreement. The theatrical records of this period are notoriously imprecise and muddled. The provenance and ownership of early plays are notoriously difficult to prove. Companies of players owned certain plays, as did the managers of the London theatres. There was a great deal of movement between companies, and actors sometimes brought plays with them. Companies also sold plays to one another.

Various inferior plays have been ascribed to Shakespeare as juvenile work, written when he first became acquainted with the stage. Other, more mature, plays have been described as later versions of his apprentice work. Perhaps his first plays have simply disappeared, lost in the voracious maw of time and forgetfulness. Certain surviving plays bear traces of the young Shakespeare's additions and interpolations. In his first years he may have worked as a reviser of botched or incomplete plays. He may simply have revived old plays by adding new colour. There may, in other words, be a great deal more Shakespeare than is currently included in scholarly editions. Did he collaborate with other dramatists? It is impossible to tell. In his early years he may not even have been particularly "Shakespearian."

The supposition must be that he began to write long before he came to London—poetry, if not drama, came instinctively and easily to him. Given the large number of plays that have been ascribed to him, it is also fair to assume that he began writing drama soon after first joining the theatre as an actor. His earliest known plays are so expert in construction and so plausible in speech that it is hard to believe that they represent the first exercise of his pen, adept though that pen was. There are certain early plays that may be in part or in whole his work. There was an early version of *Hamlet*, and perhaps of *Pericles*. There are other plays which bear the unmistakable impress of Shakespeare's imagination, *Edmund Ironside* and *Edward the Third*. They are well shaped and confident, with a steady mastery of the verse line and a fine ear for invective and declamation. They lack the Shakespearian timbre or tone, but even Shakespeare had to begin somewhere. And there are the strangest moments of recognition—of half-familiar cadences and half-shaped images—as if the shadow of Shakespeare had passed over the page. Textual analysis also suggests that *The Troublesome Raigne of King John* and *Edmund Ironside* were both written by the same person, a "young writer, glowing but dimly in the predawn darkness of Elizabethan drama, just before the morning stars sung together."³ There is one other question that has never satisfactorily been laid to rest. Who else could have written them?

Their inclusion in any list of tentative Shakespearian titles is not surprising, since in many instances they represent the germ or seed from which his more recognisable plays emerge. Nor is it inconceivable that he revised his apprentice work at a later date. It is generally accepted that he continued to revise his plays all his life, keeping in mind the demands of performance and contemporaneity. The suggestion has been rejected by some editors and textual scholars, on the very good grounds that it would make their task of publishing a "definitive" edition of any play quite impossible. But there is every reason to believe that the plays currently available in print offer only a provisional version of the plays actually performed.

So we see Shakespeare attending the plays of John Lyly and George Peele as well as watching the first performances of *Tamburlaine*. He knew *The Spanish Tragedy* very well. He was all too aware of Marlowe's brilliant success. Contemporary literature was also around him. The manuscript of the first three books of Edmund Spenser's *The Faerie Queene* was in London, and the second edition of Holinshed's *Chronicles* had just been published. If he now felt impelled to write for the stage, all these sources and influences were at hand. We also have the alleged "early" plays by Shakespeare that, at a conservative estimate, account for three years of his writing. Indeed they all fall within the period 1587 to 1590. During this period, too, the pamphleteer Robert Greene mounted a number of attacks upon an unnamed dramatist, whom he considered to be both unlearned and a plagiarist of other men's styles. Who was that particular dramatist?

CHAPTER 28

I See Sir. You Are Eaten Up with Passion

obert Greene himself was one of the "university wits," a friend to both Nashe and Marlowe, who like many of his Oxbridge contemporaries was obliged to earn his living by hack-work. He was very popular at the time–plays like *The Honourable History of Friar Bacon and Friar Bungay* and *The History of Orlando Furioso* were "box-office successes" for Philip Henslowe at the Rose Theatre. His pamphlets are still considered to be unrivalled accounts of the life of sixteenth-century London. But he was sensitive to slights and extremely envious of his talented contemporaries.

He first attacked Shakespeare overtly in 1592. But earlier and more circumspect criticisms were also directed against him and Thomas Kyd. In 1587 Greene condemned those "scabd Iades" who among other things "write or publish anie thing . . . [which] is distild out of ballets."[1] The argument still continues whether the plot of *Titus Andronicus* is derived from a ballad. It was a slight and fleeting reference, but suggestive. In the following year Greene's companion and fellow wit, Thomas Nashe, continued the assault with an attack upon those writers who "seek with slanderous reproaches to carp at all, being often-times most unlearned of all."[2] Kyd and Shakespeare were the only "unlearned" playwrights who had achieved success upon the public stage by this time. In 1589 Greene composed a romance entitled *Menaphon* in which a "countrey-Author" "can serve to make a pretie speech" but his style is "stufft with prettie Similes and far-fetched metaphors."[3] These would become characteristic criticisms of Shakespeare's style.

In the preface to *Menaphon*, Nashe amplified the attack. In 1589, Shakespeare was twenty-five years old. Nashe had just come down from Cambridge, and had decided to live upon his wits; he was the son of a curate from Lowestoft, and his subsequent career seems to fulfil the Greek proverb—son of a priest, grandson of the devil. He colluded with his friend Greene, and soon carved out a career for himself as a satirist and pamphleteer, poet and writer of occasional plays. He was well acquainted with Shakespeare; he hovered in the immediate vicinity of Lord Strange and the Earl of Southampton, looking for patronage and praise, and did not always evince the benign spirit of his contemporary. He was three years younger than Shakespeare and seems to have possessed the hardness or cruelty of early ambition; he resented the success of Shakespeare, and wished to rival or even surpass it. He never could accomplish that goal, and quickly became a bitter and disappointed young man. He was incarcerated in Newgate and died at the age of thirty-four or thirty-five.

In the preface of 1589 Nashe first attacks certain unlearned writers who are happy to appropriate the work of Ovid and of Plutarch and "vaunt" it as their own. "It is a common practice now a daies," Nashe writes, "amongst a sort of shifting companions, that runne through every arte and thrive by none, to leave the trade of *Noverint* wherto they were borne, and busie themselves with indeuors of Art, that could scarcelie latinize their neck-verse if they should haue neede." The trade of Noverint was that of the law-clerk, to which we have tentatively assigned Shakespeare in his youth. The charge that he could scarcely Latinise may be an anticipation of Jonson's remark about "small Latin and less Greek," with the obvious implication that this unnamed writer had not attended university. Nashe goes on to remark that "yet English Seneca read by candle light yeeldes manie good sentences, as *Bloud is a begger*, and so foorth; and if you entreat him faire in a frostie morning, he will afford whole *Hamlets*, I should say handfuls, of tragical speeches. But o griefe! Tempus edax rerum, where's that will last always?" So whom is Nashe attacking? The reference to "English Seneca"—the unnamed writer did not have enough Latin to read it in the original—would yield the thunderous melodrama of *Titus Andronicus*. The reference to *Hamlet* is self-explanatory, and in its original form this play may very well have tried to out-Seneca Seneca. And the quotation? "*Tempus edax rerum*" appears in *The Troublesome Raigne of King John*, the clear forerunner of Shakespeare's more famous *King John*. It is now also a critical commonplace that Shake-speare adapted Ovid and Plutarch.

There is then a description of those dramatists who "intermeddle with Italian translations, wherein how poorelie they have plotted," a plausible al-lusion to one of the earliest of Shakespeare's extant plays, *The Two Gentle-men of Verona*. The playwright is also deemed to "borrow invention of Ariosto"; the plot of *The Taming of a Shrew* derives in part from *I Suppositi* of Ariosto. It concludes with a reference to those who "bodge up a blanke verse with ifs and ands"; then, on a more personal note, they are accused of "having starched their beards most curiouslie." There are later references to starched beards, as well as other allusions to law-clerking and schoolmas-tering as the unfortunate attributes of a certain country writer. It is an in-teresting mixture, out of which seems to emerge the elusive form of Shakespeare—indeterminate, not yet full shaped, not yet wholly familiar or recognisable, but Shakespeare.

There are many other specific references, rushing headlong over one an-other in Nashe's cryptic and densely allusive prose. "To be or not to be" is ascribed to Cicero's "*id aut esse aut non esse*." The author is accused of copy-ing Kyd and of trying to "outbrave" Greene and Marlowe with his own brand "of a bragging blank verse." Can we see also in a reference to "kilcow-conceipt" a nod to Shakespeare's alleged origins in a butcher's shop? The conclusion must be that these allusions are all pointing in the same direction, to the unnamed author who by 1589 had written early versions of *Titus An-dronicus*, *The Taming of a Shrew*, *King John* and *Hamlet*. Who else might it have been? It was a relatively small world with a limited number of occu-pants, and there are very few other candidates as the targets for the combined scorn of Greene and of Nashe.

In 1590 Robert Greene returned to the attack. In *Never Too Late* he abuses an actor whom he names Roscius, after the famous Roman player. "Why Roscius, art thou proud with Esops crow, being pranct with the glorie of others feathers? Of thyself thou canst say nothing . . ."[4] He repeats this attack two years later, when he refers to his opponent as "Shake-scene." But common sense would suggest that this was a long-running campaign inau-gurated by a "university wit" who believed himself to be unfairly criticised or neglected in favour of an "unlearned" and imitative "countrey-Author"—who, it seems, never once responded to the attacks upon him.

If the intended target is indeed Shakespeare, then we have evidence that he had a distinctive presence in the London theatrical world by the late 1580s.

This means that he had begun writing for the stage very soon after his first arrival in London. The fact that he is also named as "Roscius" suggests that he had already won some acclaim for his skills as an actor. Scholars and critics disagree about any and every piece of evidence; but there is an old saying that, when doctors disagree, the patient must walk away. The figure walking away from us may be the young Shakespeare.

CHAPTER 29

*W*hy *S*hould *I* *N*ot *N*ow *H*ave the *L*ike *S*uccesses?

*S*o we can create a plausible chronology of this earliest period. In 1587, when part of the Queen's Men, Shakespeare wrote an early version of *Hamlet*. This juvenile *Hamlet* has disappeared–except that from Nashe's account of 1589 we know it contained the words "to be or not to be," as well as a ghost crying out "Revenge!" There is a long tradition of anecdotal evidence that Shakespeare played that ghost, which would also make sense of Nashe's otherwise incomprehensible aside on the unnamed writer–"if you entreat him faire in a frostie morning."

Was *King Leir*, also written in 1587, an earlier version of Shakespeare's tragedy? It begins with the famous division of the kingdom, but then diverges from the later version; there are more elements of conventional romance, derived from the popular stories of the period. In particular *King Leir* has a happy ending in which Leir and his good daughter are reunited. *King Leir* was performed by the Queen's Men at a time when it is conjectured that Shakespeare was part of that company, and it is in many respects an accomplished and inventive piece of work. But it is so utterly unlike anything written even by the young Shakespeare that his authorship must be seriously in question. Another possible form of transmission suggests itself. If Shakespeare did indeed act in it, the plot and characters of the original may have lodged in his imagination. In the other early dramas related to Shakespeare, there is a notable consonance between lines and scenes. There is no such resemblance between *Leir* and *Lear*, except for the basic premise of the plot. So it seems likely that, on this occasion, Shakespeare was reviving an old story without much reference to the original play. *King Leir* is utterly unlike *King Lear*.

There is a third play that can be dated to 1587, if only because of a reference to it in *Tarlton's Jests*. "At the Bull in Bishops-gate was a play of Henry the fift, where in the judge was to take a box on the eare; and because he was absent that should take the blow, Tarlton himselfe, ever forward to please, took upon him to play the same judge, beside his owne part of the clowne." The Bull here is the Red Bull; the clown, Tarlton, died in 1588 and so this version of *King Henry V* must predate that time. Tarlton was also a member of the Queen's Men, so the associations are clear enough. *The Famous Victories of Henry V*, "as it was plaide by the Queenes Maiesties Players," has survived in an edition published in 1593. It is not a particularly graceful or elegant piece of work, but it does contain scenes and characters that were later taken up by Shakespeare in the two parts of *Henry IV* and in *Henry V*. In particular the "low" acquaintances of Prince Harry, Falstaff and Bardolph and the others, are anticipated in the crude but effective humour of Ned and Tom, Dericke and John Cobler, in *The Famous Victories*. Other incidents in Shakespeare's plays are also based upon scenes in this earlier drama. Again, as in the case of *King Leir*, it seems likely that he acted as a member of the Queen's Men in *The Famous Victories* and then at a later date employed the elements of the plot that most appealed to him.

There are other intriguing productions that, from internal and external evidence, we may ascribe approximately to 1588. One of the most significant is *The Taming of a Shrew*, which without doubt is the model or forerunner of *The Taming of the Shrew*. There are of course differences between *A Shrew* and *The Shrew*. *A Shrew* is set in Greece rather than Italy, employs different names for most of the characters and is little more than half the length of the more famous play. But there are also strong resemblances, not least in the storyline, and a large number of verbal parallels—including exact repetitions of such recondite phrases as "beat me to death with a bottom of a brown thread." The conclusions are clear enough. Either Shakespeare took over lines and scenes from the work of an unnamed and unknown dramatist, or he was improving upon his own original. On the principle that the simplest explanation is the most likely, we can suggest that Shakespeare's

The Taming of the Shrew was a revision and revival of one of his first successes. The later version is immeasurably deeper and richer than the
original; the poetry is more accomplished, and the characterisation more assured. Since they were published some twenty-nine years apart, the author
certainly had time and opportunity to re-create or reinvent the text. We may
use a simile drawn from another art. *A Shrew* is a drawing, while *The Shrew*
is an oil-painting. But the difference in execution and composition, the difference between a sketch and a masterpiece, cannot conceal the underlying
resemblance. This was obvious enough to the publishers and printers involved in producing editions of both plays; they were both licensed under
the same copyright. The publisher of *A Shrew* went on to print editions of
The Rape of Lucrece and the first part of *Henry IV*, so he retained his Shakespearian connections.

The most intriguing factor, however, in this early play of Shakespeare is
the habit of purloining Marlowe's lines; most of the interpolations were removed at a later date, when they were no longer considered timely, but to a
large extent they characterise *A Shrew*. The two parts of *Tamburlaine* had
been performed in 1587, and when *A Shrew*'s Fernando (aka Petruchio) feeds
Kate from the point of his dagger, he is satirising a similar scene in Marlowe.
The young Shakespeare also continually parodies the language of *Doctor
Faustus*, which strongly suggests that it was the successor of *Tamburlaine* on
the stage in 1588. There is the old proverb about imitation being the sincer-
est form of flattery, and from the evidence of *A Shrew* Shakespeare was
mightily impressed by Marlowe's rhetorical verse. But it is clear that he already had a highly developed sense of the ridiculous, and realised that the
bravura of Marlovian poetry might seem inept in a less rarefied context. At a
later date he would contrast the high rhetoric of the heroic protagonists with
the low demotic of the ordinary crowd. The young Shakespeare had, in other
words, an instinctive comic gift.

In both versions of the drama he also reveals a highly theatrical sensibility. The play is set within a play; the themes of disguise, of changing costume,
are central to his genius; his characters are very good fantasists who change
identity with great ease. They are all, in a word, performers. The whole
essence of the wooing between Kate and Petruchio is performance. There is
here a plethora of words. The young Shakespeare loved word-play of every
kind, as if he could not curb his exuberance. He loved quoting bits of Italian,
introducing Latin tags, making classical allusions. For all these reasons the

play celebrates itself. It celebrates its being in the world, far beyond any possible "meanings" that have been attached to it over the centuries.

The Taming of a Shrew was in turn satirised by Nashe and Greene in *Menaphon*, published in 1589, and in a play entitled *A Knack to Know a Knave*, reputed to be the fruit of their collaboration. We must imagine an atmosphere of rivalry and slanging which, depending on local circumstances, was variously good-humoured or bitter. Each young dramatist quoted from the others' works, and generally added to the highly coloured and even frenetic atmosphere of London's early drama. Only Shakespeare, however, seems to have quoted so extensively from his rival Marlowe; the evidence of *A Shrew* in fact suggests that there was some reason for his being accused, by Greene, of decking himself in borrowed plumes. It is all very high-spirited stuff, and *A Shrew* is nothing if not swift and vivacious, but the egregious theft of Marlowe's lines suggests that he did not intend the play to be taken very seriously. It was simply an entertainment of the hour. Yet, like many English farces, it proved to be a popular success.

If he could already triumph in comedy, there was no reason why he should not have tried his hand at history. Two of the other plays emerging in 1588, plausibly attributed to the young dramatist, are *Edmund Ironside* and *The Troublesome Raigne of King John*. *Edmund Ironside* has been the subject of much scholarly dispute,[1] the controversy further inflamed by the fact that a manuscript version of the play can be located in the Manuscript Division of the British Library. It is written in a neat legal hand, on partly lined paper also used for legal documents, and displays several of Shakespeare's characteristic quirks of spelling and orthography. The eager student may call up the document, and gaze with wild surmise on the ink possibly drawn from Shakespeare's quill. Like the mask of Agamemnon and the Shroud of Turin, however, the relics of the great dead are the cause only of bitter rivalries and contradictory opinions. Palaeography is not necessarily an exact science.

The play itself concerns Edmund II, best known for his spirited defence of England against Canute in the early eleventh century. Canute and Edmund are seen in conflict, military and rhetorical, but their high intentions are often thwarted by the machinations of the evil Edricus. When the play ends in concord Edricus, in uncanny anticipation of Malvolio, stalks off the stage with the words "By heaven I'll be revenged on both of you." The part of Edmund may have been meant for Edward Alleyn, fresh from his success as Tamburlaine and Faustus. The drama is in any case fluent and powerful, with a steady attention both to rhetorical effect and to ingenuity of plotting. It still seems fresh upon the page which, by any standard, must be a criterion for its authorship. It was not immediately licensed for performance, however, because the spirited dispute between two archbishops in the play was considered indecorous in a period when the clergy were lampooning each other in the religious squabble known as the "Martin Marprelate Controversy." It was not in fact performed until the 1630s.

It is in essence a revenge tragedy, on the model of *The Spanish Tragedy*, complete with the amputation of hands and the mutilation of noses. It also marks, in Edricus, the first appearance of the theatrical Shakespearian villain:

> They cannot so dissemble as I can
> Cloak, cozen, cog and flatter with the king
> Crouch and seem courteous, promise and protest . . .

The genuine Shakespearian note once more emerges, the words an obvious preliminary to those of Richard III. *Edmund Ironside* has been described as the first English history play, but in fact that honour can be claimed by the unknown play on the exploits of Henry V staged at the Red Bull. But *Edmund Ironside* is the first history play derived from an imaginative reading of historical sources; the story is in part based upon Holinshed's *Chronicles*, the source from which *King Leir* also springs. It uses Ovid. It uses Plutarch. It uses Spenser. It is permeated by legal and biblical phraseology in a manner to which successive generations of Shakespearian scholars have become accustomed. It incorporates "low" comedy in prose beside high rhetoric in verse, placing both in an intriguing perspective. It shares the same misunderstandings of classical mythology as does the work of the young Shakespeare. It uses the imagery of "butchery" for the first time in English drama, imagery which became something of a Shakespearian speciality. It has the phrase "all hail," and the immediate reference to Judas, which is a hallmark of Shakespeare's plays.[2] There is also an odd interpolation on the subject of the parting of a newly wedded couple:

> as sadly as the late espoused man
> Grieves to depart from his new-married wife.
> How many sighs I fetched at my depart
> How many times I turned to come again . . .

All the characteristics conspire to make one pertinent question. Who else but the young Shakespeare could possibly have written it in 1588? Marlowe, Kyd, or Greene? None seems so appropriate or so convincing as Shakespeare himself.

Edmund Ironside can be adduced, then, as evidence of the young Shakespeare's talent for re-creating historical narrative on stage. Other dramatists copied him, Marlowe's *Edward II* being the most famous example, but none had his instinctive ability to create memorable action out of the sometimes laboured descriptions of the chroniclers. He was able to depict character in expressive speech, to summarise the manifold causes of action with significant detail, and to invent memorable plots. His greatest and earliest gift, however, was perhaps the introduction of comedy as a respite from tragical or violent action. He had a perfect "ear" for variation and change.

These early plays are not admitted into the official Shakespeare "canon." Many scholars believe there is no evidence, external or internal, to indicate who wrote them. Could it be simply that they are not considered sufficiently "Shakespearian"? But Shakespeare himself was not *immediately* "Shakespearian." Early Wilde was not "Wildean," and the young Browning was not in the pattern of the mature Browning. Shakespeare's plays were published long after they were written and performed; many were not printed until after his death. He had time, in other words, to revise and embellish.

His earliest plays are written in the approved "new" style of his contemporaries; they are fluent, even if on occasions they show facility rather than inventiveness. They use end-stopped declamatory verse with Ovidian and Senecan flourishes; they include Latin tags and general classical allusiveness. They are also written with great spirit and bravura, as if the words and cadences emerged effortlessly from some source of overflowing energy and confidence. But he was also learning his craft all the time, and the astonishing fact of his early development is the speed of his progress. He learnt from the reactions of the audience, and the responses of the players; the range of his language was immeasurably enlarged and deepened as he experimented with the various forms of drama. He was highly attuned to the language all around him—the poems, the plays, the pamphlets, the orations, the speech of the street—and he absorbed everything. There was perhaps no greater assimilator in the history of English drama.

It has also been plausibly conjectured that in 1588 Shakespeare wrote another play, based upon the chronicles, which was later published as *The Troublesome Raigne of John King of England*. Shakespeare's *King John* is certainly closely modelled upon it, to the extent that it can best be seen as a revision or adaptation of the older play. There is not one scene in *King John* which is not based upon an original scene in *The Troublesome Raigne*. One nineteenth-century critic remarked that "Shakespeare has no doubt kept so closely to the lines of the older play because it was a favourite with the audience."[3] It is much more likely, however, that he kept closely to the earlier scenes because he had written them. Otherwise once more we are presented with the strange anomaly of Shakespeare extensively purloining the work of an unknown and unnamed writer and passing it off under his own name. He even copied the historical errors of the original.

The later publishers of *The Troublesome Raigne*, in 1611 and in 1622, were in no doubt about the matter; they accredited it as the work of "W Sh" and "W. SHAKESPEARE" without ever being corrected. It is sometimes suggested that sixteenth-century and early seventeenth-century publishers were in some way incompetent or negligent, and that they regularly put false names on their title pages. This is in fact not the case. They were stringently regulated by their guild, the Stationers' Company, and could incur large fines for any breach of standards. There were of course occasional rogue printers who would try to pass off inferior work as that of "W.S" or some other suggestive name, but the printer of the 1611 edition of *The Troublesome Raigne*, Valentine Simms, was well known to Shakespeare and was responsible for the first editions of four of his plays. He would not have put "W Sh" on a book without some warrant for doing so.

The play itself takes its place in the continuing rivalry between the playwrights of the period. It is written in two parts, imitating Marlowe's *Tamburlaine* of the previous year. But its address to "the Gentlemen Readers," printed as a prologue in imitation of the prologue to *Tamburlaine*, criticises "the Scythian Tamburlaine" as an "Infidel" and thus an inappropriate subject for the stage of a Christian country. Where in his own prologue Marlowe scoffs at the "jigging veins of rhyming mother-wits," the author of *The Troublesome Raigne* is at some pains to compose many such rhymes. *The Troublesome Raigne* was in turn parodied by Nashe in the following year. All this was part of the battle of the young writers, which in this period was conducted at a level of comic aggression and burlesque. It gives Shakespeare a context, however, and a character.

But the extant play does provide difficulties of identification and interpretation that, incidentally, throw light upon the dramatic conditions of the period. There is one scene in *The Troublesome Raigne*, concerning the pillaging of an abbey for its gold, which is utterly unlike anything Shakespeare ever wrote. It is a comic scene, but of a very degraded kind. So we might infer that someone else added this scene—perhaps the comic actor who played one of the parts. It was quite usual for the comedians to write their own lines. The fact that Shakespeare did not include this scene in his revised *King John* suggests that it was not his work. So we have a play of mixed parentage.

We can then see the genesis of his drama in three separate but related circumstances. He wrote several early dramas that he later revised; he acted in certain plays, particularly when he was a member of the Queen's Men, which he then recalled and re-created in his own versions; he collaborated with other dramatists and actors. It is a muddle that cannot at this late date be resolved, but it has at least the virtue of indicating the confused and confusing circumstances in which Shakespeare emerged.

CHAPTER 30

O Barbarous and Bloody Spectacle

here is little argument that the young Shakespeare did indeed write most of *Titus Andronicus*, a stirring classical melodrama, a blood-and-thunder piece designed for the popular market of the public playhouse. The first act was almost certainly composed by George Peele and Shakespeare was brought in to finish the work, another example of early collaboration. It is just possible that Shakespeare wrote the entire play, having decided to imitate Peele's ceremonial and processional style, although the motive for doing so is unclear.

Titus Andronicus is a play that attempts to beat Kyd and Marlowe at their own game, a revenge tragedy on a large and bloody scale. Shakespeare borrows structure and detail from Kyd's *The Spanish Tragedy*, and renders them more colourful and theatrical; already his sense of stagecraft is much more assured than that of his older contemporary. He took his stage villain, Aaron, from the model of Barabas in Marlowe's *The Jew of Malta*; but he made him much more wicked. He echoes Marlowe all the time, just as he had explicitly done in *The Taming of a Shrew*. The drama has lashings of Ovid and Virgil, as if to prove the point that Shakespeare had also been given a classical education. He quotes lines from Seneca in the approved fashion of the day, and at one point a copy of Ovid's *Metamorphoses* is brought on stage like some memorial to his schooldays. But in dramatising Ovid, as it were, he is engaged in quite a new enterprise. He is in a sense dramatising poetry itself. He was developing his own earliest gifts.

Titus Andronicus has violent deaths, and equally violent mutilations and amputations. The heroine, Lavinia, has her tongue cut out and her hands lopped off. She is then obliged to write down the name of her murderer with her remaining stumps, holding a stick in her mouth. The right hand of Titus is cut off on stage. The horror reaches a climax in the concluding scene when the wicked queen eats the flesh of her two sons, baked in a pie, before being stabbed to death by Titus, who is himself murdered. It is so extravagant a drama—and one still very shocking to a contemporary audience—that it has been supposed that Shakespeare was parodying the worst excesses of the genre. But there is no evidence at all for that assumption. It would also run against all the practice of the sixteenth-century stage, where the revenge tragedy was still too novel and exciting a form to be ridiculed in that self-reflecting manner. It is unlikely, for example, that an Elizabethan audience would have laughed at the sight of Lavinia with her hands chopped off; it was still a punishment deployed in public places. There is a case for saying that Shakespeare pushed the spectacle of bloodshed to its extremes precisely because he was writing for citizens inured to violent and painful deaths. He wished his audience to sup its full of horrors, and he entered the spirit of the proceedings with such gusto and relish that he forgot or abandoned any sense of theatrical decorum. It was a case of declamation rather than explanation. It may of course be doubted whether such a sense of decorum existed in public playhouses that could also be used for bear-baiting and bull-baiting. Everything was permitted at this early stage in public and professional drama; there were no rules and no conventions.

His is in any case the pure joy of invention, beyond the boundaries of comedy or tragedy. He is captured by the sheer enthusiasm for display and rhetoric and spectacle. That is why he wrote fluently and quickly, even borrowing a line verbatim from *The Troublesome Raigne* in the process. There were a few dramaturgical errors and inconsistencies, but we may recall the words of the German critic A.W. Schlegel when writing of *Titus Andronicus*. "It is even highly probable," he suggested, "that he must have made several failures before he succeeded in getting into the right path. Genius is in a certain sense infallible, and has nothing to learn; but art is to be learned, and must be acquired by practice and experience."[1]

Titus Andronicus was in any case not seen as a "failure" at the time. A

hugely popular play, still praised and performed thirty years after its first production, it conferred upon the young Shakespeare reputation and prestige.
The actual date of the first production cannot now be verified; it might have
been first performed under the title of *tittus & vespacia* before being revised
three or four years later. It had music and spectacle. It required a large cast
for the various ritual and processional scenes. It was so scenically interesting,
in fact, that it inspired the first known drawing of a Shakespearian production; this was executed by Henry Peacham, the author of *The Complete
Gentleman*, but it is not at all clear whether it is a record of a stage performance or of some idealised reconstruction. The action and the attitudes,
however, can be taken as authentic of Elizabethan acting.

It is a curious fact that the earliest productions of writers and dramatists
contain the seeds of their future works, as if in embryo, so that in *Titus Andronicus* we can see the first stirrings of Caliban and Coriolanus, Macbeth and
Lear, all as it were vying for attention. On more than one occasion Shakespeare adverts to the "prophetic soul." Great writers are much more likely to
be inspired by their unknown future than by their known and constricted
past. Expectation, rather than experience, fuelled his genius.

And then, as seems to have been his custom, he revised the play in later
years for different actors or for different productions. He even added an entire scene that has very little relation to the plot but does bear upon the revelation of character. It seems likely that he had a ready and instinctive grasp
of stagecraft before he turned his attention to expression. Unlike his contemporaries he was already possessed by a firm idea of characters in action
and of characters in response to action. When they emerged from his pen
they were already engaged in the game.

So from a possible early version of *Hamlet* to *Titus Andronicus* we have some
six or seven plays which might have been composed by the young Shakespeare in the first two years after his arrival in London–among them *The Famous Victories of Henry the Fifth*, *The Taming of a Shrew*, *Edmund Ironside*
and *The Troublesome Raigne of King John*. It has been objected in the past that
he could not possibly have written so many plays in so short a space of
time–at any reckoning, some three or four a year. But that is completely to
misapprehend the conditions of the sixteenth-century theatre. He was not a
modern dramatist. The wonder is that he did not write more. Indeed other
plays, or parts of plays, have been ascribed to him. Plays were composed,

performed and discarded at an astonishingly rapid rate—with seven or eight new plays performed by each of the companies in any one season. Contemporaries like Robert Greene produced them on demand, and were lucky if their works had a dramatic life of a month or a week. They were not considered to be literature in any sense. In addition Shakespeare wished to make his name, and fortune, in the theatre. Comparisons with his later rate of production are not appropriate. He wrote quickly, and furiously, filled with the first momentum of his genius.

There is a portrait of a young man known as the Grafton Portrait, from its ownership by the Duke of Grafton in the 1700s. In this picture the age of the sitter is given as twenty-four, and the date of composition is 1588. On the back has been written "W + S." Its association with Shakespeare might be easily dismissed as wishful thinking, except that the young man bears a striking resemblance to the engraving of the older Shakespeare in the First Folio. The mouth and jaw are the same, as are the ridge of the nose and the almond-shaped eyes. The whole set of the expression is the same. This young man is dark-haired, slim and good-looking (in no way precluding the image of the somewhat stout and bald gentleman of later years); he is dressed in fashionable doublet and collar, but his expression is alert if also somewhat pensive. He is one who could, if necessary, take on the romantic lead. It has been suggested that the young Shakespeare, at the age of twenty-four in 1588, could not possibly have afforded such fashionable and expensive clothing. And how could he or his father have paid the portraitist? But if he were already a successful dramatist, what then? It is in any case a glorious supposition.

CHAPTER 31

Ɔle ꟿeuer Ꝑawse Ꟑgaine.
ꟿeuer Ꝅtand Ꝅtill

So a picture emerges of the young dramatist, still in his mid-twenties but already achieving considerable popular success with a multifarious range of histories, comedies and melodramas. He turned his hand to anything with the expedition and confidence of one who seems able to give his words wings. He wrote; he collaborated with others. The qualities with which he was later associated, abundance and copiousness, were evident from the beginning. Yet he was also earning his living as an actor, a "hired man" who was already playing demanding roles. He had moved to Lord Strange's Men by 1588, confirming Henslowe's later note that the company owned a play entitled "harey the vi." In the early months of 1589 they were travelling in the country. But there is a lacuna in the records, and it is impossible to trace the course of their theatrical journeys. They were back in London by the autumn of that year at the very latest, however, where they are recorded as playing at the Cross Keys Inn.

There had been some public controversy over certain farces referring to religious disputes of the time, and the Lord Mayor of London summoned the Admiral's Men and Lord Strange's Men to prohibit them from performing in the city. It was an indication of the constant tension between the civic authorities and the playing companies. A letter from the Lord Mayor, of 6 November, declared that the Admiral's Men had obeyed the request but that Lord Strange's Men "in very Contemptuous manner departing from me,

went to the Crosse keys and played that afternoon, to the greate offence of
the better sorte that knewe they were prohibited." As a result "I coulde do no
lesse but this evening Comitt some of them to one of the Compters."[1] It is
possible that Shakespeare was one of those consigned to prison.

Lord Strange's Men then proceeded from the Cross Keys, where they
were now banned, to the Curtain, which was outside the jurisdiction of the
city authorities. The Curtain was their "summer" house, but it was fortu-
nately empty in this period. In the early months of 1590 they were performing such entertainments as *Vetus Comoedia* while their rivals, the Admiral's
Men, were playing beside them at the Theatre. But by late 1590 they were
collaborating again. In the performances given at court before the queen, in
December 1590 and February 1591, the company is officially named
Strange's in one document and Admiral's in another. They had become indistinguishable, in other words, and together they would have had the resources to mount the large and lavish productions that were never rivalled in
later years. And this combined company was the one in which Shakespeare
and his principal history plays were to be found.

But where was he to be found in a more local sense? John Aubrey described the young dramatist as "the more to be admired because he was not a
company-keeper; lived in Shoreditch; wouldn't be debauched; and if invited
to, writ he was in pain." He acquired this information at second hand, but it
was accurate enough. Shoreditch was the neighbourhood where actors and
playwrights consorted together in the same lodgings and taverns. There were
even specific streets where the actors were located. This was the pattern of
habitation in sixteenth-century London, where trades and tradesmen congregated. Shakespeare lived where he worked, close to the playhouses in which
he was engaged, a neighbour of his fellow actors and their families.

Among Shakespeare's neighbours in Shoreditch in the late 1580s were
Cuthbert and Richard Burbage, together with their respective families, living
in Holywell Street. The comedian Richard Tarlton resided in the same street
with a woman of dubious reputation known as Em Ball. Gabriel Spencer, the
actor later murdered by Ben Jonson in a brawl, lived in Hog Lane. The Beeston family also lived in this lane. A few yards down the thoroughfare, in a
small enclave known as Norton Folgate, lived Christopher Marlowe and
Robert Greene. Thomas Watson, the playwright, also lived there.

If Shakespeare had wished to be "debauch'd" there were plenty of opportunities in that neighbourhood. The presence of the theatres attracted
inns and brothels. It was in Hog Lane that Watson and Marlowe were in-

volved in a murderous fight with the son of an innkeeper, for which they
were committed to Newgate. In *The Trimming of Thomas Nashe*, the neighbourhood is described as one where "poore Scholers and souldiers wander in
backe lanes and the out-shiftes of the Citie with never a rag to their backes"
in the society of "Aqua vitae sellers and stocking menders" together with
prostitutes "sodden & perboyled with French surfets"; there were fortune-
tellers and cobblers and citizens on the search for "bowzing and beere-
bathing." When Shakespeare introduced the "low life" of his plays, the
pimps and the pandars and the prostitutes, he knew at first hand of what he
wrote. There was a row of houses along both sides of Shoreditch High Street
and it is possible that the young Shakespeare lodged in one of them, within a
few yards of the old stone-and-wood church of St. Leonard where were
eventually buried many of the players with whom he worked. If he had not
returned to Stratford before his death, this might have been his last resting
place. It was famous for its peal of bells.

By late 1590 the Admiral's Men were once again playing at the Theatre and
Lord Strange's Men at the Curtain; there is evidence, for example, that the
former acted *Dead Man's Fortune* at one theatre and the latter performed *The
Seven Deadly Sins* at the other. Shakespeare was working alongside the greatest tragedians of his generation, Alleyn and Burbage, as well as assorted
comics and character actors. It was a highly combustible mixture of individual talents, and there is much historical evidence of violence, argument
and affray between actors, between actors and public, between actors and
managers. One incident occurred in the winter of 1590, when the widow of
John Brayne—who, as we have seen, was one of the original owners and
builders of the Theatre—fell into dispute with James Burbage over the division of the takings. The widow and her friends arrived at the gallery entrance, one November night, and demanded their share of the money.
Burbage then described her as a "murdering whore" and went on to say, according to later court testimony, "hang her hor" and "she getteth nothing
here." Richard Burbage, the tragic actor, then came forward with a broom-
stick in his hand and began to beat the widow's men. They had come for a
moiety of the takings, he said, "but I have I think deliuered a moytie wt this
& sent them packing." When someone spoke out in defence of Mrs. Brayne,
"Ry. Burbage scornfully & disdainfullye playing wt this depotes Nose sayd
that yf he delt in the matter he wold beate him also and did chalendge the

field of him at that tyme."[2] It is part of the rumbustious texture of the sixteenth-century London world and would deserve no notice here, were it not
for the fact that certain scholars have traced the presence of this quarrel in
Shakespeare's rewriting of *King John*. Shakespeare of course often introduced contemporary material for the sake of his audience. In this production
it is likely that Richard Burbage played the quasi-heroic figure of the bastard
Faulconbridge. To have Burbage playing himself–as it were–as well as
Faulconbridge would have been the cause of some amusement. We can never
hope to recover the full range of allusions that Shakespeare introduced
within his drama, but it is important to realise that they are nonetheless embedded in his texts.

A theatrical quarrel of more serious consequence took place six months
later, in the spring of 1591, when Edward Alleyn was engaged in a dispute
with James Burbage. The precise cause and nature of their controversy are
not known, but no doubt it had something to do with money. Burbage may
have been treating his actors in the same high-handed manner which he had
shown to the widow Brayne. The consequence was that Alleyn decamped to
the Rose, the theatre on the other side of the Thames that was owned and
managed by Philip Henslowe. He also took with him a large part of the combined Admiral's and Strange's company of players as well as certain playbooks and costumes. Richard Burbage of course stayed in the northern
suburbs, in the theatres owned by his father, together with a group of players who had not wished to set up with Alleyn in a new playhouse. Among
those who stayed with Burbage were John Sincler, known as Sinklo, Henry
Condell, Nicholas Tooley, and Christopher Beeston. All of them, with the
exception of Tooley, would also work with Shakespeare for the rest of his
life. It is interesting that, in his revision of *King John*, Shakespeare gives
Richard Burbage the most heroic part in the play. From the evidence of the
surviving playbooks, too, it can be assumed that he was one of those who decided to stay with the Burbages and the others at the Theatre. They were
eventually granted the patronage of the Earl of Pembroke, and became
known as Pembroke's Men.

Shakespeare no doubt decided to remain with Burbage and his men because he would then be the principal writer of the company. It was gratifying
to have a company at hand to give expression to his vision of the world. As
resident playwright he seems also to have brought some of his plays with
him, as if he exercised a proprietorial right over them. This was unusual,
since the plays generally belonged to the companies or to the managers of the

playhouses, but it suggests that even at this early stage he was not lacking a certain business acumen or professional expertise. That is how Burbage's players were able to perform *Titus Andronicus* and *The Taming of a Shrew.*

They also performed two other plays, *The First Part of the Contention of the Two Famous Houses of York and Lancaster* and *The True Tragedy of Richard Duke of York*, which anticipate the second and third parts of *Henry VI.* They may in fact have been written before the separation between Alleyn and Burbage. Another form of contention now surrounds these two early dramas, predictably between those who believe that they were written and subsequently revised by the young Shakespeare, those who argue that they were composed by one or two unknown and unnamed dramatists, and those who insist that they are later reconstructions. The first supposition seems the most likely. Both plays were published by reputable stationers, and a later combined edition of 1619 is declared to be "Written by William Shakespeare, Gent." *The First Part of the Contention* anticipates the second part of *Henry VI* in almost every respect, from whole scenes to individual lines and the smallest phrases. *The True Tragedy* bears an equally strong resemblance to the third part of the historical trilogy. The order of the scenes is the same; the long speeches are the same; the dialogue is the same. There can scarcely be any doubt that they are the originals of, and models for, the later and more accomplished plays.

There are certain scholars, however, who suggest that *The First Part of the Contention* and *The True Tragedy* actually came later and were in effect "memorial reconstructions" of Shakespeare's own plays. By "memorial reconstruction" is meant the theory that a group of actors, who had played in both parts of *Henry VI*, came together and tried to recall the words and scenes of the plays so that they might act or publish them for their own purposes. They remembered what they could, and invented the rest. The texts themselves do not bear out this interesting hypothesis. Many of the longer speeches are remembered word for word while other shorter scenes and passages are not remembered at all. It is odd that, despite their lapses of memory, they were able to produce coherent plays that manifest integrity of plot, language and imagery. Which inspired actor, for example, produced the line "Et tu Brute, wilt thou stab Caesar too?" He could not have been "reconstructing" *Julius Caesar* because it had not yet been written.

The simple response, to textual evidence such as this, is to agree that the young Shakespeare wrote these early plays and then over the course of time revised them for performance. The overwhelming similarity between *The*

Contention and *The True Tragedy* and the second and third parts of *Henry VI* rests on the fact that they were all written by the same person with the same skills and preoccupations. There is no evidence for any theatrical conspiracy, and it is hard to imagine an occasion when it would be deemed necessary. Who were these actors who patched up plays already known to be composed by Shakespeare? To what company did they belong? And why was no action taken to prevent their publishing their speculative and illicit ventures? It is scarcely likely that, in 1619, Shakespeare's name would be attached to the republication of their fraudulent endeavours. The theory defies common logic.

It is significant, too, that these plays represent further ventures into the genre of the history play that he had already fashioned in *The Troublesome Raigne of King John* and *Edmund Ironside*. He returned to the chronicles for much of his information, and again produced an historical spectacle complete with processions and battles. He knew that he excelled in this kind of work, and he knew also that it was extraordinarily popular.

All of the formidable qualities of the second and third parts of *Henry VI* are to be found in *The First Part of the Contention* and *The True Tragedy*. There is in all of them a truly epic breadth of scale with wars and rebellions, battles on the field and confrontations in the presence chamber; there is the poetry of power and of pathos, as well as the more martial clangour of duel and dispute; there are fights at sea and on land; there are murders and a plentiful supply of severed heads; there are death-beds and scenes of black magic; there is comedy and melodrama, farce and tragedy. Shakespeare invents passages of history when it suits his dramatic purpose. He revises, excises and enlarges historical episodes in the same spirit. It is clear that the young dramatist was revelling in his ability to invent paradigmatic action and to orchestrate great scenes of battle or procession. From the beginning he had a fluent and fertile dramatic imagination, charged with ritual and spectacle. The public stage was not then fixed; it was fast and fluid, capable of accommodating a wide range of effects. There was no dramatic theory about historical drama; playwrights learned from each other, and plays copied other plays. Shakespeare was still imitating Marlowe and Greene at this early date in his career, to such an extent that one or two scholars have ascribed these plays to them. This is most unlikely. The best analogy at this later date is with the historical films of Sergei Eisenstein, in particular the two parts of *Ivan the Terrible* where grave ritual and grotesque farce are held together in a context of overwhelming majesty. We may imagine the Shakespearian actors to have been as stylised, in action and in delivery, as the performers of the early

Russian cinema. The plays represented a ritualised and emblematic society where matters of heraldry and genealogy were of immense importance. They themselves are a form of ritual, like a religious ceremony assisted by chanting and incantation.

Shakespeare was an apologist for royal power. He makes the Catholic distinction between the priest and his office–the weak priest or king must still be obeyed because of the sacredness of his role. His sympathies may be found also in the fact that he describes the followers of Jack Cade as a "rabble-ment," quite different from the presentation of them in the chronicles. Cade was the leader of the disaffected multitude who in 1450 constituted the "Kentish Rebellion" against the government of Henry VI. It was an unsuccessful uprising, yet Cade himself is vilified by Shakespeare in a manner wholly at odds with his immediate sources. Shakespeare seems to have been averse to any kind of popular movement. In particular he ridicules the illiteracy of the London artisanal class, as if to be literate (as he was) was a singular mark of distinction and separation from the mass. He felt himself to be apart.

But there is a curious paradox here, one which he and his audience may have observed. The sixteenth-century theatre is a democratising force. Common players assume the roles of monarchs. On the space of the stage itself nobles and commoners are sometimes engaged within a shared action. There is no dramatic difference between the varying ranks of society. In the history plays Shakespeare creates ironic associations and parallels between the chivalric action of the nobles and the comic action of the commoners, as if he were testing the true potential of the theatre. It is a complicated point, perhaps, but one that suggests the subversive or revolutionary potential of the stage. It was in essence a populist medium.

In revising at a later date *The First Part of the Contention of the Two Famous Houses of York and Lancaster* and *The True Tragedy of Richard Duke of York*, he changed the sentence structure of certain scenes, added or excised stray lines and even words, removed local London detail and furnished more set speeches. He did not touch the actual structures of the plays but merely embellished and elaborated upon them. He also widened and deepened the characterisation. In the process of revising *The True Tragedy*, for example, he significantly added to the part of the Duke of York. It is most likely that when Shakespeare effected these revisions he already had in mind, or had written, *The Tragedy of King Richard III*. In *The True Tragedy* Richard compares himself to "the aspiring Catalin," Catiline being a noble conspirator against the Roman Republic, but in the revised version Richard compares himself more villainously to "the murtherous Macheuill."

Shakespeare also changed the parts in order to complement the actors. He altered the characterisation of Jack Cade, for example, to incorporate the talents of Will Kempe, who had become the principal comic of his company; he added the detail that Cade is a wild morris-dancer, at which dance Kempe was known for his skills. In the revised version of the play, too, the stage-directions refer to "Sinklo," "Sink." and "Sin."; this was not a character in the play but, rather, the name of the actor John Sinklo or Sincler, who was well known for his extreme slenderness. This suggests that Shakespeare was rewriting the part with Sincler fully in mind and eye.

These revisions and alterations were no doubt part of his practice with all of his drama. It is only through chance or fortune that copies of *The First Part of the Contention* and *The True Tragedy, Edmund Ironside* and *The Taming of a Shrew*, have survived. Shakespeare was also learning and changing his craft in another sense. His later historical dramas, in particular the two parts of *Henry IV*, display much more subtlety and inwardness both in their characterisation and in their action. The demonstrative and oratorical mode of the earliest plays is subdued in favour of Falstaff's wit and the old king's melancholy. It has even been suggested that Shakespeare's histories led him directly towards his experiments with tragedy and that one form cannot really be separated from the other. Certainly Shakespeare himself does not seem to have distinguished between them. The cry of "*Et tu, Brute*" in the drama appropriately entitled *The True Tragedy* points in that direction; the English history plays lead to *Julius Caesar*, which in turn proceeds towards *Hamlet*.

Part IV

The Earl of

Pembroke's Men

pendeſt on ſo meane a ſtay. Baſe minded men all three
of you,if by my miſerie you be not warnd:for vnto none
of you (like mee) ſought thoſe burres to cleaue : thoſe
Puppets (I meane)that ſpake from our mouths, thoſe
Anticks garniſht in our colours. Is it not ſtrange,that
I,to whom they all haue beene beholding: is it not like
that you,to whome they all haue beene beholding, ſhall
(were yee in that caſe as I am now) bee both at once of
them forſaken ': Yes truſt them not : for there is an vp-
ſtart Crow, beautified with our feathers, that with his
Tygers hart wrapt in a Players hyde, ſuppoſes he is as
well able to bombaſt out a blanke verſe as the beſt of
you : and beeing an abſolute Iohannes fac totum,is in
his owne conceit the onely Shake-ſcene in a countrey.
O that I might intreat your rare wits to be imploied in
more profitable courſes : & let thoſe Apes imitate your
paſt excellence, and neuer more acquaint them with
your admired inuentions. I knowe the beſt huſband of
                                                      you

Robert Greene's autobiographical pamphlet, *Groats-Worth
of Witte*, calls Shakespeare "an vpstart Crow, beautified
with our feathers, that with his Tygers hart wrapt in a
Players hyde, supposes he is as well able to bombast out a
blanke verse as the best of you."

CHAPTER 32

Among the Buzzing Pleased Multitude

hakespeare followed public taste, but he also helped to create it. He wrote ten plays devoted to the subject of English history, far more than any of his contemporaries, and we can infer that it was for him an agreeable and accommodating subject. But, as is often the case with literary genius, the imagination of the age helped to inspire him. This in a sense was the first period of secular history in England. The plays of an earlier date presented sacred history from Creation to Doom, but from the mid-sixteenth century onwards the twin forces of the Reformation and Renaissance learning persuaded scholars and writers to look beyond the eschatology of the Church. If human will rather than divine providence was the source of significant event, then drama had found a new subject. It could be said that Shakespeare was present at the invention of human motive and human purpose in English history.

Hall's *The Union of the Two Noble and Illustre Families of Lancaster and York* had been published in 1548, and the first edition of Holinshed's *The Chronicles of England, Scotland and Ireland* followed in 1577. These were the books that Shakespeare devoured, although he seemed to favour Holinshed's more popular account of the past. If we wish to see Shakespeare as a characteristically or even quintessentially English writer, this appetite for historical re-creation affords some evidence for that identification. Schelling described the history play as a distinctively English genre. It did not last for ever, of course, but faded after approximately twenty years of successful performance; coincidentally or not, history plays really only lasted while Shakespeare continued to write them.

The extent of his popularity, by 1591, can be measured in the praise bestowed upon him by Edmund Spenser. It is perfectly possible that the poet had already met the young dramatist on the occasion of Spenser's infrequent visits to London and the court. All forms of social intercourse were within a small and interconnected community. Spenser was acquainted with Lady Strange (it was once asserted that she was his "cousin") and he could have been introduced to Shakespeare in the context of the Stanley and Derby families. In 1591 Spenser dedicated *The Teares of the Muses* to Lady Strange, in which dedication he spoke of her "private bands of affinity, which it hath pleased your ladyship to acknowledge." In *The Teares of the Muses* he refers to the learned comedies that are staged in "the painted theatres" and that delight "the listeners." He could have seen one or two of Shakespeare's plays at court when he came to Westminster during the Christmas season of 1590; he may in fact have seen *The Contention* and *The True Tragedy*. This will help to explain the lines in his poem *Colin Clout's Come Home Again*, when he possibly refers to Shakespeare in the guise of Aetion—from the Greek meaning "like an eagle":

> A gentler shepherd may nowhere be found:
> Whose Muse, full of high thought's invention,
> Doth like himself heroically sound.

What name, other than "shake-spear," does "heroically sound"? It is also highly appropriate for one who had written *The Troublesome Raigne of King John* as well as *The First Part of the Contention* and *The True Tragedy*. In truth it fits no other writer of the period. *Colin Clout*, written in draft form by the end of 1591, also includes Lady Strange as Amaryllis and Lord Strange as Amyntas. So the young Shakespeare is implicitly placed in noble company and therefore perhaps in noble society. It has been objected that at this date the young Shakespeare had written little or nothing of any consequence. This narrative has suggested that, on the contrary, he had already written a great deal that was popular and successful. What could be more natural than that he should be honoured by a poet who was part of the same culture and whose own epic of national identity and salvation, *The Faerie Queene*, was even then being published? In 1591, also, was published Spenser's poem *The*

Teares of the Muses, that alludes to "our pleasant Willy." This poet is possessed by a "gentle spirit" and from his pen "large streams of honey and sweet nectar flow." This would later become the standard description of Shakespeare's sugared verses.

By 1591 he was already so successful that he must have been conveying funds to his wife and family; whether he appeared in person is another matter. He may have entrusted his moneys to the carrier. But the matters of his home town still concerned him. His father's affairs in particular continued to exercise him. He was thoroughly informed, for example, of his father's decision to file a bill of complaint in the Queen's Bench at Westminster, in the late summer of 1588, to regain possession of the house in Wilmcote from their recalcitrant relative Edmund Lambert. The case was meant to be heard in 1590 but was then dropped or settled out of court, only to be revived eight years later. It has even been suggested that Shakespeare himself may have had to appear at Westminster to further his father's case; the court document twice refers to John and Mary Shakespeare "*simulcum Willielmo Shackespere filio suo,*" together with William Shakespeare their son.

The fact that John Shakespeare pressed his case at Westminster suggests that he was not without funds. He also stood surety of £10 on behalf of a neighbour, and forfeited what was in fact a considerable sum. He was engaged in other acts of litigation. He was sued for £10 by another Stratford neighbour, arrested, released and then rearrested; then with the aid of a local lawyer, William Court, he took the case to the Queen's Bench. We cannot assume, then, that Shakespeare left his family in any condition of penury.

John Shakespeare's affairs were not confined to Westminster. He had been engaged in a dispute with one of his tenants, William Burbage, over a sum of £7. There were also further problems associated with John Shakespeare's faith. In the spring of 1592 he was prominent on a list of Stratford townspeople who refused to attend church or, in the words of the investigation, "all such as refused obstinately to resort to the church."[1] The religious commissioners were used to various excuses for non-attendance and remarked that "it is said that these come not to church for fear of process of debt"—the church being a public and visible place where a debtor might be located—but this hardly applies to Shakespeare's father. In the same year he was present on two local juries, in the full light of day. It is significant, then, that in his drama Shakespeare adopts a very lenient attitude towards oath-taking and oath-breaking, as if neither was of very much account. This was part of his recusant family's experience, obliged to affirm or to utter what they did not necessarily believe. Or, as Hamlet says, "words, words, words." Among the nine recusants who appeared on the list beside "Mr. John Shackspeare" were three men with the names of Fluellen, Bardolph and Court; these names reappear in *Henry V*. Shakespeare paid some attention to his father's tribulations. Like Blake and Chaucer, he used real names in unreal situations. It was a private joke.

So Shakespeare stayed with Burbage's men at the Theatre, while the rest of Lord Strange's Men decamped with Alleyn to the Rose. But in 1592 the future of the London theatre was not all clear or secure for any theatrical company. At the beginning of June there was a riot among apprentices, who had gathered in Southwark to see a play; the affray spread to the other side of the river, and as a consequence the Privy Council issued an order to ban all drama and to close the theatres for three months. When in July Lord Strange's Men begged the Privy Council to consider reopening the Rose, they threw an interesting light on the condition of all the players at this time. They were obliged to tour in the country, as a result of the closing of the London theatres, but "thearbie our chardge [is] intolerable, in travellinge the Countrie" so that they were close "to division and seperacion" whereby they would be "undone." They also argued for the opening of the Rose as "a greate relief to the poore watermen theare" who had lost their custom.[2] By the first week in August the lords of the Privy Council were pleased to grant their request on the condition that London was "free from infection of sickness." But even as they issued their consent the plague was emerging once more in the city, and by 13 August it was "daily increasing in London."[3] Bartholomew Fair was banned. And there would be no more stage plays for the duration of the epidemic.

Burbage's men were in the same parlous condition as their colleagues over the water. They could not work in London and, their livelihoods threatened, they were obliged to tour the country. It may well have been at this juncture that Burbage sought the patronage of Henry Herbert, the second Earl of Pembroke, to lend an air of respectability to the group of strolling players that included the young Shakespeare. In the stage directions of the playbooks owned by Pembroke's Men there is the notation of "Will," given no last name. One theatrical historian has suggested that he was "evidently a boy,"[4] but in fact there is no indication of his age.

So we see Shakespeare moving from the Queen's Men to Lord Strange's Men and then onward to Pembroke's, before he found his final home in the Lord Chamberlain's Men. It did not mean that he was a "freelance" in the modern sense of that word, as some scholars have suggested, but rather that he followed old acquaintances and fellow actors as one company grew out of another. He was loyal, as well as immensely hard-working.

CHAPTER 33

An't Please Your Honor, Players

n the summer of 1592 the newly formed Pembroke's Men were obliged to leave London. The available records suggest that the plague of this year was particularly virulent in the neighbourhood of Shoreditch where Burbage, Shakespeare and other players lived. The exact route of this late summer tour is not completely known, but there is a record of Pembroke's Men playing at Leicester as one "stop" in a more extended tour that must have included Coventry, Warwick—and Stratford-upon-Avon. We may say with some confidence that Shakespeare was reunited with his family in the late summer of 1592.

Shakespeare and his companions travelled in a wagon, the players packed in with the baskets containing the costumes and with the essential stage properties. One of the actors of Pembroke's Men, mortally ill in that summer, was obliged to sell his share of "apparell newe boughte."[1] They might manage, at best, approximately thirty miles per day. It was an uncomfortable and overcrowded mode of travelling, but the alternative was to walk. One of the stage directions in *The Taming of a Shrew* is "Enter two of the players with packs at their backs, and a boy." It is possible that some players took their horses with them, but the cost of upkeep on an extended tour was very high. They lodged at inns for the night, and played there for the price of their beds and suppers. This manner of life, difficult and uncertain in many respects, did have the virtue of encouraging a sense of fraternity among the actors. They were an extended family. It may even have become, for Shakespeare, a welcome substitute for his existing one.

They took with them trumpets and drums, to announce their arrival in every new town. They had to present the burgesses with a paper authorising them to perform, and a letter or some authority from the Earl of Pembroke to prove that they were not sturdy beggars to be whipped out of town. The mayor or chief magistrate then asked them to perform before a selected audience, for which a reward would generally be given. Only then were they granted permission to play in the inn-yards or in the guildhall. There were purpose-built playhouses, however, in larger places such as Bristol and York.

So Shakespeare came to know Ipswich and Coventry, Norwich and Gloucester, in the course of approximately twenty years of intermittent travelling "on the road." The company with which he was associated for most of his career, the Lord Chamberlain's Men, travelled extensively in East Anglia and Kent but they also journeyed to Carlisle and Newcastle upon Tyne, Plymouth and Exeter, Winchester and Southampton. They visited altogether some eighty towns and thirty noble households, even making the journey up to Edinburgh. This was an important aspect of Shakespeare's experience of the world. In the summer and autumn of 1592 it may have been the only viable means of earning a living.

But Pembroke's Men were not simply a group of travelling players. They were invited to perform before the queen during this Christmas season, a signal honour for a company so recently established. They attained this degree of recognition in part because of the acting of Richard Burbage; but their success may have also been connected with the plays which they performed. Among these, as we have seen, were *The Taming of a Shrew*, *Titus Andronicus* and the two plays on the reign of Henry VI. We may now conclude that Shakespeare had achieved some renown on his own part, perhaps among his fellows rather than the spectators who flocked to see the plays, not least because he was bitterly attacked in this year by Robert Greene.

In the autumn of 1592 Greene's autobiographical pamphlet, *Groatsworth of Witte, bought with a million of Repentance*, condemned "that only Shake-scene in a countrey" who "supposes he is able to bombast out a blank verse as the best of you." This suggests an element of rivalry and competitiveness in Shakespeare's nature. The "best of you" refers to the university playwrights, among them Marlowe, Nashe and Greene himself. It was, in other words, a continuation of that war of words which Nashe and Greene had begun three years before.

Greene describes his rival as one of "those Puppets (I meane) that spake from our mouths, those Anticks garnisht in our colours." He is saying that Shake-scene was a player—moreover a player who had acted in the dramas of Greene and his contemporaries—and therefore not worthy of serious consideration. Because the young Shakespeare was one of the few who attained the dual role of actor and playwright, Greene berates him as "an absolute Johannes factotum" or jack-of-all-trades. He also intimates that, having supplied Shakespeare with lines (either acted or purloined), he had on his death-bed now been "forsaken." "Trust them not," he warns, and calls Shakespeare an "vpstart Crow beautified with our feathers" whose "Tygers hart" (an allusion to *The True Tragedy of Richard, Duke of York*) is "wrapt inn a Players hyde." Accused of being an unlearned ("vpstart") plagiarist, Shakespeare would have questioned "unlearned"—although he had not attended university, his plays are stuffed with classical allusions—but he could hardly deny the charge of plagiarism; his early plays were bedecked with lines and echoes from Marlowe.

The charge throws a suggestive light on a little fable that Greene included in his pamphlet, which immediately succeeded the assault upon "Shake-scene" and concerned the ant and the grasshopper. Greene compared himself to the grasshopper, and we are left to wonder who the ant might be. The ant was prudent and thrifty, taking up "what winters prouision was scattered in the way" where the grasshopper was unthrifty and careless. When winter came the grasshopper, quite without provisions, begged help from the comfortably ensconced ant. But the ant scorned his requests for aid, and blamed the grasshopper for his lack of effort and refusal to work. The grasshopper characterised the ant in these terms:

> The greedy miser thirsteth still for gaine,
> His thrift is theft, his weale works others woe . . .

The charge is again that of theft or plagiarism, but the ant is also condemned as a "greedy miser." There is also an indirect allusion to "an Vsurer." In a later period of his life, as we shall see, Shakespeare hoarded essential provisions at time of dearth; he also acted as a money-lender or money-broker on certain occasions and he possessed a healthy respect for money, as his own commercial speculations will prove. So Greene's attack, over-heated and exaggerated as it is, might well have been recognised as a further assault upon Shakespeare's character. In this account he is thrifty to the point of miserliness, hard-working and inclined to scorn those who are not. "Toyling labour," the ant states, "hates an idle guest." It is a plausible description of the young man on the rise in London. It is certainly true that, in his drama, Shakespeare continually satirises indolence and self-indulgence.

There is another anecdote in the same pamphlet when Greene, under the pseudonym of Roberto, is approached by a player of rich and fashionable appearance. He confesses to being once a "country Author" but, as Greene says, "I tooke you rather for a Gentleman of great liuing, for if by outward habit men should be censured, I tell you, you would be taken for a substantiall man." The newly elevated actor agrees, and confesses that "my very share in playing apparel will not be sold for two hundred pounds." "Truly," Greene replies, "'tis straunge that you should so prosper in that vayne practise, for that it seems to me your voice is nothing gratious." By "gratious" is here meant courtly or refined. So perhaps he was a quondam "country Author" still with a country accent. The passage may or may not refer to Shakespeare, becoming affluent and successful, but it is at least an indication of how actors were deemed to prosper in London.

There is some dispute whether Greene actually wrote this death-bed "repentance," or whether it was passed off under his name. It may have been written by Nashe, Greene's colleague, or perhaps by Henry Chettle. Chettle was a printer and minor dramatist who supervised the publication of Greene's pamphlet. He was also an occasional poet and "dresser" or reviser of other men's plays who inhabited the purlieus of sixteenth-century London literary society; if there had been a Grub Street, he would have been a part of it. Shakespeare was offended by Greene's portrait of him, as well he might be, and he remonstrated with Chettle, who then wrote an apology, in a pamphlet published at the end of 1592, in which he stated that "I am as sorry, as if the originall fault had been my fault." Of Shakespeare he writes that "my self haue seene his demeanor no lesse ciuil than he excellent in the qualitie he professes: Beside, divers of worship haue reported his vprightnes of dealing, which argues his honesty, and his fa[ce]tious grace in writing, which approues his Art." In describing Shakespeare's "facetious" gift he was not employing the adjective in its modern sense; it was instead the compliment that Cicero had applied to Plautus's sprightly and fluent wit. Shakespeare's professed "qualitie" was that of actor, but the "divers of worship" who supported him are not known. It confirms, at least, that he was already recognised and admired by certain eminent people. He was also himself influential enough, at this date, to elicit an apology from Chettle.

We are now entering a period when Shakespeare's plays can be securely placed if not precisely dated. And we find what we would expect to find–that he is already a superlative writer of comedies and of histories, of farce and of tragical matter. He was indeed the "Johannes factotum," the "jack-of-all-trades," of Greene's description. The Shakespearian authorship of only one play is debated, *Edward the Third*, but the others are universally recognised as part of Shakespeare's work. In the early 1590s we may notice in particular *The Two Gentlemen of Verona*, *The Comedy of Errors* and *Richard III*.

The Two Gentlemen of Verona is one of the first of Shakespeare's comedies, composed soon after *The Taming of a Shrew*. Its best scenes bring on a clown, Launce, and his dog; Launce alternately berates and pleads with his dog, but the dog says nothing. It is suggestive of the early sixteenth-century interludes, which also included dogs as comic "props," and in that sense *The Two Gentlemen of Verona* has very ancient roots indeed. It is a rather febrile drama, with a very silly ending, but it breathes the spirit of comedy like the lop-sided grin of a clown. There are no records of any performance, which has led some scholars to speculate that it was material only for private performance. This seems most unlikely, however, since the broadly comic scenes are expressly designed for the groundlings of the public playhouses: "My Mother weeping: my Father wayling: my Sister crying: our Maid howling: our Catte wringing her hands, and all our house in a great perplexitie, yet did not this cruell-hearted Curre shedde one teare: he is a stone, a very pibble stone, and has no more pitty in him then a dogge" (571– 6).

It seems to have been written quickly–but then, under the circumstances of the time, all of his early plays were composed in that fashion. "A fine volly of words, gentlemen," as one character puts it, "& quickly shot off" (656). The same images are repeated, and the same comparisons are made. There are several inconsistencies and contradictions that show evident sign of haste or, perhaps, separate stages of composition. The Emperor suddenly becomes a Duke, and two very different characters are given the same name. In *The Two Gentlemen of Verona*, Speed, in Milan, says to Launce: "Welcome to Padua!" It has been argued that the comic passages concerning the man and the dog, easily detachable from the text, were written at a later date. It is most probable that they were added for the performance of a specific clown–Will Kempe comes immediately to mind–and thus emphasise the extent to which Shakespeare was obliged to improvise. He changed his scripts according to change of cast. One of Kempe's famous routines was to heave his leg over his staff, and pretend to urinate like a dog. And he would have danced his famous jig at the end of the proceedings.

An early date for this play can also be conjectured from the fact that Shakespeare imitates, or borrows, passages from the fashionable playwrights of the 1580s. He takes character and dialogue from John Lyly, a romantic plot from Robert Greene, and lines from Thomas Kyd. It can be argued that he is satirising the romantic drama of the 1580s, but he is at the same time heavily indebted to it. *The Two Gentlemen of Verona* is part of the atmosphere of its period, and influences upon it can be traced to Sir Philip Sidney's *Arcadia*, Arthur Brooke's poem entitled *The Tragicall Historye of Romeus and Juliet*, George Puttenham's *Arte of English Poesie* and the courtly literature of the period that Shakespeare seems to have devoured. There is even some evidence that he had read Marlowe's *Hero and Leander* in manuscript form.

From the evidence of the play the young writer is half in love with music, of which he shows a distinct technical knowledge, and is already enamoured of the sonnet form. There are other distinct or distinctive Shakespearian aspects–or, rather, aspects that at a later date can be deemed to be Shakespearian. He places romance and farce so close together that they cannot ultimately be distinguished; the lover is followed on stage by the clown, and Launce's affection for his dog seems stronger than that of the romantic rivals' for their mistress. All forms of human experience are juxtaposed by Shakespeare, but his tendency is to deflate the heroic and the romantic with broad comedy. We will come to recognise that Shakespeare was a profoundly unsentimental person. In *The Two Gentlemen of Verona*, also, action in the world is subtly confused with play-acting; here, for the first time in Shakespeare's drama, emerges the figure of the girl dressed as a boy that would become such a token of his art. The play also evinces immense verbal resource, with the principal characters trying out various forms of address with the sole intention of displaying the dramatist's own skill. It shows a boundless invention and exuberance, in a language filled with puns and rhymes. No other writer of his age was so fluent and so various.

Here, as in *Titus Andronicus*, we also see the germs or seeds of his later work. The contrast between the court and the forest is one that he would fully exploit, as he began imaginatively to enlarge the English stage beyond the confines of unified time and space. The scene of elopement in the play here prefigures *Romeo and Juliet*. There are elements of Shakespeare's imagination—preoccupations, perhaps—that did not change.

It seems almost inevitable that he turned quickly to *The Comedy of Errors*, another comedy in a hurry. At one point he mixes up the names of the characters from both plays, as if *The Two Gentlemen of Verona* was still on his mind. All of the characters in the play are in a hurry. The author was in a hurry. In her diary Virginia Woolf once confessed that "I never yet knew how amazing his stretch & speed & word coining power is, until I felt it utterly outpace & outrace my own . . . even the less known & worser plays are written at a speed that is quicker than anybody else's quickest; & the words drop so fast one can't pick them up."[2] There is a stage-direction in *The Comedy of Errors*, probably added by Shakespeare himself, concerning an exit: "Runne all out, as fast as may be."

The Comedy of Errors is a mad play about suspected madness and mistaken identity, with two sets of twins being continually misrecognised to farcical effect. Shakespeare here went back to his earliest dramatic reading, in the plays of Plautus he had studied as a schoolboy, but characteristically goes a stage further in complication and intrigue. It is in terms of structure, however, a perfectly "correct" Roman play. Unusually among his plays it observes the "unities" of time and place as adumbrated by Aristotle, with a single action occurring in a single place during the course of a single day. It was played upon a stage with three doors, or "houses," in a row like the set of some classical comedy. It is as if he had decided to prove, to his university-educated contemporaries, that he was not as unlearned as they assumed.

So *The Comedy of Errors* is for him an exercise in ingenuity as much as in comedy. His is a predominantly verbal humour, rapid, elaborate and ingenious. It is, as Coleridge put it, "in exactest consonance with the philosophical principles and character of farce."[3] In that respect it requires a writer of the highest intelligence and sensitivity to maintain the pace and direction of the action. It might be seen as a slightly derivative and old-fashioned play, written by a schoolmaster of genius, since there are also elements of the morality play in its composition. As a schoolboy Shakespeare used the volume of Plautus edited by Lambinus, in which there are manifold references to various "errors." Hence perhaps the title. But the play is not entirely derived from memories of the classroom. He is still close to Marlowe and to Lyly, from whom he lifts lines and situations. T. S. Eliot once suggested that bad poets borrow while good poets steal; Shakespeare managed to do both.

It has the distinction of being Shakespeare's shortest play, but it is not without its subtleties of characterisation. We see here what might be called the natural bent of Shakespeare's imagination, with the superiority of servants over their masters and the natural good sense of women contrasted with the wilful obtuseness of men. There also appears, in this comedy of twinship, the theme of self-division that runs through much of Shakespeare's mature drama:

> . . . oh how comes it,
> That thou art then estranged from thy selfe? (500–1)

The fact that these lines are uttered by a wife, who believes that she has been abandoned by her husband, may add a private note of self-communing. In this play, as in so many others of Shakespeare, a family is reunited after many vicissitudes, and lost children are restored.

Self-estrangement has become so obvious a topic of Shakespearean commentary that it is often forgotten that it is peculiar to, and symptomatic of, his genius. Whether Shakespeare divined within himself the play of contraries, or whether it was the fruit of observation, is an open question. As a country boy come to London, as a player with aspirations to gentility, as a writer as well as an actor, he had ample scope for contemplation. We also have the interesting spectacle of an utterly practical and business-like man who was able to create a world of passion and of dream. That is perhaps the greatest mystery of all. He had within himself legions. He saw the human truth in any argument or controversy. All the evidence of his plays suggests that if he expressed a truth, or even an opinion, an opposing truth or opinion would then occur to him—to which he would immediately give assent. That was for him the natural condition of being a dramatist. It has often been noticed that in the plays there is no sense of Shakespeare's personality, and that the characters themselves do all the thinking. It has also been suggested that there is a consistent and characteristic "doubleness" within the plays, whereby heroic or mighty action is duplicated by the fools and clowns. There are also occasions when an action can be interpreted in two different ways, or a passion such as sexual jealousy can seem both justified and unjustified. But doubleness is not the right word. Kings and clowns are all part of the essential singularity of his vision.

CHAPTER 34

They Thought It Good You Heare a Play

n 1591 and 1592 it is likely that the young Shakespeare was working on more than one play at once for Pembroke's Men. There is no reason why he could not move from comedy to history or tragedy, since he mingles these within individual scenes and even speeches. *The Tragedy of King Richard III* seems to have occurred to Shakespeare as he was completing *The True Tragedy of Richard, Duke of York.* The character emerges in the earlier drama but in subsequent revision, as we have observed, Shakespeare deepened and darkened the portrait in anticipation of the more accomplished play. It was a role for Burbage himself.

Richard Burbage did indeed become the principal interpreter of Shakespeare's plays for the rest of the dramatist's life. The recognised leader of the company, he specialised in heroic or tragic roles. It was written of him that

> whatever is commendable in the grave orator is most exquisitely perfect in him; for by a full and significant action of body he charms our attention. Sit in a full theatre, and you will think you see so many lines drawn from the circumference of so many ears while the actor is centre . . . for what we see him personate we think truly done before us.[1]

It was he who played the first Lear, the first Hamlet and the first Othello. It is also likely that he introduced Romeo and Macbeth, Coriolanus and Prospero, Henry V and Antony, to the English stage. No other actor in the world has ever achieved so much. The naturalness and liveliness of his "personation" are often mentioned. He was considered to be a Proteus of changing identity, "so wholly transforming himself into his Part, and putting off himself with his Cloathes, as he never (not so much as in the Tyring-house) assum'd himself again until the Play was done . . . never falling in his Part when he had done speaking, but with his looks and gestures maintaining it still unto the heighth."[2] He was perhaps Shakespeare's most familiar companion. The dramatist left him money to purchase a ring, but the names of Burbage's children are perhaps a better token of their intimacy. He had a daughter named Juliet, who died young; he had a son called William and another daughter named Anne.

And so we see Burbage, at the age of twenty-one, walking onto the stage as Richard III. The medieval Vice was the traditional way of representing evil. Yet Richard seems to emerge fully armed even as Shakespeare thought of him, as if he had come from his imagination even as he had ripped his way out of his mother's womb. For the first time on the English stage the Vice is capable of growth and change: Richard experiences the first faint stirrings of conscience on the eve of the battle of Bosworth. It is only momentary, but his powerful lines prefigure the agonies of Macbeth and Othello: "What do I feare? my selfe? theres none else by."

Shakespeare was too great a dramatist to rest with the conventions. He had to reinvent the paths of human consciousness in order to stay true to his interior vision. He had transcended his sources and influences–Hall, Holinshed, Seneca with the rest–by combining them in fresh and unexpected ways. The high chant of formal rhetoric is mixed with comic asides, the melodramatic with the erotic. The rough wooing of Lady Anne springs to mind, although it is hard to think of any Shakespearian scene between the sexes that is not touched by malice or competition. He had not forgotten his lessons from Marlowe, and there are echoes of *Tamburlaine* and *The Jew of Malta* in *Richard III*.

Now it was Marlowe's turn to learn from him. It is generally agreed that his *Edward II* derives part of its inspiration from Shakespeare's play. And why should it not be so? The theatre was a place of continual imitation. *The Tragedy of King Richard III* was the longest and most ambitious play that Shakespeare had written. (Only *Hamlet* is longer.) It moves from one climax of invention and feeling to the next, never slackening its pace. In this play Shakespeare blossoms and unfolds. He loves the villainy and malice of the crook-back. He exults in them. There is an atmosphere of mystery and of prophecy—of ancient archetypes and mythical encounters—that raises English history to a new level of significance and meaning. That was one of Shakespeare's great gifts to English drama.

Richard III quickly became popular, with an almost unprecedented eight reprints of the quarto text, three of these after Shakespeare's death. The despairing cry, "A horse, a horse, my kingdome for a horse," was parodied and repeated in a hundred different contexts. Thus we have "A man! A man! A kingdom for a man!" (*Scourge of Villanie*, 1598), "A boate! A boate! A full hundred marks for a boate!" (*Eastward Ho!*, 1605) and "A foole! A foole! My coxcomb for a foole!" (*Parasitaster*, 1606). It would not be at all surprising to discover that it became a popular catchphrase on the streets of London.

We can only speculate about Burbage's performance as Richard III. There is, however, one small clue: "The king is angrie, see, he gnawes his lip." Catesby notices this mannerism, but it is one that Burbage also employed in the part of Othello. "Alas," Desdemona asks, "why gnaw you so your neather lip?" There is a reminder of Burbage's power as an actor in an anecdote in the diary of a citizen called John Manningham.

Vpon a tyme when Burbidge played Richard III there was a citizen grone soe farr in liking with him, that before shee went from the play shee appointed him to come that night vnto hir by the name of Richard the Third. Shakespeare ouerhearing their conclusion went before, was intertained and at his game ere Burbidge came. The message being brought that Richard the Third was at the dore, Shakespeare caused returne to be made that William the Conqueror was before Richard the Third.[3]

It is an unproven and unprovable story, but the anecdote was repeated in the mid-eighteenth century within Thomas Wilkes's *A General View of the Stage*. Wilkes could not have copied it from Manningham's diary, since that diary did not emerge until the nineteenth century. It would be reasonable to assume that the young Shakespeare was not immune to the delights of London life, although this anecdote emphasises his quick-wittedness rather more than his lechery.

So there are two comedies, and one history, that can plausibly be attributed to Shakespeare's connection with Pembroke's Men and to his early association with Richard Burbage. And then there is the unsettled question of *Ed-*

ward the Third. Many scholars believe that it was not written by Shakespeare, but it has elements of his early genius, not least in the choice of sonorous phrase:

> . . . poison shows worst in a golden cup;
> Dark night seems darker by the lightning flash;
> Lilies that fester smell far worse than weeds.

The last line reappears in the ninety-fourth of Shakespeare's sonnets, and bears all the marks of Shakespeare's profoundly dualistic imagination.

The fact that certain scenes in the play, particularly those concerning the wooing of the Countess of Salisbury by the monarch, are more accomplished than others, has raised the question once more of collaboration with unnamed dramatists. Shakespeare is supposed, at various times of his career, to have collaborated with Jonson and Fletcher, Peele and Munday, Nashe and Middleton. There is no reason at all why he should not have done so. It has been estimated that between one-half and two-thirds of all plays written during Shakespeare's lifetime were composed by more than one hand. Some plays were written by as many as four or five different authors. That is why plays tended to be the property of the company or the playhouse rather than of an individual. The emphasis was upon speedy and efficient production. It is even possible that writers formed groups or syndicates for the writing of dramas, on the same pattern as the roving bands of medieval illuminators, the members of which specialised in different aspects of the art of painting. Collaboration between dramatists was a familiar and conventional procedure, in other words, with various acts going to various hands or plot and sub-plot being given separate treatment. There were some writers who specialised in comedy, others in pathos. Shakespeare was the exception, perhaps, in the sense that he excelled in all branches of the dramatic art. He may have been exceptional, too, in retaining proprietorship of his own plays. There is of course also the possibility that passages or scenes were added to his plays at a later date by other writers. This may have happened, for example, with *Macbeth* and with *Othello*.

Collaboration in its most extreme form is represented by the extant manuscript of a play entitled *Sir Thomas More*, that has been tentatively dated to the early 1590s. It is the one play in which there is evidence of Shakespeare's handwriting. The authenticity of this fragment of 147 lines, written in what has become known as "Hand D," has been disputed by palaeographers over the years. But the weight of proof now seems to tilt in Shakespeare's favour; the spellings, the orthography, the abbreviations, all bear his characteristics. The key is variability. Shakespeare's spelling, and his formation of letters, change all the time. He capitalises the letter "c," and tends to use old-fashioned spelling; he veers between a light secretary hand and a heavier legal hand. There are signs of haste and, in the course of that rapidity, a certain indecision.

In the scene that Shakespeare was called upon to write, the titular hero of the drama, Thomas More, speaks to certain citizens of London about to riot against the presence of foreigners in the city. It is likely that, after the success of the scenes of rebellion in *The First Part of the Contention*, he was considered to be "good" at crowds. We may refine this further by noting that Shakespeare excelled at scenes in which authority confronts disorder where, by the use of colloquialisms and other devices, the figure of authority is able to communicate with the discomfited crowd. Once more it suggests the duality of his genius.

He is also believed to have written a passage in which More soliloquises on the dangers of greatness; again it appears that the dramatist already had a reputation for meditative reflection by renowned or noble characters. The history plays would have left just such an impression. The chief author of *Sir Thomas More* was Anthony Munday, but one of the other collaborators has been identified as Henry Chettle–the same Chettle who was obliged to apologise for Greene's animadversions on Shakespeare in *Groats-worth of Witte*. If it was a small world, it was also forgiving.

Sir Thomas More seems not to have been performed, perhaps because it was too close in matter to certain London riots of 1592, and is now remarkable only for the presence of Shakespeare's handwriting. The subject of Shakespeare's handwriting is in itself important, since there is now no other means of tracing his physical presence in the world. We might note, for example, that in each of six of his authenticated signatures he spells his surname differently. He abbreviates it, too, as if he were not happy with it. It becomes "Shakp" or "Shakspe" or "Shaksper." The brevity may, of course, equally be a sign of speed or impatience. The best analysis of one signature suggests that its inscriber "must have been capable of wielding the pen with dexterity and speed. The firm control of the pen in forming the sweeping curves in the surname is indeed remarkable . . . a free and rapid, though careless, hand."[4]

The differences in the spelling of his surname can of course be ascribed to the loose and uncertain orthography of the period rather than to any perceived lack of identity, but it does at least suggest that his presence in the world was not fully determined. In a mortgage deed and a purchase deed, signed within hours or even minutes of each other, he signs his name in two completely different ways. It is even supposed by some calligraphers that the three signatures on his will are written by three different people, since the dissimilarities "are almost beyond explanation."[5] The author, as if by some act of magic, has disappeared!

CHAPTER 35

There's a Great Spirit Gone. Thus Did I Desire It

t the beginning of 1593 Pembroke's Men resumed playing at the Theatre. Shakespeare's early plays were part of their repertory. The playbooks or official texts of *Titus Andronicus*, *The True Tragedy of the Duke of York* and *The Taming of a Shrew*, when they were eventually published in volume form, all advertise the fact that these plays were "sundry times acted by the Right honourable the Earle of Pembrook his seruants." In the playbooks of *The True Tragedie* and *The First Part of the Contention* there are very precise stage-directions that suggest the intervention of the author.

But they could not have performed in London for very long. On 21 January, as a result of an epidemic of the plague, the Privy Council wrote to the Lord Mayor ordering him to prohibit "all plays, baiting of bears, bulls, bowling and any other like occasions to assemble any numbers of people together." So Shakespeare and his companions were obliged once more to leave the capital. They travelled west to Ludlow, part of the Earl of Pembroke's territory, by way of places such as Bath and Bewdley. At Bath they received 16 shillings, less 2 shillings' recompense for a bow they had broken. Perhaps it was one of those mentioned in the stage direction of *The True Tragedie of Richard Duke of Yorke*, "Enter two keepers with bows and arrows." In Bewdley they were awarded 20 shillings as "my Lord President his players." The Earl of Pembroke was known officially as President of Wales. In Ludlow they received the same sum, but were also granted "a quart of white wine and sugar." In Shrewsbury it was advertised that "my Lord President's players" were "coming to this town"; here they received no less than 40 shillings.

When they returned to London later in 1593 they were less fortunate. The Theatre, and the other playhouses, were still closed by "the sickness." It was late June, or early July, and the summer heat was approaching. In this year the epidemic disorder killed fifteen thousand Londoners, more than one-tenth of the population. While on tour in Bath, Edward Alleyn wrote to his wife instructing her "every evening throwe water before your dore and in your bakesid [back of the house] and haue in your windowes good store of rue and herbe of grace."[1]

Something else was happening in London. Threats against French, Dutch and Belgian immigrants had been pasted or nailed on the streets. On 5 May a bitterly xenophobic poem of fifty-three lines had been placed on the walls of the Dutch churchyard. It had been signed "Tamburlaine." Not unnaturally, perhaps, these attacks were considered to be the work of professional writers. So the authors of these "lewd and malicious libels" were to be arrested and examined; if they refused to confess "you shal by auctorities hereof put them to the torture in Bridewel, and by th'extremitie thereof."[2] One of the first arrested was the author of *The Spanish Tragedy*, Thomas Kyd, who was duly put to the torture. He named Christopher Marlowe as a blasphemer. It has been suggested that the entire affair was an elaborate trap by the authorities to snare Kyd and, through Kyd, to detain Marlowe himself.[3] Marlowe was called and examined by the Privy Council for two days; he was then released, on condition that he reported daily to their lordships. Ten days later he was dead, stabbed through the eye as a result of an apparent brawl in Deptford. Kyd himself died in the following year. It is hard to overestimate the impact of these events on the fraternity of players. One of their leading playwrights had been killed, in most suspicious circumstances, and another had been tortured almost to death at the instigation of the Privy Council. It was a series of shocking events, of which no one could see the outcome. The uncertainty and anxiety were intense, the fearfulness rendered even worse by the prevalence of the plague and the closure of the theatres.

But there was one other consideration for Shakespeare. The death of Marlowe occurred while he was on tour with Pembroke's Men, but the report reached him soon enough. This was for him a climactic event. The dramatic poet whom he most admired and imitated was dead. To put it more bluntly, his principal competitor was dead. From this time forward he would have a clear run. It is perhaps not surprising that his great lyrical plays—*Romeo and Juliet*, *A Midsummer Night's Dream*, *Love's Labour's Lost* and *Richard II*—emerge in the succeeding four years. In these plays he exorcises, and surpasses, Marlowe's poetical spirit. The untimely death of Marlowe left Shakespeare as the principal playwright of note in late sixteenth-century London.

The continuation of the plague throughout the summer, however, obliged Pembroke's Men to tour again. They sold their text of Marlowe's *Edward the Second* to a stationer, William Jones, no doubt to raise a modest but necessary sum. The sensation of his death might encourage sales. Then they travelled into the south of England, where they played at Rye for the relatively small sum of 13*s* 4*d*. They came back to London in August, and disbanded. They were bankrupt and could no longer cover their costs. On 28 September Henslowe wrote to Edward Alleyn, who was also still "on the road": "As for my lord of Pembroke's, which you desire to know where they may be, they are all at home, and have been this five or six weeks; for they cannot save their charges with travel, as I hear, and were fain to pawn the apparel."[4]

So Shakespeare was out of employment. But it is not to be believed that such an enterprising and energetic young man would remain idle for very long. With the closure of the theatres at the beginning of the year he must already have been considering the future. Who could tell if, or when, the plague would abate? Would the doors of the London theatres be closed for ever? He must have given serious thought to a possible change in the direction of his career, since in this period he began work on a long poem. From an early stage, too, he may have had in mind the possible benefits accruing from a wealthy patron. Such a patron might offer him employment, in the lean time of the theatres, as well as gifts. Thus in the summer of 1593 his old Stratford acquaintance, Richard Field, published a volume entitled *Venus and Adonis*. It was priced at about 6 pence, and sold at the sign of the White Greyhound in the haunt of booksellers at Paul's Churchyard. Field's shop was no doubt Shakespeare's haunt, also, where he would have found the new books of the day—among them George Puttenham's *The Arte of English Poesie*. That treatise had recommended the six-line stanza for English narrative poems, precisely the form that Shakespeare employed in *Venus and Adonis*. In Field's shop he would have seen fresh copies of Plutarch's *Lives* as translated by Sir Thomas North but, equally significantly, he would have been able to read and perhaps to borrow Field's new edition of Ovid. He took two lines from that poet as his epigraph for *Venus and Adonis*. The little shop in Paul's Churchyard, smelling of ink and paper, helped to give birth to one of the most fluent and eloquent of all English narrative poems.

No author was named on its title-page, but its dedication was signed "Your Honour's in all duty, William Shakespeare"; the dedicatee himself was a young nobleman by the name of Henry Wriothesley, Earl of Southampton. This dedication is the first example of Shakespeare's non-dramatic prose to have survived.

The first sentence alone reveals his mastery of cadence and of emphasis.

> Right Honourable, I know not how I shall offend in dedicating my vn-polisht lines to your Lordship, nor how the worlde will censure mee for choosing so strong a proppe to support so weake a burthen, onelye if your Honour seeme but pleased, I account my selfe highly praised, and vowe to take aduantage of all idle houres, till I have honoured you with some grauer labour.

He continues by calling this poem "the first heire of my inuention." None of his plays had yet been published under his own name, and anonymous play-books would certainly not count as evidence of his "invention." He seems, curiously enough, to distance himself from his career in the theatre. His epigraph from Ovid begins with the phrase "*Vilia miretur vulgus*" which, in Marlowe's translation, reads "Let base-conceited wits admire vile things." "*Vilia*" can also mean "common shows," of which the public drama was a notable example in sixteenth-century London. Shakespeare says that he will be led by Apollo to the springs of the Muses, thus severing his connection with the "*vilia*" of the playhouses. Biographers have suggested that the lines represent a certain ambiguity, or uncertainty, about his role as a playwright and actor. Neither was, after all, the profession of a gentleman. But it is more likely that Shakespeare was indulging in special pleading. With the dedication to *Venus and Adonis* he was simply entering his new role as poet, and aspirant to noble patronage, by means of a flourish. He was making a good impression. And it should never be forgotten that, throughout his life, Shakespeare remained very much an actor assuming the necessary or congenial part.

Southampton was then twenty years old, having completed the formalities of an education at St. John's College, Cambridge, and at Gray's Inn. He came from a noble Catholic family but, on the death of his father, he had become a ward of Lord Burghley the Lord Treasurer. At the age of sixteen he had been repeatedly pressed to marry Burghley's granddaughter, but had refused. *Venus and Adonis*, the story of the unwelcome wooing of a pretty boy by an older woman, might even have been conceived for Southampton. It might be seen as a follow-up to a poem entitled *Narcissus*, in which one of Burghley's secretaries had indirectly chided Southampton for his solitary state. The young lord might plausibly be identified with Adonis because by common consent he was as beautiful as he was learned, although the magnitude of both qualities was no doubt exaggerated by the panegyrists of the time. Noble youths were always deemed more attractive than their less well-born counterparts. Like many young Elizabethans of noble descent Southampton's generosity of spirit (and of his means) was matched by instability and passionate temper; the queen herself commented that he was "one whose counsel can be of little, and experience of less use."[5]

The traffic of favours went in both directions. The dedication of *Venus and Adonis* to Southampton, and its subsequent enormous popularity, helped to create an image of the young man as a patron of learning and of poetry. In the year following its publication, for example, Nashe alluded to him as "a dere lover and cherisher you are, as well of the lovers of Poets, as of Poets themselves."[6] In the heated world of court favour and court intrigue, such a reputation did Southampton no harm at all.

The poem is part of a genre of erotic narrative poems largely taken out of Ovid. Shakespeare would have read about the ill-starred pair in the first part of Spenser's *Fairie Queene*, published three years before, and of course Marlowe's *Hero and Leander* had been circulating in manuscript for a similar period. Lodge had published *Glaucus and Scilla*, and Drayton was about to offer *Endimion and Phoebe* to the world. The works of Shakespeare should not be taken out of their context, since it is there they acquire their true meaning. He borrowed the stanzaic form from Lodge, and may have found his theme in Marlowe, but he wrote the poem in part to emphasise his learning. One of his principal sources, therefore, was Ovid's *Metamorphoses*. As with the composition of *The Comedy of Errors*, he wished to demonstrate that he could deploy classical sources with as much brilliance as Marlowe or, even, as Spenser. The attack by Greene upon him, satirising him as a country bumpkin, may in part have provoked his invention. But he was still not averse to outright stealing from other places. The description of the horse of Adonis, often cited as a testimony to Shakespeare's knowledge of equine matters, is cribbed almost verbatim from a translation by Joshua Sylvester of *Divine Weekes and Workes* by Guillaume du Bartas.

Venus and Adonis was immensely popular. Only one copy of the 1593 edition survives; the first print-run had been read literally to disintegration. There were no fewer than eleven editions over the next twenty-five years, and there may have been other reprints that have simply vanished. It was in his lifetime far more popular than any of his plays, and did more to secure his literary reputation than any drama. His instinct to compose such a narrative poem, especially at a time of theatrical dearth, was undoubtedly the right one.

It is in essence a dramatic narrative that, like Shakespeare's plays, hovers between comic and serious matter. Half the lines are conceived as dialogue or dramatic oratory. The confrontation between the lascivious Venus and the frigid Adonis becomes the subject of quintessential English pantomime:

> She sincketh downe, still hanging by his necke,
> He on her belly fall's, she on her backe.

But the farce is succeeded by the solemn obsequies on the dead boy. Shakespeare cannot stay with one mood for very long. It repays reading aloud, and in Chaucerian fashion it may have been performed by Shakespeare as a private entertainment. It moves rapidly and energetically; Shakespeare is both adept and nimble, attentive and consoling. It was remarkable for what was known as its wantonness. Although it was not half as pornographic as some of the poems then being circulated in manuscript, it earned a rebuke from John Davies as "bawdy Geare."[7] Thomas Middleton included it in a list of "wanton pamphlets" and a contemporary versifier suggested that

> Who list read lust there's Venus and Adonis
> True model of a most lascivious leatcher.[8]

Venus and Adonis is a poem concerning overpowering lust for a young male, considerably more passionate even than Thomas Mann's *Death in Venice*, and it seems obvious to the reader that Shakespeare took great delight and pleasure in writing it. Erotic literature is perhaps the one genre in which the author's personal tastes and preoccupations are vital to its success and effectiveness. But at the same time it would be unwise to attribute such feelings of personal passion to Shakespeare. He is eloquent, of course, but he is also detached. Passion is an element within his repertory of effects. The reader is given the curious impression that the author is there and yet not there. To feel so much, and yet be able to mock that feeling–that is the mark of a sublime intellect. It is perhaps also why the poem has often been considered as an extension of Shakespeare's dramatic imagination. There has never been a more fluent, or more artful, English writer.

Venus and Adonis became particularly popular among the students of the universities and of the Inns, who read it individually or perhaps even in groups. In 1601 Gabriel Harvey could still write that "the younger sort take much delight in Shakespeare's *Venus and Adonis*." He was by no means the anonymous or unremarked writer he is often assumed as being. *Venus and Adonis* itself became almost a byword for poetry itself. In Peele's *Merry Conceited Jests* the tapster of the inn at Pie Corner was "much given to poetry, for he had ingrossed the Knight of the Sunne, *Venus and Adonis*, and other pamphlets." It was called "the best book in the world,"[9] and a play of 1608, *The Dumb Knight*, has the following dialogue. "I pray you, sir, what book do you read?" "A book that never an orator's clerk in this kingdom but is beholden unto; it is called, Maid's Philosophy, or *Venus and Adonis*." We may say, with some certainty, that Shakespeare now was one of the most famous poets in the country. He was not the faceless man in the crowd, or the unnoticed stranger in a corner of the inn.

CHAPTER 36

That Hath a Mint of Phrases
in His Braine

✦

Shakespeare and Southampton could have met in, or through, the playhouse. Southampton became a regular attender of plays. Indeed it seems to have been his principal London recreation. There were other connections. In the year after the publication of *Venus and Adonis* Southampton's mother, the Countess of Southampton, married Sir Thomas Heneage; Heneage was Treasurer of the Queen's Chamber, and therefore responsible for arranging payment for the players at court. It is a tenuous connection, perhaps, but in the small and overcrowded world of the English court an interesting one.

The poet and the earl might also have met through the ministrations of Lord Strange; Southampton was an intimate friend of Lord Strange's younger brother, who was himself an amateur playwright. What could be more natural than that the young earl should be introduced to the most promising author of the day? And one, too, whom he had seen act? Lord Strange and the Earl of Southampton were also part of that group of Catholic sympathisers which Lord Burghley suspected, and indeed Southampton was considered by many to be "the great hope of Catholic resistance."[1] Shakespeare was well adapted to such a group. The young earl was also, by a complicated set of circumstances, related by marriage to the Ardens of Stratford. Shakespeare could therefore have claimed a further connection. It is also intriguing to note that Southampton's erstwhile spiritual adviser, the poet and Jesuit Robert Southwell, was also related to the Arden family. It has plausibly been suggested that Shakespeare read, and copied from, some of Southwell's poetry. A poem by Southwell, "Saint Peter's Complaint," was preceded by an epistle "To my worthy good cousin, Master W.S" from "Your loving cousin, R.S." There are affinities and unwritten alliances that are now largely hidden from view.

There is also a possibility that they met through the agency of Southampton's tutor in French and Italian, John Florio. Florio, born in London, was the child of Protestant refugees out of Italy. He was an excellent linguist, a capable scholar, and a somewhat censorious lover of the drama; he professed that he was living in a "stirring time, and pregnant prime of inuention when euerie bramble is fruitefull."[2] This "stirring time" was Shakespeare's time. Florio also translated Montaigne into English, and in that work provided phrases and allusions for *King Lear* and *The Tempest*. Now all but forgotten, Florio was a contemporary of great significance to Shakespeare himself. Shakespeare's comedies of this period are Italianate in setting, if not in sentiment, and their atmosphere can plausibly be attributed to the influence of Florio upon the dramatist eleven years his junior. There are occasions when Shakespeare seems to evince so specific a knowledge of Italy that it is believed by some that he must have travelled to that country in his youthful days. But, again, the presence of Florio may account for that knowledge. Florio helped other dramatists also. In the preliminaries to his *Volpone*, set in Venice, Ben Jonson wrote an autograph dedication to Florio "the ayde of his Muses." Florio also possessed a great library, filled with Italian books. We need look no further for the Italian sources that have been identified in Shakespeare's plays. Shakespeare borrowed many phrases and images from Florio's Italian dictionary, *A World of Words*—"it were labour lost to speak of love," Florio writes—and he may have composed an introductory sonnet to Florio's *Second Frutes*, published in 1591. Florio is one of those somewhat elusive figures who appear from time to time in Shakespeare's biography, whose significance is out of all proportion to their visibility.

There are many connections, then, between Shakespeare and Southampton. That they did meet is certain. Shakespeare's second dedication to Southampton, in *The Rape of Lucrece*, is sure evidence of greater intimacy. It has also been assumed that he addressed his sonnets to some noble youth, but the case is more uncertain. One recently discovered portrait does nothing to resolve the controversy over the matter. It was painted in the early 1590s and shows a young person dressed in a somewhat effeminate manner complete with rouge, lipstick, a double earring and a long tress of hair. For many years it was mistitled as a portrait of "Lady Norton," but in more recent times it has been identified as a portrait of Southampton. If Southampton were in fact the recipient of Shakespeare's love sonnets, as some have suggested, then his androgynous appearance might afford some reason for the poet's attentions.

There is also the possibility that for a short time in 1593 Shakespeare became secretary to Southampton. There is a comic scene in *Edward the Third*, between the king and his private secretary, which suggests the ironic presence of some shared experience. He may have worked for the young nobleman at Southampton House, along Chancery Lane, but there are many scholars who have found buried allusions to the family estate at Titchfield in Hampshire in the texts of the plays of this period.[3] It would have been more sensible and appropriate to have removed to the country at the time of plague in London. It may have been here that Shakespeare wrote his second long narrative poem, *The Rape of Lucrece*, that was dedicated to Southampton.

It was not at all unusual for young writers to be pressed into the service of noblemen. Thomas Kyd had for a while become secretary to the Earl of Sussex; Lyly had been secretary to the Earl of Oxford, and Spenser had been in similar employment with the Bishop of Rochester. In fact at a later date Southampton enlisted the poet and dramatist Thomas Heywood into his household in precisely that role. Shakespeare's own employment is an unprovable hypothesis, but it does no violence to the chronology or to Shakespeare's known expertise in matters of composition and handwriting. He would have made an excellent secretary.

It is a matter of historical record that, at a dinner in Oxford in 1593, Southampton sat with the four principal patrons of the English theatre–the Earl of Essex, Lord Strange, the Earl of Pembroke and the Lord Admiral Howard. No account of Elizabethan society, or the Elizabethan theatre, can omit this almost claustrophobic sense of belonging. That claustrophobia, or closeness of association, is echoed in a play that Shakespeare wrote during this period. *Love's Labour's Lost* is something of a puzzle. It seems in part to be a satire on some of Shakespeare's more notable contemporaries, and is so highly allusive and ironic that it hardly seems designed for the public playhouses. It has sometimes been assumed that it was commissioned in some sense by Southampton, and there has even been speculation that it was first performed in Southampton House or at Titchfield. In a ground-plan for Titchfield House there is an upstairs chamber designated as the "Playhouse Room," just to the left of the main entrance.

With its cast of young noblemen and noble ladies, its affected pedants and its schoolmasters, its nimble wits and its dunces, it has been variously interpreted as a playful satire upon Southampton and his circle, upon Lord Strange and his supporters, upon Thomas Nashe, upon John Florio, upon Sir Walter Raleigh and the notorious "school of night." There are references to a thundering rival poet, George Chapman, and to other Elizabethan notables who are now less well known than the characters in the play. And it may indeed refer to all of them. But if it is so densely allusive a play, then it could really only have been intended for a very knowing audience. Shakespeare even went back to the work of John Lyly, the court dramatist par excellence, for the tone and structure of his play. He was also thinking of Sir Philip Sidney's sonnet sequence, *Astrophil and Stella*. This was the courtly and noble milieu in which his mind and imagination were working. It was played before Queen Elizabeth in 1597, and Southampton staged it for the royal family of King James I at Southampton House eight years later. Southampton had a particular, and perhaps proprietorial, interest in the play. Yet it was not only a coterie drama. It was also performed at a public theatre, and there is a poem of 1598 which begins:

> LOVES LABOR LOST, I once did see a Play
> Yclepèd [called] so . . .

The essential plot is a simple one. Ferdinand, King of Navarre, persuades three of his courtiers to join him in three years of study during which they will renounce all contact with women. At the same time, however, the Princess of France and three of her noblewomen arrive in his kingdom, with predictable results. The King and his nobles fall in love, and forswear their oaths. At the close of the play a messenger arrives to announce the death of the Princess's father, and all the revels are ended. It is a strong yet slender thread upon which to hang a range of allusions, characters and witticisms as well as assorted comic business. The range of parallels and references is indeed a wide one. The dramatic court is loosely established upon the real court of Navarre, from whom Shakespeare even borrowed the names of his courtiers. The names of Berowne, Longauille and Dumaine are taken from the Duc de Biron, the Duc de Longueville and the Duc de Mayenne. It is unlikely that Shakespeare was alluding to the internecine rivalries of French politics; it is much more probable that he found the names in contemporary pamphlets and lifted them out of their immediate context. That was his characteristic practice, which may be described as one of inspired opportunism. The character of Armado, who is described as "an affected Spanish Braggart," seems to be based upon Gabriel Harvey, a notably affected scholar and poet. There is little doubt that his page, Moth, is a caricature of Thomas Nashe; when Armado calls Moth "my tender Iuuenal" it is a pun on Nashe's assumption of the role of the Roman satirist Juvenal. The joke is that Harvey and Nashe were in fact bitter enemies, and for several years engaged in a pamphlet war with one another. To have them appear on stage as a Spanish grandee and his witty page was a stroke of great comic invention. Shakespeare had a keen eye for the vagaries of his contemporaries. It is also relevant, perhaps, that in this period Nashe was vying with Shakespeare for the patronage of Southampton. His was a good-humoured way of dealing with a rival.

The part of Holofernes, or "Pedant" as he is described in the list of characters, is no less clearly based upon John Florio; he talks as if he had swallowed Florio's dictionary, quotes some of its definitions and also employs Italian phrases to be found in Florio's *Second Frutes*. There are other connections with the life of the time. To give the name "Ferdinand" to the King of Navarre is to pay passing reference to Ferdinando, Lord Strange, who may have watched the play in the company of Southampton. There is also a reference in the text to "the school of night," although some scholars believe it to be the "scowl" or "suit" or "stile" of night. If it is indeed a school it is likely to be a reference to the scholarly coterie around Sir Walter Raleigh, whose adventures in alchemy and speculation led to their being known as a "school of atheism."

Love's Labour's Lost is written in Shakespeare's most artificial style, reminiscent of the sonnets and the longer poetic narratives that he had written or was in the process of writing. Of all Shakespeare's plays, it is the most heavily rhymed; the use of rhyme in couplets, in particular, emphasises the closed nature of the experience that the play offers. It is a world of artifice in which pattern and symmetry are the single most noticeable features. But the word "wit" is also used more than forty times. It is a world of play. That is why it is also a play of puns. As evidence of Shakespeare's dramatic and linguistic virtuosity it is little short of a wonder. As he rushes forward in composition, he sometimes stumbles on an image which he will recall later. Will Kempe, playing the clown Costard, utters the line: "My sweet ounce of mans flesh, my in-conie Iew" (865) in anticipation of *The Merchant of Venice*.

In Thomas Mann's novel *Doctor Faustus*, the composer Adrian Leverkuhn conceives this play, in musical terms, as "a revival of *opéra bouffe* in a spirit of the most artificial mockery and parody of the artificial; something highly playful and highly precious." The narrator of the novel describes it as "Leverkuhn's exuberant youthful composition,"[4] like the play itself. Yet *Love's Labour's Lost* is almost *opéra bouffe* already. With its extravagance and lasciviousness, its rush of inventiveness, its prolificity, its ornamentation and decoration, its rapid changes of verse-scheme, its general testing of sixteenth-century English to the very bounds and limits of its capacity, it is one of the cleverest plays ever written. As one of the French courtiers admits of female wit (2010–11):

> . . . their conceites haue winges,
> Fleeter then Arrowes, bullets, wind, thought, swifter thinges.

Shakespeare wrote some sonnets for the play itself, and these were later incorporated within an anthology, *The Passionate Pilgrim*, which included two of Shakespeare's "real" sonnets. The "dark lady" of those sonnets seems to have some connection with one of the Princess's entourage, Rosaline, who is described as being "as blacke as Ebonie" (1487). The connections are there. Whether they are real, or fanciful, is another matter.

Any interpretation is made more complicated by the evident fact that, after its first performances in 1593, Shakespeare revised the play before its presentation at the court of Elizabeth five years later. Many references would have been deleted or changed, and much additional material included. When the text of the play performed before the queen was published, it declared itself to be "Newly corrected and augmented *By W. Shakespere*." The printer did not always mark Shakespeare's changes, however. It seems that the dramatist added material in the margins of his papers, or inserted additional sheets, while only lightly marking the passages to be deleted. So it is that, in the quarto text, two alternative versions of speeches may be printed one after the other.

The puzzle of *Love's Labour's Lost* is rendered more puzzling by references to a sequel entitled *Love's Labour's Won*. It is part of an inventory of Shakespeare's plays compiled by a contemporary in 1598, and a bookseller's catalogue of 1603 proves that it was printed and sold. But it has entirely disappeared. There have been attempts to identify it with *The Taming of the Shrew* and with *As You Like It*, but the difference in title remains a clear obstacle. We must simply assume that it is a "lost" play by Shakespeare, to be placed with another "lost" play entitled *Cardenio*.

Shakespeare was at ease with his courtly audience, and with the composition of the gentle comedy of *Love's Labour's Lost* he played the role of a privileged servant. He knew the formalities and informalities of court life, just as he knew the exact tone with which noblemen addressed each other. He was at home with the learning of the period, and with the most important scholars and literary men around him. He was, in other words, part of one of the inner circles of Elizabethan society. There are also allusions in *Love's Labour's Lost* to the military campaigns of the Earl of Essex—to the extent that one biographer has suggested that the play is in part a tribute to him[5]—and of course Southampton himself was a close ally of Essex in the world of court intrigue. If Shakespeare was not part of "Essex's affinity," to use the formal word for the noble earl's friends and associates, he was well acquainted with those who were. We may note in a similar spirit of kinship that if Shakespeare was not himself a recusant, he was in close association with fervent adherents to the old faith. Within this cluster of interests—Essex, Southampton, Strange, Roman Catholicism—his own affinities lay.

Part V

The Lord Chamberlain's Men

Kemps nine daies vvonder.

Performed in a daunce from
London to Norwich.

Containing the pleasure, paines and kinde entertainment
of *William Kemp* betweene *London* and that Citty
in his late Morrice.

Wherein is somewhat set downe worth note; to reprooue
the slaunders spred of him: many things merry,
nothing hurtfull.

Written by himselfe to satisfie his friends.

LONDON
Printed by *E. A.* for *Nicholas Ling*, and are to be
solde at his shop at the west doore of Saint
Paules Church. 1600.

The *Nine Daies Wonder* of William Kempe, whose dance routines were as famous as
his clowning and acting. He morris-danced all the way from London to Norwich.

CHAPTER 37

Stay, Goe, Doe What You Will

Shakespeare *did not stay* within Southampton's immediate circle. With the disintegration of Pembroke's Men in the late summer of 1593, and perhaps after a short period as Southampton's secretary at the time of the plague, he joined another theatrical company. The sequence of attributions in the playbooks of his drama suggests very strongly that he served briefly with the Earl of Sussex's Men until the formation of the Lord Chamberlain's Men in the following year. If he had in fact joined Sussex's Men soon after leaving Pembroke's, then he is likely to have toured with them in the autumn and winter of 1593. They were at York in late August, moving on to Newcastle and to Winchester. At the beginning of 1594 they had returned to London, where the theatres had been permitted to reopen for the Christmas season. They performed Shakespeare's *Titus Andronicus* on three occasions at the Rose before the theatres were again closed down as a result of the plague. In his diary Henslowe registered it as "ne," but the significance of this is unclear. It cannot mean "new," as is sometimes supposed, since one play is twice given the same notation. It may mean that the play has been newly licensed by the Master of Revels, the censor of the period, or it may mean that it was new to a particular company's repertory. Other theatrical historians have supposed that it is an abbreviation for Newington Butts. The most likely meaning, in the context of *Titus Andronicus*, is that it was newly revised from an original play entitled by Henslowe *tittus & vespacia* and performed by Lord Strange's Men three years before.

On the last day of performance, 6 February, *Titus Andronicus* was entered on the Stationers' Register for publication. Shakespeare had brought it with him from Strange's Men to Pembroke's Men, and then from Pembroke's Men to Sussex's Men; on his joining the Lord Chamberlain's Men, in the summer of 1594, the new company performed his play once more. If we follow the successive productions of the play, we are also following Shakespeare's own trajectory. The publication of *Titus Andronicus* immediately after the theatres were closed down suggests that Shakespeare saw a chance to make some profit out of a successful venture; the publisher or stationer, John Danter, by chance Nashe's friend and landlord, also issued a ballad on the same subject as a way of gaining some additional pennies.

In the Easter season of 1594, the theatres were again opened for a short period. For eight evenings Sussex's Men joined with the Queen's Men to perform at the Rose, their combined forces perhaps signalling the hard times of the previous months, and in the first week of April *King Leir* was performed on two occasions. This was the play in which Shakespeare acted and which at a later date he transformed utterly.

He changed his address in this period, and in the available records he is found to be living in Bishopsgate rather than in Shoreditch. The two neighbourhoods are in fact only a short distance apart—no more than five minutes' walk—but Bishopsgate was a more salubrious area, with less taint of the brothel and the low tavern. He was part of the parish of St. Helen's, Bishopsgate, just by the wall in the north of the city, and close to the church that was reputed to have been founded by the Emperor Constantine. This was the church where he was obliged to worship, and where he would surrender a metal token at the communion table as a sign of his presence. In the assessment roll of the parish he is listed nineteenth, and the relatively small valuation of 13*s* 4*d* reflects the value of his furniture and his books. He lodged in a set of chambers within one of the tenements here.

It was a residential area favoured by the richer merchants, among whose number could be counted Sir John Crosby and Sir Thomas Gresham. Crosby Place was in the parish, a late fifteenth-century mansion in which Richard III had lodged when he was Lord Protector; Shakespeare knew it well, and set part of *The Tragedy of King Richard III* there. It had also been owned by Sir

Thomas More and, at the time of Shakespeare's residence, it was inhabited by the Lord Mayor. The parish was also a harbour for several families of French or Flemish origin, and in fact there was a slightly less agreeable area known as "Petty France." At a later date he would lodge with a Huguenot family in Silver Street; he preferred the company of what were termed "strangers" in the course of his restless London life. Another neighbour was Thomas Morley, the madrigalist and gentleman of the Chapel Royal; since Morley wrote the music for two or three of Shakespeare's songs, at some stage they became acquainted. As an actor Shakespeare would also have been trained as a singer, and in his plays he displays a technical knowledge of musical terms. Is it too much to speculate that he and Morley joined in the universal Elizabethan pastime of music-making?

John Stow, the sixteenth-century London topographer, described the parish as containing "divers fair and large built houses for merchants and such like . . . many fair tenements, divers fair inns, large for receipt of travellers, and some houses for men of worship." There was a new water conduit in the neighbourhood which, in the sanitary conditions of the period, was of great local benefit. So Bishopsgate had certain advantages over Shoreditch. The large inns here—among them the Bull, the Green Dragon and the Wrestlers—were well known for their commodious quarters. One of them, the Bull, had its own public stage where the Queen's Men used to perform.

If Shakespeare was not quite yet a "man of worship," in Stow's sense, he was travelling ineluctably in that direction. His move to Bishopsgate may in fact have coincided with his admission into the Lord Chamberlain's Men, in which he also progressed from "hired man" to "sharer." The company was established in the spring of 1594 by Lord Hunsdon, the Lord Chamberlain, who wanted to bring order into the general confusion of the London playing companies. The connection of the companies and the court should never be forgotten, since the principal purpose of the players was theoretically to provide entertainment for Her Majesty. The quality and continuity of that entertainment were now in jeopardy. The plague and the subsequent closure of the theatres had affected all of the companies. Some of them, like the Queen's Men, had divided. In April Lord Strange had died, under mysterious circumstances, and Lord Strange's Men came under the less certain patronage of his widow. So it became the Lord Chamberlain's business to provide a durable and reliable source for the queen's entertainment.

And so Hunsdon advanced an ambitious scheme. He established a duopoly in the city. He would patronise a new company to be called the Lord

Chamberlain's Men while his son-in-law, Charles Howard, the Lord High Admiral, would patronise and support a group of players to be known as the Lord Admiral's Men. The Lord Admiral's Men would be led by Edward Alleyn, and would perform at the Rose in Southwark owned by Philip Henslowe; the Lord Chamberlain's Men would be led by Richard Burbage, and would perform at James Burbage's theatres at Shoreditch. One troupe would command the south of the river, in other words, and the other would dominate the northern suburbs. As a concession to the civic authorities, who were not happy to see playhouses formally established in the suburbs, Hunsdon agreed that no inns would be employed for the staging of the drama. It was a very neat arrangement that, in its pristine form, did not last for very long.

Hunsdon acquired the players for his new venture by poaching the best actors from a variety of companies–among them Lord Strange's Men, the Queen's Men and Sussex's Men. From Sussex's Men, he took William Shakespeare. Several of the players in Sussex's Men went over to the Lord Chamberlain's with Shakespeare; among them we find John Sincler and Richard Burbage himself. There seems to have been one other division of the spoils. When the Lord Admiral's Men took Alleyn they were also granted the bulk of Marlowe's dramas. When Shakespeare joined the Lord Chamberlain's, he brought with him all of his plays. This was their great advantage. From this time forward the Lord Chamberlain's Men were the sole producers of Shakespeare's drama. In the whole course of his career only they ever performed his plays. Soon after their union, in fact, they were performing *Titus Andronicus*, *The Taming of a Shrew* and a play called *Hamlet*. At the time of their formation they may also have inherited plays from other companies. They may have given these plays, such as *Hamlet* and *King Leir*, to their resident playwright for the purposes of reshaping and rewriting for the new cast of players. It is also likely that, in these circumstances, Shakespeare would feel moved to rewrite his own earlier plays for the new company. It was, after all, a fresh start. The company was an innovation. It deserved new-minted texts. It has been estimated that 90 per cent of their plays have not survived the trials of time and usage; certainly almost half of their extant texts are by Shakespeare himself, which at least testifies to his endurance and popularity. They were saved and reissued; the others were simply discarded and forgotten.

CHAPTER 38

We Few, We Happy Few, We Band of Brothers

his extraordinary group of players, known as the Lord Chamberlain's Men, became Shakespeare's good companions for the rest of his life. He wrote for, and acted with, them only. They were his colleagues but, on the evidence of wills and other documents, they were also his intimate friends. They were also the most enduring company in English theatrical history, maintaining a recognisable identity from 1594 until 1642, a period of almost fifty years in which they performed the greatest plays in the history of world theatre.

We know the identity of some of them. Apart from Richard Burbage there were Augustine Phillips, Thomas Pope, George Bryan, John Heminges, John Sincler, William Sly, Richard Cowley, John Duke and the comedian Will Kempe. Heminges seems to have had a reputation for his business acumen as well as his acting; he became the financial manager of the company, and was named frequently as the overseer or trustee in his fellows' wills. He died a wealthy and respectable citizen, given the title of "Gent." in the confirmation of his arms by the College of Heraldry; he was also a "sidesman" or official in the parish of St. Mary Aldermanbury, an indication that the status of the acting profession had risen considerably during Shakespeare's lifetime. Heminges may well have played older character parts, such as Polonius and Capulet.

Augustine Phillips was another actor who, like Heminges and Shakespeare, was granted a coat of arms. He also died a wealthy man, with a country estate at Mortlake. He was a leading member of the company, and it was he who was once called in front of the Privy Council to represent his fellows. He seems to have been primarily a "straight" player, acting as "second" to Richard Burbage in parts such as Cassius and Claudio; but he could also entertain the audiences with farcical comedy. There is a notation in the Stationers' Register of spring 1595 for "Phillips his gigg of the slyppers"—a "gig" or "jig" being an interlude of music, dancing and comic repartee. An Elizabethan actor had to be versatile. He had to be able to dance, to sing, to play an instrument, and if necessary to fight a convincing duel upon the stage. Thomas Pope, for example, was an excellent acrobat and clown as well as a player; he, too, took out a coat of arms. John Sincler, known as "Sinklo," was a man of extraordinary thinness and as a result of his uncommon appearance played a number of comic roles including Pinch in *The Comedy of Errors* and Justice Shallow in the second part of *Henry IV*. He is also likely to have played such parts as the apothecary in *Romeo and Juliet*. It is clear, in fact, that Shakespeare created several roles with Sincler in mind.

Yet the most versatile comic actor in the company was undoubtedly William Kempe. The most famous clown in the country, he was small and stout, especially with padding or "bombasting," but quick and nimble on his feet. He was well known, in particular, for his gigs and his morris-dancing. There are many references and allusions to his dances. When not dressing up as a female street-seller he wore the costume of a country clown; he had shaggy and unruly hair; his humour was farcical and often obscene; he had a great gift for extempore repartee, or "gagging," with the audience. He could "make a scurvy face" and "draw his mouth awry,"[1] indicating that comic routines have not necessarily changed very much over the centuries. The humour of the Elizabethan stage, and indeed the humour of the medieval mysteries and interludes, survives still in farce and in pantomime. It is one of the unchanging features of the English imagination.

Kempe would often perform his own "routines" during the course of the play, and thus temporarily bring the action to a halt. Hamlet complains of the habit in his directions to the players, when he instructs them to "let those that play your clownes speake no more then is set downe for them, for there be of them that wil themselues laugh, to set on some quantitie of barraine spectators to laugh to" (1767–9). This was a direct hit against Kempe, who had just left the Lord Chamberlain's Men after some disagreement with his fellows. The quarrel may have been over just such a matter of comic performance. It is possible that in an earlier version of *Hamlet* Kempe "gagged" too often in his role as the clown and gravedigger; there would be a certain poetical justice in reprimanding him in a later version of the same play.

At an earlier date, however, other playwrights welcomed his dances and improvisations. It saved them the labour of invention. There are even indications that they would mark Kempe's entry in the playbooks, and then leave the rest to him. In one version of *Hamlet* (in this play, as in so many others, there is evidence of continual revision) Shakespeare even quotes some of Kempe's catchphrases—"cannot you stay till I eat my porridge?" as well as "My coat wants a cullisen [scutcheon]" and "Your beer is sour," the last line no doubt delivered with the mouth famously "awry." There is no doubt, too, that when they first worked together Shakespeare fashioned parts specifically for Kempe. In a similar spirit of professionalism Mozart wrote operatic roles for specific singers, and often would not write an aria until he had heard the voice of the singer who would take the part. So when Grumio saws cheese with a dagger, or when Cade dances a morris or laps up drink from the earth, Shakespeare had Kempe's drolleries very much in mind. Kempe played Bottom in *A Midsummer Night's Dream* and Dogberry in *Much Ado About Nothing*. He played Falstaff in the two parts of *Henry IV*. In the second play there is a stage direction, "Enter Will," a few lines before Falstaff begins singing a ballad "When Arthur first in court. . . ." So Kempe was cued to enter, no doubt to the delight of the audience, a minute or two before breaking into song. At the end of the play Kempe appeared upon the stage, still dressed as Falstaff, and asks the audience: "If my tongue cannot intreate you to acquite mee, will you commaund me to vse my legges?" This is the cue for a jig, in which the rest of the players are likely to have joined. Shakespeare would have danced with him, too, and in that "merry moment"—to use an Elizabethan expression—we gain an authentic glimpse of the Elizabethan theatre.

In this same epilogue Shakespeare promises a further episode in the story "with Sir Iohn in it." But in the succeeding play, *Henry V*, Falstaff mysteriously disappears and his death off-stage is merely described. There have been many critical and artistic interpretations for this absence, but the true reason may be more prosaic. In the interval between *Henry IV, Part Two* and *Henry V*, Will Kempe had left the company. Without the star comic player, there was no point in bringing back Falstaff. There was no one to play him. It is best to remember that the plays of Shakespeare are dependent upon theatrical circumstance. It may go against the current grain of interpretation to see

Falstaff as a wholly comic character, complete with dances and extemporal quips; but, again, it is part of the more strident nature of the Elizabethan theatre. Falstaff's wooden stick, red face and great belly would have immediately reminded the audience of the stock figure of the clown; anachronistically, Falstaff has more than a trace of Punch about him. But the clown was also a theatrical version of the Lord of Misrule, and what better description could there be of Falstaff himself?

When Kempe left the Lord Chamberlain's Men he performed a "wonder" by dancing all the way from London to Norwich, and described himself in a pamphlet as "Caualiero Kempe, head-master of Morrice-dauncers, high Head-borough of heighs, and onely tricker of your Trill-lilles and best bel-shangles betweene Sion and mount Surrey"[2]–a sentence suggesting that some elements of English humour have been lost for ever. If he had indeed left after a disagreement with the Lord Chamberlain's Men it gives added resonance to his address to "My notable Shakerags" in the same pamphlet, by which name he subsumes all of his enemies or "witles beetles-heads" and "block-headships" who had been spreading rumours and slanders about him. In the same place he refers to "a penny Poet whose first making was the miserable stolne story of Macdoel, or Macdobeth, or Macsomewhat: for I am sure a Mac it was." It is generally assumed that he is not referring to Shakespeare's *Macbeth* but, rather, to a ballad on the same subject. Nevertheless it is an interesting allusion.

In the company of the Lord Chamberlain's Men there were some sixteen actors, including five or six boys who played the female parts. Although there was no guild of actors in sixteenth-century London these boys served an unofficial "apprenticeship"; their training was not fixed at the seven years required in other trades, and its length seems to have varied from three years to twelve years. The boys had a "master" in one of the older actors, with whom they lodged and by whom they were instructed. One contract reveals that the boy, or in fact the boy's parents, paid a specified sum of £8 so that he could be taken into service; the master then promised to pay his charge 4 pence a day and to teach him "in playinge of interludes and plaies." The ambition of these stripling players was to rise into the profession by degrees, and if possible become an integral part of the company with whom they were trained. As the wills and estates of Shakespeare's fellow actors prove, it was about to become a very lucrative employment indeed. The boys were generally treated as part of the master actor's family, and were often held in great affection by their theatrical parents. Edward Alleyn's wife wrote to her husband, when he was on tour, asking if "Nicke and Jeames be well & commend them." Shakespeare could not have had an apprentice because, unlike some of his colleagues, he belonged to no guild.

It is generally believed that only boys played the female roles on the Elizabethan stage, but there is some cause to doubt that assumption. Young adult males possibly took on the mature role of Cleopatra, for example, where the resources of even the most skilful boy might prove ineffectual. That there were very accomplished child actors is not in doubt. In Shakespeare's company we know that there was a tall fair one and a short dark-haired one, simply because there are references in the texts to that effect. There is a remarkable sequence of comedies in which two girls vie for theatrical attention—Helena and Hermia in *A Midsummer Night's Dream*, Portia and Nerissa in *The Merchant of Venice*, Beatrice and Hero in *Much Ado About Nothing*, Rosalind and Celia in *As You Like It*, Olivia and Viola in *Twelfth Night*. It seems likely that the same gifted pair of boys played all of these parts, providing further evidence of the extent to which Shakespeare's art was defined by the potential of his company.

There are other influences. The members of the company may have suggested to Shakespeare stories that were suitable for dramatisation; they may have lent him books and the texts of old plays. In rehearsal, too, there would undoubtedly have been suggestions from the actors on the revision of a scene or dialogue. His was not a case of single-handed or single-minded invention. There can be no doubt at all that the Lord Chamberlain's Men helped to create Shakespeare as an "author."

As well as the actors and apprentices in the Lord Chamberlain's Men there was a book-keeper who also acted as prompter with perhaps an assistant stage-keeper, a wardrobe-keeper or "tireman," stage musicians, a carpenter or two, "gatherers" who collected the money at the doors before each performance, and of course stagehands. There were differences in status and income among them, the most important distinction being that between "sharer" and "hired man." A "sharer," as Shakespeare was in the Lord Chamberlain's Men, put up a sum of £50 on joining the company. He was then eligible for a share in its income, once a portion of the receipts for each performance had been paid to the owner of the playhouse and to the rest of the company. It was a theatrical version of the "joint stock company" which played so large a part in the economics of the late sixteenth century. At a later date Shakespeare also became a "house-keeper," when he was part of the group who owned the Globe playhouse. It was a way of cutting out the "middle men" or theatrical entrepreneurs such as Henslowe; since the house-keepers took half of the proceeds from the gallery, it proved to be highly profitable.

Each of the nine "sharers" in the company was also one of the principal actors, and it has been estimated that their roles took up some 90 or 95 per cent of the dialogue in each play; the "hired men" were minor actors who played only the smaller roles that could be learned without undue delay or extensive rehearsal. It seems likely that the "sharers" made their decisions, financial or artistic, by means of majority voting. Heminges and Shakespeare were no doubt known for their business acumen, and it is more than likely that the advice of Shakespeare was sought on new plays and new playwrights. He is credited, for example, with bringing the plays of Ben Jonson to his company. According to Nicholas Rowe the Lord Chamberlain's Men were about to reject *Every Man in His Humour* "when Shakespear luckily cast his Eye upon it, and found something so well in it as to engage him first to read it through." The story may be apocryphal but it accurately reflects his task of "reading through" new plays for their dramatic potential. The "sharers" were also required to arrange rehearsals, purchase costumes, put up playbills, plan for future productions and engage in all the general administration which a busy theatre requires. They paid for all those involved in the theatre, of course, from book-keeper to gatherer; they also paid for new plays and new costumes as well as the costs of licensing plays with the Master of Revels. They were also obliged, by Elizabethan custom, to give money to the needy poor of the parish.

It was a society of friends and colleagues, in other words, with common interests and common obligations. It was an extended family, with the actors living in the same neighbourhood. The actors married into one another's immediate families, too, uniting with various sisters, daughters and widows. In their wills they left money, and various tokens, to one another. It was a family that played together and stayed together. They were "ffellowes," to use the word they themselves employed.

They were also zealous and industrious. Alone among the companies of the period the Lord Chamberlain's Men avoided serious trouble with the civic authorities and stayed out of prison. When one contemporary satirist exonerated certain actors from his aspersions, calling them "sober, discreet, properly learned honest householders and citizens well thought of among their neighbours at home,"[3] it was of just such men as Shakespeare and Heminges that he was writing. In a volume entitled *Historia Histrionica* they are described as "Men of grave and sober Behaviour."[4] More than any other company of their generation they helped to elevate the status of actor beyond that of the vagabond and the acrobat.

ℒord ℋow 𝒜rt 𝒞hou 𝒞hanged

he actual nature of their acting is still not fully understood. There is some argument, for example, over the rival claims of traditionalism and realism in the Elizabethan theatre. Did the actors rely upon formal techniques of oratory and gesture or were they exploiting a new vein of naturalism in their movement and their delivery? The published reports of Burbage, for example, tend to emphasise his naturalness and fluency. His method was described as "personation," and was deemed to be the way of projecting an individual character "to the life" or "with lively action." It was a way of "counterfeiting" passions that avoided what was known as "pantomimick action."

Shakespeare often alludes to what was clearly considered to be an old-fashioned style of acting–when actors sawed the air with their arms, stamped upon the stage, interrupted their speeches with sighs, and rolled their eyes to signify fear. The old mode of walking across the stage was strutting. The word "ham," used as a description of bad acting, comes from the visibility of the ham-string of the leg. Strutting was apparently accompanied by ranting. It is what Thomas Nashe described as "ruff raff roaring, with thwick, thwack, thirlery bouncing."[1]

Burbage's style could then be described as a drift away from external symbolism towards imitation. In an earlier period the essential purpose of the actor had been to represent passion; it seems likely that Burbage and his colleagues had initiated or exploited a style of acting in which the player tried to feel or express that passion. This new emphasis can be identified with the new role of individualism in social and political life, displacing any sense of symbolic or divinely appointed hierarchy.

It may well be that some new art of emotive or emotional action, employed by Burbage and his colleagues, would help to explain the impact of Shakespeare's plays upon his contemporaries. He may have written in a new "inward" style precisely because there were players who could readily create such effects. Shakespeare differs from his predecessors in the amount of self-awareness that his characters possess. This, too, may have been a consequence of a new style of acting. Yet it should also be remembered that the company performed many plays other than those of Shakespeare, plays that were written to accord with more conventional styles of action and gesticulation.

Of course the definition of what is "natural" changes with every generation. In the sixteenth century there were "Marks, or Rules, to fix the Standards of what is *Natural*."[2] All that can be said with any precision of Shakespeare, in this respect, is that he understood the technical language of the psychology of his period. It was required of actors, in the words of a contemporary dramatist, to "frame each person" so that "you may his nature rightly know."[3] By "nature" he meant the dominant humour, sanguine or phlegmatic, choleric or melancholic, which in turn would seem to require some traditional representation. The aim of the sixteenth-century actor was to impersonate a specific passion or range of passions as they impinged upon an individual temperament; the majority of characters and situations on the Elizabethan stage, for example, are concerned with the tension between reason and passion in human behaviour with all its potentially comic or tragic consequences. It was also important for the actor to be able to enact "reversals" or "transitions" in which one passion suddenly gave way to another. The actors played a part, and not a character. That was why the art of "doubling" had become so important, and why boy actors were perfectly acceptable in female roles; the spectators were aware of the difference in sex, but they were more concerned with the action and the story. That is why there is very little, if any, "motivation" or "development" in a modern sense. Why is Iago malicious? Why did Lear divide his kingdom? Why is Leontes jealous? These are not questions to be asked. There was no appetite for realism as it is presently understood, which is why Shakespeare was able to set his plays in distant and enchanted places with no loss of power.

So a modern audience would no doubt be surprised by the amount of formality involved in all types of Elizabethan acting. It might find the acting at times risible or grotesque. The fact that at the Globe and elsewhere so many plays were produced and acted so quickly, with as many as six plays in a single week, does suggest that there were elements of "shorthand" in the performance which the actors adopted quite naturally.

Improvisation was known as "thribbling." The players would cluster, or confront one another, in traditional formal arrangements. There were orthodox ways of signalling love or hate, jealousy or distrust. The actor would find it perfectly natural to address the audience in aside or soliloquy, but in a formal rather than confidential or colloquial way. The great set speeches were recited rather than impersonated, and would have been accompanied by traditional gestures. The only general lighting effect was daylight, and so facial expressions would have been exaggerated and deliberate. The actor was advised to "looke directly in his fellowes face."[4] A spectator of *Othello* in 1610 recalled of Desdemona that "at last, lying on her bed, killed by her husband, she implored the pity of the spectators in her death with the face alone."[5] Yet all of these effects would have been accompanied at the Globe by soaring poetry and words so enthralling that they took the audience with wonder.

The other consideration must rest with the size of the audience, to be numbered in thousands rather than hundreds. There could be no attempt at intimacy. The action was vivid, strident and compelling. It is clear enough that some of the surviving texts are long, and that the actors would have spoken very quickly to compress the plot within two or even three hours. Action, too, was brisk as well as lively. Without the aid of artificial tools, their voices were open and full, their speech distinctive and resonant. The word "acting" itself derives from the behaviour of the orator, and some of those oratorical gifts were still required. That is why Richard Flecknoe stated that Burbage "had all the parts of an excellent orator (animating his words with speaking, and speech with action)."[6] Burbage knew, for example, how to change the pitch or tone of his voice; he was trained to abbreviate or lengthen syllables to register the stress of emotion. His delivery itself may have been rhythmic or "musical," distinctly at odds with the rhythms of contemporary speech. Shakespeare often uses the effect of very brief sentences, one after another, in a rhetorical device known as "stichomythia." This required a highly theatricalised version of dialogue. There was no such thing as a "normal" voice in the Elizabethan theatre, and it is extremely unlikely that the modern tones of "dialogue" were ever heard upon its stage.

Action and gesture, as any orator knew, were as important as voice. The technique was known as "visible eloquence" or "eloquence of the body." This encompassed "a gracious and bewitching kinde of action,"[7] using the head, the hands and the body as part of the total performance. Much of the audience was not able to see the actor's face, except occasionally, so the player was obliged to perform with his body. To lower the head was a form of modesty. To strike the forehead was a sign either of shame or admiration. Wreathed arms were a sign of contemplation. There was a frown of anger and a frown of love. Dejection of spirit was noted by the pulling down of the hat over the eyes. The hand in motion must travel from left to right. There were in fact fifty-nine different gestures of the hands, to signify various states ranging from indignation to disputation. Thus in Hamlet's soliloquy he would have extended his right hand for "To be" and then the negative left hand for "or not to be"; he would bring them together in the deliberative mode for "that is the question." Shylock would have his fists closed for the most important scenes. The physicality of the acting was an important—perhaps the most important—aspect of the total theatrical effect. As the classical physician Galen had taught the Elizabethans, there was a vital union between mind and body. It was believed that the four humours actually changed the body and the physiognomy; sorrow literally contracted the heart and congealed the blood. When an actor suddenly changed his dominant passion in a "reversal," everything about him changed. It was an act of self-transcendence, associated with the legendary figure of Proteus, and an act of magic. It was believed also that the overflowing animal spirits of the actor could affect the spirits of the audience. To act meant to act upon the spectators. That is why the Puritans considered the playhouses to be such dangerous places.

We may speculate, then, that the acting of the Lord Chamberlain's Men did not represent a complete break with the conventions or the traditions of the theatre. A completely new or revolutionary style would have attracted adverse comment. Of course the audience was unlikely to be aware of any distinction between the "artificial" and the "real"; it could not have occurred to them to wonder, in these first days of the public theatre, whether a particular play was real or unreal. Whatever moved their passions was real enough. For the Lord Chamberlain's Men, therefore, it was a question of adding new techniques and attitudes to the old ones. It was no doubt characterised by a mingling of formality and naturalism which would look decidedly odd in a modern theatre but might have been exciting or "realistic" for the late sixteenth-century audience. It is a combination that can never, and will never, be repeated.

CHAPTER 40

Bid Me Discourse,
I Will Inchaunt Thine Eare

*I*t *is interesting* to contemplate Shakespeare as actor. At grammar school he would have had some rudimentary training in oratory, and one educationalist described the requirement for schoolboys "to pronounce with pleasing and apt modulation, tempered with variety."[1] The emphasis was upon "sweete pronunciation" which, given Shakespeare's general disposition and reputation, would seem to have been one of his attributes. Like his colleagues he must have possessed a truly phenomenal memory, having had to learn literally hundreds of parts. There was a section of rhetoric, taught at school, which dealt with precisely this matter. It was called mnemonics.

He remained an actor for more than twenty years, a longevity that required considerable energy and resilience. He knew that actors were recommended to exercise the body, to practise moderation in meat and drink, and to sing plainsong. He was originally taught to sing and to dance, possibly to play a musical instrument and to tumble like an acrobat. English actors were well known, on the continent, for their skills in "dancing and jumping"[2] as well as music. They performed in English in such countries as Germany and Denmark, but they were still widely admired. English actors were generally believed to "excel all other in the worlde,"[3] a statement that may be true still. Shakespeare was also taught how to wrestle. He learned to fence, too, in what were highly realistic bouts with rapier and dagger or broadsword. Actors were often trained at the fencing school of Rocco Bonetti, in Blackfriars, and Shakespeare may well have attended. There are a great many stage-fights in his plays; no other dramatist of the period used them so frequently or with such dramatic effect, which suggests some particular interest on his part. His audiences were in any case thoroughly acquainted with the art of fencing in all of its forms. It was an aspect of daily life. Most males above the age of eighteen would carry a dagger.

There has been endless speculation about the roles Shakespeare played, ranging from Caesar in *Julius Caesar* to the Friar in *Romeo and Juliet*, from Pandarus in *Troilus and Cressida* to Orsino in *Twelfth Night*. It has been suggested that he played the Chorus as well as the Friar in *Romeo and Juliet* and Egeon in *The Comedy of Errors;* he was Brabantio in *Othello* and Albany in *King Lear*. Theatrical legend has claimed over the centuries that he played the Ghost in *Hamlet* and the part of Adam, the aged retainer, in *As You Like It*. He is also presumed to have enjoyed "kingly" roles. It is supposed that he played the king in both parts of *Henry IV*. We can speculate that he was the monarch in *Henry VI*, *King John*, *Henry IV* and *Cymbeline* as well as the dukes of *The Comedy of Errors* and *A Midsummer Night's Dream*. We may expect, then, an authoritative and even regal bearing with resonant voice. He seems also to have impersonated dignity and old age. There is a preoccupation with encroaching old age in the sonnets–was he exorcising his fear by acting it out? He is said to have played "a decrepit old man, he wore a long beard, and appeared so weak and drooping and unable to walk, that he was forced to be supported and carried by another person."[4] If the account is not wholly apocryphal, this would be Adam in *As You Like It*. These characters also have a tendency to be of, but somehow apart from, the action. One biographer has described it as a "blend of centrality and detachment,"[5] which seems curiously like Shakespeare's general bearing in the world. No doubt, in the process of composition, he had a pretty shrewd idea of what parts he himself would play.

He rarely played comic roles, and might have "doubled" two or three minor parts rather than the central or principal part. It is sometimes suggested that he would say the first line, or the last line, of the play: an attractive idea, but one that could not always have been possible. It does seem likely, however, that he took on the character of prologue and epilogue or chorus in those plays where they were introduced. In that sense he was what the French called the "orator" of the company, coming on stage at the beginning or end of the play to represent all of the players. This was the role of Molière, the author and actor who most resembles Shakespeare, at the Palais-Royal Théâtre. It has been said of Molière that he "was all actor from his feet to his head; it seemed as though he had several voices; everything in him spoke; and by a step, a smile, a glance of the eye or the shaking of the head he suggested more things than the greatest talker could have said in an hour."[6] Given the difference in nationality and culture, this seems like an approximate description of Shakespeare himself.

It would also be sensible to suppose that Shakespeare played those roles in which he could simultaneously watch or "direct" the other actors in rehearsal, rather like the conductor of an orchestra. In many of the parts to which he has speculatively been assigned, he would remain on stage for much of the action. He may have choreographed the exits and the entrances, for example, and given a structure to the duelling scenes. Molière was also considered to be a highly skilful trainer of other actors, and one colleague said that he could make a stick act. Perhaps Shakespeare had the same gift.

It is well enough known that the authors themselves did on occasions intervene. In the Induction to *Cynthia's Revels* Jonson alludes to the author's "presence in the tiring-house, to prompt us aloud, stamp at the book-holder, swear for our properties, curse the poor tireman, rail the music out of tune, and swear for every venial trespass we commit." Shakespeare is unlikely to have sworn or stamped–Jonson himself is a much more likely candidate for that role–but as actor as well as author he is likely to have intervened in the first staging of his dramas.

There was a long theatrical tradition that Shakespeare instructed the actors in the performance of their parts. A chronicler of Sir William Davenant's company of players, formed at the time of the Restoration, records that the part of Henry VIII in *All Is True* was "rightly and justly done by Mr. *Betterton*, he being instructed in it by Sir *William*, who had it from Old Mr. Lowen, that had his Instructions from Mr. Shakespear himself." When Thomas Betterton also acted Hamlet, "Sir *William* (having seen Mr. Taylor of the *Black-Fryars* Company Act it, who being Instructed by the Author Mr. *Shaksepear*) taught Mr. *Betterton* in every Particle of it."[7] Stage traditions of this kind often contain more than a grain of truth.

There are conflicting reports about the quality of Shakespeare's acting. John Aubrey reports that he "did act exceeding well," and Henry Chettle described him as "excelent in the qualitie he professes." Nicholas Rowe, on the other hand, believes that he was no "extraordinary" actor and that "the top of his performance was the Ghost in his own *Hamlet*."[8] At the end of the seventeenth century it is reported that Shakespeare "as I have heard, was a much better Poet than Player."[9] Yet he was fully employed by the most important theatrical company of his generation, acting for more than twenty years in parts large and small. He must, if nothing else, have been a resourceful actor. The testimony of his contemporary, Henry Chettle, is perhaps the most accurate.

His progress through the ranks of the theatrical and literary world might have earned him barbs from his more envious contemporaries. A volume dedicated to the memory of Robert Greene contained an attack upon those who had "Eclipst his fame and Purloyned his Plumes."[10] A play of 1593 on the theme of Guy of Warwick has the following piece of dialogue. "I' faith Sir I was born in England at Stratford upon Avon in Warwickshire . . . I have a fine finical name, I can tell ye, for my name is Sparrow . . . but I am a high mounting lofty minded Sparrow."[11] It may be coincidence, but it may not. "Sparrow" was close in pronunciation to "spear," and was a slang word given to a lecher; sparrows were known for their lust. The Stratford man who calls himself a "bird of Venus" (the author of *Venus and Adonis*) has got his wife with child, and then abandoned her in Warwickshire. We may also recall the story of William the Conqueror coming before Richard Burbage. In a play of this period, too, Shakespeare is mildly lampooned as a character named Prickshafte. So there is a tendency, to put it no stronger, to associate Shakespeare with lustfulness.

He is also called "finical," meaning finicky or fastidious, and we may recall Aubrey's testimony that in Shoreditch Shakespeare would not be "debauched" with his colleagues. The reference here is to carousing or drinking, not to sexual misdemeanours, and so we gain a picture of a man given to lustfulness but fastidious in other particulars. By curious chance this consorts well with the imagery of the plays where there are plentiful references to bawdiness, but also evidence of a general sensitivity to unpleasant sights or smells.

Further suggestions of Shakespeare's amorousness emerge in a curious doggerel poem, with a prose prologue, entitled *Willobie His Avisa*. It purports to be written by Henry Willobie, who was related by marriage to a friend of William Shakespeare, Sir Thomas Russell, although the connection may be fortuitous. The poem concerns an innkeeper's wife, Avisa, who is pursued by several extra-marital suitors. One of them, "H.W.," is helped by a friend named "W.S" or, in a punning reference, "Will." The relevant portion of the text suggests that "W.S" was possessed by a similar passion. H.W.

> bewrayeth the secresy of his disease vnto his familiar frend W.S who not long before had tryed the curtesy of the like passion, and was now newly recouered of the like infection; yet finding his frend let bloud in the same vaine, he took pleasure for a tyme to see him bleed . . . for that he would now secretly laugh at his frends folly, that had giuen occasion not long before vnto others to laugh at his owne.

The writer continues: "in vewing a far off the course of this louing Comedy, he determined to see whether it would sort to a happier end for this new actor, then it did for the old player."[12]

It is one of those Elizabethan prose riddles that may admit to several meanings. One theory suggests that the innkeeper's daughter is in fact an emblem for Elizabeth herself. But the essential situation, of "H.W." and "W.S" in pursuit of the same young woman, is close enough to the plot of the "Dark Lady" sonnets to suggest parallels. "H.W." may be Henry Wriothesley, Earl of Southampton, and "W.S" or "Will" or "the old player" may be Shakespeare. The suggestion of lustfulness, and of resulting venereal disease, is also part of the speculation. If there were a "true story" behind the sonnets, this passage would seem to confirm that "W.S" was not immune to the favours of young women. All must remain speculation, however, with the words of the poem's preface that "there is some thing under these false names and showes that hath bene done truely."

There were in this period the usual assaults upon Shakespeare's propensity for plagiarism as well as amorousness. But the charge of plagiarism was formulaic, a ritualised insult in the world of the theatre. Imitation and borrowing were part of the craft of composition. It is the normal story of influence and gradual change. The great eighteenth-century phrenologist, Franz Joseph Gall, believed that the mental organ for robbery was the same as the organ for the formation of dramatic plots; this may be one explanation. It should also be remembered that as an actor Shakespeare was obliged to learn the lines of other dramatists, including those of Marlowe himself, and he may have reproduced them inadvertently. But he had no interest in inventing plots or incidents; for these he went to his multifarious sources, the narratives of which he borrowed wholesale. He would sometimes copy a source line by line, and even word for word, when he knew that he could not surpass it. His interest lay in reimagining events and characters.

But Shakespeare seems primarily to have borrowed from himself. He was a self-plagiarist who reused phrases, scenes and situations. The phrase "go to thy cold bed and warm thee" occurs in both *The Taming of the Shrew* and *King Lear*; it is a small example, but it is indicative of how a particular set of words was retained in his memory over many years. In his late plays he can sometimes revert to an earlier style, as if all stages of his growth were still within him. He will use the same scenario—that, for example, of a father reading the purloined letter of a son—again and again. In *The Two Gentlemen of Verona* there are anticipations of scenes and events in *Romeo and Juliet*, *The Merchant of Venice*, *Twelfth Night* and *As You Like It*. There are also many scenic and structural parallels between the plays; there are strong resemblances between *As You Like It* and *King Lear*, for example, as well as between *A Midsummer Night's Dream* and *The Tempest*. That was how his imagination worked. It took on archetypal forms. In the process of imitating himself, however, he also revises himself; he knew by instinct what was worthy to be preserved, so that there is a continuing process of self-distillation.

Expensive 17th-century gloves were often perfumed and 'garnished with embroiderie and goldsmith's wourke'. Shakespeare's father was a glover, described as a 'whittawer' or dresser of 'tawed' or untanned white leather.

As a small child, Shakespeare would have learned with the aid of a hornbook. On it were printed the alphabet, the vowels, certain syllables and the Lord's Prayer.

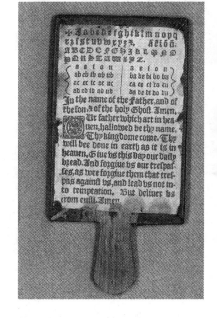

The Guild Chapel in Stratford today.
No one can know the feelings of Shakespeare's father who had been obliged
to give instructions to cover the medieval wall paintings with limewash.

Queen Elizabeth I. Initially she worked towards a middle way in religion, but after her throne was threatened by Catholic supporters of Mary Queen of Scots she sanctioned even more vigorous policies against recusants who refused to submit to the Anglican Church. This portrait dates from 1588, the year the Spanish sent their Armada against her.

Edmund Campion.
In 1580, he took part in a Jesuit undercover mission secretly to celebrate mass and rally English Catholics. It is possible that Shakespeare's father was one such clandestine Catholic. Reformers in the Anglican Church had become increasingly influential: Campion was tortured and executed, while the rituals of the old faith were gradually crushed.

Lord Strange –
Ferdinando Stanley, later the fifth
Earl of Derby – was a Catholic or
crypto-Catholic nobleman, with a
reputation for learning and artistry.
Shakespeare joined his group of
players around 1587. Lord Strange
died in 1594 – possibly poisoned.

When Shakespeare first came to
London, the most sensational
plays were *The Spanish Tragedy*
and *Tamburlane*. The three young
playwrights – Shakespeare, Kyd and
Marlowe – possibly collaborated
while working under the patronage
of Lord Strange.

Christopher Marlowe when an
undergraduate at Cambridge.
Shakespeare seems to have kept
out of the imbroglios in which
Kyd and Marlowe so dangerously
dabbled.

Titus Andronicus by William Shakespeare. Originally done for Lord Strange's Men, it was performed by many other companies including the Earl of Pembroke's, the Earl of Sussex's and the Lord Chamberlain's.

The Spanish Tragedy by Thomas Kyd: Shakespeare acted in it and Ben Jonson revised it.

The Spanish Tragedy:

Or,

Hieronimo is mad againe.

Containing the lamentable end of *Don Horatio*, and *Belimperia*; With the pitifull Death of Hieronimo,

Newly Corrected, Amended, and Enlarged with new Additions, as it hath of late beene divers times Acted.

LONDON
Printed by *Augustine Mathewes*, for *Francis Grove*, and are to bee fold at his Shoppe, neere the Sarazens Head, upon Snovv-hill. 1633.

Shakespeare dedicated both *Venus and Adonis* and *The Rape of Lucrece* to the young Earl of Southampton, Henry Wriothesley (below), who was said to be as beautiful as he was learned.

TO THE RIGHT
HONOVRABLE, HENRY
VVriothesley, Earle of Southhampton,
and Baron of Titchfield.

T HE loue I dedicate to your Lordſhip is without end: wherof this Pamphlet without beginning is but a ſuperfluous Moity. The warrant I haue of your Honourable diſpoſition, not the worth of my vntutord Lines makes it aſſured of acceptance. VVhat I haue done is yours, what I haue to doe is yours, being part in all I haue, deuoted yours. VVere my worth greater, my duety would ſhew greater, meane time, as it is, it is bound to your Lordſhip; To whom I wiſh long life ſtill lengthned with all happineſſe.

Your Lordſhips in all duety.

William Shakeſpeare.

A 2

It has been suggested that Henry Wriothesley was also the Mr W.H. of the sonnets, but a more plausible candidate is the young William Herbert, whose father the Earl of Pembroke was the patron of one of the acting companies which had employed Shakespeare and whose mother Mary was the presiding spirit of a literary coterie.

William Herbert
in later life.

Mary Herbert,
Countess of Pembroke
and sister of
Philip Sidney.

The Swan Theatre in Paris Garden. Theatres were outside the jurisdiction of the London authorities: the Swan, the Rose and the Globe were south of the Thames; the Curtain and the Theatre in Shoreditch north of the city.

Middle Temple Hall, where *Twelfth Night* was performed.

The image of 'Death with Dominion over London'. Whenever plague struck the city, which was almost every summer, the theatres closed and the players went on tour round the country.

CHAPTER 41

Doth Rauish Like
Inchaunting Harmonie

he Lord Chamberlain's Men began performing in June 1594, but before that date Shakespeare had completed his second long narrative poem. *The Rape of Lucrece* may have been written at Titchfield, while the writer was working under the auspices of the Earl of Southampton, and it is in any case dedicated to the young earl in effusive terms. "The loue I dedicate to your Lordship," Shakespeare writes, "is without end." He goes on to claim that "what I haue done is yours, what I haue to doe is yours, being part in all I haue, deuoted yours." What he had "done" was to compose a poem on the rape of Lucrece, the wife of Collatine, by Sextus Tarquinius. The mythical event is dated 509 BC, and has been used as an explanation for the rise of the Roman Republic. Shakespeare obtained his theme from the *Fasti* of Ovid and from the Roman history of Livy. They were standard grammar-school texts with which he was well acquainted. There is no direct copying of Ovid's Latin, however. He takes the plot but not the poetry. This suggests one method by which he worked. He took up a copy of the *Fasti*, read it quickly, and then put it down without further reference to it. He needed only the raw materials to excite his imagination.

The history is not, however, what interests the poet. Shakespeare is concerned with the play of feeling between the two protagonists, as Tarquin prepares himself to rape the lady and then, after the deed, slinks away. The poem is chiefly remarkable for Lucrece's sorrowful meditations after the event, in the course of which she determines to kill herself in front of her husband. The energy and fluency of Shakespeare's verse are again immediately apparent. The poem, like his drama, begins *in medias res* with a rushing speed and it maintains its dramatic momentum throughout. He even introduces the word "Actor" into the proceedings. Shakespeare renders everything instinct with palpitating life. *The Rape of Lucrece* is extravagant in diction, elaborate in cadence, filled with paradoxes and oppositions, epithets and exclamations, conceits and images; it has a vaunting rhythm and an arresting rhyme-scheme. It is, in other words, a high-spirited performance in which Shakespeare displays all of his excitement and eloquence. Once more the pleasure of the reader is equalled only by the pleasure of the writer.

The general movement of Shakespeare's dramatic verse can be characterised as one from formal regularity to irregularity. Rhymes, for example, become much less common. In his later plays, too, he pitches the natural stress of English speech against the melodious form of the iambic pentameter; he introduces parentheses, exclamations and "run on" lines that continue the cadence past its usual conclusion. He will also complete a sentence in the middle of the line, with a caesura, thus imitating the more irregular and disjunctive passages of thought and expression within his characters. There has been traced a characteristic curve in Shakespeare's composition, a rhythmic evolution that reflects the unceasing development of the music of his being. As Pasternak observed, "rhythm is the basis of Shakespeare's texts";[1] he composed, and imagined, in cadences; his head was filled with cadences, waiting to be born.

The Rape of Lucrece can also be seen as a mine of gold for Shakespeare's later dramas; he becomes fascinated by the idea of the unquiet conscience and by the murder of innocence. The poem may also be the forerunner of murders in the bed, among them those of Duncan and Desdemona. The musings of Tarquin, the rapist, might almost be read as the inner history of Richard III for which there is no space on the stage. It is the procedure of the great writer—Shakespeare knew what interested him, and what preoccupied him, only after he had written it down.

The dedication of *Lucrece* may solve a problem concerning Shakespeare's financial status at this time. Where did he obtain the £50 that was needed as his premium to become a "sharer" in the Lord Chamberlain's Men? Much of his income must by now have travelled back to Stratford in order to support a wife and young family. It may be that the fee was waived on the understanding that he would write a certain number of plays each year; he may have bequeathed to the Lord Chamberlain's Men the ownership of the plays he had already written. Or he may have been lent or given the money. There is a report by Nicholas Rowe that "my Lord Southampton, at one time, gave him a thousand Pounds, to enable him to go through with a Purchase which he heard he had a mind to." Rowe had acquired the story from one "who was probably very well acquainted with his Affairs."[2] Southampton was notably generous, but the sum seems extravagant even by his profligate standards. There is no indication that Shakespeare ever possessed, or invested, so large an amount of money at any one time. In fact "a thousand pounds" is a conventionally hyperbolic expression used by Shakespeare himself; it is the sum Falstaff believes that he will receive after Hal's coronation. We may conjecture a figure nearer £50 or £100. The young earl may have rewarded the author of *Lucrece* and *Venus and Adonis* with this more modest sum.

There is another intriguing connection between *The Rape of Lucrece* and a noble family. It has been suggested that the poem was conceived and written under the auspices–or at least under the influence–of Mary Herbert, Countess of Pembroke.[3] She was the sister of Sir Philip Sidney, and had in direct tribute cultivated her brother's own literary ideals within her circle. She completed his poetic rendering of the psalms, and was herself a notable translator. She had also created an informal network of literary patronage, and under her direction three neo-classical tragedies were written or translated from the French. Mary Herbert herself translated one of them. Each of these tragedies concentrated upon the sufferings of noble heroines, among them Cleopatra and Cornelia, and in deference to Mary Herbert takes an almost "feminist" reading of women betrayed by a hostile male world. *The Rape of Lucrece* is very much part of this tradition. It is not otherwise clear why Shakespeare would have chosen such an apparently unpromising subject. Samuel Daniel wrote a poem, *The Complaint of Rosamond*, and dedicated it to the Countess of Pembroke; this poem also expresses the sorrows of a suffering woman. Shakespeare borrowed Daniel's rhyme-royal stanza for his own narrative. In the same fashion the dramatic eloquence of Shakespeare's poem also aligns it with the neo-classical tragedies that were part of Mary Herbert's literary circle. So the connections are there. It should be recalled that Shakespeare was for a period a member of Pembroke's Men, and it is known that Mary Herbert took a personal interest in the players. One of the actors named her as a trustee in his will. The association lends further significance to Shakespeare's early sonnets, which may have been commissioned by Mary Herbert.

The Rape of Lucrece itself was almost as popular with the reading public as the earlier *Venus and Adonis*. It was reissued in six separate editions during Shakespeare's lifetime, and in two after his death; in the year of its publication it is mentioned in several poems and eulogies. A university play of the period exclaims: "Who loves not *Adon's* love, or *Lucrece* rape!" A reference in William Covell's *Polimanteia* claims "Lucrecia" by "sweet Shakespeare" to be "all-praise-worthy," and an elegy on Lady Helen Branch of 1594 includes among "our greater poets . . . you that have writ of chaste Lucretia."[4] "The younger sort take much delight in Shakespeare's Venus and Adonis," Gabriel Harvey wrote, "but his Lucrece" is considered "to please the wiser sort."[5] In poetical anthologies of the period it was extensively quoted and in *England's Parnassus* of 1600, for example, no fewer than thirty-nine passages were extracted for the delectation of the readers.

This in turn raises an interesting, if unanswerable, question. Why at the age of thirty did Shakespeare effectively give up his career as a poet and turn back to play-writing? From the extensive comment and praise that he received for his two narrative poems, his future and fame as England's principal poet would seem to be assured; in one essay on the English tongue, written in 1595, he is placed in the same company as Chaucer and Spenser. But he chose another path. Perhaps he considered that his life with the Lord Chamberlain's Men offered him financial security, away from the perilous world of private patronage; in this, his judgement proved to be correct. As Jonson wrote in *The Poetaster*, "Name me a profest *poet*, that his *poetrie* did ever afford so much as a competencie." Shakespeare wanted more than a "competency." In any case he loved the work of acting and play-writing at the heart of his own company. Otherwise he would not have chosen to continue it.

Yet the larger reason must reside in the promptings of his own genius; his instinct and judgement informed him that drama was his peculiar skill and particular speciality. Attention must also be paid to the urgency of his literary ambition and inventiveness. He had already excelled at stage comedy, at melodrama and at history. Where else might his genius take him? He knew well enough that he could write poetic narratives with ease and fluency, but the form did not challenge him in the same fundamental way as the newly emerging drama. As Donne said in a private letter, "The Spanish proverb informes me, that he is a fool which cannot make one Sonnet, and he is mad which makes two."[6] He may have found it just too easy, which is perhaps why he carries his poetic effects to excess and why in *Venus and Adonis* he interleaves lyrical pathos with deliberate farce. He was even then beginning a sonnet sequence that would test the medium to breaking point, but it was not enough. He could perhaps have settled for a life as a "gentleman-poet," like Michael Drayton, but that also was not enough.

CHAPTER 42

To Fill the World with Words

oon after the formation of the Lord Chamberlain's Men Shakespeare and his fellows began a shared run with the Lord Admiral's Men at the playhouse in Newington Butts. This association with their principal rivals did not last for long; it was a very wet summer and the takings were low. After about ten days the Lord Admiral's Men decamped to the Rose.

The unique position of the two companies in the Elizabethan theatre of course created competition and rivalry. When the Lord Chamberlain's Men put on Shakespeare's plays of *Richard III* and *Henry V*, the Lord Admiral's Men retaliated with *Richard Crookback* and their own version of *Henry the Fifth*. The Admiral's Men performed *The Famous Wars of Henry the First* as a crowd-puller to rival Shakespeare's episodes of *Henry IV*. When that was not successful they tried once more with *The True and Honourable History of the Life of Sir John Oldcastle*, an echo of Falstaff's original name of Oldcastle. But the traffic was not always in one direction. When the Lord Admiral's Men staged at least seven plays on biblical subjects, the Lord Chamberlain's Men replied with *Hester and Ahasuerus* and other similar dramas. The Admiral's Men performed two plays on the life of Cardinal Wolsey at the Rose, a theme that Shakespeare would later take up in *All Is True*; the Admiral's Men also played a version of *Troilus and Cressida* at the same theatre, before Shakespeare had written his own variation upon an identical theme. While one group had *The Merry Wives of Windsor*, the other staged a drama concerning the wives of Abingdon. Heywood's *A Woman Killed with Kindness* vied at the Rose with *Othello* at the Globe, and they were no doubt viewed in the same light by the audiences who went from one theatre to the other. Two plays on the subject of Robin Hood, written by Munday and Chettle, were proving very popular at the Rose in 1598; Shakespeare retaliated with the sylvan romance *As You Like It*. So there was a constant cross-fertilisation of themes and ideas between the companies, fuelled by fashion and inspired by rivalry. The success of *Hamlet* provoked the Lord Admiral's Men into reviving another revenge drama, *The Spanish Tragedy*, with special additions written by Ben Jonson. The popularity of Shakespeare's play in fact unleashed a whole sequence of imitations such as *Hoffman, or A Revenge for a Father* and *The Atheist's Tragedy, or The Honest Man's Revenge*. It was not unusual for playgoers to attend the various productions of these theatrical rivals, and compare notes on their respective strengths. Was Burbage superior to Alleyn in such-and-such a role? Was Mr. Shakespeare—he had become "Mr." on the playbills when he became a "sharer"—as excellent as Kyd?

After appearing at Newington Butts the Lord Chamberlain's Men toured parts of the country, including Wiltshire and Berkshire, before returning to London for the winter season. On 8 October Lord Hunsdon, their patron, wrote to the Lord Mayor requesting him to allow his servants to play in the City; his new company were already at the Cross Keys in Gracechurch Street, and he wished to prolong their engagement. It is curious that they were not using the Theatre or the Curtain, but it is likely either that the playhouses were in a state of disrepair or that they were not considered suitable venues for the darker winter season. Hunsdon promised that they would begin at two in the afternoon rather than at four, and that they would use no drums or trumpets to advertise their presence. The Lord Mayor and his colleagues gave way to the Lord Chamberlain's wishes, but this was the last time that any playing company ever used a city inn. The Lord Chamberlain's Men also performed at court this winter, and played on two occasions before Elizabeth; on 26 and 28 December they attended her at her palace in Greenwich.

The actors did not simply arrive, with their costumes and instruments. They first had to rehearse the plays intended for Her Majesty's pleasure before the Master of the Revels, Edmund Tilney. His suite of apartments and offices was in the former Hospital of St. John in Clerkenwell; by one of those strange coincidences of London life, Clerkenwell had once been the site of the London mystery plays. Since the company performed at the playhouses during the afternoon, these royal rehearsals must have taken place early in the morning or late at night. The chandler's bill for the Office of the Revels records large payments for candles, coal and firewood. Tilney would act as censor, removing those lines that might be indelicate or offensive to the royal ear. He also loaned the company more sumptuous costumes if they were needed; at the court, some of their dresses and cloaks might have seemed threadbare. There are references to the actors borrowing "the monarch's gown," to save embarrassment before the great original, and "armor for knightly combatants" in case they were ridiculed by the more martial courtiers. The Master of the Revels also lent them "apt houses made of canvas," "necessaries for hunters" and "a device for thunder and lightning."[1]

When all was settled they took a boat downriver from one of the London wharves or "stairs," with an attendant barge for their costumes and devices. The great hall at Greenwich had been cleared for the performance; the stage was at one end, decked out with perspective scenery devised by the Office of the Revels, and the royal dais was at the other. The hall, on this later winter afternoon and evening, was illuminated by candles and torches. The musicians were placed on the wooden balcony above the stage, and the actors could use the passage behind the screen as their "tiring-room." The audience, invited at royal discretion, assembled in their formal robes before the arrival of the queen herself. It was the most fashionable entertainment of the year, and it would have been natural for Shakespeare and his fellows to experience a little nervousness. The names of the plays they performed on this occasion are not recorded, but it has been suggested that the queen witnessed *Love's Labour's Lost* as well as *Romeo and Juliet*. What better fillip for an ageing queen than tales of young lovers?

The Lord Chamberlain's Men were a success, and became something of a royal favourite. The extant records show that on this first occasion the Lord Admiral's Men performed three times, and the Lord Chamberlain's Men played twice, but in later years the Lord Chamberlain's Men were called more often. In the winter season of 1596 and 1597, for example, the Lord Chamberlain's Men played six times and the Lord Admiral's Men did not appear at all. A reference to William Shakespeare occurs in the payment for the royal entertainment at Greenwich in 1594, when £20 was granted to "William Kemp, William Shakespeare and Richard Burbage" for "two comedies showed before Her Majesty in Christmas time last." It is an indication of Shakespeare's seniority in the company that he should be listed before the principal actor–unless, of course, he was the principal actor. It suggests in any case that he was a leading member at the time of its inception, and already active in the company's business. The entry in the treasurer's account has the distinction of being the only official reference to Shakespeare's connection with the stage.

On the night of the last day they performed at Greenwich, 28 December 1594, the Lord Chamberlain's Men also gave a performance of *The Comedy of Errors* in the hall of Gray's Inn. The play was part of the Christmas revels of that Inn, presided over by a lord of misrule known as "the Prince of Purpoole." Shakespeare may have been chosen as the dramatist through his association with Southampton; Southampton was a member of Gray's Inn. The play of twins and of mistaken identity, with all the complications of evidence involved, was naturally popular among students of the English law. For the purposes of the Inn, Shakespeare also revised *The Comedy of Errors*. He introduced more legalisms and two trial scenes. A special stage had been built for the production, as well as "Scaffolds to be reared to the top of the House, to increase Expectation." So there was to be an element of spectacle in the proceedings. But the play hardly received a fair hearing. The numbers of invited guests were so large, and the event so badly managed, that the entertainments had to be curtailed. The senior members of the Inner Temple, who had been invited by their colleagues, left the hall "discontented and displeased"; spectators then invaded the stage to the obvious detriment of the players. A report in *Gesta Grayorum* concludes that "that Night was begun, and continued to the end, in nothing but Confusion and Errors; whereupon it was ever afterwards called, *The Night of Errors*." Two days later the members held a "mock trial," one of the enduring features of the Inns, at which "a Company of base and common Fellows" from "Shoreditch" was berated for making up "our Disorders with a Play of Errors and Confusions."[2] It was not a serious rebuke, and the allusion to the "base and common" actors is an arch legal joke. The person blamed for the fiasco was in fact a member and "orator" of the Inn, Francis Bacon, a keen spectator of the drama and a writer sometimes deemed to have composed Shakespeare's plays himself. The contemporaneity of the two men has itself led to "nothing but confusion and errors." Shakespeare has been accused of writing Bacon, and Bacon accused of writing Shakespeare, while a third party has been held responsible for the productions of both men.

The connection between the legal Inns and the drama is a very close one. Many of the poets and dramatists of the age were attached to one of the four Inns of Court–Lincoln's Inn, Gray's Inn, the Middle Temple and the Inner

Temple–and it has plausibly been asserted that formal English drama itself originated in those surroundings. One of the earliest of English tragedies, *Gorboduc*, was written by two members of the Inner Temple and first performed at the Inns of Court. The "moots" or mock trials, as well as the legal debates and dialogues that were performed by the students, bear an interesting relation to the short interludes of the early sixteenth century. The Inns were also famous for their organisation of masques and pageants; the writers of these masques then began to write for the boy actors of the private theatres, St. Paul's and Blackfriars. The Middle and the Inner Temple were next door to the theatre at Blackfriars. There is contiguity as well as continuity.

The legal ceremonies at the courts in Westminster Hall of course involved their own kind of theatre. Lawyers, like actors, had to learn the arts of rhetoric and of performance. It was known as "putting the case." In the course of their disputations the students of law were instructed to assume the voices of different characters in order to promulgate different arguments; they were taught how to frame narratives that might include improbabilities or impossibilities in order to lend conviction to their *suasoria* and *controversia*. At a certain stage in their respective developments, then, the set speeches of English drama and the oratorical persuasions of English law looked very much alike. In sixteenth-century London, as in fifth-century BC Athens, public performance was always seen in terms of competition and contest.

In certain of his plays Shakespeare introduces references and allusions that were understood only by the students of the law; they in fact formed a large or at least recognisable part of his audience. They were the "coming men," trained to be the judges and administrators and diplomats of the next generation. Many of Shakespeare's own friends and acquaintances came from that circle. It was also widely reported, and believed, that the members of the Inns harboured papistical tendencies; Lord Burghley was obliged in 1585 to write to the treasurer of Gray's Inn, for example, complaining that "to our great grief we have understood that not only some seminary popish priests have heretofore been harboured in Gray's Inn but also have their assemblies and masses."[3]

The members of the Inns were known as "Afternoon's Men" for their habit of frequenting the playhouse in those hours, and were described by one contemporary as the "clamorous fry" who stood with the groundlings in the pit or "filled up the private rooms of greater price."[4] A moralist, William Prynne, stated that "this is one of the first things they learne as soone as they are admitted, to see Stage-playes."[5] One judgement in the civic courts charges a member of Gray's Inn "for that he brought a disordered company of gentlemen of the Inns of Court"[6] to the playhouse. They were clamorous because they hissed and booed with their fellows in the pit, but they were also known for shouting out themes or topics to be addressed by the actors; the actors would then extemporise comically or wittily. This was an extension of their practice at their "moots" in the Inns, and is again an indication of the association between law and drama in London.

It is important to understand this connection, if only to bring life to Shakespeare's use of law and of legal terms in his plays and in his poetry. A drama like *The Merchant of Venice* can be properly understood only in this context, with the civil law of Portia pitted against the common law of Shylock. It is one of the defining structures of Shakespeare's imagination.

CHAPTER 43

See, See, They Joyne, Embrace, and Seeme to Kisse

✢

he new company had the benefit of new, or almost new, plays. It is clear enough that Shakespeare revised *The Comedy of Errors*, and it is likely that he "improved" the other plays he had already written. But it is also worth noting the new vein of romantic drama that Shakespeare began at this time, the principal plays of this period being *Romeo and Juliet*, *Richard II*, *Love's Labour's Lost* and *A Midsummer Night's Dream*. The precise order cannot now be ascertained and, in any case, it is not of much consequence. The general tendency of his art is of much more significance. The hard edges of the early Italianate comedies, and the ornate rhetoric of the first history plays, now give way to extended lyricism and to more tender or perhaps just more complex characters. He was assured of a range of actors who could convey every mood and every sentiment. He was now the single most important dramatic poet of the period, and he had the incalculable advantage of a stable group of actors for whom to write.

We may plausibly imagine the cast list of *Romeo and Juliet*. We know that Will Kempe played Peter, the bawdy servant of the Capulets, and that Richard Burbage played the leading role of Romeo. One of the boys played Juliet, and another boy–or perhaps an older actor–played the garrulous Nurse. It is generally assumed that Shakespeare played the part of the Friar and the Chorus, as we have seen, but Dryden, in "Defence of the Epilogue"

to *The Conquest of Granada* (1670), says that "Shakespeare showed the best
of his skill in Mercutio, and he said himself that he was forced to kill him in
the third Act, to prevent being killed by him." Mercutio is the bawdy, gallant,
quicksilver friend of Romeo whose speech on the activities of Queen Mab is
one of the most eloquent and fanciful in all of Shakespeare; his is the soaring
spirit, buoyant and fantastical, unfettered by ideals and delusions, which
Shakespeare had to kill in order to make way for the romantic tragedy of the
play's conclusion. Such a free spirit does not consort well with a tale of love's
woe. There is melancholy as well as bawdry in Mercutio's speeches, and it becomes clear that much of that melancholy springs from sexual disgust. Dryden believed that this voice was closest to that of the dramatist himself, who
could not delineate a tragedy without introducing farcical elements and who
evinces all the manifestations of the same disgust. Mercutio has been described by some critics as heartless, even cold, but then so has been Shakespeare. That is perhaps why even in the midst of this lamentable tragedy
there is more than a trace of *commedia dell'arte*; it has even been surmised
that there were certain scenes staged in dumb-show.

The mood and imagery of the play is that of summer lightning, flashing
across the sky (892–3):

> Too like the lightning which doth cease to bee
> Ere one can say, it lightens, sweete goodnight . . .

Shakespeare had heard the phrase "Gallop apace" in Marlowe's *Edward the
Second*, and had remembered it; he gives it to Juliet as she yearns for the end
of the day. "Enter Juliet," Shakespeare puts in a stage-direction, "somewhat
fast, and embraceth Romeo." It is a play of youthfulness, of youthful impul-
siveness and of youthful extravagance; it is a play of dancing and of sword-
play, both measuring out an arena of energy with sudden violence and swift
transitions. In this play he incorporates sudden changes of mood and of
thought; he follows the quicksilver thread of consciousness in expression.
But if it is seized by transitoriness it is also touched by mystery. As Juliet and
her Nurse converse on Romeo, an unnamed and unknown voice off-stage
calls out "Juliet"; it is as if some guardian spirit were entreating her.

It has often been stated that *Romeo and Juliet* are all that lovers were, and
all that lovers ever will be, but it is important to notice the sheer artistry with
which Shakespeare entwines them. They echo each other's speech, as if they

saw their souls shining in each other's faces, and in one wonderful passage a formal sonnet emerges out of their dialogue like Aphrodite rising out of the sea (666–9):

> If I prophane with my vnworthiest hand,
>   This holy shrine, the gentler sin is this,
> My lips two blushing Pylgrims readie stand
> To smooth that rough touch with a tender kis.

This had never been achieved on the English stage before, and must have been as miraculous for the first auditors as it has been for subsequent generations. Shakespeare had taken the conventions and traditions of courtly love poetry, and had dramatised them for London audiences that had probably never picked up a sonnet sequence from the stationers' stalls. There are other themes that seem to exfoliate through Shakespeare's drama–the theme of banishment, of inequality in love, of honour and reputation–but the dramatic invocation of love remains the central and abiding impression.

The play ends in a house of tears, but that is where all dreams end. It concluded formally with a funeral procession, one of the standard spectacles of Elizabethan drama, but the dirge was succeeded by a merry jig. This was assisted by the presence of Will Kempe in the final tragic scene. He accompanied Romeo to his rendezvous with mortality at the tomb, and no doubt clowned his way through the soliloquies on dust and death. It is another indication of the essential stridency of Elizabethan drama, where there is no necessary composure or middle tone. All extremes are possible. *Romeo and Juliet* can be interpreted as a comedy as much as a tragedy, but of course it can also represent both.

Shakespeare had taken the story from a poem by Arthur Brooke, entitled *The Tragicall Historye of Romeus and Juliet*, but he condensed it; he shortened the time span, from nine months into five days, and imposed upon the narrative a careful and intricate pattern of symmetries. More significantly, perhaps, he alters the moral scheme and burden of the narrative by overtly sympathising with the lovers. That is the difference between poetry and drama. The religious imagery of the play has often been discussed, in particular its atmosphere of the old faith. Any play set in Italy is bound to be mingled with Catholicism, of course, but there is a larger point. It is characteristic of those who have forsworn their faith to cling to its vocabulary, and never more so than when describing the profane. Shakespeare also introduced far more bawdry and comedy, giving Mercutio in particular a greater role. He also changed Juliet's age from sixteen, in Brooke's poem, to thirteen. He was aware that he was thereby catering to the lasciviousness of the citizens, but he was a shameless master of effects. He recognised, too, that the crowds would enjoy the sword-fight that opens *Romeo and Juliet*.

The play was successful, therefore, and on the title page of the first published text it is referred to as one "that hath been often (with great applause) plaid publiquely." The phrases of Romeo and of Juliet were on everyone's lips. The students of Oxford University, at a later date, wore through by intensive studying and copying the pages of *Romeo and Juliet* in a chained edition of the First Folio. There were two versions published in Shakespeare's lifetime. The first is considerably shorter than the second, and is likely to have been the text actually used by the performers. In this version there is even a joke about the actor ("faintly" speaking the prologue "without-booke") who needed the prompter to help him through it. In asides like this, the life of the Elizabethan stage revives. The second version seems to be transcribed from Shakespeare's own papers, before the text had been altered and condensed in the course of rehearsals or in the process of rewriting. After the play was performed he added some passages, for example, and reassigned certain lines to other characters; he seems to have elaborated on Mercutio's Queen Mab speech by inserting words in the margin of his copy, which the printer mistook for a prose addition. There are also minor inconsistencies in stage-directions and speech prefixes.

But this was undoubtedly his usual procedure: to alter, expand or cut, after seeing the play in performance. It is exactly what any playwright would do. And then he went on to the next venture, a more overt comedy in which star-crossed lovers eventually find fulfilment.

It has been suggested that *A Midsummer Night's Dream* was written in order to celebrate the marriage of Southampton's widowed mother, Mary, Countess of Southampton, to Sir Thomas Heneage. It took place on 2 May 1594, and was perhaps celebrated by the dramatist in the summer of that year. This may seem a trifle early for so accomplished a play, but it is not beyond the bounds of possibility. The play itself seems to bear witness to the terrible summer of that year–"very wet and wonderful cold"[1] according to Simon Forman–in the long complaint by Titania that "the seasons alter" (462). But other noble marriages have been identified as the occasion for this paean to the married state. At the beginning of 1595 the new Earl of Derby, William Stanley, married Lady Elizabeth de Vere. They both had a connection with Shakespeare. William Stanley had inherited the earldom on the sudden death of the Earl of Derby, who was Shakespeare's patron, Lord Strange, and Lady Elizabeth had been the intended bride of Southampton. The associations are not the most auspicious, however, and a more plausible candidate for the occasion must be the marriage of Thomas Berkeley and Elizabeth Carey at Blackfriars on 19 February 1596. The bride was the granddaughter of Lord Hunsdon, the Lord Chamberlain, and it seems a suitable occasion for him to deploy his players. Previously she had been the intended spouse for William Herbert, heir to the earldom of Pembroke, and there is evidence to suggest that the earliest of Shakespeare's sonnets were designed to encourage that match. So he might have been considered the perfect dramatist to celebrate her eventual union. It is ironic that historians, looking for the wedding that *A Midsummer Night's Dream* might celebrate, have found no fewer than three possibilities. But the world in which Shakespeare moved was a small one, in which affinities are not hard to find, and in any event these real Elizabethan marriages make no difference to *A Midsummer Night's Dream*.

With its woodland setting, its noble protagonists, and its fairies, it can be deemed wholly Shakespearian; this is the "sweet Shakespeare" of contemporaneous discourse, the Shakespeare of burlesque humour and lyricism and dream. All of his reading, of Chaucer and of Ovid, of Seneca and of Marlowe, of Lyly and of Spenser, combines to create an enchanted landscape—where the mythical Theseus and Hippolyta celebrate their marriage, where Oberon and Titania, king and queen of the fairies, squabble over the possession of a changeling child, where Bottom and his country players put on an entertainment, and where star-crossed lovers are allowed at the close to fall into one another's arms. The moon is the mistress of these proceedings, and all within her silver empire are touched by mystery. It is a play of patterns and of symmetries, of music and of harmony restored. One of its great delights lies within the formality and fluency of its design.

There are three plays of Shakespeare that seem to be without a primary "source": *Love's Labour's Lost*, *The Tempest* and *A Midsummer Night's Dream*. All of them are highly patterned, in a manner that seems intrinsic to the English imagination;[2] they are all carefully and symmetrically structured, all touched by mystery or enchantment—two of them have elements of the supernatural—and all include dramatic entertainments within their overall structure as if in parody of the somewhat artificial plots. They are a window into Shakespeare's art and thus, perhaps, into the English imagination itself. *A Midsummer Night's Dream* is his first great contemplation of drama itself, so fresh and novel an art that it could elicit extremes of wonder and surprise. Anything might be achieved within it.

Like all Shakespeare's plays of this period *A Midsummer Night's Dream* is composed in a highly wrought and polished English, where lyrical grace is not incompatible with a hundred different rhetorical "schemes." The play is suffused with the atmosphere of dream, as its title suggests, and yet it is a magnificent piece of theatre. The characters sleep upon the stage, and when they awake they find themselves transformed. What is the connection between the theatre and the dream? In dreams nothing is real, nothing is burdened with responsibility, nothing has meaning. This mimics Shakespeare's attitude towards the drama itself. In plays, and in dreams, problems are expressed and resolved by means other than rational intelligence. It has often been said that a sense of the mystery of life is intrinsic to tragedy. But it is also part of Shakespearian comedy, where the irrational and the penumbral are of more consequence than that which is known or understood. The motives and impulses of his creations are not governed by the laws of reason or of conscience but by shape-shifting fancy and intuition.

A Midsummer Night's Dream is the occasion, too, for Theseus's remarks upon the imagination itself when he suggests (1707–8) that:

> The lunatick, the louer, and the Poet
> Are of imagination all compact.

It is all the more interesting on the assumption that Shakespeare himself played the part of Theseus. It is doubly interesting when an examination of the text reveals that the lines upon the imagination were added later, in the margins of his papers, as a kind of after-thought. We might, then, fruitfully speculate upon the nature of Shakespeare's imagination.

CHAPTER 44

What Zeale. What Furie. Hath Inspirde Thee Now?

His was in part a bookish imagination. There are times when he had the sources open beside him, and transcribed passages almost line for line; yet somehow, in the alchemy of his imagination, all seems changed. Words and cadences, when they pass through the medium of Shakespeare, are charged with superabundant life. To work on existing material–to pull out its associations and implications–was profoundly congenial to him. That is why he was prepared to revise his own work, as well as that of other dramatists, in the course of his professional career.

On occasions he read several books on the same topic, and their texts combined somewhere within him to create a new reality. There are times when he relied upon books rather than upon his own immediate experience. In his creation of the trickster in *The Winter's Tale*, Autolycus, he borrowed from one of Robert Greene's urban pamphlets, *Second Cony-Catching*, rather than employing his own observations of city life. He had learnt in his schooldays that one of the first characteristics of invention was imitation, and he was an imitator of genius. He possessed a most retentive memory as well, and could summon up phrases and quotations from his childhood reading; he could effortlessly revert to outworn dramatic or rhetorical styles.

He worked on words, not necessarily on thoughts or images. Words elicited more words from him in an act of sympathetic magic. But then one word called forth another word of quite opposite intent. In the second part of *Henry IV* there is just such a transition (412–14):

> JUSTICE: There is not a white haire in your face, but should haue his effect of grauity.
>
> FALSTAFF: His effect of grauy, grauie, grauie.

The collocation of gravity and gravy amply testifies to the mood of the play and, more importantly, the sensibility of Shakespeare. On an earlier occasion he was reading Arthur Golding's translation of Ovid, in preparation for *Titus Andronicus*, and read the line "desyrde his presence too thentent"; the last word became transmogrified into "the Thracian Tyrant in his Tent" (138). A particular word seems to elicit from him a cluster of words, in this case alliterative; the connection is often one of sound rather than of sense. Geese are constantly associated with disease, the eagle with the weasel. There are other strange synaptic leaps. Turkeys and pistols are often associated, no doubt because of the common linkage with cock. For some reason he connects peacocks with fish and with lice in the same compound of images. On twelve occasions the word "hum" is intimately connected with death, as in *Othello* (2936–7):

> DESDEMONA: If you say so, I hope you will not kill me.
>
> OTHELLO: Hum.

And in *Cymbeline* (1760–1):

> CLOTEN: Humh.
>
> PISANIO: Ile write to my Lord she's dead.

It is as if language was muttering to itself.

Yet words flew so freely from him that he distrusted them; on many occasions he revealed suspicions about their duplicity and inauthenticity. There were times, even, when fluency disgusted him. The finest poetry may be feigning; the oaths pledged on stage may be hypocritical. "Alas, I tooke greate paines to studie it," Viola says in *Twelfth Night* (471–3), "and 'tis Poeticall." "It is the more like to be feigned," Olivia replies, "I pray you keep it in." That is perhaps why there are many plays in which Shakespeare emphasised the artificiality and unreality of his drama; his narratives were meant to be improbable, even impossible.

It seems likely, also, that he did not know what he was writing until he had written it. He discovered his meaning only after he had conceived it in words. There is a wonderful remark of Coleridge's in *Table Talk* of 7 April, 1833, that "in Shakespeare one sentence begets the next naturally; the meaning is all inwoven. He goes on kindling like a meteor through the dark atmosphere." He explored the consequences of his words by seeing how a metaphor or an image might emerge from them and take on its own life; how one word would by assonance or alliteration suggest another; how the cadence of a sentence or a verse would curve in one direction rather than another. The most perceptive account of Shakespeare's method occurs, perhaps surprisingly, in a late eighteenth-century treatise. In *A Specimen of a Commentary on Shakespeare*, published in 1794, Walter Whiter remarks on the power of association that leads Shakespeare to link words and ideas "by a principle of union unperceived by himself, and independent of the subject to which they are applied." He does not know what guides his hand, in other words, or what force impels him. The meaning is somehow innate within the words themselves.

There have been many studies of his imagery, from which various conclusions have been drawn–that he was fastidious, sensitive to smells and to noise, that he engaged in outdoor sports, that he knew the natural life of the countryside very well, and so on. In the interplay of his imagery, we chance upon strange conjunctions; he associates violets with stealing, and books with love. His imagination is awash with centaurs and shipwrecks and dreams, part of the magical world that always surrounded him. But it is perhaps more appropriate to note that his images are the womb or source of further images which spring forth effortlessly. Each play has a continuous stream of images or metaphors that are intrinsic to that play. They convey a unity of feeling rather than one of meaning, rather in the way that film-music works in the cinema. There is a cohesiveness, an internal harmony, within each play; it touches even the most minor character, and places all of the protagonists together in the same circle of enchantment. In *A Midsummer Night's Dream* the rude mechanicals are quite unlike the fairies, but they partake of the same reality. They have been touched by the same lightning.

Yet that lightning was for Shakespeare a source of perpetual novelty and surprise. He did not necessarily know what was within himself. His imagination quickened as it proceeded along its ordained course; a scene will suddenly appear that elicits a powerful response, or a character emerges who will proceed to steal the best lines. There is a precise moment in *Henry IV* when Pistol develops the characteristic of quoting or misquoting lines from old dramas. It must have delighted Shakespeare, since from that moment Pistol does nothing—or hardly anything—but that. The Wife of Bath came up and took Chaucer unawares; Sam Weller popped up from nowhere in *The Pickwick Papers*. It is the same process.

A complementary path can also be traced in the shape of his career. He began as an ambitious and prolific dramatist, ready to take on any subject and any form. He excelled in melodrama as well as history, in farce as well as lyrical pathos. He could do everything. He seemed to have a natural genius for comedy, in which he could improvise effortlessly, but he learned very quickly how to employ other materials. It was only in the course of writing his plays, however, that he managed to discover his vision. It had been waiting for him all along, but he did not properly find it until the middle stage of his life. It was only then that he became truly "Shakespearian." It may even be that, in the later years, he astounded and terrified himself with these great acts of creation.

Thus Leaning on Mine Elbow
I Begin

✦

John Keats wrote that the poetical character "is not itself–it has no self–it is every thing and nothing–It has no character–it enjoys light and shade; it lives in gusto, be it foul or fair, high or low, rich or poor, mean or elevated." And thus "a Poet is the most unpoetical of any thing in existence; because he has no Identity–he is continually in [forming] and filling some other Body."

All of Shakespeare's characters have an exultant and self-sufficient energy that lifts them above the realm of nature. That is why the greatest tragic characters are also close to comedy. Their expansiveness and self-assertion provoke delight. It is also why Shakespeare betrays no real interest in motive. His characters are fully alive as soon as they come upon the stage, and no excuse for their conduct is ever necessary. He will even excise their motives, outlined in his sources, simply to augment their inward or obsessive energy. They become mysterious and more challenging, provoking the audience to wonder or alarm. There are other occasions when motive has to be inferred from conduct; the characters have acquired a reality so strong that you must try to see around them.

Their speech and action are all of a piece, and their utterances are so knit together that they manifest a complete and coherent spirit or soul. The very cadence of the voices creates a unique and identifiable personality. In the second scene of the play, on the occasion of his first appearance upon the stage, the rhythms of Othello are deeply embedded in the structure of the verse with a series of half-lines—"'Tis better as it is . . . Let him do his spite . . . Not I, I must be found . . . What is the news? . . . What's the matter, think you?" It is the rhythm of Othello's being.

As far as the great tragic heroes are concerned, there is a corresponding belief in the ruling power of the self. Their destiny does not lie in the stars, in some abstract notion of Fate or, least of all, in some scheme of divine providence. Their movement is so irresistible, their inner life so powerful, that they gather momentum as the drama proceeds. Even in their fall they are wonderful.

Genius must find its time, too, and can quicken only in the general atmosphere of its period. It has been claimed, for example, that the sixteenth century was the age of the adventurer and of the striving individual. We see him first, on the English stage, in Faustus and in Tamburlaine. In that interim between the imperatives of a sixteenth-century religious culture and the claims of "society" in the seventeenth century, the individual being emerged as the object of speculation and enquiry in Montaigne's work no less than in Marlowe's. This was also the Shakespearian moment.

Shakespeare's major protagonists have all the strength and vitality of their creator. Their capacity for life is astonishing. They have a mental, as well as a physical, energy. Even Macbeth retains a mysterious optimism. They are at one with the forces of the universe. Shakespeare's true villains are pessimists, denying human energy and the capacity for human greatness. They are self-absorbed and melancholy, the enemies of movement and vitality. And here, if anywhere, the true sympathies of Shakespeare's own nature can be found. Studies of his imagery have also shown that he was in love with movement in all of its forms, as if only in that quick sway and acceleration could he catch the vital life of things.

There was, naturally and inevitably, a particle of himself in all of his characters; that is what brings them alive. He is the source of their being. He adverts to that fact in the plays themselves. Richard III declares that "a thousand harts are great within my bosome," and in *Richard II* Aumerle cries out: "I have a thousand spirits in one breast"; in the same play the king himself reveals that "play I in one person many people." It is an odd but insistent emphasis. As Hazlitt said of Shakespeare, "He had only to think of any thing in order to become that thing, with all the circumstances belonging to it."[1] He had a preternaturally sensitive imagination, which could clothe itself in the being of another. This gift or capacity expresses itself in terms of another insistent Shakespearian theme. I am not what I am. Who is it that can tell me who I am?

Since there is an element of Shakespeare in all the myriad heroes and heroines of his plays, they must also remain fundamentally mysterious. They are not governed by rational choices; their logic is always the logic of intuition and of dream. Their dilemma often concerns the role that they must play, and the part they must assume in the world. It is the secret of his heroines. His characters are witty, and cryptic, and whimsical. They are sometimes inscrutable, and more than a little fantastical. As Ophelia remarks to her father of Hamlet's behaviour, "I doe not knowe, my Lord, what I should thinke" (517). They partake of their maker. That is also why Shakespeare's characters still seem "modern," since they are based upon diversity and indeterminacy. It is sometimes said that he invented individual consciousness on the stage but it would be more true to say that, taking his cue from Montaigne, he conveyed the idea of consciousness as unfixed and unstable. This was almost certainly not a deliberate ploy on his part but, rather, the natural expression of his own genius.

It also reflects an actor's consciousness. As the hero of Sartre's novel *Les Mains Sales* reveals, "You think I am in despair. Not at all. I am acting the comedy of despair." It has been remarked that in Shakespeare's plays the language of self-knowledge is the language of acting; by impersonating others he became more himself. Or, to put it another way, Shakespeare understood himself by becoming someone other. He often resorts to metaphors of the stage, and one of his favourite phrases is "to play the part." His lovers learn to perform and improvise before one another. His most interesting characters are actors at heart. No other dramatist of his age maintains such an emphasis. He did not owe this interest to the fact that he was a player; rather, he became an actor because he already possessed that interest. His plays, with the possible exception of those of Molière, are the most entirely suited to the theatre in the history of world drama.

In the speech by Theseus on the nature of imagination, in *A Midsummer Night's Dream*, there is an apparently fluent and straightforward passage (1715–1717):

> . . . the Poets penne
> Turnes them to shapes, and giues to ayery nothing,
> A locall habitation, and a name.

But in the vocabulary of the Elizabethan drama "shape" was the name for the actor's costume, "habitation" for his place upon the stage, and "name" for the scroll on the actor's chest revealing his identity.

When in his speech Hamlet adverts to "this goodly frame the Earth," to this "sterill Promontory" and "this Maiesticall Roofe, fretted with golden fire" his audience would know that he was referring in turn to the walls of the theatre, to the bare stage, and to the roof of the pent-house above his head spangled with stars. The theatre was the occasion for the speech. Shakespeare is saturated with the language of the stage. Who would dream, in all his talk of "shaddowes," that "shadow" was a technical term for the actor? Thus at the close of *A Midsummer Night's Dream*, when Robin Goodfellow declares that "If we shadowes haue offended" he is speaking for the cast. When the actor playing Buckingham in *All Is True* declares that "I am the shadow of poore Buckingham" (258) he is making an overtly theatrical reference. The connection also lends resonance to Macbeth's remark that "Life's but a walking Shadow, a poore Player" (2004). In one of Shakespeare's most theatrical plays, *Richard II*, there is a constant interplay between shadow as reflection of what is real and shadow as insubstantiality or unreality itself. There are shadows everywhere in Shakespeare's plays. There is also a curious fact about shadows that he understood very well: however insubstantial they may be, they lend depth and delight to any view.

Shakespeare sees his characters as an actor would, not as a poet. It is noticeable, for example, how many of his characters blush. That is for the stage. Dickens said that he had only to imagine a character, and that character would appear before him. Shakespeare had the same power *in excelsis*. And the central point is that Shakespeare sees before him not just the character but the actor playing the character. That is why he, of all contemporary playwrights, had the surest command of stagecraft. It was an instinct. He saw gestures; he saw groups of actors moving across the stage. There are some scenes that are dominated by one gesture or by a series of parallel gestures, such as kneeling or sitting on the ground as a token of abasement. Characteristically, a scene with many characters will be preceded by a scene with few characters, both as a principle of contrast and as a means of giving time for the larger cast to be assembled. He also gave 95 per cent of the lines to the fourteen principal actors in the company; this was partly a matter of seniority, but it was also the carefully planned economy of a practical manager. It permitted rehearsals to go ahead without the presence of the hired men.

One stage direction in *Timon of Athens* has all the marks of Shakespeare's imaginative vision: "Then comes dropping after all Apemantus discontentedly like himselfe." In *Antony and Cleopatra* there is the direction: "Enter the Guard rustling in." He hears, as well as sees, the players. In such business, as he himself wrote, action is eloquence. He must have visualised the costumes also since, in Elizabethan drama, clothes made the man (or woman). There are scenes in which he ordains the use of masks, or of clothing all in black. The visual imagery of the play was of the utmost importance. That is why he was aware of the passage of time and of daylight across the open stage, so that he wrote shadowy scenes for the hour when the shadows begin to deepen across London itself. In the last act of *Romeo and Juliet* Romeo and his servant enter "with a Torch"; in the last act of *Othello*, the Moor enters "with a light." So each scene or episode has its own form and tempo, with the overriding emphasis being given to the continuity and the coherence of the action. That is why in the Folio he is described as "the Famous Scenicke Poet," and why Tolstoy believed that Shakespeare's principal gift lay in his "masterly development of the scenes."[2]

It has become clear that he saw certain performers, Kempe or Burbage, Cowley or Sincler, in the roles he had assigned to them in his imagination. Most of the actors had their own particular speciality, at which he aimed his art. He heard their voices; he knew in advance their individual presence upon the stage. Why does Gertrude say that Hamlet is "fat and scant of breath" (3508) when fighting Laertes, if Burbage himself were not inclined to perspire during the duelling scene? There is no other indication of Hamlet's weight. The development of Burbage as an actor had a direct influence upon the growing depth and complexity of Shakespeare's tragic heroes. They also gradually age with Burbage. Shakespeare wrote progressively more challenging parts for Kempe, too, leading him up to the supreme achievement of Bottom in *A Midsummer Night's Dream*, where his genius for clowning is touched by lyricism and by mystery.

It is possible that a character would somehow acquire added qualities by virtue of being performed by one particular actor. It was reported by Charles Gildon in 1694, for example, that "I am assur'd from very good hands, that the person that acted Iago was in much esteem for a comedian, which made Shakespeare put several words and expressions into his part (perhaps not agreeable to his character)."[3] Inadvertently, perhaps, *Othello* has therefore been sometimes considered as a form of *commedia dell'arte*.

There are some theatrical historians who have explained the development of his art in terms of different players and different venues. It has been asserted, for example, that he wrote the "cheerful" comedies of his early period for Kempe and composed the "bitter-sweet" comedies of his middle years for Kempe's successor. It is an argument that has the undoubted advantage of being incapable of proof. It does have the merit of emphasising, however, the close bond between play and players. There were no doubt also occasions when Shakespeare took up suggestions from his fellow actors, on matters of staging or even speech.

It is clear enough that Shakespeare gave much thought to doubling, where one actor played more than one part; obviously he had to ensure that the same characters were not on stage at the same time which, with a cast of twenty-one actors perhaps playing in some sixty different parts, was in itself a feat of theatrical memory. But in doubling he could also create some wonderful effects. Thus the doubling of Cordelia and the Fool in *King Lear*—the Fool mysteriously disappears when Lear's good and faithful daughter reappears in the plot—allowed for deeper ironies beyond the reach of words. He also created parts for himself, as we have observed, and in each of the plays there will be one character that he intended to perform. The character may not have resembled him at all, but he is the one Shakespeare wished to play.

His amenability to actors is evident elsewhere. It has been remarked by generations of actors that his lines, once remembered, remain in the memory; they are, to use the word of the great nineteenth-century actor, Edmund Kean, "stickable." This of course was an enormous advantage for the first players, who might have to repeat several plays on various occasions during one theatrical "season." The words are also attuned to the movement of the human voice, as if Shakespeare could hear what he was writing down. They possess a natural speech emphasis, quite unlike the stiffness of Kyd or of Marlowe. Actors have, in addition, commented upon the fact that the cue for movement or stage business is implicit within the dialogue itself. He was also able to exploit the dramatic possibilities of silence in many of the plays. He used off-stage cries or sounds to suggest turns in the plot, like the knocking at the gate in *Macbeth* or the shouts of the crowd in *Julius Caesar*. There never has been a more professional or accomplished master of all the devices of the stage.

As an actor, too, he was in intimate communion with the audience. His purpose was to please the spectators, and every episode in the play was designed to engage their attention. There are passages of dialogue which are clearly meant to signal, to those parts of the audience who might not be able to see clearly, what is happening upon the stage. When Macbeth calls out "Why sinkes that Caldron," he is telling the spectators that the vessel is now going through the trap-door. Ben Jonson wrote his plays ultimately to be read; Shakespeare wrote his for performance.

If there is a certain modesty in this, it is a virtue he learned early. He was obliged, after all, to act in many ill-written plays composed by his contemporaries; the greatest dramatist of the age had to subdue himself, and bring to life, the words of deeply inferior playwrights. He went from *King Lear* to Barnaby Barnes's *The Devil's Charter* in one season and, in another, from *The Taming of a Shrew* to *The Ranger's Comedy*. In a lifetime of reticence and self-effacement it is perhaps the greatest act of self-abnegation that Shakespeare ever endured; it may account for his occasional expressions of dissatisfaction with his chosen profession.

Fluency or fluidity is also the form of his thought. He delights in pairs, in doubleness, in oppositions. He cannot conceive a thought or sentiment without reversing it. Søren Kierkegaard, the Danish philosopher who had a preternatural sense of style and tone, perhaps expressed it best when he declared that the "art of writing lines, replies, which express a passion with full tone and complete imaginative intensity, and in which you can none the less catch the resonance of its opposite—this is an art which no poet has practised except the unique poet, Shakespeare."[4] He is preoccupied by change and contrast, as if only in the play of differences can the life of the world be expressed. The clown continues his farce as Romeo enters the tomb of Juliet and as Hamlet stands by the grave of Ophelia. In the quick changes of the stage the solemn councils of the court are followed by the pantomimic revels of the Boar's Head Tavern in Eastcheap. The King and the Fool are true companions in the storm. Tolstoy complained that these scenes in *King Lear* were barren of meaning or consolation but, for Shakespeare, there is no meaning other than these two bare figures upon the stage. Lear can no more exist without the Fool than the Fool can exist without Lear. Thus is the spirit of difference, and of opposition, played out. In the most sublime reaches of Shakespeare's art there is no morality at all. There is only the soaring human will in consort with the imagination.

The dispassionate nature of his genius, the almost impersonal intensity of his art, persuaded many eighteenth-century critics that he was kin to nature itself; he had the same indifference to the life of his creations. There is no reason to believe that he was deeply disturbed or troubled by the death of Desdemona, for example–deeply excited, of course, because he was involved in all the power and momentum of his expressiveness. But not deeply moved. It may have been remarked that he was particularly cheerful that day.

CHAPTER 46

So Musicall a Discord,
Such Sweete Thunder

t is in the spirit of change and difference, too, that the plays are best understood. They seem positively to invite conflicting notions of their meaning so that *Henry V*, for example, can be played as heroic epic or as cruel bombast. Shakespeare's art is open to both interpretations equally. The nature of Hamlet is eternally in question. The ending of *King Lear* is endlessly debated. The purpose of *Troilus and Cressida* is now all but lost in the fog of conflicting critical commentaries. In that play he establishes a code of value, through the speeches of Ulysses, which is then undermined or ignored by all of the characters in the play.

Shakespeare grew up with a profound sense of ambiguity. It is one of the informing principles both of his life and of his art. In the plays themselves the themes and situations are endlessly mirrored in the plots and sub-plots, so that the reader or spectator is presented with a series of variations on the same subject without any one of them given pre-eminence. Shakespeare will begin two or three stories at once, all of which share the same trajectory. The bond between Hamlet and his father, for example, is echoed both in the relations between Laertes and Polonius and in the kinship between Fortinbras and his father. Certain characters, generally one from a high and one from a low estate, seem deliberately to parallel or parody one another; they are paired visually and scenically.

Shakespeare uses all the tricks of Elizabethan stagecraft, including simultaneous staging, in order to show that the dramatic world is mixed and uncertain. Entire plays seem to be made up of parallels and contrasts and echoes. All of his characters have mixed natures. Despite the apparently orchestrated harmony of his endings, there are in fact very few genuine resolutions of the action. The closing scenes are deliberately rendered ambiguous, with one character generally excluded from the happy picture of reconciliation. That is why some critics have agreed with Tolstoy that Shakespeare really had "nothing to say." He simply showed action and rhetoric upon the stage for the purposes of spectacle and entertainment. Yet generations of readers have also been affected by his apparent profundity. There has never been a great English dramatist whose art has remained fundamentally so mysterious. That is why he retains all of his power.

The stuff of Shakespeare is endlessly variable, but the connections or associations become darker. The comic servants of the first dramas become Iago or Malvolio; the clown of the early comedies becomes the Fool of *King Lear* or the gravedigger of *Hamlet*; the sexual jealousies within *The Merry Wives of Windsor* turn murderous in *Othello*; the joyous misrule of Falstaff becomes rancid and acrimonious in Thersites or in Timon. His imagination was drawn to the same patterns again and again. The same rushing power, the same imaginative *furia*, is evident in all of them. You can often tell, in little asides or allusions, that Shakespeare is thinking of the next play even as he is completing the one to hand. In *Macbeth*, for example, there is a clear signal of *Antony and Cleopatra*. The language of *Henry V* anticipates that of *Julius Caesar*. The plays are all of a piece and are best seen in relation to each other.

The majority of the plays open *in medias res*, as if a conversation had already been taking place which the audience has just joined. It is part of Shakespeare's fluency that he creates a world already in process. The art of Elizabethan stagecraft is the art of the entrance, since there are no formal divisions into acts, and in Shakespeare the players enter from an ongoing world which is fully alive in some enchanted space elsewhere. The action is conceived as a sequence of intense episodes; but his pacing, his sense of variety and change, are so fluent that this action proceeds without impediment or hesitation. It is a continuous stream, mimicking the process and activity of life itself.

It has become apparent that Shakespeare was a master dramatist who was also a consummately practical man of the theatre—or, rather, he was a master dramatist because he was a practical man of the theatre. He was actor, playwright, sharer in the proceeds and, eventually, part-owner of the theatre itself. He seems to have ensured that all of the cast were used in his plays, and it is possible that he kept extra costs to a minimum. Hence the conspicuous absence of expensive "special effects" in his drama. Such effects do in any case distract the audience from a plot based upon human conflict. The great advantage of his position, however, lies in the fact that he was able to write very much as he wished; he was not a hired writer obliged to accede to the pressures and fashions of the moment. Once his popularity and success had been assured in his early days with the Lord Chamberlain's Men, he was able to strike out in whatever direction he wished. This in part explains the boldness and variety of his drama. If he wished to write a play with a Moor as the tragic hero, or a play with an enchanted island for its setting, the rest of the company were prepared to trust his judgement. As long as he provided two or three plays each year, his "fellows" were satisfied.

His whole social, financial and imaginative life was therefore implicated in the stage. There was no one in his period with the same range of connections; he was uniquely theatrical. There were other playwrights, for example, who were not concerned to have their work performed. George Chapman grandly declared: that "I see not mine own plays."[1] But Shakespeare was present at every part of the life of his plays, from the first words written down in a fury to the last words refined at rehearsal. When they were acted he knew every sigh or shout they elicited from the audience.

There were other tasks to perform. It was he who perused plays submitted for approval by other writers, and it was no doubt his task to revise and generally to prepare manuscripts for performance. He was asked to rewrite difficult passages or introduce a speech at an opportune moment. He provided prologues or epilogues for the revival of old plays, and rewrote contentious passages to avoid the censorship of the Master of the Revels. He was a swift worker. It should always be remembered that the great majority of the plays written in this period have wholly disappeared. Within the hundreds that have been lost, there will have been many touches of genuine Shakespeare.

His role as a company man may help to explain why he was not perhaps concerned with the publication of his plays in his own lifetime. The fellowship of the players was so intense that the plays themselves may have been considered to be in a sense common property, a communal effort that should remain within the community. It would have been considered inappropriate, and against the spirit of their fellowship, for him to cause to be published these works under his own name. One contract survives for another drama- tist in which it is stipulated that the author "should not suffer any play made or to be made or composed by him" to be printed "without the license from the said company or the major part of them."[2] Shakespeare's agreement is unlikely to have taken the form of a contract, but he felt a deep obligation to give them his work. The great virtue of this informal understanding was that the company preserved his plays; the work of no other playwright, with the possible exception of Jonson, was kept intact in this manner.

The difference between Shakespeare and Jonson is in any case instruc- tive. Jonson was willing to introduce himself as an author, as an individual outside the bounds of any company or fellowship; Shakespeare, of an older generation, was much more at ease in the collaborative and guild-like venture of the Lord Chamberlain's Men where the individual was subsumed within the group. His status was much closer to that of a craftsman than an "artist" in any modern sense. It was only after his death that his fellow professionals, in an act of group piety, formally published his plays.

CHAPTER 47

I Understand a Fury in Your Words

rom the evidence of the manuscript of *Sir Thomas More* Shakespeare wrote at extreme speed and intensity; he seems to have been able to summon up the energy and the inspiration at will, with the words and cadences emerging from some deep well of his being. He left some lines unfinished in the rapidity and restlessness of creation. In *Timon of Athens* the protagonist is described as begging "so many" talents; Shakespeare clearly meant to add an exact figure at a later stage. But he simply had to get on. He hardly ever punctuated, preferring to rely instead upon the roll and rush of creation. In some instances he seems to have left spaces between his words, where punctuation marks could be inserted after the fit had passed. He did not mark act or scene divisions. Ludwig Wittgenstein gained the impression that his verses were "dashed off by someone who could permit himself anything, so to speak."[1] Samuel Johnson remarked that the endings of his plays were sometimes written with undue haste, as if the exigencies of the moment forced him to hurry.

It seems likely that he wrote on loose sheets of paper, and he may have embarked upon separate scenes as his inclination took him. He might, for example, have completed the first episodes and the last episodes before turning his attention to the intervening scenes. There is a report by Ben Jonson, in his notebooks, of a contemporary writer, that may bear some relation to this. He was one who when "he hath set himself to writing he would join night and day and press upon himself without release, not minding it till he fainted."[2] If this is a description of Shakespeare, however, it is odd that Jonson does not name him.

There are of course more precise descriptions of his practice from his contemporaries. John Heminges and Henry Condell concluded, in their joint preface to the First Folio, that "His mind and hand went together: And what he thought, he vttered with that easinesse, that wee haue scarse receiued from him a blot in his papers." That may not be altogether true, but Heminges and Condell were concerned to emphasise the extraordinary facility of his invention. His ease or "easinesse," too, was part of the wondrous effect; the verse flows naturally and instinctively from each character.

Ben Jonson was less sanguine about his fluency. In *Timber, or Discoveries Made upon Men and Matter* he wrote that

> I remember, the Players have often mentioned it as an honour to Shakespeare, that in his writing, (whatsoever he penn'd) hee never blotted out line. My answer hath beene, would he had blotted a thousand. Which they thought a malevolent speech. I had not told posterity this, but for their ignorance, who choose that circumstance to commend their friend by, wherein he most faulted.

He goes on to conclude that "hee flow'd with that facility, that sometime it was necessary he should be stop'd; *Sufflaminandus erat*; as Augustus said of *Haterius*. His wit was in his owne power; would the rule of it have beene so too." Shakespeare may not have been the most prolific of his contemporaries–Thomas Heywood seems to have written wholly or in part some 220 plays–but it is clear enough that he had a reputation for rapid and inspired composition.

So we may plausibly see him at work, sitting in a standard panel-backed chair at his table. If he had a study, it was one that he had fitted up for himself in the sequence of London lodgings that he rented. It is sometimes suggested that he returned to his house in Stratford in order to compose without noise or disturbance, but this seems most unlikely. He wrote where he was, close to the theatre and close to the actors. It is doubtful if, in the *furia* of composition, noise or circumstance affected him. It is likely in any case that, as a result of his various employments in the theatre, he was obliged to write at night; there are various references in the plays to "oil-dried lamps," to candles, and to "the smoakie light" that is "fed with stinking Tallow" (*Cymbeline*, 632–3).

He would have possessed a small "desk box" together with pen-case, pen-knife and inkwell; he is also likely to have owned a book-chest and a book-rest for the proper perusal of the bulky histories and anthologies from which he gathered his material. He may also have made notes in what were known as "table-books" or bound notebooks; Hamlet calls for "my tables" to "set it downe" (725). He could have jotted down notes or passages that occurred to him in the course of the day; other writers have found that walking through the busy streets can materially aid inspiration.

When he sat down at his desk he wrote on thick, coarse paper with sharpened pens or pencils; he used the conventional quill of goose-feathers, firm and reliable. He wrote on both sides of the folio-sized paper–paper was expensive–with approximately fifty lines on each side; in the left margin were the speech-prefixes and, in the right margin, the hasty stage-directions. He would often omit the name of the speaker, in his rush to go on, and only add it at a later stage.

Time is a fluid and capacious medium in his plays. He shortened or lengthened it at will so that it would fit the scale of his plots. He was so enveloped in the medium of the play that he created his own time within it; there is "stage time" and "real time" which only occasionally correspond. In *Julius Caesar* the passage of a month, between the Night of Lupercal and the eve of the Ides of March, takes place within one impassioned night. This is not Newtonian time but medieval time, shaped by sacred meaning. In *Othello* and *Romeo and Juliet* there is the presence of what has become known as "double time," accommodating both the swift passage of event and the slow growth of feeling; the success of the device is manifest in the fact that no audience seems to notice it.

He was, as we have seen, generally in a hurry to complete a play. But this emphasis upon his fluency and facility must be tempered by his evident hesitations and revisions. He often seems to pause in mid-verse, as it were, pen held over paper, ready to strike out a word or improve it with a better one. There are occasions when he loses his way with a speech or passage of verse, and so returns to the beginning and tries all over again. It is a question of mustering the right impetus and fury. In his earliest plays there is at times evidence of "padding," when he runs out of inspiration or energy; but these *longueurs* occur far less frequently in the plays of his maturity. More often than not he works at white heat. There are moments when he does not know whether he was writing prose or verse. In the second part of *Henry IV*, for example, Falstaff delivers some lines that could be printed in either mode. In

Timon of Athens some of the original prose actually rhymed. His phrases are filled with the natural cadence of the English pentameter and the discrimination between poetry and prose might have seemed to him unimportant. There are occasions in which he runs verse lines together in order to save space; the lines of songs are joined together for the same reason. In the manuscript of *Sir Thomas More* he compresses three and half lines of verse into two lines of prose, just so that he can finish a speech at the end of the page. Again the formal difference between prose and poetry melts away in his compulsion to set it all down. It could in fact be argued that his texts were always in a fluid and incomplete state, waiting for the actors to lend them emphasis and meaning.

There are, as a result, confusions. He sometimes muddled names, or gave characters different names in the course of the same play. Characters are also given different descriptions or professions; in *Coriolanus* Cominius is at one moment a consul and at the next a general. There are often loose ends, when a plot line is begun but never completed. There are inconsistencies of time and place. The space of nineteen years is suddenly contracted to fourteen years in succeeding scenes of *Measure for Measure*, suggesting that he did not necessarily write scenes consecutively; otherwise he would have remembered the span of time from one scene to the next. A character suddenly "forgets" information that he or she has just imparted, or asks the same question on separate occasions. In *Julius Caesar* Brutus receives the first news of Portia's death having just announced the same fact to Cassius; he also gives inconsistent answers to the same question. Shakespeare was in the process of creating Brutus's character, and may inadvertently have left both first and second thoughts upon the page. At the close of *Timon of Athens* Timon's epitaph says in one line, "Seek not my name" and in the next line continues "Here lie I, Timon." Again it is an example of Shakespeare trying out two versions, both of which somehow survived for the printer to translate into type and therefore to posterity. When in his famous soliloquy at the beginning of the third act Hamlet (1617–18) describes death as

> The vndiscouer'd country, from whose borne
> No trauiler returnes . . .

he seems to have forgotten that he has already seen his father's ghost. The speech "To be, or not to be" is probably an interpolation within the text. It may have been a speech that Shakespeare composed for an earlier version of

Hamlet or for another play altogether; it may have been a speech he jotted down in a table-book for unspecified later use. It was in any case too good to abandon, and so he placed it in this version of *Hamlet*.

His stage-directions are a good indication of his method. Sometimes they are misplaced. He abbreviates or omits them in a haphazard manner, as if the speed and urgency of his composition drove all before them. The fact that he did not write coherent notes or systematic directions is a sure sign that he knew he would be engaged in the rehearsals at some later time. All would then be made clear. He forgets to "exit" some characters, an omission that would of course have been picked up at just such a rehearsal. Sometimes he hopelessly confuses the speech-prefixes of minor characters, so that it becomes difficult to tell who is addressing whom. In *King John* the French king is sometimes known as Philip and sometimes Lewis. Shakespeare introduces characters who never speak at all; he may have intended them to play a part but in the quick working of his invention forgot about them entirely. In *Much Ado About Nothing* Leonato apparently has a wife called Innogen, but she never makes an appearance. The name reappears in *Cymbeline*. Sometimes he will add the stage-direction "with others," and only gradually will the members of this unknown assembly reveal themselves in individual parts. Some of his plays seem too long for conventional or average performance. It has been suggested that these are reading versions of his dramas, but it is more probable that they are examples of allowing his invention to advance unimpeded. He had in any case no need to curb his flowing pen; he knew that cuts could be made in rehearsal. As an epistle at the beginning of Beaumont and Fletcher's published works testifies in 1647, "When these comedies and tragedies were presented on the stage, the actors omitted some scenes and passages, with the authors' consent, as occasion led them." There is no reason to believe that Shakespeare reacted any differently.

It is sometimes suggested that his hesitations and inconsistencies are the mark of every dramatist. But that is not necessarily the case. Molière, for example, has practically none. They are much more the token of Shakespeare's uniquely fluid imagination and fluency of language. He was neither a cautious nor a deliberate artist. As the Poet confesses in *Timon of Athens* (21–5):

> Our Poesie is as a Goume, which ouses
> From whence 'tis nourisht: the fire i'th'Flint
> Shewes not, till it be strooke: our gentle flame

> Prouokes it selfe, and like the currant flyes
> Each bound it chafes.

Poetry creates itself in the act of being created; it needs no external stimulus but provokes itself and streams forth with its own insistent momentum. He was always, as it were, in a state of suspenseful attention, not knowing precisely where he was going. That may help to explain his more than usually erratic spellings; in the manuscript of *Sir Thomas More*, for example, there are five different spellings of "sheriff " in five consecutive lines. The name of "More" is spelled in three different ways in the same line. It is as if he wished his meaning to be indeterminate, to be open to any and every interpretation. This was also his professional method, leaving as much as possible to the process of rehearsal and the interpretation of the player. But the effect of course is further to heighten what has been called his "invisibility" as if the words, like the oozing gum, came from some natural source.

Yet there is an apparent paradox here. In the course of revision or rewriting, he often changes the most minute details out of some general desire to polish the verse still brighter. It may have been an instinctive, and for him a barely noticed, process; but of course there were occasions when he changed the general tenor of a scene. It has already been noticed that Shakespeare continued to revise his plays throughout his career. The new Oxford edition of his plays, for example, prints two versions of *King Lear* composed at different times. All the evidence suggests that some of his more accomplished dramas, such as *The Taming of the Shrew* and *King John*, are rewritten versions of his earlier originals. *Othello* was revised in order to augment the part of Emilia; she needed to be more sympathetic in order to avert any dissatisfaction in the audience at her giving Iago the handkerchief. Iago must be the sole architect of evil in the play. Shakespeare presumably registered the ambivalent reaction of the first audiences to her role, and changed the text accordingly. There are interpolations in many of the plays; the diversion upon the misfortunes of the players in *Hamlet* is one example. In *Romeo and Juliet* the speech beginning "The grey eyed morne smiles on the frowning night" is transferred from Romeo to Friar Lawrence in a significant change of emphasis. In *Love's Labour's Lost* Berowne gives two different versions of the same speech, one much more lyrical than the other; one was presumably added in the margin, or on a separate piece of paper, at a later date without the printer noticing that the other had been cancelled.

This is a very common phenomenon in the plays of Shakespeare. There are single lines that contain intact Shakespeare's first and second thoughts. In the second quarto of *Romeo and Juliet*, for example, there exists the strange and unmetrical line "Rauenous douefeatherd rauen, woluishrauening lamb"; here the process of his thought from ravenous through dove to raven is made clear; if the editor removes the first "Rauenous," a certain sense emerges. The ending of *Troilus and Cressida* has been heavily restructured, and it can in fact fairly be claimed that there are few plays in which there is no evidence of rewriting or structural revision. He often cut lines at a later date. In the two sequences of history plays, concerning Henry VI and Henry IV respectively, there is some evidence that he added speeches which would knit the plays together and thus provide a more unified structure of action. He added material for plays to be performed at court, and was sometimes obliged to rewrite existing material. Thus Oldcastle became, in a later version, Falstaff. He also changed material to accommodate the changing cast of players. This need not necessarily negate the impression given by his contemporaries that he wrote speedily and easily; it implies only his plays were always in a provisional or fluid shape. It is clear enough that at some point he generally went back over what he had written. It may have been at the moment of making a fair copy for his earliest manuscript pages; it may have been at the time he revised a play for a new season of performances.

One example may stand for many. In *Hamlet* his first version of the Player Queen's speech runs:

> For women feare too much, euen as they loue,
> And womens feare and loue hold quantitie,
> Eyther none, in neither ought, or in extremitie.

But this was too prolix and confusing, so he tightened up the verses in a succeeding version (1888–9):

> For womens feare and loue, holds quantitie,
> In neither ought, or in extremity.

He would have had to ensure that these changes met with the approval of the actors, who of course would have had to learn the new lines; he must also have made certain that the revisions were not so drastic that the play had to be resubmitted to the Master of Revels for approval. Within these constraints, therefore, his plays were never fixed or finished; he was continually remaking them and, to the horror of editors who would prefer a definitive text, we may fairly assume that each play was slightly different at every performance.

There were ideas and projects that he abandoned as unpromising or unworkable. And of course he changed his mind about plot and characterisation as he went along. He had already read around the subject, perhaps over a period of weeks or even months, and the principal lines of action were clear to him. It is not necessary to suppose that he kept elaborate synopses or schemes before he began composition, and it is in fact more likely that he retained the entire play in his capacious memory. The play hovered in the air, as it were, in inchoate shape. That is why he could change direction as he wrote; he could alter motive and character, create fresh scenes and provoke new debates. In his speech-prefixes stock names slowly give way to personal names as Shakespeare deepens and extends their characterisation; in *All's Well That Ends Well*, for example, "Clown" becomes "Lavatch" and "Steward" becomes "Rynaldo." They are coming to life in front of him.

He lost interest in certain plot lines after he had introduced them. Nothing, for example, is made of the Princess's early demands for the territory of Aquitaine in *Love's Labour's Lost*. The business between Lorenzo and Bassanio in *The Merchant of Venice* is left unresolved. In that play, too, it is clear that Shakespeare gained interest in Shylock while at the same time noticeably losing enthusiasm for Antonio. Antonio opens the play in an intriguingly melancholy style, but thereafter is never properly developed. The public context of *Coriolanus* is rapidly succeeded by private communings; the character of Hamlet is transformed in the last two acts of the play. Of course it could be argued that these were long-considered decisions on Shakespeare's part, but they bear all the hallmarks of improvisation and spontaneous invention.

So Shaken as We Are,
So Wan with Care

n the summer of 1595 the Lord Chamberlain's Men went on tour. In June they were at Ipswich and at Cambridge, in each place receiving the not inconsiderable sum of 40 shillings. There had been a time when a university town such as Cambridge had shunned the presence of common players, but their status and prestige had risen. William Shakespeare already had, as we have seen, an eager audience among the educated young; it is not too much to suggest that he might have been a "draw" for the members of the various colleges.

They had left London for the very good reason that the theatres had once again been closed. There had been a number of food riots, over the soaring costs of fish and butter, in the late spring and early summer; there were twelve affrays in June alone. The apprentices had taken over the market in Southwark, and then subsequently the market at Billingsgate, to sell the staples of food at what they considered to be an appropriate rate. Then, on 29 June, a thousand London apprentices marched on Tower Hill to pillage the shops of the gun-makers there, clearly with nefarious intent. The pillories in Cheapside had been torn down, and a makeshift gallows was erected outside the house of the Lord Mayor. There were pamphlets circulated on the "rebellious tumults" and in subsequent legal proceedings the apprentices were charged with attempting to "take the sword of auchtoryte"[1] from the mayor and aldermen of the city. Five of their leaders were hanged, drawn and quartered, thus incurring an unusually severe punishment. So London was placed under the Elizabethan version of martial law, and of course the theatres were out of action.

The Lord Chamberlain's Men had in any case begun their career in London during a generally troubled period. One alderman complained to the Privy Council in 1596 of the "great dearth of victual which hath been continued now these three years, besides three years' plague before."[2] Weavers' apprentices were part of the summer riots of 1595, and a silk weaver was incarcerated in Bedlam for accusing the mayor of insanity. In *A Midsummer Night's Dream* Bottom, the leader of the artisans, is himself a weaver. It has been suggested that Shakespeare was transforming violence into farce and comedy. Certainly this would resemble his practice on other occasions. There are, of course, many other contemporary allusions in his plays that are now irrecoverable. He may also have taken advantage of the interval of closure to travel back to Stratford: there is a local record of "Mr. Shaxpere" purchasing "one book" from "Jone Perat"[3] at the end of August. Aubrey reports on unknown authority that he "was wont to goe to his native Country once a yeare."[4]

When the company resumed acting in London at the end of August the Lord Mayor demanded that their resident theatres, the Curtain and the Theatre, should be pulled down in order to avoid the threatening presence of crowds and disorder in that neighbourhood. The virtues of the players, however, were more widely appreciated by the gentry than the City fathers. At the beginning of December Sir Edward Hoby wrote to his first cousin, Sir Robert Cecil, member of the Privy Council, asking "your grace to visit Canon Row; where as late as it shall please you a gate for your supper shall be open, and King Richard present himself to your view."[5] This may allude to a late-night performance of *The Tragedy of King Richard III* but it has generally been interpreted as referring to *The Tragedy of King Richard II* that had just lately been written. It is in certain respects a contentious play, concerned as it is with the forced abdication and murder of a legitimate sovereign, and Cecil may have been invited to check its suitability for the court. The scenes directly concerned with those events may have been acted within the lifetime of Elizabeth I, but they were never printed in the period. That would have incurred too great a risk.

The censored play was a popular success, however, with three quarto editions printed in the space of two years; the last two of them included the name of William Shakespeare as author. Its popularity may in fact have helped to promote the life of Richard II in the public imagination. There is a letter from Raleigh to Robert Cecil written in the summer of 1597, shortly before the publication of the play in quarto form, in which he states that "I acquainted my L: generall [the Earl of Essex] with your letter to mee & your kynd acceptance of your enterteynemente, hee was also wonderfull merry at ye consait of Richard the 2."[6] Here the name of the dead king is a joking pseudonym for the living queen.

Shakespeare wrote *The Tragedy of King Richard II* in verse, and it has all the splendour of his lyric impulse. That is why it is associated with *A Midsummer Night's Dream* as well as *Romeo and Juliet*. The verse shimmers and soars as the history of England is mingled with enchantment—not the enchantment of legend or of faery, but of a theatrical and lyrical sovereign who laments the end of his reign in soliloquies of dust and desolation. He is the monarch of metaphor and simile. His is in every sense a wonderful performance. Shakespeare has followed the symbolic logic of his dramaturgy by combining king and actor in one role, with all the spectacle and vainglory the combination implies. That is why it is also a play of ritual and rhetoric, with elaborate effects of staging as well as language. Richard finds his deepest being while musing upon his role or part within the world. He is depicted here as a highly self-conscious and dramatic monarch; he is the only person in the play to be granted soliloquies while his enemy and supplanter, Henry Bolingbroke, remains resolutely unyielding and external. The declining king seems to grow in interest as he approaches his defeat and death—or, rather, Shakespeare becomes more interested in his temperament and situation. At the beginning of the play he is depicted as somewhat callous and avaricious but, as he figuratively and literally bends lower to the earth, he inspires some of Shakespeare's greatest verse. The dramatist is always engaged by failure, especially failure on such a cosmic scale. It summons up all the grace and sympathy of his nature, which may in part be connected with some tenderness towards his father, and in this play he proves himself beyond doubt to be the master of pathos.

It may be that the role of the declining king was played by Shakespeare himself, while the part of Bolingbroke was taken by Burbage. Yet, characteristically, Shakespeare does not judge between the deposed monarch and his supplanter. Henry Bolingbroke emerges as the victor, but there is no hero in this race. That is why Shakespeare only alludes to the possibility that Richard II was responsible for the murder of his uncle, Thomas of Woodstock, Duke of Gloucester, even though it was the pivotal plot of a very successful contemporary play entitled *Thomas of Woodstock*, which may have been part of the Lord Chamberlain's repertory; it is clear that Shakespeare relied upon the audience's knowledge of it as a preliminary to his own less partisan drama. It was not a question of right or wrong; it was a question of magnificence. The English loved spectacle and rhetoric; they loved sweet and powerful orations. That was what the sixteenth-century stage was about.

It has been surmised that there is some lost source play for *Richard II*, but the material for the tragedy was already to hand. There were of course the chronicles of Hall and of Holinshed, from whom he lifts some lines almost verbatim. But there was also the particular example of Samuel Daniel's *The Civile Warres betweene the two houses of Lancaster and Yorke*, published in 1595, although it is not altogether clear who borrowed from whom. Daniel was a poet of courtly, rather than theatrical, circles; his sonnet sequence, *Delia*, had been published in 1592 and had some influence upon Shakespeare's own ventures in that medium. There was a further association with the dramatist. Until this time Daniel had been part of the household of the Countess of Pembroke, at Wilton; he was tutor to her son, William Herbert, with whom Shakespeare may have had a direct connection through those same sonnets. Daniel was also the brother-in-law of John Florio, whom Shakespeare knew well. He was also an enthusiastic supporter of the Earl of Essex; once more the Essex affinity emerges in this narrative.

If Shakespeare borrowed from Daniel, then in turn the poet borrowed from the dramatist; some effects from *Antony and Cleopatra* become part of Daniel's verse drama on the same theme. So there was, in a sense, a meeting of minds. Samuel Daniel is an image of what Shakespeare might have been—a writer of obscure country origins who, by dint of learning and skill, fashioned a career for himself as poet and retainer. There is even the story that, in 1599, Elizabeth had chosen him as unofficial poet laureate in succession to Edmund Spenser; whatever the truth of the matter, there is no doubt that Daniel was considered highly at court.

The Lord Chamberlain's Men returned to that court for the Christmas season of 1595 about three weeks after their performance at the house of Sir Edward Hoby in Canon Row. It is not known whether they played *Richard II* before the ageing queen. Six years later she told a visitor to Greenwich Palace that "I am Richard the Second, know ye not that?" and complained that the tragedy "was played fortie times in open streets and houses." It is not clear what she meant by "open streets" but by "houses" she must have been alluding to private performances of the play, indirectly providing further evidence that the players were indeed hired by nobles or rich men. So, at the very least, she was aware of the play's existence. Could it have been acted at court at the end of the year?

There was a gap in their performances from 28 December to 6 January, in which interval they travelled to Rutland. In the household of Sir John Harington, at Burley-on-the-Hill, the Lord Chamberlain's Men gave a performance of an old favourite, *Titus Andronicus*, as part of the New Year celebrations of 1596. They acted on the evening of their arrival, and left on the following day. Presumably they were well rewarded. It may seem unusual for an entire company to travel over a hundred miles into the heart of Rutland, in order to give one performance of an old play, but as is so often the case in the sixteenth century there are relations and affinities that help to explain the journey. Sir John Harington was an intimate friend of the same Hoby of Canon Row, with whom he had been at Eton. In addition the French tutor in the household, Monsieur Le Doux, was later financed by the Earl of Essex on various expeditions to the continent as an intelligence agent. The mystery deepens in the knowledge that Anthony Bacon's confidential secretary, Jaques Petit, was also at Burley-on-the-Hill this Christmas and was according to one report posing as Monsieur Le Doux's valet.[7] It was he who wrote a letter describing the performance of *Titus Andronicus*.

So we have Shakespeare and his company paying an especial favour, or tribute, to one of Essex's affinity. It reaffirms the suggestion that Shakespeare himself was close to the circle of Essex's supporters, most notable among them the young Earl of Southampton. The familial association between Hoby and Cecil—Hoby's maternal uncle was William Cecil, Lord Burghley—renders this whole network of friends and relations even more significant, especially since in this period Essex and the Cecils were on friendly terms. Shakespeare, if only briefly, was moving in a world of confidential agents and secret missions, of plot and counter-plot. It was a world that many of his contemporaries, Christopher Marlowe chief among them, knew very well. It must have been a world that Shakespeare himself understood.

So there is an air of unfamiliarity, and perhaps mystery, about his appearance in the grand house at Rutland. It has even been suggested that "Monsieur Le Doux" was a pseudonym for an English secret agent, and perhaps even a pseudonym for a resolutely undead Christopher Marlowe.[8] On a more prosaic note we may simply record that Jaques Petit said in his letter that "*on a aussi joué la tragédie de Titus Andronicus mais la monstre a plus valu que le sujet.*"[9] The "*monstre*" or spectacle was more interesting than the plot. The same might be said of this particular gathering. The stage of Rutland is suddenly lit, and Shakespeare is glimpsed in the company of people with whom he is not ordinarily associated. If ever there was a "secret Shakespeare," as a hundred biographies testify, it lies in obscure moments such as these.

C H A P T E R 4 9

Ah, No, No, No, It Is Mine Onely Sonne

The immediate problems of the Lord Chamberlain's Men had not been lifted by royal or noble favour. The city authorities still seemed eager to close down the Theatre and the Curtain, and James Burbage had already been making plans to convert part of Blackfriars into a roofed playhouse; since Blackfriars was a "liberty," an area where the City's powers of arrest did not run, it was not under official jurisdiction. Burbage had also been involved in difficult negotiations with the landlord of the Theatre, Giles Allen, who wished to profit from the success of the playhouse. He increased the ground rent from £14 to £24 per annum, and Burbage agreed that Allen would eventually be able to take possession of the building after a number of years. But Allen seems to have gone too far in his demand that the Theatre become his property after only five years; Burbage demurred, and began to invest in Blackfriars. Throughout the summer of 1596 he was engaged in tearing down tenements, and converting an old stone building known as the "Frater" or refectory in the precincts of the ancient monastery. It was his insurance policy. He even arranged that his master carpenter, Peter Streete, should move down to the river in order to be close to the site.

On 23 July 1596 Henry Carey, Lord Hunsdon, at the age of seventy, died at Somerset House. His successor as Lord Chamberlain, Lord Cobham, was much less sympathetic to the theatrical profession; one of his ancestors,

Sir John Oldcastle, had been mocked in the first part of *King Henry IV*. So relations between the Lord Chamberlain and the Lord Chamberlain's Men were not necessarily benevolent. The players may even have feared that Cobham would support the Lord Mayor's request permanently to close down the public playhouses. As Thomas Nashe put it in a letter of this time: "howeuer in there old Lords tyme they thought there state settled, it is now so uncertayne they cannot build upon it."[1] The players had begun a tour of Kent soon after Hunsdon's death–they were playing at the market hall of Faversham on 1 August–but once more they found themselves in an insecure profession.

A few days after playing in Faversham, however, Shakespeare suffered a greater blow. His son of eleven years, Hamnet Shakespeare, died. There is every reason to suppose that Shakespeare hastened from Kent to Stratford, for the funeral on 11 August. The death of a young son can have many and various effects. Did Shakespeare feel any sense of guilt, or responsibility, at having left his family in Stratford? And how did he respond to his grieving wife, who had been obliged to care for the children without his presence? The questions cannot be answered, of course. There are some powerful lines in the second part of *Henry IV*, written shortly after these events, when Northumberland's wife blames his absence for the death of their son (985–6). The child

> Threw many a Northward looke, to see his father
> Bring vp his powers, but he did long in vaine.

Many of Shakespeare's later plays have the pervasive theme of families reunited and love restored. In *The Winter's Tale* the son, Mamillius, dies as the result of his father's conduct; the boy who plays this part doubled as Perdita, the daughter who at the end of the play is restored to her errant father. In her form and figure the dead son is also revived.

The death of children was much more common in the sixteenth than in the twenty-first century. Elizabethan families were also more "extended," with various cousins and other kin, so that sudden death had a natural buttress against prolonged or severe grief. It is not necessary to fall into the delusion that sixteenth-century parents were less caring or less emotional than their successors, but it is important to note that the death of a child was not an unusual experience. The cause of the death of Shakespeare's son is not known, although at the end of this year Stratford suffered a severe rise in mortality from typhus and dysentery. Hamnet's twin sister Judith, however, lived to the great age of seventy.

So Shakespeare had lost his only son, the recipient of his inheritance. In the sixteenth century the blood line was charged with significance, and in his subsequent will he went to elaborate lengths to provide for an ultimate male heir, suggesting that the matter still provoked his attention and concern. He had lost the image of himself.

It is of course impossible to gauge the effect upon the dramatist. He may, or may not, have become inconsolable. He may have sought refuge, as so many others have done, in hard and relentless work. The plays of this period have nevertheless been interpreted in the light of this dead son. One critic has described *Romeo and Juliet* as a "dirge for the son's death";[2] this stretches chronology, if not credulity. In James Joyce's *Ulysses* Stephen Dedalus declares that his "boyson's death is the death-scene of young Arthur in King John. Hamlet, the black prince, is Hamnet Shakespeare." Indeed it cannot be wholly coincidental that Shakespeare was drawn at a later date to the tragedy of Hamlet, Prince of Denmark, who is haunted by the spectre of his dead father. In *Twelfth Night*, the story of identical twins—boy and girl—is resolved by the miraculous reappearance of the male child from apparent death. The twin is restored to life. In the period immediately following Hamnet's death, as Stephen Dedalus noted, Shakespeare also rewrote the play concerning King John. One of his additions is a lament by Constance on the untimely death of her young son, which begins (1398–1405):

> Greefe fils the roome vp of my absent childe:
> Lies in his bed, walkes vp and downe with me,
> Puts on his pretty lookes, repeats his words,
> Remembers me of all his gracious parts,
> Stuffes out his vacant garments with his forme;
> Then, haue I reason to be fond of griefe?
> Fareyouwell: had you such a losse as I,
> I could giue better comfort then you doe.

It may not be appropriate to draw strong lines between the art and the life but, in such a case as this, it defies common sense to pretend that Constance's lament has nothing whatever to do with Shakespeare's loss of Hamnet.

The comicall History of the Merchant of Venice, or otherwise called the Iewe of Venyce, written in this same period for the Lord Chamberlain's Men, begins in mournful tone. It is one of the strangest, and most arresting, openings in Shakespeare:

> In sooth I know not why I am so sad,
> It wearies me, you say it wearies you . .

It is often assumed that Shakespeare himself played this part of Antonio, implicitly enamoured of his friend Bassanio. Antonio appears at crucial moments of action, but he is generally a lower-keyed figure who in rehearsals could have guided the others. The play does not linger on his sentimental tragedy, however, but mounts higher with the story of Shylock and his bloody bargain.

It was Shakespeare's practice to combine elements from what would seem irreconcilable sources, and thereby create new forms of harmony. For *The Merchant of Venice* he no doubt plundered an old stage drama, *The Jew*, which had been played at the Bull Theatre almost twenty years before; a spectator there described it as representing "the greedinesse of worldly chusers and bloody mindes of Usurers."[3] That itself is a reasonable if brief summary of Shakespeare's play. It would have been just like Shakespeare's ordinary practice—to take an ancient "potboiler," which he must have seen and remembered, and to infuse it with fresh life. He had also witnessed *The Jew of Malta*, since the role of Shylock is in part based upon that of Marlowe's Barabas; the instinct for imitation is implicated in the desire to outwrite his dead rival. The story of Shylock acted as the catalyst, whereby these two plays came together in new and unusual combination. He also makes use of an Italian story from Ser Giovanni's *Il Pecorone*; it had not been translated into English at this time, and so we are led to the conjecture either that Shakespeare could read Italian or that he picked up the story at second hand. He remembered, too, the story of the Argonauts from his schoolboy reading of Ovid. There are of course other sources, many of them now unknown or forgotten, part of the texture of Shakespeare's mind; but with the plays, the Italian story and the school reading of set texts, we may gain some inkling of the combinatory power of Shakespeare's imagination.

The character of Shylock has provoked so many different interpretations that he has turned into the Wandering Jew, progressing through a thousand theses and critical studies. He may have been the model for Dickens's Fagin but, unlike the entrepreneur of Saffron Hill, he could never become a caricature; he is too filled with life and spirit, too linguistically resourceful, to be conventionalised. He is altogether too powerful and perplexing a figure. It is almost as if Shakespeare fully intended to create a character drawing upon conventional prejudices about an alien race, but found that he was unable to sympathise with such a figure. He simply could not write a stereotype. He would later explore the nobility of an alien or "outsider" in *Othello*. It is likely that the sound and appearance of Shylock led Shakespeare forward, without the dramatist really knowing in which direction he was going. That is why he is perhaps, like so many of Shakespeare's principal figures, beyond interpretation. He is beyond good and evil. He is simply a magnificent and extravagant stage representation.

But we must never forget the stridency of the Elizabethan theatre. Shylock would have been played with a red wig and bottle nose. The play is, after all, entitled the "comicall History." The play retains strong elements of the *commedia dell'arte*, and can indeed be seen in part as a grotesque comedy which includes the figures of the Pantaloon, the Dottore, the first and second lovers, and of course the zanies or buffoons. But Shakespeare cannot use any dramatic convention without in some way changing it. In *The Merchant of Venice* the usual rules of the *commedia dell'arte* are subverted. The fact that it also incorporates fanciful elements from other sources, such as Portia's riddle of the caskets, only serves to emphasise the highly theatrical and dream-like world in which it is set. There was perhaps a masque introduced in the course of the narrative, which in turn suggests that at least one version of the play was designed to be performed at Burbage's newly refurbished Blackfriars; an indoor playhouse was the appropriate setting for an elegant entertainment of that sort. There are, indeed, images of music throughout the play which reach the peak of their crescendo in the last scene at Belmont (2340–4):

> . . . looke how the floore of heauen
> Is thick inlayed with pattens of bright gold,
> There's not the smallest orbe which thou beholdst
> But in his motion like an Angell sings.

All of the scenes are wrapped in the greater unreality of sixteenth-century theatrical convention, which veered closer towards nineteenth-century melodrama or pantomime than twentieth-century naturalistic theatre.

· · ·

There were a small number of Jews in sixteenth-century London, as well as ostensible converts from Judaism known as Marranos, generally living and working under assumed names. In 1594, only two years before the first production of *The Merchant of Venice*, the Earl of Essex had been instrumental in the apprehension, torture and death of Roderigo Lopez, a Jewish doctor accused of attempting to poison the queen. There is an allusion to that affair in the play itself. But the stage image of Jews essentially came from the mystery plays, where they were pilloried as the tormentors of Jesus. In the dramatic cycle Herod was played in a red wig, for example; it represents the origin of the clown in pantomime. It was the costume of Barabas in Marlowe's *The Jew of Malta*. It is, in effect, the image with which Shakespeare was obliged to work. Yet out of the character he created something infinitely more interesting and sympathetic than the stock type. As a result Shylock has entered the imagination of the world.

CHAPTER 50

What Are You? A Gentleman

ess than three months after Hamnet's death, John Shakespeare was awarded a coat of arms by the Garter King of Arms. He became a gentleman, and of course his son would share that appellation by inheritance. It is more than likely, in fact, that Shakespeare himself was responsible for the renewal of an application that his father had made—and then dropped—twenty-eight years before. The cost of obtaining the coat of arms had then seemed prohibitive but, in the milder climate of Shakespeare's new-found affluence, that impediment had gone. It is difficult to be sure of the time needed to procure such a suit, but Shakespeare must have entered his father's submission before Hamnet's death. It would have been fitting and appropriate for Shakespeare to wish to pass on his new status to his only son, a natural succession that Hamnet's death frustrated.

The coat of arms was a rebus, or pun on the name of Shakespeare. On the grant of arms an heraldic drawing was sketched at the top of the page; it showed a falcon, holding a spear, perched above a shield and crest. The falcon is displaying its wings, in the action known as "shaking."[1] The motto included here, *"Non sainz droict,"* means "Not without right." The shaken spear was of gold tipped with silver, as if it were some courtly or ceremonial staff, and the falcon itself was considered to be a noble bird. The livery of the Earl of Southampton contained four falcons, and it is possible that Shakespeare was claiming some kind of relationship with him. The whole device is somewhat assertive, and no doubt reflected the conviction of the Shakespeare males (or at least of one of them) that they were indeed gentlemen.

The Garter King of Arms had granted these arms to John Shakespeare "being solicited and by credible report informed" that his "parentes & late Grandfather for his faithfull & valeant service were advaunced & rewarded by the most Prudent Prince King Henry the seventh of famous memorie."[2] This seems to have been sheer invention on the Shakespeares' part; there is no record of any Shakespeare being honoured by Henry VII. But it may have been one of those "family stories" that are believed without necessarily being investigated.

Shakespeare seems to have been preoccupied with heraldry. In *Richard II* he displays considerable technical knowledge of the subject, while Katherine says in *The Taming of the Shrew* (1028–30):

> If you strike me, you are no Gentleman,
> And if no Gentleman, why then no armes.

To which Petruchio replies:

> A Herald Kate? Oh put me in thy bookes.

There is in the same play an episode clearly taken from a volume of heraldry, Gerard Legh's *Accedens of Armory*,[3] suggesting that Shakespeare was reading such books as early as the 1580s. He wished to demonstrate, and to publicise to the world, his "gentle" state. It was a way of setting himself apart from the still ambiguous reputation enjoyed by most players. It was also an indirect way of associating himself with the Ardens of his mother's line. In a more immediate sense he was restoring his family's reputation after the sudden and perplexing withdrawal of John Shakespeare from public business.

At this late date it may seem a mere contrivance, an honorific without meaning, but in the late sixteenth century it was a sign and emblem of true identity. It afforded the bearer proper individuality as well as a secure place within the general hierarchy of the community. By combining emblem and reality, spectacle and decoration, heraldry truly became a Tudor obsession. There were no fewer than seven standard texts on the subject. In this, at least, Shakespeare was very much a man of his age. The world of his drama is that of the great house or of the court; none of his central protagonists is "low born," to use the phrase of the time, but is a gentleman, a lord or a monarch.

The only exceptions are the protagonists of *The Merry Wives of Windsor*, citizens all. The common people are, in the mass, described by him as "the rabble."

But John Shakespeare's right to bear arms was not without critics. From the late 1590s onwards the York Herald, Sir Ralph Brooke, had challenged the decisions of the Garter King of Arms, Sir William Dethick, in granting arms to apparently unworthy recipients. There were accusations of malfeasance, if not explicitly of fraud and bribery. In Brooke's list of twenty-three "mean persons" who had been granted arms wrongly, the name of Shakespeare came fifth. The qualities of the recipient were called into question, to which William Dethick replied that "the man was a magistrate of Stratford-upon-Avon: a Justice of the Peace. He married the daughter and heir of Arden, of a good substance and ability." There is at least one false note in this defence. Mary Arden was the daughter and heir of a very obscure branch of the Arden family, and it is likely that the Shakespeares exaggerated her ancestry. As in their former claim of a forefather rewarded by Henry VII, the ambition outran the reality.

The fact that the dispute had become public knowledge must have been an irritant, to put it mildly, to Shakespeare, whose assertive emblem and motto had now been cast into doubt. This did not prevent him, however, from applying three years later for the Shakespeare arms to be impaled with the arms of the Arden family. He may have done this "to please his Mother, and to be partly proud" (35–6), as the citizen says of Coriolanus, but it suggests the persistence and quality of his interest in such matters.

He also received some barbed criticism from a dramatic colleague. In *Every Man out of His Humour* Ben Jonson introduces a vainglorious rustic, Sogliardo, who acquires a coat of arms. "I can write myself a gentleman now," he says; "here's my patent, it cost me thirty pounds, by this breath." The arms include a boar's head to which an appropriate motto is suggested, "Not without mustard." This has generally been taken, not without reason, as an allusion to Shakespeare's "Not without right." The mustard may also refer to the bright gold of the Shakespearian coat. So his newly found eminence did not go without some malicious comment.

Yet, characteristically enough, Shakespeare was also able to satirise his own pretensions. In *Twelfth Night*, performed in the period when Brooke was challenging Dethick's bestowal of arms upon the Shakespeares, the steward Malvolio has pretensions to gentility. He is persuaded to wear yellow stockings "cross-gartered"–with a garter crossing on each leg–and his lower body would therefore have been seen as a grotesque parody of Shakespeare's coat of arms.[4] These arms were also yellow, with a black diagonal band. Malvolio is by far the most deluded and ridiculous character in the entire play, and in the cross-gartering episode he ambles and simpers upon the stage in a caricature of gentility. "Some are borne great . . . Some atcheeue greatnesse," he declares. "And some haue greatnesse thrust vpon them" (1516–20). If Shakespeare played the part of Malvolio, as seems to be likely, the joke could not have been more explicit. It would have come naturally to Shakespeare—to parody his pretensions to gentility at the same time as he pursued them with the utmost seriousness, to mock that which was most important to him. It was a part of his instinctive ambivalence in all the affairs of the world.

CHAPTER 51

His Companies Vnletter'd, Rude, and Shallow

❦

James Burbage's plan to convert part of Blackfriars into a private theatre, and thus circumvent the authority of the City fathers, was not advancing. In the early winter of 1596 it was criticised by thirty-one residents in the immediate vicinity. Their petition objected to the erection of "a common playhouse . . . which will grow to be a very great annoyance and trouble, not only to all the noblemen and gentlemen there-about inhabiting, but also a general inconvenience to all the inhabitants of the said precinct, by reason of the gathering together of all manner of lewd and vagrant persons." There were allusions to "the great pestering and filling-up of the same precinct,"[1] and to the loud sound of drums and trumpets coming from the stage.

Another piece of playhouse business was responsible for Shakespeare's next entry in the public records. He had played some part in aborted negoti-ations for the Lord Chamberlain's Men to use Francis Langley's theatre, the Swan, on Bankside. It was a readily available alternative to the Curtain and the disputed Theatre. The Swan had been erected by Langley two years be-fore in the neighbourhood of Paris Garden. It was the latest, and grandest, of the public theatres. There is a famous drawing of it by Johannes de Witt, and such was the ubiquity of this print that for many years it was taken as the model of all the sixteenth-century playhouses. Since each playhouse differed from every other, it was an unwarrantable assumption. In his notes de Witt explains that the Swan is "the largest and most magnificent" of the London playhouses, capable of holding three thousand spectators; it was constructed of "a mass of flint stones (of which there is a prodigious supply in Britain), and supported by wooden columns painted in such excellent imitation of marble that it is able to deceive even the most cunning." He also disclosed that "its form resembles that of a Roman work."[2] Langley's intent was that of somewhat cheap magnificence. Despite its exterior lustre, however, the Swan never achieved any great theatrical eminence. If the Lord Chamberlain's Men had moved there, in the winter of 1596, its theatrical history would have been very different.

The connection between Shakespeare and Langley is to be found in a petition of a certain William Wayte who, in the autumn of 1596, named them both–together with Dorothy Soer and Anne Lee–in a writ *ob metum mortis*. Wayte was alleging that he stood in danger of death or grave physical harm from Shakespeare and others. This was a legal device for the completion of a writ, however, and did not necessarily mean that Shakespeare had threatened to kill him. It transpired that Francis Langley himself had previously taken out a writ against Wayte and his stepfather, William Gardiner; Gardiner, Justice of the Peace with special jurisdiction in Paris Garden, had a reputation in the district for corruption and general chicanery, and had apparently sought to close down the Swan Theatre. Wayte may have encountered some kind of resistance from Shakespeare and his co-defendants while in fact attempting to do so. But that is supposition. We only know for certain that Shakespeare was somehow involved with the imbroglio. It has in fact been suggested by some theatrical scholars that the Lord Chamberlain's Men played at the Swan for a short season, but there is no evidence of this except for a stray reference in Thomas Dekker's *Satiromastix*–"My name's Hamlet revenge: thou hast been at Paris Garden, hast not?"

It is perhaps worth noting that Langley himself enjoyed a somewhat dubious reputation as a money-broker and minor civic official who had managed to accumulate a large fortune; he had been charged by the Attorney General, in no less a tribunal than the Star Chamber, of violence and of extortion. Sharp practice has always been a London speciality. He had purchased the manor of Paris Garden in order to build and let out tenements, and of course there were also brothels in that particular neighbourhood. One of those named in the petition, Dorothy Soer, owned property in Paris Garden Lane and gave her name to cheap lodgings known as "Soer's Rents" or "Sore's Rents." It is more than likely that some of the tenements in that lane were of low repute.

Shakespeare may even have lived among them. The eighteenth-century scholar, Edmond Malone, has left a note stating that "from a paper now before me, which formerly belonged to Edward Alleyn, the player, our poet appears to have lived in Southwark, near the Bear garden, in 1596."[3] That paper has never been recovered. But whatever the date of Shakespeare's removal to the south bank of the Thames, Wayte's petition reveals one salient fact. Shakespeare was associated with people not altogether dissimilar to the comic pimps and bawds of his plays. He was thoroughly acquainted with the "low life" of London. It was an inevitable and inalienable part of his profession as a player. The fact is often forgotten in accounts of "gentle" Shakespeare but it is undoubtedly true that he knew at first hand the depths, as well as the heights, of urban life.

And then, for the winter season, he was once more in front of the queen. The Lord Chamberlain's Men gave six performances at court, among them of *The Merchant of Venice* and *King John*. It is also possible that Falstaff made his appearance before the sovereign, in the first part of *Henry IV*. There is a long-enduring story that Elizabeth was so taken with the comic rogue that she requested a play be written in which Falstaff falls in love; the requests of Elizabeth were never lightly refused, and so appeared *The Merry Wives of Windsor*. It is a charming, if unconfirmed, story.

The nature of *The Hystorie of Henry the Fourth*, otherwise known as the first part of *Henry IV*, has also been the subject of debate. It is not clear whether Shakespeare wrote it with Part Two in mind, or whether the narrative grew under his hand. The first part did in any case provoke controversy of another kind. The Lord Chamberlain, Sir William Brooke, Lord Cobham, had been alerted to the fact that the play's principal comic character was named Sir John Oldcastle. He may well have first seen the play in the presence of the queen at court. He was related to the original Oldcastle, and was not pleased with the farce surrounding the theatrical namesake. The real Oldcastle had been a supporter of the Lollards who had led an abortive insurrection against Henry V; subsequently he had been executed for treason. But he was considered by many to have been a proto-Protestant, and thus an early martyr to the cause of Reformation. His descendant did not approve of his presentation as a thief, braggart, coward and drunkard.

So Cobham wrote to the Master of the Revels, Edmund Tilney, who in turn passed on the complaint to Shakespeare's company; Shakespeare was then obliged in the second part of the play to change the name of his comic hero, from Oldcastle to Falstaff, and publicly to disavow his original creation. It is not clear why in the beginning Shakespeare chose the name of Oldcastle. It has been suggested that Shakespeare's "secret" Catholic sympathies led him to lampoon this Lollard and anti-Catholic. In his *Church History* Thomas Fuller writes of Shakespeare's original use of Oldcastle, "but it matters as little what *petulant Poets* as what *malicious Papists* have written against him." But it seems unlikely that any overt Catholic bias entered the play. The name of Oldcastle had already appeared in *The Famous Victories of Henry the Fifth*, and Shakespeare may simply have borrowed it without considering the connection with Cobham.

It was in any case changed, and not without a certain humiliation on Shakespeare's part. In an epilogue to the second part of *Henry IV* he himself came upon the stage and announced that "for any thing I knowe Falstaffe shall die of a sweat, vnlesse already a be killd with your harde opinions; for Oldecastle died a Martyre, and this is not the man . . ." (3224–7). Then he danced, and afterwards knelt for the applause.

The connection was not wholly erased, however. In a letter to Robert Cecil the Earl of Essex gave out the news that a certain lady was "maryed to Sir Jo. Falstaff"–this was the Court nickname now given to Lord Cobham. The name of Oldcastle was also still associated with *Henry IV*, and in fact the Lord Chamberlain's Men played for the Burgundian ambassador a play entitled *Sir John Old Castell*. Shakespeare's inventions have a habit of lingering in the air.

Oldcastle, or Falstaff, is at the centre of the play. He is the presiding deity of the London taverns who takes the young Prince Hal, heir to the throne, within his paternal and capacious embrace; he is discomfited only when Hal, on becoming sovereign, repudiates him in bitter terms. Hal has been compared to Shakespeare in that respect, disowning such supposed drinking companions as Robert Greene and Thomas Nashe. It may be significant that Greene had a wife known as "Doll" and that Falstaff's weakness is for a prostitute known as Doll Tere-Sheete, but this may be coincidental. In any case Falstaff is too large, too monumental, to be identified with anyone in life. He is as mythical as the Green Man.

He has become perhaps the most recognisable of all Shakespearian characters; he now appears in a thousand different contexts, from novel to grand opera. He became famous almost as soon as he appeared upon the stage. One poem notes "but let Falstaff come" and "you scarce shall have a roome" in the theatre, and another celebrates how long "Falstaff from cracking nuts hath kept the throng":[4] when Falstaff came on stage the audience were silent with anticipation. It was indeed the presence of Falstaff that rendered these plays so popular; the first part of *Henry IV* was reprinted more frequently than any other of Shakespeare's plays. The first quarto edition was read so often and so widely that it survives only in fragments; there were three reprintings in the first year of publication.

The boisterous, extravagant, rhapsodical figure was at once recognised as a national type; he seemed to be as English as beef-pudding and beer, a great deflator of authority and pomposity, a drinker to excess, a rogue who concealed his crimes with wit and bravado. He is an enemy of seriousness in all of its forms, and thus represents one salient aspect of the English imagination. He is filled with good humour and good nature, even when he is leading conscripted soldiers to their certain death, and in that sense he is above mere censure; he is like one of the Homeric gods whose divinity is in no way impeded by their wilful behaviour. He is free from malice, free from self-consciousness; he is in fact free from everything. He is the thorn to the rose, the jester to the king, the shadow to the flame. His instinct for bawdry and subversion are part of his language that parodies the rhetoric of others and follows its own anarchic chain of associations; we have already seen how he translates "gravitie" into "gravie." Whatever can be thought of, Falstaff says. Shakespeare took comedy as far as it can possibly go.

He was played by William Kempe, the pre-eminent clown in England, and Inigo Jones gives a fine contemporaneous description of "a Sir John fall staff" with "a roabe of russet Girt low . . . a great belley . . . great heade and balde" and "buskins to shew a great swollen leg."[5] He was great in every respect, therefore, and Kempe provided the perfect model of the comic fat man. The actor was also famous for his jigs, and so he would have set Falstaff dancing and singing on the stage. He is in any case conceived in great theatricality and, as William Hazlitt puts it, "he is an actor in himself almost as much as upon the stage."[6]

Inigo Jones's coincidental spelling of "fall staff" makes a phallic pun not unlike those connected with shake-spear, and it has been suggested by the more analytical critics that in Falstaff Shakespeare is creating an alter ego through which all his unruly energy, all his defiance and instinct for subversion, can be channelled. Behind the face of Falstaff we can see Shakespeare smiling. Falstaff deflates the claims of history and of heroism on every level, even as his creator was writing plays about those subjects. How can the creator of *Henry V* also be the writer who revels in Falstaff's unheroic antics upon the battlefield, with his parodies of martial ardour and even his parody of death itself? In that sense Falstaff is the essence of Shakespeare, cut free of all ideological and traditional notions. He and his creator go soaring into the empyrean, where there are no earthly values. It would of course be absurd and anachronistic to portray Shakespeare as a nihilist; nevertheless the dissolute and antinomian Falstaff is powerful and energetic because he has the power and energy of Shakespeare somewhere within him. It is also worth observing that in the first part of *Henry IV* there are certain words of Warwickshire dialect, among them "a micher" (one who sulks by straying from home), a "dowlas" and "God saue the mark" (from ancient Mercia, of which Warwickshire was a part). In a play concerned with fathers and with father figures, Shakespeare seems instinctively to revert to the language of his ancestors.

Hegel said that the great characters of Shakespeare are "free artists of themselves" engaged in fresh and perpetual self-invention; they are surprised by their own genius, just as Shakespeare was surprised when the words of Falstaff issued from his pen. He did not know where the words came from; he just knew that they came. It has become unfashionable in recent years to discuss Shakespeare's characters as if they somehow had an independent existence, outside the boundaries of the play; but it was not unfashionable at the time. Falstaff and his comic colleagues proved so successful that they were brought back by Shakespeare, for an encore, in *The Merry Wives of Windsor*.

There is perhaps a further connection between Falstaff and Shakespeare. The relation of the fat knight to Prince Hal has often been taken as a comic version of the relationship between Shakespeare and the "young man" of the sonnets in which infatuation is succeeded by betrayal. The twin "act" of older and younger man in that sonnet sequence has also been related to Shakespeare's longing for his dead son. These were some of the forces in his life that, in this period, propelled him towards a supreme poetic achievement.

You Haue Not the Booke of Riddles About You, Haue You?

re *Shake-speares Sonnets* authentic representations of Shake-speare's inner experience, or are they exercises in the dramatic art? Or do they exist in some ambiguous world where both art and experience cannot be distinguished? Could they have begun as testimonies to real people and real actions, and then slowly changed into a poetic performance to be judged on its own terms?

There were many models for their composition. Shakespeare was entering a crowded arena where poets and poetasters regularly published sequences of sonnets to various real or unreal recipients. The unofficial publication of Sir Philip Sidney's *Astrophil and Stella*, in 1591, was an indication of the demand for such works; the pirated edition was withdrawn but in its preface the sonnets were described by Nashe as "a paper stage strewed with pearl . . . whiles the tragicomedy of love is performed by starlight."[1] This suggests the overwhelming theatricality or artificiality of the genre, for which the expression of private passion was by no means a necessary condition. They were primarily designed to display the wit and ingenuity of the poet, and to test his ability in handling delicate metres or sustained conceits. The publication of Sidney's collection was followed by Samuel Daniel's *Delia*, Barnaby Barnes's *Parthenophil and Parthenophe*, William Percy's *Coelia*, Drayton's collection of fifty sonnets entitled *Idea's Mirror*, Bartholomew Griffin's *Fidessa*, Henry Constable's *Diana* and a host of other imitators. Sonneteering had become the English literary fashion.

Many of these sonneteers characteristically make use of legal imagery in the course of their poetical love-making. This may perhaps be part of their vocabulary as members of the various Inns of Court, but it suggests some instinctive doubling of law and love in sixteenth-century England. Shakespeare's own sonnets are filled with the language and imagery of the law. But his mercantile and legalistic mind is at odds with his generous muse, just as his plays often stage the contention of faith and scepticism; from that strife emerges his greatness.

Of course he may not have wanted his sonnets to be printed; there was, after all, an interval of approximately fifteen years between composition and publication. Like Fulke Greville, whose sonnet sequence *Caelica* languished in a drawer, he may have considered them to be private exercises for a select audience. But this does not imply that they are accounts of an authentic passion; Fulke Greville's poems are governed by a literary rather than a real mistress.

One sonneteer, Giles Fletcher, admitted that he had embarked upon the poetic enterprise, "only to try my humour";[2] that may also be the explanation for Shakespeare's performance. There is evidence that throughout his career he was inclined to experiment with different forms of literature simply to prove that he could successfully adapt them to his purposes; there was a strong streak of competitiveness in his nature, already manifested in his overreaching of Marlowe and of Kyd, and the sonnet had in this period become the paramount test of poetic ability. So Shakespeare used many of the stock themes—the beauty of the beloved, the cruelty of the beloved, the wish to confer upon him or her the immortality of great verse, the pretence of age in the poet, and so on—and gave them a dramatic emphasis while at the same time handling the form of the sonnet superbly well. He sat down and wrote the best sonnets of all.

The first of them are overtly addressed to a young man, who is encouraged to marry and to breed so that his beauteous image may persist in the world. There has been endless speculation about the recipient of this loving advice, and for many biographers the palm must be awarded to the Earl of Southampton. He had refused to marry Lady Elizabeth deVere, granddaughter of Lord Burghley, and that is supposed to be the occasion for the early sonnets–commissioned, so it is said, by his irate mother. But this imbroglio occurred in 1591, an early date for the composition of the sonnets, and by the more likely date of 1595 Southampton had begun a notorious liaison with Elizabeth Vernon.

A more appropriate candidate appears to be William Herbert, the future Earl of Pembroke. In 1595, at the age of fifteen, he was being urged by his immediate family to marry the daughter of Sir George Carey; but he refused to do so. This might have been the spur for Shakespeare's early sonnets. Since William Herbert's father was the patron of the company for which Shakespeare acted and wrote plays, it would have been natural for him to ask Shakespeare to provide some poetical persuasion. The poems, alternatively, may have been written at the instigation of William Herbert's mother, the illustrious Mary Herbert; she was the sister of Sir Philip Sidney, and the presiding spirit of a literary coterie in which Shakespeare played a part.

There was another fruitless marriage plan for William Herbert, concocted by his family in 1597, which could have provided a similar opportunity. But the reluctance of the fifteen-year-old Herbert seems a better context for Shakespeare's advice. It may also help to clear up the confusion concerning the publisher's later dedication to "Mr. W.H." Could this not be William Herbert, surreptitiously addressed? It would help to explain Ben Jonson's cryptic dedication to Herbert on the publication of his *Epigrammes* in 1616, "when I made them, I had nothing in my conscience, to expressing of which I did need a cypher."

William Herbert entered Shakespeare's life at an opportune moment, but the connections between them can only be puzzled out of inference and speculation. The First Folio of Shakespeare's works was dedicated to him, and to his brother, Philip, Earl of Montgomery, and in the course of that dedication the author is described to the Pembrokes as "your seruant, *Shakespeare*." Of the plays, it is stated that the Pembroke brothers "haue prosequuted both them, and their Author liuing, with so much favour" and that "you will use the indulgence toward them, you have done vnto their parent." There is also a reference to their lordships' "liking of the seuerall parts, when they were acted." This implies some deep reserve of affection, and respect, towards Shakespeare. It has sometimes been suggested that noblemen so eminent as the Pembroke brothers would not have formed any attachment for an actor and playwright, but that is not the case. William Herbert, in particular, was to lament the death of Richard Burbage in 1619 and to write from Whitehall to the Earl of Carlisle that "there was a great supper to the French Ambassador this night here, and even now all the Company are at the play, which I being tender-harted could not endure to see so soone after the loss of my old acquaintance Burbadg."[3] The loss of his other old acquaintance, William Shakespeare, three years before, had no doubt aroused similar sentiments.

There have been many attempts to construct a coherent narrative out of Shakespeare's sonnet sequence. The first seventeen are overtly concerned with pressing matrimony upon the sweet boy whom the poet addresses, but thereafter the sonnets assume a more intimate and familiar tone. The young man is addressed as the poet's beloved with all the range of contrary feelings that such a position might inspire. The poet promises to confer immortality upon him but then bewails his own incapacities; the poet adores him but then reproaches him with cruelty and neglect; the poet even forgives him for stealing the poet's mistress.

Then the sequence once more changes direction and sentiment, with the final twenty-seven sonnets concerned with the perfidy of a "Dark Lady," by whom the poet is obsessed. The sonnets are also caught up in the soul of the time, with the politics and pageantry of the period, with its informers and flatterers, with its spies and its courtiers, all invoking the panoply of the Elizabethan state lying behind the impassioned speech of the poet to his beloved.

Certain sequences are united by mood and tone rather than by story, and there are various lacunae that make interpretation more like supposition. It is not even clear that the sonnets are addressed to the same persons throughout. One of them, No. 145, appears to have been written to Anne Hathaway at a much earlier date, and there may be other unknown recipients. And of course many of them may have been addressed to no one in particular. In certain places Shakespeare seems to be taking on the conventional themes of sonneteering—the eternal conflicts between Body and Soul, Love and Reason, are just two examples—in implicit competition or rivalry with other poets. The last sonnets on the theme of the "Dark Lady" have been read as an exercise in anti-sonneteering, in which the conventions of the form are used to overturn the usual subject matter. There are hints of supreme dramatic levity here, in the sheer triumph of inventiveness that these sonnets evince. Shakespeare was already well known for his gift of dramatic soliloquy—it was one of his additions to the play on Sir Thomas More—and it is perfectly natural that he should take that form of internal debate and project it upon a sequence of poems. He was trying out different possibilities within the range of human feeling. We might say that, in the sonnets, he imagined what it would be like to be in the situations he describes. If a consummate actor wrote poetry, this is what it would be like.

There are very clear associations between the sonnets and some of the earlier plays, which seem to clinch the argument that Shakespeare began his sequence in the mid-1590s at the time when the fashion for sonneteering was at its height. There are particular associations with *The Comedy of Errors*, *The Two Gentlemen of Verona*, *Love's Labour's Lost* and the disputed *Edward the Third*. A dramatic replay of the scenario in the poems, where a compromised poet seeks the love of a high-born young man, occurs in the relationship between Helena and Bertram in *All's Well That Ends Well*; it is one of the patterns that Shakespeare's imagination formed. There are of course complete sonnets in *Love's Labour's Lost*, suggesting the complementarity of Shakespeare's invention; in that play there is also a dark beauty, Rosaline, who may or may not be related to the unfaithful lady of the poetic sequence. We can only say with certainty that Shakespeare was playing with the dramatic possibilities of a black mistress. In *The Two Gentlemen of Verona*, also, Valentine renounces Silvia for the sake of his friendship with Proteus; it is another formative situation replicated in the sonnets. When in the ninety-third sonnet the narrator refers to himself behaving "like a deceived husband," he is following the pattern of many of Shakespeare's plays.

The poems are perhaps best seen as a performance. All of them are informed by a shaping will, evincing an almost impersonal authority and command of the medium. Shakespeare seems to have been able to "think" and write in quatrains without effort, which presupposes a very high degree of poetic intelligence. No one would have read such a sequence for autobiographical revelations–they were quite foreign to the genre–and at this late date it would be anachronistic to look for any outpouring of private passion or private anguish. It was in fact only in the early nineteenth century, at the time of the Romantic invention of the poetic selfhood, that the sonnets were considered to be vehicles for personal expression. We may recall Donne's words on his own love poetry: "You know my uttermost when it was best, and even then I did best when I had least truth for my subjects."[4] It is of some interest that, on five occasions in his plays, Shakespeare associates poetry with "feigning." So on the sonnets themselves we may remark with the Clown in *As You Like It* (1582) that "the truest poetrie is the most faining."

• • •

What had perhaps begun as a private exercise, commissioned by the Pembrokes, then became an enduring project; sonnets were added at intervals, some of them being dated as late as 1603, until they were finally arranged for publication by Shakespeare himself. In fact the first reference to Shakespeare writing "sugred Sonnets among his private friends"[5] appeared in 1598. Some of them were then printed in an anthology of 1599, entitled *The Passionate Pilgrime by W. Shakespeare*; it was suggested at a later date that Shakespeare had been "much offended" with the publisher of this unofficial or pirated edition "that altogether unknowne to him presumed to make so bold with his name."[6] Shakespeare may have been particularly irate because the volumes contained other, manifestly inferior, poems that were not composed by him.

He also added some sonnets at a late stage, and cancelled others, shaping them all into some semblance of dramatic unity. There is evidence of revision, in at least four of the sonnets, which was undertaken later with the purpose of unifying the sequence. There is also a confluence of what scholars called "early rare words" and "early late words"; this mixture suggests that Shakespeare first worked on the sonnets in the early and mid-1590s and then went back to them for the purposes of revision in the early seventeenth century. Other sonnets seem to have been added at intervals between those dates. This intermittent composition also throws doubt upon the presence of any coherent story of love and betrayal within the sequence.

In the first publication of 1609 the sonnets were followed by a longer poem, "A Lover's Complaint"; that was also standard procedure in the style of Spenser's *Amoretti* and Daniel's *Delia*. The whole exercise was perhaps for him a way of asserting his worth as a poet. The question that has exercised scholars for many generations—are these ventures in dramatic rhetoric or are they impassioned messages to a lover?—becomes therefore unanswerable. And that is perhaps what is most significant. Wherever we look in Shakespeare's work, we see the impossibility of assigning purpose or unassailable meaning.

This of course flies in the face of those who have looked for parallels in Shakespeare's private life for the characters in the poems. The references to a rival poet, claiming the favour of the young man, have been interpreted as allusions to Samuel Daniel, Christopher Marlowe, Barnaby Barnes, George Chapman and assorted other versifiers. The "lovely Boy" and object of the poet's passion has been identified with the earl of Southampton. In the late sixteenth century, however, the impropriety of addressing a young earl in that manner would have been quite apparent; to accuse him of dissoluteness and infidelity, as Shakespeare accuses the unnamed recipient, would have been unthinkable. The "Dark Lady" has been variously identified as Mary Fitton, Emilia Lanier, and a black prostitute from Turnmill Street in Clerkenwell. Elaborate stories have been written, therefore, about Emilia Lanier abandoning Shakespeare for a passionate affair with Southampton; the suggestion has been made that the whole experience of loss was then darkened by the threat of contracting venereal disease from this faithless woman. It is very dramatic, but it is not art. It seems to have been forgotten by these clandestine biographers that one of the conventions of the sonnet sequence consisted in the poet magnanimously awarding his mistress to his close friend. Shakespeare was following the tradition in his own explosive way. The fact that the collection was greeted with almost universal silence on its publication in 1609 suggests that there was no inkling of controversy or private scandal connected with it; it is, in fact, likely that the audience of the day found the poems slightly old-fashioned.

Emilia Lanier was certainly well known to Shakespeare. She was the young mistress of Lord Hunsdon who had been the patron of the Lord Chamberlain's Men, and was also related to Robert Johnson, a musician who collaborated with the dramatist on several occasions. She was a poet, too, who at a later date dedicated one of her volumes to the Countess of Pembroke. Born Emilia Bassano, she was the illegitimate daughter of Baptist Bassano, one of a Jewish family from Venice who had become the court musicians. He had died early and, in her youth, Emilia had become the ward of the Countess of Kent before attending court where she "had been favoured much of Her Majesty and many noblemen." Among those noblemen was the old Lord Hunsdon, fifty years her senior; but, when she became pregnant, she was married off "for colour" to a "minstrel"[7] named Alphonse Lanier.

Members of the Bassano family accompanied the performances of Shakespeare's plays in the royal palaces. They were dark-skinned Venetians, and some of Emilia's relatives were described as "black men." It may not be entirely coincidental, therefore, that Shakespeare wrote a play about a Jewish family in Venice and that one of the central characters is named as Bassanio. Here we may remark upon Shakespeare's manner of invention. Baptist Bassano is split into two. He becomes Shylock, the Venetian Jewish merchant, and also the Venetian Bassanio. Shakespeare loved the process of self-division. There may of course be some association, too, with *Othello*, also set in

Venice. And there is the connection already noted with Rosaline of *Love's Labour's Lost* who is described as being "black as ebony."

Emilia Lanier née Bassano appears most clearly in the historical record by way of the journals of Simon Forman, the Elizabethan magus whom she consulted over the fortunes of her husband. It is also clear that the good doctor seduced her, and that he was neither the first nor the last to do so. It cannot be known if she ever became Shakespeare's lover and, even if she was, whether she is memorialised as the faithless lady of the sonnets. There is, however, one suggestive detail. Simon Forman notes that Emilia Lanier has a mole below her throat; in *Cymbeline* Shakespeare describes a mole under the breast of the beautiful (and chaste) Imogen.

CHAPTER 53

You Would Plucke Out the Hart of My Mistery

Instead of speculating about the personages addressed, it is more appropriate to speculate about the speaker. In the only sense that matters Shakespeare addresses the sonnets to himself; his muse here is midwife rather than mother. That is why he continually transforms his love of a person to love of an idea or essence. The poems themselves are maintained within a very direct form of address, a piercing eloquence that is controlled, convincing and fluent. They show great strength of mind, well ordered and well sorted. They display enormous self-confidence as well as inordinate cleverness. The speaker is heavily addicted to puns. There is the occasional tincture of false modesty, but the tone is generally enterprising and bold. The speaker takes a great deal of pride in his performance, and is insistent that his poetry will confer everlasting fame. The poems represent a narrator who is sexually alert and eager, but who is also capable of intense infatuation and no less extreme sexual jealousy. This is not necessarily William Shakespeare; it is William Shakespeare as poet.

It would be wrong to argue, of course, that the plethora of outside parallels means that there is no parallel at all. It is certainly possible that elements of Shakespeare's emotional life entered the poems just as they entered the plays. We may note, for example, the strain of keen competitiveness within his nature. He seems to have been charged by the prospect of literary challenge and by the presence of literary rivalry. It is most plausible, then, that he invented or concocted the idea of a rival poet as a spur to his invention; the idea of "a better spirit" gave him a sense of limitation which he could then transcend.

It is interesting that throughout his career he never once praised a fellow dramatist. He was highly ambitious, energetic and resourceful. Who else would have conceived of the great range of history plays at such a young age? In his earlier plays he thrived upon parody of the fashionable authors, such as Marlowe and Lyly, which can of course be interpreted as a form of aggression. He was very good at creating slyly or openly aggressive characters, such as Richard III and Iago. It is intriguing that much of the dialogue in his plays takes the form of competition or contest of wit. There is much scorn and impatience, anger and fretfulness, in the sonnets. Shakespeare was spurred on by his predecessors, by his "sources," in the continuing pursuit of mastery. It should be added that Shakespeare did not become the most eminent dramatist in London by chance or accident; he actively wished for it.

This may have some connection with another persistent tone in the sonnets, where the narrator seems to be essentially a solitary. It is significant that the "beloved," if one existed, is never mentioned by name—especially given the fact that Shakespeare assures him that he will be rendered immortal. Shakespeare wanted the world to honour and remember his love rather than any recipient of it. In the sonnets Shakespeare is musing essentially upon the true nature of the selfhood. His subject was his own self, and in that cunning and witty solipsism others were lovable in so far as they loved him.

We may recall Aubrey's remark that, in Shoreditch, he declined to join the "debauchery" of his colleagues. For most of his professional life he lived in lodgings, away from his family. No letters survive. He may have written very few. There are few reminiscences of him and he was of course singularly reticent about himself. Was he shy, or reserved, or aloof? One or all of these terms may fit his being in the world. We have also found him by report to be amorous, witty, fastidious and fluent. There is no necessary discrepancy. It should be recalled that he played his own role in the world with supreme success; he invested with great joyfulness those characters who, like Falstaff, create and re-create themselves for any conceivable situation.

It is also the mark of his powerful presence, and authority, that he is utterly and uniquely "Shakespearian" in all of the themes and moods inherent within the sonnets. This may sound like the merest commonplace, but it is a phenomenon worthy of contemplation. There is no other writer quite with his consistent and continuing identity through comedy and tragedy, verse and prose, romance and history. He plagiarises himself; he parodies himself. His plangent words in the sonnets on love and obsession echo those of Richard II immured in prison; whenever Shakespeare is inclined towards meditation, he reverts to the idiom of that player-king. There are so many echoes of *Twelfth Night* in the sonnets that the strident figure of the man/woman Viola might almost be considered to be the master/mistress of the sequence.

There is a phrase in the 121st sonnet, the words of which echo through his plays, "I am that I am." It is of course a repetition of God's words to Moses on Mount Horeb. But the phrase may also be compared to Iago's remark that "I am not what I am." Shakespeare is both everything and nothing. He is many and yet no one. It might almost be a definition of the creative principle itself, which is essentially a principle of organisation without values or ideals. Virginia Woolf described Shakespeare as "serenely absent-present"[1] and that strange counterpoise seems to summarise the evanescent yet ubiquitous shape of his genius in his works. His presence is conspicuous by its absence. He had an excess of selflessness, a negative so deep that it became a positive. This may have been at first a matter of instinct, or of vital necessity, but at some point it became part of a deliberate pattern.

There is, therefore, the mystery of his invisibility, his self-effacement and self-depreciation. We may plausibly imagine that he accommodated himself to every situation and to every person whom he encountered. He had no "morality" in the conventional sense, since morals are determined by dislike and antipathy. There is nothing of personal vanity or personal eccentricity about him.

In his sonnets, too, there is the occasional element of self-abasement and even self-disgust. It is the key to part of the meaning of the sequence. Knowing himself guilty, he was drawn to those who would hurt him. And then, baffled by that injury (even if it were only indifference), he seeks solace in thought. For most of his life he was Shakespeare the player rather than Shakespeare the gentleman, and the taint of the public theatre never completely left him. In the 110th sonnet the narrator regrets that he has "made my selfe a motley to the view," and in the following sonnet he laments "that my name receiues a brand" from the element in which he works. There are many critics who have therefore detected in Shakespeare a revulsion from the stage and a distaste for the business of writing, and acting in, plays. One of his persistent metaphors for human futility and pretension is the theatre. When he compares one of his characters to an actor, the allusion is generally negative.

This is particularly true of his later plays. How much this was a common-place of the age, and how much a reflection of Shakespeare's true attitude, is difficult to discern. It may have been a piece of rhythmic grumbling, not to be taken very seriously. If we assume it to be genuine, it is one of the indications of his divided self. If he felt scorn, he felt at the same time what it was to be scorned.

The poems to his "black mistress" contain allusions to sexual disgust and sexual jealousy that are also to be found in his drama. There is a hint of homosexual passion in *The Merchant of Venice*, *Twelfth Night*, *Othello* and elsewhere—a passion not unlike that evinced by the writer of the sonnets to his favoured boy. There are also the veiled references to venereal disease in connection with the "Dark Lady." Shakespeare's sonnets are suffused with sexual humour and sexual innuendo. The language of the poems is itself sexual, quick, energetic, ambiguous, amoral. From the evidence of the drama alone it would be clear that he was preoccupied with sexuality in all of its forms. He outrivals Chaucer and the eighteenth century novelists in his command of smut and bawdry. He is the most salacious of all the Elizabethan dramatists, in an area where there was already stiff competition. There are more than thirteen hundred sexual allusions in the plays, as well as the repeated use of sexual slang.[2] There are sixty-six terms for the female vagina, among them "ruff," "scut," "crack," "lock," "salmon's tail" and "clack dish." There are a host of words for the male penis as well as insistent references to sodomy, buggery and fellatio. In *Love's Labour's Lost* Armado declares that he allows his royal master "with his royall finger thus" to "dallie with my excrement" (1700).

Shakespeare is never more lively, or more alert, or more witty, than in dealing with sexual matters. They are such a pervasive presence that they quite overshadow the ending of *The Merchant of Venice*, for example, where a number of obscene puns dominate the closing dialogue. The English crowd has always enjoyed sexual farce and obscenity, and he knew that such comedy would please the spectators of both "higher" and "lower" sort. But in his plays sexual puns and sexual allusions are more than just a dramatic device; they are part of the very fabric and texture of his language. His writing is quick with sexual meanings.

It could be argued that this is in part the sexual expressiveness of a celibate, or a faithful if absent husband, but common sense suggests otherwise. The printed reminiscences (or gossip) of his contemporaries strongly indicate that he had a reputation for philandering. He may have been "pricked out," as he puts it, for women's pleasure in a world where sex itself was a dark and dangerous force. The writer of the sonnets seems to have been touched by the fear and horror of venereal disease, and some biographers have even suggested that Shakespeare himself died from a related venereal condition. Nothing in Shakespeare's life or character would exclude the possibility.

The Elizabethan age was one of great and open promiscuity. London women were known throughout Europe for their friendliness, and travellers professed to be astonished by the freedom and lewdness of conversation between the sexes. It was not only in the capital, however, that sexual activity was commonplace. It has been recorded that, out of a population of forty thousand adults in the county of Essex, some fifteen thousand were brought before the church courts for sexual offences in the period between 1558 and 1603.[3] This is an astonishingly high number, and can only reflect upon the even more obvious opportunities and attractions of the city.

It was not always a clean or hygienic period in matters pertaining to the body, at least from a modern perspective, and the sexual act veered between mud wrestling and perfumed coupling. In order to avoid the more unpleasant sights and odours, it was customary for men and women to have sexual congress almost fully clothed. It was in many respects a short and furtive act, a mere spilling of animal spirits. In certain of the sonnets that act provokes shame and disgust. Hamlet is a misogynist. Loathing for the act of sex is apparent in *Measure for Measure* and in *King Lear*, in *Timon of Athens* and in *Troilus and Cressida*. This is of course a function of the plot, and cannot be taken as an expression of Shakespeare's opinions on the matter (assuming that he had any at all), but it is a mirror of the reality all around him.

The poet's passionate attachment to the young man of the sonnets, whether real or assumed, suggests that Shakespeare had an understanding of devoted male friendships. We have already noticed the presence of such friendships in the plays. It is also the case that Shakespeare was a "born" actor, and it has become apparent through the ages that actors are often possessed by an ambiguous sexuality. A great actor must always have a uniquely sensitive and yielding temperament, capable of assuming a thousand different moods, and psychologists have often assumed this to be a "feminine" component inherited from love or imitation of the mother. We do not need to go far down the by-ways of psychology to find this an eminently sensible observation. From

the time of the Greek dramas of the fifth century BC, actors have been classified as wanton or effeminate, and in the late sixteenth century London
preachers and moralists inveighed against the uncertain sexuality of the players. Acting was also deemed to be unnatural, an attempt to escape from nature and an act of defiance against God. It does not prove anything about
Shakespeare, but it does help to explain the context and society in which he
worked.

In his writing he knew what it was like to be both Cleopatra and Antony,
both Juliet and Romeo. He became Rosalind and Celia, Beatrice and Mistress
Quickly. More than any of his contemporaries he created memorable female
roles. This does not imply that he was in any sense homosexual but suggests,
rather, an unfixed or floating sexual identity. He had the capacity to be both
female and male, and the scope of his art must have affected his life in the
world. We may recall here the recently discovered portrait of the Earl of
Southampton apparently dressed as a woman. In the late sixteenth century it
was considered natural and appropriate that high-born males should assert
the feminine aspect of their natures; it was a part of the Renaissance human-
ism considered essential for "gentle" conduct. The concept of divine an-
drogyny was an element in the popular and fashionable teaching inspired by
Renaissance Platonists. This is the proper context in which to understand
Shakespeare's invocation of the "master-mistress" of his passion. His was
not an invitation to sodomy, which remained a capital offence in sixteenth-
century England together with heresy and sorcery. Even arguably homosexual poets such as Marlowe draped their allusions in appropriately classical
garb. It has also been demonstrated that, in sixteenth-century texts, what may
be described as theoretical homosexuality was considered to be a predilection
of the noble and the well-born; so it would not have been unthinkable for the
"gentle" Shakespeare to make poetical allusions to the subject. It was a love
not of the phallus, but of the mind.

It is instructive to compare the women in his plays with the "Dark Lady"
of the sonnets. His comic heroines are lively and self-assured, which may
also be an implicit reference to their sexual vitality; they have enormous
powers of will, in a world where "will" also meant sexual power and potency.
Will Shakespeare was fully aware of this. But there are other females touched
by more desperate and dangerous forces. Ted Hughes has noticed in the
plays evidence of Shakespeare's loathing of the lustful female together with
an "obsession with chastity."[4] This may be true of the late plays, where Miranda and Perdita and Imogen are altogether non-sensual beings. But it is not

clear in these accounts whether the preoccupations of Shakespeare have been confused with those of his commentators. There is really no typical Shakespearian woman, in other words, and it is perhaps more interesting to study the responses they elicit from men. The most obvious and most common reaction is one of sexual jealousy, whether Othello at Desdemona or Leontes at Hermione. This is also the dramatic situation of the sonnets. There is much suspected betrayal and some real infidelity. It has become a commonplace of Shakespearian biography, of course, that Shakespeare suspected his absent wife of unfaithfulness. It is plausible but unprovable. We can only say that infidelity, true or false, plays as large a part in the plots of his plays as in the sequence of the sonnets.

It is of course true that most of Shakespeare's plays involve the promise and the problems of love, in all its forms, and that his is the most profound treatment of love in the English language. It is natural and inevitable, therefore, that he should be preoccupied with sexual, as part of amatory, relationships. But that does not explain why sex is often treated with shame, horror and disgust. In his treatment of love he frequently uses the metaphors of warfare. The only couple who seem to be happily married in the plays are Claudius and Gertrude in *Hamlet* although, of course, Macbeth and his wife are not without fondness for each other. But these fortunate pairs are hardly what in the modern world would be called "role-models." Unhappy love and amatory conflict are the staple of drama, and dramatic convenience does not necessarily reflect Shakespeare's personal misgivings. There is no need to introduce a poignant autobiographical note.

CHAPTER 54

And to Be Short, What Not, That's Sweete and Happie

James Burbage had died at the end of January 1597, and was buried in the little church of Shoreditch in the presence of his family and of the players. It has been assumed by some that he expired from disappointment or depression at the failure of his scheme to convert the Blackfriars refectory into a playhouse, but he was probably too tough and experienced a manager to succumb to local difficulties. He was in any case past his mid-sixties, and in sixteenth-century terms had reached an advanced age. He left everything to his two sons who had continued in their father's theatrical business. He gave the Theatre to Cuthbert Burbage, company sharer but not an actor, and the Blackfriars property to Richard Burbage, actor and company sharer; both properties may have seemed to his sons at the time to be the theatrical equivalent of the poisoned chalice, especially since Cuthbert was still not able to reach a satisfactory agreement with the landlord of the Theatre. The ground lease was set to expire in April 1597; Giles Allen agreed to an extension of the lease, but then objected to Richard Burbage as one of its guarantors. So it seems that in the late spring and early summer of 1597 the Lord Chamberlain's Men performed at the Curtain, while dispute continued over the now deserted Theatre. It was at the Curtain that the two completed parts of *Henry IV* were played.

• • •

Richard Burbage, the actor for whom Shakespeare wrote some of his greatest parts.

Both Burbage and Shakespeare were 'poached' by the Lord Chamberlain, Henry Carey, the first Lord Hunsdon, to join the players known as the Lord Chamberlain's Men. Henry Carey was succeeded as Lord Chamberlain first by Lord Cobham and then by George Carey – 'the actors' winter under Cobham's rule turned to glorious summer with the son of their former patron and supporter'.

George Carey, the second Lord Hunsdon (centre), with other Knights of the Garter, taking part in the procession known as *Eliza Triumphans*.

Falstaff and the hostess
(Mistress Quickly).

Procession of the Knights of the Garter
at Windsor, 1576.

Windsor Castle in the 1560s.

It was said that Queen Elizabeth was so taken with Falstaff that she requested a drama in which the comic rogue falls in love. *The Merry Wives* was written for the Garter Feast celebrating the election of Lord Hunsdon as a Knight of the Garter, and was set in Windsor because the new Knights were ceremonially installed at St George's Chapel, Windsor Castle.

John Gerard's *The Herball or Generall Historie of Plantes* was published in the year that Shakespeare bought New Place, a large house in his home town of Stratford. Shakespeare had a countryman's knowledge of flowers and plants.

Visscher's panorama of London shows St Paul's church on the north bank, the Globe Theatre and the bear garden on the south bank and, to the east, Southwark and London Bridge.

A printing shop of the 16th century.

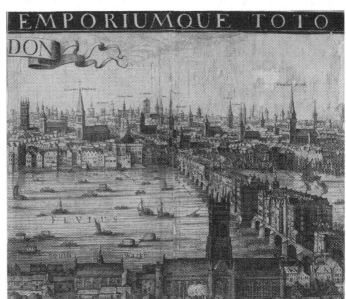

SVÆ 24   1·5·8·8·

The engraving which appeared on the title page of the First Folio (facing page, top left) was by Martin Droeshout. The artist was only fifteen at the time of Shakespeare's death, so is unlikely to have drawn him from life; but the compilers of the First Folio knew Shakespeare well and presumably thought it was an adequate likeness.

Similarly, the monument (facing page, top right) over his tomb must have been acceptable to his family who commissioned it. Shakespeare has a little beard in the sculpture, which according to one scholar looks like a 'self-satisfied pork butcher'.

He might almost be playing Shylock when he wears an ear-ring (facing page, below). This painting, like other late portraits, seems to be based on the Droeshout likeness.

The exception is the so-called Grafton Portrait (above) which is dated 1588. Do the features resemble those in the Folio engraving of 1623? It is tempting to see this 24-year-old as the young Shakespeare.

Mr. WILLIAM
SHAKESPEARES
COMEDIES,
HISTORIES, &
TRAGEDIES.

Published according to the True Originall Copies.

LONDON
Printed by Isaac Iaggard, and Ed. Blount. 1623

Robert Devereux, the Earl of Essex, with whom Shakespeare had 'an affinity'. He loved the theatre and brought the Lord Chamberlain's Men close to danger when he rebelled against the Queen in 1601. He was executed and the Earl of Southampton, to whom Shakespeare had dedicated poetry, was imprisoned.

Southampton in the Tower with his cat.

After Elizabeth's death, the new king released Southampton from prison. James VI of Scotland and I of England had a superstitious fear of witchcraft and a cultivated interest in the theatre. Shakespeare, who served him as a King's Man, wrote *Macbeth* in the aftermath of the Gunpowder Plot.

Shakespeare had in fact stopped work upon the second part of *Henry IV* in order to concentrate upon *The Merry Wives of Windsor*. It is generally supposed that this latest comedy was written for the Garter Feast celebrated at Whitehall on 23 April 1597. Specifically it was a feast held in honour of the election of George Carey, Lord Hunsdon, as Knight of the Garter; he had just been appointed Lord Chamberlain after the death of Lord Cobham and had become the patron of the Lord Chamberlain's Men. The actors' winter under Cobham's rule had turned to glorious summer with the son of their former patron and supporter. The first Lord Hunsdon had been a welcome patron, and it seemed likely that his son would carry on that honourable tradition. It is reported that the queen asked for a drama about Falstaff in love, as we have already observed, and it is further reported that Shakespeare wrote the play in two weeks. Lord Hunsdon doubtless relayed the royal request, and Shakespeare immediately set to work. It is clear enough, given the number of their performances at court, that the Lord Chamberlain's Men were singled out for royal attention. Shakespeare may not have been court poet, but he was certainly favourite dramatist.

The Merry Wives of Windsor was set in Windsor simply because the new knights were ceremonially installed at St. George's Chapel, Windsor Castle. There is no indication of any full-length drama being presented at such Garter celebrations, but the masque at the end of the play in which Mistress Quickly, absurdly disguised as the Fairy Queen, trips a measure, might have been perfomed at the castle rather than at the feast in Westminster Palace. A fortnight seems a reasonable time for its composition, together with other incidental stories or pieces of dialogue. Shakespeare then subsequently wrote the rest of the play to lead to this celebratory climax.

The characters of Falstaff and Shallow, Pistol and Bardolph, were just too good to relinquish; by dint of popular applause they came back. In the first printed edition the principal attraction is made clear in the description of "an excellent and pleasant conceited commedie of Sir John Faulstof and the merry wyves of Windesor." Shakespeare may also have included material that he was unable to use in the history plays themselves. He was thrifty in such matters. He also added a contemporary note. One of the exasperated husbands in the play, concerned about his wife's possible adultery with Falstaff, takes on the assumed name of "Brooke." It seems to be a clear if harmless hit against the Brooke family whose *paterfamilias*, Lord Cobham, had recently died. Yet it may also be a hit against Sir Ralph Brooke, the York Herald who was disputing the Shakespeares' right to bear arms. Whatever the truth of the matter Shakespeare was obliged by the Master of the Revels to turn "Brooke" into "Broome." The joke is in any case lost upon posterity. There were other jokes, one about a German count who had been made a knight *in absentia*, suggesting that Shakespeare still had an eye for contemporaneous affairs.

The fact that the drama flowed so fluently from his pen suggests that it was an emanation from his natural wit—which means, in turn, that it can be interpreted as a traditional English comedy. Here are all the ingredients of English humour—a continual bawdiness of intention, a salacious narrative, and a man farcically dressed in "drag" as Falstaff escapes detection by posing as the fat woman of Brentford. There is also a comic Frenchman and, in true native style, a sudden turn towards supernaturalism at the end. More importantly, perhaps, sexual desire is continually transformed into farce. It is the stuff of a thousand English comedies, and in this place the sexual innuendo and the blue joke find their *locus classicus*. Others have noticed how in the play the English language is twisted and turned in a hundred different ways, in the mouths of a Frenchman and a Welshman, but this is only another aspect of the variability and variety of Shakespeare's style when he is writing at the height of his invention. Words themselves become farcical in a world where improbability and incongruity are the only standards. In one sense *The Merry Wives of Windsor* resembles the "citizens' plays" that had become very popular, but it is governed by a more genial spirit. By setting it in a country town, outside London, Shakespeare avoids the kind of urban satire that Jonson and Dekker employed.

The comedy would have been a gift to his players, too, with the emphasis on mistaken identities and sudden changes of plot. If Kempe continued to play Falstaff, he would have proved a singular "hit" dressed up as the fat woman of Brentford; the spare Sinklo would have played Slender. It has often been supposed that Shakespeare borrowed his comic plots from Italian drama, but in the crossing they have suffered a sea-change. It is characteristic of the English imagination, of which he is the greatest exemplar, to incorporate and to alter foreign models.

Part VI
New Place

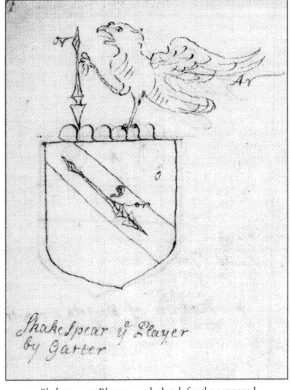

Shakespear ye Player

by Garter

Shakespear ye Player: rough sketch for the proposed
coat-of-arms.

CHAPTER 55

Therefore Am I
of an Honourable House

n the early days of May 1597, Shakespeare purchased one of the largest houses in Stratford. It was called New Place and had been erected at the end of the fifteenth century by the most celebrated former resident of the town, Sir Hugh Clopton. Its ownership set the seal on Shakespeare's standing in the place of his birth. Its frontage was some 60 feet, its depth some 70 feet, and it reached a height of 28 feet. Shakespeare's new house was made of brick upon a stone foundation, gabled, and with bay windows on the eastern or garden side. The topographer, John Leland, had called it a "pretty house of brick and timber,"[1] and to the people of Stratford it was known as the "Great House." As a boy Shakespeare had passed it every day, on his way to school, and it impressed itself on his imagination as a most desirable residence. It represented his childhood dream of prosperity. It was exactly the same spirit that persuaded Charles Dickens to buy Gad's Hill Place in Kent; that house was for him, too, the measure of his childhood longing for success and notability. "If you work hard," John Dickens had told his son, "you may one day own such a house." These were perhaps also the words of John Shakespeare.

It was on the corner of Chapel Street and Chapel Lane, a commodious residence with its servants' quarters at the front looking over Chapel Street; behind these was an enclosed courtyard and the main house. It was a prosperous, but not necessarily a quiet, neighbourhood. Chapel Street had many

good houses, but Chapel Lane was squalid and malodorous; there were pig-
sties and common dunghills there, together with mud-walls and thatched
barns. New Place itself stood immediately opposite the Falcon hostelry, and
the local cheese market took place just outside the front door. Further down
the street, on the other side of the lane, was the guild chapel and schoolroom
where he had spent his early years. He had come back to the very site of his
childhood.

He purchased the house and grounds for "sixty pounds in silver," representing the first large investment he had ever made. In this he differed from
his theatrical colleagues who tended to make their first investments in
London property for themselves and their families. It is an indication that
Shakespeare still readily and naturally identified himself with his native
town; in London he remained, to use a Greek term, a resident alien. It may
be doubted, however, whether he was really at home anywhere.

The deeds mention this sum of £60 but the complication of Elizabethan
property negotiations is such that the actual cost was probably twice as much.
Before Shakespeare bought it, however, the property had been described as
"in great ruin and decay, and unrepaired, and it doth still remain unrepaired."
It was going cheap, in other words, and Shakespeare saw a likely opportunity
for investment. According to a Clopton descendant Shakespeare "repair'd
and modell'd it to his own mind."[2] He ordered stone to fulfil his vision. The
building work must have been extensive, therefore, and almost instinctively
found its way into the play he was writing at the time. In the second part of
Henry IV there are three references to the building of a house, with its plots
and models and costs.

It comprised at least ten rooms (there were ten fireplaces that were taxed
at a later date), with two gardens and two barns; a later reference to two orchards may mean that Shakespeare and his family converted part of the gardens to more practical use. A similar if less spacious house, two doors away
from Shakespeare's dwelling, contained a hall, a parlour bedchamber, a
"great chamber" and two other chambers beside a kitchen and cellar. Was
there also in New Place a study, or perhaps even a library, for the master of
the house? On this, of course, the public records are silent. But if Shakespeare now returned more often to Stratford, as some people surmise, then
he would have required a place to read and to write.

He enlarged the garden by buying additional land and by demolishing a
cottage. There were two ancient wells here, which can still be seen on the

now empty site. Shakespeare was at ease in these surroundings, on his frequent or infrequent returns to Stratford. It is very likely that he owned a copy of John Gerard's *The Herball or generall historie of plantes*, which was published in the year he purchased New Place. In that compendium of garden lore there is a reference to a blue-petalled speedwell that the Welsh called "*fluellen*." Fluellen was the name he gave to the Welsh captain in *Henry V*. He is also supposed to have planted a mulberry tree in the garden, from which in later years an inexhaustible supply of wood was provided to cater for "tourist" items such as paperweights and walking sticks. If he did indeed plant a mulberry tree, he would have done so twelve years after the purchase of the house; in 1609 a Frenchman named Verton distributed young mulberry plants through the midland counties at the request of James I. There were also fruitful grape-vines here. A few years after Shakespeare's death a local dignitary asked to be given from New Place "2 or 3 of the fairest of those budes on some few shutes of the last yeares vines."

The two barns were used to store corn and barley although, in these years of harvest failures and short supplies, Shakespeare might be deemed guilty of hoarding such materials. The year of his house purchase was the fourth year of bad harvests, and the grain shortage was such that its price had risen fourfold. Shakespeare was always an astute businessman. Some historians have described him as one of the first "venture capitalists" in an emerging "market economy," ready to trade in cash or credit, but this is perhaps too theoretical an interpretation for what must have been for him a sensible speculation. A few months after his purchase of New Place he was recorded as hoarding 10 quarters, or 80 bushels, of malt; this was no doubt used for the purposes of brewing by Mrs. Shakespeare or her daughters, but it provoked censure.

There is a curious story concerning the Underhills, a family of Catholic recusants from whom Shakespeare bought the house. William Underhill was a devoted Catholic who was often fined and "presented" for recusancy. He seems to have been forced to sell New Place as a result of debt, which again is testimony to Shakespeare's business acumen rather than to any religious sympathy on his part. Two months after relinquishing New Place, Underhill died in mysterious circumstances; it transpired that he had been poisoned by his son and heir, Fulke Underhill, who was later executed for the crime. By strange chance a former owner of New Place, William Bott, was accused of murdering his daughter by poison on the premises; he gave her ratsbane, according to a witness, and she "swelled to death."[3] It can be surmised that Shakespeare was not superstitious about the possibility of unlucky or unhappy houses.

That house itself has long gone, having been levelled to the ground by a subsequent owner who was tired of unannounced visitors coming to his door and asking to view the surroundings of the late dramatist. But there survives one description from a small boy of Stratford in the late seventeenth century; he recalled "a small kind of Green Court before they entered the House . . . fronted with brick, with plain windows, Consisting of common panes of Glass set in lead, as at this time."[4] There are also some early eighteenth-century sketches, the work of George Vertue, who seems to be relying on the testimony of the descendants of Shakespeare's sister. The principal drawing does indeed show a dwelling that might easily be described as the "Great House." Certainly it was grand enough for Henrietta Maria, the wife of Charles I, to keep her court here for three weeks in the summer of 1643. We might see it at this time, and no doubt before, as a stronghold for monarchists. It should be recalled that Shakespeare was only thirty-three years old when he became the owner of this substantial property. His advance had been rapid indeed. New Place should be seen, then, in connection with the grant of arms to Shakespeare's family. It was a way of demonstrating the dramatist's gentility to his neighbours. It banished the normal associations surrounding a London player, and confirmed his status as one of the richest of Stratford's inhabitants.

CHAPTER 56

Pirates May Make Cheape Penyworths of Their Pillage

In the summer of this year, a theatrical scandal threatened to take away the livelihood of all players. In July 1597, the Earl of Pembroke's Men performed a satirical play entitled *The Isle of Dogs* at the Swan in Paris Garden. It lampooned various members of the administration and thus elicited the wrath of the authorities. It was considered to be a "lewd plaie" stuffed with "seditious and sclanderous matter."[1] One of the authors, and certain of the players, were arrested and imprisoned for three months. The part-author was in fact the young Ben Jonson; he had also acted in the production, and was promptly despatched to the Marshalsea. Jonson was twenty-five at the time, and *The Isle of Dogs* was the first play he had written or had helped to write; his was certainly a fiery baptism. He later recalled "the tyme of his close imprisonment" when "his judges could gett nothing of him to all their demands but I and No."[2] It is difficult to imagine Shakespeare in such unpleasant circumstances, but he would not have dreamed of writing anything remotely seditious or slanderous. He was not a rebel or incendiary; he was firmly within the boundaries of the Elizabethan polity.

The Privy Council then demanded that "no plaies shalbe used within London . . . during this tyme of sommer" and furthermore that "those playhouses that are erected and built only for suche purposes shal be plucked downe."[3] It was one of those announcements that flew in the face of all urban realities—equivalent to the proclamations demanding a halt in the growth of the city itself—and was never properly enforced. Tudor edicts sometimes give the impression of being rhetorical gestures rather than legal requirements. It is possible that the declaration was aimed at the Swan since it demanded the destruction of those playhouses that were erected "only" for the performance of plays. Henslowe at the Rose, for example, might argue that his venue was also used for other forms of entertainment; in any case he continued as if nothing untoward had happened. The justices of Middlesex and Surrey specifically ordered the owners of the Curtain Theatre "to pluck downe quite the stages, galleries and roomes" but again the order was not obeyed. If the Lord Chamberlain's Men were still playing here, as seems likely, they could shelter in the shadow of their great patron.

They did, however, decide to go on tour. In August they went down to the fishing port of Rye, built on a sandstone hill, and then journeyed to Dover; from there they moved on in September to Marlborough, Faversham, Bath and Bristol. There is every reason to believe that Shakespeare was with them on their travels.

The "inhibition" upon playing in London was lifted in October, and the Lord Chamberlain's Men returned to the Curtain. It may have been in this season that "Curtaine plaudeties"[4] were heard for performances of *Romeo and Juliet*, which was one of three plays by Shakespeare published this year in volume form. They were three of his most popular dramas, and it is likely that they were all being performed in this period. Publication would then be a way of exploiting their success in a different market. In August *The Tragedie of King Richard the Second* appeared on the book stalls. It proved such a success that two further editions were published in the succeeding year. It was followed in October by *The Tragedy of King Richard the Third*. This play was reprinted four more times in Shakespeare's lifetime. Then in the following month *Romeo and Juliet* appeared in volume form.

There is a difference, however, in the nature of the publications. The first two were published by Andrew Wise and printed by Valentine Simms, but *An Excellent Conceited Tragedie of Romeo and Juliet* was simply printed by John Danter without a named publisher. Earlier that year Danter's presses had been raided by the authorities and Danter charged with printing *The Jesus Psalter* "and other things without aucthoritie."[5] This edition of *Romeo and Juliet* was one of those printed without requisite authority. Two years later another edition appeared under the title of *The Most Excellent and Lamentable Tragedie, of Romeo and Iuliet* with the addition, "Newly corrected, augmented, and amended." This amplified edition was printed from the text used by the playhouse–there is a direction for "Will Kempe"–which may imply that the author did not have his own version of the play. Danter's premises were raided in the spring of 1597, and it seems very likely that the Lord Chamberlain's Men then gave *Richard II* and *Richard III* to Andrew Wise as a way of pre-empting any other possible thefts. In subsequent years they employed a printer, James Roberts, to place "blocking" entries in the Stationers' Register; he would register a manuscript with the proviso that it could not be printed "without licence first had from the right honorable the Lord Chamberlain" or some such wording.

It seems likely that the version of *Romeo and Juliet* used by Danter was a corrupt or maimed text. It could, for example, have been the product of a hack writer working with someone who knew the play well and who had seen it many times in performance. Such a person might have been Thomas Nashe, who was associated both with the Lord Chamberlain's Men and with the printer John Danter.[6] Another candidate as midwife for the corrupted text is Henry Chettle, the dramatist who had clashed with Shakespeare over Greene's remarks about the "upstart Crow." Chettle participated in the writing of forty-nine plays in the course of his short life; he was one of a number of Elizabethan writers who lived literally from hand to mouth, working incessantly for the voracious medium of the public theatre. A contemporary traveller remarked that "there be, in my opinion, more Playes in London then in all the partes of the worlde I have seene,"[7] and it is calculated that between 1538 and 1642 some three thousand plays were written and performed.

There are six editions of Shakespeare's plays that have been described by some textual scholars as "bad quartos"–*The Contention*, *The True Tragedy*, *Henry the Fifth*, *The Merry Wives of Windsor*, and the first quartos of *Hamlet* and *Romeo and Juliet*. They are significantly shorter than the versions eventually published in the Folio or collected edition of Shakespeare's plays that was published after his death. In these quartos lines are paraphrased, characters are omitted, and scenes are placed in a different order from other versions. It may be that an adapter shortened them, for purposes now unknown, and that adapter may even have been Shakespeare himself. It is generally agreed that the Folio edition is transcribed from Shakespeare's "foul papers" or manuscripts, however, while the shorter quartos reflect an actual performance of the play; the stage-directions are often unusually full and vivid. In the same spirit of performance the cuts in the shorter quartos are designed to add pace and simplicity to the plot, removing undue complexity or awkwardness of staging. The poetry goes, where it is not germane to the story, and extraneous dialogue or characterisation is also removed.

It is not at all clear who was responsible for these adaptations. They might have been put together by a book-keeper or even by Shakespeare himself. It has also been suggested, as we have seen, that they were the product of "memorial reconstruction" by certain of the actors involved in the original production. The nature and purpose of such an activity, however, remain unclear. It has even been proposed that the plays were the product of certain members of the audience who, wishing to pirate them, transcribed them in shorthand or what was then known as brachygraphy. One playwright complains of a pirated edition that was produced "by Stenography . . . scarce one word trew."[8] Given the relatively strict conditions of publication, however, the hypothesis seems untenable.

There is of course no reason to call these six shorter plays "bad" quartos; they are simply different. They do illustrate, however, the somewhat brutal way in which Shakespeare's texts could be treated. At the time of first rehearsal or first performance whole soliloquies could be taken out, lines reassigned and scenes transposed for the sake of narrative efficiency. If they were indeed performed in that fashion, Shakespeare must have concurred in the changes. His position as an eminently practical and pragmatic man of the theatre once more becomes clear.

CHAPTER 57

No More Words, We Beseech You

By becoming resident playwright of the Lord Chamberlain's Men, Shakespeare had avoided the unhappy fate of those freelance dramatists who lived upon their increasingly frayed wits. There were not many of them, and they were all known to one another. In the manner of such things the now respectable and "gentle" Shakespeare would have been the object of some scorn and derision, as well as implicit envy, in their tavern sessions. The writers were employed either by the actors or by the managers of the theatre; they wrote singly or in groups, according to the exigency of the moment. The diaries of Philip Henslowe at the Swan reveal that, of the eighty-nine plays he supervised, thirty-four were written by a single author and the other fifty-five were the result of collaborative enterprise. Collaboration was the single most important method of providing a play. That is one reason why we never read of "author" or "playwright" concerned with any play before 1598. In an earlier period the actors themselves had written the plays, so little did the text matter compared to the spectacle and action. In *Histriomastix* the actors arrive in a town and proclaim their play, at which point they are asked: "What's your playes name? Maisters whose men are ye?" The identity of the author is not a question.

The writer or writers might have proposed the story, or the story might have been suggested to them by the actors or theatre managers; they would then set to work on the "plot" or narrative scheme which, proving successful, they would fashion into the play itself. They tended to write in instalments, being paid for each stage of their delivery. "I haue hard fyue sheets of a playe," one member of the Admiral's Men wrote to Henslowe, "& I dow not doute but it wyll be a verye good playe." But the playwright admitted that they were "not so fayr written all as I could wish."[1]

It is of the greatest importance to note that these men were the first of their kind. There were no rules. There had never existed professional writers before, by which is meant writers who were dependent upon the commercial market for their success or failure. Chettle, Nashe and Shakespeare—whether they knew it or not—were the harbingers of a new literary culture.

The playwrights finished their "sheets" quickly. It was the literary equivalent of factory farming, and Jonson was scorned when he admitted to spending five weeks on a play. They were also called upon to augment or revise existing plays, and to adapt them to different casts and circumstances. New plays were needed all the time but, equally importantly, new kinds of play were constantly in demand. In this recently created world of play-making and play-going there were instant fashions and fancies. For a decade the fashion had been for history plays, revenge tragedies and pastoral comedies; they were then supplanted by comedies of "humours" and city comedies; the city comedies became more and more concerned with sex, and satires also came to the fore. Then there was a fashion for Roman plays. There was a vogue for plays concerned with rulers in disguise. There was a period when romances and plays containing masques became popular. Shakespeare himself was not immune to these changes of direction, and we will see how his own plays were subtly attuned to the demands of the moment.

That is why play-writing was also considered to be the most lucrative employment for any writer of the period. The average rate for a new play was approximately £6, and it can be estimated that the most successful or popular playwrights were able to compose at least five plays each year. Their annual income, therefore, was more than twice as much as they could have earned as schoolmasters. There were others who were not so fortunate, however, and were reduced to menial literary employment for the sake of a bottle of wine and a few shillings. It was an energetic, boisterous, drunken and on occasions violent world that naturally spilled over into the circles of the theatrical profession.

There was no question, then, of creating an eminent "career" out of writing for the playhouses; these men were not established poets such as

Samuel Daniel or Edmund Spenser, patronised by royalty and financed by nobility. They were journeymen or workmen. Whether Shakespeare considered himself in this light is an open question. His pursuit of armigerous status suggests that he had higher aspirations, but in the actual practice of his trade he was no doubt as pragmatic and as workmanlike as any of his contemporaries.

There was, however, one great change in the printing and publication of Shakespeare's plays. On 10 March 1598, the volume edition of *A Pleasant Conceited Comedie called Loues labors lost* was issued as newly "corrected and augmented" by "W. Shakspere." This was the first of his plays in which he was announced as the author, and heralded the growing importance of his name in the dissemination of his work to the public. He had managed to fight his way through the general anonymity of the play-writing profession and had become an identifiable "author." In the same year new quarto versions of *Richard II* and *Richard III* proclaimed that they, unlike their anonymous predecessors, had been composed solely by "William Shake-speare." In the following year the spurious volume, *The Passionate Pilgrim*, also made use of Shakespeare's name as an evident attraction for the reading public. It is sometimes suggested that the Lord Chamberlain's Men sold these plays to their respective publishers as a ploy for raising much-needed finance. This is most unlikely; plays were by no means a large part of any publisher's stock and would not have commanded extraordinarily high prices. It is much more likely that publication of the plays was a way of advertising them in periods when they were simultaneously being performed on the public stage.

The publication of *Love's Labour's Lost* can be seen, however, as a highly significant event in the creation of the modern conception of the writer. It was not the least of Shakespeare's accomplishments to elevate, and perhaps even to create, the status and the reputation of the commercial author. After the spring of 1598 the number of his plays entering publication, with his name attached to them, multiplied. It has also been suggested by theatrical historians that from this time forward dramatists became more "aggressive"[2] about their roles and reputations with players and publishers alike. The author may have come out of the printing press rather than the theatre, as this narrative suggests, but the literary and cultural identity of the individual writer could no longer be ignored.

It may not be coincidence that in the autumn of the same year there appears the first public praise for Shakespeare as a dramatist rather than as a poet. In *Palladis Tamia: Wits Treasury* Francis Meres remarks that "as *Plau-*

tus and *Seneca* are accounted the best for Comedy and Tragedy among the Latines: so Shakespeare among the English is the most excellent in both kinds for the stage." Among Shakespeare's comedies he mentions "*Midsummers night dreame* & his *Merchant of Venice*" and, among the tragedies, he refers to *King John* and *Romeo and Juliet*. He augments his praise by declaring that "I say that the Muses would speak with *Shakespeares* fine filed phrase, if they would speake Englishe."[3] He goes on to mention Shakespeare's name in five other passages. This is high praise, only slightly modified by the general extravagance of Meres's encomia. It signals Shakespeare's eminence in his profession and the fact that as an author he can now legitimately claim a place beside "*Philip Sidney, Spencer, Daniel, Drayton*" and the other poets whom Meres mentions. Shakespeare had made the profession of dramatist culturally respectable, in a way unimaginable even twenty years before.

Meres had recently published a sermon entitled *God's Arithmetic* and in the same year as *Palladis Tamia* he brought out a pious book entitled *Granado's Devotion*; later he became a rector in Rutland. So Shakespeare now appealed to the "godly" as well as to the "lower sort" who filled the pit of the playhouses. Meres was severe on the generally dissolute lives of Marlowe, Peele and Greene but placed Shakespeare himself in the more elevated company of Sidney and Daniel and Spenser. The publication of *Palladis Tamia* marked a very important stage in Shakespeare's literary reputation, also, since from this time forward begins the serious commentary upon his plays.

There is a curious addendum to Meres's praise. Among the comedies of Shakespeare he identifies is one entitled *Loue labours wonnne*. The name also emerges in a publisher's catalogue at a later date. No such play survives. It has been suggested that it is an alternative title for an existing play, such as *Much Ado About Nothing*, but it may well be one of those Shakespearian productions that, like the mysterious play *Cardenio*, has been lost in the abysm of time.

Shortly after Meres published his comments the scholar and close friend of Edmund Spenser, Gabriel Harvey, inserted a note in his newly purchased copy of Speght's edition of Chaucer. He wrote that "the younger sort takes much delight in Shakespeares Venus, & Adonis: but his Lucrece, & his tragedie of Hamlet, Prince of Denmark, haue it in them, to please the wiser sort." He then includes Shakespeare among a group of "flourishing metricians"[4] including Samuel Daniel and his friend Edmund Spenser. Leaving aside the apparently early date for the production of *Hamlet*, and the fact that Harvey seems to regard that play as a text to be read, this is also significant praise from a representative of what might be called Elizabethan high poetics. Harvey had already scorned the lives and works of the jobbing playwrights of the period, in particular Thomas Nashe and Robert Greene, but in this private notation he places Shakespeare in much more elevated company—including that of his beloved Spenser.

There is one other piece of evidence that confirms Shakespeare's standing among the "younger sort." In this period some students at St. John's College, Cambridge, devised a trilogy of satirical plays on current literary fashions. They have become known as the *Parnassus Plays* and the second of them, *The Second Part of the Returne from Parnassus*, has a considerable interest for the student of Shakespeare. In this play a feeble character named Gullio, who may or may not be a satirical portrait of Southampton, sings aloud the praises of Shakespeare to the amusement of the more alert Ingenioso. "We shall have nothing but pure Shakspeare," Ingenioso declares at an outpouring by Gullio, "and shreds of poetrie that he hath gathered at the theators." When Ingenioso is obliged to attend to Gullio's verses he cries out, sarcastically, "Sweete Mr. Shakspeare!" and "Marke, Romeo and Juliet! O monstrous theft!" Gullio then goes on to ask: "Let mee heare Mr. Shakspear's veyne" which suggests that his "vein" was well enough known to be admired, imitated and occasionally disparaged. "Let this duncified world esteeme of Spencer and Chaucer," Gullio goes on, "I'le worship sweet Mr. Shakspeare, and to honour him will lay his Venus and Adonis under my pillowe."[5] There is no doubt, then, that Shakespeare was indeed the "fashion." Another character in the *Parnassus* trilogy seems designed to be a parody of the dramatist himself. Studioso is both playwright and schoolteacher, and he speaks in the accents of Shakespeare with plentiful natural analogies and melodious conceits. A recognisably Shakespearian style could be parodied in front of an audience, who would know precisely the object of the parody.

In 1599 a student of another Cambridge college, Queens', wrote an encomium on "honie-tong'd Shakespeare" in which he praises the two long poems, *Venus and Adonis* and *The Rape of Lucrece*, as well as *Romeo and Juliet*. That same play was also mentioned in *The Second Part of the Returne from Parnassus*, which suggests that it was very popular indeed among the young scholars of the university. Shakespeare was known for his "sweetness," but the next play of the *Parnassus* trilogy also mentions *Richard III*. The fact that

Gabriel Harvey names *Hamlet* as one of his principal productions suggests that the dramatist was now being taken seriously on a number of levels. In the same year John Marston satirises a contemporary from whose lips flow "naught but pure *Iuliat and Romio*."[6] All in all, Shakespeare had become a phenomenon.

CHAPTER 58

A Loyall, Just and Upright Gentleman

Shakespeare's purchase of New Place located the dramatist firmly at the centre of Stratford's life. His wife and daughters moved into their newly refurbished residence, and perhaps looked forward to spending more time with the head of the household. He was of course *de facto* the guiding hand of the family's own finances. He must have been instrumental in November 1597, for example, for re-entering at Westminster Hall the Shakespeares' suit for the recovery of Arden property in his mother's native village of Wilmcote; they were pressing their case against their relatives, the Lamberts, who had refused to hand over a house there. It was a difficult and somewhat technical legal challenge, apparently hanging upon a dispute over actual payment of, or promise to pay, the sum of £40. In the deposition John and Mary Shakespeare are described as "*of small wealthe and verey fewe frendes and alyance.*"[1] It may have been "small wealth" that persuaded John Shakespeare, in this same year, to sell a strip of land beside his property in Henley Street to a neighbour for the sum of 50 shillings.

The witnesses brought forward in the case against the Lamberts were in fact colleagues of William, rather than John, Shakespeare, which argues the dramatist's personal investment in the matter. Amongst this tangled procedure it is clear that the Shakespeares were assiduously and energetically pursuing their case, to the extent that John Lambert accused them of harassment. He claimed that they "doe now trowble and moleste this defendante by unjuste sutes in law";[2] "sutes" implies that he was being accused in other courts as well. The case dragged on for more than two and a half years, eventually to be settled, apparently in Lambert's favour, out of court. In the course of the proceedings, however, the Shakespeares were rebuked for "wasting Chancery's time."[3] It is an indication of how far Shakespeare would go in defence of family honour and in pursuit of family property. He may have been relentless in such matters. He forfeited 40 acres with the loss of the Wilmcote property, but soon enough he was buying up more Stratford land.

At the very beginning of 1598 the bailiff of Stratford, Abraham Sturley, was ready to approach Shakespeare with news of a likely investment. He had informed a close relative, Richard Quiney, alderman, "that our countriman mr Shaksper is willinge to disburse some monei vpon some od yardeland or other att Shottri or neare about vs; he thinketh it a veri fitt patterne to move him to deale in the matter of our tithes." Sturley went on to say that "Bi the instruccions you can geve him thereof, we thinke it a faire mark for him to shoote att, and not unpossible to hitt. It obtained would advance him in deede, and would do vs muche good."[4]

So the new owner of New Place was already a gentleman of financial consequence in Stratford. It seems likely that he was being asked to consider the purchase of the house and land of his wife's stepmother, Joan Hathaway, in Shottery; the old woman died in the following year, leaving 2½ yardlands (a yardland being approximately 30 acres) as well as the farmhouse now known as "Anne Hathaway's Cottage." He was also considered to be in the market for the purchase of "tithes," money in lieu of a percentage of crops or farm-stock on land possessed by tithe-holders; it had once been a religious obligation which had become a matter of lay ownership.

It is not clear which particular tithes Quiney and Sturley had in mind—although they were the "farmers" of the "Clopton tithe-hay"—but the essential point is that Shakespeare did not take up their offer. He did not in fact purchase tithes until 1605, which suggests a measure of prudence on his part. In the 1590s, Stratford was in a condition of economic and social depression. In the same letter Abraham Sturley notes that "our neighbours are grown, with the wants they feel through the dearness of corn, malcontent." The succession of bad harvests had weakened the financial strength of the town, and there had been two recent widespread and devastating fires that had further depressed the price of property. It was one of the reasons why Shakespeare had been able to purchase New Place so cheaply. Richard Quiney was in fact in London on pressing local business when he received the letter from Abraham Sturley. As alderman he had been charged with the responsibility of pleading Stratford's case with the national administration. The town asked to be made exempt from certain taxes, and wished to be given more ample provision from a fire-relief fund.

And then later in the year Richard Quiney decided to approach Shakespeare on another matter. He needed a loan on behalf of the Stratford Corporation. Who else to ask but the man who was arguably now the wealthiest householder in Stratford? So in October 1598, from his London lodgings at the Bell Inn in Carter Lane, he wrote a letter to his "Loveinge Countreyman" declaring that "I am bolde of yowe as of a ffrende, craveing yowre helpe with xxx li [£30] . . . Yowe shall ffrende me muche in helpeinge me out of all the debettes I owe in London, I thancke god, & muche quiet my mynde." He then noted that he had gone to "Cowrte" at Richmond over Stratford affairs and pledged that Shakespeare "shall neither loase creddytt nor monney by me, the Lord wyllinge . . . & yf we Bargaine farther yowe shalbe the paiemaster yowre self." It seems likely that Richard Quiney needed the money to sustain his advocacy of Stratford's business in the capital. News of his attempts to borrow money from Shakespeare reached Stratford itself, and eleven days later (the speed of the post was not great) Abraham Sturley wrote to him saying that he had heard "our countriman Mr. Wm Shak. would procure vs monei, which I will like of as I shall heare when, and wheare, and howe."[5] It does not take an over-sensitive ear to detect a note of scepticism or caution on Sturley's part. Did Shakespeare have a reputation for meanness or avariciousness? It is not an impossible assumption. He took small debtors to court. Yet it is more likely that his financial reputation, if such it was, was that of canniness rather than avarice. The idea that Shakespeare would "procure" the requisite sum suggests that Shakespeare may have been ready to deal with a money-lender on Quiney's behalf. There have even been suggestions that, like his father, Shakespeare himself acted as a part-time money-lender. In the conditions of the time, and in the absence of banks, this was not an unusual activity for a wealthy man. It will seem inappropriate only to those who hold an excessively romantic opinion of eminent writers.

The letter to Shakespeare was in fact never sent, and was later found among Quiney's papers. Perhaps the alderman had decided to pay a call on his countryman. But where was he to find him? In November 1597 the dramatist had failed to pay 5 shillings in property tax to the collectors of St. Helen's Bishopsgate. He was one of those who were "dead, departed, and gone out of the said ward." It may be that he had already removed to Southwark, out of the reach of the Bishopsgate collectors. In the following year, 1598, he was listed again by the parish authorities for non-payment of 13*s* 4*d*. He had certainly moved to Southwark by 1600, for in that year he is reported to the officers of the Bishop of Winchester for having still failed to pay his property tax. The Bishop of Winchester had jurisdiction over that area of Southwark known as the Clink. It was a common enough offence but it is still difficult to understand why the wealthy Shakespeare seems deliberately to have withheld payment of a standard tax. Was it laziness or meanness? Or did he feel that he had discharged his obligations by paying taxes in Stratford? Did he not consider himself to be thoroughly "settled" in London? Did he feel that he owed London nothing or, perhaps more likely, that he owed the world nothing?

Part VII
The Globe

The Globe Theatre on Bankside.

ℭ Pretty Plot, Well Chosen to Build Vpon

n the summer of 1598 there were still demands from the civic authorities and indeed from the members of the Privy Council that the
theatres should be "plucked down" as a result of the "lewd matters
that are handled on the stages."[1] This had become something of an occu-
pational hazard, and the playhouses simply ignored the injunctions. Given
the undoubted popularity of plays and playhouses there was also going to be
competition, official or unofficial, springing up to challenge the two established companies. The Earl of Pembroke's Men had put on *The Isle of Dogs*
at the Swan, as we have seen, before being disbanded.

New theatres were about to be erected in the city and northern suburbs,
also, among them the Fortune and the newly refurbished Boar's Head. In addition, the boys' companies were soon to be in operation again. In the following year an indoor playhouse was opened in the precincts of St. Paul's
grammar school, where the children of St. Paul's performed two plays by a
new writer, who referred to himself as the "barking satirist," John Marston.
The competition demonstrated the vitality of theatrical life in London, but it
was an annoyance to the already established players. Nevertheless the Lord
Chamberlain's Men were still at the Curtain, and the Admiral's Men across
the river at the Rose. There is no record of the players touring in this year,
so it can be supposed that Shakespeare and the rest of the company were
playing in the capital. We know that they were performing Ben Jonson's new

play, *Every Man in His Humour*, in the autumn of 1598. So Shakespeare acted in a drama written by one whom posterity has declared to be his "rival." Reports of such rivalry are always greatly exaggerated by various partisans. We may place them against the testimony that Shakespeare became godfather to one of Jonson's children.

The wayward, obstinate and bad-tempered character of Ben Jonson is well enough known. But it is often forgotten that he was a supreme literary artist who wrote for the play-going public only on his own terms. Unlike Shakespeare he was not born to please. He had genuine faith and pride in his achievement, however, and ensured that his dramas were properly collected and published. His opinion about Shakespeare's work seems to have been one of admiration only slightly modified by misgivings about what he considered to be his excessive fluency and his dramatic "absurdities." Jonson was a classicist by inclination and by training. He recognised Shakespeare's genius but considered it prone to extravagance and unrealism. "In reading some bombast speeches of Macbeth," according to John Dryden, "which are not to be understood, he [Ben Jonson] used to say that it was horrour."[2] There are also reports of conversations between the two men at the Mermaid Tavern. The tavern itself lay back from Bread Street, with passage entries from Cheapside and Friday Street. Since Jonson had a reputation for a loose tongue, flowing with sexual innuendoes and sexual gossip, these dialogues were perhaps not always very edifying; we have seen that Shakespeare himself was not averse to bawdry. Modern auditors would no doubt be shocked. "Many were the *wit-combates* betwixt him and Ben Johnson," wrote Thomas Fuller in his *Worthies of England*:

> which two I behold like a Spanish great Gallion and an English man of War; Master Johnson (like the former) was built far higher in Learning; Solid but Slow in his performances. Shake-spear, with the English-man of War, lesser in bulk but lighter in sailing, could turn with all tides, tack about and take advantage of all winds, by the quickness of his Wit and Invention.[3]

This itself is a pleasing invention. Fuller has captured something of the spirit of both men but, having been born as late as 1608, can hardly be cited as a witness.

In this period Sir Walter Raleigh established a "Mermaid Club" that met on the first Friday of every month; among its members, according to one of

Ben Jonson's early editors, were Shakespeare, Beaumont, Fletcher, Donne and Jonson himself. Beaumont wrote some verses to Jonson in which he remarks:

> What things have we seen
> Done at the "Mermaid"? Heard words that have been
> So nimble, and so full of subtle flame . . .[4]

Whether any of those "words" came from Shakespeare is open to doubt. Among the members of the Mermaid Club, however, was Edward Blount; Blount was one of the publishers of Shakespeare's First Folio. So there are connections. Jonson at this time was an avowed Catholic who used to meet his co-religionists at the Mermaid. The previous owner of the Mermaid had been the Catholic printer John Rastell, who was also brother-in-law of Sir Thomas More. Certain associations cling to specific sites. At a later date Shakespeare purchased a house harbouring Catholic associations; one of his co-purchasers was the landlord of the Mermaid, William Johnson.

Very shortly after the production of *Every Man in His Humour* Jonson became involved in an argument with an actor and erstwhile colleague from the Admiral's Men, Gabriel Spencer. The quarrel may have arisen from Jonson's recent defection to the Lord Chamberlain's Men, or it may have been entirely personal. Whatever the cause a duel was fought in the fields of Shoreditch, close to the Theatre, and Spencer was killed by Jonson's sword. The playwright only saved himself from the gallows by pleading benefit of clergy—that is, by proving he was literate and could read. His thumb was branded with the letter "T," for Tyburn, so that he would not escape a second conviction.

In this same period Burbage and Shakespeare, together with their colleagues, had arrived at an important decision which would also have consequences for the young Ben Jonson. Their negotiations concerning the lease with the landlord of the Theatre had got precisely nowhere. They had read the existing contract very carefully, over the period of these strained discussions, and its wording seemed to offer a solution. The landlord owned the land upon which the Theatre stood, but he did not own the theatre itself. So he could keep the land, and they would take away the theatre. They literally moved it. Three days after Christmas 1598, on a day of heavy snow, the

Burbage brothers, Cuthbert and Richard, and their mother, together with twelve workmen and their surveyor and carpenter, Peter Streete, arrived in front of the Theatre in Shoreditch. The aggrieved landlord, Giles Allen, has left a picturesque description of the extraordinary scene.

The Burbages and their cohorts did "ryotouslye assemble themselves" armed with "swords daggers billes axes and such like," whereupon they "attempted to pull downe the sayd Theater." Allen alleges that diverse people asked them "to desist from their unlawfull enterpryse," but the Burbages violently resisted their objections and then began "pulling breaking and throwing downe the sayd Theater in verye outragious violent and riotous sort." In the course of this operation they were responsible for "the great desturbance and terrefyeing" of the local inhabitants of Shoreditch.[5] It is interesting how Tudor legalese encourages melodrama; it was a dramatic society on every level.

The great and terrifying disturbance, if such it was, lasted for some four days. Within that period the Burbages and their employees took down the playhouse's old timbers and loaded them onto wagons; the tiring-house, the beams, the galleries, were all taken up and transported across the river by ferry or by means of London Bridge. There is no reference to the ironwork that was also employed in its construction, although they are unlikely to have left such a valuable asset on site. Much had to be discarded, however, as a result of the speed of the operation. The appurtenances of the Theatre were then deposited south of the river on some land that the Burbages had recently leased for thirty-one years. The plot of ground was a little to the east of the Rose, in the pleasure grounds of Southwark, but further back from the Thames. Ben Jonson described the area as "flanked with a ditch and forced out of a marsh."[6] It would have been filled with tidal waters, ooze and garbage. At the time of its redevelopment by the Lord Chamberlain's Men it comprised seven gardens, a house, and a row of tenements that held fifteen people.

In these watery and insalubrious surroundings the Globe would rise. It was a bold and enterprising decision. The landlord of the plot where the Globe was erected, Nicholas Brend, was in fact brother-in-law of the queen's Treasurer of the Chamber. So he had impeccable references. But the trustees engaged in the negotiation also throw a little light on the intricate social networks of Elizabethan society. One of them, a goldsmith called Thomas Savage, came from the town of Rufford in Lancashire—where it has been deemed that the juvenile Shakespeare was once in the employment of Sir Thomas

Hesketh as schoolmaster and actor. Savage's wife was a member of the extended Hesketh family. It may simply be coincidence, in a relatively small society, but it is suggestive. The other trustee was a merchant named William Leveson, who became a part of the colonial enterprise to Virginia that also involved the Earl of Southampton. Two of Shakespeare's early patrons, therefore, can be glimpsed in the dramatist's later career.

Giles Allen was obviously surprised and angered by the sudden disappearance of the playhouse. He sued the Burbages for £800 in damages, and the litigation lasted for two years through various courts and tribunals. But the Burbages had in fact behaved within the strict interpretation of the law, and Allen received no compensation.

The building work on the new theatre, however, did not proceed as quickly as had been anticipated. So the Burbages spread the financial responsibility. They created five "sharers" who between them would put up half the costs, and who would in return become "house-keepers" or part owners of the new theatre. One of those sharers was William Shakespeare, who now had the advantage of owning one-tenth of the theatre in which he acted and for which he wrote. It was the most complete association possible between playwright and playhouse. His other sharers were the principal actors of the Lord Chamberlain's Men, Will Kempe and Thomas Pope, John Heminges and Augustine Phillips. They had all grown moderately wealthy out of their new-found profession.

Peter Streete contracted to finish the construction of the Globe within twenty-eight weeks, although that may be an example of perennial builders' optimism. Strong foundations had to be laid, since the Globe was erected on watery soil; wooden piles were driven into the Southwark earth, and a ditch had to be bridged to allow public access. This operation would have taken some sixteen weeks. By May 1599 a legal document refers to a "*domus*" with an attached garden in the parish of St. Saviour's, Southwark, "*in occupatione Willielmi Shakespeare et aliorum*"–in the occupation of Shakespeare and others, the prominence given to the dramatist's name suggesting that he was considered to be the first mover in this enterprise. Intriguingly enough "*domus*" may be interpreted to mean either the theatre itself or a house adjoining that structure. A picture of Shakespeare living in a house beside the playhouse proper is not inconceivable.

CHAPTER 60

Thou Knowest My Lodging.
Get Me Inke and Paper

here is no doubt that Shakespeare lived south of the river, but his exact location is not known. The immediate vicinity of the Globe Playhouse was described by John Stow's editors in the eighteenth century as a "long straggling Place, with Ditches on each side, the Passage to the Houses being over little Bridges, with little Garden Plotts before them."[1] It was no more salubrious in the period when Shakespeare himself moved to Southwark. Nevertheless it was important for him to be close to the centre of all his activities. Here he joined his colleagues from the Globe, Thomas Pope and Augustine Phillips; Phillips lived with his large family close to the river. Southwark was in fact something of an actors' district. Shakespeare also had, as neighbours, Edward Alleyn and Philip Henslowe, who already possessed extensive interests in the vicinity. Henslowe's address was "on the bank sid right over against the clink,"[2] the "clink" itself being the small underground bishop's prison by the river.

Shakespeare himself could have taken up temporary residence at one of the three hundred inns of the neighbourhood. The Elephant was on the corner of Horseshoe Alley, for example, just a few yards from the Globe. In *Twelfth Night*, written a year or two after his removal to that district, Antonio remarks (1467–8):

In the South Suburbes at the Elephant
Is best to lodge . . .

But this may be no more than a local joke. If he had lived in the liberty of the Clink, as the records of non-payment of property tax imply, then he would have inhabited the long street which runs beside the Thames just north of Winchester Palace Park. This was the street in which Henslowe also dwelled. In a memorandum, quoted by the eighteenth-century scholar Edmond Malone but no longer extant, Alleyn records that Shakespeare lived close to the Bear-Garden, and in fact the distance is only a few hundred yards. Edmond Malone further claims that Shakespeare lived in this neighbourhood until 1608, a residence of some ten years. For a peripatetic dramatist, that is a long sojourn indeed. He might almost have been described as a gentleman of Southwark rather than as a gentleman of Stratford.

The history of Southwark had for many hundreds of years been associated with public entertainment. A gladiator's trident has been found here, which suggests that a Roman arena was once constructed in the vicinity of the Globe. In the years immediately preceding the late sixteenth century, however, the area was known for bull-baiting and bear-baiting, for exhibitions of wrestling and acrobatics. It was also the venue for various forms of drama. When the priests of St. Mary Overie (now known as Southwark Cathedral) were singing "*Dirige*" for the soul of Henry VIII in 1547, their prayers were interrupted by the noise of players performing in the neighbourhood. Thirty-one years later the Privy Council was still complaining to the Surrey justices about the prevalence of play-acting in the same vicinity. The evidence suggests that Paris Garden itself had been used as the venue for medieval "folk festivals," under which quaint term we may include a great many crude entertainments as well as cruel and violent sports.

Chief among those sports has always been animal-baiting. It was a peculiar love of the English, and conducted with a ferocity that horrified continental visitors. A Venetian traveller noted two hundred dogs in "traps," ready to be set upon bulls and wild bears. There was another sport in which a blind bear was tormented by men with whips; occasionally the maddened animal was known to break free of its chain and run among the crowd. When Shakespeare includes the famous stage-direction in *The Winter's Tale*, "Exit, pursued by a bear," the audience would have been able to picture the scene quite precisely.

There was a bull-ring in Southwark by 1542 at the latest, and a new bull-ring was being built on Bankside in the 1550s. Shakespeare would have heard the roaring from his lodgings by the Clink. The cost of admission was a penny, with an additional penny for a good place in the galleries. In 1594 Edward Alleyn secured the lease of the bear-baiting ring at Paris Garden, in the neighbourhood of the Globe, for £200. A few years later he and Henslowe purchased the office of mastership of the "Queen's Games of Bulls and Bears." The bear-pits were an adjunct, not a cheap alternative, to the playhouses. On Thursday and Sunday of each week, the theatres were closed and the animal-pits opened. At a slightly later date Alleyn and Henslowe built the Hope Playhouse, close to the Globe, which was both theatre and animal-pit; the bears were baited on Tuesday and Thursday, plays performed on every other day (except Sunday). It was the same business, run by the same operatives. The reek of the animals must have sullied the actors' costumes. It is a condition of London life that the atmosphere of a neighbourhood lingers like some fugitive odour in the air; we can say with some certainty, therefore, that Shakespeare lived and worked in a parish characterised by violence and casual cruelty. That is perhaps why Southwark provided more soldiers for the realm than any other area apart from the city of London itself. More than a third of its householders were watermen, and watermen were well known throughout England for their abusive behaviour and foul language.

There was a "sanctuary" at Paris Garden from the early fifteenth century, and the neighbourhood had a history of criminal association and criminal practice. It had also been a haven for many and varied groups of immigrants, known as "aliens," among them Dutch and Fleming. The topography of the neighbourhood is perhaps then predictable. There were larger houses and gardens for the more notable residents, such as Henslowe and Alleyn (and perhaps Shakespeare himself), but for the rest it was an area of packed tenements and swarming streets, of stables and alleys. What were known as the "stink-trades" were also congregated here, brewing and tanning among them. There was a busy ferry-crossing at Paris Garden Stairs, transporting passengers over to Blackfriars on the opposite bank. But even here the generally rough reputation of the neighbourhood intervened. A civic edict of the sixteenth century ordered wherrymen to moor their boats on the northern bank at night to ensure that "thieves and other misdoers shall not be carried"[3] to the brothels and taverns of Southwark. There were indeed many brothels, some of them owned by the ubiquitous business partners Alleyn and Henslowe. Henslowe's playhouse, the Rose, was named after a well-known house of assignation in the vicinity. They were, you might say, all-round entertainers. And Shakespeare knew them well.

It may seem odd that Alleyn and Henslowe were also vestrymen of the church of St. Saviour's, and that Henslowe became churchwarden. Yet in a more youthful and enterprising society, established upon the active pursuit of profit, such dual allegiances were not unusual. Prostitutes had been known as "Winchester Geese," after the Bishop of Winchester's manor in which they operated. One inn and brothel was called the Cardinal's Hat, not necessarily because of any ecclesiastical connection but because red was deemed to be the proper colour for the tip of the penis. The sacred and the secular were still thoroughly mingled. Only after the parliamentary wars was the effort made to separate them.

It is of course easy to exaggerate the stench and horrors of the south bank. There were fields and woods within easy reach of the busy streets, and the herbalist John Gerard was agreeably surprised by the number of flowers he observed in the water ditches of the neighbourhood. In Paris Garden Lane, for example, he found the "water yarrow" and "plentie" of "water gilloflower."[4] So it was not an altogether disagreeable area. Demographic surveys also suggest that its inhabitants did not move away from it in any significant numbers; like Londoners elsewhere, they were happy to remain in the familiar neighbourhood. So life in Southwark was not necessarily insupportable, only colourful and occasionally inconvenient. It was always a lively and active area. Why else should Shakespeare choose to remain there for so long? In twenty-first century London, people do not choose to move out of Soho. Southwark, then, was the centre of genuine and teeming life.

CHAPTER 61

Ƈhis ꟿide and ꟿniuersall Ƈheatre

nd so the new Globe arose. It was considered at the time to be the most splendid of all the London theatres. Its name implies that it was the theatre of the world itself and, as the arena in which *Othello* and *King Lear*, *Macbeth* and *Julius Caesar*, were first performed, it can lay some claim to that title. It has been suggested that Peter Streete, carpenter and builder, followed the precepts of Vitruvius in designing this space. The book of Vitruvius known as *Architectura* was available in England at the time, but it is highly unlikely that Streete ever consulted it. His immediate model is more likely to have been that of the animal-baiting ring, with which he and his contemporaries were intensely familiar. Nevertheless its design has been interpreted as a copy of the amphitheatre of the antique world, or of the holier circles of primeval Britain. That circular shape has also been supposed to suggest the womb or the embrace of encircling maternal arms. It even bears a passing resemblance to the magician's circle, in which bright visions might appear. But no wooden building in the sixteenth century could be entirely circular. It was in fact polygonal in shape, accommodating some fourteen sides, with three galleries surrounding the stage and the open yard or "pit."

The Globe's structure was of timber, made up of prefabricated oak posts (some of them over 30 feet long) infilled with wattle-and-daub and with a finished exterior of white plaster; its roof was thatched. It is possible that the plaster was designed to resemble stone, so that the building of the theatre was itself theatrical. The playhouse was 100 feet in diameter, and is supposed to have held some 3,300 people. Each of the two lower galleries could hold one thousand people. It was in other words very tightly packed with Elizabethan bodies, accommodating audiences two or three times the size of those in a modern London theatre. Indeed the atmosphere would have been more like that of a football stadium than a playhouse. It also had some elements of the funfair.

It has been supposed that the Globe had a "sign" for ready identification above the stage or perhaps above the principal entrance. That would be quite usual in Elizabethan London and, if it existed at all, stray references suggest that it was an image of Hercules holding a globe upon his shoulders. The Shakespearian scholar, Edmond Malone, has stated that the playhouse also displayed a motto above its entrance or within its interior–"*Totus mundus agit histrionem*," which may be translated as "The whole world plays the actor." The interior would have been colourful if not gaudy, with classical motifs and statuary prominent among the paintings and decorations. We know well enough from other interiors, with their satyrs and herms, their paintings of gods and goddesses, that the Elizabethans loved bright patterning and intricate carving. Nothing was too extravagant or too elaborate. At the Globe the wood was painted to resemble marble or jasper, and there were various hangings or tapestries to add to the impression of pseudo-classical luxury. The colours were vivid, with much gilt and gold, and the general effect was one of elaborate splendour. The theatre, after all, was a world of artifice in what was already a highly scenic and ritualistic culture. It vied with the court as the central point of ritual and display. It was the very fulcrum of art as demonstration.

The stage itself was just under 50 feet in width. It was so placed that it stayed out of direct sunlight, and remained in shadow for the duration of the afternoon's performances. When an actor stepped forward to the front of the stage, however, his face would have been significantly lightened. It had two exits/entrances, one on either side; between them was the curtained "discovery" space in which characters might be found asleep, dead, or privately employed; it could be used, for example, as a tomb or a study. Jutting out upon the stage itself was a canopy held up by two wooden pillars. This was also known as the "heavens," and was decorated with stars and planets against a celestial blue background; the pillars are also supposed to have defined "front stage" and "rear stage." It was an exceedingly simple arrangement, taken from classical stagecraft, and was designed to emphasise the bodily presence of the actor. On the level above the stage was a balcony employed by the musicians, and hired sometimes by the most privileged of the audience; but it could also be used as part of the theatrical stage. When a general appeared on the ramparts of a city, or when a lover climbed up to his mistress's bedchamber, this was the space that was used. Beneath the stage was the area known as "hell." A trap-door allowed personages magically to ascend or descend, but it was also the area where the "props" were kept. There does not seem to have been any machinery in the Globe, however, for tricks of "flying" or descending upon the stage. This would not become available to Shakespeare, and the players, until they began to use an indoors playhouse at Blackfriars.

On the stage of the Globe an actor would enter at one door and exit at another. When a character or characters left the stage, they would not be the first to appear in the subsequent scene. These were important principles, designed to lend the impression of a dramatic world in process; theatrical life continued, as it were, "behind the scene." There was an illusion of a flowing imaginative world, of which the actors on the stage were the visible token. It is also an indication of the formal fluency of Elizabethan drama, depending as it does upon contrast and symmetry, balance and opposition, of finely poised forces. The wide space allowed for speed and flexibility of plot. It is possible that the words were spoken much more quickly than in any modern performance. There were no acts, only scenes signalled by the various exits and entrances of the actors themselves. Act breaks were not introduced until approximately 1607. After a general exit, for example, a stage-property might be carried on by stagehands (wearing their blue livery) before other characters entered. The Elizabethan stage was not self-conscious about its procedures, the mechanics of stage "business," and of course neither were the plays themselves. There was no appetite for realism, or naturalism, in any of its current senses.

The drama of the Globe, then, was largely built upon a succession of scenes. The sequence of scenes conforms to the English love of interdependent units, a series of variations upon a theme that encourages variety rather than concentration and heterogeneity rather than intensity. That is why a new entrance was always significant, and why it is heavily emphasised in the stage-directions. "Enter Cassandra with her hair aboute her eares . . . Enter a Troian in his night-gowne all vnready . . . Enter Godfrey as newly landed & halfe naked . . . Enter Charles all wet with his sword . . . Enter Ercole with a letter . . ." These were defining moments in the creation of a scene. They represented purpose and character, setting in motion the subsequent action. The presence of the actor, what was known as "the ability of body," was the paramount element of the dramatic entertainment. It is also possible that the player sometimes made his entry from the yard, perhaps from one of the entrances to the theatre, and then vaulted onto the stage.

The actor would come forward, and then deliver his lines to the audience. He did not enter a particular location; he entered in order to address or confront another actor. Speakers were also separated from non-speakers in the dramatic space. There were set patterns for scenes of greeting and of parting; there were stage conventions for kneeling and embracing. There were no doubt also accepted theatrical codes for asides and soliloquies, perhaps a particular placing of the body on stage. At the close of the performance the highest-ranking character left on stage delivered the final lines. The audience loved processions and marches and dumb-shows; it loved colour and display. There is a large element of ceremony or ritual about this theatre, in other words, which remained an important part in its staging.

It was a general setting, a blank space that actor and playwright could manipulate with perfect imaginative freedom. It has been suggested by some theatrical historians that place cards were set up to inform the audience of a particular setting, but this is perhaps too prescriptive. It was enough for the actor to announce his location. And of course the nature of the costumes also determined the nature of place. The green garment of a forester would signify a wood, a set of gaoler's keys a prison. Costume was a most important theatrical device. In a visual culture it was the key to all levels of society and all forms of occupation. Elizabethan actors, and audiences, also delighted in disguise as a plot device. More was spent on costumes than on texts or actors' salaries, and the inventory of the company wardrobe includes robes, cloaks, jerkins, doublets, breeches, tunics and nightshirts. And of course there was always a need for armour. In one of his inventories Henslowe also lists a range of more exotic costumes—a suit for a ghost and a senator's gown, a coat for Herod as well as apparel for a devil and a witch. A good wardrobe master kept cast-offs and oddments of clothes, and there is reason to believe that the companies were sometimes given the remnants of a nobleman's wardrobe of worn-out clothes and garments that had gone out of fashion. Clothing also determined the identity of the character. There were conventional costumes for the Jew and the Italian, the doctor and the merchant. A canvas suit indicated a sailor, and a blue coat was the token of a servant. Virgins wore white, and doctors were dressed in scarlet gowns. The female characters sometimes wore masks, as an overtly theatrical way of disguising their fundamentally male identity. In that sense the Elizabethan theatre has affiliations with classical Greek and Japanese drama.

There was no scenery as such, but on occasions painted cloths were used. In Henslowe's theatrical accounts there is a description of "a clothe of the Sone & Moone." They were not naturalistic, but were designed to convey an atmosphere or to suggest a theme. When romances were to be played, for example, there were cloths painted with cupids. When tragedies were to be performed, the stage was hung in black draperies.

There were a few stage-properties for each production, notably beds or tables and chairs. Allusions in play texts to trees may refer to the two pillars, holding up the canopy, which could be employed for a multitude of purposes. Realism was not an issue. Stools were left on stage for histrionic use; an actor might wish to sit upon them or to brandish them at an opponent. A scaffold could double as a monument or a pulpit. The list of properties for the Lord Admiral's Men has survived; among them are noted a rock, a cave, a tomb, a bedstead, a bay tree, a boar's head, a lion's skin, a black dog and a wooden leg. Bladders of sheep's blood were readily available for murders and battle scenes. It has been calculated, however, that 80 per cent of Shakespearian scenes written for the Globe needed no props at all.[1] Shakespeare was content with a bare space in which to create his dramatic narratives. It is a very clear indication of his bounding imaginative energy.

CHAPTER 62

Then Let the Trumpets Sound

ords were not the only theatrical reality. There was much music. The little group of musicians in the balcony, no more than six or seven, would have included a trumpeter and a drummer, as well as players of horns, recorders, "hoboyes" or "haut-boys" and lutes. There are also reports of actors playing instruments upon the stage itself. Alleyn was a lutanist, for example, and on his death Augustine Phillips bequeathed a bass viol, bandore, cittern and lute. The players certainly performed songs and ballads on stage, and they were chosen in part for the quality of their voices. Certain plays must have resembled "musicals" rather than dramas. Music was associated on the stage with sleep and healing, with love and death. It was employed as a prelude to supernatural visitations. And of course it accompanied the numerous dances of Shakespearian drama. In the combination of music and movement we may glimpse the harmony of the spheres.

Many of the lyrics of the songs in Shakespeare's plays were written by the dramatist himself, and there is evidence in his later life of collaboration with such skilled musicians as Thomas Morley and Robert Johnson. Morley had been his neighbour in Bishopsgate, and was also part of the circle around the Countess of Pembroke; so there were many opportunities for their meeting. It was Morley who wrote the musical setting for one of Shakespeare's most famous songs, "It was a lover and his lass."

Robert Johnson was related, as we have seen, to Emilia Lanier, who through her influence had him indentured to Sir George Carey; he collaborated extensively with Shakespeare in the music of the late plays. Johnson is largely remembered for two songs from *The Tempest*, "Full fathom five" and "Where the bee sucks," but at the time he played a not inconsiderable role in the staging and effects of dramas such as *Cymbeline* and *The Winter's Tale*. It is significant that when Shakespeare does import songs from other sources, however, he generally chooses the popular ballad material of sixteenth-century England. These were the ballads he had heard in childhood.

From the references in his drama it is clear that Shakespeare had a technical knowledge of music and of musical terms. This was almost a commonplace skill in the period, where music-making was an indispensable aspect of social life; sight-reading of music was a familiar accomplishment. All the evidence suggests that Shakespeare possessed an acute and sensitive ear. He was a hater of discord in all its forms, even though his plays thrive upon a kind of harmonious discord. He would in any case have been required to sing, and perhaps also to play an instrument, upon the stage. His characters frequently burst into song, among them such unlikely vocalists as Hamlet and Iago, and there are endless references in his plays to the power and sweetness of music. The songs of Ophelia and of Desdemona are employed to touch the scenes of tragedy with eternal harmonies. The music of *The Winter's Tale* and of *The Tempest* is an important part of their meaning. It can be argued, in fact, that Shakespeare was the first English dramatist to make song an integral part of the drama, apart from the anonymous chants of the medieval Mysteries, and can thus be seen as the begetter of the musical theatre. In that, as in so many other matters, he was a divining rod for the nation's genius. It is worth remarking that he was the contemporary of two of the greatest composers in the history of English music, William Byrd and Orlando Gibbons. It was an epoch of profound musical accomplishment. It has been said that England was once "a nest of singing birds," and it was a matter of particular comment among foreign visitors that music was closely woven within London stage performances.

Towards the end of Shakespeare's career, the "outdoor" playhouses were being replaced by "indoor" theatres. In those quieter surroundings, there was music between the recently introduced "acts"–in fact acts may have been devised solely for the purpose of affording musical accompaniments–and there was often a musical performance before the play actually began. Conditions at the Globe, in the open air and in front of a larger and more restive audience, were not conducive to such refined entertainment.

The stage itself was full of noises. Plays were acccompanied by the simulated sound of horses' hooves and of birdsong, of bells and of cannons. Voices off-stage amplified battle scenes with cries of "Kill, kill, kill," loud shouts, shrieks and general clamour. There were fireworks available, for lightning, and smoke was used to imitate fog or mist. When the directions called for "thunder" a sheet of metal was shaken vigorously, and squibs were let off, behind the scene. The sound of pebbles in a drum could counterfeit the sea, and a piece of canvas tied to a wheel could mimic the wind. The sound of dried peas upon a metal sheet would substitute for rain.

Lighting was another source of stage-effects. Torches or tapers were used to signify night. There were certain scenes where supernumeraries would come upon the stage carrying candles as an indication of a night-time banquet or meeting. On occasions lights were placed behind bottles of coloured water to provide sinister or supernatural illumination. In the late sixteenth century the stage was the centre of public enchantment.

CHAPTER 63

Why There You Touch the Life of Our Designe

※

he repertoire of the Lord Chamberlain's Men at the Globe was extensive and various. Quite apart from Shakespeare's plays they seem to have owned approximately one hundred other dramas ranging from *Cloth Breeches and Velvet Hose* to *Stuhlweissenburg*, from *The London Prodigal* to *The Fair Maid of Bristol*. In all of these plays it is likely that Shakespeare played his part. It is not clear how long it required to stage a revival, but it took between two and three weeks to prepare a new play. Since on average fifteen new plays were performed each year, the schedule of business was extremely tight. The records of the Globe have not survived but related material from the Rose suggests that the players there gave 150 performances of thirty separate plays during one winter season. In any week a different play was performed each afternoon. Nothing can better capture the vitality and excitement of the new medium. The constant demand was for novelty.

There was a tested procedure for the production of these new plays. The author or authors, as we have noted, would approach the playhouse with a skeleton narrative for a new play. On the basis of this scenario the playhouse might commission the drama, with a series of part payments followed by the remainder when a satisfactory manuscript or "book-of-the-play" was delivered. At the time of its final delivery the players met in order to listen to the playwright reading out the entire text. There is a note in Philip Henslowe's diary, in May 1602, for two shillings "layd owt for the companye when they read the playe of Jeffa for wine at the tavern." It may have been at this juncture, or slightly later, that the "book-keeper" prepared a "plot" or outline of the action in which the names of the actors, the stage-props required, and the requisite stage-noises, were written down. But by far the most important function of the "plot" was to list the sequence of entries, and thus the number of scenes. It was a way of adjusting the play, in other words, to the available resources and numbers of the company. One task, for example, was carefully to allot the roles to individual actors so that "doubling" (one actor taking two parts) became easily achieved. The player, however skilled, could not be in two places on the same stage. The plot was divided into individual scenes by the simple expedient of a line ruled across the various columns, and each scene began with the direction "Enter." This was also placed on pasteboard and hung in the tiring-house behind the stage as an *aide-memoire* to players.

A member of the company, perhaps the book-keeper himself, also copied down the individual actor's parts on a "scroll" or long strips of paper. It was this that the player carried about with him and memorised. One of those given to Edward Alleyn, for the part of Orlando in Robert Greene's *Orlando Furioso*, has survived. It is made up of fourteen half-sheets of paper pasted together so that it forms a continuous roll some 17 feet in length and 6 inches in width. The speeches are given "cues" in the last words of the previous speaker, and there are occasional directions.

The author's original manuscript became the "play-book," known also as the "Book." It was used to adapt the manuscript for theatrical performance, but such was the speed and professionalism of the theatrical company that in practice little was done. In certain circumstances stage-action was simplified and speeches shortened. But these were rare interventions. The more usual notes were simply concerned with the traffic of the stage. The author's list of characters, for example, was substituted by the names of individual actors. The stage-properties, and the "noises off," were incorporated. The author's own stage-directions were occasionally revised; entrances, for example, were marked earlier so that the actor had more time to cross the stage. Other stage-directions by the author were left, although they must often have been ignored. His vision was no longer important. It had become a collective reality.

It seems likely that the "book-keeper" also superintended the rehearsals of the play, with prompt-copy in hand, and also acted as prompter during the

performance itself. The prompter did not perform his modern task of whis-
pering lines to an actor who was "out"; his role was to co-ordinate entrances
and expedite the use of properties and "noises off." There is a reference in
Ben Jonson's *Every Man in His Humour* to a choleric gentleman who "would
swear like an Elephant, and stamp and stare (God blesse us) like a play-house
book-keeper when the actors misse their entrance." We may only conclude
that the book-keeper was sometimes also the prompter, and sometimes not.
The player himself, however, was assisted neither by prompter nor by book-
keeper. Once he was on the stage he relied upon his own resources and his
own professionalism, as well as the support of the rest of the players, who no
doubt covered any lapse of memory or mistake in timing.

Before any play could be performed, the finished text had to be despatched to
the Master of the Revels in Clerkenwell for possible alteration and censorship. For a fee, which rose steadily through the years from 7 shillings to £1,
the Master licensed each drama for public performance. With his signature
appended to the manuscript it became the "allowed" book, available for performance throughout England. It was a most important document indeed
and one that in ordinary circumstances the company would keep within its
possession.

Obvious allusions to current events were of course examined very carefully by the Master of the Revels. Any challenge to the established authorities, overt or implied, was taken out. As the authors and actors of *The Isle
of Dogs* discovered, there were also civil penalties for public disrespect. That
is why the deposition scene of the monarch in *Richard II* was removed during
Elizabeth's lifetime. To the book of *Sir Thomas More* the Master of the Revels has added: "Leave out the insurrection wholy & the cause thereoff"; the
caution was necessary in a period when the threat of civic violence in
London was strong. Blasphemy was of course forbidden. One manuscript is
marked by the command to remove "Oathes, prophaness & publick Ribaldry."[1] The evidence, however, suggests that relations between the theatrical companies and the Revels Office were generally good. They were, in a
sense, in the same business.

Assuming that all the formalities and the stage-mechanics had been satisfactorily completed, a play could be performed upon the stage within a few
weeks of its being handed to the company. There was a premium on speed
and professional competency. The rehearsals of new plays, and of revivals,

occurred in the morning. There was no director in the contemporary sense but, as has been suggested, the book-keeper may have played that role in many productions. There is the strong probability that Shakespeare himself performed that duty when his own plays were in rehearsal. It would be the natural thing to do. An excellent dancer such as Will Kempe was responsible for the choreography, and a musician such as Augustine Phillips arranged the music.

A German traveller noted, on a visit to London in 1606, that the players were "daily instructed, as it were in a school, so that even the most eminent actors have to allow themselves to be taught their places by the dramatists."[2] This may have been a misunderstanding, so common in foreign reports of sixteenth-century London, since it is unlikely that an eminent actor would have endured direction from a young or minor playwright. But it would have been different with Shakespeare. Evidence to that effect comes in Richard Flecknoe's *Short Discourse of the English Stage*, published in 1664, in which he describes how in the time of Shakespeare and Jonson "it was the happiness of the Actors of those Times to have such Poets as these to instruct them, and write for them; and no less of those Poets to have such docile and excellent Actors to Act their Playes as a *Field* and *Burbidge*."[3] They were not directed; they were "instructed."

The actors had the "scrolls" of their own lines, but no complete script. They memorised or part-memorised their words before beginning the rehearsal itself. It can be inferred that approximately thirteen principal actors and boys were gathered together on this occasion. The smaller roles need not have been rehearsed. At this stage jokes were added or taken out, difficulties of action overcome, and obscurities of plot or dialogue clarified. At this point, too, the problems attendant on "doubling" were resolved. This was often done unobtrusively, but there were occasions when the Elizabethan players revelled in the artificiality of the procedure. Doubling was an obvious excuse for comedy as well as mystery. It also provided the actor with an opportunity to display his virtuosity and versatility, and it has been calculated that a player needed the time of just twenty-seven lines to change roles. In certain plays Shakespeare will allow precisely that amount of time for the transformation. There were occasions, too, when the audience revelled in "doubling." When an actor dies on stage as one character, but then re-emerges as another living—this must often have been the cue for shouts of approval.

There is every reason to believe that actors and writers in rehearsal behaved very differently from their modern counterparts, who seem to be held in thrall to their director. In contrast the Elizabethan actor suggested lines, or ways of delivering lines, and may even have helped to invent new scenes to assist the progress of the plot. In the "epistle" to a publication of the plays of Beaumont and Fletcher it is announced that "when these *Comedies* and *Tragedies* were presented on the Stage, the *Actours* omitted some *Scenes* and Passages (with the *Authour's* consent) as occasion led them."[4] The plays of Shakespeare were not treated very differently. The play is not a piece of writing, but a collaborative event; it is never finished, in other words, but subject to a continuous and inevitable process of change. There was in the sixteenth century a well-understood set of stage conventions, however, which helped the process of rehearsal; there were principles of movement and gesture that the good actor would have known instinctively. It is interesting, for example, that exits are rarely mentioned in stage texts; it was assumed that competent performers would know exactly when to leave the stage.

A general "run" of a new play was between four to six weeks, played at intervals, but of course there were always revivals and reworkings whenever the occasion required them. The general business of the day would include rehearsals in the morning, playing in the afternoon, and the learning of innumerable lines in the evening. In the case of Shakespeare this was complemented by the necessity of writing plays in relatively quick succession. He was continually, and exhaustingly, occupied. J. M. W. Turner once said that the secret of genius was "hard work," a sentiment with which Shakespeare would have agreed.

CHAPTER 64

See How the Giddy Multitude Doe Point

veryone knew when the playhouse was open. A flag was flown from the roof, announcing the news, and a trumpet was blown to alert those in the vicinity. Playbills advertising the forthcoming entertainment had already been pasted onto walls and posts, as well as the doors of the Globe itself. These "bills" gave the time and place, title and company, as well as sensationalist details to attract the public—"the pittiefull murther . . . the extreame crueltie . . . the most deserved death" and so on. The play itself began with three "flourishes" from the small orchestra, designed in part to still the ever restless audience. Then there came upon the stage the "prologue," attired in a long black velvet cloak, false beard and a wreath of bay-leaves. It was he who introduced the play and pleaded for the audience's attention.

At the end of the play, after the epilogue had been concluded, the next and forthcoming drama was announced to the audience. There then followed the prayers for the monarch, when all the actors knelt upon the stage. And then there came the jig. Its name suggests a merry folk dance, but its provenance goes wider. The stage jig was a comic afterpiece accompanied by dancing, lasting for approximately twenty minutes, in which some or all of the players joined. Its principal exponents were of course the comedians in the company who, like Will Kempe, gained a reputation for their extempore dancing; they turned like a "gig," or top, and sang ribald or personal songs.

The jigs often included folk dances and ballads as well as what are euphemistically termed "figure dances" by the comedians and boys. They were characterised and criticised for their bawdiness, described variously as "a nasty bawdy Iigge" and "obscaene and light Iigges."[1]

Shakespeare's comedies generally end with a wedding rather than with a marriage (the auspices are rarely favourable), and the couples are in a sense unconsummated; that consummation may have been depicted in the jig. And it was a jig in which Shakespeare himself would have joined. In many instances it seems to have been the most popular part of the afternoon's entertainment, "called for" by the impatient audience at the end of the play. The crowd could also demand the performance of a favourite jig such as "master Kemps Newe jigge of the kitchen stuffe woman" or "a ballad of Cuttinge George and his hostis."[2]

It is not at all clear when, or even whether, the performance of jigs was discontinued at the Globe. It is sometimes conjectured that Will Kempe's departure from the Lord Chamberlain's Men in 1599 was the signal for their demise. When a playgoer, Thomas Platter, refers to a jig at the end of a performance of *Julius Caesar* at the Globe in that year he was apparently chronicling one of its last appearances. But at the close of *Twelfth Night*, written and performed in 1601, a clown is left on stage with a song. Where there is a song, there is a dance. There is in fact no real evidence to suggest that the jig came to a sudden or inglorious end in the Bankside theatre. Why remove one of the most popular entertainments that the theatre could provide? Ben Jonson may have complained about the jig but Jonson was not an enthusiast for populist theatre in any of its forms. It certainly flourished in the theatres of the northern London suburbs for many years. It seems unlikely that the "southern" theatres, catering for a similar audience, would discontinue the practice. The jig served a great purpose, not unlike that of the satyr plays which were performed at the end of the dramatic trilogies in fifth-century BC Athens. It was part of the dramatic celebration. It may seem inappropriate after the last scenes of *King Lear* or *Othello*, but there is somehow a dramatic rightness about ending any play with a song and a dance. It suggests that the drama is an aspect of human joy. The original meaning of *"mimesis,"* the word for mimicry or imitation, is "expression in dance." It is perhaps the oldest form of human activity or human game.

The experience of the play has in fact been described as that of a ritual, in which the stage represents a heightened reality not unlike the gestures and movements of a Catholic priest at the altar. It is almost commonplace to suggest that the Elizabethan drama, emerging to full life after the reformation of religion under the Anglican supremacy of Henry and Elizabeth, served as a substitute for the rituals of the old English faith. It fulfilled the audience's appetite for significant action and iconic form. The Globe announced itself to be a cosmos in miniature, like the operations of the Mass. It is well known that ecclesiastical vestments were sold to the players, when their sacredness fell out of use, and that Puritan moralists denounced Roman Catholicism as "Mimic superstition."[3] A company of Catholic travelling players performed *King Lear* in the households of Yorkshire recusants. Shakespearian tragedy, in particular, has some deep affinity with the experience of Catholic worship and the sacrifice of the Mass. Simon Callow, the English actor, has suggested in a modern context that "Catholicism (and its English variant) is another great manufactory of actors . . ."[4] So there is a connection. But the historical argument can be taken too far. The stage may have been inclined to ritual but, throughout the period of Shakespeare's career, it also became an arena for the presentation of human character and of individual striving.

The play began at two o'clock in the winter, and three o'clock in the summer. Its average length was approximately two hours, some plays perhaps thirty or forty minutes longer. Since the length of *Hamlet* and of *Bartholomew Fair* is some four thousand lines, the actors in these and plays of similar length must have spoken very rapidly indeed. The average length of an Elizabethan play, lasting the conventional two hours, is 2,500 lines. Shakespeare's plays average 2,671 lines; as always he stays close to accepted stage procedure. He was in every sense a professional.

The Globe has often been considered to be a summer theatre, but the records show that it was also used in the months of winter. Elizabethan audiences wrapped up more warmly than their modern counterparts, and were in any case hardier, so that the chilly temperatures would not have discouraged them. Playgoers were drawn from all classes, except from the vagrant and the very poorest who could scarcely earn or even beg enough to eat. It is a matter of common sense that there were more middling than lower people, to use a distinction of the period, and that it would be mainly "gentry" and their consorts who would have the leisure or opportunity to spend their afternoons in this fashion. Among this latter class would be included "all Martial men . . . all Students of Artes and Sciences, and by our English custome, all Innes of Court men, professors of the Law."[5] To this list must be appended courtiers and assorted noblemen; London merchants and their wives, as well as apprentices, may be added on the presumption that some of them were willing or able to break off their business for two or three hours. The important point is that the Globe was not filled only with the plebeians of sixteenth-century London, as is sometimes suggested, and there was thus no need for Shakespeare to write "down" to his audience.

There was of course one division, between those who paid a penny for the pit and those who paid a penny more for a seat in the galleries. In the galleries "each man sate downe without respecting of persons, for he that first comes is first seated."[6] As a general rule the porters and carters and apprentices would have been content with their standing room in the pit; these were described as the "under-standers." The pit itself was paved with ash and industrial "slag," such as clinker, with a plentiful covering of hazelnut shells, and probably sloped downward towards the stage. The gentlemen and the richer Londoners (with their ladies) would have preferred the relative comfort of a wooden bench. Once they had paid for their token they could proceed either to the left or right in order to enter the galleries. Yet no doubt it was more random and haphazard than this neat formula would imply. It is possible, for example, that the groundlings did not necessarily stand at all. They may have been able to sit upon rushes strewn across the yard. Some of them, according to Thomas Dekker in *The Gull's Hornbook*, brought with them a "tripos or three-footed stool."[7]

It has also been inferred that the "stinkards," or lower classes of Londoners, congregated at suburban theatres such as the Red Bull and the Fortune; these theatres then become harbingers of the music halls of the East End in the late nineteenth century. But such segregation is very doubtful. When Stephen Gosson disparaged the playhouse audience for being a loose assemblage of "Tailers, Tinkers, Cordwayners, Saylers, olde Men, yong Men, Women, Boyes, Girles and such like"[8] it is clear that the "such like" included a very wide spectrum of humanity indeed. The Globe did truly encompass the human world, or at least that portion of it residing in late sixteenth-century London.

CHAPTER 65

And Here We Wander in Illusions

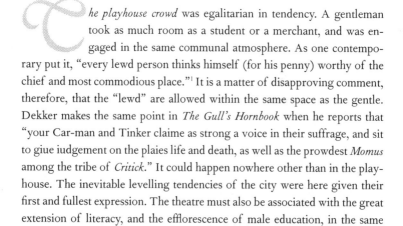

he playhouse crowd was egalitarian in tendency. A gentleman took as much room as a student or a merchant, and was engaged in the same communal atmosphere. As one contemporary put it, "every lewd person thinks himself (for his penny) worthy of the chief and most commodious place."[1] It is a matter of disapproving comment, therefore, that the "lewd" are allowed within the same space as the gentle. Dekker makes the same point in *The Gull's Hornbook* when he reports that "your Car-man and Tinker claime as strong a voice in their suffrage, and sit to giue iudgement on the plaies life and death, as well as the prowdest *Momus* among the tribe of *Critick*." It could happen nowhere other than in the playhouse. The inevitable levelling tendencies of the city were here given their first and fullest expression. The theatre must also be associated with the great extension of literacy, and the efflorescence of male education, in the same period. All these things worked together to make Shakespeare's plays what they were. His audience was eager, alert and excited by this new form of entertainment.

Shakespeare's plays are often very demanding, as modern playgoers know, but sixteenth-century audiences were equally capable of picking up the intricacies of the rhetoric as well as the harmonies of the verse. Some of Shakespeare's more recondite phrases would have passed over them, as they baffle even the most highly educated contemporary audience, but the Elizabethans understood the plots and were able to appreciate the contemporary allusions. Of course scholars of a later age have detected in Shakespeare's plays a subtlety of theme and intention that may well have escaped Elizabethan audiences. But it may be asked whether these are the inventions of the scholars rather than the dramatist. Shakespeare relied upon the audience and, with such devices as the soliloquy, extended the play towards it; the drama did not comprehend a completely independent world, but needed to be authenticated by the various responses of the crowd.

Some of those responses were very noisy indeed. In 1601 John Marston characterised hostile comments as "Mew, blirt, ha, ha, light Chatty stuff,"[2] while at the Fortune the noise was described as that "of Rables, Apple-wives and Chimney-boyes" whose "shrill confused Ecchoes loud doe cry."[3] Shakespeare himself evoked the behaviour of playgoers through the description of Casca in *Julius Caesar*, "If the tag-ragge people did not clap him, and hisse him, according as he pleas'd, and displeas'd them, as they vse to doe the Players in the Theatre, I am no true man" (334–7). Since *Julius Caesar* was played at the Globe, rather than the Theatre, he could not be accused of attacking this particular audience.

"Mew" was a favourite signal of displeasure, from which we get the more recent expression "cat-call." The audiences in the galleries might stand up during a particularly exciting duel or battle, urging on the participants. They would applaud individual speeches. There were hisses and shouts, tears and applause, but all these responses were part of an intense emotional engagement with the play itself. It is almost impossible to replicate the experience of the first theatres. It was an astounding reality, quite unlike anything ever seen before. The mystery plays on the streets, or the interludes in the halls, offered no true comparison. In modern terms the sixteenth-century theatre was television and cinema, street festival and circus, all in one.

There was of course much eating and drinking during the course of the performance, and sellers went around with oranges, apples, nuts, gingerbread and bottled beer. There is a description of a nervous playwright who is so fearful of his play's reception "that a bottle of ale cannot be opened but he thinks somebody hisses."[4] There was a "tap room," or bar, attached to the Globe itself. Pipes of tobacco could be purchased for 3 pence, and one contemporary moralist noted with disquiet that these pipes were offered even to the women. There was no doubt casual or opportunistic prostitution and pickpocketing. Wherever there are large groups of people in London, there are bound to be thieves and ladies of the game. That is the nature of the city. On a more genteel note there are reports that books were for sale in the Globe, with the cry of "Buy a new book!" There was of course no interval, so refreshments were consumed throughout the duration of the play.

Stories of fights and riots in the theatre are essentially of the eighteenth century. The worst that is noted of the sixteenth-century playhouse is the occasional hurling of fruit or nuts at the stage, particularly if the players were late to begin. It was still too novel and exciting an experience, too much a matter of general interest, for a London crowd to permit violent interruption. There was such a thing as "the justice of the street," and no doubt it was visited upon anyone who interfered with the playgoers' pleasure. The plays of Shakespeare were not attended by raucous scenes, or by the yells and shouts of drunken apprentices. It is worth remarking in this context that English drama began its precipitous decline in the late seventeenth century precisely when the theatres became more private and apparently more refined places.

In *Every Man out of His Humour* Ben Jonson wrote of "attentive auditors"; he considered himself to be poet as much as playwright and wished for an understanding or listening audience. The published descriptions of plays by contemporary playgoers are not generally revealing about the level of sensibility in the playhouse. The fact that most audiences were accustomed to listening to sermons, however, must have helped to shape their response. That is why they tend to describe the individual characters and actions, and on occasions the moral lessons that might be adduced from them.

There were, however, some very attentive playgoers who would bring with them "table-books," in which they would note down significant passages. It should be remembered that poetry was still considered to be a matter of speech rather than of writing. So any alert Elizabethan would have been highly sensitive to the range and nuance of the spoken word. There would have been little or no difficulty, for example, in following some of Shakespeare's more complex speeches. If there had been any problems of comprehension, he would not have written them in the way he did.

But there was a significant part of the audience derided by Jonson in *A Staple of News* as "Nut-crackers, that only come for sight." It is as well to remember the Elizabethan addiction to spectacle and to display. There is also Volumnia's advice to Coriolanus (1859–60) that

> Action is eloquence, and the eyes of th'ignorant
> More learned then the eares . . .

There has been much speculation about the relative importance of sight and hearing in the Elizabethan theatre, with the usual assumption that the more intelligent members of the audience listened while the others watched. Volumnia's words are those of a patrician, who may well have been hissed by the audience, and cannot be taken for Shakespeare's own thoughts on the matter. Indeed it is clear enough that in his later plays Shakespeare actually augmented the spectacle in his drama. He knew very well that it was an essential element of stage illusion, and an important contribution to the excitement and satisfaction of the playgoers. He never lost his desire to impress and to entertain. He never shared Jonson's low opinion of the popular theatre. Indeed he was in large part responsible for creating that theatre.

It seems likely, however, that there was no real distinction between sight and hearing as agents of understanding. The whole point of the drama is that it represented a mingling of both, a synaesthetic experience which in the words of one playgoer combined "*Ingeniousness* of the Speech" with "the *Gracefulness* of the *Action*."[5] The life of the drama consisted in character and movement.

The finances of the Globe were carefully reckoned before the venture began, and Peter Streete would have been asked to accommodate the largest possible audience. For the first performance of the new play, on the day of the Globe's opening, prices were doubled. But the general run of performances was at fixed prices. It has been calculated that between 1580 and 1642 playgoers made fifty million separate visits to the London theatres; the Globe became a thriving business from which all parties might do well. In any one year there would have been £1,500 to share among all the actors, giving them an approximate annual income of £70. In addition it has been estimated that the house-keepers at the Globe earned between them £280 per annum. On Shakespeare's death his one share in the Globe had an income of £25, therefore, while his share in the Blackfriars playhouse earned him £90.

There has been much speculation about Shakespeare's own income, deriving money as he did from his writing, his acting, his position as a "sharer" and his new status as "house-keeper" or part owner of the Globe. There have been differing estimates, perhaps set off by a notebook entry by John Ward in the early 1660s that the dramatist "had an allowance so large" that he "spent att the Rate of a 1000l. a year as I have heard."[6] This is surely a wild exaggeration. From the reckoning of all the sources of income, we reach a more likely figure of approximately £250 per annum. This was during a period when the average wage for a schoolmaster was £20, and for a journeyman labourer £8. In his will Shakespeare left bequests to the value of £350 and an estate worth £1,200. He was not spectacularly rich, as some have suggested, but he was very affluent.

CHAPTER 66

Sweete Smoke of Rhetorike

horoscope was consulted to determine the exact day for the opening of the Globe. The play chosen for that auspicious occasion
was *Julius Caesar* and, from allusions in the text itself, it is clear
that it was first performed on the afternoon of 12 June 1599. This was the day
of the summer solstice and the appearance of a new moon.[1] A new moon was
deemed by astrologers to be the most opportune time "to open a new
house."[2] There was a high tide at Southwark early that afternoon, which
helped to expedite the journey of the playgoers coming from the north of the
river. That evening, after sunset, Venus and Jupiter appeared in the sky.
These may seem to be matters of arcane calculation but to the actors and
playgoers of the late sixteenth century they were very significant indeed. It
has been demonstrated, for example, that the axis of the Globe is 48 degrees
east of true north, and so was in fact in direct alignment with the midsummer
sunrise. Astrological lore was a familiar and formative influence upon all the
affairs of daily life. It is also the context for the supernatural visitations and
prognostications in *Julius Caesar* itself.

There is other evidence of the play's summer opening. In June 1599 the
takings at Philip Henslowe's Rose, neighbour to the new Globe, registered
a sharp fall which must have been the result of new competition. It is a matter of record that Henslowe and the actor-manager Alleyn soon decided to
depart with the Admiral's Men from the Rose, and to resume acting at the

newly built Fortune in the northern suburbs. The proximity to the Lord Chamberlain's Men had been bad for business. Henslowe was too good a manager to lose an asset, however, and he leased out the Rose to Worcester's Men.

Julius Caesar was Shakespeare's first Roman play, attuned to the gaudy "classicism" of the Globe interior. A Roman setting, complete with marbled pillars, needed a Roman play. The stage-directions for *"thunder"* and for *"thunder and lightning"* also provided an opportunity to display the sound effects of the new theatre. Unlike the extravagant playhouse, however, the play itself is a triumph of simple diction and chaste rhetoric; it is as if Shakespeare had somehow been able to assume the Roman virtues and to adopt the Roman style. His deployment of forensic oratory is so skilled that it might have been composed by a classical rhetorician. He had the ability to blend himself with different states of man. In the very cadence and syntax of the words, he is Caesar. He exists within the formal periods of Brutus's prose and within the self-serving mellifluousness of Antony's verse.

The novelty of the new playhouse also aroused Shakespeare's ambitions, since in this play there is a more subtle sense of character, of motive, and of consequence. The emphasis is not so much upon event as upon personality. The action is so skilfully balanced that it becomes impossible to apportion praise or blame with any certainty. Is Brutus deluded or glorious? Is Caesar matchless or fundamentally flawed? Shakespeare seems almost deliberately to have established a new kind of protagonist, whose character is not immediately apparent or transparent to the audience. Shakespeare always finds it difficult to defend those things towards which he is most sympathetic, and in this particular play the distrust of the new is matched only by scepticism about the old. It is a play of oppositions and of contrasts in which there is no final resolution. In this same spirit it can be seen as a history play or as a revenge tragedy, or as both combined. It is a new kind of drama. He knows the sources, North's translation of Plutarch principal among them, but he changes their emphasis and direction. He invents Caesar's deafness, too, as well as the scene in which Brutus and his co-conspirators steep themselves in the murdered Caesar's blood. There were other Roman plays in the period, written by Shakespeare's contemporaries, but they were content to give the historical narratives a spectacular and theatrical decoration. Shakespeare goes to the heart of the matter.

· · ·

Ben Jonson resented its production, not least since it came from the pen of a man who had "little Latin." Jonson's play, *Every Man out of His Humour*, was performed later in the same year and within it are references to *Julius Caesar* which may be construed as playful or sarcastic. At one point the dying fall of "*Et tu, Brute!*" is satirised; this in itself is a clear indication that the original phrase was now known to playgoers. Among Shakespeare's audience in 1599 were two young men who knew very well the nature of betrayal. A letter of the period reveals that "my Lord Southampton and Lord Rutland come not to the Court . . . They pass away the tyme in London merely in going to plaies every day."[3]

There is a reference to *Julius Caesar* in *Henry V*, which was composed a few months after. There are also references in *Henry V* to the expedition by the Earl of Essex to Ireland that was rumoured to have failed by the summer of 1599 and ended in disgrace that autumn; so *Henry V* is likely to have been written before those dates. Whatever the question of date, however, the two plays are complementary. The English history is just as much an exercise in ambiguity, in opposition and contrast, as *Julius Caesar*; but it is screwed to an even higher pitch. Is Henry a bullying thug or a great leader of men? Is he made of valour or formed from ice and snow? Is he an image of authority or a figure fit for ridicule? The scenes of military prowess and achievement are framed by a comic plot that subtly deflates this heroic tale of success. The king's speech beginning "Once more vnto the Breach, deare friends . . ." (1038) is immediately succeeded by the braggart Bardolph's "On, on, on, on, on, to the breach . . ." (1073). The burlesque may not have been deliberate. Shakespeare did not have to stop and think about it. He did it naturally and instinctively. It was as inevitable as a pianist using both the black and the white keys.

On the character and motives of the king, black or white, it is possible that Shakespeare himself was not sure. But, clothed in the shimmering veil of Henry's rhetoric, they do not matter; Shakespeare was entranced by the idea of magnificence, and there is nothing like the exercise of power to create memorable lines and powerful scenes. Henry overbears judgement; he transcends or dissolves questions of morality. As William Hazlitt said in discussing *Coriolanus*, "the language of poetry is the language of power."[4] It is not of much consequence whether that power is nobly or ignobly used. The imagination itself is a form of power, and will incline towards any sympathetic object. That is why the presence of Henry, even in the comic scenes, is continually invoked. It is worth remarking, too, that the cadences of Henry's speech are uncannily similar to those of Richard III.

When Shakespeare follows Holinshed, his principal source, he runs the risk of tedium; when he follows his instincts, he is sublime. His "Muse of Fire" rises into the air, and his imagery is concerned with soaring. The long speeches are rich in texture and strident in delivery. There is one phrase, however, that has a more particular resonance. At one point the Chorus of the drama, generally performed by Shakespeare himself, beseeches the audience to sit and watch, "Minding true things, by what their Mock'ries bee" (1780). It is a true indication of Shakespeare's imaginative sensibility. Whereas most craftsmen judge the false according to their knowledge of the genuine, Shakespeare works the other way round.

Henry V is in fact the culmination of Shakespeare's preoccupation with kingship. Shakespeare invented the role of the player king. Certainly, more than any other dramatist before or since, he popularised the role of sovereign and managed infinitely to extend its range, while the imagery of the player king is unique to him. In his history plays, of course, the part of the monarch is the most significant and effective on the stage; but there are also Lear, Macbeth, Duncan, Claudius, Ferdinand, Cymbeline, Leontes and a host of noble rulers. He uses the word "crown" 380 times, and Edmond Malone commented perceptively that "when he means to represent any quality of the mind as eminently perfect, he furnishes the imaginary being whom he personifies, with a crown."[5] One of his abiding images is that of the king as sun and, in his dramaturgy, he loves what is stately and what is grand. He was concerned with tragic narratives only in so far as they were concerned with persons of high degree; tragedies of "low life," which were written in this period, held no interest for him. But kings appear in his comedies as well as in his tragedies. They may not always be portrayed in a flattering light, but nevertheless he evinces collaborative sympathy with them. It is notable that in his tragedies the person of highest rank speaks the last lines of the play, and in his later comedies it is always the king or principal nobleman who pronounces the verdict upon what might be called the final state of play. There is a prince in the concluding scene of thirteen out of his sixteen comedies.

It should not be forgotten that throughout his career he was a regular receiver of court favours and that in the latter part of his life he wore the royal livery as the king's true servant. There was of course a Renaissance tradition of the courtier as actor and, as John Donne wrote, "Plays were not so like Courts, as Courts are like plays."[6] In turn the tone and attitude of Shakespeare's sonnets prompted the late Victorian critic and biographer, Frank Harris, to describe him as a snob. That is not the correct description for a man of infinite sympathies. A writer who can create Mistress Quickly and Doll Tearsheet is not a snob. But he was possessed, or obsessed, by the inwardness of the ruler rather than the ruled. The role of monarch seems to spring naturally and instinctively from his imagination, and one close student of Shakespeare's imagery has pointed out "how continually he associates dreaming with kingship."[7] Did he enjoy fantasies and day-dreams of power? There is indeed a natural consonance between the player and the king, both dressed in robes of magnificence and both obliged to play a part. It may have been one reason why Shakespeare was attracted to the profession of acting in the first place.

Among his contemporaries he was well known for playing kingly parts upon the stage. In 1610 John Davies wrote a set of verses to "our English Terence, Mr. Will Shake-speare" in which he declared that

> Some say (good Will) which I, in sport, do sing,
> Had'st thou not plaid some Kingly parts in sport,
> Thou hadst bin a companion for a King.[8]

The assumption seems to be that his manners would have been gracious and "gentle" enough to enjoy high companionship, had it not been for the fact that he was an actor. In another poem the same author considered that "the *stage* doth staine pure gentle *bloud*." In *Measure for Measure* there is an implicit comparison between the powers of the playwright and the power of the ruler of Vienna, guiding and moving human affairs from a distance.

Shakespeare did indeed play "kingly parts." It is surmised that he played Henry VI in the trilogy of that name, and Richard II against Burbage's Bolingbroke. Long theatrical tradition maintains that he played the ghost of the dead king in *Hamlet*, and that he might have doubled as the usurping king. The assumption of these parts was no doubt the result of an instinctive grace and authority, deepened by the theatrical assumption of *gravitas*, but it may also be evidence of some natural predilection. He had a noble bearing and a graceful manner. Yet, somewhere within him, there is always the voice of Bardolph mocking the king.

He is unlikely to have played the king in *Henry V*. That role was reserved for Burbage. Shakespeare is much more likely to have taken on the part of the Chorus, addressing the playgoers as "Gentles all" and referring to "this Woodden O" of the Globe in which the action of the play is about to take place. It is an appropriate opening to be spoken by Shakespeare himself; he is, for example, alternately deferential and self-confident. The persona of this Chorus has often been compared with the persona of the sonnets, and there is indeed some resemblance in that powerful combination of enormous pride in creative achievement and personal self-abnegation. And so he paces upon the stage with sovereign words:

> A Kingdome for a Stage, Princes to Act
> And Monarchs to behold the swelling Scene.

If we accept the pattern of *Julius Caesar*, followed by *Henry* V, we may note in their composition the harbinger of Shakespeare's great tragedies.

CHAPTER 67

Well Bandied Both, a Set of Wit Well Played

f *the two comedies* written at this time, *Much Ado About Nothing* and *As You Like It*, the evidence suggests that *Much Ado About Nothing* was written first. It may indeed have been performed at the Curtain, with Will Kempe in the immortal role of Dogberry, before the Lord Chamberlain's Men removed to the Globe. Shakespeare's plays were being launched and performed even as the Globe was being constructed. *Much Ado About Nothing* remains one of Shakespeare's most popular plays, largely because of the wit combats of Beatrice and Benedick. "Let but Beatrice and Benedicke be seen," one versifier wrote in 1640, "the Cockpit, Galleries, Boxes are all full."[1] Theirs is a wit of high order, anticipating Congreve and Wilde, subtly shadowed by the farcical humour of Dogberry and his cohorts.

The entire play in fact provides a significant insight into the range and nature of Elizabethan comedy, consisting of fast repartee, complicated wordplay, extravagant conceits, endless sexual innuendo and what can only be described as a form of reckless melancholy. The Elizabethan age seems always to be on the edge of despair or dissolution, with the prospect of everything crashing down in flames; hence all the bravura and defiance of its major players.

The title of the play itself is indicative of its plot, in which the protagonists are led forward by a series of false reports and mistaken impressions. It has also a predictably bawdy significance since "nothing" was a slang word for the female genitals. It is a play of improbabilities and coincidences lovingly embraced by Shakespeare, who seems to have countenanced everything for the sake of theatrical effect. It resembles one of those light dances often mentioned in the text, the cinque pace or the Scotch jig, where the swiftness and the delicacy of the pattern are paramount. We may recall here the Elizabethan love of artifice for its own sake.

As You Like It was certainly performed at the Globe, not at the Curtain; Jaques's speech, beginning "All the world's a stage," makes reference to the motto of the Globe on the world as a player. Perhaps more importantly, the character of Touchstone was played by a relatively new recruit to the Lord Chamberlain's Men. The part was written for Robert Armin, comedian and musician, who was the replacement for Will Kempe. Kempe left the company at a point in 1599 with some ill-humour. It may have been suggested that his own brand of foolery would seem somewhat old-fashioned in the changed circumstances of the Globe, or he may have become disenchanted with the range of parts created for him. From various veiled references and allusions it seems that Shakespeare did not instinctively appreciate the type of humour in which Kempe himself was the star performer (and even, on occasions, writer). Kempe was too obstreperous and unpredictable; he insisted on making his personality central to his role. In turn Kempe may not have recognised the subtleties of Shakespeare's art, being more used to an earlier generation of the theatre where writers were mere hired hacks. They represented a clash of two cultures. In any case, in Kempe's own words, he "danced out of the world" or globe.

Whatever the circumstances of Kempe's departure, the Lord Chamberlain's Men decided to replace him with a new kind of comic player. Armin had begun the world as apprentice to a goldsmith in Lombard Street, but very quickly earned some kind of reputation as a dramatist and ballad writer. He wrote such popular plays as *The History of the Two Maids of More-clacke* and *A Nest of Ninnies*. Even if his principal career was as comic actor, he never gave up his profession as a writer; so he manifested some instinctive sympathy with Shakespeare that Kempe had lacked. He has even been described by one theatrical historian as an "intellectual."[2] Certainly he knew Latin and Italian. He became a member of Lord Chandos's Men, and must then have gained his reputation as a comic player or a natural wit. One of his publications was credited to "Clonnico de Curtanio Snuffe," which intimates that he was Snuff the clown at the Curtain, followed by a later edition in which he is described as "Clonnico del Mondo Snuffe"[3] or Snuff at the Globe itself. He was also known as Pink. There are two possibilities. He was already in the employment of the Lord Chamberlain's Men, and simply took over from Will Kempe. He certainly assumed the role of Dogberry at a later date, since he is described in one source as "his Constableship."[4] Or it may be that Armin was performing with Lord Chandos's Men at the Curtain, and replaced Kempe on his departure at the end of 1599.

It is worth remarking that Shakespeare started writing parts for "fools" only after Armin had joined the company. Since Armin was also known for his singing voice, Shakespeare wrote many songs for him. From Touchstone forward emerge the fools who break into song. It is a moot point whether Shakespeare fashioned his new "fools" in the image of Armin, or whether Armin's persona was fashioned by Shakespeare. No doubt both elements were at work in the creation of Touchstone and Feste, the Fool in *King Lear* and the gravedigger in *Hamlet*. With their mixture of melancholy and whimsicality, song and learning, mimicry and word-play, wit and proverb, satire and philosophy, they are of a distinctive and instantly recognisable type. Their costumes are motley, and their language is motley.

Armin had studied what were known as "natural fools" and with his instinctive skills in mimicry he had learned to imitate them; so he brought a self-consciousness or interiority to the role of clown that Kempe himself never provided. He did not "ad lib" or make impromptu jokes in the manner of his predecessor; he studied each role with care, and differentiated one from another. That was why he was important to Shakespeare's dramaturgy. Since Armin played the part of the foul-mouthed and pustular Thersites in *Troilus and Cressida*, it is clear enough that he could undertake what at a later date would be called "character parts." He may have played Casca in *Julius Caesar*, for example, and Caliban in *The Tempest*. This also makes a difference to the interpretation of Shakespeare's drama. It is sometimes supposed that Menenius in *Coriolanus* is the voice of good sense or worldly wisdom; but if he were played by Armin, as has been suggested, he would have become a grotesque.

So he first appears as Touchstone in *As You Like It*, proclaimed as "Nature's naturall." He does not wear the conventional russet outfit of the clown but instead the fool's costume of motley that included a long coat woven of green and yellow, an eared hood and a baton. For Armin Shakespeare invented the character of Touchstone, without relying upon his usual multifarious sources. He also gave Armin an extensive part, the third largest in the play, with 320 lines of dialogue. In the third act he sings snatches of a song, "Wind away, Be gone, I say," before he runs off the stage with Audrey. He probably doubled as Amiens–Armin/Amiens–with more lyrical ballads from the repertoire. There are in fact more songs in *As You Like It* than in any other Shakespearian play, and they are clearly related to the use of Armin as counter-tenor. When, a year later, Armin played the Clown in *Twelfth Night* he is given a significant compliment (1244–5):

> This fellow is wise enough to play the foole,
> And to do that well, craues a kinde of wit.

Given the enclosure riots of the period, and the general fear of those who lived in forests as "outlaws" and "robbers," it would have been relatively easy to turn *As You Like It* into a satirical portrait of greed and corruption; but he chose another path. By adopting the plot of Thomas Lodge's *Rosalynde*, he writes charming pastoral satire with the additional figures of Jaques and Touchstone to lend comic depth to the proceedings. He was a literate man who preferred romance to reality. The forest prompts the characters, not into rapine or violence, but into poetry and song. It is a haven for generosity of spirit and for melancholy musing, a place where love is celebrated and confirmed; it is a locale in which the audience witnesses the conversion of evil to good as well as supernatural visitations. The spell of enchantment is upon everything.

CHAPTER 68

Now. One the Better: Then. Another Best

✻

et it was in many respects a hard and disenchanted age. Satire was very much in the air. Given the macabre atmosphere around the declining queen, it could hardly fail to be so. The final stages of an *ancien régime* always provoke black humour. It was the age of Donne's satires and of such books as Lodge's *Wits Miserie and the Worlds Madness*.

On I June 1599 the Archbishop of Canterbury banned all satire in verse. The Privy Council ordered that the number of plays be restricted. But the new vogue for satire came directly to involve Shakespeare in what is known as the "Poets' War." Like all internecine conflicts its origins are uncertain, and have as a result been endlessly debated. We may trace a source or origin, however, in John Marston's association with the Middle Temple and with the choirboys of St. Paul's who performed dramas in their singing-school by the cathedral.

John Marston had acquired a reputation as a precocious satirist, especially of those older writers who had attained success or renown. One of his earliest productions, *The Metamorphosis of Pygmalion's Image*, was a burlesque upon *Venus and Adonis*. His satire at Shakespeare's expense, however, did not prevent him from borrowing or copying extensively from the work of the older dramatist. Marston is a familiar type. Shakespeare already knew him; as a member of the Middle Temple Marston's father had stood surety for Shakespeare's cousin, Thomas Greene, to become a member of that institution. For the members of the Middle Temple, in late 1598 or early 1599, Marston wrote a satirical play, *Histriomastix*, in which he glances unfavourably at both Shakespeare and Jonson.

Ben Jonson, never one to ignore or forgive an offence, then parodied Marston in *Every Man out of his Humour*. He had some reason to be sensitive. He had already been touched by Shakespeare. In *Henry V* the character of Nym continually repeats "That's the humour of it," a direct echo of Jonson's favourite theatrical device. In *As You Like It* the character of Jaques, melancholy and voluble in his "humorous sadness," has often been taken as a satirical if good-humoured presentation of Jonson himself.

Jonson was a less endearing humorist. In *Cynthia's Revels*, in 1600, he pilloried Marston as well as his play-writing colleague, Thomas Dekker; one was "a light, voluptuous reveller" and the other "a strange arrogating puff." In his next play, *The Poetaster*, he ridiculed Marston as a hack poet and plagiarist. Marston eventually counter-attacked with *What You Will*, in which Jonson was lampooned as an arrogant and insolent failure. In his aggressive manner Jonson then challenged Marston to a duel; since he was already branded on the thumb for murder, this was a foolhardy strategy. He probably guessed, however, that Marston would decline the challenge. Jonson then sought his man in the taverns of London, and found him. Marston pulled a pistol, whereupon Jonson took it from him and thrashed him with it. That is the story that went around London. Jonson repeated it later.

Dekker had already returned to the fray in *Satiromastix* in which Shakespeare is gently lampooned as the lecherous playwright Sir Adam Prickshaft but in which Jonson is more cruelly ridiculed as a failed court dramatist. The Lord Chamberlain's Men nevertheless agreed to perform Dekker's *Satiromastix*. At this point the literary feud ceased to be the "Poets' War" and became known as the "War of the Theatres."

The problem came with the boy-actors. Both Marston and Dekker had written their satirical and cynical plays for the Children of St. Paul's. The boys' companies had a long history, and in the early years of the reign of Elizabeth they were the dominant force in the London theatre. The rise of the public playhouses had somewhat dimmed their lustre but, in this era of satire in the late 1590s, they had returned to popularity. They performed a large number of "railing plays," and one contemporary condemned those "committing their bitternesse, and liberall invectives against all estates, to the mouthes of Children, supposing their juniority to be a priviledge for any rayling, be it never so violent."[1] The connection between boys and adult satire was an aspect of a larger tradition. It is in part the legacy of the boys' dramas written by John Lyly a generation before, which deployed a setting of classical history and legend. *Cynthia's Revels* and *Poetaster*, among other plays of the Poets' War, used similar classical settings. It is also likely that the connection of the boys' companies with court and Church, as well as their status as private companies, rendered them relatively immune to the usual condemnations of the civic authorities and the Privy Council. The experience of watching children playing adult parts was in any case quite a different thing. They could, as it were, mock adults in a different key. To be a boy, and to play an adult passion, is to throw that passion in sharper perspective. The emotion, or obsession, is more purely defined. In a theatrical culture which encouraged unreality and artifice, the mimicry of the boy-players was thus doubly attractive.

But why did the Lord Chamberlain's Men agree to perform Dekker's *Satiromastix* in which Ben Jonson is caricatured? The immediate cause is not hard to discern. Jonson had begun writing for the Children of the Chapel Royal at Blackfriars. He and the adult players may have been involved in some kind of quarrel or conflict in connection with their productions of *Every Man in His Humour* and *Every Man out of His Humour*. It is perhaps more likely that the Lord Chamberlain's Men had rejected a new play offered to them by Jonson. Had he expected *Cynthia's Revels* to be performed at the Globe? There was another irritant, however. The boys' companies readily asserted their "gentle" associations and the exclusiveness of the private theatres. The playwrights who wrote for them took some delight in mocking the "common players" of the public playhouses. And this is what Jonson did. In the plays he wrote for performance at Blackfriars he ridiculed the "common actors," "the decayed dead arras in a public theatre" and those who "will press forth on common stages." He also accused the actors of being "licentious, rogues, libertines, flat libertines."[2] The players of the Globe took their revenge.

It is even possible that Shakespeare wrote a scene for *Satiromastix* in which Horace, aka Jonson, comically labours over the composition of an ode. The author of the *Parnassus* trilogy refers to that "pestilent fellow," Ben Jonson, and to the fact that "our fellow Shakespeare hath giuen him a purge that made him beray his credit."[3] In a prologue later written for *Poetaster*, Jonson ruefully berated "some better natures" who had been persuaded to "run in that vile line." At the time, however, Jonson was not so sanguine. In *Poetaster* itself he had attacked the Globe for ribaldry and its actors for hypocrisy and stupidity. But one of them in particular is addressed as "proud": "You grow rich, do you, and purchase?"[4] The same actor is also mocked for his coat of arms, when it is made clear that his real pedigree is listed in the Statute of Rogues and Vagabonds that controlled the activities of players. It was in the autumn of 1599 that the Shakespeares had sought to impale their arms with those of the noble family of the Ardens.

Shakespeare did not reply directly. That was not his way. Instead he refers to the whole controversy in *Hamlet*, the play most notably established upon the devices of the theatre. Rosencrantz remarks to Hamlet that "there is Sir an ayrie of Children, little Yases [an eyas was a young hawk], that crye out on the top of question; and are most tyrannically clap't for't; these are now the fashion, and so be-ratle the common Stages (so they call them)" that as a consequence there was "for a while no mony bid for argument, vnlesse the Poet and the Player went to Cuffes in the Question" (1269–85). Hamlet's uncharacteristically reasonable response is that the boys should not disparage the "common players" when, at a later stage, they were likely to become them.

The whole controversy faded away, and soon enough the major antagonists were working together once more. It had elements of "ado" about "nothing," too, in the sense that Richard Burbage himself had leased the Blackfriars Playhouse to the Children of the Chapel Royal; the owner of the Globe was making money from his apparent rivals, and it is possible that the "war" was in part an advertising opportunity for the sake of attracting more custom. The nature of Elizabethan society in any case encouraged sudden "flares" followed by equally sudden reconciliations. The rumblings of the controversy, however, can still faintly be heard in *Twelfth Night* and *Troilus and Cressida*.

At the end of the century there was a positive rush of Shakespeare's plays to the printers, which is some indication of his prevailing popularity. In the autumn of 1599 there were new editions of *Romeo and Juliet* and of the first part of *Henry IV*; there was also another edition of *Venus and Adonis*, suggesting that his standing as a poet was still as high as that of playwright. At the beginning of 1600, in fact, a "staying entry" was placed in the Stationers' Register for "A booke called *Amours* by J.D. with certain *other sonnetes* by W.S." In the previous year, as we have seen, some of Shakespeare's sonnets had been pirated for a volume entitled *The Passionate Pilgrim*. It may have been that Shakespeare wanted his real work to be duly registered and noted.

The new edition of *Romeo and Juliet* was described as "Newly corrected, augmented and amended," while the new edition of *Henry IV* was described as being "Newly corrected by William Shake-speare." It may have simply been an advertising device, to persuade readers of the "newness" of the edition. In the same period the Admiral's Men, about to move into the recently built Fortune, were also advertising their wares by publishing the works they owned. The two companies, the Lord Chamberlain's Men and the Admiral's Men, had a virtual monopoly on play texts as well as on plays. But in the phrase "newly corrected" there is at least a suggestion that Shakespeare was actually revising and rewriting his plays ahead of publication. His name was in any case at a premium, and had gone beyond the usual bounds of the universities and the legal Inns. In the summer of 1600 *The Merchant of Venice*, *Henry V*, *Much Ado About Nothing* and *As You Like It* were placed in the Stationers' Register "to be stayed," so that the very latest plays would at least in theory soon become available. It certainly meant that the Lord Chamberlain's Men, no doubt including Shakespeare himself, were eager to safeguard what was becoming more valuable literary property. These entries were followed by *A Midsummer Night's Dream* and the second part of *Henry IV*, credited as being "written by master Shakspere." Curiously enough *Julius Caesar* was not registered at all. This might suggest that the play was less than successful on the public stage, but there is a more pertinent explanation. Towards the end of Elizabeth's reign it was not considered prudent or appropriate to publish a play in which a ruler is assassinated by his courtiers.

The number of Shakespeare's plays published through 1599 and 1600 also suggests that the printed versions were becoming a staple part of the city's literary currency, akin to pamphlets and to sermons. For a previous generation they had been catchpenny curiosities. Now they were regularly to be found on the bookstalls. Shakespeare was in the air. The Countess of Southampton was making playful allusions to Falstaff in the same year as verses were being written by admirers "Ad Gulielmum Shakespeare" in which he is praised as "honie-tongued."[5]

It was not an easy time, however, for the companies. In June 1600, the Privy Council limited playing time to two performances a week. The order did not preclude royal performances, of course, and the Lord Chamberlain's Men played twice before the queen during the Christmas season. They were, however, about to encounter royal disapproval.

CHAPTER 69

I Must Become a Borrower
of the Night

he official documents of the case tell their own story. "The Erle of Essex is charged with high Treason, namely, That he plotted and practised with the Pope and king of Spaine for the disposing and settling to himself Aswell the Crowne of England, as of the kingdome of Ireland." In one count of the indictment he was charged with "permitting of that most treasonous booke of Henry the fourth to be printed and published . . . also the Erle himself being so often present at the playing thereof, and with great applause giving countenance and lyking to the same."[1] The treasonous book was John Hayward's account of the abdication and murder of Richard II. The drama that the Earl of Essex greeted with great applause was Shakespeare's play of the same name. It would seem, therefore, that Shakespeare was somehow implicated in treason and conspiracy. Essex had planned an uprising on the streets of London that would be a prelude to the invasion of the court, ostensibly to protect the monarch from her advisers. Yet the main purpose of the rebellion was to protect Essex himself who, after his failure in Ireland, had been placed under house arrest and was fearful of even more serious consequences.

It is well enough known that Shakespeare was connected with the Essex "circle." His past and present associations with Southampton, with Lord Strange, with the Countess of Pembroke, with Samuel Daniel, with Sir John Harington, and with others, make this clear. But the events of early 1601 might have placed him in real jeopardy. The Earl of Essex believed himself to be the victim of manifold court plots organised by Sir Robert Cecil, and decided to strike first lest he be struck. So, together with such followers and supporters as the Earl of Southampton, he determined to seize the court itself. He would then free the queen of her advisers, and eventually secure the succession of James I. He had ill-advisedly believed that the populace of London would rise up and take sides with him when he declared his intentions. One way of alerting the populace was to stage a play at the Globe on the day before the insurrection.

On that day, Saturday 7 February 1601, some of Essex's supporters— among them Lord Monteagle, Sir Christopher Blount and Sir Charles Percy— dined at Gunter's eating house by the Temple. Lord Monteagle was a staunch Roman Catholic, but he was a loyalist who would later be instrumental in uncovering the "gunpowder plot"; Sir Christopher Blount had formerly been the Earl of Leicester's Master of Horse and was Essex's stepfather; Sir Charles Percy was the scion of a famous Catholic family from the North of England. After dinner they took a wherry across the Thames and walked into the Globe Theatre before the start of that afternoon's play. It was an especially commissioned performance. On the day before some of their number had visited the same theatre, "tellyng them [the players] that the play wold be of Harry the Fourth,"[2] the monarch who had deposed Richard II. In a later account of Essex's treason, written by Francis Bacon, the play is described as "the play of deposing King Richard the second";[3] in other words it contained the scenes of Richard's forced abdication that had not appeared in the printed version of the drama. The intention of Essex's supporters was clear enough. The power of the theatre could be used to justify their removal of Elizabeth. It could be used, too, to strengthen their resolve. Whatever the excuses and tergiversations of the Earl of Essex later, it was a clear case of "imagining" the sovereign's death.

One of the players, Augustine Phillips, later deposed that he "and hys fellows were determyned to have played some other play, holdyng that play of Kyng Richard to be so old & so long out of vse as that they shold have small or no Company at yt."[4] This was simply an excuse, born out of fear. *Love's Labour's Lost* and *The Comedy of Errors*, plays written before *Richard II*, were both performed at much later dates. At which point it seems that one of Essex's allies, Sir Gilly Meyrick, offered to pay 40 shillings for this uniquely commissioned production. The players acquiesced, and accepted the offer. In hindsight this was not a wise decision, since they could have been implicated in the charge of treason. They may have had no advance notice of Essex's plans and could have claimed that they innocently took part in the production; yet in the highly charged atmosphere of the time, when rumour and counter-rumour were flying about the city, this was highly unlikely. They were afraid. They could hardly have done it simply for the additional payment of 40 shillings. It is much more likely that they were bullied and ca-joled, perhaps even threatened, by these grandees. Note that the lords were reported "telling," not asking, the Lord Chamberlain's Men to perform that play. It is an indication of the ready professionalism of the players, however, that they were able to reproduce the play from memory after a long period in abeyance. *Richard II* had been written and played six years before and, al-though it had no doubt been revived in the interim, its reconstruction at such short notice is still a very remarkable achievement.

In the event Essex's uprising failed disastrously. The people did not rise to his banner, as he had hoped, and the earl (together with Southampton and other followers) was besieged in his house along the Strand. He surrendered, was tried and eventually executed. Southampton would have followed him to the block, but for the pleas of his mother to the queen. Instead the young no-bleman was indefinitely incarcerated in the Tower. Such was the fate of Eliz-abeth's enemies and false friends.

Of course the production of the play had not gone unnoticed by the au-thorities. Augustine Phillips, who seems to have been equivalent to the busi-ness manager of the company, was ordered to appear before an examining committee of three chief justices. There he explained the circumstances, and the payment of 40 shillings. It should be remembered that, four years before, the actors and writers of *The Isle of Dogs* had been summarily imprisoned and perhaps even tortured for performing a "seditious" play. On this hypo-thetically more dangerous occasion, however, the Lord Chamberlain's Men were relieved of any fine or penalty. They were effectively "let off" with perhaps a reprimand.

Many theatrical historians have puzzled over this lenity. But if the Lord Chamberlain's Men had indeed been threatened and cajoled by the plotters, the members of the committee may well have decided to exercise clemency. Tudor law is often regarded as inconsistent and draconian, but there was still a measure of fair play and common sense in its decisions. The players also had a reliable patron in the Lord Chamberlain, a loyal and trusted servant of the queen to whom he was also closely related. If they had been charged with treachery would not the shadow of suspicion, however unjustified, have fallen upon him also? That was unthinkable. Others have suggested that the good report of Francis Bacon, a friend of the players, saved the company. It is also evident that Elizabeth herself regarded the Lord Chamberlain's Men with particular favour–especially, perhaps primarily, because of their Shakespearian repertoire. So, by the grace of God and Her Majesty, Shakespeare and his fellows avoided the prison or even the gallows. In fact, a week after Phillips's interrogation, the Lord Chamberlain's Men were once more playing before the queen. On the day after that performance, Essex was beheaded.

CHAPTER 70

ᒥut ᕯ ᑬm in ᒥheir ᗷosomes

he affairs of Stratford also claimed Shakespeare's attention. For a moment his wife, Anne, re-enters the historical record in a minor role. The will of a neighbouring husbandman, Thomas Whittington of Shottery, left 40 shillings to the poor of Stratford "that is in the hand of Anne Shaxspere, wyf unto Mr. Wyllyam Shaxpere, and is due debt unto me."[1] It has been suggested that Anne Shakespeare had been forced to borrow money from Whittington, whom she had known since childhood, because her husband was not maintaining her in proper fashion. This is most unlikely. She was ensconced in New Place, one of the most valuable properties in the town, and it would have been a disgrace to the name and reputation of the whole Shakespeare family if she had not been given the means both for its upkeep and for her standing in the town. All the evidence suggests that Shakespeare, far from being a negligent or parsimonious husband, regularly sent relatively large sums of money to his family. What other way would there have been of maintaining appearances, one of the essential characteristics of a sixteenth-century gentleman? The will in fact means only that Anne Shakespeare owed Whittington 40 shillings in a technical sense; it is likely that he gave the sum to her for safe-keeping, confirming the impression of her as a reliable and trustworthy housekeeper.

There is one small episode of the period that also merits attention. At a slightly later date William Shakespeare sued a Stratford apothecary, Philip

Rogers, for non-payment upon a consignment of malt. He had sold 20 bushels, at a price of 38 shillings, and then lent Rogers a further 2 shillings. Rogers himself had repaid only 6 shillings of the total amount, and so Shakespeare went to court for the remainder with a further demand for 10 shillings in damages. Nothing more is known of the case, and so it is likely that Rogers made reparations. It testifies, if nothing else, to Shakespeare's strong sense of financial justice. It also suggests that Anne Shakespeare, in charge of domestic arrangements, ran something of a small household business in Stratford itself.

There were in fact alarms and excursions in the town which find a strange reflection in the drama that Shakespeare was about to compose. At the beginning of 1601 the lord of the manor of Stratford, Sir Edward Greville, had challenged the rights of the borough by enclosing some common land. Six of the town's aldermen, among them Shakespeare's acquaintance Richard Quiney, then levelled the hedges that marked the enclosures; whereupon Greville accused them of riot. Quiney and Shakespeare's cousin, Thomas Greene, travelled to London to enlist the advice and assistance of the Attorney General; among those who had signed a statement concerning the town's rights was John Shakespeare. But no immediate aid was forthcoming. Quiney was elected bailiff that autumn, against the wishes of Greville, and the whole affair turned into an aggressive confrontation between the two parties. There are reports of "minaces" and of "braweling,"[2] and in the spring of 1602 Quiney was attacked in an affray and wounded. He died soon after. It is a nasty story of rivalries between the local people and the avaricious lord. It has its counterparts in other country towns where the problem of enclosures had arisen, but in this case it implicated people well known to Shakespeare. It is not stretching credulity too far to see something of this local drama in the plot of *Coriolanus*, whereby the tribunes of the people are matched against a haughty and domineering patrician.[3] Yet, even here, it is impossible to say that Shakespeare takes "sides." He needed this detachment from the events around him in order to invest so much energy in his imagined drama.

CHAPTER 71

And So in Spite of Death Thou Doest Suruiue

꙳

On 8 September 1601, John Shakespeare was buried in the old church at Stratford. His son was undoubtedly present, and walked in procession with the new bailiff Richard Quiney. John Shakespeare was in his seventies but seems to have left no will. By natural right, therefore, Shakespeare inherited the double-house in Henley Street as well as agricultural land belonging to his father. John Shakespeare was in fact more prosperous than is generally assumed. He may have characterised himself as a man of small wealth in the Westminster courts, but the reality was very different. In the following year, Shakespeare began to invest a great deal of money amounting to approximately £500.

He kept the house, where his widowed mother continued to live in the company of her daughter, Joan Hart, and her daughter's family. Joan Hart had married a local hatter, William Hart, but remained in the family dwelling to look after her mother. Shakespeare seems to have left his mother's affairs in her hands, since the Harts looked after Mary Shakespeare's estate upon her death seven years later.

The death of John Shakespeare himself has been considered a defining event in his son's progress. It has been characteristically associated with the writing of *Hamlet*, for example, a play that was composed during the obligatory period of mourning. In the first scene the ghost of Hamlet's father comes back from the flames of purgatory, a wholly Catholic territory, in order to haunt the earth. The available evidence supports the belief that Shakespeare himself played the part of the dead father. It is a suggestive impersonation, adding to the fact that the title of the play invokes the name of his own dead son. In this period fathers and sons are deeply implicated in the workings of his imagination. In this play, too, the inheritance from father to son is riven and brutally distracted. It is also Shakespeare's longest play, and it has been calculated to require a playing time of four and a half hours—far too long to be performed entire in the sixteenth century, even if the playing time were stretched to the maximum. It suggests that he wished, or was determined, to include all its connections and associations. We must not use the anachronistic vocabulary of obsession or compulsion in this matter. We can only say, with certainty, that there was much for Shakespeare to dramatise.

Richard Burbage played the titular hero. It was a part in which he could excel, and proves to an almost excessive degree that the art of Elizabethan drama was the art of character. There is an allusion to Burbage's acting of Hamlet in a poem of 1604, which describes how the apparent madness of the prince was signified by Burbage sucking on a pen as if it were a tobacco pipe and drinking from an inkpot as if it were a bottle of ale. It seems to have been a memorable piece of stage "business." If we were to provide a Jingle-like anatomy of Hamlet's changing passions, however, it would read something like this. In turn Hamlet displays himself as ironic, sincere, obedient, despairing, disgusted, welcoming, questioning, disgusted, speculative, impetuous, angry, scholarly, antic, jocular, actorish, despairing, of mimic disposition, sarcastic, welcoming, speculative, despairing, exuberant, self-punishing, changeable (very), confused, contemptuous, actorish, courteous, playful, threatening, hesitant, fierce, scornful, rhetorical, bewildered, soul-searching, macabre, furious, mocking, stoical, parodic, and resigned. It has become well known as a part to challenge actors; to play it competently, by general consent, they have to drag into the light parts of their personality they thought they had lost.

Shakespeare was known to be the master of soliloquy long before *Hamlet*—it was one of his "strengths" that could be called upon in patching up a play such as *Sir Thomas More*—but in this play he refines his art to the extent that the soliloquy seems to become the index of evolving consciousness. It is no longer a summary of "this is what I am" but, rather, of "this is what I am becoming." It has been remarked that, in the same period, the growth of literacy was leading to a great extension of letters and private diaries; writing itself encouraged "introspection and reflection."[1] This throws new light on the often noticed allusions to books in *Hamlet*.

But can we speak of interiority on the Elizabethan stage, where a whole set of theatrical conventions determined staging and acting? It is perhaps with *Hamlet* that it first becomes possible to do so. For the first time it is not anachronistic to discuss the "character" of Hamlet even if it remains utterly mysterious, not least to Hamlet himself. Julius Caesar and Henry V live in a world of circumstance and event; they are lodged, as it were, in a real world. Hamlet's reality, in contrast, is almost entirely self-created. His soliloquies often have a dubious relation to the action of the plot, which is why they can be added or removed in the various versions of the play without any noticeable interruption to the story. Nevertheless Hamlet remains the very pivot of the narrative. Like his creator, his centre is nowhere and his circumference is everywhere.

Hamlet has no reason to exist except as a projection from Shakespeare. He is a master of every mood and subject to none. He is possessed by an extraordinary mental agility and energy. He has many voices, but it is hard to locate any central or defining voice. No one is so free with words and yet so secretive about himself. He is addicted to puns and to word-play, but his obscenities are matched by what Sigmund Freud called his "sexual coldness."[2] The play is invaded by the theme of duality and doubleness, of appearing to be what you are not. That is why it is also suffused with the spirit of playing. It is not too much to say that *Hamlet* could only have been written by a consummate actor.

It soon became one of Shakespeare's most celebrated dramas. It seems to have the singular distinction of being the only play performed, during Shakespeare's lifetime, at both the universities of Oxford and Cambridge. This was a sea-change in the academic response to contemporary vernacular drama. Before this period plays in English were considered to be below serious consideration. Sir Thomas Bodley banned plays from his new library at Oxford, stating that they were "of very unworthy matters" and that the keeper and underkeepers of the library "should Disdain to seek out . . . Haply some Plays may be worthy the Keeping: But hardly one in Forty."[3] He was probably correct about the proportion, but *Hamlet* itself was certainly considered to be "worthy." There is a reference in 1604, stating that "faith, it should please all, like Prince Hamlet."[4] Three years later, it was performed off the coast of Sierra Leone by a group of seamen. *Hamlet* was referred to in private, and diplomatic, correspondence. The young John Marston paid the ultimate compliment of copying from it with a remarkably similar revenge tragedy entitled *Antonio's Revenge*. It has in fact been suggested that the order of composition should be reversed, and that Shakespeare copied Marston's play. There is no reason why he should not have been inspired by an ingenious original to produce a compelling masterpiece of his own. He had been doing it all his life.

Yet the origins of *Hamlet* are much more complicated than that. There was a true and "original" *Hamlet* on the public stage by 1589, since it is mentioned by Nashe in that year. There was also a version of *Hamlet* being performed by the combined forces of the Lord Chamberlain's Men and the Admiral's Men in the summer of 1594 at Newington Butts; this production is confirmed by the notes of Philip Henslowe. At some point between 1598 and 1601, the remark being privately transcribed in a book, Gabriel Harvey referred to Shakespeare and "his tragedie of Hamlet, Prince of Denmarke."⁵

The complex matter is further complicated by the presence of a printed version of the play, issued in quarto form in 1603. It has generally been described as a "bad" quarto, but at a length of 2,500 lines it is in fact a perfectly good acting version of the long drama marred by stylistic infelicities. The publishers, Nicholas Ling and John Trundell, had known associations with Shakespeare's plays and with the Lord Chamberlain's Men, so there is no question of its being a "pirated" edition. On the title page it is described as "By William Shake-speare."

A second edition was published in the following year and, with twelve hundred extra lines, was advertised as "newly imprinted and enlarged" according to "the true and perfect copy." In the first version Hamlet is younger, and some of the names are different; Polonius, for example, is called Corambis. More importantly, perhaps, in the first version Gertrude becomes convinced of her second husband's guilt and colludes with her son. The first and shorter drama is an exhilarating and exciting piece of work, in no way inferior as a stage production to the second version. The second version is more rhetorical and deliberate, with much greater attention paid to the text itself.

The most likely explanation for these different versions seems to be that Shakespeare took an old play of *Hamlet* and fashioned it into new and surprising shape for the performance at Newington Butts in 1594. This is the version printed as the first quarto. Then, at a later stage, he revised it for a new production at the Globe in 1601. This is the second quarto. It should be noted that Shakespeare then seems to have revised *Hamlet* for a third time, adding and subtracting material for a version that became the Folio edition of the play published in 1623.

The purists insist that the less than perfect text of *Hamlet* is "corrupted" by actors' reports or faulty shorthand reporting; and that the second edition was Shakespeare's attempt to supplant a botched job. Other scholars believe that the first text was a version of Shakespeare's early work, hasty and jejune as it may sometimes be, and that the second version is evidence of Shakespeare's habit of revision. One image is of Shakespeare as perfectionist, producing more or less the orthodox canon of the plays as printed in "good" quartos. The other image is of Shakespeare in a continuous state of evolution, moving between early versions and revised versions, short versions and long versions. The latter alternative seems more plausible.

There is one other piece of literature that emerged in 1601. Attached to a volume celebrating "the love and merit of the true-noble knight, Sir John Salisburie" were sets of verses written by "the beste and chiefest of our moderne writers." Sir John Salisbury had been knighted in the summer of 1601 for his services in helping to suppress the Essex rebellion. Among these verses was Shakespeare's poem now known as "The Phoenix and Turtle," as complex and as riddling a piece of work as anything to be found in *Hamlet*. On a mundane level Shakespeare may have been happy to disassociate himself from the Essex episode, in which *Richard II* had been so unfortunately imbroiled. But it is also possible that the poem had originally been written in 1586 when Salisbury had married Ursula Stanley, half-sister to Lord Strange.

But the poem itself rises above its immediate circumstances. It is a threnody upon the indivisibility of lovers and the divine union of love:

> Beautie, Truth, and Raritie,
> Grace in all simplicitie,
> Here enclosde, in cinders lie.

It has been treated as an allegorical work or, in more modern terms, as an exercise in "pure" poetry rising unbidden and entire from the depths of Shakespeare's being, a pearl of great price fashioned instinctively by experience and suffering. In its riddling complexity it bears more than a passing resemblance to the contemporaneous poetry of John Donne. Although Shakespeare sometimes seems more inclined to poetical miscellanies and ancient English ballads, there is no reason why he should not have heard or read Donne's poetry in manuscript. Donne was known to the Countess of Pembroke. He had been a member of Lincoln's Inn and had also served with the Earl of Essex; he can be said to have moved in the same London circles as Shakespeare himself. This was also the milieu in which Donne's poems were circulating in manuscript, and there seem to be echoes of his work both in *King Lear* and in *Two Noble Kinsmen*. There are connections between the personages of Shakespeare's world that are now lost to view.

CHAPTER 72

I Am (Quoth He) Expected of My Friends

fter the death of his father Shakespeare's visits to Stratford, in order to see his widowed mother as well as his wife and family, are likely to have become more frequent. It was a slow process of readjustment, or reorientation, that would finally result in his living for long periods of time in his home town. It represents the return of the native, one of the most characteristic passages of human experience. In his later plays, too, Shakespeare celebrates the reunification of families and the reconciliation of old differences. There is one other additional fact to add to this homecoming, which is to be found in Oxford.

The association with Shakespeare and Oxford is not well understood—there are somewhat implausible suggestions that he used the Bodleian Library that was established in 1602—but it is clear enough that he habitually stopped at Oxford on his journeys between London and Stratford. We know this from three separate sources. One was a diary kept by an Oxford antiquary, Thomas Hearne, in which he states that Shakespeare "always spent some time at the Crown tavern in Oxford kept by one Davenant." Thirty years later Alexander Pope, who could not have known of Hearne's diary, has the same story to the effect that

Shakespeare often baited at the Crown Inn or Tavern in Oxford, in his journey to and from London. The landlady was a woman of great beauty

and sprightly wit; and her husband, Mr. John Davenant, (afterwards
mayor of that city) a grave melancholy man, who as well as his wife used
much to delight in Shakespeare's pleasant company.[1]

Aubrey completes the story with the note that "Shakespeare did comonly in
his journey lye at this house in Oxon: where he was exceedingly respected."[2]

John and Jennet Davenant were a London couple–Davenant was a wine-
importer living in Maiden Lane–who had somehow become acquainted with
Shakespeare. One contemporary stated that Davenant was "an admirer and
lover of plays and play-makers, especially Shakespeare."[3] In 1601, after six of
their children had died at birth or in early infancy, they decided to move to
the healthier atmosphere of Oxford. Here they managed a tavern, then
known simply as the Tavern, a four-storeyed building on the east side of
Cornmarket. It was not an inn, which could take in travellers, but a place for
convivial drinking. If Shakespeare did indeed stay with the Davenants, as
seems very likely, he would have done so as a guest rather than a customer.
The air seems to have been beneficial, and the Davenants acquired a family
of seven healthy children. Their first-born son, Robert, recalls Shakespeare
covering him with "a hundred kisses."[4] Their second son William, apparently
named after Shakespeare and the dramatist's godson, has left a more equivocal story.

Hearne and Pope both confirm that William Davenant claimed to be
Shakespeare's illegitimate son as well as his godson. As Hearne notes in a
bracket, "In all probability he [Shakespeare] got him." They both retold the
story of how the boy was once asked by an elderly townsman why he was
running home; he replied "to see my godfather Shakespeare." To which the
old gentleman replied, "That's a good boy, but have a care that you don't take
God's name in vain."[5]

The story was no doubt apocryphal, and had in fact been applied to
others beside Shakespeare, but at the time it reinforced the general belief that
the dramatist was something of a philanderer. William Davenant, in later
life, did nothing to dispel the rumour that he was Shakespeare's illegitimate
son: he continued to advertise the fact with pride. As Aubrey noted, "that notion of Sir William's being more than a poetical child only of Shakespeare
was common in town."[6] Since William Davenant was himself a poet and
playwright, he may have had some slight excuse for defaming his mother and
claiming such distinguished parentage. He did indeed serve Shakespeare
well. He himself revised *Macbeth* and *The Tempest*, with the assistance of

John Dryden, and helped to maintain the continuity of Shakespearian drama; he was also instrumental in the revival of nine plays after the restoration of the monarchy in 1660.

Murals from the sixteenth century have been uncovered at the Crown, one of them with the monogram of "IHS" which is the characteristic Catholic sign of Christ. William Davenant himself was in later life a Catholic and a Royalist. So Shakespeare stayed in congenial company. Davenant was also said to have a semblance of Shakespeare's "open Countenance" but the resemblance could not have been exact; he had lost his nose as a result of mercury treatment for syphilis. As a contemporary noted, "the want of a Nose gives an odd Cast to the Face."[7] Certainly he inherited nothing of Shakespeare's genius.

It is interesting to speculate, however, about the physical appearance of Shakespeare then in his mid-forties. The slimness, if not the sprightliness, of youth had long gone. He had been a handsome and well-shaped man, according to Aubrey's report, but by now he must have become a little portly. It is not inconceivable that he actually became rather fat. His auburn or chestnut hair had withered on the vine, and it is likely that his cranium was already as bare as it appears in the Droeshout engraving which decorates the frontispiece of the Folio. From that engraving, too, we gain some acquaintance with his full lips, his straight and sensitive nose, his watchful eyes. The beard he sported in his earlier life has gone, leaving behind a small moustache. A professional phrenologist has concluded, from the shape of the head, that the dramatist was possessed of "ideality, wonder, wit, imitation, benevolence, and veneration" with "small destructiveness and acquisitiveness." His cranium also evinces "great susceptibility, activity, quickness and love of action."[8]

There is no doubt that he would have dressed well; his neatness and general cleanliness are well attested from his work. The standard dress of an Elizabethan gentleman included a bejewelled and quilted silk doublet, with a ruff for formal occasions; the doublet was covered with a jerkin, manufactured perhaps of fine leather or costly cloth. He wore breeches, an Elizabethan form of short trousers, that were fastened at the doublet and tied at the knees. The codpiece, plumped up by stiff packing, was out of favour by the end of the century. The shirt beneath his doublet was of cambric or of lawn. It could be tied or worn open at the front; in some apocryphal portraits of Shakespeare the wide collars of the shirt are draped over the doublet. The tail of the shirt was used as a form of underwear. He sported silk stockings and variously coloured leather "pumps" or shoes, with heels and soles of cork. He owned a cloak, reaching anywhere from the waist to the ankles and characteristically worn over one shoulder. And he carried a sword, as the mark of a gentleman. He had a tall hat; the higher the hat, the higher the social status. Dress was an essential aspect of late Tudor society. As one instructor on the art of being a gentleman put it, "The sum of a hundred pounde is not to be accompted much in these dayes to be bestowed of apparell for one gentleman."[9] There is no reason to believe that Shakespeare was strident or ostentatious in his dress—far from it—but he would have been as elegant as the best of his contemporaries.

The Droeshout image, approved by Shakespeare's colleagues after the playwright's death as a fitting accompaniment to the collected edition of the plays, is perhaps the closest to a true resemblance. Martin Droeshout could not have been working from life, since he was only fifteen at the time of Shakespeare's death. But he was part of a dynasty of Flemish artists living in London. His father, Michael Droeshout, had been an engraver and his uncle, Martin Droeshout, was a painter. It is possible, then, that the younger Martin Droeshout based his engraving upon an earlier likeness now lost. It is also relatively close to the image adorning the monument above Shakespeare's tomb in the church at Stratford. That bust shows Shakespeare with a beard, which suggests that he grew it or shaved it according to mood.

The sculpture has been described by one Shakespearian as resembling that of "a self-satisfied pork butcher."[10] That it is a good likeness is not in doubt, however, because an early chronicler of Shakespeare's Stratford believed that "the head was evidently taken from a death-mask."[11] It must have been acceptable to Shakespeare's immediate family, who commissioned it. It was executed by Gerard Johnson, a Dutch artist who lived near the Globe in Southwark. He had ample opportunity, therefore, to study his subject. There is no reason why a great writer should not resemble a pork butcher, satisfied or otherwise, and it is at least ironic that later accounts did make him a butcher's apprentice. He may have possessed that corpulent and ruddy glow that seems to be peculiar to English butchers. And why should he not look satisfied?

There are other portraits which claim some attention from posterity, if only because the quest for Shakespeare's face is an unending one. They all provide varying degrees of resemblance. One painting, now known as the "Chandos portrait" (*c*.1610), depicts a man in his early forties wearing a black silk doublet; he is of muddy or swarthy complexion, and his black curls lend him a gypsy or continental appearance. He is also wearing a gold earring. It was once suggested, half in earnest, that it was a portrait of Shakespeare dressed to play Shylock. The painting itself has a long and complicated history, which is as much as to say that its provenance is uncertain.

A more refined and noble image presents itself in the painting known as the "Janssen portrait" (*c*.1620), in which a sensitive face surmounts an exquisite doublet. The "Felton portrait" (*c*. eighteenth century) is executed on a small wood panel, and displays a man in his thirties with an enormous forehead but no other distinguished or distinguishing characteristics. The "Flower portrait" is close to the Droeshout engraving, and has led some scholars to believe that it is in fact the lost original for the Folio engraving; it is dated 1609, and has been painted on top of a Madonna of the fifteenth century. But there have been arguments over the authenticity of the dating. And so the matter rests. All of these paintings have a family resemblance, but all of them may be derived from Droeshout.

The one notable exception would seem to be the Grafton portrait (*c*. 1588), which has already been described in the context of Shakespeare's own life. It shows a young and fashionably dressed man in his early twenties, and was previously dismissed on the grounds that the young Shakespeare could not have been so affluent at such an early stage of his career. That is no longer a reasonable supposition, as we have seen, and so the merits of the painting can be taken on their own. If it is placed next to the Droeshout engraving, a consonance of youth and middle age begins to emerge. All of these representations, hovering in the realm of uncertainty and conjecture, resemble Shakespeare in more than a pictographic sense; they are a token of his elusiveness in the world. They also suggest that the appearance of the man may have been quite different from any mental or cultural image of Shakespeare that currently exists. He may have been swarthy. He may have worn an earring. He may in later life even have been fat.

CHAPTER 73

My Lord This Is But the Play. Theyre But in Jest

❧

e can see him in another sense. On 2 February 1602, he walked from the landing-stage by the Thames a few yards northwards to the hall of the Middle Temple. It was here that a new play, *Twelfth Night*, was to be performed by the Lord Chamberlain's Men in front of the members of that Inn. There is an account of it by one of them, John Manningham, in his diary. "At our feast wee had a play called 'Twelue Night, or what you will' much like the commedy of errores, or Menechmi in Plautus, but most like and neere to that in Italian called *Inganni*."[1] He then goes on to describe the gulling of Malvolio. It is a brief but interesting entry, revealing the game of source-hunting to be an old one. It might even lead to the speculation that Shakespeare expected the sources of his plays to be known to the more knowledgeable among the audience, and that his departure from such sources was part of the drama's effect.

The work to which Manningham refers is *Gl'Inganni* by Curzio Gonzaga, an Italian play that had not been translated into English. It is likely, then, that Shakespeare had some knowledge of Italian. He had a professional attitude towards reading, and probably never opened a book without hoping to extract something from it. In any case Shakespeare always departed from his sources when he deemed it necessary to do so, elaborating them and pushing them further into romance and fantastic improbability.

The fact that Manningham compared *Twelfth Night* to *The Comedy of*

Errors suggests that there were playgoers who were familiar with a number of Shakespeare's plays; this, in itself, is a serious measure of his reputation. But they may not have been in the majority. The audience in the hall of the Middle Temple was presumably rowdy and quite possibly drunken. If they wished for bawdy humour and broad farce, then *Twelfth Night* would have satisfied them. It took its name from the "Twelfth Day" festivals that were well known for their riotousness, and it had an effervescent mood of continual gaiety that did not dip once. The story of Sir Toby Belch and Sir Andrew Aguecheek, of Malvolio and Feste, was awash with innuendo and suggestion. The fact that Viola dressed as a boy, while being acted by a boy, added an element of sexual *frisson* that would not have been lost upon the members of the Inn. It may be that the convention of boys playing female roles was in fact the context for obscenity and suggestion that do not appear in the written texts. The language of the wooing scenes was in any case erotically charged, and might well have been complemented by "wanton" gestures. The layers of strange multisexual loving delighted Shakespeare.

There are also numerous legal puns and quibbles in *Twelfth Night* that would have found responsive hearers. A literal interpretation of the title, of course, would imply that it had first been performed on the afternoon of 6 January 1602. So it is unlikely that the performance in the Middle Temple was the first. It would have suited the Globe, and there are remarkably few stage-properties to be accommodated.

It can be assumed that Armin played Feste, and as a result Feste is given four songs, three of which have entered the national repertoire—"O Mistris mine where are you roming?," "Come away, come away death," and "When that I was and a little tine boy." *Twelfth Night* is suffused with music. It begins and ends in music. Shakespeare has used the advent of Armin, and perhaps the acoustic resources of the Globe, to explore a new range of theatrical effect. It is more than possible that the dramatist himself played Malvolio; as has already been suggested, Malvolio's crossed yellow garters may have been a farcical version of Shakespeare's own coat of arms.[2] There are many topical allusions in *Twelfth Night*, but one of the most prominent must surely concern the scenes between Feste and Malvolio. Feste represents the spirit of festival and entertainment, for example, whereas the rancorous Malvolio is described as a Puritan. Their conflict represents one of the oldest and most divisive controversies of the period, with the Puritan faction ranged against plays and playhouses as agents of the devil.

The Puritans opposed the playhouses on a number of levels. Playhouses competed with the pulpits in the matter of public instruction or, as one moralist put it, "the Playe houses are pestered when the churches are naked."[3] The dramas were considered to be the entertainment of idle people, gapers and lookers-on who ought to be more profitably employed in the afternoons. The actors were deemed to encourage ready emotionalism; they relied upon sexuality and sexual innuendo, especially with the pretty boys dressed as girls who excited lascivious passions; they were subversive of hierarchies, dressed as princes in one scene and as commoners in the next. They were in any case acting, counterfeiting God's image; it was a form of primitive idolatry, that only papists could enjoy.

It is also possible to go from the general to the particular. It has been suggested that Malvolio was based upon a "real" original, one Sir William Knollys, the Comptroller of the Royal Household, but all such allusions have long since been lost. Yet there can be no doubt that Shakespeare often had certain contemporaries in mind, when inventing characters, and that the actors deliberately impersonated them in their parts. He never knowingly neglected a source of amusement for the London crowd.

That popular success meant that he had become a relatively affluent man. It may be that his purse had been enlarged by his father's recent death but, whatever the source of his funds, he paid the large amount of £320 for more Stratford land. On 1 May 1602, he purchased from John and William Combe 107 acres of arable land and 20 acres of pasture in the hamlets of Bishopstone and Welcombe. He knew the Combes very well, and he knew the land in question very well. He was now, in the words of his Hamlet, "spacious in the possession of durt" (3356–7). It is doubtful whether he took so ironical an attitude towards his own property. Three years later he purchased even more land. Earlier in *Hamlet* he betrays his interest in the subject, when the prince of Denmark holds up a skull, and remarks that "this fellowe might be in's time a great buyer of Land, with his Statuts, his recognisances, his fines, his double vouchers, his recoueries" (3072–4). The buying of land in the late sixteenth century was indeed a tiresome and complex business; it was natural for Shakespeare to express his frustration, even through the mouth of the melancholy Dane. In the autumn of 1602 he also bought a plot of half an acre of land, with a cottage and cottage garden, in Chapel Lane just behind his grand house of New Place. The cottage may have been intended for a servant and family, or even for a gardener. Or could it possibly have been a place in which he might seclude himself?

He was clearly aiming for local respectability as well as prosperity. The corporation of Stratford, however, were not necessarily sympathetic to the sources of his wealth. At the end of this year they formally forbade the performance of plays or interludes in the guildhall. It was a manifestation of the regional Puritanism that affected other districts of the country. The fact that he began to spend more time, and money, in Stratford suggests that he was not much concerned about such matters. His life as dramatist, and his life as townsman, were separate and not to be confused.

Part VIII
The King's Men

MISCHEEFES MYSTERIE:
OR,
Treasons Master-peece,
The Powder-plot.

Inuented by hellish Malice, preuented by heauenly
Mercy : truely related.

And from the Latine of the learned and reuerend Doctour
HERRING *tranflated, and very much dilated.*

By IOHN VICARS.

James I depicted on the title page of *Mischeefes Mysterie
or Treasons Master-peece, the Powder-plot*. Shakespeare's *Macbeth*
was written during the aftermath of the attempt by
Robert Catesby with Guy Fawkes and other conspirators
to blow up king and parliament.

$\mathcal{H}$ee $\mathcal{I}$s $\mathcal{S}$omething $\mathcal{P}$eeuish $\mathcal{T}$hat $\mathcal{W}$ay

*S*hakespeare *was on stage* when the Lord Chamberlain's Men played their last parts before the ageing queen. They performed at White-hall on 26 December 1602 and at Richmond on 7 February 1603. Six weeks later Elizabeth was dead, worn out by age and power. In the last stages of her life she had refused to lie down and rest but had stood for days, her finger in her mouth, pondering upon the fate of sovereigns. The theatres had been closed five days before her death, since plays were not appropriate in the dying time.

By many, including the imprisoned Southampton, she was considered to be a tyrant who had exercised power for too long. Shakespeare was at the time criticised for writing no encomium on the dead queen–not one "sable teare" dropped from his "honied muse" as part of the national exequies. He had been asked to sing the "Rape" of Elizabeth "done by that Tarquin, Death,"[1] with reference to his earlier *Rape of Lucrece*, but he declined the honour. There was a ballad of the moment exhorting "you poets all"[2] to lament the queen. Shakespeare was at the head of the list of the poets in-voked, among them Ben Jonson, but he made no response. In truth he had no real reason to mourn the queen's passing. She had beheaded Essex and several members of Essex's affinity whom Shakespeare knew very well.

Yet he was not altogether silent. He did produce in this period one work that cogently reflects the somewhat rancid and fearful atmosphere at the court of the dying queen. It was not an exequy, but a play entitled *Troilus and Cressida* in which all the certainties and pieties of court life are treated as material for jest and black humour. It has been surmised that the failure of the Essex rebellion in 1601 helped to create the atmosphere of gloom and discomfiture that pervades the play. It has even been suggested that there are allusions to the Earl of Essex within the text, where he is to be seen as Achilles skulking in his tent. There have been traced parallels among the other Greeks with various members of Elizabeth's *ancien régime* such as Cecil and Walsingham—but one hypocritical and self-serving courtier looks very much like another.

It is unlikely that the censor would have forbidden publication of the play, in any case, since it is set in the ancient and mythical period surrounding the fall of Troy. It was a period favoured by Elizabethan poets and dramatists, and only four years before George Chapman's translation of seven books of Homer's *Iliad* had been published. Yet the publisher of *Troilus and Cressida* in the Stationers' Register, James Roberts, is given the right to print "when he hath gotten sufficient aucthority for yt," an unusual phrase that suggests some problem with its licensing.

The legend of Troy was one of the most popular of all the classical stories that circulated in Elizabethan England; it was the stuff of Homer and of Virgil. London itself was considered by many antiquarians to be New Troy, "Troynovaunt," founded by the lineage of the refugees from the fallen city. Yet in *Troilus and Cressida* Shakespeare sets out deliberately to subvert the legends. It is a play in which the orthodox pieties of Trojan courage and Greek valour are quite overturned, revealing a callous, brutal and hypocritical reality underlying the acts of both sides. There are no values except those that are traded by time and fashion; traded is here the operative word, since every value is a commodity to be bought and sold in the market-place. This may indeed be a form of displaced patriotism. Shakespeare was prohibited from lamenting the condition of his own country on the London stage, but the presentation of the ancient world was treated with considerable leniency by the censors. What could be more natural than to vent his conservative fury in a safer context?

Troilus and Cressida is a savage and satirical comedy upon the themes of love and war, treating them both as false and fickle. The love between Troilus and Cressida is exposed as counterfeit, or temporary, when Cressida is seduced by a Greek warrior. It is in part Shakespeare's revision of Chaucer's poem *Troilus and Criseyde*, in which he supplants medieval grace and good humour with the language and vocabulary of a harsh and unsettled time. The diction itself is highly Latinised, with many "hard" words as well as an odd or convoluted syntax. As in *Julius Caesar* Shakespeare wished to give the verbal impression of an alien and classical world, and it is not too much to speculate that in *Troilus and Cressida* he tried to make English resemble what he considered to be Greek. He may also have been trying to rival Chapman's translations of Homer. It has been remarked that his was an envious muse. He had to outdo Chaucer as well as Chapman, to rewrite the heroic myth of the Greeks and the Romans.

But in *Troilus and Cressida* the pertinence of satire and sarcasm, raillery and buffoonery, cannot be doubted. It is unlikely to have been performed in the queen's presence, but it was played at the Globe. The entry in the Stationers' Register states that the play will be "as yt is acted by my Lord Chamberlens Men" and the printed version, published some six years later, declares that this is the play "as it was acted by the Kings Maiesties seruants at the Globe." So *Troilus and Cressida* was played during the reign of Elizabeth, and during the succeeding reign of James I. This suggests that it was a popular play, perhaps pandering to the popular dislike of the Greeks as opposed to the Trojans who were the presumed ancestors of Londoners. It has been argued that at some point it was performed at one of the Inns of Court.[3] A prologue and an epilogue were composed for that occasion, the latter of which has a private air of salaciousness. This would account for an "epistle" written for the quarto version in which the play is described as "a new play, neuer stal'd with the Stage, neuer clapper-clawd with the palmes of the vulgar" or "the smoaky breath of the multitude." If Shakespeare had revised the play for the particular delectation of a legal audience, then it could pass by convenient fiction as a "new play."

Nevertheless it remains Shakespeare's most savage drama, with the possible exception of *Timon of Athens*, and has prompted more romantic biographers into assuming that the dramatist suffered some kind of "nervous breakdown" in the middle of composition. Nothing could be further from the truth. He was never more sharp-eyed. There is a slight confusion among his publishers, however. The quarto edition describes it as a "Historie" but the "epistle" to that quarto refers to it as a comedy; in turn the later Folio version refers to it as a "Tragedie." This suggests some uncertainty concerning its final or ultimate tone.

That is why it is a mistake to attribute some kind of private motive behind Shakespeare's choice of material. Nothing in his life and career gives any reason to suggest that he chose a theme or story with any specific intention other than to entertain. He had no "message." The most likely explanation for his choice of the Trojan wars lies within the context of theatrical competition. In 1596 the Admiral's Men performed a play that Henslowe simply noted as "troye."[4] Three years later Thomas Dekker and Henry Chettle were paid for a play entitled "Troyeles & creasse daye" and then, at a later date, for one entitled "Agamemnon" (first listed as "troylles & Creseda"). So the fate of the unfortunate Trojan pair were elements in the new theatrical environment. It seems highly likely, then, that the Lord Chamberlain's Men asked Shakespeare to provide a drama upon the same theme. As soon as he began to write, however, the power of his genius colluded with the forces of his age to produce a complete statement. His words were magnetic. All the particles of a decaying court culture, a decaying world of individual heroism and nobility, flew towards them.

CHAPTER 75

𝔍. But the Case 𝔍s Alter'd

✣

he queen was dead. Long live the king! Elizabeth had died at two in the morning of 24 March 1603; nine hours later, a crowd of courtiers and nobles who had assembled on the west side of the High Cross in Cheapside listened to a proclamation by Cecil and then shouted out "God save King James!" As one courtier put it, quoting a psalm, "We had heaviness in the night but joy in the morning." The news was brought to the prisoners in the Tower of London and Southampton, among them, rejoiced. Southampton had been condemned to life imprisonment for his part in the ill-fated Essex rebellion, but he was quickly released from his confinement by the new king.

King James had made a slow procession from Scotland, and did not arrive at his palace in Greenwich until 13 May. Then, six days later, letters patent were issued "*pro Laurentio Fletcher et Willielmo Shakespeare . . .*" permitting them to perform as "well for the recreation of our loving subjects, as for our solace and pleasure when we shall think good to see them," both "within their now usual house called *The Globe*" and all the other towns and boroughs of the kingdom. They were no longer to be known as the Lord Chamberlain's Men. They were the King's Men. A few months later they were appointed "grooms of the chamber" and their social status therefore greatly improved. They were given the right, indeed the duty, of wearing the royal livery of red doublet, hose and cloak. Shakespeare was placed first in the list, by the Master of the Great Wardrobe, for receiving 4½ yards of scarlet cloth for his uniform.

It is perhaps odd to consider Shakespeare as a royal servant, following in procession on ceremonial occasions, but there is no reason to believe that he questioned the privilege. It was, in a real sense, the height of his social accomplishment. Gone were the days when players were classified with strolling vagrants, and were often turned back by the aldermen of various towns. Gone, too, were the days when the actors were merely tolerated rather than welcomed in the capital. The new king, very early in his reign, had bestowed his favours upon them. Before the reign of James, the Globe players had been called upon to perform at court on approximately three occasions each year; in the first ten years of his reign they were asked to play fourteen times each year. So the court was a source of profit, as well as patronage, to the King's Men.

There were of course those of a jealous disposition. A play by Francis Beaumont on the subject of social climbing, *The Woman Hater*, struck a glancing blow at Shakespeare's elevation with the remark that "another payre you shall see, that were heire apparent legges to a Glover, these legges hope shortly to bee honourable." Shakespeare's modest origins were by now well known.

It is significant that William Shakespeare and Laurence Fletcher were first mentioned in the letters patent. Fletcher, hitherto never mentioned as one of the Globe players, had in fact been leader of a group of Scottish actors who had in previous years been patronised and welcomed by James when he was James VI of Scotland; he had even protected them against the depredations of the Kirk. Fletcher had been known as "comedyan to his majestie." So he travelled south with the new English monarch and, as the sovereign's true servant, had been placed with the new company of the King's Men. The fact that he is named before Shakespeare in the letters patent suggests, however, that by common consent Shakespeare was the leader or principal man of the Globe players.

Many of Shakespeare's earlier plays were now revived for royal performance. The King's Men put on new productions of *The Comedy of Errors*, *Hamlet*, *The Merry Wives of Windsor*, *Love's Labour's Lost*, *Henry V* and *The Merchant of Venice*. If James had not previously been acquainted with the work of Shakespeare, the oversight was now remedied. He seems particularly to have enjoyed *The Merchant of Venice*; he asked for it to be performed again, perhaps because the legal scene between Portia and Shylock satisfied his own taste for disputation. But it is more significant that all of Shakespeare's new plays—those written after 1603, in other words—were performed at least once before the king. Some of them were performed several times. The records of payment demonstrate that, whenever the King's Men performed at court, the king himself watched the proceedings.

The presence of the new monarch, then, had an effect upon the dramatist's art. It could hardly be otherwise. The London theatre always had to look towards the sources of power and of patronage. The monarch was the lord of the spectacle. So it is no real cause of wonder to discover that, after the accession of James, Shakespeare was ready to shape certain of his plays to reveal the figure of the king somewhere in the design. This is the case with *Macbeth* and, to a certain extent, with *Measure for Measure*. The plays reflect, for example, James's well-known fear of witchcraft—especially the form of magic aimed against a ruling sovereign. They reflect his fear of crowds, and his habitual dislike of Puritans. The ruling family's great liking for masques also affects the staging of tableaux and dumb-shows in Shakespeare's last plays, where music and dance play a large part in the concluding action.

But the King's Men could not stay in London to enjoy their privileged position. The plague had returned to the city. John Stow later estimated that, out of a population of approximately two hundred thousand, some thirty-eight thousand died. After this date, the references to plague in Shakespeare's plays take on a much darker hue than hitherto; there are references to death tokens and to plague sores. It was not some local difficulty but a pressing and ominous reality; at a conservative estimate some seven years of Shakespeare's career were affected by what was known as "the death." Contemporary Londoners believed that the plague came from planetary influences, blasting the air with fever. Yet of course, though Londoners did not know it, the rats and their fleas had come back.

The king eventually granted his new players some £30 for "mayntenaunce and releife" during the epidemic, but it was still necessary for them to go on tour. By the end of May 1603, the King's Men had begun their travels to the plague-free regions of Maldon, Ipswich, Coventry, Shrewsbury, Bath and Oxford where, among other of Shakespeare's dramas, they played *Hamlet*. It was in this year, too, that the first quarto of *Hamlet* was published; from its relative shortness, it may have been a version of the play prepared for this particular tour. The journey to Maldon and Ipswich is likely to have been conducted by sea. They travelled many hundreds of miles. They visited more towns than can now be shown in the official records, and must have given more than fifty performances. There is also a possibility that Shakespeare visited Stratford, since it is less than twenty miles from Coventry. It is certain, however, that he would not have remained in London.

The plague was particularly prevalent in Southwark. In Shakespeare's own parish more than two and a half thousand people died within the space of six months. Two of Shakespeare's old colleagues, William Kempe and Thomas Pope, expired; they had both been residents of Southwark. So the epidemic fury sent Shakespeare away. At some point in this period, he left the Bankside shore and moved to another part of London. He changed his address from Southwark to the more fashionable and affluent neighbourhood of Silver Street, between Cripplegate and Cheapside. He was once more a lodger, living in a house at the corner of Silver Street and Muggle (Monkswell) Street as a tenant of a Huguenot family called the Mountjoys. Christopher Mountjoy was a wig-maker and "tire-maker," a maker of ornamental headdresses; he catered for the theatrical trade as well as for private patrons, and he was no doubt associated with the King's Men in a professional capacity.

His was a large and commodious house of three storeys with jettied upper floor and attics; there is an image of it in the Agas map of London, executed in 1560, where even on a small scale it looks relatively imposing. Mountjoy's shop was at ground level, shielded from the weather by a "pentice" or roof, with the living apartments above. Silver Street itself, as its name implies, was a rich street. John Stow described it as containing "divers fair houses." It was also famous for its wig-makers such as Mountjoy himself. In *The Silent Woman* a wife's hair is said to be "made" in Silver Street. Here Shakespeare shared the house with Mountjoy, his wife and daughter, as well as three apprentices and a servant called Joan. He was perhaps reminded of the time when he lived above a shop in Henley Street, also in the company of apprentices. By the standards of the period, however, this was a relatively small and quiet establishment. But it was not without its internal disharmonies. Madame Mountjoy had been conducting an affair with a local tradesman, and had consulted Simon Forman about a possible pregnancy. Her daughter was being pursued by one of the apprentices, with the active encouragement of Shakespeare himself.

When Shakespeare had resided in Southwark he had been close to the theatre, and subject to the appearance of uninvited colleagues and friends.

But he was by no means isolated in Silver Street. He was close to his old Stratford friend, the publisher Richard Field; Mrs. Field, herself a Huguenot, worshipped at the same French church as Madame Mountjoy. In certain respects late sixteenth-century London still resembled a small town or village. He was also a few yards from the bookstalls of St. Paul's Churchyard, where he would have seen his own plays on sale for sixpence. He could have picked up the short version of *The Tragicall Historie of Hamlet, Prince of Denmarke* at Nicholas Ling's new shop by St. Dunstan's in the West near St. Paul's in Fleet Street.

The subject of booksellers was close to Shakespeare. He needed books, expensive though the majority of them were, to furnish his art. By 1600 there were some hundred publishers as well as a score of printers and an indeterminate number of booksellers. The figures can only be approximate since one man or shop might combine two or three of these separate trades. All printers were, for example, in some degree also publishers; but not all publishers were printers. Many of the booksellers were established in Paternoster Row, that quarter of the city behind St. Paul's Cathedral where the trade clustered, and there were at least seventeen bookshops in St. Paul's Churchyard itself. The area remained the centre of the book-publishing business until the fire-storms of the Second World War entirely destroyed it. It was a relatively small trade, compared to the printing and publishing business of such continental centres as Bruges and Antwerp, but it was well established and well organised. The London publishers were skilful and professional with relatively high standards of type-setting, proof-reading and printing. The publication of plays, Shakespeare's among them, comprised only a very small part of their overall trade. Books of sermons and of meditations, as well as books of history and domestic etiquette, sold far more. But sales must be set in perspective. The most popular books had an approximate print-run of 1,250 copies.

Close to Paternoster Row stood Stationers' Hall, the centre of the guild of the publishers, printers and booksellers where were placed the registers of the books published and licensed in the city. They were inspected for any offence against state or religion, and were then duly entered at the cost of 6 pence. Although many books were not entered, any registered book was deemed to be under the copyright of the publisher. Severe penalties were imposed upon any breaches of copyright, which included fines and confiscations as well as the more serious punishment of the printing press being broken up. So it seems unlikely that many of Shakespeare's plays emerged in "pirated" form, as has sometimes been suggested. But in the case of these plays there was a long history of transference from one publisher to another. John Busby registered *The Merry Wives of Windsor*, for example, and on the same day transferred it to Arthur Johnson, who promptly published it. Andrew Wise registered and published three of the history plays in the late 1590s, and then five years later transferred them to Matthew Law. There are other publishers involved in the transmission of Shakespeare's texts—Nicholas Ling, John Danter, Thomas Millington, James Roberts and Edward Blount among them. They were tradesmen principally, concerned to earn a profit, and were in no sense "patrons" of the dramatist.

Close to his new neighbourhood, too, was John Heminges; he rented a house in Addle Street owned by Thomas Savage, the goldsmith who was also a trustee of the Globe. Another colleague from the playhouse, Henry Condell, lived in the same parish as Heminges. In that sense the area was an extension of Shakespeare's theatrical family. It seems very likely that he was the godfather to John Heminges's son, William, who was christened in the autumn of 1603 at the church of St. Mary's Aldermanbury a few yards away from Silver Street. If the three friends sometimes travelled together to the Globe, it was a matter of a few hundred yards' walk to the wherries that would carry them over the Thames.

It has sometimes been surmised, however, that Shakespeare's removal from Southwark was also a sign of some growing detachment from the life of the playhouse—and that, at some point in this period, he gave up acting without of course abandoning his career as dramatist. He is listed among the players for Ben Jonson's *Sejanus* in 1603, but is not mentioned as playing in the production of the same dramatist's *Volpone* in 1605. This is a significant omission, if in that interval there lies the decision to leave the stage. He had invested heavily in Stratford land, and did not need an actor's income. He also earned money from his share in the Globe, as well as from his plays. He was forty years of age, middle-aged in Elizabethan terms, and may have tired of the endless activity of the stage. And was it right, for a landed gentleman, still to tread the boards? From 1603 to 1616, his company was engaged in a great deal of provincial travelling. Touring cannot have been a pursuit he still welcomed. He may have preferred to confine his travels to the route between London and Stratford, making the journey from Silver Street to New Place unencumbered by an actor's duties.

Silver Street was itself not immune to the plague. In the course of the epidemic a royal musician, Henry Sandon, died together with his daughter.

A painter, William Linley, succumbed with his wife. The porter of the Barber Surgeons' Hall, nearby in Monkwell Street, also expired. So it is likely that in the summer and autumn of 1603 Shakespeare was either residing in Stratford or taking part in what would have been his last provincial tour.

The doors of the London theatres were of course shut for most of this year. The playhouses were automatically closed when mortality from the plague reached thirty a week, and the outbreak of 1603 far surpassed that figure. By October the companies had returned from their touring, and were hoping that the theatres might reopen. In a letter from their house on Bankside Edward Alleyn's wife wrote to her husband, staying at Bexhill, "my own self (your self) and my mother, and the whole house, are in good health, and about us the Sickness doth cease, and is likely more and more, by God's help, to cease. *All the companies be come home*, and are well, for aught we know . . ."[1]

Yet all cannot have been entirely well, since the King's Men then decamped to the estate of Augustine Phillips in plague-free Mortlake by the Thames. In this small riverine town also lived John Dee, the magus and scientist whose predictions and exploits had made him famous in late sixteenth-century society. He had even been consulted by Queen Elizabeth. It is possible that the actors encountered the notorious Doctor Dee during their residence in Mortlake. It would at least give a context to the persistent reports that Shakespeare in part modelled the character of Prospero on this contemporary magician.

The removal of Phillips from London did not delay his death. In the spring of 1604 he died at Mortlake, bequeathing "to my ffellowe William Shakespeare a Thirty shillings peece in gould." To a former apprentice Phillips left a purple cloak, a sword and a dagger; to a newer apprentice he bequeathed his musical instruments. Shakespeare heads the list of colleagues and house-keepers in the will, however, a prominence which suggests that Phillips had an especial attachment to him.

Phillips may have acted towards the close of 1603, however, when the King's Men performed for the first time before their new patron. From Mortlake they were obliged to travel to Wilton, the Earl of Pembroke's estate near Salisbury in Wiltshire, where on 2 December they played for the sovereign. John Heminges was paid £30 "for the paynes and expenses of himself and the rest of the company in coming from Mortelake in the countie of Surrie unto the court aforesaid and there presenting before his majestie one playe."[2] There have been numerous reports that a letter once existed, written by the Countess of Pembroke from Wilton House. She is supposed to have counselled her son to come with the king from Salisbury, in order to see a performance of *As You Like It*; she also mentioned the fact that "we have the man Shakespeare with us." The letter has disappeared, but the story lingers. It is not necessarily apocryphal, and the remark has the appropriate ring of *noblesse oblige*. But it cannot now be substantiated. There are even reports of an "amicable" letter from King James himself to the dramatist, but this is beyond conjecture. It may have been the Earl of Pembroke, however, who recommended that the Lord Chamberlain's Men be given royal patronage; he had been closely involved with Shakespeare and Burbage, as we have seen, and he had also become a confidant of the new king.

From Wilton, the king and his retinue moved to Hampton Court. The King's Men moved with them. They would not return to London until the early spring. One courtier observed that at Hampton Court "we had every night a publicke play in the great halle, at which the King was ever present, and liked or disliked as he saw cause: but it seems he takes no extraordinary pleasure in them. The Queene and Prince were more the players frendes, for on other nights they had them privately."[3] So the king was perhaps not enamoured of the drama. He was himself of a theatrical disposition, and went to some pains to announce his majesty in dramatic and symbolic way; his long delayed "entry" into London proceeded under great triumphal arches designed to renew the example of Rome. It is likely, then, that he viewed theatrical representations as but a shadow of the real spectacle of power and authority. The fact remains, however, that the players performed before him far more frequently than they ever performed before his predecessor. In this period, too, the dramatist himself was being described as "*Friendly Shakespeare*" in whose plays "the *Commedian* rides when the *Tragedian* stands on Tip-toe," and thus manages "to please all."[4] "All" included the new sovereign.

Ɔ Will a Round Unvarnish'd Tale Deliuer

✳

he king entered London, as into his kingdom, on 15 March 1604. It was a triumphant occasion, not least because it was a celebration of the fact that the epidemic plague had finally retreated from the city. It was for this occasion that Shakespeare and his fellows had been given the 4½ yards of scarlet cloth, so they are likely to have been part of the ceremonial procession through the streets of London from the Tower to Westminster. It was an historic walk by Shakespeare through the city that had nourished him. It is possible that he, or one of his colleagues, made a speech at one of the triumphal arches; their rival, Edward Alleyn, made an oration as the "Genius" or guiding spirit of the city. It may have been Alleyn's last performance, since in this year he retired from the acting profession. The pageants at Bishopsgate and Fenchurch Street were devised respectively by Thomas Dekker and Ben Jonson. Dekker seems to have borrowed from Shakespeare in his address to the king:

> This little world of men; this pretious Stone,
> That sets out Europe . . .

Since Thomas Middleton was also brought in to provide some suitable verses for the occasion, the absence of Shakespeare from this cast-list of royal panegyrists is somewhat puzzling. He could hardly have declined the honour. It may have been implicitly understood, however, that he was not that kind of writer. There were seven triumphal gates, created in the style of Roman arches by Stephen Harrison; there were fountains, and flames, and living statuary. Shakespeare himself adopted the device of a statue coming alive, at a later date, in *The Winter's Tale*. It was a thoroughly theatrical occasion, complete with all the crowds and noise that the new king detested.

The King's Men were called upon to perform other royal services in this first full year of the new king's reign. Twelve of them were appointed grooms of the chamber in the summer of 1604, when in August they were charged with the entertainment of the Spanish Ambassador Extraordinary and his retinue of 234 gentlemen who had come to London in order to negotiate the signing of a peace treaty; they had taken up residence for eighteen days in Somerset House, which had become the palace of the queen. The duties of Shakespeare and his colleagues are not detailed, and it is even possible that Shakespeare himself avoided attendance; if he was no longer an actor, there might be no need for him. The players were there, however, to look decorative and to fulfil their role as courtiers. They may even have been asked to perform; but there are no records of any play being staged, and each of them was paid what seems to have been a bare minimum of 2 shillings per day.

The King's Men were travelling in the spring and summer of 1604; they visited Oxford, for example, in May and June. It is unlikely, as we have seen, that Shakespeare now travelled with them. During this period he completed two plays that were performed at court towards the close of 1604; *Othello* and *Measure for Measure* were staged respectively in November and December of this year. Since the public theatres had been allowed to open again in April, one or both of these plays had first been shown at the Globe. They were the first productions of the King's Men after their return from Hampton Court. It has been suggested that *Othello* and *Measure for Measure* are both dark plays for a dark time, born of the plague and the queen's death, with the tragedy of Othello and Desdemona preceding the bitter and forlorn story of Angelo and Isabella. But in fact they seem to have been written in a period of general rejoicing at the new king's accession, with Shakespeare reaching the pinnacle of his social eminence.

The King's Men were acting as courtiers for the Ambassador Extraordinary of Spain in the period when Othello "the Moor" was being created.

The "Moor" himself is of Spanish origin while two of the other characters in the play, Roderigo and Iago, have recognisably Spanish names. Even in the period when Shakespeare was writing there was a concerted Spanish effort to expel the very large population of Moors from their country. The Moors, like the Jews, were the victims of European racial prejudice. There was also a large colony of Moors in London, refugees from Spanish persecution. Elizabeth I issued an edict against "the great number of negars and blackamoors which are crept into the realm since the troubles between Her Highness and the King of Spain."

In 1600 a Moorish ambassador for the King of Barbary came to Elizabeth's court, and became an object of fascinated attention. There is ample reason for Shakespeare to have seen, and even spoken with, him. He played before him at court, during the Christmas season. The Moor sat for his portrait during this visit, too, and the image of this dignified if somewhat withdrawn figure must have impressed itself upon Shakespeare's conception of Othello. At the age of forty-two he looks haunted, forever watchful. It is a mistake to consider Othello to be of African or West Indian origin, as is often the case in modern productions. He was of Moorish stock, olive-skinned, and Shakespeare portrays him as "black" for the purposes of theatrical emphasis and symbolism. In Shylock Shakespeare had created a character of some complexity; by the time he came upon Othello, he had become even more interested in the role and nature of the scapegoat. But it would be a mistake to assume that he had any overt humanitarian purpose. Instead he had a keen eye and ear for theatrical intrigue.

There are other contemporary matters that must be seen in the context of *Othello*, if only because they would have been known to every member of the audience who witnessed the first production. King James had a pronounced sympathy for the Spanish state; that is why Shakespeare and his fellows were entertaining the Ambassador Extraordinary in Somerset House. But there was also a well-attested story publicised throughout Europe that the previous king of Spain, Philip II, was an insanely jealous husband who had strangled his wife in her bed. What is more, he had become suspicious of her when she had inadvertently dropped her handkerchief. These parallels are too close to be coincidental. The fact that Cyprus becomes the scene of the tragic action of *Othello* is also explicable in these terms. Cyprus was once a Venetian protectorate but had been occupied by Turkish forces for more than thirty years, and thus posed a threat to Spanish as well as Venetian interests in the region. King James himself had written a poem upon the subject. So Shakespeare was deliberately reflecting the interests and preoccupations of the sovereign. During the present reign of Philip III, too, Spain was at odds with the republic of Venice. It would be too much to claim, as some commentators have done, that Othello "represents" Spain and that Desdemona "represents" Venice. Yet it is undoubtedly true that Shakespeare's imagination, magnetised, as it were, around Spain, had drawn in everything. He had become, for the purposes of this play, a vessel for all things Spanish.

So it would be wrong to state that Shakespeare never wrote a play concerning contemporary life. *Othello* was a very modern drama, refracting all the circumstances of the period. Shakespeare also read some recently published translations that suited his purpose–among them *A Geographical Historie of Africa* and Pliny's *Historie of the World*. He also read Sir Lewis Lewkenor's *The Commonwealth and Government of Venice*. These books were published in 1600, 1601 and 1599 respectively, so we may plausibly imagine Shakespeare as a haunter of bookstalls, picking up any recently printed volumes as a spur to his creativity. The booksellers pointed out their recent acquisitions, and his noble patrons may have informed him of the latest fashionable volume. But there was a pattern to his reading. The evidence of *Othello* suggests that, when he had hit upon a theme, he opened those books that were directly relevant to it. He was searching for local "colour" but also for the circumstantial detail and the significant phrase.

The question of Shakespeare's learning has vexed many commentators. Its extent can perhaps be measured in the simple statement that he learned as much as he needed to learn. He had no wasted or superfluous knowledge. He was familiar with the classics of the schoolroom, as we have seen, and for his own dramatic purposes used Ovid and Virgil, Terence and Plautus. He could read Latin, and possibly even a smattering of Greek, but he preferred to use translations wherever possible. He read North's translation of Plutarch rather than Plutarch himself, for example, and read Golding's translation of Ovid's *Metamorphoses* rather than the great original. He would have been obliged, however, to read Plautus and Ovid's *Fasti* in Latin. He was not interested in these texts for their own sake, only for what they inspired within him. He was of course thoroughly familiar with all of his source material, whether it be out of Plutarch or Holinshed. This may also come under the rubric of useful learning. He was not a scholar, an antiquarian or a philosopher. He was a dramatist. He seems in fact to have distrusted philosophy, rational discourse and sententiousness in all of its forms. Abstract language was his abhorrence. He trusted only language imbued with action and with character, with time and with place.

It is possible that he could read both French and Italian, but he preferred to use translations wherever possible. It is not a question of laziness but of efficiency. The fact that he preferred English versions of foreign stories also suggests that he was not particularly interested in the "otherness" of other cultures. It was his habit to search through books, old or new, looking for that which his imagination could use. He seems on occasions to have read the summaries of the text in the margin rather than the text itself. His knowledge of popular botany, medicine, astrology, astronomy, and other matters, is extensive rather than profound; his alertness and power of assimilation were unique, so that he seems to know "more" than his contemporaries. He picked up everything.

We may make an informed guess about the books he assimilated. Among them are William Painter's *Palace of Pleasure*, Geoffrey Fenton's *Certaine Tragicall Discourses*, Bandello's *Novelle*, Giraldi Cinthio's *Gli Hecatommithi*, George Whetstone's *Heptameron*, Arthur Brooke's *Tragicall Historye of Romeus and Juliet* and the anonymous *A Hundreth Mery Tales*. They are what might be called "light" contemporary reading. He seems to have had a particular affection for anthologies of romance stories and for the new Italian novels, and it has already been noted how closely his work followed the model of the popular romances. But he also read the English poets, principal among them Edmund Spenser and Geoffrey Chaucer; he seems to have sensed, justifiably, that these were his real predecessors. He also seems to have read poetical miscellanies such as *The Paradyse of Daynty Devises* and *A Gorgious Gallery of Gallant Inventions*. There is some hint, too, that he read contemporary poets such as Donne and Southwell in manuscript form. He may have read those plays by his contemporaries that had emerged in print, although it is always possible that he preferred to watch them. He was acquainted with Montaigne and with Machiavelli, but such knowledge was commonplace at the time. It is unlikely that he studied them with any great attention.

He may have owned a library or carried his store of books with him in a book-chest. He mentions libraries only twice in his published work. Yet he could have used the libraries of patrons, such as Southampton or Pembroke, and of course he might have lingered and read in Richard Field's bookshop. He must have had one or two books physically close to him, however, since there are occasions when he quotes long passages almost verbatim from Plutarch and from Holinshed. Various books have emerged over the last three centuries, bearing Shakespeare's signature, but the chances of forgery and fakery are high. The most plausible and likely candidate for inclusion among Shakespeare's books, however, is the signed edition of Lambarde's *Archaionomia* mentioned earlier. It would not seem appropriate material for a forger, unlike the works of Ovid or of Plutarch, and the volume does indeed chime with Shakespeare's youthful legal interests. So there may be a true connection.

When he read his primary source narrative for *Othello*, Giraldi Cinthio's *Hecatommithi*, he must have been struck—inspired, rather—by its first sentence. "*Fu gia in Venezia un Moro.*" There was a Moor in Venice. Venice had been the site of his first outcast, in the person of Shylock. Othello was another example of the dispersed and dispossessed, the wanderers of the earth. There was a Moor in Venice. Cinthio's narrative is a prose tale, but something within it stirred all the powers of Shakespeare's sympathetic imagination. He immensely deepened and broadened the story, so that the first two acts of the play in particular bear very little resemblance to any possible originals. A measure of his contribution is to be found in the fact that all the names of the characters, apart from that of Desdemona, were formulated by him. He also revised his play, giving Desdemona more pathos and credibility, and, because he must have realised in performance that Emilia, the wife of Iago, had become too unsympathetic a creation, he gave her more dialogue with Desdemona so that she gained in sympathy.

The play, with the title of *The Moor of Venis* by "Shaxberd," was performed for the king and his court on 1 November 1604 in the Banqueting House at Whitehall. It was not written for private performance, of course, and it had already been played at the Globe and in the guildhalls of the company's provincial tours. Richard Burbage, as Othello, would have "blacked up." There was no occasion for subtlety in the presentation. A versifier later commented upon Burbage's role as "the grieved Moor." One curiosity concerns the part of Othello. When Ben Jonson described Shakespeare's own character he considered that he "was (indeed) honest, and of an open, and free nature."[1] He is quoting almost verbatim from Iago's description of Othello (677–8):

> The Moore is of a free and open nature,
> That thinkes men honest, that but seeme to be so.

It may be an inadvertent recollection on Jonson's part, but does it suggest that Shakespeare was in some sense "like" Othello? The theme of sexual jealousy runs deeply through many of Shakespeare's plays. Could Jonson have known that Shakespeare harboured suspicions about his wife in Stratford? It has become a well-known theory, promulgated among others by James Joyce and Anthony Burgess, but it must remain wholly theoretical. It might just as well be said that, because both Julius Caesar and Othello suffer from epilepsy, Shakespeare was personally acquainted with the disorder.

If a boy played Desdemona, he must have been a skilful and remarkable actor. He had to suggest a certain eroticism within Desdemona's innocence; as the German philosopher Heinrich Heine put it, "What repels me most every time are Othello's references to his wife's moist palm."[2] The boy actor would also have had a good voice, able to sing popular ballads. Since Desdemona's willow song is absent from the first published version of the play, however, it is likely that for some performances he was unavailable for the part.

It might come as a surprise to contemporary audiences that Iago, customarily seen as the epitome of evil in modern productions, was initially played by the company's resident clown and fool, Robert Armin. Iago was in the comic mode, and spoke to the audience in his confidential soliloquies. Charles Gildon, at the end of the seventeenth century, disclosed that

> I'm assur'd from very good hands, that the Person that Acted Iago was in much esteem for a Comoedian, which made Shakespeare put several words, and expressions into his part (perhaps not so agreeable to his Character) to make the Audience laugh, who had not yet learnt to endure to be serious a whole Play.[3]

Iago's role as comedian also fits the essentially comic structure of the play itself. Of course Gildon is alluding here to the sexual bawdry and innuendo in which Iago indulges with Desdemona, but he is being less than fair to Shakespeare. The dramatist loved sexual slang, and would not have considered it as writing "down" to any audience. It was a part of his imagination. As for being "serious" for "a whole Play" there is not one drama of Shakespeare's which aspires to that unity of mood or tone. Comedy and tragedy were equal parts of his art.

There are elements of Roman new comedy and Italian learned comedy in this play with the presence of the zany and the cuckold who is also the

Spanish braggart. But again they are here enriched beyond measure. Shakespeare used "types" as a matter of course, but they were simply the structure upon which he built. It is also worth observing that *Othello* is unique in being a tragedy largely established upon comic formulae. That may even have been the task that Shakespeare set himself. He establishes a comic structure, in which the locales of Venice and Cyprus have little connection with the main action, but then all begins to go awry. In the process he manages to enter the very rhythm of his characters in the world. They are deeply embedded in their language, with their own particular vocabulary and even cadence, so that we can as it were see Shakespeare living and breathing in unison with them. It is a miracle of transference. And we can feel the propulsion of his imagination. When a character mentions the "enchafed flood," the immediate response is that the Turkish fleet be not "ensheltered and embayed"; the syllables push him forward into new paths of thought.

It has been suggested that in some way Iago is a refraction of the dramatist, an unmoved mover whose intellectual agility far outruns any moral conscientiousness, but in fact he is closer to the medieval Vice who stirred up trouble with the unwitting connivance of the audience. No doubt, however, Shakespeare derived great pleasure from creating a villain who orchestrates his victims like a dramatist while at the same time proclaiming his honesty and sympathy on every occasion.

CHAPTER 77

Why, Sir, What's Your Conceit in That?

❧

hree days after the performance of *Othello* in the Banqueting House, *The Merry Wives of Windsor* was performed in the same setting. There is a description of the king attending a performance. When the king entered

> the cornets and trumpets to the number of fifteen or twenty began to play very well a sort of recitative, and then after his Majesty had seated himself under a canopy alone . . . he caused the ambassadors to sit below him on two stools, while the great officers of the crown and courts of law sat upon benches.[1]

But the hall, with "ten heights of degrees for people to stand upon,"[2] seems by general consent to have been too large for comfort. It was 100 feet long, with 292 glass windows. It had been erected by Elizabeth twenty-three years before, and King James described it as an "old, rotten and slight-built shed."[3] The Great Hall at court was prepared, instead, for the production of Shakespeare's second new play of the year, *Measure for Measure*.

Before that event, however, another play was to emerge from the King's Men only to disappear very rapidly. It was entitled *Gowry* and purported to be a dramatic version of the "Gowrie conspiracy" against James four years before. The play no doubt celebrated the courage and virtue of the new sovereign but, despite its patriotic tone, it was deemed unsuitable for public performance. One courtier wrote on 18 December that

> The Tragedy of Gowrie, with all actions and actors, hath been twice represented by the King's Players, with exceeding concourse of all sorts of people; but whether the matter or manner be not well handled, or that it be thought unfit that princes should be played on the stage in their lifetime, I hear that some great councellors are much displeased with it, and so it is thought it shall be forbidden.[4]

It was indeed considered to be unfit, and the play disappeared never to rise again. The courtier had hit upon the right explanation. It was considered *lèse-majesté* to portray a reigning monarch upon the public stage, in whatever circumstances. It served only to emphasise the theatricality of the king's role. The author of the forbidden play remains unknown, although it is not beyond conjecture that Shakespeare may have contributed to it.

James could not have been wholly displeased by his players since, a week later, they performed before him *Measure for Measure*. In this play a ruler, Duke Vincentio, disliking crowds and noise of "applause, and Aues vehement," pretends to absent himself from his land in order better to survey it. In his absence a rigidly puritanical deputy, Angelo, proves himself unworthy of his superior's trust. There are enough contemporary allusions here to have occasioned volumes of commentary, not least the resemblance between the Duke and King James himself. The king was known to dislike crowds and "Aues" to the same degree as the imaginary ruler. The unflattering portrayal of the Puritan, Angelo, must be seen in reference to the current controversies involving those sectarians in the new kingdom. That, at least, is how contemporary playgoers would have viewed it. Earlier that year, for example, the king had been presented by the country's foremost Puritans with a "Millenary Petition," containing proposals on dogma and ritual that the king rebuffed. The conclusion of the play, in which the Duke redeems those who have been judged guilty, can also be said to reflect current controversies over the privileges of the king. James believed that Parliament depended upon royal grace, and the ending of *Measure for Measure* can be construed as maintaining the divine right of kings. The title of the play itself may be taken from a sentence from James's own treatise on divine right, *Basilikon Doron*, in which he writes: "And, above all, let the measure of your love to everyone be according to the measure of his virtue." The King's Men were precisely that, the sovereign's servants, and part of their role was to advertise the virtues of their patron. Since the play is also set in Catholic Vienna, with a Catholic nun as the principal female and the Duke disguising himself as a Catholic friar, Shakespeare seems to be reflecting the increased level of tolerance for those who professed the old faith. It is pertinent, perhaps, that in this play as in *Romeo and Juliet* and in *Much Ado About Nothing*, the friar counsels deceit or concealment for the sake of a greater good. Shakespeare seems always to have been preternaturally alert to the prevailing atmosphere of his time. He was such a sensitive instrument in the world that he could not help but reflect everything.

Shakespeare derived some of the story of *Measure for Measure* from the same source as *Othello*. This suggests that he had riffled through Cinthio's *Hecatommithi* in search of likely plots. An anthology of stories, such as this one, was a mine of gold. When he found this particular plot to be of interest, he looked up an earlier dramatisation of it–George Whetstone's *Promos and Cassandra*, written in 1578–to see if there were any extra scenes or characters he might borrow. There were more immediate models to hand, also, since the theme of the ruler in disguise was a popular one in the London playhouses. It is important to grasp the immediacy of Shakespeare's inspiration. If there were two or three plays using a plot or character that had proved popular, the chances are that he would use them. Even though *Measure for Measure* is ostensibly set in Vienna, its real setting is early seventeenth-century London with its stews and suburbs, bawds and pandars. It is the world of Southwark and the Globe. *Measure for Measure* is in part a sketch for *King Lear* and *The Tempest*; here the Duke abandons the governance of his dukedom, but the space from this play to *King Lear* is measured in the shift from comedy to tragedy. It is also worth noticing that the first scenes of the play are also the most inventive. That is frequently the case in Shakespeare's dramaturgy, where he is often most spirited and emboldened at the beginning of each enterprise.

At court, the day after the performance of *Measure for Measure*, the Earl of Pembroke helped to assemble and present a masque with music entitled *Juno and Hymenaeus*. The text has not survived, but Pembroke may have obtained some assistance from the king's leading dramatist. Then, on the next day, *The*

Comedy of Errors was performed. This was followed on 7 January with *Henry V*. It was something of a Shakespeare festival, marked a day later by a special production of *Love's Labour's Lost* at the London house of the Earl of Southampton. This was the play that seems to bear references to the Southampton coterie or "circle" which in previous years had included some of the king's most fervent supporters. Sir Walter Cope, the Chamberlain of the Exchequer, wrote to Robert Cecil earlier in the month that

> I have sent and bene all thys morning huntyng for players Juglers & Such kinde of Creaturs, but fynde them harde to finde, wherfore Leavinge notes for them to seeke me, Burbage ys come, & Sayes ther ys no new playe that the queen hath not seene, but they have Revyved an olde one, Cawled Loves Labore Lost, which for wytte & mirthe he sayes will please her exceedingly. And Thys ys appointed to be playd to Morowe night at my Lord of Sowthamptons . . . Burbage ys my messenger Ready attending your pleasure.[5]

"Burbage" here is likely to be Cuthbert rather than Richard. It is highly unlikely that the leading tragedian of the day would be employed as a "messenger" between two servants of the state, although the association of players with "Juglers & Such kinde of Creaturs" shows little respect for the social standing of the theatrical profession.

The epistle is interesting for the fact that it also marks a definite occasion when Shakespeare's "old" plays can be enumerated. We can calculate that in the last two years he had written *Othello* and *Measure for Measure*, and that in the succeeding nine years he would write twelve more plays. It is sometimes assumed that this represents a general or gentle decline in his production of new drama as a result of age or debility but, on the assumption that he began his playwriting career in 1586 or 1587, then the rate of composition remains approximately the same throughout his life. The fact that the plays to be written include *King Lear*, *Macbeth* and *The Tempest* is clear enough proof that there was no loss of power.

The performance of *Love's Labour's Lost* in the second week of January was noted by Dudley Carleton when he remarked that "It seems we shall have Christmas all the yeare and therefore I shall never be owt of matter. The last nights revels were kept at my Lord of Cranbornes . . . and the like two nights before at my Lord of Southamptons."[6] Then, in the following month, there

were two performances of *The Merchant of Venice*. No contemporary dramatist had ever been so honoured by the ruling family. In this year, too, the
fourth quarto of *Richard III* was published; the play was still successful almost
fifteen years after its first performance.

Another play, of curious construction and tone, seems to date from this
period. *All's Well That Ends Well* is generally considered to be a comedy, but
it is one dressed in sombre hues. The plot of the infatuated orphan, Helena,
pursuing the fatuous and disdainful Count Bertram is not the most edifying;
it might almost be a sourly dramatic version of the relationship between the
lover and the beloved proposed in the sonnets, with the "lascivious" Bertram
as an image of the "Lasciuious grace" of the poems' recipient. When Helena
writes a letter, it takes the form of a sonnet. But the play does have a re-
deeming character in the portrayal of the elderly Countess of Rossillion, described by George Bernard Shaw as "the most beautiful old woman's part
ever written." A certain unevenness of tone in the writing prompted Coleridge to speculate that the play "was written at two different, and rather distinct periods of the poet's life,"[7] and it used to be believed that it was a
rewriting of the early play *Loue labours wonne* attributed to Shakespeare. Yet
it is best to accept the play as a complete and coherent achievement.

Shakespeare adopted the plot from an anthology of stories, William
Painter's *Palace of Pleasure*, but the original or parent source is Boccaccio's
Decameron. This was a book from which Chaucer also purloined some of his
plots. Shakespeare intensified the action while at the same time introducing
riddling complications that display his sheer love of invention. He provides
plots and sub-plots that work in parallel, and in part parody one another. He
creates patterns of imagery that are like the shadows of paper-lace upon a
wall. He has also invented the character of Parolles, the military braggart, a
creature of prolific and meaningless words who can now be firmly identified
as a Shakespearian "type." Shakespeare loved those who dwelled in a wilder-
ness of words.

It is a difficult play in the sense that in characteristic fashion Shakespeare
conflates several disparate elements, with the folk tale vying with realistic
comedy and the elements of fable coexisting with the elements of farce. The
verse itself is often very difficult, with meaning wrestling against syntax and
cadence. Helena laments "the poorer borne," for example (182–5),

Whose baser starres do shut vs vp in wishes,
Might with effects of them follow our friends,
And shew what we alone must thinke, which neuer
Returnes vs thankes.

It is a demanding poetry once more recalling that of Shakespeare's contemporary John Donne. It is even possible that there was in this period a fashion for difficult poetry, which Shakespeare mastered just as he mastered every other form. It is a difficult play but it is also a dry play, an abortive exercise in comic form. We do not need to suppose any great crisis in Shakespeare's creative or personal life, as some biographers have suggested, in order to explain this loss of power. A dark thought took wing into a dark valley which, once thoroughly investigated, proved barren and boring. That is all.

CHAPTER 78

The Bitter Disposition of the Time

✦

n 24 July, 1605, Shakespeare invested £440 in tithes or, as the official document states, "one half of all tythes of corne and grayne aryseing within the townes villages and fieldes of Old Stratford, Byshopton and Welcombe" as well as "half of all tythes of wooll and lambe, and of all small and privy tythes."[1] A tithe had originally been a tenth part of the produce from the land, paid by farmer or tenant to the Church; this archaic form of tribute had then been passed to the Stratford Corporation at the time of the Reformation. Shakespeare was leasing his tithes from the corporation for a period of thirty-one years. At this late date it sounds a complicated matter, but at the time it was a conventional and familiar way of securing a reasonable income. The sum laid out by Shakespeare was in fact a very large one, and he could not raise the whole amount at one time; a year later he still owed some £20 to the vendor, Ralph Hubaud. He expected an annual return on his investment of something like £60, which was in itself a reasonable income. There were, however, one or two additional costs. He collected the tithes but was obliged to pay an annual fee of £17 to the Corporation of Stratford for the privilege. Nevertheless he still gathered a large amount.

The fact that his tithe lease ran for thirty-one years is evidence that he was intent upon securing his family's future after his death. It was a question of social, as well as financial, status. As the owner of tithes he was classified as a "lay rector," and had earned the right to be buried within the rails of the chancel of Stratford Church; it was a right that was taken up at his behest or on his behalf. Meanwhile his purchase of New Place had given him the right to a reserved pew in the church. He seems always to have been concerned about his precise social standing in his old town. It was in this period, too, that he rented out the eastern part of the family house in Henley Street to brewers by the name of Hiccox.

The transaction concerning the tithes was witnessed by two friends who would at a later date be named in his will, Anthony Nash of Welcombe and the lawyer Francis Collins. It is a mark of the invisibility of Shakespeare's Stratford life that little is known of these gentlemen, who played an intimate and familiar part in the dramatist's commercial affairs. They were part of a world very different from that of the players and playgoers, but he was equally at home in their company.

His prosperity did not go unremarked and in a fictional "biography" published this year of a notorious highwayman, Gamaliel Ratsey, there are references to actors who "are grown so wealthy that they have expected to be knighted, or at least to be cojunct in authority and to sit with men of great worship." There is also a clear allusion to Shakespeare in the remark that "thou shalt learne to be *frugall* . . . to make thy hand a stranger to thy pocket . . . and when thou feelest thy purse well-lined, buy thee some *Place* or lordship in the country, that growing weary of playing thy mony may there bring thee to dignitie and reputation."[2] The anonymous writer goes on to say that "I haue heard indeede, of some that haue gone to London very meanly, and haue come in time to be exceeding wealthy." This fits Shakespeare's case exactly. The little volume seems to have been written by someone who knew of Shakespeare's affairs, and it is interesting that he should emphasise the dramatist's obvious thrift as well as his success.

The wealthy player is described as "weary of playing," too, which confirms the evidence that Shakespeare had retired from the stage by 1603 or 1604. The purchase of tithes, as we have seen, ensured that he had an annual and independent income larger than that of a player. It is doubly unlikely, then, that he was on tour with the King's Men in autumn and winter of this year. They were travelling again out of necessity, since a new onset of the plague meant that the theatres were closed from the middle of October to the middle of December. Among the plays they took with them were *Othello* and *Measure for Measure* as well as Ben Jonson's *Volpone*. They seem to have travelled as far west as Barnstaple, taking in Oxford and Saffron Walden en route, and may indeed have stayed in the provinces until the Globe was re-opened on 15 December. Just eleven days later, they performed before the king.

They were playing in uncertain times, and to a king who was reported to be in a state of alarm and anxiety. In early November the conspiracy popularly known as the "Gunpowder Plot" was revealed to the world, with its ambitious and unprecedented attempt to blow up king and Parliament. It led to renewed suspicion and persecution of Roman Catholics, of course, nowhere more fiercely than in Stratford and Warwickshire. The leading conspirator, Robert Catesby, was a Warwickshire man. The conspirators met in that county, and one of them had even rented Clopton House just outside Stratford to be close to his colleagues. In the immediate aftermath of the discovery of 5 November the bailiff of Stratford seized a cloak-bag "full of copes, vestments, crosses, crucifixes, chalices and other massing relics." It was supposed "to be delivered to one George Badger there."[3] George Badger was the woollen-draper who lived next door to the Shakespeares in Henley Street. Shakespeare knew him very well indeed, and would have quickly been informed by his family of the calamity that had fallen upon him.

New legislation was passed by the Parliament against Catholic recusants, and the king himself, according to the Venetian ambassador, declared: "I shall most certainly be obliged to stain my hands with their blood, though sorely against my will . . ."[4] For the Shakespeare family in Stratford, it was an uncertain time. In the spring of the following year, Susannah Shakespeare was cited for her failure to receive holy communion that Easter. She is listed with some well-known Catholic recusants in the town, among them Shakespeare's old friend Hamnet Sadler—the godfather of his dead son. The danger of her position must have been emphasised to her by someone close to her, since the word "*dismissa*" was later placed against her entry. She must have outwardly conformed by taking communion. Three years later, however, Richard Shakespeare, the dramatist's brother, was taken before the bawdry court at Stratford for some unspecified offence; he was fined 12 pence, for the use of the Stratford poor, which suggests that he was found guilty of breaking the Sabbath.

The response of Shakespeare to the turbulent events of 1605 was to write a play of apparently conservative and orthodox intent. *Macbeth* was concerned with the terrible consequences of murdering a divinely appointed sovereign, and within the drama itself there are even references to the trials of the conspirators in the spring of 1606. There are allusions to "equivocation," a concept which appeared at the trial of the Jesuit Father Henry Garnet, who was subsequently hanged. When Lady Macduff remarks, on the subject of treason, "every one that do's so, is a Traitor, and must be hang'd" (1512) there may have been applause and cheers among the audience of the Globe. In *Macbeth*, too, there is an invocation of the Stuart dynasty, with reference to the kings who will rule England as well as Scotland. Since the play is also steeped in King James's favourite subject, witchcraft, there can be no doubt that it was purposefully designed to appeal to the new monarch. The witches of *Macbeth* can be said to plot against the lawful king, with their intimations of Macbeth's greatness, and just fifteen years previously some Scottish witches had been tried for conspiring against James himself. The parallel is clear. In the previous year, too, King James had been greeted by three sibyls at the gates of an Oxford college and hailed as the true descendant of Banquo. That is no doubt why Shakespeare, in direct contrast with the source, refuses to connect Banquo with the Macbeths' plot against Duncan. Shakespeare was adapting James's own suppositions and beliefs into memorable theatre. He was in a sense sanctifying them and turning them into myth.

Yet Shakespeare wrote with only one eye upon the king. *Macbeth* was also designed to entertain everyone else. It ushers on to the stage ghosts as well as bloodshed and magic. What could be more appealing to an early seventeenth-century audience than royalty and mystery combined? The scene at the banquet, in which Banquo's ghost appears to Macbeth, mightily impressed itself upon Shakespeare's contemporaries. It is a play that acquired an almost Celtic sense of doom and the supernatural. That is why actors refuse to name it *Macbeth*, but to this day continue to call it "the Scottish play." It is as if Shakespeare, deep in his Scottish sources, was possessed by a new form of imagination; it is a tribute to his extraordinary sensitivity and to his unconscious powers of assimilation.

Macbeth is one of the shortest plays that Shakespeare ever wrote—in fact only *The Comedy of Errors* is shorter—and has a playing time of approximately two hours. It is also remarkably free of oaths and profanities, as a result of a measure passed by Parliament in March 1603; a parliamentary act to "restrain the abuses of players" forbade irreverence or blasphemy on the public stage. It has been suggested that the relative brevity of the play is an indication of the king's span of attention, but this is unlikely. It may have been the result of cuts by the Master of the Revels. More likely, however, is that the play itself demanded this length. The intensity and concentration of the fatal action require a series of drumbeats. Although the slight ambiguity in the respective roles of Macbeth and Lady Macbeth suggests that Shakespeare may have begun the play without knowing which of them would kill the king, there is a consistency of effect. The verse is shaped and pared down so that it becomes echoic; it is almost relentless in its pace, and there are images throughout of rushing action. "Time" is mentioned on forty-four occasions. There are no puns, and only one "comic" scene in which the Porter responds to the knocking at the gate; it is hardly comic, however, since the Porter is modelled upon the keeper of Hell's gates and the elaborate references in the Porter's monologue to the details of the recent conspiracy are pervaded by a chilling gallows' humour.

The Porter is indeed an image of the Hell Porter in the mystery plays, and it has been well observed that the banqueting scene in the play is related to the scene of feasting in that part of the mystery cycle entitled "The Death of Herod." The death and doom of the ancient plays survive in Shakespeare's dramaturgy, as another layer of darkness and supernatural fear. Shakespeare is much more concerned with the ancient forces of the earth than with the omens of the sky. *Macbeth* is a poem of the night. Yet, in any discussion of Macbeth himself, the concept of darkness is not required. He is the most vital and energetic character within the play, a natural force, surpassing any conventional notion of good and evil. He partakes of the sublime. Like many of Shakespeare's tragic protagonists, he seems actively to seek out his fate.

Since the play is mentioned in a production by the Children of St. Paul's in early July 1606, it must have been performed at the Globe before that date. So *Macbeth* was played during the season that ran from Easter on 21 April until the middle of July, when once more the playhouses were closed as a result of the plague. The King's Men remained in the neighbourhood of London for a short period, however, in order to entertain King Christian of Denmark, who was the brother-in-law of James; he remained in England from 15 July to 11 August, and Heminges was paid for "three playes before his Majestie and the kinge of Denmarke at Greenwich and Hampton Court." It has plausibly been asserted that one of these plays was *Macbeth*, performed before the royal parties in the early days of August.

It is not at all clear, however, that King Christian and his hosts attended to the great drama. The Danish king was a heavy drinker, who on one evening was carried out of the entertainments in a state of insensibility. Everyone seemed to follow his example, according to Sir John Harington, and the English nobles "wallow in beastly delights" while their ladies "roll in intoxication." He added that "I ne'er did see such lack of good order, discretion and sobriety. The Gunpowder fright is got out of all our heads . . ."[5] The men fell down and the women were sick, an apt token of the change that had taken place since the days of Elizabeth. If it was a new society, it was not necessarily a more decorous one.

After their royal performances the King's Men began a season of touring in Kent, where they played at Dover, Maidstone and Faversham. They also journeyed to Saffron Walden, Leicester, Oxford, and Marlborough. It is tempting to believe that Shakespeare was with them when they visited Dover, at the beginning of October, if only because of the important presence of that town in his next play. But such explicit connections are dangerous. There is no reason to suppose that Shakespeare travelled with them, and every reason to believe that he was engaged elsewhere. In the course of this year, after all, he completed the writing of *King Lear*.

CHAPTER 79

Oh You Go Farre

here is ample evidence for the first performance of *King Lear* at the court on 26 December 1606. On the title page of the first quarto publication, it is announced that "yt was played before the Kinges Maiestie at Whitehall vppon St. Stephans night in Christmas Hollidayes." The title page is also singular for the name of "Mr. William Shakspeare" blazoned across the top in type larger than the rest. It is a clear sign of his eminence and what a later age would call "name recognition." It was also a way of distinguishing this play from the old *King Leir* published in 1605.

There were clear associations with *Macbeth*, the play composed immediately before it. Both dramas were concerned with what might be called the mythological history of Britain, but both have some contemporary import. The folly of Lear's division of his kingdom had been amply demonstrated, in a period when King James was intent upon unifying the separate kingdoms of Scotland and England into the one realm of Great Britain. In the third act the word "English" had been substituted by "Brittish." King James had warned his son, in *Basilikon Doron*, that "by deuiding your kingdoms, yee shall leaue the seed of diuision and discord among your posteritie." *King Lear* might be described as a meditation upon that theme. A political decision is once more lent a theatrical and even mythological dimension. In *Lear*, as in *Macbeth*, there are invocations of the medieval mystery cycle. Lear becomes the sacred figure who is mocked and buffeted. The use of British mythology once more prompted Shakespeare into calling up the powers of ancient drama. He was aiming for a total theatrical effect. If the regality of Lear was emphasised upon the stage, perhaps by the wearing of a crown, then his innate authority would have been sustained by James's own assertion of divine right. It renders Lear's decline and fall all the more fearful for a contemporaneous audience. The spectator must be thoroughly possessed by the idea of sacred kingship fully to appreciate the play.

The casting can in part be reconstructed. Richard Burbage excelled as Lear, and indeed it was reported that the old king "lived in him." Robert Armin played the Fool, and perhaps Cordelia. It seems to be a strange "doubling" but it would explain the fact that the Fool mysteriously disappears at the end of the third act, at which point Cordelia emerges. The idea of Cordelia played by a comic actor, however, does not suit modern taste. It is easier to imagine a boy in the part. We may also envisage Burbage and Armin upon the stage, contesting against the storm–or, rather, fighting to be heard against the noise of kettle-drums, squibs, and cannon balls being rolled in metal trays.

The young Shakespeare may have acted in an early production of the old play of *King Leir*. It has been suggested that the first *King Leir* was part of his own juvenile work, but it is more probable that he recalled his youthful involvement in it and then completely rewrote it for the King's Men. In preparation he read Holinshed and Sir Philip Sidney's *Arcadia*. He must also have been reading Florio's translation of Montaigne, since one hundred new words in that volume re-emerge in *King Lear*. He was immensely susceptible to the sound and rhythm of words, to the extent that after first encountering them he could effortlessly reduplicate them.

He also read an account of some spiritual malpractice by Jesuit priests in Samuel Harsnett's *A Declaration of Egregious Popish Impostures*. It was an account that had some resonance after the discovery of the Gunpowder Plot, but for Shakespeare it had a specific interest. Among the Jesuit priests, who were accused of feigning ceremonies of exorcism on some impressionable chambermaids, were Thomas Cottam and Robert Debdale. Cottam was the brother of the Stratford schoolmaster, John Cottam, to whom, many years before, Shakespeare probably owed his introduction to the Lancastrian recusant families of Hoghton Tower and Rufford Hall. Robert Debdale had been a neighbour of the Hathaways at Shottery and, being of an age with Shakespeare, may well have attended the Stratford school with him. So it is likely that Shakespeare turned to Harsnett's account for news of his contemporaries, and only by accident or indirection discovered material that would be of use in *King Lear*.

We may picture his mind and imagination as a vast assimilator, picking up trifles that were later polished until they glowed. He incorporates so many disparate elements, and conflates so many inconsistent sources, that it is impossible to gauge what attitude he takes towards the unfolding drama of King Lear. He is so absorbed by the matter to hand that there is neither opportunity nor occasion to dispense judgement except of the most blatant theatrical kind. The drama has no ultimate "meaning." In a play filled with rage and death, this may be the hardest lesson of all. Yet it may contain redemption. To watch *King Lear* is to approach the recognition that there is indeed no meaning to life and that there are limits to human understanding. So we lay down a heavy burden and are made humble. That is what Shakespearian tragedy accomplishes for us.

We glimpse here the insistent and instinctive patterns of his imagination that have nothing to do with homilies or sermons. He moved forward quickly with chiming words and themes, parallel phrases and situations, contrasting characters and events, working out their destinies. He improvised; he was surprised by his characters. He picked material from anywhere and everywhere. The feigning of madness by "poor Tom," for example, is amplified by allusions to Samuel Harsnett's account of apparent diabolic possession; in front of large crowds the Jesuit priests summoned forth various unclean spirits from the bodies of the women. Shakespeare uses the names of the devils that were invoked on this occasion. He also borrows the language of possession. It was a way of intimating that Tom's madness is feigned, just as the Jesuit priests are engaged in what Harsnett describes as "the feat of juggling and deluding the people by counterfeit miracles." But is there not some deeper connection between the theatre and these rites of exorcism, in front of an awed and astonished crowd? It is as if the "mimic superstition" of the papists was somehow replicated or complemented by the illusions of the playhouse. The invocation of Roman Catholic superstition, far from lancing Tom's folly, somehow increases the sacredness of Lear's terror. It may also have led Shakespeare to contemplate the nature of illusion itself. Even when the powers of the Jesuit priests are feigned, they seem to be effective.

That is why many scholars have deemed *King Lear* to be a mystery play in all but name, an echo of Catholic ritual satisfying the liturgical and iconographic hunger of those who professed the old religion. The desire for ceremony outlives the faith that first employed it. In fact there may be grace and redemption in the ceremony itself. It is certainly true that in 1609 and 1610 a group of Catholic actors performed *King Lear* in various sympathetic houses in Yorkshire. It would be absurd to suggest that this was a deliberate strategy on Shakespeare's part. It is more likely that the forces of his nature comprehended sacred, as well as secular, realities and that this reversion to old imagery was wholly instinctive.

There is another possible "source" for the play. An old courtier and "Gentleman Pensioner," Brian Annesley, was suffering from senility. Two of his daughters wished him to be declared insane, and thus "altogether unfit to govern himself or his estate."[1] But a third daughter, by the name of Cordell or Cordelia, pleaded on her father's behalf to Lord Cecil. After her father's death in the summer of 1604, in fact, Cordell inherited most of his property. Cordell Annesley then went on to marry Sir William Harvey, Southampton's stepfather. The case was well known, even beyond the Southampton circle, and indeed it may have prompted the revival of the old version of *King Leir* in 1605. It was a common enough occurrence for a contemporary sensation to be staged in the playhouses. It could have been performed by the Queen's Men at the Red Bull, for example, a playhouse that had been built in 1605 for just such popular or populist drama with what Thomas Dekker called its "unlettered" audience "of porters and carters."[2]

But *King Lear* leaves its sources far behind. Shakespeare removes the Christian allusions of the earlier drama, and gives it a thoroughly pagan atmosphere. This is a play in which the gods have turned silent. Shakespeare also strips away the romance elements, and fashions his plot out of disloyalty and ingratitude. The happy finale of the original *King Leir*, for example, is abandoned here for the numinous and tragic end of the protagonists. He invented the death of Cordelia cradled in her father's arms, a scene not to be found in any of the sources. The unremitting horror of that conclusion has prompted one eminent critic, Frank Kermode, to postulate the play's "unsparing cruelty" and "an almost sadistic attitude to the spectator."[3] Certainly the death of Cordelia would have come as an unhappy surprise to anyone acquainted only with the old play. *King Lear* is deeper and darker than any presumed original, with the forces of transcendence somewhere at work within it.

There are images throughout the play of the human body being wracked and tortured, as if Shakespeare were invoking the image of the Divine Human torn and dismembered. By slow degrees the wheel is turned, and all is thrown into agony and confusion. The play also elicits some of Shake-speare's most enduring preoccupations, particularly that of the father and daughter. The family, and conflict within the family, are the bases of the play itself. Indeed the family is at the centre of Shakespeare's dramaturgy; more than any other contemporary dramatist he is concerned with familial conflict. The action of *King Lear* itself exists only within the context of domestic hos-tility and rage. Lear and Cordelia are reunited, if not necessarily reconciled, and anticipate the family reunions of the later plays where in particular father and daughter achieve a living harmony—whether it be Pericles and Marina, Leontes and Perdita, Prospero and Miranda, Cymbeline and Imogen. The Latinate sonority of the daughters' names suggests, too, that they are in part formal or primal figures of filial love. In the earlier plays, by contrast, fathers and daughters are at odds—Capulet and Juliet, Shylock and Jessica, Leonato and Hero, Brabantio and Desdemona, Egeus and Hermia, Baptista and Katherina, are the most prominent examples. It is a pattern too persistent to be altogether neglected. In the late plays, when Shakespeare himself was reaching the end of his life, an ageing father is reunited with a long-absent daughter; there may be feelings of guilt and shame associated with this ab-sence, but all is forgiven. There are rarely mothers and daughters in Shake-speare's plays. The essential bond is father and daughter. It may not be the pattern of his life, but it is clearly the pattern of his imagination.

There is another aspect of his dramaturgy that generally goes unre-marked. In modern drama the accepted context is one of naturalism, which certain playwrights then work up into formality or ritual. In the early seven-teenth century the essential context was one of ritualism and formality, to which Shakespeare might then add touches of realism or naturalism. We must reverse all modern expectations, therefore, if we are properly to com-prehend *King Lear*.

There are many differences between the quarto and the folio editions of the play, to such an extent that the authoritative Oxford collection of Shake-speare's drama prints two separate versions as if they were indeed two dis-tinct plays. The quarto play was entitled *The History of King Lear*, and the folio play *The Tragedy of King Lear*. It seems that the first version was re-vised some five years after it was performed, and at that stage the newly fash-ionable act and scene divisions were introduced. The late folio omits three hundred lines of the early quarto, and adds a further one hundred "new" lines. In the quarto version there is a clear indication that Cordelia is leading a French army on English soil, where in the folio version the emphasis is upon domestic rather than foreign imbroglios. Cordelia is a stronger presence in the quarto than in the folio.

Since certain of the omitted lines reveal the presence of a French army on English soil, they may have been removed at the behest of the Master of the Revels. But it is much more likely that Shakespeare was responding to dramatic imperatives; the earlier version did not sufficiently isolate and clarify the figure of Lear. It scattered interest and effect, which could more usefully be focused upon the single tragic individual. It is the difference, perhaps, between the "history" and the "tragedy" on the respective title-pages. The later version is a more concise and more concentrated play, with greater attention to the pace of the action. The hundreds of minor changes between the two versions, compatible with a rewriting at speed by a dramatist absorbed in his work, also reveal the work of a thoroughly dramatic imagination, intent upon wholly theatrical effects. They prove beyond any possible doubt that Shakespeare was not averse to extensive revision and rewriting of his material, when occasion demanded it. His was always a work in progress.

CHAPTER 80

My Life Hath in This Line Some Interest

❖

Shakespeare had returned to Stratford by the summer of 1607, at the very latest, in order to attend the marriage of his oldest daughter. Susannah Shakespeare, named as a recusant in the previous year, had now outwardly conformed; this may have been to facilitate the wedding itself. In any case she was marrying a man of Puritan belief, John Hall, so there was no great religious prejudice in the family itself.

On 5 June William Shakespeare processed with his family to the church where at the altar, in ritual fashion, he relinquished his daughter to her new husband. In the marriage settlement he had promised them the 127 acres of Old Stratford he had purchased from the Combes five years before. There is every reason to suppose that Susannah was his favourite child. Certainly she was singled out in his will for preferential treatment. She may in fact have inherited something of his spirit, and was described on her tombstone as being "Witty above her sexe" and "Wise to salvation." The memorialist added that "something of Shakespeare was in that," so at the time she must have been recognised as in some ways resembling her father. She could also sign her own name, a skill which her sister Judith did not possess.

Her spouse, John Hall, was a doctor. Since in his later drama Shakespeare himself displays the utmost respect for doctors, the union no doubt had his blessing. The bridegroom was only eleven years younger than Shakespeare himself, and so Susannah was marrying a figure of some authority not unlike her father. He had been born in Bedfordshire, and had attended Queens' College, Cambridge, where he received a bachelor's and a master's degree. He had travelled in France for a period, and had set up practice at Stratford some years before his betrothal. The newly married couple lived in New Place for a period after the wedding, but it is possible that they soon purchased a house a few hundred yards away in the area designated on the maps as "Old Town." A timber-framed house of the period still survives, and has become known as "Hall's Croft." But the Halls returned to New Place after Shakespeare's death.

Hall became a confidant of Shakespeare, travelling with him to London on occasions, and "proving" his father-in-law's will. He kept a medical diary or case-book, which was published after his death with the somewhat exotic title of *Select Observations on English Bodies*. Here we find evidence that Doctor Hall tended his own family. When Susannah was suffering from the torments of the colic, for example, "I appointed to inject a Pint of Sack made hot. This presently brought forth a great deal of Wind, and freed her from all Pain." In her youth their daughter, Elizabeth, suffered serious spasmodic pain. Her father rubbed spices into her back, and massaged her head with almond oil until she was "delivered from Death." Hall believed in herbal cures, in other words, and treated other patients with pearl, powder of leaf gold and other precious minerals. He used emetics and purgatives to good effect. One happy patient wrote that "In regard I kno by experience: that hee is most excellent In that arte."[1] It can be supposed that he also treated his father-in-law, in Shakespeare's declining years, although no record of his ministrations has been recovered.

It is interesting, however, that in his previous plays Shakespeare had used the language and terminology of what might be called folk medicine, with allusions to wormwood and ratsbane, syrup and balsam, but from the time of his friendship with his son-in-law he introduced a more exotic range of medicines such as hebenon and coloquintida, mallow and mandragora. In *All's Well That Ends Well* he writes of the fistula and alludes to Galen and Paracelsus; in *Pericles* the doctor, Cerimon, revives Thaisa with "the blest infusions that dwels in Vegetiues, in Mettals, Stones" (1239–40). It is hard to escape the conclusion that his interest in such matters was quickened by his son-in-law's successful remedies. When in *Troilus and Cressida* Thersites recites a list of maladies, including cold palsies and sciatica, he might have been reading from Dr. Hall's case-book.

There is also proof in this case-book that Hall was by no means an extreme Puritan. He successfully treated a Catholic priest and noted that "beyond all expectation the Catholicke was cured," adding in Latin "*Deo gratias.*" We may imagine him to have been a moderate Puritan, married to a recusant and therefore content to overlook religious differences.

There were other births and deaths in the immediate Shakespeare family. The register of St. Leonard's Shoreditch records the birth, on 12 July 1607, of "Edward Shakesbye, the sonne of Edward Shakesbye, was baptised the same day–morefilds." The fact that he was baptised on the same day as his birth suggests that there was some urgency about the matter, and indeed a month later the baby died. On 12 August he was buried in St. Giles Cripplegate, where the register duly notes "Edward sonne of Edward Shackspeere, Player:base-borne." The infant was the son of Shakespeare's younger brother. The name "Edward" in the church registers is a transcription error for "Edmund," and is a common enough confusion in documents of the period; the mistake was prompted by the unfortunate child's own name.

So we can deduce that Edmund Shakespeare had travelled to London and had taken up the profession of "Player," imitating the career of his famous brother. Whether he had taken up the profession on his brother's advice, or whether he had simply followed his example, is not known. The fact that his son was baptised in Shoreditch and buried in Cripplegate must mean that Edmund was living in the northern suburbs, and that he was probably playing at the Curtain Theatre. He was living very close to Shakespeare's lodgings in Silver Street, in fact, and it is even possible that he shared them with him. There is no official record of his marriage, so he had also sired a bastard son. This was a not uncommon phenomenon in early seventeenth-century London but it does suggest that Edmund Shakespeare, now in his mid-twenties, was living a somewhat irregular existence as a player.

There are other domestic events to record. On 14 October 1607, in the parish church of Stratford, the son of Richard Tyler was baptised as "William"; it is possible that William Shakespeare was his godfather. Tyler, two years younger than Shakespeare, was a friend and neighbour of the dramatist. He was also no doubt at school with him. He was bequeathed a ring in the first draft of Shakespeare's will. Richard Tyler was a prosperous yeoman and gentleman, living in Sheep Street, who had held civic office and had been elected as churchwarden. In an official document he is described as "a man of honest Conversacion & quiet & peacable Carryage amongst his neighbours & towards all people."[2] Very little else is known about Tyler, but he may stand as representative of Shakespeare's Stratford acquaintances. They were generally prosperous, some of them being tradesmen and some of them being, like Tyler, "gentlemen." They were "honest" and "quiet" and "peaceable," very much the model of the English townsman of this period. And Shakespeare remained on affectionate terms with them all his life. It is hard not to suspect that they were comfortable and welcome company after the vivid and more excitable ambience of London. Shakespeare could relax with them, converse with them, drink with them, without the constant press of theatrical business. Four days after the baptism of little William Tyler in the parish church, Shakespeare's nephew, Richard Hathaway, baker, was married at the same altar. If the laws of family life applied to the Shakespeares, then the dramatist would have been present for that occasion also.

These rituals were taking place in the immediate aftermath of great local disturbance. The "Midlands Rising" was punctuated by savage enclosure riots directed against the larger landowners. The problems were particularly acute in the Forest of Arden where the enclosers had "turn'd so much of woodland into tillage . . . that they produce corn to furnish other counties." The ironworks in the region had also "destroyed prodigious quantities of wood,"[3] and the old commons had been transformed into privately owned pasturage. No one denied that the land was the property of the landowner; the rioters were protesting against the overthrow of centuries of traditional usage. There was also anger and dismay at continuing food shortages, a dearth which in the popular mind was associated with the pace of enclosures.

The rising began on the eve of May Day and quickly spread throughout the Midland counties until it became a summer of insurrection. The king issued a royal proclamation deploring the fact that "many of the meanest sort of people have presumed lately to assemble themselves riotously in multitudes."[4] The rebellion was only halted after savagely repressive measures by the authorities; the military killed scores of protesters, and many of those captured were hanged, drawn and quartered. The problems were, almost literally, on Shakespeare's doorstep and they entered at least one of his subsequent dramas.

In the winter season of this year, stretching from December 1607 to February 1608, the King's Men staged thirteen plays at the court for the benefit of the royal family. The names of these plays have not been recorded, but it is a fair assumption that one of them was the drama entitled *The Tragedie of Antony and Cleopatra*. In Samuel Daniel's verse drama *Cleopatra*, reissued in this year, there is a detailed and expressive description of the dying Antony being hoisted onto Cleopatra's "monument." This had not appeared in the earlier version of Daniel's play, printed in 1594, and suggests that Daniel had witnessed a performance of Shakespeare's scene in which, according to the stage-directions, "They heaue Antony aloft to Cleopatra." It has all the marks of a visual, rather than a verbal, memory. Since the theatres were closed from July onwards by reason of the plague, the likelihood must be that Daniel saw the play at the Globe in the late spring or early summer of 1607. It was restaged that Christmas for the benefit of the sovereign.

It is possible, however, that the audiences of the time remained unmoved by *Antony and Cleopatra*. With the exception of the allusion by Samuel Daniel, there is no recorded comment on its production. It was not published in Shakespeare's lifetime—and nor indeed was that other Roman drama, *Coriolanus*. If they had not been included in the Folio edition of Shakespeare's works, there would be no surviving text.

For *Antony and Cleopatra* Shakespeare borrowed from Plutarch and from Horace, from Montaigne and from Pliny. It says something about the effect of the theatre and the permanence of theatrical memory that this doomed love between Antony and Cleopatra, together with the assassination of Julius Caesar, have become the two most famous episodes of Roman history. With the magniloquent verse of *Antony and Cleopatra*, in particular, Shakespeare has reinvented the last years of republican Rome. The language of passion and aspiration dominates this play. It valorises everything, with the billowing rhetoric of the Egyptians contrasted with the high Roman rhetoric of time and duty. It is the oration conceived as poem. By some unerring insight, too, he has divined the essential characteristics of the protagonists. Octavius Caesar here bears all the incipient greatness and ruthlessness of the ruler who would become Augustus, the first emperor in Roman history.

Shakespeare's imagination seems to have been stirred by the vastness of the enterprise he is enacting; there are images of the world and of immensity, with the main protagonists in the early stage of becoming deities. Antony and Cleopatra could have echoed the emperor Vespasian's words upon his death-bed, "I am afraid I am turning into a god." But they embrace that fate; they long for metamorphosis. No play has so wide a stage, with so many scenes and with so many messengers from the boundaries of the known world–except that there are no boundaries and no limits, in this evocation of immensity. It is a pageant, a moving tableau, a procession. That is why Antony and Cleopatra are intensely theatrical creations, admiring their images as if they had been projected by some conjuror upon a linen screen.

CHAPTER 81

ℭhat $train Agen,
Ic Had a Dying Fall

ᛗ

n the last day of 1607, Edmund Shakespeare was buried. It was
a time of almost unbearable cold. By the middle of December
the Thames had frozen solid so that "many persons did walk
halfway over the Thames upon the ice, and by the thirtieth of December the
multitude . . . passed over the Thames in divers places."[1] A small tent city
sprang up on the ice, with wrestling bouts and football matches, barbers'
shops and eating-houses, trading upon the novelty of the silent and immobile
river.

On 31 December Edmund Shakespeare was carried to the church on the
southern bank of the Thames. The entry in the burial register of St. Saviour's reads: "1607 December 31 Edmond Shakespeare, a player, in the
Church." And then a note by the sexton runs: "1607 December 31 Edmund
Shakespeare, a player, buried in the church with a forenoon knell of the great
bell, 20s." The money for the bell no doubt came from the purse of his
brother, who in the bitter cold accompanied the coffin to the burial place. It
is possible, probable even, that Edmund died of the plague. He had followed
his infant son within six months.

And then, in the spring of 1608, an entry in the Stationers' Register
records a play that, unlike *Antony and Cleopatra*, became hugely popular in
Shakespeare's lifetime. In the published version of 1609 *Pericles* is identified
as "diuers and sundry times acted by his Maiesties Seruants at the Globe on

the Banck-side." So it must have been played at that theatre in the spring of the previous year, since the theatres were subsequently closed for eighteen months. The Venetian Ambassador took the French Ambassador to a performance, and a Venetian contemporary noted that "All the ambassadors who have come to England have gone to the play."[2] One versifier compared large London crowds "of gentles mixed with grooms"[3] with those who swarmed to see *Pericles*. Its edition in quarto was reprinted five times. It was quoted incessantly, and had the distinction of being dismissed by Ben Jonson as a "mouldy tale."[4] It was, of course, more successful than anything Jonson himself had ever written.

There is some disagreement over the form and nature of *Pericles* as well as the other late plays which share an abiding interest in music and spectacle. A convenient term is that of romance, since in this period there was a revival of what might be described as the cult of romance. The king's oldest son, Henry, was being compared with the legendary Arthur; this in turn inspired a new fashion for chivalry and legendary adventure on the pattern of Malory and Spenser. This was not of course a sufficient condition for the creation of *Pericles*, but it is a contributing factor. There was also a tradition of stage plays taken from medieval gestes, but the medieval context of *Pericles* is wider than that of knights and battles.

It is often suggested that Shakespeare had entered an "experimental" phase with *Pericles* and subsequent plays, but he himself would not have recognised or understood the term. It would also be a mistake to impose upon him principles or standards which a later generation would describe as "aesthetic." He did not have an aesthetic view of the drama at all, but a practical and empirical one. *Pericles* is an example. It is a play of extremities, of foul and fair closely joined. The most lubricious and bawdy prose is placed beside some of Shakespeare's most plangent verse, so that all seems to cohere as if by miracle. The great dirge to the sea deeps gives way to an image of prostitutes that "with continuall action, are euen as good as rotten" (1532–3).

The play attests in particular to Shakespeare's long affection for the religious plays of his childhood. The last mystery cycle was played in Coventry as late as 1579, well within the purview of the young Shakespeare. It is not necessary that he should have seen the mystery plays–although in the course of a Stratford boyhood it is likely that he did–only that he should have come from a culture in which they played a central role. They were part of the spirit of place.

Such paradigmatic events as "the Agony" and "the Betrayal" are redeployed in a number of Shakespeare's plays, and *Pericles* in particular inhabits a world of vision and of supernatural intervention, where the spiritualised hero must endure much suffering before being blessed. The visitation of the goddess Diana here replaces the more usual appearance of the Virgin Mary, but the meaning is the same. Indeed the play of St. Mary Magdalene to be found in the Digby Manuscript bears many parallels with Shakespeare's drama, including the birth of a child at sea during a storm, and the miraculous restoration of the unhappy mother. It is a matter of record that the Catholic players who had performed in the recusant households of Yorkshire included *Pericles* in their repertoire, and that the play was also included in a booklist belonging to the English Jesuit College at St. Omer in France.[5] It must have been deeply congenial to the adherents of the old religion.

Shakespeare seems deliberately to re-create the tone and atmosphere of the early medieval romances, too, on the very good and practical grounds that they could still have a startling effect upon their spectators. Longinus wrote of the *Odyssey*, "Homer shows that, as genius ebbs, it is the love of romance that characterises old age."[6] The Shakespearian romances may be an indication of advancing age but not of ebbing inspiration. His late plays are unique in the history of Elizabethan drama. With their combination of music, spectacle and vision, they fulfil all the conditions of older drama while at the same time providing a wholly contemporaneous interest in narrative and adventure. The medieval atmosphere of *Pericles* is in fact deliberately created with the appearance of the fourteenth-century poet John Gower as Chorus, at the beginning of every act. Gower's Chorus lends the play the form of ritual, exactly the effect that was intended. Ritual is another element involved in the enchanted atmosphere of romance.

After Shakespeare's death his fellow actors excluded *Pericles* from the Folio edition of his works in 1623. They seem to have taken the view that it was in part a collaboration and therefore did not fit an attribution to William Shakespeare. Most historians and textual scholars agree that much of the play was written by a second playwright, but there are also scenes and passages that are undoubtedly and authentically composed by Shakespeare. The identity of the second dramatist has been a matter of speculation, but one candidate emerges above all others. At some point in 1608 a playwright in his mid-thirties, George Wilkins, published a novelisation of the play entitled *The Painfull Aduentures of Pericles Prince of Tyre*. The novel is so close to the play, and is so intimate with its structure, that it has generally been agreed that Wilkins himself collaborated with Shakespeare in the composition of the drama. Wilkins was writing his novel from memory, his "foul papers" being now in the possession of the King's Men, and it is likely that the play proved so popular in the spring months of 1608 that Wilkins rushed into publication during the period when the playhouses were closed once more.

In the years between 1604 and 1608 Wilkins wrote other works of a popular nature, among them plays and prose narratives. The King's Men had performed his *The Miseries of Inforst Mariage* in the year before, so the connection between him and Shakespeare was already there. Wilkins wrote the first sections of *Pericles*, and parts of the other acts, while Shakespeare wrote the rest. It should also be noted here, given the fact that *Pericles* has often been considered to be a "Catholic" play, that Wilkins himself adhered to the old faith.

It might be wondered why the older and much more famous dramatist would condescend to work with a tyro. But Shakespeare was a man of the theatre. He was competent and practical, no doubt ready to work with anyone for the good of the company. It is not at all likely that the collaborators sat down together with their principal sources, Gower's *Confessio Amantis* and Laurence Twine's *The Patterne of Painefulle Aduentures*, before sharing out the plot of *Pericles*. It is much more likely that Wilkins suggested the idea of the play and himself devised the plot. His earlier venture with the King's Men had been relatively successful, and he was already trying his hand at prose romances. The company might have considered him to be a promising dramatist. After essaying a first version of *Pericles*, however, he may have discovered himself to be unequal to the task. He may have been in trouble with the authorities, or even briefly imprisoned. He may simply have run out of invention. So the work was handed to Shakespeare for completion. Shakespeare could on occasions act as a superior "play doctor" bringing together all the themes and strands of a plot. His imagination seems, in fact, to have been quickened by the last sections of *Pericles*, in which the restoration of Marina and the resolution of family loss are the important motifs. He added significantly to these scenes, and tended to leave the earlier stage business as it was. Since the play was extraordinarily popular, he made the right decision.

The prospect of Wilkins being arrested or imprisoned is no biographical fantasy. George Wilkins was a tavern-keeper and brothel-owner whose establishment was on the corner of Turnmill Street and Cow Cross Street. At the beginning of the twenty-first century, the site is still that of a flourishing public house. Wilkins had a reputation for violence and was regularly cited in the proceedings of Middlesex sessions court, particularly for assaults against the young female prostitutes whom he employed. He was accused, for example, of "kikkinge a woman on the Belly which was then greate with childe."[7] One of the guarantors of Wilkins on this occasion was Henry Gosson, of St. Lawrence Pountney; it was Gosson who issued the play of *Pericles* in quarto form. It seems probable that Wilkins obtained the play for him from the King's Men. Since he had written much of it, he may have had some claim to proprietorship. It might be added that, at a later date, Wilkins was convicted of being a thief and of harbouring criminals in his inn.

Shakespeare may also have been acquainted with Wilkins's father, a poet and well-known Londoner, who had died of the plague five years before. But it is also likely that Shakespeare encountered Wilkins through the agency of the Mountjoys; when the daughter of the house married one of the apprentices, Stephen Belott, the young couple became tenants of Wilkins at his inn on the corner of Turnmill Street. Belott himself had been well acquainted with Wilkins, and had eaten meals at his establishment. It was the most notorious of all London quarters, filled with brothels and cheap taverns, but it was also one of the most interesting. This was the world in which Shakespeare encountered his collaborator. It is not unusual to find Shakespeare in what might be called "low" company—he has been discovered before with the landladies of Southwark in an affray—and it is not even occasion for surprise. Even when wealthy and successful, he fitted himself to any kind of society.

Part IX

Blackfriars

Ben Jonson's *Oberon, the Fairy Prince* (1611): designs by Inigo Jones.
The style and staging of plays changed with the move to "indoors"
theatres such as Blackfriars.

CHAPTER 82

As in a Theatre the Eies of Men

✦

ince the doors of the playhouses were shut for eighteen months, from the summer of 1608, it may seem a strange time for the King's Men to be engaged in a very expensive theatrical speculation. Nevertheless at the beginning of August 1608, just when the theatres had closed down, Shakespeare and six of his colleagues leased the Blackfriars Theatre for a period of twenty-one years. The Children of the Chapel Royal had been disbanded, after a particularly contentious production that had scandalised the French Ambassador, and so their venue was available for hire.

Each "sharer" among the King's Men paid a seventh part of the annual rent of £40 to Cuthbert Burbage. There was also the cost of necessary repairs. Very little had been done during the last years of the childrens' occupancy, and the playhouse "ran far into decay for want of reparations."[1] It may have seemed a tempting prospect, but the King's Men must also have had great faith in the long-term financial health of the London drama. It may be that they were also trying to circumvent the ban on public playing at a time of plague by using a "private" playhouse; there is a note of a reward from the king in January 1609 "for their private practise in the time of infeccon."[2] This suggests that they did perform plays, under the cover that they were rehearsing for the court dramas of the Christmas season.

Their purchase is in any case a measure of the supremacy of the King's Men in the London theatre. No adult company had ever leased an indoors theatre, and no adult company had ever before played within the walls of the city. The playhouse was in a wealthy and respectable neighbourhood, too, close to the playgoing members of the Inns of Court. Ben Jonson lived here as did Shakespeare's friend, Richard Field; it was also a haven of painters' studios and the workshops of feather-makers. It is also worth observing that no other company had ever boasted the proprietorship of two theatres, or extended itself to the purchase of an indoors "winter" theatre and an outdoors "summer" theatre. As it turned out, the financial gamble of the new "sharers" paid off, and their profit at the Blackfriars playhouse was almost twice that of their profit from the Globe.

The cost of a token at the Blackfriars playhouse was 6 pence for the gallery, contrasted with a penny or 2 pence for the Globe. A shilling purchased a bench in the pit, closer to the level of the stage, and a half-crown bought a box. Gallants and devotees could hire a stool and sit upon the stage for 2 shillings; this was a habit apparently detested by the actors themselves, for obvious reasons, but it seems to have made economic sense. There was no standing room. Yet the Blackfriars Theatre had attractions of its own. Its use of music, in a closed space, was more elaborate. It had indoor illumination, with candles or torches, and was much more appropriate for formal and masque-like effects. The candles were hung from candelabra which could be lowered for "mending" or trimming, but for afternoon performances the windows allowed natural light to enter the proceedings. There was no curtain and there were no "footlights"; the auditorium was as brightly illuminated as the stage.

It has often been suggested that Shakespeare's dramaturgy changed after the removal to the Blackfriars Theatre, and that he increased the spectacular and the ritual elements of his drama. It is an interesting supposition but of course his use of Blackfriars postdates the highly ritualistic *Pericles*, which was performed at the Globe; it should also be remembered that in subsequent years his drama was to be seen at the Globe as well as at Blackfriars. There was no sudden or wholesale change in his art. Yet he was a skilful and professional man of the stage, and he made some alterations for the production of his plays in the private theatre. It is even possible that he added songs and music to old "favourites" such as *Macbeth*. The intimacy of the new theatre, which held some seven hundred spectators instead of the thousands at the Globe, may also have prompted him to make some changes in action and in dialogue. Many of these changes were not noted in the published versions of the plays, and are thus irrecoverable.

The King's Men also now commissioned from other dramatists plays that were more suitable for the smaller space of Blackfriars. From this time forward, for example, most of Ben Jonson's dramas were written for the company. Jonson's success as a writer of court masques, and his previous career as the writer of plays for the children's company, made him eminently suitable for the more refined audiences of the indoor playhouse. He wrote *The Alchemist* for this audience, succeeded by plays such as *Catiline* and *The Magnetic Lady*. At this juncture, also, the King's Men employed the play-writing skills of Francis Beaumont and John Fletcher; they had written all their plays for the private theatres, and were obvious candidates for the Blackfriars stage. Fletcher collaborated with Shakespeare in the older dramatist's final works. It may in fact have been Shakespeare who discerned his talent and urged his colleagues to hire him. Beaumont and Fletcher's *Philaster* bears a striking resemblance to Shakespeare's *Cymbeline*, but it is not clear which came first. The important point, however, is that they were both written for the conditions of the new theatre. Indeed in later years the King's Men would become associated with, and identified by, the Blackfriars playhouse as their principal centre of operations.

There is one other change that is associated with the use of indoor playhouses. From 1609 onwards the plays of the King's Men were divided into acts and intervals. Earlier dramas, when published after this date, have also been artificially divided into acts. It had become the new convention, dependent entirely upon the new conditions of the indoors playhouse where musical interludes became more significant; there was also the necessity of trimming the candles, for which the interval gave a convenient opportunity. Intervals had in any case already been introduced into the performances at court and at the Inns. They had become the token of a more "polite" attitude towards the experience of play-going. They were the fashion.

It is only to be expected that Shakespeare himself accepted the theatrical innovation in his last plays, and that he handled it expertly. He even revised the structure of some of his earlier plays, such as *A Midsummer Night's Dream* and *King Lear*, in order to accommodate the use of acts; in the latter case, particularly, he used the opportunity of restaging to make large revisions to the play itself. But there is no clear or general transformation. All of his subsequent plays could have been performed either at the Globe or at Blackfriars.

Coriolanus may be a case in point. It is a play that seems naturally to form itself into acts, and the sound of cornets is demanded on two occasions. Cornets were generally supplied in private playhouses. But *Coriolanus* also calls for trumpets, a Globe speciality, and some of the play's staging would suggest the larger arena of the public playhouse. So he composed it with both stages in mind. There were other Roman plays in the period, *Sejanus* and *Catiline* among them, but no one had previously treated the theme of Coriolanus, the Roman nobleman who refused to co-operate with the plebeians, and was exiled from the city only to return with an enemy army. Shakespeare had known the story from his schoolboy reading, and invoked the name of Coriolanus in the very early play of *Titus Andronicus*. He was one of the figures of Shakespeare's imagination. Shakespeare found the general story in North's translation of Plutarch's *The Lives of the Noble Grecians and Romanes*, one of his most constantly used and prolific source-books. By curious chance a paper survives, noting that a copy of North's translation was borrowed from the library of Ferdinando Stanley; it was loaned to one "Wilhelmi" by Ferdinando's wife, Alice, and returned in 1611.

Shakespeare proceeded to intensify the drama of Plutarch's central characters. There is a spareness in the language that is reminiscent of *Julius Caesar*, another Roman play in which a mighty figure is raised and pulled down. There are passages, however, where he seems undecided between verse and prose; in the cauldron of creation, they were indistinguishable. He had also become more interested in the theatrical possibilities of a particular flaw or weakness in character, whether amorousness in Antony or pride in Coriolanus. Yet as with all of Shakespeare's most important figures, Coriolanus is conceived in ambiguity. The rules or standards of interpretation are never clear, and there is no possibility of any final judgement. Like his maker, he remains opaque. He exists; he sings his high chant; and then he is ended.

Yet the play is affected by all the pressures of the time. The great insurrection in the Midlands of the previous year had been bloodily suppressed, but the summer of 1608 was marked by dearth and famine. On 2 June the king issued "A Proclamation for the preuenting and remedying of the dearth of Graine, and other Victuals" but it had only limited effectiveness. The people were starving from want of bread, and it is not at all surprising that the first scene of *Coriolanus* concerns the plight of the Roman citizens who are "all resolu'd rather to dy then to famish." The first citizen declares that they must "revenge this with our Pikes, ere we become Rakes. For the Gods know, I speake this in hunger for Bread, not in thirst for Reuenge" (19–22). Yet it would be wrong to consider Shakespeare as fundamentally sympathetic to their cause. In *Coriolanus* the crowd is portrayed as fickle and ever changeable, as light and as variable as the wind. In what seems to be an unconscious token of his attitude Shakespeare writes the stage-direction, "Enter a rabble of Plebeians." They are contrasted with the Roman nobles who in a fit of anachronism he calls "all the Gentry." The tribunes of the people are not treated by Shakespeare with any great respect, either. His opinion was shared by King James, who castigated the parliamentarians who failed to pass his expenses as "Tribunes of the people, whose mouths could not be stopped."[3] As a servant of the king, too, Shakespeare could not be seen to condone insurrection or rebellion. All of his instincts would in any case have been against it. He could draw attention to the plight of the poorer people without bread, while at the same time firmly withholding assent from their campaign of violence. That is what happens in *Coriolanus*.

There are other significant aspects to the play's topicality. The first citizen launches a direct assault upon hoarding, and upon those who "Suffer vs to famish, and their Store-houses cramm'd with Graine" (76–77). It so happens that Shakespeare himself had already been noted for the storage of 80 bushels of malt at New Place, as we have seen, and there is no reason to doubt that he continued to store or hoard quantities of corn or malt. So through the irate voice of the first citizen he adverts to himself. It is a most extraordinary act of theatrical impersonality, suggesting very forcefully that his imagination was not violated by sentiment of any kind. He could even see himself without fellow feeling. When it is also noticed that some of the charges against the Midlands rioters are here replicated as charges against the nobleman, Coriolanus, then we realise that the events of the day have been displaced and reordered in an immense act of creative endeavour. Everything is changed. It is not a question of impartiality, or of refusing to take sides. It is a natural and instinctive process of the imagination. It is not a matter of determining where Shakespeare's sympathies lie, weighing up the relative merits of the people and the senatorial aristocracy. It is a question of recognising that Shakespeare had no sympathies at all. There is no need to "take sides" when the characters are doing it for you.

Which is as much as to say that his sympathies, such as they were, lay entirely with the unfolding of the drama. It might even be suggested that the food riots at the beginning of the play (not present in the source, which merely describes the popular clamour of the Romans against usury) may simply have been Shakespeare's way of arresting the attention of his audience. It was a way of allowing them access to the world of ancient Rome. It was a way of gaining their imaginative assent by presenting something topical and familiar. Certainly the theme of dearth disappears from the gathering drama. Once it had achieved its purpose, it was forgotten. It is an important token of Shakespeare's true response to the world, which may well have been one of utter calmness and even of disinterest.

It has sometimes been surmised that he treats Coriolanus himself with a respect not untinged with admiration. He seems to be aware of his follies but forgives them for the sake of the character he presents to the audience. And that is the important point. The dramatist is intent upon presenting a character of power. Individual power is theatrical. Power misused and abused is also dramatic. Coriolanus is a thing of power; when he ceases to be that, he ceases to exist. That is the only reason Shakespeare chose him out of Plutarch. In a very interesting essay on *Coriolanus* William Hazlitt asserts that "the imagination is an exaggerating and exclusive faculty . . . which seeks the greatest quantity of present excitement by inequality and disproportion." Thus poetry puts "the one above the infinite many, might before right."[4] So the position of Coriolanus, reviled by the mass and exiled from Rome only to vow a terrible vengeance, is infinitely dramatic and elicits from Shakespeare some of his finest poetry.

CHAPTER 83

And Sorrow Ebs. Being Blown with Wind of Words

⟨ornament⟩

ne of the most powerful figures in *Coriolanus* is the mother of the eponymous hero, Volumnia, who has sometimes been considered to be a portrait of Shakespeare's own mother. One Danish critic, Georg Brandes, described Volumnia as the "sublime mother-form."[1] By curious coincidence Mary Arden died in the late summer of 1608, even as *Coriolanus* was being written, and on 9 September was buried in the parish church. She had outlived her husband and four of her children; whether the evident success of her oldest son compensated for the losses among her other children, is an open question. She had seen him rise to eminence in his dual profession as actor and writer, and purchase one of the grandest houses in the town. There is every reason to believe that she was proud of his achievements, and perhaps somewhat over-awed by them. We may recall here the admonitory words of Coriolanus to himself, that he must stand (2946–7)

> As if a man were Author of himself,
> And knew no other kin.

His mother had been occupying the old house in Henley Street together with Shakespeare's sister, Joan Hart, who continued to live there after Shakespeare's own death.

Shakespeare must have visited his mother there before her death. It has even been suggested that *Coriolanus* was written at Stratford because of the large supply of stage-directions in the published text. Thus there is written, "In this Mutinie, the Tribunes, the Aediles and the People are beat in" and "Martius followes them to gates, and is shut in." The argument postulates that he did not intend to be present for any of the rehearsals of the first performances, and so had to be more than usually explicit in his directions for the actors. It is a possible circumstance.

Just before his mother's death Shakespeare sued a Stratford neighbour, John Addenbrooke, for debt in the borough court; the sum of £6 was not forthcoming and so Shakespeare sued Addenbrooke's "surety" for the money. The case continued for ten months, a clear sign of Shakespeare's determination in such matters. In October he stood as godfather to the infant son of the alderman, Henry Walker, who was christened as William; he left the child a bequest in his will. It is important to note that Shakespeare could be accepted as a godfather only if he had outwardly conformed to the Church of England. There were clear rules on this matter, particularly since the godfather was charged with the spiritual education of the child. No nonconformist or recusant would have been permitted in that role. Before the ceremony, Shakespeare would also have received holy communion as a token of his orthodox faith. As the child of a recusant household, attached to the old faith but conforming to the observances of the new, he would have grown up with a profound sense of doubt. That is why ambiguity became one of the informing principles of his art. And why should it not be a mark of his behaviour in the world?

This raises the vexed question of his religion, endlessly debated through the centuries. It is true that he used the language and the structure of the old faith in his drama, but that does not imply that he espoused Catholicism. His parents are likely to have been of the old faith, but he did not necessarily take it with him into his adulthood. The old religion was part of the landscape of his imagination, not of his belief. As Thomas Carlyle stated, "this glorious Elizabethan Era with its Shakspeare, as the outcome and flowerage of all which had preceded it, is itself attributable to the Catholicism of the Middle Ages."[2]

There have been many studies of the association between Catholicism and the theatre itself, at the time "most of our present English *actors* (as I am credibly informed) being professed *Papists*."[3] William Prynne's asseveration does not help to untangle Shakespeare's private allegiances, however, and at most suggests that as an actor and dramatist he might have evinced a certain sympathy with the old faith. It must be said that there are a large number of friars and nuns, handled with gentle circumspection, within his drama; his contemporaries, in contrast, tended to treat them as an object of scorn or obloquy. There are also incidental references to Catholic rituals, services and beliefs that suggest some previous acquaintance with them; there are allusions to purgatory, to holy water, to the sacrament of penance, to the Blessed Virgin, and so on. They are all perfectly explicable on the understanding that the young Shakespeare was brought up in a household that professed the old faith. But his interest in ritual and sacramental observance was also part of his interest in the theatre. It was an aspect of his concern for the panoply of power, whether sacred or spiritual. He summons the pagan deities, for example, as frequently as he invokes the Christian God.

His own adult beliefs are much more difficult to estimate. It is possible that he was, in the language of the period, a "church papist"; he outwardly conformed, as in the ceremony of christening, but secretly remained a Catholic. This was a perfectly conventional stance at the time. There is also the statement, by Richard Davies, the Archdeacon of Coventry, that he "dyed a papist."[4] The archdeacon was a zealous Anglican, and would not have passed on this report with any great pleasure. It is not known how he received the information, but it is not necessarily inauthentic. It can be taken to mean that Shakespeare was given the sacrament of extreme unction at the time of his death. But this may have been at the instigation, or even the insistence, of his recusant family. He may have been too weak and too sick to comprehend the matter. Yet it is also sometimes the case that lapsed or quondam Catholics will, in extremis, embrace the possibility of redemption.

So there is only evidence by default. He seems to have avoided attending Anglican worship. There is no record for him in the token books (to prove that he had received holy communion) or vestry minute books of Southwark; he may have moved in with the Mountjoys since, as a member of a Huguenot household, he was not bound to attend the Anglican service. But, on the other hand, there is also no reference to him in any of the prolific records of Catholic recusants. He made no protest and incurred no fine. Once more he becomes invisible. That invisibility, or ambiguity, is reflected in his work itself. Despite the myriad allusions to the old faith, Shakespeare in no sense declares himself. In the tragedies, for example, the religious imperatives of piety and consolation are withheld; these are worlds with no god. He never adverts to any particular religious controversy, unlike the satirists of the contemporaneous theatre. It should be added that there is also very little sign of religious sensibility in Elizabethan drama as a whole; it is as if the dramaturge, having been banished from temple and church, shook the dust from his feet and built his own temple in the unhallowed ground without. The safest and most likely conclusion, however, must be that despite his manifold Catholic connections Shakespeare professed no particular faith. The church bells did not summon him to worship. They reminded him of decay and of time past. Just as he was a man without opinions, so he was a man without beliefs. He subdued his nature to whatever in the drama confronted him. He was, in that sense, above faith.

Nevertheless he was godfather in this year to another William, baptised in the font of Stratford Church. William Greene was the child of Thomas and Laetitia Greene, who were in fact residing at New Place during this period. Thomas Greene was a local lawyer who had been educated at the Middle Temple, an institution with which Shakespeare was very well acquainted, and he had moved to Stratford in 1601. At some point he moved with his wife into New Place as a tenant, sharing the household with Anne Shakespeare and her daughters. It may have been a way for Shakespeare of easing the burden of costs. The fact that they named their son William is, in any case, an indication of harmony with the master of the house.

The continuance of the plague meant that, in the summer and autumn of 1608, the King's Men were obliged to tour the provinces with their new plays. They were at Coventry at the end of October, and also at Marlborough, but the rest of their progress is unknown. They were back in London, however, for the court performances of that year. They performed twelve plays at Whitehall, but the titles are not recorded.

It is more than likely that Shakespeare's most recent plays, *Pericles* and *Coriolanus*, were among them. But there is one other candidate for inclusion in this period. *Timon of Athens* is a play of strange clamour and majesty. It is the story of a man whose lavish generosity is not reciprocated and who, as a result, falls into a state of savage misanthropy. It has been suggested that it comes close to a fable or morality play, with Timon as a type rather than a character. But that is to misinterpret Shakespeare's subtlety. There is no conflict here between good and evil, only between variously mixed natures.

The play cannot be securely dated. It is one of those free-floating dramas, without much contemporary reference and no record of contemporary performance, which could be placed anywhere in the early seventeenth century. It may be unfinished or have been abandoned. There are passages of dialogue that need revision, and certain elements of the plot are left suspended. His texts were always in a fluid and incomplete state but, to paraphrase *Animal Farm*, some are more incomplete than others. It is also possible that it represents a "first draft" by the dramatist, and that he was content to leave it at that point. There is also a theory that the play survives at various stages of composition, with some scenes "roughed out" and others almost finished. If that is the case, then it is a Shakespearian document of the utmost interest; it shows, as it were, the painterly "washes" of Shakespeare's imagination. On this occasion he created a structure and sketched out the balance of plot and sub-plot, adding incident and detail, but he paid relatively little attention to the role of the minor characters. None of these observations necessarily implies that the play was not performed. Even in its incomplete state it is a fluent and powerful piece of theatre. There is no record of any contemporary productions, but that in itself is not conclusive.

The immediate source of the play was once more North's translation of Plutarch, and indirectly we may see Shakespeare's process of association. The story of Timon is related in Plutarch's life of Antony, which Shakespeare studied for *Antony and Cleopatra*. In Plutarch's work Alcibiades is the figure complementary to Coriolanus, the subject of Shakespeare's previous drama. Alcibiades plays a large part in *Timon of Athens*. So there is a set of connections leading Shakespeare forward. He moved from one classical figure to another, all part of the immediate arena of his imaginative concerns. He was also influenced by an academic comedy, entitled *Timon*, which might have been performed at the Inns of Court. This drama may have played some part in the composition of *King Lear* as well, and so acted as a powerful spur to Shakespeare's imagination.

It is also surmised that *Timon of Athens* was in part the result of a collaboration with the young dramatist Thomas Middleton, who by his midtwenties was already well known for his verse and for his satirical city comedies. Shakespeare's collaboration with Middleton resembled that with a co-author, perhaps George Wilkins, over *Pericles*. Shakespeare was happy to contribute scenes, or whole acts, while leaving intact the somewhat jejune work of his collaborators. It is as if he did not care very much about the finished article, as long as it was performable. In this respect he was acting as a professional man of the theatre rather than as an "artist" in the modern sense. It may well be that each dramatist wrote his selection of scenes independently, and that they were brought together only in the process of rehearsal. For this reason his colleagues did not originally intend to place *Timon of Athens* in the Folio edition of his collected plays. It was only included when a sudden gap (the result of problems over the publication of *Troilus and Cressida*) had to be filled. The King's Men did not consider the play to be really "by" Shakespeare. As a result of its placing in the Folio, however, it has remained forever in the canon. The legacy and reputation of even the most eminent writers can sometimes be secured by accident.

CHAPTER 84

And Beautie Making Beautifull Old Rime

⁂

The plague raged through London for the entire year of 1609. Dekker lamented the condition of the period when "Pleasure itself finds now no pleasure but in sighing and bewayling the Miseries of the Time." He recorded that "play-houses stand (like Tavernes that have cast out their Maisters) the dores locked up, the Flagges (like their Bushes) taken down; or rather like houses lately infected, from whence the affrighted dwellers are fled, in hope to live better in the Country." And he added that "Playing vacations are diseases now as common and as hurtful to them as the Foul Evil to a Northern Man or the Pox to a Frenchman."[1] The King's Men were once more on a provincial tour to escape the miasma of the capital. They visited, among other places, Ipswich, New Romney and Hythe. For much of this journey they sailed around the coast.

Shakespeare, probably relieved of his acting duties, was certainly now considering a permanent removal to Stratford. His tenant or house-guest, Thomas Greene, was urgently enquiring whether a new house would be ready for him by the spring of 1610. This suggests that a date for Shakespeare's return had been agreed. But in this year, too, Shakespeare had business finished and unfinished in Stratford. In June 1609, for example, he settled his dispute over debt with John Addenbrooke. In the records of the Stratford court Shakespeare himself is described as "*generosus, nuper in curia domini Jacobi, nunc Regis Anglie.*"[2] He was, in translation, a gentleman recently at the court of James, now King of England. His status as the king's servant was very well known in Stratford. He was something of a resident dignitary. In this year, too, he and Thomas Greene sent a suit of complaint to the Lord Chancellor over some matters concerning the Stratford tithes which Shakespeare had been granted. Later in the year his brother, Gilbert, had to appear in court for some unspecified offence; to judge from those cited with him, he had some violent companions in the neighbourhood.

Shakespeare had not finished accumulating land in the vicinity. In the following year he bought for £100 a further 20 acres from the Combe family, adding to his previous purchase of 127 acres eight years before. In this period his brother-in-law, Bartholomew Hathaway, paid £200 for the farm and farmhouse at Shottery where Anne Hathaway had been brought up. It was their real family home. It is likely that Shakespeare helped his relative to find that large sum. One astute scholar of Shakespeare's imagery has noted that in *Cymbeline*, the play he was composing in this period, there is a continual vein of allusion to "buying and selling, value and exchange, every kind of payment,"[3] as if Shakespeare's mind was running upon such matters even without his realising it.

He may also have needed the seclusion of New Place to arrange in shape and order the sonnets he had written on various occasions in the past. Now that his mother was dead, he may have felt able to publish their somewhat scandalous content. It is not certain whether he considered the sensibilities of his wife–unless he believed, as many scholars have since maintained, that the contents would be understood to be manifest fiction. Deprived of income from the closed theatres, he may also have considered this an opportune moment to sell the manuscripts to a publisher.

They were duly published in 1609 under the title "SHAKE-SPEARES SONNETS Neuer Before Imprinted." They were printed by George Eld and were to be sold for 5*d* a copy, by John Wright whose shop was at Christ Church gate on Newgate Street. The dedication was signed by Thomas Thorpe, the publisher, rather than by Shakespeare himself. It must be the most famous dedication in all literary history, consisting of the mysterious and much debated lines.

TO THE ONLIE BEGETTER OF THESE INSVING SONNETS MR.
W H ALL HAPPINESSE AND THAT ETERNITIE PROMISED BY

OVR EVER LIVING POET WISHETH THE WELL-WISHING
ADVENTVRER IN SETTING FORTH. TT.

It is not at all clear what is meant by this. Who or what is the "begetter"?
The inspirer of the sonnets, or the person who provided them to the pub-
lisher? And who is "Mr. W H"? Could it be Henry Wriothesley, Earl of
Southampton? But then why are the initials reversed? Is it William Herbert,
Earl of Pembroke, who may have been the recipient of the early sonnets? It
is unlikely that a nobleman would be addressed as "Mr." Could it be William
Hathaway? Or might it be Sir William Harvey, who had previously been
married to the Countess of Southampton? It might even be a misprint for
"Mr. W SH." It is also possible that Thorpe misunderstood Shakespeare's
original dedication to "W H," and added "Mr." as an afterthought. Like all
good historical problems, the interpretations are endless and endlessly intriguing. Who is the "adventurer" and to what obscure or dangerous corner
of the world is he "setting forth"? Could this also be another reference to
William Herbert, Earl of Pembroke, who in the spring of this year became a
member of the consortium known as the King's Virginia Company?

It is sometimes suggested that Thomas Thorpe was a "pirate" printer
who came across Shakespeare's poems clandestinely and published them
without authorisation. But there is no record of Shakespeare's protest, and
there is no sign that they were withdrawn from sale or subsequently "corrected" for an authorised edition. It is much more likely that Shakespeare
himself was responsible for their collection and publication. The order of
the poems is expertly arranged, and who else would have such a complete
collection of the sonnets in manuscript? They were an enduring project,
continued over several years. No one else would have owned all of the
material available to the poet himself. In 1612, three years after publication,
Thomas Heywood reported that Shakespeare had indeed published his sonnets "in his owne name."[4] Then, two years later, William Drummond
recorded that Shakespeare had "lately published"[5] his work on the subject of
love.

There is no reason to doubt this contemporary testimony. Thomas
Thorpe himself was a respectable publisher who had issued works by Jonson
and by Marston, and who also had close connections with the theatrical
world. In recent years he had published authorised versions of *Sejanus* and
Volpone, performed by the King's Men, as well as *Eastward Ho!* It is most improbable that he would print a pirated edition of poems by the most famous

dramatist of the age. It would have been a grave lapse of duty in the eyes of his colleagues in the Stationers' Company, and open him to severe censure.

It has been stated with some authority that by 1609 the fashion for sonnet sequences had passed, and that at this late date the passionate expression of even the most famous dramatist might not find favour. It is true that the early seventeenth-century world was fuelled by sudden fads and fashions. It was a time of constant novelty and inventiveness in which there was little room for old styles and old themes. But the first years of the reign of James had inaugurated a new range of sonneteering, and in particular a kind of roguish or epigrammatic "anti-poetry" of which the sonnets to the Dark Lady are a good example. It was not necessarily a bad time to be published.

Edward Alleyn purchased a copy of the Sonnets in the summer of 1609 (if the reference is not a later forgery), but the little volume does not seem to have been overwhelmingly popular. There was to be no further edition until 1640, long after the death of the poet. In contrast, Michael Drayton's sonnet sequence was reprinted on nine separate occasions. There was, however, some reaction to Shakespeare's publication. The young George Herbert condemned the sequence for indecency, and one early reader appended in his first edition "What a heap of wretched Infidel Stuff."[6] The complaint has not been upheld by posterity, but at the time it may have been provoked by the unflattering references to the Dark Lady or to the homo-erotic tone of some of the earlier sonnets.

However long Shakespeare remained in Stratford, he had returned to London for the Christmas season at court. He was no longer acting but he was still responsible for rewriting and general supervision of the plays set before the king. In the chamber accounts of Whitehall it is noted that the King's Men played no less than thirteen times. One of those plays was the newly written *Cymbeline*.

It is a play that might have been composed for the newly purchased Blackfriars Theatre which, after a respite in the plague, opened a few weeks later in February 1610. There were a number of stage devices, including the descent of Jupiter "in Thunder and Lightning, sitting vppon an Eagle: hee throwes a Thunder-bolt. The Ghostes fall on their knees." There was no mechanism for these effects at the Globe, so we may assume the likely venue to have been the private playhouse. Such gaudy interventions emphasise how carefully and deliberately Shakespeare staged his dramas for the new conditions of performance. There is "Solemne Musicke" and a jaunty parade of spirits, all adding to the atmosphere of intimate spectacle that the Blackfriars playhouse encouraged. This is also the play in which Imogen wakes up beside a headless corpse, and believes it to be the body of her husband. No artifice is too obvious, no illusion too theatrical, in this most pantomimic of plays. Shakespeare has taken a potential tragedy and elevated it to the status of melodrama. In this last phase of his career he was pre-eminently a showman.

Samuel Johnson did not admire *Cymbeline*.

> To remark the folly of the fiction, the absurdity of the conduct, the confusion of the names and manners of different times, and the impossibility of the events in any system of life, were to waste criticism upon unresisting imbecility, upon faults too evident for detection, and too gross for aggravation.

If we rename folly as fancy, and absurdity as deliberate farce, then we may come to a better understanding of the play than the eighteenth-century critic. Shakespeare delighted in its "impossibility" because he was writing a play which was in part masque and in part romance. It was entirely suited to its period, at a time when Jacobean spectacle had reached new heights of artificiality. It was a play without a subject, except that of its own intricacy.

Shakespeare went back to the legendary history of Britain and to the plays of his childhood, even to the plays in which he had been cast as a young actor, summoning up the spirit of old romance; in the sequence of spectacle and vision towards the end of the play, he even employed an antique style in homage rather than in burlesque. Plays of this kind had become very popular on the London stage, with dramas such as Beaumont's and Fletcher's recent *Philaster* and the revival of the favourite *Mucedorus*. But, in *Cymbeline* Shakespeare out-runs them all with the sheer arbitrariness and extravagance of his invention. There was also a vogue for plays concerning the British past, perhaps reflecting the new king's concern for a united Britain. Throughout this play, in fact, can be detected the pressure of James's sovereignty in small allusions and details. There is one other detail. Imogen, disguised as a boy, claims that her master is one "Richard du Champ." This is of course Richard Field in a French guise. Field had been the publisher of *The*

Rape of Lucrece and *Venus and Adonis*, in whose atmosphere of musical solemnity *Cymbeline* itself is bathed. Shakespeare here is making a playful allusion to his old friend.

The presence of Imogen is a reminder that in *Cymbeline* for the last time Shakespeare uses the device of the girl dressed as charming boy, when in reality she is a boy actor all along, with an attendant atmosphere of sexual bawdry and innuendo; it is a transformation so much associated with his plays that with some justice we may call it Shakespearian. No other dramatist employed the devices of cross-dressing so frequently or so overtly as Shakespeare. It is clear why he was so enamoured of it. It is ingenious and strange, allowing much subtle play and allusiveness. It offers rich comic possibilities, but it also invokes the spirit of sexual liberty. It is perverse and pervasive, representing the licence of Shakespeare's imagination.

There are other echoes and allusions to his previous plays in *Cymbeline*, suggesting that the full force of his creation is deployed somewhere within it. There are invocations of *Othello* and *Titus Andronicus*, most strongly, but also of *Macbeth* and *King Lear*. A speech in the play closely parallels one of the sonnets which he was revising for publication.

In these last plays (which he did not necessarily know were his last) he was opening the gates. What is important in *Cymbeline* is the note of sustained feeling, what Hazlitt describes as "the force of natural association, a particular train of thought suggesting different inflections of the same predominant feeling,"[7] which is evidence of continuous excitement in the process of writing. He uses the broken language of passion and of intimate feeling with many asides and colloquialisms, ellipses and elisions; he even seems to transcribe the language of thought itself, as it is turning into expression. His language rises upwards in endless ascent, with the soaring of the cadence matched with aspiring feeling and unforced fluency. The Jacobean audiences were entranced by it. They sucked up extravagant words like sweets.

The music for *Cymbeline* was especially written by the court lutanist, Robert Johnson, who had been brought in by the King's Men to arrange the musical settings for the Blackfriars plays. One of the songs from the play, "Hark, hark, the lark," survives in a manuscript score which may be Johnson's own.

Two brothers are about to sing a dirge, the justly celebrated "Feare no more the heate o'th' Sun," when one of them explains that "our voyces Haue got the mannish cracke" (2188). The other then adds, in parentheses, "I cannot sing: Ile weepe, and word it with thee" (2191). It is clear that the voices of the two child actors had unexpectedly broken and, without replacements for them, the apology was added at a late stage of rehearsal. Shakespeare was accustomed to last-minute revisions, and in this broken music we discern the circumstances of the time.

CHAPTER 85

So There's My Riddle.
One That's Dead Is Quicke

n the spring of 1611 Simon Forman, the Elizabethan doctor and magus, made notes upon the productions he had seen recently. He was among the thousands at the Globe who had gone to performances of *Macbeth*, *Cymbeline* and a brand-new play entitled *The Winter's Tale*. Of *Macbeth* Forman principally noted the supernatural events and the prodigies. It seems from his account that the most extraordinary and effective scene was that in which Banquo's ghost appears at the banquet. The witches obviously had a sensational effect, too, but from Forman's account it is clear that they were played as "3 women feiries or Nimphes,"[1] perhaps by the boy actors. Forman made a professional note to himself when he observed "Also howe Makbetes quen did Rise in the night in her slepe, & walke and talked and confessed all, & the doctor noted her wordes."[2] Forman also watched *Cymbeline*, for which he gives a bald summary of events; the spectacle of "a cave" impressed itself upon his imagination, so it must have been a striking effect somewhere within the "discovery space" of the stage. Forman is circumspect about *The Winter's Tale*, although it is clear that the character who most entertained him was Autolycus "the Rog that cam in all tattered like coll pixci." The part was no doubt played to great effect by Robert Armin, and led to Forman appending a note to "beware of trustinge feined beggars or fawninge fellous."[3]

Shakespeare had been writing *The Winter's Tale* in the preceding year, and its overwhelmingly pastoral setting has suggested to some critics that he wrote it at New Place in Stratford. The same reasoning would suggest that he wrote *The Tempest* while temporarily residing on an island in the Mediterranean. *The Winter's Tale* is a play that could have been performed at the Blackfriars playhouse as well as the Globe; since they remained open for ten months of this year, 1611, it is likely to have been presented at both the indoor and outdoor theatres. The elaborately staged drama is crowned by the ultimate scene in which the supposed statue of Hermione is miraculously restored to life in front of her astonished husband and daughter. It is an exhilarating theatrical moment. Shakespeare may have previously seen it in action at two royal events. During the king's entry into London in 1604, and during his opening of the New Exchange in 1609, statues also stirred into life and spoke. It may in fact have been one of the boys from the King's Men who performed the feat at the New Exchange. Once Shakespeare had seen it, however, he had to use it.

The play was closer to a musical comedy than any previously written by him; there are six songs, five of them sung by Armin as Autolycus, with Robert Johnson as the very likely composer of the music. One song demands a trio. There are also two elaborate dances, by satyrs and by shepherds, which would have been closer to masque than popular folk dance. Music would also have been heard as the enchanted statue begins to move. It is perhaps indicative of the play's appeal that it was performed at court on an unprecedented six occasions. It was better than a masque. It was a full-scale entertainment, drama and ritual all in one. Yet, as Forman suggests, it also pleased the great crowds at the Globe. Many of the scenes relied upon spectacle as much as sense. One long scene, one of the longest in all of Shakespeare's works, depicts a sheep-shearing festival which becomes an image of timeless popular ritual. And there is the famous stage-direction in the third Act (1309–10):

> This is the Chace,
> I am gone for euer.
> *(Exit pursued by a Beare)*

The bear was a familiar feature of Bankside, of course, and dancing or performing bears were also very common in the streets of London. But it is doubtful that the King's Men used or borrowed a real animal from their colleagues in the baiting arena. It would have been more comic to have an actor in a costume. But the sudden and apparently random use of the animal testifies to Shakespeare's extraordinary grasp of stage business. The appearance of the bear marks the transition in this play from the direst tragedy to the most whimsical comedy, and just such a diversion prepares the audience for the change in pace and tone. The pursuit of the old man by the bear is, of course, terrible and comic all at once. It is a symbol of the play itself.

As in all romances, or musical comedies, the passions in *The Winter's Tale* are strident and ill-concealed. The principal themes are of insane jealousy followed by guilt and remorse; the unhappy and separated protagonists are then reunited in a scene of ultimate forgiveness and reconciliation. It is a play that induces happiness, and awakens hope, in its spectators. It is perhaps not coincidental that it was performed on the anniversary of the Gunpowder Plot, and then again after the catastrophic death of James's elder son and heir. *The Winter's Tale* was something of a public benefit, a device to remove mourning. In this play the human and the natural come together, in the great ongoing rhythm of life itself. The poetry of the dialogue follows the natural fluencies and hesitations of thought itself; it is instinct with the life of the mind.

The principal source of the play is Robert Greene's prose romance *Pandosto*, from which Shakespeare takes much of the material for his first three acts. It will be remembered that Greene was the author who, just before his death, had attacked "Shake-scene" in *Groats-worth of Witte*. Among other charges he accused him of plagiarism. Now, eighteen years later, Shakespeare was extracting matter from the dead man's most popular work, making the whole plot more fanciful and more unreal. He may have permitted himself a moment of satisfaction. And then he called it a winter's tale, an idle story, an old fable, a fireside extravagance. Shakespeare was not a sentimental man.

In this year, too, there were third editions of no fewer than three of his plays—*Titus Andronicus*, *Hamlet* and *Pericles*. These were plays from all the stages of Shakespeare's career, from the very early *Titus* to the very late *Pericles*. He was now being recognised and measured by his total achievement. He could delight the royal family, please the audiences of Oxford, and entertain the great crowds at the Globe. It seems clear, in retrospect at least, that he had reached the very pinnacle of his career. And now he was on everyone's lips. One author, writing upon the standards of "true writing," refers to Shakespeare as one from whom "wee gather the most warrantable English."[4] In a letter of 1613 Leonard Digges, the stepson of Shakespeare's executor, wrote of a "Booke of Sonets which with Spaniards here is accounted of their lope de Vega as in Englande wee sholde our Will Shakespeare."[5] Note that here he is "our" Shakespeare, already treated as a representative of the national literature.

For the winter season in late 1611 he returned to court with two new plays. In the revels accounts there are references, on 5 November, to "A play Called ye winters nightes Tale." Four days before, "Hallomas nyght was presented att Whithall before ye kinges Maiestie a play Called the Tempest."[6] No significance can be read into the date of All Hallows, 1 November, when the poor would sing for soul-cakes. Yet there remains an air of enchantment, not unmixed with melancholy, about Shakespeare's last completed play. He would collaborate with other dramatists in future productions, lending his skills and experience to the work of others, but *The Tempest* has the distinction of being the final work he wrote alone.

As in *Pericles* and *The Winter's Tale* there are large elements of masque and music in *The Tempest*. It seems very likely that he wrote the play for production in the indoors playhouse of Blackfriars. It is very specifically designed for intervals between the acts, particularly that between the fourth and fifth act, when music would be played. Ariel and Prospero leave the stage together at the end of the fourth act, and then enter together at the beginning of the fifth. This would not have been possible at the Globe, where action was continuous and uninterrupted.

Shakespeare's imagination was always roused by the sea. It is no accident, therefore, that he was drawn to the recently published accounts of colonial voyages. Two years previously, some colonists on their way to Jamestown, in Virginia, were blown by a severe storm onto the Bermudas. Shakespeare had read their adventures. He had also read a book entitled *A True and Sincere declaration of the purpose and ends of the Plantation begun in Virginia* as well as Silvester Jourdain's *A Discovery of the Bermudas, otherwise called the Ile of Divels*, both published in 1610. He was already acquainted with some of the principal members of the Virginia Company, such as the

Earl of Pembroke, and he had ready access to first-hand accounts of mutiny and insubordination among some of the colonists. He read Montaigne's essay, "Of the Canniballes," in Florio's translation. He remembered Marlowe's *Faustus*, and his schoolboy reading of Ovid and of the storm in Virgil's *Aeneid*. There was a riding-master in London called Prospero. So all these things came together, stirred by the report of a great storm.

The Tempest begins with a great shipwreck with its *"tempestuous noise of Thunder and Lightning"* and the entrance of the mariners *"wet."* From this first scene onward, Shakespeare explores in a wholly practical sense all the possibilities of the indoors stage. It is a play of almost continuous spectacle. There are songs with *"solemne and strange Musicke,"* in a drama that is accompanied by music composed once more by Robert Johnson. The late plays could easily be identified as works "by Shakespeare and Johnson." The elaborate effects of magic and the supernatural are also accompanied by instruments, as, for example, in the scene where the spirits enter *"in seuerall strange shapes, bringing in a Table and a Banket; and dance about it with gentle actions of salutations."* And there was of course now the almost obligatory inclusion of the masque, heralded once more by music and by the goddess Juno's descent upon the stage. Then enter *"certaine Reapers (properly habited:) they ioyne with the Nimphes, in a gracefull dance,"* until they are dismissed by Prospero with the utterance of some of the most famous lines in all of Shakespeare (1612–14):

> . . . we are such stuffe
> As dreames are made on; and our little life
> Is rounded with a sleepe.

Shakespeare has created the most artificial of all plays that becomes a meditation upon artifice itself. *The Tempest* also has the distinction of using a classical form, with the unities of time and place, for the purpose of conveying completely non-classical, which is to say magical, effects. It is as if he were, like Prospero, writing a lesson in theatrical enchantment. It is sometimes concluded that Prospero is an image of Shakespeare himself, renouncing his "potent art" at the close of a successful theatrical career. But that seems an unwarranted supposition. There is no reason to believe that Shakespeare deemed his theatrical career to be at an end. The model for Prospero might in any case have been Doctor John Dee, the magus of Mortlake (where

Shakespeare once stayed) who declared that he had burned his books of magic.

It is also sometimes suggested that at this late date Shakespeare was becoming disengaged from, or disenchanted with, the theatre; but the careful crafting of *The Tempest* suggests that he was still closely involved in all aspects of the drama. There is no sense of an ending.

When Men Were Fond,
I Smild, and Wondred How

Shakespeare returned to Stratford in the early months of 1612 to bury his brother, Gilbert, in the old church. Gilbert Shakespeare was two and half years younger; he had never married, living with his sister and her husband in the family home of Henley Street where he may have continued his father's trade as glover. He was literate, and well enough acquainted with business to act on his brother's behalf in the purchase of Stratford land. There was now one surviving brother, Richard Shakespeare, who also continued to live as a bachelor in Henley Street; but he, too, would die before Shakespeare himself. It would be a strange man who, under these circumstances, did not consider the limits of his own mortality. It was a shrinking family, emphasised by the fact that Shakespeare had no male descendants direct or indirect.

He was back in London three months later, when he was asked to testify in a case concerning the Mountjoy family of Silver Street with whom he had lodged. The case had been brought by one of Mountjoy's apprentices, Stephen Belott, who had married Mary Mountjoy but had still not received from Mountjoy himself the dowry that he had been promised. So he called William Shakespeare to testify on his behalf. The case was heard at the Court of Requests, at Westminster, on 11 May. Shakespeare was described as "of Stratford-upon-Avon," which suggests that he had no residence in London during this period. He had been called as a witness because, as it transpired, he had acted as an intermediary between Belott and the Mountjoys in the matter of the marriage and the dowry.

A maidservant, Joan Johnson, declared the Mountjoys had encouraged "the shewe of goodwill betweene the plaintiff [Belott] and defendants daughter Marye." She also recalled Shakespeare's role in the affair. "And as she Remembreth the defendant [Mountjoy] did send and perswade one mr Shakespeare that laye in the house to perswade the plaintiff to the same marriadge." It would seem, then, that Shakespeare had some skill as a "persuader" in affairs of the heart. A friend of the family, Daniel Nicholas, then amplified the picture of Shakespeare with his testimony that

> Shakespeare told this deponent [Nicholas] that the defendant told him that yf the plaintiff would Marrye the said Marye his daughter he would geve him the plaintiff A some of money with her for A porcion in Marriadge with her. And that yf he the plaintiff did not marry with her the said Marye and shee with the plaintiff shee should never coste him the defendant her ffather A groate, Whereuppon And in Regard Mr. Shakespeare hadd tould them that they should have A some of money for A porcion from the father they Weare made suer by mr Shakespeare by gevinge there Consent, and agreed to marrye.

It is not clear if these are the exact words that Shakespeare used to Nicholas on this occasion; given the interval of eight years, it is unlikely. But it is clear that he played an intimate part in all the arrangements for the marriage portion, and in fact took upon himself the task of match-making. To be "made sure" was to perform a troth plight, pledging marriage one to another.

The testimony of Shakespeare himself, as transcribed in the court, is non-committal. This must have been a peculiarly sensitive moment, assuming that Shakespeare still retained the trust of Mountjoy himself. He was in practice being asked to testify against him. So there is a measure of caution in his reported testimony. It is most interesting, however, as the only recorded transcript of Shakespeare's voice. The dramatist stated that "he knoweth the parties plaintiff and deffendant and hath known them bothe as he now remembrethe for the space of tenne yeres or thereabouts." Stephen Belott "did well and honestly behave himselfe" and was a "very good and industrious servant in the said service," although Shakespeare had never heard him state that he "had gott any great profitt and comodytye by the service." Perhaps this was in answer to a question about Belott's recompense from

Mountjoy. Mrs. Mountjoy had been the one to solicit Shakespeare's help in the marriage when she did "entreat" him "to move and perswade" Stephen Belott. He testified that she and her husband did "sundrye tymes saye and reporte that the said complainant was a very honest fellow."

It seems that at some point Belott had then asked Daniel Nicholas to get some specific answer from Shakespeare about "how muche and what" Mountjoy was promising him on marriage to Mary. Shakespeare then replied, according to Nicholas, "that he promised yf the plaintiff would marrye with Marye . . . he the defendant [Mountjoy] would by his promise as he Remembered geve the plaintiff with her in marriadge about the some of ffyftye poundes in money and Certayn houshould stuffe." But in subsequent questioning Shakespeare was extremely vague. He recalled that a dowry of some kind had been promised but, in contrast to Nicholas, he could not remember the sum "nor when to be payed." Nor could he remember any occasion when Mountjoy "promised the plaintiff twoe hundered poundes with his daughter Marye at the tyme of his decease." Nor could Shakespeare describe "what implementes and necessaries of houshold stuff" Mountjoy gave with his daughter. In fact Belott and his new wife had received only the sum of £10, and some old furniture. It seems that Mrs. Mountjoy had urged her husband to be more generous, but she had died in 1606. From Belott's point of view, it was all very unsatisfactory. And Shakespeare had not been of any help. He could not remember any details of any conversations. It might even be concluded that he was being deliberately vague or forgetful, for the sake of his old friendship with Mountjoy.

A second hearing took place on 19 June, when Shakespeare's memory would have been further put to the test, but Shakespeare did not appear on that occasion. Like many such cases it grumbled on without any definite conclusion. It was referred to arbitration, and Belott was awarded a little over £6, but no payment by Mountjoy is recorded. The details of this ancient case are no longer of any consequence, except in so far as they help to illuminate Shakespeare's life in the ordinary world. He seems to have been willing to act as a "go-between" in delicate marital negotiations, no doubt because he had a reputation for finesse in such matters. He was clearly not a forbidding or unapproachable man; quite the contrary. But when called to account for his actions he becomes non-committal or impartial, maintaining a studied neutrality. He withdraws; he becomes almost invisible.

CHAPTER 87

Let Time Shape, and There an End

here is a curious mention of a play performed at Whitehall on 8 June 1612, in front of the Ambassador of the Duke of Savoy. It was entitled *Cardenna*. It was then performed again at court in the following year, under the title of *Cardenno*. It is curious because, at a later date, a play was registered for publication under the title of "*The History of Cardenio* by Mr. Fletcher & Shakespeare." It is well known that in this period Shakespeare and Fletcher were indeed collaborating upon dramas for the King's Men. The fruits of their joint endeavours were to include *All Is True* and *The Two Noble Kinsmen*. It may be that Shakespeare had entered semi-retirement and that Fletcher had in fact taken over from Shakespeare as the company's principal dramatist. *Cardenio* would then have as much claim to authenticity as the two other plays which have now formally entered the Shakespearian canon. But *Cardenio* has not survived. It is a lost play. It may have been derived from the first part of Cervantes's *Don Quixote*, in which the character of Cardenio emerges, and in 1758 Lewis Theobald, a distinguished editor of Shakespeare's works, published a play on the story of Cardenio which he claimed to be "revised and adapted" from a manuscript in his possession "written originally by W. Shakespeare." No trace of the manuscript has been found.

If Shakespeare did indeed play a part in writing *Cardenio* in 1612, it is the only drama of that year with which he can be associated. All subsequent plays would also be collaborative works. So there is clear evidence of a diminution of activity, the reasons for which are unclear. It may have been encroaching ill-health; it may have been the pleasures of Stratford and of retirement; it may simply have been the loss or lack of inspiration. He may have done as much as he had ever wanted to do. It is not an unusual scene in the last years or months of a writer's life. He did not necessarily "know" that he would be dead within three years; when his imagination dimmed, death may have intervened naturally.

There was one unwanted and unwarranted publication, however, in this year. The printer William Jaggard brought out a third edition of *The Passionate Pilgrim* in which five of Shakespeare's poems, purloined for the occasion, were added to much inferior stuff and the whole advertised as "by W. Shakespeare." One of the authors whose work had been pirated for this collection, Thomas Heywood, then complained of the "manifest injury" done to him. He went on to claim that "the Author," or Shakespeare himself, was "I know much offended with M. *Jaggard* (that altogether unknowne to him) presumed to make so bold with his name."[1] Shakespeare's remonstrances must have had some effect, because a second title-page was added without any attribution to him. It is a trivial incident that displays the extent of Shakespeare's literary fame.

In his preface to *The White Devil*, published this year, John Webster adverts to "the right happy and copious industry of M. *Shake-speare*, M. *Decker* & M. *Heywood*."[2] It may seem odd at this late date to include Shakespeare with such manifestly inferior writers, but the disparity would not have occurred to anyone at the time. Contemporaries lack the subtle discrimination of posterity. In this case the emphasis is being placed upon the three dramatists' fluency and speed of production. Ben Jonson had said as much in the same year, with his address to the reader in *The Alchemist* in which he disparaged those dramatists who "to gain the opinion of copy"[3] or facility, will not check or polish their invention. Jonson's disguised complaint was that Shakespeare had written too much. It is not likely to have been a criticism upheld by the audiences of the period.

From Christmas 1612 through to 20 May 1613, the King's Men played continually at court as well as Blackfriars and the Globe. Among the royal performances were those of *Much Ado About Nothing*, *The Tempest*, *The Winter's Tale*, *Othello* and *Cardenio*. For the betrothal and marriage of King

James's daughter, Princess Elizabeth, the King's Men played on no fewer than fourteen occasions. For these performances they received the large sum of £153 6s 8d.

Despite the evident fact that Shakespeare was writing less there is no indication that he was losing his interest in, or enthusiasm for, the theatre itself. In March 1613, for example, he completed negotiations to buy the gatehouse of Blackfriars. It was described as a "dwelling house or Tenement" partly built over "a great gate." It was against the building known as the King's Wardrobe on the west side, and on the east bordered a street that led down to Puddle Dock; the price also included a plot of ground and a wall. Part of it had once been a haberdasher's shop. He was now very close to the Blackfriars playhouse and, by means of a wherry from Puddle Dock, in easy reach of the Globe on the other side of the river. Shakespeare paid £140 for the property, of which £80 was in cash and the other £60 tied up with a kind of mortgage.

The purchase may have been purely an investment on Shakespeare's part, but then why break the habit of a lifetime and invest in London rather than in Stratford property? It may have been the propinquity to the playhouses that steered his decision. Did he still think of himself as a man of the theatre? He was now collaborating with Fletcher, and could hardly have done so from Stratford. He may simply have grown tired of living in lodgings, and wanted some permanent home in the capital. He was still only in his forties and, despite the deaths of two of his brothers, he may have had little reason to doubt his longevity.

There were, as so frequently in seventeenth-century legal transactions, complications. Shakespeare brought in with him three co-purchasers or trustees to safeguard his interest. One of them was Heminges, his colleague from the King's Men, and another was the landlord of the Mermaid Tavern, William Johnson. This suggests some familiarity on Shakespeare's part with the famous drinking-place. The third trustee was John Jackson—also an habitué of the Mermaid—whose brother-in-law, Elias James, owned a brewery by Puddle Dock Hill. They were three local men of some repute, therefore, and represent precisely the kind of society to which Shakespeare had become accustomed. It has been suggested that Shakespeare chose these trustees so that a third of the property would not automatically be inherited by his wife, as her "dower" right, and there may have been some agreement (no longer extant) on its use after his death. In 1618, two years after his death, the trustees did in fact convey the gatehouse to John Greene of Clement's

Inn and to Matthew Morrys of Stratford "in performance of the confidence and trust in them reposed by William Shakespeare deceased, late of Stretford aforesaid, gent., . . . and according to the true intent and meaning of the last will and testament of the said William Shakespeare."[4]

Morrys and Greene were part of Shakespeare's extended family. Morrys had been the confidential secretary of William Hall, who was the father of John Hall, Shakespeare's son-in-law, and had been entrusted with William Hall's books on alchemy, astrology and astronomy in order to instruct John Hall on these arcane matters. Greene was a friend and neighbour, the brother of Thomas Greene who had resided for a while in New Place. It looks very much as if these two men were acting as agents on behalf of John Hall and his wife Susannah Shakespeare. It was the only London property owned by the Shakespeare family, and the beneficiaries may have wished to make good use of it. So by means of complication and indirection Shakespeare made sure that the house reverted to his oldest daughter rather than to his wife. Any interpretation is possible, the most likely being that Anne Shakespeare had neither need nor use for a house in the capital. She never actually visited London, as far as is known, and is hardly likely to have done so after the death of her husband. Or the whole matter may have simply been a technical or legal device to expedite a quick mortgage without incurring a fine. It is all too easy to over-interpret ancient documents.

The gatehouse did have a very curious history, however, largely concerned with its role as a papist "safe-house" in times of trouble. As the former home of the black friars, before the dissolution of the monasteries, it carried some ancient spirit of place. In 1586 a neighbour complained that the house "hath sundry back-dores and bye-wayes, and many secret vaults and corners. It hath bene in tyme past suspected, and searched for papists."[5] A relative of the Lancashire Hoghtons, Katherine Carus, died here "in all her pride and popery."[6] Then in later years it was used as a hiding-place for recusant priests, and it was searched many times. In 1598 it was reported that it had "many places of secret conveyance in it" as well as "secret passages towards the water."[7] The owners admitted to being adherents of the old faith, but denied harbouring priests. The papist connection may simply be coincidental, and Shakespeare may have purchased the house for quite other reasons, but it is suggestive of a certain affection or nostalgia.

It seems that he also leased out a set of rooms in the gatehouse to John Robinson, son of a Catholic recusant who had harboured priests in Blackfriars and brother of a priest who was lodged at the English College in Rome.

Robinson's affiliations are really not in doubt, and he may in fact have acted as a "recruiting agent" for the Jesuit college at St. Omer.[8] In his will Shakespeare refers to the gatehouse "wherein one John Robinson dwelleth scituat." Some biographers suggest that Robinson was a servant rather than a tenant of Shakespeare, but the connection was in any case a close one. Robinson visited Stratford, and was one of those who attended New Place in Shakespeare's dying days. He was a witness who signed the dramatist's will. Nothing else is known of him. The cloak of Shakespeare's invisibility covers those closest to him.

There is much that is perplexing about Shakespeare's association with known or suspected recusants. A list of his acquaintance will reveal six men who suffered death for the old faith; in 1611 John Speed explicitly linked the dramatist with the Jesuit missionary, Robert Persons, as a "petulant poet" and "malicious papist"[9] intent on treasonable practice. There is a connection, glimpsed by his contemporaries, but it remains occluded.

One of Shakespeare's new neighbours was Richard Burbage, who owned a great deal of property in Blackfriars. In fact, shortly after purchasing the gatehouse, Shakespeare collaborated with his colleague in a surprising venture. They designed an *impresa* for the Earl of Rutland, to be worn by that young nobleman on the occasion of the Accession Day tilt of 24 March. An *impresa* was a badge or token which acted as a kind of cipher for the wearer's moral characteristics; it generally included an emblem, and a motto, painted upon pasteboard. Shakespeare's motto for Rutland may have been suitably cryptic. A courtier of the time noted that some of the *imprese* were so obscure "that their meaning is not yet understood, unless perchance that were their meaning, not to be understood."[10] Shakespeare was paid 44 shillings in gold pieces for the design of the device, and Burbage the same amount for constructing and painting it. The object itself has not survived, but clearly the young earl considered that Shakespeare and Burbage were the two most prominent of the courtly makers. Burbage also had a considerable reputation as a part-time artist. The Earl of Rutland may also have seen the *impresa* created by Shakespeare for the tournament of *Pericles*, and had been suitably "impressed."

It should not be a surprise that Shakespeare, at this late stage of his career, was called upon to perform relatively minor tasks. He had in his youth been called a "Johannes factotum," after all, and he may have enjoyed the opportunity of creating on a small scale. It has for some time been suspected, for example, that he composed epitaphs for his friends and colleagues—sometimes in game and sometimes in earnest. There is extant an epitaph to Elias James, the brewer whose premises were on Puddle Dock Hill. It is to be found in a manuscript that includes a poem, "Shall I die?," which has also been tentatively attributed to Shakespeare. The seventeenth-century antiquary Sir William Dugdale, who has a reputation for accuracy, stated that the epitaphs on the tombs of Sir Thomas Stanley and Sir Edward Stanley in Tonge Church "were made by William Shakespeare, the late famous tragedian."[11] They strengthen the dramatist's connection with the Stanley family, and increase our understanding of the acquaintance of "gentle" Shakespeare. It seems likely that Shakespeare also composed the epitaph for his friend and neighbour in Stratford, John Combe, and in fact Combe's tomb was constructed by the partnership of Garret and Johnson close to the Globe on Bankside. Shakespeare evinces a particular interest in, and fondness for, funereal monuments; no doubt the Combe family left the commissioning in his hands. It has also been suggested that Shakespeare's own epitaph, containing the famous curse on anyone who moves his bones, was written by the incumbent himself.

CHAPTER 88

Ɔ Ɔ(aue ℳot Ɖeseru'd ℭhis

n incident on the afternoon of Tuesday 29 June 1613 threw all
of Shakespeare's plans into confusion. The King's Men were
playing *All Is True* at the Globe, a play concerning the marital
affairs of King Henry VIII upon which Shakespeare collaborated with
Fletcher. It was a new play, having been performed only two or three times
previously. The courtier, Sir Henry Wotton, has left a complete account of
the disaster that ensued. "Now," he wrote:

> King Henry making a masque at the Cardinal Wolsey's house, and cer-
> tain cannons being shot off at his entry, some of the paper, or other stuff,
> wherewith one of them was stopped, did light on the thatch, where being
> thought at first but an idle smoke, and their eyes more attentive to the
> show, it kindled inwardly, and ran round like a train, consuming within
> less than an hour the whole house to the very grounds. This was the fatal
> period of that virtuous fabric, wherein yet nothing did perish but wood
> and straw, and a few forsaken cloaks; only one man had his breeches set
> on fire, that would perhaps have broiled him, if he had not by the benefit
> of a provident wit put it out with bottle ale.[1]

Another observer of less sardonic temper noted that "the fire catch'd & fastened upon the thatch of the house, and there burned so furiously as it con-

sumed the whole house, & all in lesse than two houres (the people having enough to doe to save themselves)."[2] A third account confirmed that all of the spectators escaped without injury "except one man who was scalded with the fire by adventuring in to save a child which otherwise had been burnt."[3]

It was a disaster for the King's Men, who had been deprived of a venue and an investment in one swift action. It might have been an enactment of Prospero's words that "the great Globe it selfe" shall "dissolue" and "Leaue not a racke behinde."

There was of course the immediate matter of rebuilding. Shakespeare owned a fourteenth part of the theatre's shares, and was therefore liable for one fourteenth of the cost; this amounted to something like £50 or £60. He still owed £60 for the mortgage on the Blackfriars gatehouse, to be paid back within six months. Even for an affluent country landowner, these were large sums of ready money. Since there is no mention of the Globe shares in his will, it is possible that he sold them as a consequence of the fire. The Globe rose again within a year, but without Shakespeare as part owner. On this, or a later, date he also sold his shares in the Blackfriars playhouse. His financial interest in the theatre had come to an end. It is possible that he gave up play-writing when he gave up his shares, a practical end to a thoroughly pragmatic career.

There was a further, private, anxiety concerning his daughter Susannah. In the summer of this year she had brought an action of defamation against a neighbour, John Lane, who had claimed that she had "the running of the raynes & had bin naught with Rafe Smith"—that she had had sexual inter-course with Rafe Smith, in other words, and had contracted gonorrhoea. In the small enclosed community of Stratford, these were controversial allega-tions indeed against the wife of a prominent doctor and daughter of a local eminence. The case was heard in the bishop's Consistory Court at Worcester Cathedral, a measure of the seriousness with which the affair was taken, but John Lane did not appear for questioning. The case brought by Susannah Shakespeare was proved, and John Lane was excommunicated.

In the latter part of 1613, in the absence of the Globe and the now almost predictable closure of Blackfriars from July to December, the King's Men toured in the late summer and autumn in Folkestone, Oxford, Shrewsbury and Stratford itself. They played fourteen times at court, and among the court performances were the two plays jointly written by William Shakespeare and John Fletcher. *All Is True* and *The Two Noble Kinsmen* were the last fruit of Shakespeare's association with the King's Men, and as such have the curious status of all last things. It is likely that Shakespeare was himself at court to receive the congratulations and thanks of his sovereign. *All Is True* was performed at the Globe, unhappily as it turned out, but it was equally well suited to the private circumstances of court performance and preeminently to the indoors playhouse at Blackfriars. In one of those rare moments of dramatic enchantment, some of the events depicted in the play actually occurred in the same great chamber of the Blackfriars where the performance was being held. The re-enactment was so astonishingly complete that there must have been a somewhat eerie feeling of historical déjà vu about the whole performance. The scene in question concerns the appearance of Henry VIII and Katherine of Aragon in a consistory court, before the papal legate, to determine whether their marriage was legal or not. It was not a divorce court, as some have alleged; if there had been no marriage, there could be no divorce. It was a solemn and sacred occasion none the less, and in *All Is True* it is imparted with a weight of dramatic spectacle and rhetoric.

This is in keeping with a play which is freighted with historical allusions, to a period only just out of reach, and which is bounded by the notion of historical majesty. Sir Henry Wotton, in his report on the fire, had noted that the play "was set forth with many extraordinary circumstances of pomp and majesty." Wotton disliked this aspect of the drama, since then the theatre seemed to become a second court. In the play there are spectacles and masques, processions and trumpeters, with elaborate stage-directions in one scene for the appearance of "short siluer wands . . . the great Seale . . . a Siluer Crosse . . . a Siluer Mace . . . two great Siluer Pillers." There were scenes in which at least twenty-three players had to be accommodated upon the stage. The whole thing must have been performed very rapidly indeed to be encompassed within the "two short hours" promised by the Prologue.

How much of this is Shakespeare's devising, and how much Fletcher's, is open to guess. Before we ascribe the excessive theatricality to the younger man, however, it should be remembered that in his earliest plays Shakespeare had a pronounced and definite taste for spectacle. This is a period when English history plays were once more becoming fashionable, and Shakespeare always had an eye for fashion. *All Is True* also gave him the opportunity of exploring the nature and character of Wolsey, and it should come as no surprise that Shakespeare should illuminate him from within and thus avoid overt partisanship or prejudice; he wonders at his magnificence, but pities him in his fall. At a time when King James was seeking peace with Spain it was natural that the Spanish queen in the play, the aggrieved Katherine, is conceived in the form of suffering virtue.

It is generally agreed that Shakespeare wrote the first two scenes of the first act, involving court intrigue as well as the appearance of the king and the cardinal. He then went on to write the first two scenes of the next two acts, sketching out the main lines for his collaborator or collaborators to follow. He also wrote the great set scene of the Consistory Court, as well as the more intimate and lubricious dialogue between Anne Boleyn and an "old lady"; these are, in a sense, his specialities. The court scene is in fact largely transcribed from his main source, Holinshed's *Chronicles*, and perhaps lacks the quick alchemy of his earlier borrowings; but the verse is forceful and supple enough to suggest no lessening of dramatic power. He wrote the scene in which Wolsey contemplates his fall, another great transition that Shakespeare had mastered in the early history plays; whenever any man fails, Shakespeare's sympathy envelops him. He also wrote the first scene of the last act which sets up the denouement. He gave a structure, and a tone, to the whole production. He may also have gone over the finished playscript, adding phrases or images here and there. There may even have been a third collaborator, the elusive Beaumount, but at this point speculation becomes useless.

There seems to be no doubt, however, that *The Two Noble Kinsmen* was the next collaboration between William Shakespeare and John Fletcher. On the title page of the first edition, published in quarto form in 1634, it is described as being "presented at the Blackfriers by the Kings Maiestie servants, with great applause: Written by the memorable Worthies of their time: Mr. John Fletcher, and Mr. William Shakspeare. Gent." It is worth noting that Fletcher's name is mentioned first.

Shakespeare once more established the essential structure of the play, by writing the whole of the first act and parts of the final three acts; he may also have gone over the completed work, rephrasing and augmenting as he saw fit. It is a reworking of "The Knight's Tale" from Geoffrey Chaucer's *The Canterbury Tales*; characteristically Shakespeare takes a more ritualistic, and Fletcher a more naturalistic, attitude towards the original source. The fact that it was not included in the Folio edition of Shakespeare's plays may suggest that it was considered to be a company, rather than an individual, play.

All Is True had escaped that fate by being the culmination of a long sequence of history plays already accredited to Shakespeare.

Two of Shakespeare's most alert and astute interpreters, however, found the signs that he had inhabited *Two Noble Kinsmen* all but overwhelming. Charles Lamb noted of its Shakespearian passages that he "mingles everything, he runs line into line, embarrasses sentences and metaphors: before one idea has burst its shell, another is hatched and clamorous for discourse."[4] Schlegel, writing on the same play, considered its "brevity and fullness of thought bordering on obscurity."[5] There are occasions when meaning seems to run away from him, losing itself among a plethora of rich phrases, and there are occasions when the language is pushed to extremity (I.i.129–31):

> But touch the ground for us no longer time
> Then a Doues motion, when the head's pluckt off:
> Tell him if he i'th blood cizd field, lay swolne
> Showing the Sun his Teeth; grinning at the Moone
> What you would doe.

There are lines that seem purely Shakespearian, as when one queen speaks of her humble suit as (I.i.184–5):

> Wrinching our holy begging in our eyes
> To make petition cleere.

There are times when the syntax is very complicated indeed, seeming to express the concept of difficulty itself. And there are occasions when Shakespeare seems to rebuke his own contorted prolixity. He had forged so supple and subtle a medium that, effectively, he could do as he liked with it. So it is perhaps worth quoting the last lines of the play, delivered as customary by the most well-born of the remaining characters on the stage. They are the words of Theseus, Duke of Athens, and they have some claim to being the last that Shakespeare ever wrote for the stage (2780–6):

> O you heavenly Charmers,
> What things you make of us? For what we lacke
> We laugh, for what we have, are sorry, still
> Are children in some kind. Let us be thankefull
> For that which is, and with you leave dispute

> That are above our question: Let's goe off,
> And beare us like the time.

In retrospect this may seem a fitting epitaph for Shakespeare's career, with its resolution and its stoicism, its subdued gaiety and its sense of transcendence.

CHAPTER 89

My Selfe Am Strook in Yeares I Must Confesse

n the spring of 1614 a preacher was staying overnight at New Place. He was supposed to preach at the Guild Chapel, next door to Shakespeare's dwelling, and the corporation paid the Shakespeare family 20 pence for the expense of "one quart of sack and one quart of clarett wine"[1] purchased to entertain the unnamed minister. It is not known if the master of the house was present on this occasion, but the likelihood must be that he spent more time in Stratford than in the gatehouse of Blackfriars. His seems to have been a kind of retirement, or semi-retirement, if only because of the evident fact that he neither wrote nor collaborated in more drama. But he still travelled to and from London.

His earliest biographer, Nicholas Rowe, states that the

> latter part of his life was spent, as all Men of good Sense will wish theirs may be, in Ease, Retirement, and the Conversation of his Friends. He had the good Fortune to gather an Estate equal to his Occasion and, in that, to his Wish; and is said to have spent some Years before his Death at his native Stratford.[2]

There is no reason to doubt the essential narrative here, although it does tend to discount the purchase of his gatehouse in Blackfriars. The reasons given for his retreat have been various. He came back because he was tired and in ill-health. He came back because he knew that he was dying. He came back in order to revise his plays for future publication. All, or none, may apply.

Nicholas Rowe reports further that "his pleasurable Wit and good Nature engag'd him in the Acquaintance, and entitled him to the Friendship, of the Gentlemen of the neighbourhood."[3] These "gentlemen" would of course include the town worthies, many of whom he had known all his life and some of whom he would remember in his will. There were the Combes, for example, who lived in the largest house in Stratford and who were among the wealthiest families in Warwickshire. There was the Nash family, large landowners, who lived next door to New Place. And there was Julius Shaw, a very prosperous dealer in wool and high bailiff of the town; he lived two doors down from New Place. There were of course many other neighbours—as well as his immediate family—living in close proximity. These were the people whom he saw every day, and with whom he exchanged greetings and small talk. Shakespeare was now much more identified with his family, and with his native background, than he had been at any time since his childhood. He had, in a sense, completed the circle. The themes of restoration and regeneration, so familiar in his late drama, could now be applied to life itself.

There were also the local dignitaries with whom he would have had an acquaintance if not necessarily a friendship. Among these were Sir Henry and Lady Rainsford, who lived at Clifford Chambers very close to Stratford. John Hall, Shakespeare's son-in-law, was their doctor; but they were also closely associated with another Warwickshire poet of note, Michael Drayton. John Hall had also once treated him with a concoction described as "syrup of violets." Drayton, like Shakespeare, had risen from obscure Warwickshire origins to distinction in English letters and, perhaps more importantly, to gentlemanly status. They had followed different paths, with Drayton achieving the most obvious literary and poetical eminence after first fashioning a career as a dramatist; he became the English "laureate" and was granted a monument in Westminster Abbey, whereas Shakespeare had to be content with one in the local church. Shakespeare alluded to Drayton's work in his drama, and Drayton himself praised Shakespeare in a set of public verses. Drayton was also a close friend of Shakespeare's "cousin," Thomas Greene, who had lived for a while in New Place. The vicar of Stratford blamed Shakespeare's death upon a "merry meeting" in Stratford between Drayton, Shakespeare and Ben Jonson. We may safely conclude that they were well acquainted, and that they saw each other in their local neighbourhood.

There was Fulke Greville, Lord Brooke, the son and heir of Fulke Greville of Beauchamps Court who had played so large a part in Stratford affairs. As a poet and dramatist Greville knew Shakespeare very well indeed, and has left a cryptic report that he was in some sense Shakespeare's "master."

There was a larger Warwickshire "circle," including men of the Middle Temple such as Greville and Greene, who felt themselves to be closely associated. The ties of territory and inheritance were very strong in early seventeenth-century England, and it was natural and inevitable that Shakespeare should return to Stratford at the close of his London career.

In the early summer of 1614, however, a "suddaine and terrible Fire" engulfed part of the town. The strength of the conflagration "was so great (the wind sitting full uppon the Towne) that it dispersed into so many places therof whereby the whole Towne was in very great daunger to have been utterly consumed."[4] Some fifty-four houses were destroyed, together with barns and outhouses and stables to the total value of £8,000. It was a calamity for the town, which had in Shakespeare's lifetime been visited twice before by a devastating fire, and a charitable subscription was set up for the victims. Shakespeare's own house, and his various properties, were not affected.

He was implicated, however, in a controversy of this year concerning the progress of enclosures upon the common land in the vicinity. He seems for the most part to have stayed away from local issues. Three years previously, the more affluent householders of Stratford raised money in order to assist the passage of a bill through Parliament "for the better Repayre of the highe waies";[5] there were seventy-one names on the list of those who had contributed, but that of Shakespeare was added later in the right-hand margin by Thomas Greene. It seems very likely that Shakespeare paid his own share at the last minute.

In the autumn of 1614, however, there was some trouble in the neighbouring hamlet of Welcombe where Shakespeare owned land. William Combe, a younger member of the family that Shakespeare knew so well, had inherited his uncle's estate in that neighbourhood. So he aligned himself with Arthur Mainwaring, the steward to the Lord Chancellor Ellesmere, in a scheme to enclose lands in Old Stratford and Welcombe. This would improve farming efficiency, but the land would be given over to pasture for sheep rather than to crops. The price of grain would consequently rise, and the rights of common grazing would be restricted. It was an old argument in which the more enterprising landowners were generally pitted against those who upheld the rights of the community. On this occasion William Combe and Mainwaring were challenged by the town council of Stratford, their most vociferous opponent being Thomas Greene. So Shakespeare's cousin was pitted against Shakespeare's friends.

Shakespeare had in the interim entered a separate agreement with Mainwaring which promised him compensation "for all such losse detriment & hinderance"[6] to his tithes as the result of the planned enclosures. Shakespeare was not ready to align himself with either party in the dispute, but was merely protecting his own financial interests. Thomas Greene had travelled to London to plead the town's case at Westminster, and in the middle of November paid a visit to his cousin "to see him howe he did."[7] So Shakespeare had returned to London, and it is likely that he was staying in Blackfriars in order to superintend the court productions of his plays in that year. Greene asked him about the plans for the enclosures and

> he [Shakespeare] told me that they assurd him they ment to inclose noe further then to gospel bushe & so upp straight (leavyng out part of the dyngles to the ffield) to the gate in Clopton hedge & take in Salisburyes peece: and that they meane in Aprill to servey the Land & then to gyve satisfaccion & not before.

So Shakespeare was very well acquainted with the plans of Combe and Mainwaring, to the extent that he knew in detail what they proposed to enclose. He was clearly also completely familiar with the topography of the area, as might be expected from one who had known it since his earliest childhood. Yet on this occasion, too, he refused to take sides in the dispute which implicated those closest to him. He assured Greene that he did not believe anything would be done, and in this belief he was joined by John Hall. His son-in-law had come with him to Blackfriars, and was present at the interview. Whether Hall had come in the role of relative, or doctor, is not known.

But, contrary to their reassurances, something was done. By the end of the year Combe and Mainwaring were planting hedges and digging ditches as a preliminary to enclosure, and Thomas Greene attended a meeting with a variety of local dignitaries. He noted that he had sent "to my Cosen Shakspear the Coppyes of all our oaths made then, alsoe a not of the Inconvenyences wold grow by the Inclosure." It is clear enough that Shakespeare's support and advice were considered to be important aspects of their campaign. When the digging and planting went ahead the Stratford corporation caused the ditches to be filled in, at which point scuffles ensued between the interested parties. Combe called the members of the Stratford council: "Puritan knaves!" But then women and children from Stratford were also conscripted to fill in the ditches.

So matters rested until the spring, when the Warwick Assizes prohibited Combe and Mainwaring from proceeding with their plans without showing good cause. Combe persisted, and went so far as to depopulate the village of Welcombe itself. Shakespeare again enters the record with a note by Thomas Greene to the effect of "W Shakespeares telling J Greene that I was not able to beare the encloseinge of Welcombe." "J" was Greene's brother. The meaning of "beare" here seems to be "bar," and the import of Shakespeare's remark then becomes clear. The process of enclosure was bound to go ahead. In this respect, he was wrong. The Chief Justice of the King's Bench eventually forbade Combe to continue his plans.

Certain historians have criticised Shakespeare's responses to the crisis of enclosures, and blamed him for not taking the side of the "commons" in the dispute over land. But he may simply have believed that the process of enclosure would be ultimately beneficial. More likely than not, however, he "believed" nothing whatever. He seems to have been incapable of taking sides in any controversy, and remained studiedly impartial in even those matters closest to him. It is hard to imagine him angry, or contemptuous, or bitter. His principal concern seems to have been with the preservation of his own finances. In any case his sentiments on the matter of enclosure suggest a resigned or fatalistic attitude towards the affairs of the world in harmony with the last lines of his last play –

> . . . Let's goe off,
> And beare us like the time.

CHAPTER 90

The Wheele Is Come Full Circle
I Am Heere

Shakespeare stayed in London from November until after Christmas. This lengthy residence in Blackfriars suggests that he was busy over theatrical matters and, despite the society of John Hall, not in particularly bad health. His presence may well have been requested by the King's Men, since his withdrawal from play-writing had considerably affected their receipts and even their reputation. They performed on eight occasions at Court during this winter season, but the Lord Chamberlain had complained that "our poets brains and inventions are grown very dry, in so much that of five new plays there is not one that pleases; and therefore they are driven to publish over their old, which stand them in best stead and bring them most profit."[1] He is describing here, at least in part, the "old" repertory of Shakespeare's plays that stood considerably higher in esteem than the "new" plays. Shakespeare was in as much demand as ever.

As we have seen, there is a theatrical tradition concerning the role of Henry VIII in *All Is True* which suggests direct supervision by Shakespeare. It was suggested in the late seventeenth century that the "part of the King was so right and justly done by Mr. Betterton, he being instructed in it by Sir William [Davenant], who had it from old Mr. Lowin, that had his instructions from Master Shakespeare himself."[2] So the line of direction descends as far as John Lowin, who was indeed a member of the King's Men in the last years of Shakespeare's life. It seems that Shakespeare coached the then young actor in his penultimate play.

Shakespeare may also have returned to London in the spring of 1615 when he and six others entered a bill of complaint against Matthew Bacon of Gray's Inn, for withholding the deeds of certain properties in Blackfriars. Yet this is the last possible recorded occasion of his stay in the city. When he returned to Stratford, he would never leave it again.

Since in the first weeks of 1616 he gave instructions for the drawing up of his will, it is likely that he began to suffer from some serious malady; he had given instructions on 18 January, and had arranged to execute it a few days later, but for some reason the appointment was postponed.[3] It has been estimated that the usual period between the making of the will and death was approximately two weeks, so Shakespeare may have experienced some form of remission or relief.

The nature of his ill-health, or his disease, has been endlessly debated. There are some who believe that he was suffering from tertiary syphilis, a not uncommon condition in the period and one to which he could undoubtedly have been exposed. Analysis of his final signatures has suggested that he had contracted a malady known as "spastic cramp," a variant of "scrivener's palsy" that affected voluminous writers. This would make it impossible for him to write at any length, and would also provide some explanation for his withdrawal from play-writing. Others have suggested that he died of alcoholism. Reference has already been made to the "merry meeting" between Shakespeare, Michael Drayton, and Ben Jonson. It is reported, by the Stratford vicar, that they "drank too hard, for Shakespeare died of a feavour there contracted."[4] This of course need not have been a sign of alcoholism.

Yet the disease may not have been of a degenerate kind at all. It may have seized him suddenly and violently, withdrawing once only to invade him with greater virulence. A seventeenth-century doctor noted that fevers were "especially prevalent in Stratford" and that 1616 was a particularly unhealthful year.[5] In the winter of 1615 and 1616 there was an epidemic of influenza; the winter itself had been "warm and tempestuous," a sure nurse of ague. There was also a small rivulet running past New Place, and it was later proven that these small streams were carriers of typhus. The supposition might then be that he was carried off by typhoid fever. The funeral was held so soon after the death that his fatal illness may have been considered to be contagious.

One reason for the postponement of the execution of the will, however, may have been the imminent marriage of his remaining daughter. Judith Shakespeare was betrothed to one of Shakespeare's family friends, Thomas Quiney, but in the following month they were excommunicated for having married in Lent without the possession of a special licence. They may have married in haste. It seems that the local vicar had been at fault, but the punishment was reserved for the participants. This was succeeded by worse news, when Quiney was brought before the bawdry court for unlawful copulation with a local girl. The girl herself, Margaret Wheeler, had died in childbirth together with her infant. Mother and child had been buried on 15 March, just a month after the marriage between Quiney and Judith Shakespeare. It must have been common knowledge and local gossip, at the time of the marriage, that a girl made pregnant by Quiney was still living in town and proclaiming the paternity of her child. It was a local disgrace, something of a humiliation touching the family of the Shakespeares, and as a result Shakespeare changed his will by striking out the name of Thomas Quiney.

The will itself was drawn up on 25 March 1616. It has sometimes been suggested that the will has been executed in Shakespeare's own hand; but this is very unlikely. It was no doubt composed or transcribed by his lawyer, Francis Collins, or by the lawyer's clerk. A preliminary will had been made in January, but this was now altered. A new first page was substituted, and there were many changes made on the second and third pages. It opens in the conventional manner with the pious declaration that "In the name of god Amen I William Shackspeare . . . in perfect health & memorie god be praysed doe make & Ordayne this my last will and testamente." It is not clear that Shakespeare was in perfect health or memory; the evidence of his final signatures suggests a weak and debilitated man.

He deals first with the case of his daughter Judith, who had recently entered such an unsatisfactory marriage with Thomas Quiney. The reference to "my sonne in L[aw]" has been crossed out, and the phrase "daughter Judyth" substituted. He left her £150 on condition that she renounced any claim to the cottage he owned in Chapel Lane close to New Place. This suggests that she and her new husband had been living there. He also bequeathed her a further £150, three years later, if she or any of her heirs were still living. Thomas Quiney could only claim this sum if he gave Judith lands valued at the same amount. It was not a large bequest, at least compared to the largesse bestowed upon her sister, and in equity she could have expected three or four times that amount. It is apparent, therefore, that Shakespeare was in some respects stern or unyielding with his younger daughter.

Shakespeare then left £30, and his clothes, to his sister. Joan Hart was also allowed to stay in Henley Street for a nominal rent, and £5 were left to each of her three sons. Unfortunately Shakespeare forgot the name of one of his nephews. He scarcely refers to his wife, but Anne Shakespeare would have been automatically entitled to one-third of his estate; there was no reason to mention her in an official document. But he does make one provision. As an afterthought in the second draft he added "Item I gyve unto my wief my second best bed with the furniture." This has aroused much speculation, principally concerned with the burning question why he did not leave her the "best" bed. In fact the "best" bed in the household was that characteristically used by guests. The "second best bed" was that reserved for the marital couple and, as such, is best seen as a testimony to their union. As one cultural historian has put it the marital bed represented "marriage, fidelity, identity itself" and was "a uniquely important possession within the household."[6] The bed may indeed have been an heirloom from the Hathaway farmhouse in Shottery. It may have been the one on which Shakespeare was lying. The fact that he added this bequest as an afterthought suggests the benevolence of his intention. He is unlikely to have wished to snub his wife at the last minute. It is of some interest, however, that he did not feel the slightest need to call his wife by the conventional testamentary phrases of "loving" or "well beloved"; he did not need, or like, conventional sentiments. Nor did he name his wife as his executrix, and instead left everything in the hands of his apparently more capable daughter. Anne Shakespeare may therefore have been incapacitated in some way.

The larger part of his bequest did indeed go to his older daughter, Susannah, and to her husband. They are nominated by Shakespeare as the ones to hold together his estate. He left the Halls "All the rest of my goods Chattels Leases plate Jewels & household stuffe whatsoever." The "leases" may have included his shares in the Globe and in Blackfriars, if he still in fact retained them. He left his daughter New Place and the two houses in Henley Street as well as the gatehouse in Blackfriars; in addition Shakespeare bequeathed her all the lands that he had gradually purchased over the last few years. The bequest was to be held entire and in turn left to the first male son of the Halls, or to the son of the second son, going down through the generations of males in the putative Shakespearian genealogy. His patriarchal instincts were clear, even though nature thwarted his intentions.

There were other gifts to relatives and to neighbours, as well as the price of three gold rings for three of his colleagues from the King's Men–Richard Burbage, John Heminges and Henry Condell. Since Heminges and Condell were the begetters of the subsequent Folio edition of his plays, the rings can be considered to be a "forget not" token. It makes it more, rather than less, likely that in Stratford he had been revising his plays for future publication.

He left £10 for the relief of the poor of Stratford, by no means an extravagant sum, and his processional sword to Thomas Combe. It has been considered odd or singular that Shakespeare mentions no books or play-manuscripts in this will, but they may have been included in the "goods" generally inherited by the Halls. They could also have formed part of an inventory that is now lost. In his own will, at a later date, John Hall refers to his "study of Bookes" which were entirely scattered to the winds. There was also a report that Shakespeare's granddaughter (he had no male heirs) "carried away with her from Stratford many of her grand-father's papers,"[7] but this cannot now be verified.

It is a sensible and business-like document, evincing Shakespeare's eminently practical temperament. It is true that other early seventeenth-century testators are more effusive in their allusions to family and friends, but they had not spent a lifetime writing plays. When one eighteenth-century antiquary complained that the will was "absolutely void of the least particle of that Spirit which Animated our Great Poet,"[8] he forgot that he was dealing with a legal document rather than a work of art. The distinction would not have been lost on Shakespeare himself. He signed the first two sheets of the will "Shakspere," and the final sheet was completed with the words "By me William Shakspeare." The surname trails off, as if the hand could hardly hold or direct the pen. These were the last words he ever wrote.

Shakespeare lingered for four weeks from March into April; if he was indeed suffering from typhoid fever, the period is right. He would have experienced insomnia, fatigue and overwhelming thirst which no amount of liquid could reasonably assuage. It is reported from no very reliable source that "he caught his death through leaving his bed when ill, because some of his old friends had called on him."[9] We have had cause to note the belief that "he dyed a Papist," which may mean that he was given extreme unction according to the old Catholic rite. As death approached, the passing bell was rung in the Stratford church. He died on 23 April and, having been born on the same day, he had just entered his fifty-third year.

He was embalmed and laid upon the bed, wrapped in flowers and herbs in the process known as "winding" the corpse. His friends and neighbours walked solemnly through New Place to view the body; the principal rooms and staircases were draped with black cloths. The corpse was then "watched" until interment. He was wrapped in a linen winding sheet and, two days later, carried down the well-worn "burying path" to the old church. It was sometimes the custom to accompany the burial procession with music. He was said to have been buried at a depth of some 17 feet; this seems a deep pit indeed but it may have been dug out of fear of contagion from the typhus. He was placed beneath the floor of the chancel, beside the north wall, as his status as lay rector and receiver of tithes required. It is likely to have been Shakespeare himself who wrote the epitaph:

> GOOD FREND FOR IESVS SAKE FORBEARE,
> TO DIGG THE DVST ENCLOASED HEARE!
> BLEST BE YE MAN YT SPARES THES STONES,
> AND CVRST BE HE YT MOVES MY BONES.

He gave the world his works, and his good fellowship, not his body or his name.

The mourners carried small bunches of rosemary or bay to throw into the grave which, to this day, is visited by thousands of admirers and pilgrims.

CHAPTER 91

Ꝍo Ꝍeare the Story of Ꝿour Ꝟife

e died as he had lived, without much sign of the world's attention. When Ben Jonson expired his funeral procession included "all of the nobility and gentry then in the town."[1] Only Shakespeare's family and closest friends followed his bier to the grave. There were scant tributes paid to his memory by other dramatists, and the commendatory verses in the Folio of 1623 are slight indeed compared to the copious verse epistles on the deaths of Jonson, Fletcher and other fashionable playwrights. There were no books by Shakespeare in Jonson's library. Shakespeare neither established nor encouraged any school of younger "disciples."

It was only after half a century that the first biographical notices appeared, and no scholar or critic bothered to discuss Shakespeare with any of his friends or contemporaries. This may preface Emerson's remark that "Shakspeare is the only biographer of Shakspeare."[2] He is one of those rare cases of a writer whose work is singularly important and influential, yet whose personality was not considered to be of any interest at all. He is obscure and elusive precisely to the extent that nobody bothered to write about him.

Yet the range of Shakespeare's influence is not hard to discern. More than seventy issues and editions of his work appeared in his lifetime. By 1660 no fewer than nineteen of his plays had been published, and by 1680 there had been three editions of his collected plays. Theatrical reports suggest that, in hard times, the King's Men supported themselves by replaying Shakespeare's "old" dramas. Other playwrights, including Massinger and Middleton, Ford and Webster, Beaumont and Fletcher, were drawn to imitate him. *Othello* and *Romeo and Juliet* were particularly influential among younger dramatists, and the figures of Hamlet and of Falstaff maintained their theatrical life and presence outside the plays in which they had originally appeared. Shakespeare also seems almost single-handedly to have maintained the status of the revenge tragedy and the romance. He was a hard writer to ignore.

On the occasion of the Shakespeare Jubilee, in the summer of 1769, a painting was hung before the windows of the room where the dramatist was supposed to have been born; it displayed the image of the sun breaking through clouds. It is a wonderful emblem of birth. But it also suggests revival and return. If at a later date that sun had shone through another window of the house in Henley Street its rays would have been refracted through a score of different names, where distinguished nineteenth-century visitors had scratched or scored their signatures upon the glass. Among them are Sir Walter Scott, and Thomas Carlyle, William Makepeace Thackeray and Charles Dickens, all of them registering the fact that they were shining within the light of Shakespeare himself.

The Folio or collected volume of his plays followed some seven years after his death. It was assembled by two of his fellows, John Heminges and Henry Condell, and was dedicated to the two Pembroke brothers. The Earl of Pembroke was Lord Chamberlain and the direct superior of the Master of the Revels. It served its purpose very well, and was for three centuries believed to represent the Shakespearian "canon" of thirty-six plays with the notable exclusion of certain collaborative ventures such as *Pericles* (later added) and *The Two Noble Kinsmen*. The fact that a list of the actors was added at the beginning suggests that this was as much a theatrical as a literary celebration. It may have been the subject of discussion among Shakespeare and his colleagues before his death, and it is even possible that some of the plays were printed from a revised transcript by the playwright himself. Many of them, however, are in the hand of a professional scrivener named Ralph

Crane who was often employed by the theatrical companies. The volume is adorned by the Droeshout engraving of the dramatist, which is indeed the only generally accepted likeness of William Shakespeare.

Acknowledgements

For ease of reference I have quoted line numbers from *The Complete Works, Original-Spelling Edition*, published by Oxford University Press (1986), easily the best modern edition of Shakespeare's plays. I would also like to express my obligation and gratitude to its editors, Stanley Wells and Gary Taylor, for providing the closest possible transcription of Shakespeare's printed words.

I would like to register a more private debt to my assistants, Thomas Wright and Murrough O'Brien, for their help in research and elucidation.

I would also like to thank Katherine Duncan-Jones and Jenny Overton for their invaluable suggestions and emendations and my editor, Penelope Hoare, for her patient work upon the typescript. All surviving errors are, of course, my own.

Notes

Chapter One

1 Quoted in David Cressy: *Birth, Marriage and Death*, page 81.

2 Jeanne Jones: *Family Life in Shakespeare's England*, page 93.

3 Robert Bearman (ed.): *The History of an English Borough*, page 92.

Chapter Two

1 Richard Wilson: *Will Power: Essays on Shakespearian Authority*, page 71.

2 ibid.

3 ibid.

Chapter Four

1 Caroline Spurgeon: *Shakespeare's Imagery*, page 93.

2 ibid., page 98.

3 Jeanne Jones: *Family Life in Shakespeare's England*, page 22.

4 ibid, page 33.

5 Keith Wrightson: *English Society 1580–1680*, page 149.

Chapter Five

1 Quoted in E.K. Chambers: *William Shakespeare: A Study of Facts and Problems*, Volume Two, page 247.

2 Quoted in Samuel Schoenbaum: *Shakespeare's Lives*, page 5.

3 Chambers: *Shakespeare: Facts and Problems*, Volume Two, page 19.

4 P. Hanks and F. Hodges: *A Dictionary of Surnames*, page 482.

5 Chambers: *Shakespeare: Facts and Problems*, Volume Two, page 375.

6 Quoted in Samuel Schoenbaum: *William Shakespeare: A Documentary Life*, page 27.

7 Wrightson: *English Society*, page 52.

8 Quoted in E.I. Fripp: *Shakespeare's Stratford*, page 64.

9 Schoenbaum: *Shakespeare: A Documentary Life*, page 14.

Chapter Six

1 Quoted in Schoenbaum: *Shakespeare: A Documentary Life*, page 15.

2 Quoted in Nathan Drake: *Shakespeare and His Times*, page 99.

3 Quoted in Mark Eccles: *Shakespeare in Warwickshire*, page 17.

Chapter Seven

1 Quoted in Mark Eccles: *Shakespeare in Warwickshire*, page 39.

2 Heinrich Mutschmann and Karl Wentersdorf: *Shakespeare and Catholicism*, page 147.

3 Information in Fripp: *Shakespeare's Stratford*, page 31.

4 Quoted in P. Collinson (ed.): "William Shakespeare's Religious Inheritance and Environment," in *Elizabethan Essays*, page 246.

5 Alexandra Walsham: *Church Papists*, page 78.

Chapter Nine

1 Quoted in Drake: *Shakespeare and His Times*, page 116.

2 Quoted in Wrightson: *English Society*, page 19.

3 Quoted in Schoenbaum: *Shakespeare: A Documentary Life*, page 36.

4 Quoted in E.I. Fripp: *Shakespeare: Man and Artist*, Volume One, page 74.

Chapter Ten

1 Quoted in Fripp: *Shakespeare: Man and Artist*, Volume One, page 65.

Chapter Eleven

1 Quoted in Chambers: *Shakespeare: Facts and Problems*, Volume Two, pages 252–3.

2 John Palmer: *Molière, His Life and Works* (London, 1930), page 35.

Chapter Twelve

1 Quoted in Chambers: *Shakespeare: Facts and Problems*, Volume Two, page 264.

2 Quoted in Fripp: *Shakespeare: Man and Artist*, Volume One, page 83.

3 Quoted in B.L. Joseph: *Elizabethan Acting*, page 28.

4 Stanley Wells: *Shakespeare For All Time*, page 14.

5 Quoted in Chambers: *Shakespeare: Facts and Problems*, Volume Two, page 264.

6 Quoted in Joseph: *Elizabethan Acting*, page 11.

7 ibid., page 12.

8 Quoted in Andrew Gurr: *Playgoing in Shakespeare's London*, page 80.

9 ibid., page 17.

10 Dennis Kay: *Shakespeare: His Life, Work and Era*, page 26.

11 Quoted in Mark Eccles: *Shakespeare in Warwickshire*, page 57.

Chapter Thirteen

1 Quoted in R. Savage (ed.): *Minutes and Accounts of the Corporation of Stratford upon Avon, 1553–1620*, Volume Two, page xlvii.

2 Nicholas Rowe: *Some Account of the Life of Mr. William Shakespeare* (London, 1848), page 17.

3 Quoted in Fripp: *Shakespeare: Man and Artist*, Volume One, page 155.

Chapter Fourteen

1 Quoted in Jonathan Bate (ed.): *The Romantics on Shakespeare*, page 304.

2 Quoted in Katherine Duncan-Jones: *Ungentle Shakespeare*, page 14.

3 Quoted in Chambers: *Shakespeare: Facts and Problems*, Volume Two, pages 252–3.

4 ibid., page 265.

5 Quoted in Schoenbaum: *Shakespeare: A Documentary Life*, page 81.

6 ibid., page 80.

7 Quoted in C.C. Stopes: *Shakespeare's Warwickshire Contemporaries*, page 23.

8 Fripp: *Shakespeare's Stratford*, page 2.

9 Quoted in Stopes: *Shakespeare's Warwickshire Contemporaries*, page 77.

Chapter Fifteen

1 T.W. Baldwin: *William Shakespeare's Small Latine and Lesse Greeke*, Volume Two, page 672.

2 Quoted in E.K. Chambers: *Shakespearean Gleanings*, page 52.

3 Richard Wilson: *Secret Shakespeare*, page 57.

4 ibid., page 58.

5 Quoted in E.A.J. Honigmann: *Shakespeare: The "Lost Years,"* page 33.

6 A. Keen and R. Lubbock: *The Annotator*, page 9.

7 Quoted in Ivor Brown: *How Shakespeare Spent the Day*, page 167.

Chapter Sixteen

1 Quoted in Fripp: *Shakespeare: Man and Artist*, Volume One, page 173.

2 Edmond Malone: *The Plays and Poems of William Shakespeare*, Volume Two, *A Life of the Poet*, page 108.

Chapter Seventeen

1 Quoted in Mark Eccles: *Shakespeare in Warwickshire*, page 66.

2 Quoted in Wells: *Shakespeare For All Time*, page 269.

3 Quoted in Schoenbaum: *Shakespeare: A Documentary Life*, page 72.

4 Quoted in Fripp: *Shakespeare: Man and Artist*, Volume One, page 191.

Chapter Eighteen

1 Quoted in Chambers: *Shakespeare: Facts and Problems*, Volume Two, page 253.

2 Quoted in Fripp: *Shakespeare: Man and Artist*, Volume One, page 195.

3 ibid., Volume Two, page 520.

Chapter Nineteen

1 Quoted in the introduction by E.I. Fripp to R. Savage (ed.): *Minutes and Accounts of the Corporation of Stratford-upon-Avon*, Volume Four, page xxi.

2 Quoted in Edwin Nungezer: *A Dictionary of Actors*, page 348.

3 Quoted in Fripp: *Shakespeare: Man and Artist*, Volume One, page 206.

4 Quoted in Andrew Gurr: *The Shakespearean Playing Companies*, page 203.

Chapter Twenty

1 Quoted in J.O. Halliwell-Phillips: *Outlines of the Life of Shakespeare*, page 79.

2 Quoted in Schoenbaum: *Shakespeare: A Documentary Life*, page 101.

3 Quoted in Liza Picard: *Elizabeth's London*, page 89.

Chapter Twenty-one

1 Timothy Mowl: *Elizabethan and Jacobean Style*, pages 13, 22 and 87.

2 Quoted in David Scott Kastan (ed.): *A Companion to Shakespeare*, page 43.

3 Quoted in Lawrence Manley: *Literature and Culture in Early Modern London*, page 431.

4 Quoted in Lawrence Manley (ed.): *London in the Age of Shakespeare*, page 106.

Chapter Twenty-two

1 Quoted in Lawrence Stone: *The Family, Sex and Marriage in England*, 1500–1800, page 520.

2 Quoted in Duncan-Jones: *Ungentle Shakespeare*, page 81.

Chapter Twenty-three

1 Quoted in Chambers: *Shakespeare: Facts and Problems*, Volume Two, page 253.

2 Quoted in John Gross (ed.): *After Shakespeare*, page 10.

3 Baldassare Castiglione: *The Courtyer* (London, 1928), page 33.

4 Quoted in Chambers: *Shakespeare: Facts and Problems*, Volume Two, page 266.

5 Quoted in Gross (ed.), *After Shakespeare*, page 7.

Chapter Twenty-four

1 Quoted in Chambers: *Shakespeare: Facts and Problems*, Volume Two, page 265.

2 Quoted in J.O. Halliwell-Phillips: *Outlines of the Life of Shakespeare*, Volume Two, page 288.

3 ibid.

4 Quoted in Chambers: *Shakespeare: Facts and Problems*, Volume Two, page 288.

5 ibid., page 296.

6 Quoted in Edward Burns (ed.): *King Henry VI, Part One*, the Arden edition (London, 2000), page 19.

7 Quoted in Charles Nicholl: *The Reckoning*, page 268.

Chapter Twenty-five

1 Quoted in Dennis Kay: *Shakespeare*, page 62.

2 Quoted in E.K. Chambers: *The Elizabethan and Caroline Stage*, Volume Four, page 123.

3 Quoted in Charles Knight: *William Shakespeare: A Biography*, page 310.

4 Quoted in Halliwell-Phillips, Volume Two, page 354.

5 Quoted in Chambers: *Shakespeare: Facts and Problems*, Volume Two, page 386.

6 ibid., page 397.

7 Quoted in Halliwell-Phillips, Volume Two, pages 355–6.

8 ibid., page 363.

9 ibid.

10 Quoted in Schoenbaum: *Shakespeare: A Documentary Life*, page 106.

11 Christine Eccles: *The Rose Theatre*, page 94.

12 Quoted in P. Whitfield White: *Theatre and Reformation*, page 49.

13 ibid., page 51.

Chapter Twenty-six

1 E.J.L. Scott (ed.): *Letter Book of Gabriel Harvey* (London, 1884), page 67.

2 Quoted in G.K. Hunter: *John Lyly: The Humanist as Courtier*, page 87.

3 Quoted in Charles Nicholl: *A Cup of News: The Life of Thomas Nashe*, page 61.

4 Quoted in F.S. Boas: *Christopher Marlowe*, page 241.

5 Quoted in Nicholl: *The Reckoning*, page 242.

6 ibid., page 474.

Chapter Twenty-seven

1 Quoted in G.L. Hosking: *The Life and Times of Edward Alleyn*, page 36.

2 See E.A.J. Honigmann: *Shakespeare: The "Lost Years,"* page 109.

3 E.B. Everitt: *The Young Shakespeare*, page 61.

Chapter Twenty-eight

1 Quoted in Eric Sams: *The Real Shakespeare*, page 163.

2 ibid., page 66.

3 ibid., page 67.

4 ibid.

Chapter Twenty-nine

1 The most notable defender is Eric Sams, in *Shakespeare's Lost Play: Edmund Ironside*.

2 I am indebted for these observations to Eric Sams.

3 Quoted in Charles Praetorius (ed.): *The Troublesome Raigne of John, King of England*, page xvi.

Chapter Thirty

1 Quoted in Bate (ed.): *The Romantics on Shakespeare*, page 543.

Chapter Thirty-one

1 Quoted in Chambers: *Shakespeare: Facts and Problems*, Volume Two, page 305.

2 Quoted in E.A.J. Honigmann (ed.): *King John*, pages xlviii–xlix (London, 1954).

Chapter Thirty-two

1 Quoted in Fripp: *Shakespeare: Man and Artist*, Volume One, page 306.

2 ibid., page 298.

3 ibid.

4 Quoted in David George: "Shakespeare and Pembroke's Men," page 312.

Chapter Thirty-three

1 Quoted in George: "Shakespeare and Pembroke's Men," page 307.

2 Quoted in Gross (ed.): *After Shakespeare*, page 23.

3 Quoted in Bate (ed.): *The Romantics on Shakespeare*, page 279.

Chapter Thirty-four

1 Quoted in Fripp: *Shakespeare: Man and Artist*, Volume Two, page 831.

2 Quoted in Nungezer: *A Dictionary of Actors*, page 78.

3 ibid., page 72.

4 Quoted in C.T. Onions and S. Lee (eds): *Shakespeare's England*, Volume One, page 301.

5 ibid., page 304.

Chapter Thirty-five

1 Quoted in Fripp: *Shakespeare: Man and Artist*, Volume One, page 347.

2 Quoted in A. Freeman: *Thomas Kyd*, page 25.

3 The best analysis of the whole episode is to be found in Charles Nicholl's masterly *The Reckoning*.

4 Quoted in Fripp: *Shakespeare: Man and Artist*, Volume One, page 369.

5 Quoted in G.P.V. Akrigg: *Shakespeare and the Earl of Southampton*, page 182.

6 Quoted in C.C. Stopes: *The Life of Henry, 3rd Earl of Southampton*, page 56.

7 Quoted in Akrigg, *Shakespeare and the Earl of Southampton*, page 197.

8 ibid.

9 Quoted in Drake: *Shakespeare and His Times*, Volume Two, page 12.

Chapter Thirty-six

1 Richard Wilson: *Secret Shakespeare*, page 134.

2 Quoted in F. Yates: *John Florio*, page 127.

3 See in particular Stewart Trotter: *Love's Labour's Found*.

4 Translation by H.T. Lowe-Parker.

5 ibid.

Chapter Thirty-eight

1 Quoted in Fripp: *Shakespeare: Man and Artist*, Volume One, page 207.

2 Quoted in Nungezer: *A Dictionary of Actors*, page 219.

3 Quoted in M.C. Bradbrook: *The Rise of the Common Player*, page 72.

4 Quoted in Irwin Smith: *Shakespeare's Blackfriars Playhouse*, page 258.

Chapter Thirty-nine

1 Quoted in M. Hattaway: *Elizabethan Popular Theatre*, page 72.

2 Quoted in Joseph: *Elizabethan Acting*, page 149.

3 Quoted in Fripp: *Shakespeare: Man and Artist*, Volume One, page 214.

4 ibid.

5 Quoted by Daniel Seltzer: "Elizabethan Acting in Othello," *Shakespeare Quarterly*, 10 (1959).

6 Quoted in M. White: *Renaissance Drama in Action*, page 59.

7 Quoted in Joseph: *Elizabethan Acting*, page 17.

Chapter Forty

1 Quoted in Joseph: *Elizabethan Acting*, page 9.

2 Quoted in P. Thomson: *Shakespeare's Theatre*, page 110.

3 Fynes Moryson: *Itinerary* (London, 1617), page 476.

4 Quoted in Chambers: *Shakespeare: Facts and Problems*, Volume Two, page 278.

5 John Southworth: *Shakespeare the Player*, page 173.

6 Quoted in J.B. Matthews: *Molière: His Life and Works*, page 39.

7 Quoted in *Shakespeare Survey*, 17, page 197.

8 Quoted in Chambers: *Shakespeare: Facts and Problems*, Volume One, page 84.

9 Quoted in Chambers: *Shakespeare: Facts and Problems*, Volume Two, page 262.

10 ibid., page 190.

11 Quoted in Michael Wood: *In Search of Shakespeare*, page 146.

12 Quoted in Chambers: *Shakespeare: Facts and Problems*, Volume Two, page 191.

Chapter Forty-one

1 Quoted in Gross (ed.): *After Shakespeare*, page 24.

2 Quoted in Schoenbaum: *Shakespeare: A Documentary Life*, page 133.

3 I am indebted for these suggestions to Rolf Soellner's essay, "Shakespeare's Lucrece and the Garnier–Pembroke Connection," *Shakespeare Studies* XV (1982).

4 Quoted in Halliwell-Phillips: *Outlines of the Life of Shakespeare*, page 119.

5 Quoted in Chambers: *Shakespeare: Facts and Problems*, Volume Two, page 197.

6 John Donne: letter to Sir Henry Goodere in *Letters to Severall Persons of Honour* (1651).

Chapter Forty-two

1 Quoted in R. Fraser: *Shakespeare: The Later Years*, page 9.
2 Quoted in R.A. Foakes (ed.): *The Comedy of Errors*, Arden edition (London, 1962), pages 116–7.
3 Quoted in Picard: *Elizabeth's London*, page 206.
4 Quoted in Fripp: *Shakespeare: Man and Artist*, Volume One, page 255.
5 Quoted in W. Nicholas Knight: *Shakespeare's Hidden Life*, page 159.
6 Quoted in Fripp: *Shakespeare: Man and Artist*, Volume One, page 255.

Chapter Forty-three

1 Quoted in Fripp: *Shakespeare: Man and Artist*, Volume One, page 393.
2 See Peter Ackroyd: *Albion* (London: 2002).

Chapter Forty-five

1 Quoted in Bate (ed.): *The Romantics on Shakespeare*, page 182.
2 Quoted in Emrys Jones: *Scenic Form in Shakespeare*, page 4.
3 Quoted in R. Dutton: *William Shakespeare: A Literary Life*, page 113.
4 Quoted in Gross (ed.): *After Shakespeare*, pages 23–4.

Chapter Forty-six

1 Quoted in Marchette Chute: *Shakespeare of London*, page 81.
2 Quoted in Richard Dutton: "The Birth of the Author," in R.B. Parker and S. Zitner (eds): *Elizabethan Theater*, page 73.

Chapter Forty-seven

1 Quoted in Gross (ed.): *After Shakespeare*, page 169.
2 Quoted in Ivor Brown: *Shakespeare and the Actors*, page 71.

Chapter Forty-eight

1 Quoted in Ian Archer: *The Pursuit of Stability*, page 1.
2 ibid., page 10.
3 Quoted in Schoenbaum: *Shakespeare's Lives*, page 462.
4 Quoted in Chambers: *Shakespeare: Facts and Problems*, Volume Two, page 253.
5 Quoted in Fripp: *Shakespeare: Man and Artist*, Volume One, page 421.
6 Quoted in Chambers: *Shakespeare: Facts and Problems*, Volume One, page 353.
7 See Peter Farey: *Deception in Deptford*, on the internet—www.users.globalnet.co.uk/~hadland/tvp/tvpintro.htm
8 ibid.
9 Quoted in Jonathan Bate (ed.): *Titus Andronicus*, Arden edition (London, 1995), pages 43–4.

Chapter Forty-nine

1 Quoted in Peter Thomson: *Shakespeare's Professional Career*, page 117.

2 Julia Kristeva: *Tales of Love*, trans. L.S. Roudiez (New York, 1987), page 9.

3 Quoted in Fripp: *Shakespeare: Man and Artist*, Volume One, page 416.

Chapter Fifty

1 I am indebted to Katherine Duncan-Jones for this observation.

2 Quoted in Mark Eccles: *Shakespeare in Warwickshire*, page 84.

3 Noted in Brian Morris (ed.): *The Taming of the Shrew*, Arden edition (London, 1981), page 84.

4 See Duncan-Jones: *Ungentle Shakespeare*, page 157. My discussion of this issue owes a great deal to her perspicacity.

Chapter Fifty-one

1 Quoted in Fripp: *Shakespeare: Man and Artist*, Volume One, pages 455–6.

2 Quoted in Schoenbaum: *Shakespeare: A Documentary Life*, page 108.

3 Quoted in Leslie Hotson: *Shakespeare versus Shallow*, page 12.

4 Quoted in J.Q. Adams: *A Life of William Shakespeare*, page 227.

5 Quoted in Park Honan: *Shakespeare: A Life*, page 220.

6 Quoted in Bate (ed.): *The Romantics on Shakespeare*, page 357.

Chapter Fifty-two

1 Quoted in Fripp: *Shakespeare: Man and Artist*, Volume One, page 248.

2 Quoted in Adams: *A Life of William Shakespeare*, page 163.

3 Quoted in Nungezer: *A Dictionary of Actors*, page 73.

4 Quoted in R. Dutton: *William Shakespeare: A Literary Life*, page 42.

5 Quoted in Chambers: *Shakespeare: Facts and Problems*, Volume One, page 559.

6 Quoted in Katherine Duncan-Jones (ed.): *Shakespeare's Sonnets*, Arden edition (London, 1997), page 2.

7 Quotations from Trotter: *Love's Labour's Found*, page 68.

Chapter Fifty-three

1 Quoted in Gross (ed.): *After Shakespeare*, page 17.

2 I am indebted for this information to Eric Partridge: *Shakespeare's Bawdy*, passim.

3 Quoted in Stone: *The Family, Sex and Marriage in England*, page 519.

4 Ted Hughes: *Shakespeare and the Goddess of Complete Being*, page 164.

Chapter Fifty-five

1 Quoted in Schoenbaum: *Shakespeare's Lives*, p.14.

2 Quoted in Schoenbaum: *Shakespeare: A Documentary Life*, page 178.

3 Quoted in Honan: *Shakespeare: A Life*, page 237.

4 Quoted in Schoenbaum: *Shakespeare: A Documentary Life*, page 178.

Chapter Fifty-six

1 Quoted in Nicholl: *A Cup of News: The Life of Thomas Nashe*, page 243.

2 ibid.

3 Quoted in Thomson: *Shakespeare's Professional Career*, page 120.

4 Quoted in Chambers: *Shakespeare: Facts and Problems*, Volume Two, page 196.

5 Quoted in Brian Gibbons (ed.): *Romeo and Juliet*, Arden edition (London, 1980), page 3.

6 I am indebted for this observation to Nicholl: *A Cup of News*, pages 242–3.

7 Fynes Moryson: *Itinerary*, page 476.

8 Quoted in Thomson: *Shakespeare's Professional Career*, page 85.

Chapter Fifty-seven

1 Quoted in Chambers: *Shakespeare: Facts and Problems*, Volume One, page 95.

2 E.A.J. Honigmann: *The Stability of Shakespeare's Texts*, page 188.

3 Quoted in Chambers: *Shakespeare: Facts and Problems*, Volume Two, page 194.

4 ibid., pages 197–8.

5 See J.B. Leishmann (ed.): *The Three Parnassus Plays*, passim.

6 Quoted in Chambers: *Shakespeare: Facts and Problems*, Volume Two, page 195.

Chapter Fifty-eight

1 Quoted in Nicholas Knight: *Shakespeare's Hidden Life*, page 199.

2 ibid., page 205.

3 ibid., page 216.

4 Quoted in E.A.J. Honigmann: *Shakespeare's Impact on His Contemporaries*, page 8.

5 ibid., pages 8–9.

Chapter Fifty-nine

1 Quoted in Kay: *Shakespeare: His Life, Work and Era*, page 191.

2 Quoted in Chambers: *Shakespeare: Facts and Problems*, Volume Two, page 211.

3 ibid., page 245.

4 Quoted in Wood: *In Search of Shakespeare*, page 326.

5 Quoted in Schoenbaum: *Shakespeare: A Documentary Life*, page 153.

6 Quoted in Garry O'Connor: *William Shakespeare: A Popular Life*, page 161.

Chapter Sixty

1 John Stow: *The Survey of London* (London, 1912), page 154.

2 Quoted in R.A. Foakes (ed.): *Henslowe's Diary*, page 277.

3 Quoted in Peter Ackroyd: *London* (London, 2000), page 690.

4 Quoted in T.F. Ordish: *Shakespeare's London*, page 129.

Chapter Sixty-one

1 See Bernard Beckerman: *Shakespeare at the Globe*, page 106.

Chapter Sixty-three

1 Quoted in Grace Ioppolo: *Revising Shakespeare*, page 213.

2 Quoted in John Southworth: *Shakespeare the Player*, page 113.

3 ibid.

4 Quoted in Chambers: *Shakespeare: Facts and Problems*, Volume One, page 97.

Chapter Sixty-four

1 Quoted in Chambers: *Shakespeare: Facts and Problems*, Volume One, page 116.

2 Quoted in C.S. Baskerville: *The Elizabethan Jig*, page 108.

3 Quoted in Stephen Greenblatt: *Shakespearean Negotiations*, page 112.

4 Simon Callow: *Charles Laughton*, page 6.

5 Barnaby Rich: *Roome for a Gentleman* (London, 1609), page 23.

6 Quoted in J.P. Collier: *The History of English Dramatic Poetry to the Time of Shakespeare*, Volume Three (London, 1931), page 145.

7 Quoted in Christine Eccles: *The Rose Theatre*, page 31.

8 Quoted in William C. Hazlitt (ed.): *The English Drama and Stage* (London, 1869), page 184.

Chapter Sixty-five

1 Quoted in M.C. Bradbrook: *John Webster*, page 21.

2 Quoted in Gurr: *Playgoing in Shakespeare's London*, page 47.

3 ibid., page 45.

4 Quoted in Onions and Lee: *Shakespeare's England*, Volume One, page 276.

5 Quoted in Joseph: *Elizabethan Acting*, page 141.

6 Quoted in Schoenbaum: *Shakespeare: A Documentary Life*, page 155.

Chapter Sixty-six

1 See S. Sohmer: *Shakespeare's Mystery Play*, pages 11–13.

2 Quoted in Wood: *In Search of Shakespeare*, page 227.

3 Quoted in Drake: *Shakespeare and His Times*, Volume Two, page 2.

4 Quoted in Bate (ed.): *The Romantics on Shakespeare*, page 282.

5 Quoted in F.D. Hoeniger (ed.): *Pericles*, Arden edition (London, 1962), page 146.

6 Quoted in G. Schmidgall: *Shakespeare and the Poet's Life*, page 125.

7 Spurgeon: *Shakespeare's Imagery*, page 190.

8 Quoted in Chambers: *Shakespeare: Facts and Problems*, Volume Two, page 214.

Chapter Sixty-seven

1 Quoted in A.R. Humphreys (ed.): *Much Ado About Nothing*, Arden edition (London, 1981), page 33.

2 D. Wiles: *Shakespeare's Clown*, page 136.

3 Quoted in Nungezer (ed.): *A Dictionary of Actors*, page 17.

4 ibid., page 19.

Chapter Sixty-eight

1 Quoted in Gurr: *Playgoing in Shakespeare's London*, page 155.

2 Quoted in Adams: *A Life of William Shakespeare*, pages 325–6.

3 Quoted in Leishmann (ed.): *The Three Parnassus Plays*, page 59.

4 Quoted in Fripp: *Shakespeare: Man and Artist*, Volume Two, page 566.

5 Quoted in Chambers: *Shakespeare: Facts and Problems*, Volume Two, page 199.

Chapter Sixty-nine

1 Quoted in Chambers: *Shakespeare: Facts and Problems*, Volume Two, page 323.

2 ibid., page 324.

3 ibid., page 326.

4 ibid., page 325.

Chapter Seventy

1 Quoted in Chambers: *Shakespeare: Facts and Problems*, Volume Two, page 42.

2 Quoted in Mark Eccles: *Shakespeare in Warwickshire*, page 99.

3 See in particular Richard Wilson: *Will Power*, pages 104–17.

Chapter Seventy-one

1 Wrightson: *English Society, 1580–1680*, page 197.

2 Quoted in Gross (ed.): *After Shakespeare*, page 162.

3 Quoted in Onions and Lee (eds): *Shakespeare's England*, Volume One, page 42.

4 Quoted in Halliwell-Phillips: *Outlines of the Life of Shakespeare*, Volume One, page 314.

5 Quoted in Chambers: *Shakespeare: Facts and Problems*, Volume Two, page 197.

Chapter Seventy-two

1 Quoted in Schoenbaum: *Shakespeare: A Documentary Life*, page 165.

2 Quoted in Honan: *Shakespeare: A Life*, page 320.

3 ibid., page 319.

4 ibid., page 320.

5 Quoted in Chambers: *Shakespeare: Facts and Problems*, Volume Two, page 177.

6 Quoted in Schoenbaum: *Shakespeare: A Documentary Life*, page 165.

7 ibid., page 166.

8 Quoted in Stephanie Nolen: *Shakespeare's Face*, page 164.

9 Onions and Lee (eds): *Shakespeare's England*, Volume Two, page 20.

10 Quoted in Duncan-Jones: *Ungentle Shakespeare*, page 197.

11 Fripp: *Shakespeare's Stratford*, page 75.

Chapter Seventy-three

1 Quoted in Chambers: *Shakespeare: Facts and Problems*, Volume Two, page 328.

2 First noticed by Katherine Duncan-Jones in *Ungentle Shakespeare*, pages 157–8.

3 Quoted in A. Cargill: *Shakespeare the Player*, page 5.

Chapter Seventy-four

1 Quoted in Chambers: *Shakespeare: Facts and Problems*, Volume Two, page 189.

2 Quoted in Duncan-Jones: *Ungentle Shakespeare*, page 165.

3 See Neville Coghill: *Shakespeare's Professional Skills*, page 78 ff.

4 Quoted in R.M. Foakes (ed.): *Henslowe's Diary*, page 47.

Chapter Seventy-five

1 Quoted in Fripp: *Shakespeare: Man and Artist*, Volume Two, page 588.

2 Quoted in Honan: *Shakespeare: A Life*, page 301.

3 ibid., page 299.

4 Quoted in Chambers: *Shakespeare:Facts and Problems*, Volume Two, pages 214–15.

Chapter Seventy-six

1 Quoted in Chambers: *Shakespeare: Facts and Problems*, Volume Two, page 210.

2 Quoted in Gross (ed.): *After Shakespeare*, page 216.

3 Quoted in Chambers: *Shakespeare: Facts and Problems*, Volume Two, page 261.

Chapter Seventy-seven

1 Quoted in Chambers: *The Jacobean and Caroline Stage*, Volume Four, page 257.

2 Quoted in Fripp: *Shakespeare: Man and Artist*, Volume Two, page 629.

3 Quoted in Ben Weinreb and Christopher Hibbert (eds): *The London Encyclopaedia* (London, 1983), page 37.

4 Quoted in Fripp: *Shakespeare: Man and Artist*, Volume Two, page 629.

5 Quoted in Chambers: *Shakespeare: Facts and Problems*, Volume Two, page 332.

6 ibid.

7 Quoted in G.K. Hunter (ed.): *All's Well That Ends Well*, Arden edition (London, 1959), page xix.

Chapter Seventy-eight

1 Quoted in Chambers: *Shakespeare: Facts and Problems*, Volume Two, page 123.

2 Quoted in Fripp: *Shakespeare: Man and Artist*, Volume Two, pages 633–4.

3 ibid., page 640.

4 Quoted in A. Dures: *English Catholicism, 1558–1642*, page 44.

5 Quoted in Fripp: *Shakespeare: Man and Artist*, Volume Two, page 654.

Chapter Seventy-nine

1 Quoted in Geoffrey Bullough: *Narrative and Dramatic Sources of Shakespeare*, Volume Five, page 270.

2 Quoted in Gurr: *Playgoing in Shakespeare's London*, page 64.

3 Frank Kermode: *Shakespeare's Language*, page 193.

Chapter Eighty

1 Quoted in Mark Eccles: *Shakespeare in Warwickshire*, page 115.

2 ibid., page 124.

3 Quoted in Richard Wilson: *Will Power*, page 81.

4 Quoted in Kermode: *Shakespeare's Language*, page 243.

Chapter Eighty-one

1 Quoted in Leeds Barroll: *Politics, Plague and Shakespeare's Theatre*, page 159.

2 Quoted in Kay: *Shakespeare: His Life, Work and Era*, page 304.

3 Quoted in Duncan-Jones: *Ungentle Shakespeare*, page 204.

4 ibid., page 205.

5 Wood: *In Search of Shakespeare*, page 310.

6 Quoted in Norman Rabkin: *Shakespeare and the Common Understanding*, page 213.

7 Quoted in Roger Prior, "The Life of George Wilkins," *Shakespeare Survey*, Volume 25 (1972), page 144.

Chapter Eighty-two

1 Quoted in Irwin Smith: *Shakespeare's Blackfriars Playhouse*, pages 247–8.

2 Quoted in Beckerman: *Shakespeare at the Globe*, page xii.

3 Quoted in Honan: *Shakespeare: A Life*, page 346.

4 Quoted in Bate (ed.): *The Romantics on Shakespeare*, pages 282–3.

Chapter Eighty-three

1 Quoted in Philip Brockbank (ed.): *Coriolanus*, Arden edition (London, 1976), page 25.

2 Quoted in Bate (ed.): *The Romantics on Shakespeare*, page 247.

3 Quoted in Mutschmann and Wentersdorf: *Shakespeare and Catholicism*, page 103.

4 Quoted in Chambers: *Shakespeare: Facts and Problems*, Volume Two, page 255.

Chapter Eighty-four

1 Quoted in Southworth: *Shakespeare the Player*, page 245.

2 Quoted in Chambers: *Shakespeare: Facts and Problems*, Volume Two, page 115.

3 Spurgeon: *Shakespeare's Imagery*, page 296.

4 Quoted in Katherine Duncan-Jones (ed.): *Shakespeare's Sonnets*, Arden edition

(London, 1997), page 35. I am indebted generally to Professor Duncan-Jones's introduction to this volume.

5 ibid., page 36.

6 ibid., page 49.

7 Quoted in Bate (ed.): *The Romantics on Shakespeare*, page 301.

Chapter Eighty-five

1 Quoted in Chambers: *Shakespeare: Facts and Problems*, Volume Two, page 337.

2 ibid., page 338.

3 ibid., page 341.

4 Quoted in Honigmann: *Shakespeare's Impact on His Contemporaries*, page 141.

5 ibid., page 143.

6 Quoted in Chambers: *Shakespeare: Facts and Problems*, Volume Two, page 342.

Chapter Eighty-six

1 Court transcript from Chambers: *Shakespeare: Facts and Problems*, Volume Two, pages 90–5.

Chapter Eighty-seven

1 Quoted in F.T. Prince (ed.): *The Poems*, Arden edition (London, 1960), page xxii.

2 Quoted in Honigmann: *Shakespeare's Impact on His Contemporaries*, page 100.

3 ibid.

4 Quoted in Schoenbaum: *Shakespeare: A Documentary Life*, page 224.

5 Quoted in Chambers: *Shakespeare: Facts and Problems*, Volume Two, page 166.

6 Quoted in Richard Wilson: *Secret Shakespeare*, page 260.

7 ibid., pages 166–7.

8 ibid., page 260.

9 ibid., page 206.

10 Quoted in Kay: *Shakespeare: His Life, Work and Era*, page 328.

11 Quoted in John Payne Collier: *The Works of William Shakespeare* (London, 1858), page ccxliv.

Chapter Eighty-eight

1 Quoted in Chambers: *Shakespeare: Facts and Problems*, Volume Two, page 344.

2 Quoted in Peter Levi: *The Life and Times of William Shakespeare*, page 330.

3 Quoted in Stanley Wells: *Shakespeare: A Dramatic Life*, page 375.

4 Quoted in Bate (ed.): *The Romantics on Shakespeare*, page 556.

5 ibid., page 557.

Chapter Eighty-nine

1 Quoted in Schoenbaum: *Shakespeare: A Documentary Life*, page 230.

2 Quoted in Chambers: *Shakespeare: Facts and Problems*, Volume Two, page 268.

3 ibid.

4 Quoted in Schoenbaum: *Shakespeare: A Documentary Life*, page 230.

5 Quoted in Mark Eccles: *Shakespeare in Warwickshire*, page 133.

6 Quoted in Schoenbaum: *Shakespeare: A Documentary Life*, page 231.

7 ibid.

Chapter Ninety

1 Quoted in Fripp: *Shakespeare: Man and Artist*, Volume Two, page 816.

2 Quoted in Duncan-Jones: *Ungentle Shakespeare*, page 259.

3 See Halliwell-Phillips: *Outlines of the Life of Shakespeare*, page 391.

4 Quoted in Chambers: *Shakespeare: Facts and Problems*, Volume Two, page 250.

5 Quoted in C.I. Elton: *William Shakespeare: His Family and Friends*, page 306.

6 Lucy Gent: *Albion's Classicism* (London, 1995), page 325.

7 Quoted in Schoenbaum: *Shakespeare: A Documentary Life*, pages 249–50.

8 ibid., page 246.

9 Quoted in Schoenbaum: *Shakespeare's Lives*, page 78.

Chapter Ninety-one

1 Quoted in Duncan-Jones: *Ungentle Shakespeare*, page 309.

2 Quoted in Schoenbaum: *Shakespeare's Lives*, page 182.

$\mathcal{B}$ibliography

I came to this study as a Shakespearian enthusiast rather than expert, and my debt to previous scholarship is as obvious as it is profound. Of the most recent biographies, I have found these most illuminating: Katherine Duncan-Jones's *Ungentle Shakespeare*, Stephen Greenblatt's *Will in the World*, Anthony Holden's *William Shakespeare*, Park Honan's *Shakespeare: A Life*, Eric Sams's *The Real Shakespeare*, Stanley Wells's *Shakespeare: A Dramatic Life*, Richard Wilson's *Will Power* and *Secret Shakespeare*, and Michael Wood's *In Search of Shakespeare*. To all these scholars and biographers I extend my thanks, as well as to those whose books are to be found in the following bibliography.

Adams, J.Q., *A Life of William Shakespeare* (London, 1923)

Akrigg, G.P.V., *Shakespeare and the Earl of Southampton* (London, 1968)

Anon., *Tarleton's Jests* (London, 1844)

Archer, I., *The Pursuit of Stability: Social Relations in Elizabethan London* (Cambridge, 1991)

Armin, R., *The Italian Taylor and His Boy* (London, 1609)

Armin, R., *Nest of Ninnies* (London, 1842)

Armstrong, E.A., *Shakespeare's Imagination* (London, 1946)

Baines, R.J., *Thomas Heywood* (Boston, 1984)

Baker, O., *In Shakespeare's Warwickshire* (London, 1937)

Baldwin, T.W., *The Organisation and Personnel of the Shakespearean Company* (Princeton, 1927)

Baldwin, T.W., *William Shakespeare Adapts a Hanging* (Princeton, 1931)

Baldwin, T.W., *William Shakespeare's Petty School* (Urbana, 1943)

Baldwin, T.W., *William Shakespeare's Small Latine and Lesse Greeke* (Urbana, 1944)

Baldwin, T.W., *William Shakespeare's Five Act Structure* (Urbana, 1947)

Barber, C.L. and Wheller, R.P., *The Whole Journey: Shakespeare's Power of Development* (Berkeley, 1981)

Barish, J., *The Antithetical Prejudice* (London, 1981)

Barroll, L., *Politics, Plague and Shakespeare's Theatre* (London, 1991)

Barton, J., *Playing Shakespeare* (London, 1984)

Baskerville, C.S., *The Elizabethan Jig and Related Song Drama* (Chicago, 1929)

Bate, Jonathan (ed.), *The Romantics on Shakespeare* (London, 1992)

Bate, Jonathan, *Shakespeare and Ovid* (Oxford, 1993)

Bate, Jonathan, *The Genius of Shakespeare* (Basingstoke and London, 1997)

Bayley, J., *Shakespeare and Tragedy* (London, 1981)

Bayne, Rev. R., *Lesser Jacobean and Caroline Dramatists* (London, 1910)

Bearman, R. (ed.), *The History of an English Borough: Stratford-upon-Avon* (Stroud, 1997)

Beckerman, Bernard, *Shakespeare at the Globe: 1599–1609* (New York, 1962)

Bednatz, J.P., *Shakespeare and the Poets' War* (New York, 2001)

Bentley, G.E., *Shakespeare: A Biographical Handbook* (New Haven, 1961)

Bevington, D., *From "Mankind" to Marlowe* (Cambridge, 1962)

Bevington, D., *Shakespeare* (Oxford, 2002)

Binns, J.W., *Intellectual Culture in Elizabethan and Jacobean England* (Leeds, 1990)

Bloom, Harold, *Shakespeare: The Invention of the Human* (London, 1999)

Bloom, J.H., *Folk-Lore, Old Customs and Superstitions in Shakespeare's Land* (London, 1930)

Boas, F.S., *Christopher Marlowe: A Biographical and Critical Study* (Oxford, 1940)

Bolt, Rodney, *History Play: The Lives and Afterlife of Christopher Marlowe* (London, 2004)

Bradbrook, M.C., *The Rise of the Common Player* (London, 1962)

Bradbrook, M.C., *Shakespeare: The Poet in His World* (London, 1978)

Bradbrook, M.C., *John Webster* (London, 1980)

Bradley, A.C., *Shakespearean Tragedy* (Basingstoke and London, 1974)

Bradley, D., *From Text to Performance in the Elizabethan Theatre* (Cambridge, 1992)

Braunmuller, A.R., *George Peele* (Boston, 1983)

Bray, A., *Homosexuality in Renaissance England* (London, 1982)

Brennan, M., *Literary Patronage in the English Renaissance* (London, 1988)

Brinkworth, E.R.C., *Shakespeare and the Bawdy Court of Stratford* (Chichester, 1972)

Brooks, D.A., *From Playhouse to Printing House* (Cambridge, 2000)

Brown, I., *How Shakespeare Spent the Day* (London, 1963)

Brown, I., *Shakespeare and the Actors* (London, 1970)

Brown, J.R., *Shakespeare's Plays in Performance* (London, 1966)

Bullough, Geoffrey, *Narrative and Dramatic Sources of Shakespeare* (London, 1957)

Burgess, Anthony, *Shakespeare* (London, 1970)

Buxton, J. (ed.), *The Poems of Michael Drayton* (London, 1953)

Callow, Simon, *Being an Actor* (London, 1984)

Callow, Simon, *Charles Laughton: A Difficult Actor* (London, 1987)

Carew Hazlitt, W. (ed.), *Shakespeare's Jest Books* (London, 1881)

Cargill, A., *Shakespeare the Player* (London, 1916)

Carlin, M., *Medieval Southwark* (London and Rio Grande, 1996)

Carlisle, C.J., *Shakespeare from the Greenroom* (Richmond, 1969)

Carson, N., *A Companion to Henslowe's Diary* (Cambridge, 1988)

Chambers, E.K., *The Elizabethan and Caroline Stage*, 7 vols. (Oxford, 1941)

Chambers, E.K., *Shakespearean Gleanings* (Oxford, 1944)

Chambers, E.K., *Sources for a Biography of Shakespeare* (Oxford, 1946)

Chambers, E.K., *William Shakespeare: A Study of Facts and Problems* (Oxford, 1930)

Chute, Marchette, *Shakespeare of London* (London, 1951)

Clemen, W., *English Tragedy before Shakespeare* (London, 1961)

Clemens, W.H., *The Development of Shakespeare's Imagery* (London, 1951)

Coghill, N., *Shakespeare's Professional Skills* (Cambridge, 1964)

Collinson, P., "William Shakespeare's Religious Inheritance and Environment" in *Elizabethan Essays*, ed. P. Collinson (London, 1994)

Collinson, P. and Craig, J. (eds.), *The Reformation in English Towns 1500–1640* (Basingstoke, 1998)

Cook, A.J., *The Privileged Playgoers of Shakespeare's London 1576–1642* (Princeton, 1981)

Craig, H., *A New Look at Shakespeare's Quartos* (Stratford, 1961)

Cressy, D., *Birth, Marriage and Death: Ritual, Religion and the Life-cycle in Tudor and Stuart England* (Oxford, 1997)

Crompton Rhodes, R., *The Stagery of Shakespeare* (Birmingham, 1922)

De Banke, C., *Shakespearean Stage Production Then and Now* (London, 1954)

De Grazia, M. and Wells, S., *The Cambridge Companion to Shakespeare* (Cambridge, 2001)

De Groot, J.H., *The Shakespeares and "the Old Faith"* (New York, 1946)

Dessen, A.C., *Elizabethan Stage Conventions and Modern Interpreters* (Cambridge, 1984)

Dessen, A.C., *Rediscovering Shakespeare's Theatrical Vocabulary* (Cambridge, 1985)

Dobson, Michael and Wells, Stanley, *The Oxford Companion to Shakespeare* (Oxford, 2001)

Dowden, E., *Shakespeare: His Mind and Art* (London, 1875)

Drake, N., *Shakespeare and His Times* (London, 1817)

Duncan-Jones, Katherine, *Ungentle Shakespeare: Scenes from His Life* (London, 2001)

Dures, A., *English Catholicism, 1558–1642* (Harlow, 1984)

Dutton, R., *William Shakespeare: A Literary Life* (Basingstoke and London, 1989)

Dutton, R., *Mastering the Revels* (Basingstoke and London, 1991)

Dutton, R., "The Birth of the Author," in Parker and Zitner (eds.), *Elizabethan Theater* (Newark, 1966)

Dutton, R., Findlay, A. and Wilson, R., *Theatre and Religion: Lancastrian Shakespeare* (Manchester, 2003)

Eccles, Christine, *The Rose Theatre* (London, 1990)

Eccles, M., *Christopher Marlowe in London* (Cambridge, MA, 1934)

Eccles, M., *Shakespeare in Warwickshire* (Madison, 1963)

Edelman, C., *Sword-Fighting in Shakespeare's Plays* (Manchester, 1992)

Edwards, P., *Shakespeare: A Writer's Progress* (Oxford, 1986)

Elizabethan Theatre, The, Vols. 1–15 (Toronto, 1969–2002)

Elton, C.I., *William Shakespeare: His Family and Friends* (London, 1904)

Elton, W.R. and Long, W.B. (eds.), *Shakespeare and Dramatic Tradition* (London, 1989)

Engle, L., *Shakespearean Pragmatism* (Chicago and London, 1993)

Everitt, E.B., *The Young Shakespeare* (Copenhagen, 1954)

Everitt, E.B. and Armstrong, R.L., *Six Early Plays* (Copenhagen, 1965)

Felver, C.S., *Robert Armin, Shakespeare's Fool* (Kent, 1961)

Fernie, E., *Shame in Shakespeare* (London, 2002)

Foakes, R.A., "The Player's Passion" in *Essays and Studies* 7 (London, 1954)

Foakes, R.A. (ed.), *Henslowe's Diary*, second edition (Cambridge, 2002)

Forrest, H.T., *Old Houses of Stratford-upon-Avon* (London, 1925)

Fox, L., *The Borough Town of Stratford-upon-Avon* (Stratford, 1953)

Fox, L., *The Early History of King Edward VI School Stratford-upon-Avon* (Oxford, 1984)

Fraser, R., *Shakespeare: The Later Years* (New York: 1992)

Freeman, A., *Thomas Kyd: Facts and Problems* (Oxford, 1967)

Fripp, Edgar I., *Shakespeare's Stratford* (Oxford, 1928)

Fripp, Edgar I., *Shakespeare's Haunts near Stratford* (Oxford, 1929)

Fripp, Edgar I., *Shakespeare: Man and Artist* (Oxford, 1938)

Frost, D.L., *The School of Shakespeare* (Cambridge, 1968)

George, David, "Shakespeare and Pembroke's Men," *Shakespeare Quarterly* 32 (1981)

Goldberg, Jonathan, *James I and the Politics of Literature* (Stanford, 1989)

Goldsmith, R.H., *Wise Fools in Shakespeare* (Michigan, 1955)

Gosson, S., *The School of Abuse* (London, 1841)

Grady, H., *Shakespeare, Machiavelli and Montaigne* (Oxford, 2002)

Gray, A., *A Chapter in the Early Life of Shakespeare* (Cambridge, 1926)

Gray, J.C. (ed.), *Mirror up to Shakespeare: Essays in Honour of G.R. Hibbard* (Toronto, 1984)

Gray, J.W., *Shakespeare's Marriage* (London, 1905)

Greenblatt, Stephen, *Shakespearean Negotiations* (Berkeley and Los Angeles, 1988)

Greenblatt, Stephen, *Will in the World: How Shakespeare Became Shakespeare* (London, 2004)

Greer, G., *Shakespeare* (Oxford, 1986)

Gross, John (ed.), *After Shakespeare: Writing Inspired by the World's Greatest Author* (Oxford, 2002)

Gurr, A., *Playgoing in Shakespeare's London* (Cambridge, 1987)

Gurr, A., *The Shakespearean Stage 1574–1642* (Cambridge, 1992)

Gurr, A., *The Shakespearean Playing Companies* (Oxford, 1996)

Haigh, C., *Reformation and Resistance in Tudor Lancashire* (Cambridge, 1975)

Haigh, C. (ed.), *The Reign of Elizabeth* (London, 1984)

Haigh, C. (ed.), *The English Reformation Revised* (Cambridge, 1987)

Halio, J.L., *The First Quarto of King Lear* (Cambridge, 1994)

Halliday, F.E., *The Life of Shakespeare* (London, 1961)

Halliwell-Phillips, J.O., *Outlines of the Life of Shakespeare* (London, 1887)

Hankins, J.E., *Backgrounds of Shakespeare's Thought* (Hassocks, 1978)

Hanks, P. and Hodges, F.A., *A Dictionary of Surnames* (London, 1988)

Hannay, M.P., *Phillip's Phoenix* (Oxford, 1990)

Happé, Peter, *English Drama Before Shakespeare* (Harlow, 1999)

Harbage, A., "Elizabethan Acting," *PMLA* LIV (Baltimore, 1939)

Harris, F., *The Man Shakespeare and His Tragic Life-Story* (London, 1911)

Hartwig, Joan, *Shakespeare's Analogical Scene* (Lincoln and London, 1983)

Hattaway, M., *Elizabethan Popular Theatre* (London, 1982)

Hattaway, M. and Braunmuller, A.R. (eds.), *The Cambridge Companion to English Renaissance Drama* (Cambridge, 1990)

Henn, T.R., *The Living Image: Shakespearean Essays* (London, 1972)

Herford, C.H. and Simpson, P., *B. Jonson: The Man and His Work* (Oxford, 1925)

Heywood, Thomas, *An Apology for Actors* (London, 1841)

Hibbard, G.B. (ed.), *The Elizabethan Theatre* (London, 1975)

Holden, Anthony, *William Shakespeare: His Life and Work* (London, 1999)

Holland, N., *Shakespeare's Personality* (London, 1989)

Holland, N., Homan, S. and Paris, B.J. (eds), *Shakespeare's Personality* (Berkeley, 1989)

Holmes, M., *Shakespeare and His Players* (London, 1972)

Honan, Park, *Shakespeare: A Life* (Oxford, 1998)

Honigmann, E.A.J., *The Stability of Shakespeare's Texts* (London, 1965)

Honigmann, E.A.J., *Shakespeare's Impact on His Contemporaries* (Basingstoke and London, 1982)

Honigmann, E.A.J., *Shakespeare: The "Lost Years"* (Manchester, 1985)

Honigmann, E.A.J., *Myriad-Minded Shakespeare* (Basingstoke and London, 1989)

Honigmann, E.A.J., *Shakespeare: Seven Tragedies Revisited* (London, 2002)

Honigmann, E.A.J. and Brock, S., *An Edition of Wills by Shakespeare and His Contemporaries in the London Theatre* (Manchester, 1993)

Hosking, G.L., *The Life and Times of Edward Alleyn* (London, 1952)

Hosley, R. (ed.), *Essays on Shakespeare and Elizabethan Drama* (London, 1963)

Hotson, L., *Shakespeare Versus Shallow* (London, 1931)

Hotson, L., *I, William Shakespeare* (London, 1937)

Hotson, L., *Shakespeare's Motley* (London, 1952)

Howard, J.E., *Shakespeare's Art of Orchestration* (Urbana, 1984)

Hughes, Ted, *Shakespeare and the Goddess of Complete Being* (London, 1992)

Hunter, G.K., *John Lyly: The Humanist as Courtier* (London, 1962)

Ingram, R.W., *John Marston* (Boston, 1978)

Ingram, W., *The Business of Playing* (Ithaca, NY, 1992)

Ioppolo, Grace, *Revising Shakespeare* (London, 1991)

Irace, Kathleen O., *Reforming the "Bad" Quartos* (Newark, 1994)

Jenkins, H., *The Life and Work of Henry Chettle* (London, 1934)

Jones, E. *The Origins of Shakespeare* (Oxford, 1977)

Jones, Emrys, *Scenic Form in Shakespeare* (Oxford, 1971)

Jones, J., *Shakespeare at Work* (Oxford, 1995)

Jones, Jeanne, *Family Life in Shakespeare's England, Stratford-upon-Avon 1570–1630* (Stroud, 1996)

Joseph, B., *The Tragic Actor* (London, 1959)

Joseph, B.L., *Elizabethan Acting* (London, 1951)

Kastan, D.S. (ed.), *A Companion to Shakespeare* (Oxford, 2000)

Kay, Dennis, *Shakespeare: His Life, Work and Era* (London, 1992)

Keen, A. and Lubbock, R., *The Annotator* (London, 1954)

Kempe, Will, *Kempe's Nine Dayes Wonder* (Dereham, 1997)

Kenny, T., *The Life and Genius of Shakespeare* (London, 1864)

Kermode, Frank, *Shakespeare's Language* (London, 2000)

Kermode, Frank, *The Age of Shakespeare* (London, 2004)

Kernan, A., *Shakespeare the King's Playwright* (Newark, 1995)

King, T.J., *Shakespearean Staging 1599–1642* (Cambridge, MA, 1971)

King, T.J., *Casting Shakespeare's Plays* (Cambridge, 1992)

Kinney, A.F., *Humanist Poetics* (Amherst, 1986)

Knight, C.S., *William Shakespeare: A Biography* (London, 1843)

Kokeritz, M., *Shakespearean Pronunciation* (New Haven, 1953)

Lake, P. and Questier, M. (eds.), *Conformity and Orthodoxy in the English Church 1560–1660* (Woodbridge, 2000)

Laroque, F., *Shakespeare's Festive World* (Cambridge, 1991)

Lee, S., *Stratford-upon-Avon from the Earliest Times to the Death of Shakespeare* (London, 1907)

Leishman, J.B. (ed.), *The Three Parnassus Plays* (London, 1949)

Lever, T., *The Herberts of Wilton* (London, 1967)

Levi, Peter, *The Life and Times of William Shakespeare* (Basingstoke and London, 1988)

Lynch, S.J., *Shakespearean Intertextuality* (Westport, CT, 1998)

Maguire, L.E., *Shakespearean Suspect Texts* (Cambridge, 1996)

Mahood, M.M., *Shakespeare's Word-Play* (London, 1957)

Malone, Edmond, *The Plays and Poems of William Shakespeare* (London, 1821)

Manley, L. (ed.), *London in the Age of Shakespeare* (London, 1986)

Manley, L., *Literature and Culture in Early Modern London* (Cambridge, 1995)

Mann, D., *The Elizabethan Player* (London and New York, 1991)

Maropodi, M. (ed.), *Shakespeare and Intertextuality* (Rome, 2000)

Matthews, J. B., *Molière: His Life and Works* (London, 1910)

McGann, Jerome, K. (ed.), *Textual Criticism and Literary Interpretation* (London, 1985)

McKerrow, R.B., *The Works of Thomas Nashe* (Oxford, 1958)

Medieval and Renaissance Drama in England, all vols. (New York, 1984–)

Mehl, D., *The Elizabethan Dumb Show* (London, 1965)

Miles, R., *Ben Jonson: His Life and Work* (London, 1986)

Miller, S.R., *The Taming of a Shrew, 1594 Quarto* (Cambridge, 1998)

Milward, P., SJ, *Shakespeare's Religious Background* (London, 1973)

Milward, P., SJ, *The Catholicism of Shakespeare's Plays* (Southampton, 1997)

Milward, P., SJ, *The Plays and the Exercises—A Hidden Source of Inspiration?* (Tokyo, 2002)

Minutes and Accounts of the Corporation of Stratford-upon-Avon, *see* Savage

Miola, R.S., *Shakespeare's Reading* (Oxford, 2000)

Mitchell, John, *Who Wrote Shakespeare?* (London, 1996)

Montrose, L., *The Purpose of Playing* (Chicago, 1996)

Mowl, Timothy, *Elizabethan and Jacobean Style* (London, 1993)

Muir, K., *The Sources of Shakespeare's Plays* (London, 1977)

Muir, K. (ed.), *Interpretations of Shakespeare* (Oxford, 1985)

Mulryne, J.R. and Shewring, Margaret (eds.), *Shakespeare's Globe Rebuilt* (Cambridge, 1997)

Mutschmann, H. and Wentersdorf, K., *Shakespeare and Catholicism* (New York, 1952)

Newdigate, B.H., *Michael Drayton and His Circle* (Oxford, 1941)

Nichol Smith, D. (ed.), *Eighteenth-Century Essays on Shakespeare* (Oxford, 1963)

Nicholas Knight, W., *Shakespeare's Hidden Life: Shakespeare at the Law 1585–1595* (New York, 1973)

Nicholl, Charles, *A Cup of News: The Life of Thomas Nashe* (London, 1984)

Nicholl, Charles, *The Reckoning: The Murder of Christopher Marlowe*, revised edition (London, 2002)

Noble, R., *Shakespeare's Use of Song* (London, 1923)

Nolen, Stephanie, *Shakespeare's Face* (London, 2003)

Nungezer, Edwin, *A Dictionary of Actors* (New York, 1971)

Nye, Robert, *The Late Mr. Shakespeare: A Novel* (London, 1998)

O'Connor, Garry, *William Shakespeare: A Popular Life* (New York and London, 2000)

Onions, C.T. and Lee, S. (eds.), *Shakespeare's England* (Oxford, 1916)

Ordish, T.F., *Shakespeare's London* (London, 2004)

Orgel, Stephen, *Imagining Shakespeare* (Basingstoke, 2003)

Ornstein, R., *A Kingdom for a Stage* (Cambridge, MA, 1972)

Orrell, J., *The Quest for Shakespeare's Globe* (Cambridge, 1983)

Parker, R.B. and Zitner, S.P. (eds.), *Elizabethan Theater: Essays in Honor of S. Schoenbaum* (Newark, 1996)

Partridge, Eric, *Shakespeare's Bawdy* (London, 1968)

Patterson, A., *Shakespeare and the Popular Voice* (London, 1989)

Payne Collier, J. (ed.), *Memoirs of Edward Alleyn* (London, 1841)

Payne Collier, J. (ed.), *The Alleyn Papers* (London, 1843)

Pearson, H., *A Life of Shakespeare* (Harmondsworth, 1942)

Perry, W. (ed.), *The Plays of Nathan Field* (Austin, 1950)

Picard, Liza, *Elizabeth's London* (London, 2003)

Pitcher, S.M., *The Case for Shakespeare's Authorship of "The Family Histories"* (New York, 1961)

Plunket Barton, (Sir) D., *Links between Shakespeare and the Law* (London, 1929)

Poel, W., *Shakespeare in the Theatre* (London, 1913)

Pollard, A.W. and Dover Wilson, J., *Shakespeare's Hand in the Play of "Sir Thomas More"* (Cambridge, 1923)

Pollock, L.A., *Parent–Child Relations from 1500–1900* (Cambridge, 1988)

Price, G.R., *Thomas Dekker* (New York, 1969)

Pringle, Roger, *The Shakespeare Houses* (Norwich, n.d.)

Rabkin, Norman, *Shakespeare and the Common Understanding* (Chicago and London, 1984)

Raleigh, W., *Shakespeare* (London, 1907)

Reay, B., *Popular Culture in Seventeenth-Century London* (London, 1985)

Rees, J., *Samuel Daniel* (Liverpool, 1964)

Reese, M.M., *Shakespeare: His World and His Work* (London, 1953)

Reynolds, G.F., *The Staging of Elizabethan Plays at the Red Bull Theatre 1605–1625* (London, 1940)

Reynolds, G.F., *On Shakespeare's Stage* (Boulder, 1967)

Ribner, I., *The English History Plays* (Princeton, NJ, 1957)

Riewald, J.G., "Some Later Elizabethan and Early Stuart Actors and Musicians," in *English Studies* xl, no. 1 (Amsterdam, 1959)

Righter, A., *Shakespeare and the Idea of Play* (London, 1962)

Roach, J.R., *The Player's Passion* (Newark, 1985)

Robertson Davies, W., *Shakespeare's Boy Actors* (London, 1939)

Rolfe, W.J., *Shakespeare's Early Life* (London, 1897)

Rowse, A.L., *Shakespeare's Southampton* (London, 1965)

Rowse, A.L., *Shakespeare the Man* (Basingstoke and London, 1973)

Salgado, G., *Eye-Witnesses of Shakespeare* (London, 1975)

Salgado, G., *The Elizabethan Underworld* (London, 1977)

Salingar, L., *Shakespeare and the Traditions of Comedy* (Cambridge, 1974)

Salingar, L., *Dramatic Form in Shakespeare and the Jacobeans* (Cambridge, 1986)

Sams, E. (ed.), *Shakespeare's Lost Play: Edmund Ironside* (London, 1985)

Sams, E., *The Real Shakespeare* (New Haven, CT, and London, 1995)

Sams, E. (ed.), *Shakespeare's "Edward III"* (London, 1996)

Savage, R. (ed.), *Minutes and Accounts of the Corporation of Stratford-upon-Avon, 1553–1620*, Vols. I–V (London, Oxford and Hertford, 1921–90)

Schmidgall, G., *Shakespeare and the Poet's Life* (Lexington, 1996)

Schoenbuaum, S., *William Shakespeare: A Documentary Life* (Oxford, 1975)

Schoenbaum, S., *Shakespeare's Lives*, new edition (Oxford, 1991)

Shaheen, N., *Biblical References in Shakespeare's Tragedies* (Newark, 1987)

Shaheen, N., *Biblical References in Shakespeare's History Plays* (Newark, 1989)

Shaheen, N., *Biblical References in Shakespeare's Comedies* (Newark, 1993)

Shakespeare Quarterly, all vols. (New York)

Shakespeare Studies, all vols. (Cincinnati)

Shakespeare Survey, all vols. (Cambridge)

Skura, H.A., *Shakespeare the Actor* (London, 1993)

Slater, A.D., *Shakespeare the Director* (Brighton, 1982)

Smart, J.S., *Shakespeare: Truth and Tradition* (London, 1928)

Smidt, K., *Unconformities in Shakespeare's History Plays* (London and Basingstoke, 1982)

Smidt, K., *Unconformities in Shakespeare's Early Comedies* (London and Basingstoke, 1986)

Smidt, K., *Unconformities in Shakespeare's Tragedies* (London and Basingstoke, 1989)

Smith, B.R., *Homosexual Desire in Shakespeare's England* (Chicago, 1991)

Smith, Irwin, *Shakespeare's Blackfriars Playhouse* (London, 1966)

Smith, L.T. (ed.), *The Itinerary of John Leland* (London, 1907)

Soellner, Rolf, "Shakespeare's Lucrece and the Garnier–Pembroke Connection," *Shakespeare Studies*, XV (1982)

Sohmer, S., *The Opening of the Globe Theatre 1599* (New York, 1999)

Sohmer, S., *Shakespeare's Mystery Play* (Manchester, 1999)

Southworth, John, *Shakespeare the Player: A Life in the Theatre* (Stroud, 2000)

Spurgeon, Caroline, *Shakespeare's Imagery* (Cambridge, 1935)

Steggle, M., *Wars of the Theatres* (Victoria, BC, 1998)

Sternfield, F.W., *Music in Shakespearean Tragedy* (London, 1963)

Stevenson, R., *Shakespeare's Religious Frontier* (The Hague, 1958)

Stone, L., *The Crisis of the Aristocracy 1558–1641* (Oxford, 1965)

Stone, L., *The Family, Sex and Marriage in England, 1500–1800* (London, 1977)

Stopes, C.C., *Shakespeare's Warwickshire Contemporaries* (Stratford, 1897)

Stopes, C.C., *Shakespeare's Family* (London, 1901)

Stopes, C.C., *The Life of Henry, 3rd Earl of Southampton* (Cambridge, 1922)

Styan, J.L., *Shakespeare's Stagecraft* (Cambridge, 1967)

Styles, P., *The Borough of Stratford-upon-Avon* (Oxford, 1946)

Taylor, G., *Reinventing Shakespeare* (London, 1989)

Taylor, G. and Jowett, J., *Shakespeare Reshaped 1606–1623* (Oxford, 1993)

Taylor, M., *Shakespeare Criticism in the Twentieth Century* (Oxford, 2001)

The Elizabethan Theatre, see *Elizabethan Theatre, The*

Thistleton Dyer, Rev. T.F., *Folk-Lore of Shakespeare* (New York, 1966)

Thomson, P., *Shakespeare's Theatre* (London, 1983)

Thomson, P., *Shakespeare's Professional Career* (Cambridge, 1992)

Thomson, P., *On Actors and Acting* (Exeter, 2000)

Trotter, Stewart, *Love's Labour's Found* (Ashford, 2002)

Tucker Brooke, C.F. (ed.), *The Shakespeare Apocrypha* (Oxford, 1929)

Turner, R.Y., *Shakespeare's Apprenticeship* (Chicago and London, 1974)

Urkowitz, S., *Shakespeare's Revision of "King Lear"* (Princeton, NJ, 1980)

Van Laan, T.F., *Role-Playing in Shakespeare* (London, 1978)

Vendler, H., *The Art of Shakespeare's Sonnets* (London, 1997)

Vickers, B. (ed.), *Shakespeare: The Critical Heritage*, 6 vols. (London, 1974–81)

Vickers, B., *The Artistry of Shakespeare's Prose* (London, 1979)

Vickers, B., *Shakespeare, Co-Author* (Oxford, 2002)

Videback, B.A., *The Stage Clown in Shakespeare's Theatre* (Westport, CT, 1996)

Waller, G., *Edmund Spenser: A Literary Life* (Basingstoke, 1994)

Walsham, A., *Church Papists* (Woodbridge, 1993)

Walton, J.K., *Lancashire, A Social History 1558-1939* (Manchester, 1987)

Weinmann, R., *Author's Pen and Actor's Voice* (Cambridge, 2000)

Weinmann, R., *Shakespeare and the Popular Tradition in the Theatre* (Baltimore, MD, 1978)

Wells, Stanley, *Re-editing Shakespeare for the Modern Reader* (London, 1984)

Wells, Stanley (ed.), *The Cambridge Companion to Shakespeare Studies* (Cambridge, 1986)

Wells, Stanley, *Shakespeare: A Dramatic Life* (London, 1994)

Wells, Stanley, *Shakespeare For All Time* (London, 2002)

Wells, Stanley and Taylor, Gary (with John Jowett and William Montgomery), *William Shakespeare: A Textual Companion* (London and New York, 1997)

Wheeler, R.B., *History and Antiquities of Stratford-upon-Avon* (Stratford, 1806)

White, M., *Renaissance Drama in Action* (London, 1998)

White, Whitfield P., *Theatre and Reformation* (London, 1992)

Wiles, D., *Shakespeare's Clown: Actor and Text in the Elizabethan Playhouse* (Cambridge, 1987)

Wilson, F.P., *Marlowe and the Early Shakespeare* (Oxford, 1953)

Wilson, I., *Shakespeare: The Evidence* (London, 1993)

Wilson, J., *The Archaeology of Shakespeare* (Stroud, 1995)

Wilson, Richard, *Will Power: Essays on Shakespearian Authority* (Detroit, MI, 1993)

Wilson, Richard, *Secret Shakespeare: Studies in Theatre, Religion and Resistance* (Manchester, 2004)

Winstanley, L., *Hamlet and the Scottish Succession* (Cambridge, 1921)

Winstanley, L., *Macbeth, King Lear and Contemporary History* (Cambridge, 1922)

Winstanley, L., *"Othello" as the Tragedy of Italy* (London, 1924)

Wood, Michael, *In Search of Shakespeare* (London, 2003)

Worthen, W.B., *The Idea of the Actor* (Princeton, NJ, 1984)

Wraight, A.D., *Christopher Marlowe and Edward Alleyn* (Chichester, 1993)

Wright, L.B., *Middle-Class Culture in Elizabethan England* (Richmond, VA, 1935)

Wrightson, Keith, *English Society 1580-1680* (London, 1982)

Yates, F., *John Florio* (Cambridge, 1934)

Young, F.B., *Mary Sydney* (London, 1912)

Index

ALSO BY PETER ACKROYD

THAMES
The Biography

In *Thames: The Biography*, Peter Ackroyd delves into the hidden byways of history, describing the river's endless allure in a journey overflowing with characters, incidents, and wry observations. *Thames: The Biography* meanders gloriously, rather like the river itself. In short, lively chapters Ackroyd writes about connections between the Thames and such historical figures as Julius Caesar and Henry VIII, and offers memorable portraits of the ordinary men and women who depend upon the river for their livelihoods. The Thames as a source of artistic inspiration comes brilliantly to life as Ackroyd invokes Chaucer, Shakespeare, Turner, Shelley, and other writers, poets, and painters who have been enchanted by its many moods and colors.

History

ALSO AVAILABLE

Albion
The Casebook of Victor Frankenstein
The Clerkenwell Tales
The Fall of Troy
The Lambs of London
The Life of Thomas More
London: The Biography
London Under: The Secret Beneath the Streets
The Plato Papers
Venice

ANCHOR BOOKS
Available wherever books are sold.
www.anchorbooks.com

Printed in the United States
by Baker & Taylor Publisher Services